Whatever Happened to the Tories

to the Tories

THE CONSERVATIVE PARTY SINCE 1945

Whatever Happened to the Tories

The Conservative Party Since 1945

Ian Gilmour and Mark Garnett

FOURTH ESTATE · *London*

First published in Great Britain in 1997 by
Fourth Estate Limited
6 Salem Road
London W2 4BU

Copyright © 1997 Ian Gilmour and Mark Garnett

1 3 5 7 9 10 8 6 4 2

A catalogue record for this book is available from the British Library.

ISBN 1–85702–475–3

Typeset by Rowland Phototypesetting Ltd, Bury St. Edmunds, Suffolk
Printed in Great Britain by Clays Ltd, St Ives plc

Contents

Acknowledgements

Many people have helped in the writing of this book. Wynne Godley, John Grigg, William Keegan, Robert Shepherd and David and Andrew Gilmour read some or most of the manuscript. We are profoundly grateful to them for giving us their time and knowledge and for making many invaluable criticisms and suggestions. Our greatest debts are to them and to Diane Craig, who has deciphered increasingly obscure hieroglyphics with her usual skill. She has also shown remarkable stamina in typing a bulky manuscript at a very busy time.

The staff of the House of Lords Library have provided their usual prompt, courteous and expert assistance. Anthony Fanshawe kindly gave us a copy of his notes of discussions with Lords Margadale and Hailsham about the leadership contest of 1963. We also owe thanks for help on particular points to Robert Atkins, Peter Carrington, Kenneth Clarke, Hugh Cudlipp, Roy Denman, Philip Goodhart, Peter Kellner, Timothy Kitson, Piers Morgan, Richard Thorpe, Brian Urquhart, William Waldegrave, Peter Walker and Dennis Walters. In addition, Alexandra Rocca and Richard Weight have unearthed valuable facts and figures. Our thanks, too, to Clive Priddle and Fourth Estate for managing to be both encouraging and stoically patient.

Finally, any student of the modern Conservative Party must acknowledge a debt to the work of Robert Blake and John Ramsden. This book aims to help fill the space between Blake's classic, sagacious, broad-brush *The Conservative Party from Peel to Thatcher* and Ramsden's richly-detailed volumes *The Age of Churchill and Eden* and *The Winds of Change: Macmillan to Heath, 1957–1975*.

Despite our debts to all of the above, the responsibility for any errors of fact or interpretation is ours alone.

Ian Gilmour
Mark Garnett

Introduction

Just before the Conservative Party Conference in 1950, nine enthusiastic young MPs published a book of essays with official blessing. The essays, covering a wide range of domestic policy issues but mainly concerned with social matters, appeared under the title *One Nation*, which the group had adopted as their collective name.

The title, suggested at the inaugural meeting by Iain Macleod, was well chosen. Recalling a passage in Benjamin Disraeli's novel *Sybil* which deplored the existence of Two Nations in Britain – the rich and the poor, 'between whom there is no intercourse and little sympathy' – it emphasised the Tory belief that society does exist and that Britain is not just a random collection of jostling individuals. In the foreword to *One Nation*, R. A. Butler picked up this theme. The Conservative Party, he wrote, had a 'long and honourable record in the field of Social Service', which refuted the Attlee Government's claims that Labour had 'a monopoly in this sphere'. The Conservatives had lost successive elections in 1945 and 1950, but their fortunes would revive provided they stayed true to Disraeli's message.[1]

Up to 1979, Conservative Governments pursued 'One Nation' policies, although the problems that had plagued Britain since 1945 resisted a lasting cure. The leaders of the 1979 Government and its successors, however, regarding the 'One-Nation' approach as another of those problems rather than as part of the solution, abandoned them. The ruling orthodoxy of these Governments became Two-Nations Conservatism. Margaret Thatcher, who while in office had admitted that she did not know what 'One-Nation' meant, in 1996 even claimed that 'One-Nation' Tories were really 'No Nation Conservatives'. Before 1979 the gap between the rich and the poor was substantial; since then it has grown much wider. After fifteen years of Two-Nations rule, the percentage of households which lacked an income from employment had doubled. In an opinion poll in November 1995 even 51 per cent of declared Conservative supporters thought that Britain was likely to become still further removed from One Nation. That view was understandable: between 1979 and 1996 the pace at which the gap widened between rich and poor was faster in the UK than in any other industrial country except New Zealand; by 1997 the range of social inequality in Britain was the same as that in Nigeria.[2]

Conservatives have never sought to produce equality, regarding it, with Jeremy Bentham, as 'a chimera'. Yet, also agreeing with Bentham, they formerly sought to diminish inequality, partly because they wanted to eliminate poverty and partly because they realised that, as David Hume put it, 'a too great disproportion among the citizens weakens any state'. Since 1979 that humane and sensible attitude has been lost. Such ideas, like international comparisons, meant little to the Conservative Right, who were overcome with admiration for what they believed Two-Nations Conservatism to have achieved.[3]

This Thatcherite triumphalism was reflected in the writings of a new generation of Conservative historians. These scholars produced a new reading of post-war history which, echoing the speeches of the new party leaders, closely resembled the existing left-wing analysis. They agreed with the socialist view that after years of compromise the Conservative Party was at last following its 'true' principles. Like their socialist counterparts, these observers added spice to their account by disparaging their party's former leaders. Every post-war Conservative Prime Minister, it emerged, had deviated from the true creed, although some were undoubtedly worse than others, and Winston Churchill needed to be handled with care. The chief villains in this melodrama, therefore, had to be Harold Macmillan and Edward Heath.

Right-wingers often claim that they have won the 'Battle of Ideas' since 1979. Yet surveys show that their policies increased the popularity of the One-Nation approach.[4] If the public was divided by the Thatcher Governments, so were Conservative MPs. Well before the crushing defeat in the 1997 general election, right-wing triumphalism had been replaced by virtual civil war in the Conservative Party. The resulting bloodshed seemed an appropriate reason for taking another look at Conservative Governments and the Conservative Party during the last half-century.

CHAPTER

I

Prologue

In October 1938 George Orwell predicted 'a sweeping win for the Conservatives' in what he assumed to be an imminent general election. Had there been such a peacetime election between 1938 and 1940, the Conservative Party would probably not have enjoyed the support of Anthony Eden. He would have stood as an Independent Conservative, and very possibly Winston Churchill would have had to do the same. The latter's constituency association at Epping gave him a vote of confidence by only three to two, and opposition to him, encouraged by Conservative Central Office, continued; unless he was prepared to support the Government, said a branch chairman (later an MP), he 'ought no longer to shelter under the goodwill and name of such a great party'. Epping might well not have readopted him.[1] In any case, had there been no war, Orwell's prediction would surely have been proved right.

Seven years later, on 5 June 1945, Orwell still thought the Conservatives would win the election the following month but with only a small majority. On the same day, the back-bencher and diarist 'Chips' Channon recorded that fellow Conservatives were confident of an overwhelming victory; evidently they did not think their party's electoral strength had changed much since 1938. Rab Butler, Harold Macmillan and Eden (who confessed to his diary his 'dislike of much [the] Tory Party stands for or pretends to stand for' and believed he had no 'party politics'), did not share the general Conservative optimism, but they were in a small minority. The *Daily Express*, which had repeated its fatuous slogan 'There will be no war' right up to the outbreak of war, got it wrong again. Lord Beaverbrook took a poll of his senior executives on the election result: only one of them 'thought the Tories were out', and on polling day, 5 July, the *Daily Express* rejoiced that 'we are winning'. In the interval of three weeks needed to collect the votes of servicemen overseas, the *Liverpool Post* was able to toast a three-figure Conservative majority well after the electors had cast their votes.[2]

The election did produce a three-figure majority, but a Labour one – which was as much of a surprise to Clement Attlee as to the *Daily*

1

Express and the *Liverpool Post*. Winning 394 seats, Labour had an overall majority of 146 and a majority of 181 over the Conservatives and their National Liberal allies. Rarely have the experts been so confounded, though they were not alone in failing to perceive what had been happening. Like many others, two new Conservative candidates, Christopher Hollis in Wiltshire and Reginald Maudling in the London suburbs, also 'quite misjudged the temper of the electorate and imagined ... that the Prime Minister who had won the war would be returned with a large majority'.[3] That, after all, was what had happened after military victories in 1918 and 1900. Yet much readily available evidence had in fact pointed to a Labour victory. By-elections had been going badly for the Conservatives. As recently as April 1945 the left-wing Commonwealth Party had gained a majority of 6,000 votes in Cheltenham, a constituency which in 1935 the Conservatives had won with 70 per cent of the vote. The Gallup poll of public opinion had been pointing the same way: for some time Labour had been well ahead in it. Public opinion polling was still new, and most people preferred to rely on their intuition, yet it was not necessary to make a close study of Gallup to pick up the change in opinion that had taken place. All that was needed was to visit the cinema. There, whenever Churchill, Roosevelt, or Stalin appeared on the newsreels (which were then invariably part of the cinema programme) the audience always gave the loudest applause to Stalin, while the achievements of the Red Army or anything to do with Russia gained far more enthusiastic acclaim than the exploits of the British or Americans.[4]

Yet Churchill was not running against Stalin, and most of the Conservatives who did notice the change in British opinion assumed that it would be more than counteracted by the general admiration of and affection for Winston Churchill as a war leader. In the event, however, Churchill's popularity did not translate into votes for the Conservative Party – or rather, it did not do so in sufficient numbers – whereas the alteration in public attitudes translated into votes for Labour. Naturally enough, two of the main reasons for that change were events between 1938 and 1945, and a perception of the 1930s which had altered since Orwell made his forecast of a Conservative landslide.

The Pre-war Record

Today the most lively memories of the 1930s are probably dole queues and Mr Chamberlain waving a piece of paper; in 1945 popular memories were similar, with the addition of the means test. A few years after his election defeat Churchill claimed that the socialists had spread 'a legend or large-scale propaganda of falsehoods' about 'the lamentable conditions' in Britain between the wars.[5] The legend was not confined to socialists and their supporters. Whatever they might have felt at the time, others, too, had come to regard the thirties, if not as a 'devil's decade', as an inglorious period in the country's history.

There was, therefore, all the more need for Churchill to remind his audience that the inter-war years had been over-denigrated and were less 'a sad period of stagnation' than one 'of almost unequalled progress and expansion in the life of the wage-earning masses throughout this island'.[6] So, contrary to the post-war vilification, the Conservative Party could be genuinely proud of its record since 1918. Of the three Conservative Prime Ministers between the wars, only Bonar Law could be called a right-wing Conservative. Stanley Baldwin could plausibly say that if he was not the leader of his party he would like to be the leader of those who did not belong to any political party, and that while he was opposed to socialism he had 'always endeavoured to make the party face left in its anti-socialism'.[7] As the young Anthony Eden wrote to *The Times* in 1930, 'So long as Mr Baldwin leads the Conservative Party, so long will its "right" wing be unable to dominate the party's counsels and narrow its purpose . . . nor, with Mr Baldwin as its leader, will the Conservative Party ever sink to become the creature of millionaire newspaper owners or a mere appendage of big business.'[8]

Down to 1931, as they were to do again later, the Conservative and Labour Parties had converged. As the economist Joseph Schumpeter later remarked, it was difficult for the first Labour Government to strike a distinctive note because 'fiscal radicalism had been (and continued to be) carried quite as far as was possible under the circumstances, by Conservative governments'.[9] Until the 1914–18 war, Labour had been a trade union and social reform party, reflecting the ordinary worker's acceptance of capitalism. It was moderate and gradualist. In 1918 it had officially become a socialist party with a socialist constitution largely drafted by Sidney Webb, but for many of the party's leaders that conversion was more outward than genuine.

The original socialist ideal was to end the class struggle by reorganising the community on a co-operative basis.[10] Co-operation was to take the place of competition. This was such a large ambition and such a difficult, not to say impossible, project that socialism in this world became rather like the next world for Christians – something which was inevitable and something to look forward to in moments of exaltation but difficult to envisage or even to hasten. In the meantime, therefore, one had to deal with this more prosaic world – and live with capitalism.

And this is what the Labour Party conspicuously did. Both the first and second Labour Governments were highly moderate, if not conservative. A capital levy which had been Labour policy was dropped when the party took office in 1924; and the budget of the Labour Chancellor, Philip Snowden, he was happy to record, 'relieved the feelings of the rich, who had feared that there might be drastic impositions upon their class'. In its programme for the 1929 election, Labour scarcely mentioned 'socialism', while a party document noted the year before that the other parties had embraced a 'tentative doctrineless socialism'.[11]

Neville Chamberlain gave the impression of looking upon the Labour Party as inferior; Baldwin had to remind him that in Parliament he was addressing an assembly of gentlemen. Yet Chamberlain was scarcely to the right of Baldwin. He was the driving force behind many of the Conservatives' pre-war social reforms and had sympathy with many of Labour's objectives. 'Hoare and I', he told his sister in 1923, 'are the only socialists in the government'; in the early thirties he hoped to move towards a 'fused party under a National name'.[12] Under Baldwin and Chamberlain, what Winston Churchill later called 'much far-reaching legislation for some of which I was personally responsible was devised and carried out' by Conservative and National governments.[13] Between the wars, over 4 million homes were built, and such great strides were made to the creation of the Welfare State that, in Paul Addison's judgement, in 1939 'the social services in Britain, taken all in all, were the most advanced in the world . . .'[14]

The two large blots on that pre-war Conservatism were unemployment and foreign policy. Between 1921 and 1940 unemployment never fell below 10 per cent and in the early 1930s was over 20 per cent. In its 1929 election manifesto Labour had given an 'unqualified pledge to deal immediately and practically' with unemployment. Unfortunately it had made no plans to do so. When Labour took office in May 1929, unemployment was 1,164,000; by July 1930 it was over two million, by December two and a half million and by July 1931 two and three-quarters. The Chancellor of the Exchequer, Philip Snowden, may have been a socialist, as L. S. Amery said, in the sense that he hated the rich; yet he was a rigid liberal nineteenth-century free trader who did not believe that socialism entailed interference with the laws of supply and demand. During the 1929 election Labour damned Lloyd George's plan to conquer unemployment by a large programme of public works as 'unsound' and 'patchwork'. In office it belatedly embarked on some public works. Otherwise all the Government did to fulfil 'its unqualified pledge to deal immediately and practically' with soaring unemployment was to appoint a committee.[15]

The Labour Government was in office during the worst slump in British and world history. Provided with a powerful demonstration that capitalism was not stable or self-adjusting, Labour ministers had a magnificent opportunity to substitute socialism, in which they professed to believe, or at least to do something innovative: they could have adopted the policies advocated by Keynes and Lloyd George before the election, or they could, as Ernest Bevin advocated, have devalued the pound. Admittedly Labour lacked a parliamentary majority but that was not the cause of its paralysis; the Liberals on whom it depended were more interventionist than Labour was. As John Paton, later a Labour MP, correctly wrote, the Government's 'timid policies' did not spring from its minority position but from wrong views. In consequence, after floundering with orthodox financial policies, it split and resigned. 'What would you think', asked Sir Oswald Mosley, the future Fascist leader who, when a Labour minister, had proposed radical measures to fight unemployment, 'of a Salvation Army who took to its heels on the day of judgement?'[16] Yet while agnosticism is not a state of mind much associated with the Salvation Army, many of the Labour Ministers were agnostic if not atheistic about socialism.

Snowden remained Chancellor long enough in the new 'National', though largely Conservative, Government to introduce an emergency budget, which Churchill described as 'the last expiring convulsion of Treasury Cobdenism', and which Keynes thought 'replete with folly and injustice', adding that its effect on unemployment would be 'disastrous'.[17] Fortunately, after the National Government's massive victory in the 1931 election, Neville Chamberlain went to the Exchequer. Whereas Snowden would have fitted snugly into the neo-Cobdenite Treasury of the 1980s and 1990s, Chamberlain would have been treated as a deluded outsider. Before the election the Government had gone off the gold standard; now free trade, high interest rates and *laissez-faire* were in turn jettisoned. F. A. Hayek was distressed: Britain, he later noted, had 'in the short space of the nine inglorious years 1931 to 1939 transformed its economic system beyond recognition'. Harold Macmillan was correspondingly delighted, believing that the idea of 'an unplanned self-adjusting economic system had been destroyed for ever'. Certainly the hallmarks of Conservative economic policy in the thirties were cheap money, protection, rationalisation of industry, control of prices and output, subsidies and agricultural marketing boards rather than competition, free trade and *laissez-faire*, which Chamberlain regarded as 'an obsolete and worn-out system'. He sought 'something more adaptable to the needs of modern industrial civilization'.[18]

The Government suffered no retribution for its flouting of nineteenth-century classical economics and its sweeping adoption of heresy. Between 1931 and 1937, manufacturing productivity rose by 20 per cent; real wages also rose, as did Britain's share of world trade. Britain recovered from the slump more rapidly than other countries. Probably only Nazi Germany and Soviet Russia did better, and few wanted to go down either of those revolutionary paths. Chamberlain thought that he, too, was making 'changes of a really revolutionary character,' yet in one important respect he clung to orthodoxy, sharing with Snowden the Treasury's obsession with balanced budgets. To reduce unemployment, Keynes had long been advocating a large scheme of public investment – Churchill had had a similar idea when President of the Board of Trade in 1909 – but Chamberlain would have none of it. In 1933 he predicted that high unemployment would continue for ten years, for which complacency he was attacked by Churchill. Two years later the Chancellor was patting himself on the back for having balanced the budget, claiming without evidence that a policy of public works to provide employment was always disappointing.[19]

Consequently little was done, although the problem was obvious to many, including Churchill: there was no serious unemployment 'here in the south', he told his constituents in 1933, but 'in the north or in the poorer working class areas' the 'cancer of unemployment is eating out the heart of the people'. He was, of course, right. While unemployment was 3 per cent in High Wycombe, it was 58 per cent in Pontypridd in Wales, 67 per cent in Jarrow and nearly 100 per cent in Shildon in County Durham. At the end of 1933 Chamberlain did introduce special measures to help areas of high unemployment, yet allocated such trifling sums for the purpose that he drew deserved ridicule from Lloyd George. Hence, although two million more people were working in 1937 than in 1932, the depressed areas remained depressed; some of them became more so. After becoming Prime Minister in 1937 Chamberlain expressed a commitment to the goal of full employment, yet three years later, at the time of Dunkirk, a million people were still unemployed.[20]

Worse still, the unemployed were not well treated. Until 1931 Unemployment Benefit was paid as a right except to those in breach of the regulations. In 1931 a stringent means test was introduced. The whole of the resources of a household were taken into account when calculating how much relief should be allowed. This meant that if a father, previously the breadwinner, lost his job, he became dependent on the earnings of his children. The system was harsh, haphazard and manifestly unfair. It produced widespread poverty, illness and malnutrition. Admittedly, the British unemployed were better off than their contemporaries on the Continent. But that was small consolation, and the depressed areas and the means test were powerful fomenters of disaffection with the Conservatives during the war and after it.[21]

Some Conservatives thought the Government should do much more to diminish hardship. Macmillan urged it not to use the recovery as an excuse for future inactivity; in his 1933 book *Reconstruction* he advocated economic planning and co-operation between workers, employers and Government. Earlier, in 1927, Macmillan, together with Oliver Stanley and Robert Boothby, had produced *Industry and the State – a Conservative View*, a book which the *Daily Mail* damned for its 'crude and hasty theories characteristic of modern Socialism'. The *Daily Mail* went on to applaud the even cruder practices of Benito Mussolini and of Oswald Mosley's blackshirts.[22]

Other Conservatives wanted the Government to move in the opposite direction to that of Boothby and Co. In 1933 Maurice Hely-Hutchinson suggested that the long-term unemployed should lose the right to vote, and Sir John Wardlaw-Milne wanted to abolish free elementary education. Both MPs were strong supporters of Chamberlain's policy of appeasement. Hely-Hutchinson told one of the Conservative rebels who had helped to bring Chamberlain down in 1940 that he and his friends were like 'parachutist troops who had descended behind the lines in Conservative uniform'. Wardlaw-Milne, who was educated privately, moved a vote of censure on Churchill's Government in 1942, wrecking his case by claiming that it would be 'a very desirable move' to make the Duke of Gloucester Commander-in-Chief, a suggestion which was not a good advertisement for an expensive education.[23]

Appeasement

The Government's appeasement policy was popular until 1939 and has more supporters today than it had in the intervening years. Some recent historians have even argued that Britain's real enemy was not Nazi Germany but Communist Russia, and therefore it was Churchill, not Chamberlain, who was wrong and bears the responsibility for Britain's loss of her Empire. That is not how pre-war foreign policy was viewed between 1940 and 1945. Appeasement, which had plainly failed, was regarded as discreditable as well as disastrous.

Anthony Eden achieved a high reputation as a strong opponent of appeasement. As his presence in the Foreign Office as a minister from 1933 to 1938 suggests, that reputation was only partly deserved; Eden's record in office was mixed. When he met Hitler, he 'rather liked him', finding that 'the man has charm'. When Hitler marched into the Rhine-land in 1936, Eden, who was by then Foreign Secretary, did little. The Rhineland has often been judged as the best occasion and place to have stopped the dictator, and a later Permanent Under-Secretary at the Foreign Office regarded Eden as 'responsible for the great and tragic "appeasement"'. However, the French were similarly passive, and Eden explained to Parliament that without stronger public support the French and Belgian governments could not have fought effectively – something he would have done well to remember twenty years later. Eden regarded Mussolini as an 'anti-Christ', which was odd if only because Hitler was a far stronger candidate for that role; but unlike Eden's meeting with Hitler, his encounter with Mussolini had not been cordial.[24]

Prime Ministers tend to think they have a natural aptitude for con-ducting foreign policy, no matter how ignorant of the subject they may be. Neville Chamberlain was no exception, even though he had been told by an acknowledged expert, his brother Austen, 'Neville, you must remember that you know nothing about foreign affairs.' Neville never did remember it; his vanity was too all-embracing for him even to contemplate the idea.[25] Also like other Prime Ministers, Chamberlain disliked the Foreign Office because it was liable to oppose his policy and give him unpalatable advice. Contrary to custom, he did not have an FO man as one of his private secretaries. And when he flew to Berchtesgaden to see Hitler in 1938, he took with him no one from the Foreign Office, nor so far as is known even a brief; he did take an adviser to Munich but ignored his advice.[26]

Anthony Eden thought Chamberlain had 'a certain fondness for dic-tators', admiring their efficiency. Fond of them or not, Chamberlain believed that he could reach agreement with Hitler and Mussolini pro-vided that Britain was properly conciliatory. Appeasement is not wrong in itself, of course: it may be the best way of settling conflicts abroad or at home. Churchill himself said after the war that 'appeasement from strength [was] magnanimous and noble'; he objected only to 'appease-ment through weakness or fear'. Chamberlain's appeasement was objec-tionable because it was at the expense of others – at the time, it cost Britain little save honour.[27]

In January 1938 President Roosevelt confided to Chamberlain his intention of holding an international conference in Washington to dis-cuss the gravity of the current situation. Not surprisingly, the British Ambassador in Washington advised 'a very quick and cordial accept-ance'.[28] Although the Roosevelt invitation might well not have come to anything, any Prime Minister less conceited and self-centred than Chamberlain would surely have taken the Ambassador's advice. Chamberlain, however, thought Roosevelt's plan 'fantastic and likely to excite the derision of Germany and Italy [who] might even use it to postpone discussions with us.'[29] Accordingly, without consulting Eden, who was abroad on holiday, Chamberlain effectively turned down Roosevelt, conveying to the President that his proposal might impede 'some improvement in the immediate future', for which Chamberlain hoped and which merely amounted to Britain giving *de facto* recognition to Mussolini's swallowing of Abyssinia and to the prospect of conversations with the Italian government. Although outraged by Chamberlain's behaviour, Eden did not resign. As Roosevelt's approach was confidential, he could hardly have done so. Instead, he resigned shortly afterwards over talks with Italy.[30]

In his diary Eden wrote that the difficulty was 'that N. believes that he is a man with a mission to come to terms with the Dictators. Indeed one of his chief objections to Roosevelt's invitation was that with its strong reference to International Law it would greatly irritate Dictator powers.'[31] Eden was unlikely to be of much help with such a mission. He favoured a stronger line with the dictators, at least with Mussolini, and he took a fairly strong line with Chamberlain himself. Hence Chamberlain was happy to see him go, hoping for a more accommodating successor in Lord Halifax.

Chamberlain's 'mission' led him to make three journeys to see the German dictator in September 1938 in an attempt to defuse the crisis caused by Hitler's insistence on incorporating the Czech Sudetenland into his Reich. In accordance with his belief in his great understanding of foreign policy, Chamberlain proposed his first visit to Hitler without consulting his Cabinet. In between his second and third flights he expressed his dismay in a broadcast to the British people that peace was threatened by 'a quarrel in a far-away country between people of whom we know nothing',[32] a remark which has brought him much obloquy and indicates the accuracy of his brother's opinion of Chamberlain's own grasp of foreign affairs. Chamberlain put an end to the immediate threat by giving Hitler what he wanted through the Munich agreement between Germany, France, Italy and Britain. The Czechs were compensated for the dismemberment of their country with a four-power guarantee of their new truncated borders. Chamberlain did not need compensation. He felt he had won Hitler's 'respect', he believed Hitler's promise that he had 'no more territorial ambitions in Europe', and he was overjoyed by Hitler's reaction to a piece of paper that he had given him. This stated that the Munich agreement was 'symbolic of the desire of our two peoples never to go to war with one another again' and that the two countries were resolved to discuss the removal of other 'possible sources of difference and thus to contribute to assure the peace of Europe'. Hitler, perhaps thinking that it would be quite unnecessary to go to war with Britain again because she would always accede to his demands, happily signed it. This worthless document was the piece of paper waved by Chamberlain when he returned to London saying that he had brought 'peace with honour. I believe it is peace for our time.'[33]

Munich soon became a by-word for shame and dishonour. Not at the time. The Munich agreement and Chamberlain himself were hugely popular. Companies bought space in the newspapers to express their gratitude. Shops sold Chamberlain dolls and sugar umbrellas. So great was the general relief and exultation that Winston Churchill (and George Orwell) feared that Chamberlain would cash in his popularity by calling a snap election. In the debate on Munich, after saying that we had sustained 'a total and unmitigated defeat', Churchill warned the Government that to hold an 'inverted khaki election' when they had a 'large working majority' would be 'an act of historic, constitutional indecency'.[34] At the end of the debate, thirty Conservatives, including Churchill and Eden, abstained.

The Munich agreement was soon afterwards defended on the grounds that it gave Britain and France time to rearm. Yet the Prime Minister did not regard Munich as (primarily) a device for gaining time; his first motive, as his biographer wrote, was the rightness of peace and the wrongness of war. When Lord Swinton told him that he thought Munich had been worthwhile because it bought a year's grace for rearmament, Chamberlain replied, 'But I have made peace.' Although Hitler's worst-yet pogrom against German Jews, the *Kristallnacht* in November, horrified Chamberlain, it did not persuade him to alter his course. Channon's comment probably mirrored the Prime Minister's attitude: 'I must say Hitler never helps, and always makes Chamberlain's task more difficult.' At the end of the year Chamberlain was still so satisfied with his diplomacy that his Christmas card consisted of a picture of an aeroplane and one word: 'Munich'.[35]

In any case, Britain did not embark on an emergency programme of rearmament after Munich; that might have annoyed Hitler. As Anthony Eden rightly said, British rearmament was still 'on a peacetime basis', whereas that of the totalitarian states was not.[36]

In early 1939 Chamberlain's confidence grew. In March, he gave an off-the-record briefing to journalists, telling them, as a jaundiced Foreign Office official put it, that the international position could now be viewed with 'comfort and optimism'. A few days later, Hitler marched into Prague. The *Daily Telegraph* denounced a 'flagrant and impudent act of unprovoked aggression', but in a curt and chillingly detached statement Chamberlain made it clear that his policy of 'general appeasement' remained in being. The Prime Minister told Parliament that he had no doubt that 'the course we took [at Munich] was right' and we must not be deflected from it. The end of Czechoslovakia, he said, 'may or may not have been inevitable'. The little matter of the British guarantee was casuistically ruled to be no longer operative.[37]

Almost immediately, however, Chamberlain found that his stoicism at the fall of Prague was not shared by the public, his party or his Foreign Secretary, Lord Halifax. Even 'Chips' Channon was shocked by Hitler's 'callous desertion of the Prime Minister'. Chamberlain again discovered that the Foreign Office had not been neutralised by Eden's departure; backed by other Cabinet ministers, Halifax forced a change of course, as he had briefly done during the Munich crisis. Britain gave guarantees to Poland, Romania, Greece and Turkey who, having seen what a guarantee had done for Czechoslovakia, could have gained very limited comfort. Understandably, Lloyd George called the guarantees 'demented pledges that cannot be redeemed'.[38]

At all events, when Hitler invaded Poland on 1 September, only a week after the signature of the Anglo-Polish Treaty which put the guarantee into legal form, the British Government displayed no eagerness to shoulder its obligations. Before the Cabinet met, the Polish Ambassador asked for help from the RAF, help which, under Article I of the Anglo-Polish Treaty, Britain was obliged to give 'at once'; yet the Ambassador's request was ignored both then and later. An instant ultimatum to Germany with a short time limit was the plain and minimum duty of the Government, yet the Cabinet wavered. The Government's prevarication, partly caused by difficulties with France, shocked and enraged the House of Commons. Only fear of a defeat in Parliament together with an actual Cabinet revolt on 2 September impelled the Prime Minister to instruct the British Ambassador in Berlin to deliver an ultimatum with a time limit of two hours at 9.00 a.m. on Sunday, 3 September. No wonder Hitler had thought that Britain and France would not fight for Poland, and that, even if they did, the war they fought would be half-hearted and brief.[39]

Shortly after the two hours were up, Chamberlain spoke to the nation on the wireless; he then addressed the House of Commons. On both occasions he was inappropriately egotistical. Because of Chamberlain's appearance and manner, Brendan Bracken, one of Churchill's very few followers in Parliament, had long called him 'the undertaker'; and Chamberlain's speeches on Britain's declaration of war were more a funeral service for his policy than a call to arms. The Prime Minister spoke as though the chief tragedy were not the national one, that Britain was having to embark upon what was likely to be a bloody war, but a personal one for him, in that his hopes for peace had been dashed. 'You can imagine', he told the British people in his broadcast, 'what a bitter blow it is to me that all my long struggle for peace has failed. Yet I can not believe that there is anything more, or anything different that I could have done, and that would have been more successful . . .' Rarely, if ever, can less inspiring words have been addressed to a nation at war. The undertaker had excelled himself.[40]

Of course Chamberlain's determination to avoid war at almost any price was shared by most people and, in view of the horrors of 1914–18, fully understandable. Hitler and the Nazis were a new phenomenon in international affairs, and many found it difficult to take their measure. The British Empire was overstretched, and the armed forces could not meet all their commitments. The other political parties were worse. Despite Munich's sacrifice of the good Czech army and their strong fortifications (and ignoring the possibility of a military revolt against Hitler in 1938), Britain was in a better position to fight Germany in 1939 than the year before. And, finally, the European Union and the United States, when confronted fifty years later by a much less formidable enemy, the Serbs, conducted themselves little better than Britain and France in the 1930s.

Yet, during the war and the years succeeding it, the excuses that could be made for Chamberlain and appeasement were forgotten. The failure and the dishonour were not. Along with unemployment, appeasement provided a fertile field for propaganda against the Conservatives from 1939 to 1945. 'The British people', Bob Boothby wrote two years after the 1945 election, 'remembered the ten years of unchallenged Tory domination before the war, which led through one national humiliation after another, to the final scenes of horror on the beaches of Dunkirk.'[41]

The Coalition

Less than a month before Dunkirk, the vote of 41 of its normal supporters against the Government and the abstention of some 60 others at the end of the Norway debate had brought about a change of Prime Minister. Chamberlain might have been able to hang on had not the Labour Party, performing its best service to the state for many years, refused to serve under him. He was succeeded by the greatest opponent of appeasement, Winston Churchill – an outcome which few wanted or expected. The King, the great bulk of the Conservative Party, most of the Labour leaders and Chamberlain himself would all have preferred Halifax. Luckily Halifax, like Churchill, preferred Churchill.

The new Prime Minister was initially unpopular with much of the Conservative parliamentary party. It feared and distrusted Churchill not merely because of his long fight against appeasement but because of his misguided opposition to the Government's liberal policy over India and his misjudgement over the Abdication crisis in 1936 when the House of Commons had refused him a hearing. The affections and allegiance of Conservative MPs still lay with Chamberlain, who remained leader of the party. As Churchill reciprocated their dislike and distrust, it was some time before the yes-men of the Tory back-benches transferred their 'yes' with any conviction to their new and very different leader.

Aware of the possible danger to his back, Churchill safeguarded his flanks. Before long he had dispersed the leading men of Munich: Halifax to Washington, Hoare to Madrid, and Simon to the Woolsack; Chamberlain died in November, when Churchill became the party leader. The sole senior survivor was the only real mediocrity among them. Sir Kingsley Wood had turned away from Chamberlain early enough for Churchill to be grateful and to keep him in high office until his death in 1943. The eclipse of the other grey men was not regretted in the country. Beachcomber had expressed the public attitude when he ironically sang in the *Daily Express*:

> Democracy gives us the men we want
> And the two that we all adore
> Are colourful, vital Kingsley Wood
> And glamorous Samuel Hoare.[42]

Yet the disappearance of the so-called 'Big Four' and of collective leadership (even if Chamberlain had been much more than *primus inter pares*) left something of a vacuum in the Conservative Party. Although Chamberlain's appeasement policy was most strongly supported by the Conservative Right,[43] the Big Four were well ahead of most of their back-benchers on home affairs. As has been seen, Chamberlain was the leading social reformer between the wars, and Hoare when Home Secretary produced a major Criminal Justice Bill, which even contained a clause abolishing judicial flogging. Despite the expected frenzied opposition from the press and many of his back-benchers, Hoare got the clause through its Committee stage before the bill was killed by the war.

Churchill could not have introduced a new collective leadership even had he wished to. He was running the war and had no time for anything else, thinking in any case that it was pointless to devote time and thought to political problems before the likely post-war world had a discernible shape. Eden was similarly occupied running the Foreign Office, even though he did add the leadership of the House of Commons to his responsibilities in 1942. Sir John Anderson, whom Churchill called the 'Home Front Prime Minister' and who was known in Whitehall as 'Jehovah', was not a Conservative. Formerly a dominant civil servant, he had only entered Parliament in 1938, standing as a National Government candidate. His election address told his constituents that he was 'not a party man' and that he preferred 'the moderate forms of socialism practised by the . . . National Government to the more extreme forms advocated in other quarters'.[44]

Nor could the friends and associates whom Churchill brought into the Government fill the gap. They had no standing in the party and no political base of their own. Lord Beaverbrook, who had tried to destroy Baldwin in 1930 and had memorably been likened to a harlot by his intended victim, was disliked and feared in all quarters of the House of Commons; MPs' hostility to him would have been all the greater had they known of Beaverbrook's activities during the 'Phoney War' when his defeatism verged on sedition, if not treason.[45] Others, such as Oliver Lyttelton and Lord Woolton, were able departmental Ministers who had little time and, at this stage at least, less taste for party politics.

Not surprisingly, many of the Chamberlainites were disgruntled; when Kingsley Wood left the War Cabinet early in 1942 (though remaining at the Treasury), they felt that there was 'not a single real Conservative' in the War Cabinet: as Churchill and Eden had opposed appeasement, they were not, Leo Amery wrote, classed 'as such'.[46] If the Chamberlainites were the real Conservatives, Churchill and Eden were happy to be thought unreal ones. Eden recorded that he and Churchill had agreed 'how little we liked [the Conservative Party] and how little it liked us'.[47]

In consequence, while the country was given a strong, inspiring lead by Churchill, the Conservative Party was scarcely led at all. Its main coalition partner was not similarly discomposed. Labour had not suffered an upheaval in 1940; instead of its leaders disappearing from public view they became suddenly prominent. With Number 10 and the Foreign Office occupied by Conservatives, the Labour members of the coalition were necessarily entrusted with largely domestic portfolios. The appointment of Ernest Bevin, the General Secretary of the Transport and General Workers Union, entrenched trade-union power and influence in Whitehall. The Labour Party's leaders had the opportunity to make a considerable impact on the country, and they took it. At the same time their position in government made a similar impact upon them.

14

The 1930s had been Labour's most discreditable decade. In the twenties, as we have seen, the two Labour Governments were scarcely, if at all, tinged with socialism. Indeed, when Winston Churchill invited his Labour predecessor as Chancellor to dine at 11 Downing Street together with Lord Haldane and P. J. Grigg, his private secretary at the Treasury whom he had inherited from Snowden, Grigg found Snowden the least 'socialistic of the three'.[48]

In the early thirties, however, Labour deviated sharply to the left. Much as the great slump and high unemployment did not breed strikes or industrial militancy, Labour's reduction after the 1931 election to a pathetic rump of fifty-two MPs – by far the smallest opposition since 1832 – did not lead to wild scenes of disorder in the House of Commons. It led instead to verbal extremism and folly. While Joseph Stalin was killing millions of Kulaks in the Ukraine, Sir Stafford Cripps lamented that we did not have 'a workers' government in this country, as they have in Russia'. Despite the experience of the two Labour Governments, the Labour Party existed, Cripps wrote, 'for no other purpose than for the economic revolution to socialism'. To ensure the success of that revolution, the Socialist Party would probably have to prolong 'the life of parliament for a further term without an election'.[49]

All this (and much more) could be ignored as the ravings of a man who was, in Hugh Dalton's words, 'becoming a dangerous political lunatic',[50] were it not that Cripps was far from alone in his lunacy. 'I associate myself with [Cripps's] conclusions,' Clement Attlee wrote. After outlining how the actual socialist paradise could not be achieved without energetic, socialist district commissioners, Attlee admitted that this might be thought rather like the Russian plan of commissars, but he was not afraid of the comparison. Conceding that he had strayed 'into autocracy to some extent' during the transition to socialism, Attlee felt there was no need to worry because there would be full 'democracy as soon as the Socialist State is in being'.[51]

Fortunately, during the thirties, the true nature of Soviet Communism had been revealed to all who did not insist on remaining blind to it. Stalin's atrocities had become known even to the British Left, some of whom excused them as a necessary price to pay for the achievement of socialism. Except by such true believers, however, the millenarian fantasies of a socialist dictatorship were abandoned and, although Cripps was urging factory workers to refuse to make armaments as late as 1937, Labour had moved back towards the centre well before 1939, a process which was completed when the Labour leaders assumed high office in the Churchill Government.[52]

Labour's return to reformism was a reversion to the twenties when, as we have seen, there had been strong continuity between the policies in Government of the two major parties. Hence there was nothing surprising about the consensus that was formed under the wartime coalition, even though the different circumstances ensured that this consensus was further to the left than its predecessor.

At first there was little to have a consensus about, except to wage war as vigorously as possible. In 1940 and 1941 the end of the war seemed too far away for peacetime problems to merit much consideration. Even in 1940, however, Churchill told the boys of his old school, Harrow, that when the war was won, one of their aims should be 'to establish a state of society where the advantages and privileges which have hitherto been enjoyed only by the few shall be far more widely shared by the many . . .'[53] 1942 saw some of the worst disasters of the war, but thoughts had begun to turn towards post-war reconstruction. By then, the peril the country faced, its almost total mobilisation, high taxation, and the belief that pre-war Britain was a much worse place than it should have been, for which its mainly rich and upper-class leaders bore the blame, had bred a strong feeling of egalitarianism and collectivism.

Though irksome to more than a few, rationing was a great leveller. Not only did it ensure a degree of equality but, combined with free school milk and vitamins for children, it brought an end to undernourishment for the third of the population which had not been properly fed before the war. The nation, the popular Minister of Food Lord Woolton said in 1941, 'had never been in better health for years'.[54]

Plainly there could be no return to the Britain of the thirties. Almost everybody except a few businessmen – such as the Director of the Confederation of British Employers, who told Sir William Beveridge that 'we did not start this war with Germany to improve our social services'[55] – accepted that Britain was fighting not only against Hitler but also for a better society. In the war for freedom against tyranny, only a few thought the freedom they were fighting for was the freedom to be permanently unemployed and to rear undernourished children in an urban slum. If Britain could so impressively combine in war, the strong feeling was that she could and should do the same in peace. Such was the background to the politicians' discussion of the problems of peacetime Britain.

This general desire for a better post-war world was focused, and seemed to be made concrete, by the Beveridge Report on *Social Insurance and Allied Services* which was published at the beginning of December 1942. It soon enjoyed a phenomenal success, selling more than 600,000 copies. Much to do with the Report was fortuitous. The inquiry which led to it either would not have taken place or would have had no very significant outcome, had not the permanent officials at the Ministry of Labour found the egotistical Beveridge an impossible colleague. The Minister, Labour's Ernest Bevin, had initially opposed an interdepartmental inquiry into Social Security; he changed his mind when he saw that it offered a way of getting rid of Beveridge, who he suggested should be its chairman. Beveridge himself did not at first see what an opportunity he had been given, and was hurt and angry at having been kicked upstairs. The Report's publication date, shortly after the victory of El Alamein had created a new mood of optimism, contributed mightily to its remarkable popularity with the public.[56]

'A revolutionary movement in the world's history', Beveridge wrote, 'is a time for revolutions, not for patching.' His proposals were not in fact revolutionary. To some extent he was articulating views that were already widely held in informed circles, and his reliance on the insurance principle was far from radical. Yet nobody could accuse him of 'patching'. His plan was all-embracing; everybody was to be included. Assuming a National Health Service, a system of family allowances for all children, and a high level of employment, Beveridge regarded his Report as merely a stage in 'a comprehensive policy of social progress' against the 'five giants on the road of reconstruction'. These giants were Want, Ignorance, Squalor, Idleness and Disease; relying on co-operation between the individual and the state, Beveridge aimed to slay all of them and, through a plan of insurance, to provide an adequate income for all citizens.[57]

The Beveridge Report put the Government in considerable difficulty. The proposals were so popular at home and would provide such valuable propaganda in Occupied Europe that they could not be rejected out of hand. Indeed, Anthony Eden had earlier thought that Social Security should be 'the first object of our policy' after the war. Yet, as Bevin acknowledged, no government could have been expected meekly to accept so far-reaching a plan without looking carefully at its recommendations and its cost.[58] Furthermore, to put the report into force straight away might have instilled doubts in our allies as to whether Britain was still concentrating her energies on winning the war. Indeed, Beveridge seemed to think, Attlee later said, that 'the war ought to stop while his plan was put into effect'.[59] The Americans might argue, Churchill's scientific adviser Lord Cherwell told him, that they were being asked to pay for Britain's social services. The Prime Minister himself, who at this time was still strongly in favour of postponing controversial questions until Hitler had been defeated, was worried that 'a dangerous optimism' about peacetime possibilities was already sprouting in the country. Reminding his colleagues of the economic difficulties the peace-time Government would face, he warned against deceiving the people by raising 'false hopes and airy visions of Utopia and Eldorado'.[60]

Bevin's idea of setting up a committee to examine the Report's proposals in detail was accepted. At the Treasury, Maynard Keynes, who had helped Beveridge, felt 'wild enthusiasm' for his general scheme and thought there was nothing in it 'which need frighten a mouse'. Nevertheless Kingsley Wood reacted to the Report as almost any Chancellor of the Exchequer – and certainly Snowden – would have done. Relentlessly negative and pessimistic about it, Wood was also far-sighted in questioning Beveridge's confidence that the general finance of his scheme could be carried without any undue difficulty. Since Beveridge's optimism was based on a naïve belief in the efficacy of state ownership and control of the means of production – only later did Beveridge become a Keynesian – the Treasury's scepticism was better founded than it knew. Wood summed up his attitude by asking Churchill in a personal note, 'Is this the time to assume that the general taxpayer has a bottomless purse?'[61] Yet the Government had to deal with the problems of the day and the immediate post-war world, not with those which might or might not be present fifty years later; the state of public opinion ruled out any possibility of the Government cold-shouldering the Beveridge plan. Post-war Reconstruction had been forced onto the political agenda.

Leo Amery thought the Report's 'main features ... were not only sound but essentially Conservative, and the cost ... by no means excessive', as did Quintin Hogg, who while serving in Egypt had seen that Beveridge had made a great impact on both officers and men in Cairo. Yet when he returned to London, Hogg found that most of the Conservative Party shared the Treasury's reservations, plaintively asking 'Where is the money coming from?' Now the old collective leadership was most missed. Without it, there was nobody to guide the people whom Baldwin had called 'Diamond Jubilee Die-hards' into the contemporary world; Butler found them a 'stupid lot'. They were prepared to accept family allowances but not much else. On the other wing of the party the newly formed Tory Reform Committee, which had some thirty-five Conservative MPs, including Hogg, Lord Hinchinbrooke and Peter Thorneycroft, wanted the Government to go much further: to accept the report and immediately set up a Ministry of Social Security. A Ministry of Social Insurance was established in October 1944.[62]

After he had read the Beveridge Report in detail early in 1943, the Prime Minister took a far more favourable view of it. Although still strongly believing that the wartime Cabinet should not seek to bind its peacetime successor, he had realised that the problems of peace could not be put aside until the war was over. The hopes and fears of the public demanded Government action, and preparations had to be made. Accordingly, in January, a Reconstruction Priorities Committee was set up; and in March Churchill set out his attitude and that of the Government in his longest broadcast of the war. He favoured the making of 'a Four Years' Plan' which 'would cover five or six large measures of a practical character', one of which would deal with National Insurance. After recalling that he had 'brought my friend Sir William Beveridge into the public service thirty-five years ago', he told his listeners that they must 'rank him and his colleagues as strong partisans of national compulsory insurance for all classes for all purposes from the cradle to the grave'. 'The best way to insure against unemployment', he continued, 'is to have no unemployment.' We could not afford 'to have idle people. Idlers at the top make idlers at the bottom.' The country 'must establish on broad and solid foundations a national Health Service ... there is no finer investment for any community than putting milk into babies.' Education, too, was of vital importance. The 'schooling of the great mass of our scholars' had to be 'progressively prolonged' and our schools and the training of teachers improved in good time. There was therefore plenty of material for a Four Years' Plan.

Meanwhile, during the war, the 'rule should be, no promises but every preparation, including, when requested, preliminary legislative preparation'. Before concluding, Churchill gave a resumé of his economic credo. 'The modern state will increasingly concern itself with the economic well-being of the nation, but it is all the more vital to revive at the earliest moment a widespread healthy and vigorous private enterprise, without which we shall never be able to provide, in the years when it is needed, the employment for our soldiers, sailors and airmen to which they are entitled after their duty has been done.'[63]

Despite the Prime Minister's sensible caution about legislating then for a post-war world, the mood of activity within the Government could not be confined to those whose energies were devoted to the prosecution of war, and the enthusiasm extended beyond Labour Ministers. In February 1944 the Conservative Minister of Health, Henry Willink, prepared a White Paper which proposed a free and comprehensive service but represented a compromise between the various interests involved; as such, it attracted criticism from all sides, but the underlying principles were not far from those eventually adopted by Aneurin Bevan in 1948. Rab Butler, who had disregarded Churchill's order not to risk causing religious controversy by bringing in a major education bill, managed to raise the school leaving age to fifteen and reorganise the funding of schools without provoking serious opposition through his great 1944

Act. This was the greatest advance in education since 1870; Butler thought it would 'have the effect of welding us into one nation ... instead of two nations as Disraeli talked about'.[64]

In May 1944 the government produced another compromise document, its White Paper on Employment Policy. Although it recognised the value of public works, its proposals stopped well short of a full endorsement of Keynesian economics. Indeed, Keynes could not understand its discussion of monetary policy, yet for him the opening words of the White Paper – 'This government accept as one of their primary aims and responsibilities the maintenance of a high and stable level of employment after the war' – were more important than the mish-mash which followed.[65] In September 1944 the coalition published another White Paper, this time accepting most of Beveridge's proposals on social insurance. Another milestone was the introduction of family allowances as part of a notable series of social policy measures unveiled to the House of Commons in November 1944. At the end of that month the Prime Minister himself pledged that the Government would press forward with the great programme of legislation 'which this remarkable coalition has framed'. Although no one could bind a future Parliament, he could not believe, he added, that 'any of us, whether in office or in opposition, who have been sponsors of this programme, will fail to march forward along the broad lines that have been set forth'.[66]

The Government was active in every field. That did not, of course, mean that Britain was 'socialist' during the war. Together with his colleagues in the Government, Attlee told Labour's National Executive, 'he held the view that the Labour party should not try to get socialist measures implemented under the guise of winning the war'. Like Churchill, Attlee well knew the difference between social reform and socialism.[67] F. A. Hayek did not. Understandably, perhaps, given his experiences before the war, he spotted the seeds of totalitarianism in even the mildest forms of collectivism. In 1944 he was disturbed by the 'drawing together' of what he called 'the socialists of the Left and Right'. It was, Hayek believed, 'conservative socialism which is the dominant trend in this country now'.[68]* He might as well have called it 'socialist conservatism'. Hayek was deploring a degree of collectivism, which was recognised to be necessary by almost everybody except free-market ideologues.

Many voters, who would have deplored Hayek's conclusions, shared

---

* In 1847, after telling Guizot, the French Prime Minister, that 'the conservative principles are applicable to the most diverse situations', the Austrian Chancellor Metternich described himself as 'a conservative socialist'.[69]

his misconception about Britain's wartime policies. Among them was Churchill's daughter, Sarah, who told her father during the election, 'Socialism as practised in the war did no one any harm, and quite a lot of people good. The children of this country have never been quite so well fed or healthy, what milk there was was shared equally, the rich did not die because their meat ration was no larger than the poor; and there is no doubt that this common sharing and feeling of sacrifice was one of the strongest bonds that unified us. So why, they say, can not this common feeling of sacrifice be made to work as effectively in peace?'[70] Social solidarity and social reform were widely and wrongly equated with socialism.

In consequence, the 1945 election was the first and last one in which 'socialism' was a popular word. 'The Labour Party', said the party's manifesto, 'is a Socialist Party, and proud of it.'[71] Labour had kept such pride to itself in 1929 (though not of course in 1935), and did so again in later elections; in 1945 it could safely flaunt the word. And the Conservatives played into their hands. Lord Woolton claimed to be the man who decided after the war that 'we would call the [Attlee] Government the "Socialist Party"', and some historians have followed him. In fact the Conservative practice of talking about 'the Socialists' and 'the Socialist Party', not the Labour Party, was already rife in 1945. In his four election broadcasts Churchill constantly referred to Labour as the Socialist Party, and in the Conservative manifesto (then, according to custom, entitled *Mr Churchill's Declaration of Policy to the Electors*) he referred in his first sentence to 'the Socialist and Sinclair Liberal Parties'. Indeed, in his third election broadcast Churchill even complained of 'the Socialist Party calling themselves the Labour Party'.[72] All this was a mistake. Because of its association with so-called 'war socialism', the word socialist had become an asset to Labour and should have been avoided by their Conservative opponents.

The Conservative manifesto was superior to Labour's *Let Us Face the Future*, which harked back to the past while promising Utopia. *Mr Churchill's Declaration of Policy to the Electors* reflected the approach which the Prime Minister had adopted during the war. Accepting that 'the plans for social progress which we are determined to carry out' required 'a much higher rate of national expenditure than before the war', it also enshrined the traditional Conservative preference for empiricism over dogma. For example, the doctrinaire cases for and against nationalisation were rejected; arrangements in each industry would be studied on their merits. The manifesto aimed 'to make an early reduction in taxation [to] stimulate energy and permit free individual choice', but in view of the necessarily high level of wartime taxation, that was not an anticipation of Newt Gingrich and the 1994 Republican 'revolution' in the United States. The priorities developed by the coalition – full employment, a National Health Service, and comprehensive social security – were of course adopted and were to be pursued by a future Conservative Government. In conclusion, the manifesto declared that the great material progress of recent generations 'must be extended and accelerated not by subordinating the individual to the authority of the state, but by providing the conditions in which no one shall be precluded by poverty, ignorance, insecurity or the selfishness of others from making the best of the gifts with which Providence has endowed him'.[73]

Unfortunately, the party did not fight the election on its manifesto. Apart from an excellent broadcast by Eden, who half hoped to lose the election, it fought it on scares, on hatred of socialism, and on Churchill's personality and achievements. The Prime Minister set the tone in his first election broadcast. There could be no doubt, he said, that 'Socialism is inseparably intertwined with Totalitarianism and the abject worship of the State . . . I declare to you from the bottom of my heart', he went on, 'that no Socialist system can be established without a political police . . . No Socialist Government conducting the entire life and industry of the country could afford to allow free, sharp, or violently-worded expressions of public discontent. They would have to fall back on some form of *Gestapo*, no doubt very humanely directed in the first instance.'[74]

That lamentable broadcast was, deservedly, not a success. Although Labour's lead narrowed during the campaign, it probably did irreparable damage.[75] Churchill's outburst was all the more extraordinary in that the country was, of course, still at war. For the Prime Minister to attempt to undermine the democratic credentials of his trusted colleagues, whom he had recently pressed to remain in a brilliantly successful coalition with him but who also would have to lead the fight against tyranny in Japan if he lost the election, was an astounding aberration. Churchill's wife, Clemmie, begged him to take out the word 'Gestapo', but he was adamant.[76]

Had Attlee, Bevin and Morrison and Cripps still held the views expressed by Cripps and Attlee in the early thirties, then there would at least have been some logic, if not wisdom, in Churchill's 'Gestapo' allegation. But after working closely with them for the last five years, Churchill knew them to be democratic patriots and was well aware that their 'socialism' was vastly nearer to Snowden's than to Stalin's or Hitler's. Not surprisingly, Churchill became depressed about his electioneering. Just before his third broadcast of the campaign, his wife wrote to their daughter, Mary, 'He thinks he has lost his "touch"'; and temporarily he had.[77]

As usual, the British electoral system magnified the extent of the Conservative defeat. The party won some 40 per cent of the national vote which, in the light of the unpopularity of the 1930s and the perceived Conservative responsibility for the war, was higher than it might have been. All the same, the Conservative defeat was, apart from 1906, the heaviest the party had suffered since 1832. After dinner at Chequers on Sunday 29 July everyone signed the Visitors Book. Churchill signed last of all, and underneath his signature he wrote: 'Finis'.[78] The future did indeed look bleak for him and the Conservative Party and correspondingly long and secure for Labour and the Attlee Government.

CHAPTER II

1945–51: 'The Road to Serfdom'?

By the time Parliament reassembled, the depleted ranks of Conservative MPs had sufficiently forgotten their leader's electoral performance to greet his entry into the Commons Chamber with the most rousing cheer of his career; they then broke into 'For he's a jolly good fellow', which the old Chamberlainite, 'Chips' Channon, feared was an 'error in taste'.* With much more cause for celebration than the Opposition, Labour joined the sing-song with a loud rendering of 'The Red Flag'. Unaware of what had happened earlier, the displaced Minister of Production, Oliver Lyttelton, was hurrying to his place on the Opposition front bench as 'The Red Flag' began. Until that moment, Lyttelton was enjoying the prospect of life without the pressures of office, but now he 'began to fear' for his country.[2]

Outside the Chamber, the coalition spirit was more prevalent, especially among the leaders. Lyttelton's patriotic misgivings were soon seen to be as unfounded as similar Tory fears after their other disaster in 1906. The foreign policy of Labour's Foreign Secretary, Bevin, was virtually indistinguishable from what Anthony Eden's would have been. Ernest Bevin, said Oliver Stanley, had learned 'The Importance of being Anthony'. And so far from Labour's home policy requiring a Nazi 'Gestapo', most of it was based on policies and ideas that had been formulated by Churchill's wartime coalition. The danger the country faced was not dictatorship, but bankruptcy.

More highly mobilised for war than any other country, Britain had incurred, in Attlee's words, an 'immense deficit' on the balance of payments.[3] Serious as this was, it did not seem to amount to an imminent crisis for the incoming Government. The war was expected to continue for at least another year and, so long as it lasted, Britain's external

---

* No doubt it was unparliamentary, but it was not unprecedented: after a stirring speech by the Younger Pitt in 1797, the House sang 'Britons, Strike Home'.[1]

deficit would largely be covered by Lend-Lease from the United States. For better or worse, however, the atomic bombs on Hiroshima and Nagasaki ended the war in a matter of days, and Truman, the new and inexperienced American President, ended Lend-Lease without warning less than a week later. Thus Britain was confronted with what Lord Keynes thought to be 'without exaggeration . . . a financial Dunkirk'.[4] Although Keynes trusted that we would recover from it, the financial equivalent of the victorious Battle of Britain which followed the real Dunkirk was to seek a loan from the United States, and this time the outcome was different: the victor was the United States.

Keynes, who was the chief British negotiator in Washington, was initially optimistic. After all, Britain's parlous situation was the result of her unique war effort. Her overseas military expenditure had exceeded America's; her economy had suffered from her war effort, whereas America's had enormously benefited; her contribution in the form of reciprocal aid to the United States had not, relative to her resources, been much less than the US contribution in the form of Lend-Lease to the British Empire; and finally Britain had spent $3 billion – which was more than half of what she received under Lend-Lease – buying arms in the United States before Lend-Lease had come into full operation and America had entered the war. In consequence, Britain had no net overseas assets, and as late as 1951 her total real wealth was no greater than it had been in 1913.[5] Here, surely, was an unanswerable case for generous treatment from an ally with whom, it was widely believed, Britain enjoyed a unique relationship.

Unfortunately, that was not how the Americans saw the position. They were not prepared even to consider a grant or an interest-free loan which Keynes considered to be necessary and justified; and among other unwelcome and unrealistic demands they insisted that sterling should become convertible into dollars a year after the loan agreement had come into force. Though onerous in the circumstances, the American terms were generous by commercial standards. (Canada's was more so: with a much smaller economy, she lent Britain one-third as much as the US.) All the same, the wartime partnership between the two countries had not been a commercial one, and many in Britain were dismayed by the deal that Keynes had negotiated. Uncle Sam, they felt, was being Uncle Scrooge. Yet, there being no realistic alternative, the Labour Government had to put aside its pride and pocket the money. The Opposition had more freedom and conspicuously used it. While the Conservative leadership enjoined abstention in the Commons vote, only 119 MPs stuck to the official line: eight voted for the loan and seventy-eight voted against it.

The negotiations and outcome of the American loan revealed that, although Britain retained (until 1947) the largest Empire ever seen, she was no longer a great power in the sense that America now was, and that while the British regarded their relationship with the United States as unique, the Americans took a less exalted view of their links with Britain. Winston Churchill called for 'a special relationship' in his Fulton Speech in March 1946. During the next fifty years British politicians assumed that Churchill's wish had been granted, and the phrase 'special relationship' was frequently on the lips of British politicians and journalists. American leaders rarely used the same rhetoric, because except in intelligence and defence they did not recognise such a relationship. Yet myths prevail because they are more acceptable than reality. The myths both of the special relationship and of Britain's continued standing as a great power lingered on – and among the Right still do. Hence British ideas and attitudes about the country's international status for long remained as out of date as its economy, its industry and the structure of its trade unions.[6]

'Convertibility' duly produced a sterling crisis and had to be abandoned within a month. By then America had begun to realise that its own self-interest demanded enlightened generosity, and its Marshall Plan for Europe soon helped to alleviate Britain's economic plight. While convertibility was far from being Labour's only crisis or blunder, the Government had considerable economic achievements to its credit. Except during the fuel crisis of 1947, full employment was maintained throughout the five years from 1946 to 1951 – average unemployment was less than 2 per cent in every year – industrial production rose by one-third during the same period, exports and investment recovered, strikes were few, productivity rose and inflation was initially low; later, however, the rise in world prices triggered by the Korean War brought an acceleration which resulted in prices during the tenure of the Labour Government rising by over one-third. Furthermore, the rise in consumption per head was held down to about one per cent a year, which was good for the country but damaging to Labour. In view of this record, the verdict of the Attlee Government's economic historian that 'the years 1945–51 set the stage for Britain's post-war economic development' seems just.[7]

In its social policy and elsewhere, the government carried out most of its 1945 election programme, some of which it would have done better to forget or at least tone down. Beveridge's proposals on National Insurance were implemented in an Act of 1946, and Aneurin Bevan secured legislation to set up a National Health Service in the same year. Against constant Treasury criticisms, ministers refused to sacrifice increased social spending – at least until April 1951, when the Chancellor Hugh Gaitskell introduced National Health charges as the defence budget soared during the Korean War.

Only over nationalisation did Labour's policies notably diverge from those outlined by the wartime coalition. Its nationalisation policy also diverged from what its leaders had originally intended. At the 1944 Party Conference the leadership's main economic resolution, which did not even mention nationalisation, was contemptuously cast aside, and a resolution from the floor, moved by the left-winger Ian Mikardo and supported by the young James Callaghan, calling for the nationalisation of all major industries, was put in its place. Congratulating Mikardo on his performance, Herbert Morrison added, 'You do realise, don't you, that you've lost us the general election?' Not even nationalisation could defeat Labour in 1945, but the issue did damage the party in later elections.[8]

Not that Labour's nationalising measures, which resulted in over a fifth of the economy being taken into public ownership, were at first acutely controversial. The Conservatives had little objection to the nationalisation of the Bank of England, which in Churchill's opinion did not 'raise any matter of principle',[9] and they did not make a great fuss over coal and the railways being taken into public ownership. Before the war, after all, they had themselves created the Central Electricity Board and set up similar corporations to run the BBC, the Tote and Civil Aviation; in 1938 they had nationalised coal deposits. And when, during the war, Oliver Lyttelton was asked by Herbert Morrison what he would do with the coal industry, Lyttelton replied, 'Nationalise it.'[10] Paradoxically, indeed, prudent nationalisation would in some ways have been a more appropriate policy for the Conservatives than for Labour; they certainly thought of it first.

When the Attlee Government nationalised Cable and Wireless, the Chancellor of the Exchequer, Hugh Dalton, exulted: 'The socialist advance continues.'[11] Herbert Morrison indulged in similar ecstasies over the nationalisation of the coal industry, urging miners and management to emancipate themselves from the crude capitalism of the past and become 'co-operators and partners in a great and worthy adventure for the common good'.[12] Yet what, if anything, Labour's nationalisation ventures had to do with socialism is hard to discern. The previous shareholders were fairly, or rather, very generously, compensated, so that the distribution of income was not altered and the capitalists were not weakened;* if anything, they were strengthened, being freed to invest in flourishing instead of declining companies. The centralised structures

---

* The total paid in compensation was £2.6 billion – the US loan was £3.75 billion.[13]

of the new nationalised industries, based on the pre-war model of the London Passenger Transport Board (itself copied by Herbert Morrison from the Conservatives' Central Electricity Board) produced managements that were no less remote from their workers than the previous capitalist regime. Workers' control was anathema to Morrison and the other architects of the new boards; there were no provisions for the introduction of industrial democracy, which was indeed heavily frowned upon; and no contribution was made to the blurring or blending of the two adversarial sides of industry. The trade unions in the nationalised industries were strengthened, but that facilitated not socialism, planning or industrial efficiency, but inflation, over-manning and strikes. The new boards did not even do much to provide good jobs for deserving socialists. With a disregard for party patronage scarcely comprehensible to those accustomed to the Walpolean habits of late twentieth-century governments, the Attlee administration stuffed its new boards with former pro-consuls, retired generals and Conservative capitalists.

All in all, therefore, Labour's nationalisations brought socialism no nearer. As Harold Macmillan said of coal nationalisation, 'this is not socialism; it is state capitalism'.[14] As such, nationalisation was an expedient to which either a Labour or a Conservative Government might legitimately resort when all else had failed – when the industry or company was moribund or bankrupt or when there was no prospect of competition – but for Labour to make it the centrepiece of its policy and the prize exhibit of 'socialism' defied all reason. (The successful socialist parties in Scandinavia were much more intelligent.) Nationalisation soon became, and stayed, deeply unpopular, yet the Labour Party clung to it for the next half-century, giving its Conservative opponents a constant and inviting target that was difficult to miss. Ironically, it was not until the orgy of privatisation in the eighties and nineties had again made state ownership popular and acceptable that Labour abandoned it.

Labour's self-inflicted wound of nationalisation was made deeper by the Government's incompetence. That coal stocks were dangerously low, largely because there were not enough miners, had long been plain to many people, including some ministers. Yet nothing was done. The minister immediately responsible, Emanuel Shinwell, was confident all would be well. 'Everybody knows', he boasted in October 1946, 'that there is going to be a serious crisis in the coal industry – except the Minister of Fuel and Power.'[15] That was virtually true; unfortunately, only four months later, in February 1947, 'everybody' was proved to be right and the Minister wrong. Shinwell blamed the disaster on the weather, the yet-to-be-nationalised railways and on 'capitalism'.[16] He was indeed unlucky with the terrible weather, but the responsibility for the crisis lay squarely with his own complacent inactivity. The restrictions imposed on industry's use of power drastically cut industrial production and exports, and in the ensuing chaos unemployment rose temporarily to about two million. The Government trumpeted its belief in economic planning; it was conspicuously unable to achieve it.

The convertibility crisis of July and August of the same year was not self-induced; it was largely imposed by the terms of the American loan. Yet it too showed the Government's inability to plan and, like coal, convertibility was mishandled. The Government's forecasts were wrong, and its attempts to mitigate, if not ward off, the sterling crisis by cutting imports and expenditure were tardy and inadequate. Nobody emerged with credit.

Two years later, a mini-recession in the United State precipitated a 30 per cent devaluation of the pound against the dollar. In both May and July 1949 the Chancellor, Sir Stafford Cripps, denied any intention of devaluing, but while he was in a Swiss sanatorium the Government decided to reverse his policy. The United States was properly warned; France and other European countries were not. Although it had been too long delayed, devaluation was an economic success – the economy was buoyant and inflation declined until the outbreak of the Korean War a year later – but it damaged both the Government's political standing and the Chancellor's moral authority.

In 1951 Labour maintained its record of having an economic crisis every other year, but this time it also had a political crisis when, in order to help pay for the rearmament caused by the war in Korea, the Chancellor, Hugh Gaitskell, insisted on introducing charges for dental care and spectacles. Aneurin Bevan (followed by Harold Wilson) resigned in protest at this desecration of 'his' free National Health Service. In reality, Bevan's differences with his colleagues went wider than false teeth and spectacles. Attlee had not offered him the Treasury or the Foreign Office when Cripps and Bevin fell ill, and he thought the scale of the Government's rearmament programme excessive. In this he was undoubtedly right. If the 1947 and 1949 crises had demonstrated London's decline in power and status relative to Washington, 1951 made that descent explicit. The strength of Britain's response to North Korea's aggression depended more on her wish to please the United States than on a sober assessment of foreign and domestic needs. The British Ambassador in Washington urged Attlee to send troops to Korea in order to confirm Britain's position as 'first in the queue' in Washington, and Gaitskell's highest priority in deciding upon the scale of rearmament was 'to show that Britain was America's best and firmest ally',[17] a demonstration which did heavy damage to the British economy. Thus the desire to confirm one British myth, that of 'the special relationship', demonstrated the falsity of the other – that Britain was still a great power.*

The British economy was the chief sufferer. In 1939–45 Britain had won the military and social war, but she had decisively lost the economic one. The failure to appreciate that fundamental fact was the chief cause of many of her post-war problems. Instead of posturing as one of the 'Big Three', we should have recognised that our economic defeat required a quite different outlook and conduct.

The Conservatives in Opposition

Labour's generous output of crises and its later nationalisation ventures gave its Conservative opponents valuable ammunition. Apart from the two short-lived minority Labour Governments of 1923–4 and 1929–31, 1945 was the first time since May 1915 that the Conservative Party was wholly excluded from office, and the 1945 parliament was the first since 1906 in which the party's main opponents had an overall majority in the House of Commons. Not surprisingly, the party was at first badly disorientated. It now had fewer than half the MPs it had had before the election, and to make matters worse the quality of the new intake was not high.

After inevitable doubt and depression, Churchill decided to stay on as leader. As he was already over seventy and would be seventy-five at the probable date of the next general election, many of his followers expected (and even hoped) that he would leave, if not straightaway, in a year or two's time. 'Will he or won't he resign?' remained for the next ten years a constant preoccupation for his front-bench colleagues and in particular for Anthony Eden who sometimes feared that the premiership might after all elude him. Although Churchill remained immensely popular among the rank and file and in the country, in 1947 his leading colleagues deputed James Stuart, the Chief Whip, to suggest that in the interests of the party he should retire. Yet, however restive they became, most of them were well aware of his strong popular support, and there

---

* Neither the Labour nor the Conservative leadership remembered Lord Curzon's prediction that the loss of India would reduce us to a third-rate power. The politicians were not so clear-sighted as Sir Henry Tizard, the brilliant scientist and defence adviser, who remarked, 'We are a great nation, but if we continue to behave like a great power we shall soon cease to be a great nation.'[18]

was anyway scant chance of a ruthless coup being led by his heir-apparent. As the years went by, Eden was increasingly frustrated by Churchill's clinging to the leadership; 'Winston', he rather obscurely told Lord Halifax in 1946, 'is like a porpoise in the bath and one of uncertain moods.'[19] Yet in any confrontation between them, Eden was a minnow easily swallowed by the porpoise.

Having seen the mistakes made by Balfour and the Conservatives after 1906 from the best of vantage points – as a Minister in the Liberal Government – Churchill was not likely to repeat them. As Evelyn Waugh noted, 'nothing could be more unfortunate for [Churchill's] reputation than for him to start a clause-by-clause heckling opposition'.[20] Instead, he adopted a cautious approach to the tasks of Opposition and to the new Government. This disappointed his back-benchers, some of whom thought he was more negligent than cautious. Both he and Eden were tired after their wartime exertions, and neither was anxious to undergo the drudgery of daily attendance at Westminster. Before long, the 1922 Committee of back-benchers and the Whips complained of their infrequent attendance; back-benchers also complained of their limited hostility to the Government.

The back-benchers' resentment of their leaders being Laodicians rather than zealots like themselves was understandable but mistaken. For at least three reasons restrained Opposition was the only sensible course for the party to follow. First, as their leader pointed out in the debate on the King's Speech, most of Labour's proposed legislation had been 'prepared by our joint exertions during the coalition'. They are, he said later in the year, 'in great measure our own Bills'.[21] Secondly, the electorate appeared to have overwhelmingly endorsed Labour's pro-posals for post-war Britain. And thirdly, there was considerable doubt as to what the Conservative attitude was or should be. The need for sensible restraint had been clearly demonstrated by its abandonment over Bevan's Health Service Bill during the first session of the Parliament. By its violent attacks on the Minister and by putting down extremist reasoned amendments on both second and third reading, the party gave the impression of being opposed to the principles of a National Health Service. This was not only contrary to party policy, it was bad politics and did considerable damage.

Churchill still took something of a coalition attitude to internal poli-tics. This did not inhibit him, however, from launching fierce attacks on the Government when necessary. He thought the problems which faced Britain after the war 'required the strength of a united people to solve and overcome'. Instead, the Government had 'raised this great schism of militant socialism in the land', and 'set themselves to establish the rule of a party and a sect within a party . . . Before they nationalised our industries', he added 'they should have nationalised themselves.'[22] Obviously such a stance precluded the Opposition from espousing any form of 'doctrinaire Conservatism', whatever that might have been, and from adopting plainly factional policies. Yet Churchill went further. He declined to commit the party to definite policies of any sort, which disappointed and irritated many of his followers. This impatience was felt mainly on the Left where the realisation was strongest that the party was still damagingly identified with the thirties, a decade which fairly or unfairly was widely deemed to have been disastrous. Hence the desire of the Left for some new and different policies to convince the voters that the party had changed and was at home in the post-war world.

Yet, like Disraeli and Balfour before him, Churchill remained sure that detailed policy-making in Opposition was a mistake: it would tie the hands of the next Conservative Government and cripple the party now. 'When an Opposition spells out its policy in detail,' he told Butler, 'the Government becomes the Opposition and attacks the Opposition which becomes the Government. So, having failed to win the sweets of office, it fails equally to enjoy the benefits of being out of office.'[23] Then at Edinburgh in April 1946 he defined Conservative policy as 'Liberty with security; stability combined with progress; the maintenance of religion, the Crown and Parliamentary Government' – which was no great help to party workers on the doorstep and sounded like a pastiche of Disraeli's celebrated speech at the Crystal Palace.[24] Nevertheless, such was the pressure from below that Eden and Oliver Stanley were able later in the year to persuade their leader that some sort of document must be produced to feed the faithful. Accordingly he set up a committee under the chairmanship of Butler to consider industrial policy.

Rab Butler had become Chairman of the Conservative Research Department shortly after the election defeat. At that time there was little to be chairman of, but Michael Fraser, whom Butler rightly described as 'the best adjutant the party has ever had',[25] and the talented Peter Goldman were soon recruited, and by the end of 1946 the Department was up to strength. The Conservative Political Centre, which had been set up under 'Cub' Alport a year earlier, worked closely with Butler, and then in 1948 the Parliamentary Secretariat which provided briefs for MPs and speeches for Shadow Ministers amalgamated with the Research Department. As the secretariat included the extraordinarily able trio of Iain Macleod, Reginald Maudling and Enoch Powell, Butler had in 1948 a unique galaxy of talent at his disposal.

Two years earlier, because of his Chairmanship of the party's Post-

War Problems Central Committee and his much-praised Education Act, Butler had been the obvious choice to chair the Industrial Committee. Like Churchill, he was chary of embarking upon detailed policy-making, though less for Churchill's reasons than because he doubted if the time was yet ripe for it; in other words, he wanted to be sure that the party was facing the right direction before it made firm commitments. The members of the Industrial Policy Committee included three future Chancellors of the Exchequer – Butler himself, Macmillan and Derick Heathcoat-Amory – Oliver Stanley, who had he lived would have been Churchill's first Chancellor in 1951, and three future Cabinet ministers, Oliver Lyttelton, David Maxwell Fyfe and David Eccles. Its findings were therefore likely to carry weight and, since most of its members were on the left of the party, of a nature likely to appeal to Butler. Both expectations were fulfilled.

The Committee's *Industrial Charter* did indeed achieve general acceptance. Churchill had played little part in it, but he placed Butler on his right hand at a dinner of shadow ministers at the Savoy, plied him with brandy and was complimentary about his work. Four days after its publication Churchill gave the charter more formal support, saying that it had been 'written in a spirit of honest and progressive realism' and was 'a broad statement of policy to which those who are opposed to the spread of rigid socialism can now rally'. Nevertheless, the charter was not yet party policy. The right-wing former chairman of the party, Ralph Assheton, privately said that it would be likely to lead to 'socialism of the worst kind', the Beaverbrook press attacked it for being left wing, and Sir Waldron Smithers, MP, who was then considered to be on the lunatic fringe of the right, but would now probably be thought a moderate Thatcherite, produced a thirty-page pamphlet entitled 'Save England'.

On the other side Harold Macmillan denied that the charter was 'pink socialism', a Central Office pamphlet pointed out that *laissez-faire* had been 'an interlude which ended long before the end of the nineteenth century', and most importantly Anthony Eden made a number of approving speeches, drafted by Reginald Maudling, an assistant secretary to the Committee. At the Party Conference at Brighton an amendment moved by Maudling, accepting the charter as 'a clear statement of the general principles of Conservative economic policy', was carried with only three dissentient votes, one of Maudling's opponents being Smithers's ideological twin, Sir Herbert Williams, who after proclaiming that there could be 'no compromise with socialism or communism' urged the Conference to 'save the Conservative Party and England'. At his hotel Churchill congratulated Butler on his victory, and in his leader's speech dutifully read out the short paragraph on the subject written by the same Reginald Maudling, who had explained to him that 'this is what the Conference adopted'.[26]

The adoption of the *Industrial Charter* was a decisive moment in Conservative post-war history. As Quintin Hogg pointed out in a book published in the same year, the Conservative Party had long criticised *laissez-faire* capitalism as 'an ungodly and rapacious scramble for ill-gotten gains, in the course of which the rich appeared to get richer and the poor poorer'. Yet because the party was now opposing Socialism whereas in the nineteenth century it had opposed Liberalism, 'its most ignorant opponents' could accuse it of being the party of *laissez-faire*. The *Industrial Charter* made such accusations unconvincing. Calling for 'a partnership between the Government, Industry and the Individual', it sought 'a system of free enterprise ... which reconciles the need for central direction with the encouragement of individual effort', and reaffirmed the commitment to full employment enshrined in the 1944 White Paper.[27]

Like Hogg's book, the *Industrial Charter* strongly opposed any further nationalisation, but did not promise to bring back into private ownership any of the industries already nationalised. This was neither as inconsistent nor as pusillanimous as it seems at first sight. In 1947 only the Bank of England, coal, the railways, electricity and gas had been taken over by Labour. In none of these industries was any genuine competition at that time present, all of them needed reorganisation, and all of them except coal would have had to be regulated if they had been denationalised. They were thus very different from other industries likely to suffer nationalisation by the Attlee Government.

In contrast with Hogg's book, the prose of the *Industrial Charter* was not exhilarating. As Margaret Thatcher later commented, it 'hardly made the pulse beat faster', although anybody whose pulse was quickened by a party policy document might well be in need of medical attention. In any case, the document was not intended to stir the blood of party activists but to demonstrate that the policy positions embraced by the party during the war were not going to be ditched in peacetime. From then on, although the Conservative Party 'still contained', as Sir Robert Rhodes James has written, 'a depressing number of reactionaries in Parliament and outside', it was unequivocally committed to a mixed economy and the rejection of unregulated capitalism. As Butler told Lord Woolton two years later, it 'placed the party on the fairway of modern economic and political thought';[28] and there it remained for some thirty years, until the leaders of the party decided that, like Herbert Williams and Waldron Smithers, they preferred the rough – though it is fair to say that by then many economists and financial journalists had redesigned the golf course.

The *Industrial Charter* was indeed, as Harold Macmillan claimed, more a restatement of Conservative principles than a radical break with the past. The National Governments of the thirties had by the standards of the time been decidedly interventionist; *laissez-faire* was thought to be old-fashioned. By 1947 the centralised war economy, the spread of Keynesian ideas and the paramount need to preserve full employment had altered the 'circumstances' which, to Conservatives, always are, or should be, of overriding importance. Hence the 'centre' of British politics had shifted from where it had stood before the war towards a greater role for Government in guiding the economy. Even though the performance of the pre-war Governments had been nowhere near as bad as was popularly believed, it was the popular perception that counted. So the party had to convince the voters that post-war Conservatism was different – a hard task. As late as 1949, a party survey suggested that memories of the thirties still created scepticism about the sincerity of its current attitudes, especially in industrial areas. This was particularly disappointing, since the *Industrial Charter* had included proposals on worker participation in decision-making which should have dispelled any misconceptions about the party. Such an enlightened attitude to factory management was well in advance of Labour Party thinking at the time – and indeed of Conservative Party thinking fifty years later. None of the authors of the *Industrial Charter* would have raised even an eyebrow at the *Protocol on Social Policy*, agreed in 1992 by all the countries in the European Union save Britain. Yet in the 1990s Conservative Ministers spent much time denouncing that innocuous document.

By the time *The Right Road for Britain* was published in July 1949, the position was drastically different. Nationalisation was already unpopular. The annual reports of the taken-over industries made gloomy reading for enthusiasts of public ownership, and Churchill felt able to claim that 'the complete failure of nationalisation is already apparent. The experiment has cost us dear . . .'[29]

No less important, by 1949 Labour had nationalised the road haulage industry and was in the throes of doing the same to iron and steel, in which it was impeded by the House of Lords. Both road haulage and iron and steel were in a different category from the previous targets for state ownership. Whereas few people (if anybody) would have risked their money to buy back coal, railways, electricity or gas (which had anyway been municipally, not privately, owned before) there would be little difficulty in finding owners for steel or road haulage. Furthermore, unlike the previous victims, denationalised road haulage and steel would not suffer from lack of competition. There was therefore a clear difference of principle between them and their predecessors which demanded different treatment. To leave coal, railways, gas and electricity under state control was in accordance with Conservative conduct before the war and with political and economic reality. On the other hand, not to promise to denationalise steel and road transport would have given the green light to Labour to threaten to nationalise any other industry which took its fancy. Not surprisingly therefore, *The Right Road* undertook to return road transport and steel to private hands. As for the others, where it was not practicable to denationalise, Eden promised, they would decentralise. He conceded that it was a poor substitute for free enterprise, 'but once the eggs have been scrambled, it is not at all easy to get them back in their shells'.[30]

The Right Road, which had a foreword by the leader evoking Disraeli and Lord Randolph Churchill, was considerably more polemical than its predecessor. The *Industrial Charter* had been measured in tone primarily because it was addressed to opinion-formers and also because the next election was still far off. By 1949, the 1945 Parliament was drawing to a close, and the nationalisation controversies had sharpened party conflict, as had Labour's succession of crises. At the same time the country's tolerance of continued austerity and controls – in some spheres even greater than during the war – was wearing thin. At least one of the reasons for the Government's hair-shirt attitude was praiseworthy: its desire to curb consumption at home in order to permit exports to boom. But Ministers also seemed to think that austerity – Macmillan called it 'fish and Cripps'[31] – was laudable in itself, that it was a proper and indispensable part of the socialist uniform. Indeed, with the failure of nationalisation to achieve its proclaimed objective of creating a new industrial climate and spirit among the nationalised work force and the palpable inability of the Government to plan the economy, austerity seemed to be just about the only socialist garment available. At all events, controls and the drabness of everyday life were increasingly resented, which provided the Tories with a promising election issue. So promising was it that the Government, in the person of thirty-two-year-old Harold Wilson, President of the Board of Trade, tried to blunt or pre-empt it by lighting a bonfire of controls on 5 November 1948. That move was only partially successful since many controls escaped the flames. So, for most of the time, did wage restraint; real wages scarcely rose under the Attlee Governments, although real earnings did.[32] A full explanation of the continued need for sacrifice would have laid bare Britain's reduced international status, a confession that the Government was not ready to make because, like the Conservative Opposition, it did not recognise the true situation. The way was open, therefore, for the Conservatives to blame austerity exclusively on the 'discredited' socialist experiment. By magnifying the differences between the parties, they could harvest the votes of those who, surfeited with high-minded sacrifice, hungered for fewer controls and lower taxes. *The Right Road* caught this mood, and with its publication the party's policy-making exercise was complete in good time for the election.

Although sharp in tone, *The Right Road* was moderate in content. The wartime consensus was still intact and would remain so, whoever won the election. This consensus was not fixed; it evolved. Much the greater part of it originated under Churchill's coalition; it moved in a Labour direction in the immediate post-war years and then back in a Conservative direction from 1948 onwards. It was not, of course, a full-scale agreement or a party truce but an unwritten and unspoken understanding that the party battle, like eighteenth-century fighting, was a limited war and did not extend to the fundamentals of a welfare state, the maintenance of full employment or the continuance of Britain as a great power. As Churchill put it in 1954, 'party differences are now in practice mainly those of emphasis'.[33]

Much, though, as even limited war can cause heavy casualties, the limited party war did not preclude bitter words, unfair criticisms and outrageous allegations not just from extreme partisans on the outside wings of their parties but from centrist politicians. The Conservative Shadow Ministers were often harsh in their language and unreasonable in their attacks – Eden was an exception. Yet Oliver Stanley, Harold Macmillan and others were models of eighteenth-century politeness compared to some Labour Ministers. In 1946 the Attorney General, Sir Harold Shawcross, who later in life moved to the far right of politics, displayed the arrogance of office by boasting, 'We are the masters at the moment – and not only for the moment, but for a very long time to come.'[34] Emmanuel Shinwell and Aneurin Bevan waged a verbal class war, contending that only the workers mattered. 'We know that you, the organised workers of this country, are our friends,' Shinwell told the conference of the Electrical Trades Union in 1947. 'As for the rest, they do not matter a tinker's curse.' Not to be outdone, Bevan, whose wartime criticisms of the Government had led to Churchill writing him off as 'a squalid nuisance', told a Manchester audience of his 'deep burning hatred for the Tory Party'. So far as he was concerned, he added, 'they are lower than vermin'. Such self-indulgent extremism angered Attlee and could only aid Labour's opponents, yet at the 1949 Party Conference both men continued in the same vein: predicting or threatening civil war if the Conservatives won the election. Even the (by now) highly respectable Stafford Cripps foolishly echoed Churchill's 'Gestapo' speech, claiming that a Conservative victory would inevitably lead to a totalitarian Britain.[35]

Organisational Reform

While the party's thinkers had been restoring its sense of direction, its 'doers' had also been revived and rejuvenated. During the war, the party organisation had been run down and the flow of Conservative propaganda had dried up. Believing that the war effort and the need for national unity superseded all other activities and considerations, the Conservatives interpreted the electoral truce which had been agreed by the three parties in September 1939 as a general political truce. Labour, on the other hand, lived by the letter rather than the spirit and confined its observance of the agreement to not putting up official party candidates at by-elections. It energetically continued all other party business, thereby showing that while it takes two to make peace it only takes one to make a truce. Hence Labour was very much better prepared for the election when it came than were their opponents.[36]

In July 1946, Churchill appointed Lord Woolton as the new Party Chairman. Woolton had been a non-party Minister of Food (late of Reconstruction) in the coalition, and only joined the Conservatives the day after their defeat, a gesture which greatly touched Churchill. Woolton's lack of a Conservative history – he had a left-wing background – was an asset in helping the party to live down its unpopular past, and he was altogether an excellent choice. Apart from being a successful businessman and a very good speaker, he had a genius for publicity and had been a popular figure during the war, acquiring the nickname of 'Uncle Fred'. He charmed party conferences, and used his authority to launch ambitious campaigns for funding and new members. At Brighton in October 1947 he appealed for £1 million, a target exceeded before the end of the year. A recruitment drive begun at Blackpool the previous year (when Woolton was new to the job) brought in over 200,000 recruits to the party, and a further initiative of April 1948 was directed at a million new members. Woolton soon got them. His reputation and popularity grew so tall, according to Woolton himself, that Churchill 'felt resentment against the amount of power that had come to me'. True or not, Churchill did try to get rid of him in 1952–3, but was frustrated by Woolton's enlistment of other party bigwigs to plead his cause; eventually Woolton outstayed Churchill.[37]

Woolton was a high-spending Chairman whose efforts ensured that by 1950 the Conservatives had more than twice as many constituency agents as Labour. In order to pay for them, he instituted a quota system, as recommended by a party committee, under which constituency parties were asked to contribute a sum proportional to the number of local Tory voters. The natural result was that those providing the money wanted to know how it was spent. Another party committee, under the far from radical Henry Brooke, responded by recommending more openness about the party's finances and the publication of accounts. No accounts were published, however. The party received so much more money from industrial sources and the City than it did from individual party members in the constituencies that to reveal it would have been embarrassing. Furthermore, questions would then have been asked about who the large donors were and what they got, or hoped to get, in return. Hence slightly shady secrecy was prudent for the party. Luckily Labour was not at that time in a good position to throw stones. Its Trade Disputes Act had substituted 'contracting-in' for 'contracting-out'. All trade unionists now had to pay the party a political levy unless they specifically asked not to, a change which brought Labour another 2,000,000 contributors.[38] Without stopping the rival parties attacking one another on the subject of finance, the presence of mutual disreputability did serve to dampen the conflict.

More edifying was the question of election expenses. Before the war Conservative candidates were expected to subsidise the activities of their local associations, a system which ensured the prevalence of rich men on the Tory benches. In 1925 Duff Cooper journeyed to Stroud in search of a seat and was relieved to find that instead of a barrage of questions on agriculture, which he was ill-equipped to answer, the association only 'enquired concerning my health, my religion and the amount I was prepared to contribute to local expenses'; later, after winning the Westminster by-election in 1931, he had to contribute only £100 a year to that wealthy constituency. The young Quintin Hogg was less fortunate, finding that £500 a year was the normal tariff for a safe seat, although one constituency demanded £3,000. During the war he condemned 'the virtual sale of safe seats' as 'a festering sore in the Conservative Party'.[39]

In 1944, a candidate's maximum contribution was fixed at £100 a year plus half the election expenses; under this provision nearly all the candidates to fight the 1950 election, including Edward Heath, Iain Macleod, Reginald Maudling and Enoch Powell, were chosen, thus providing men not only of powerful intellect but from a wider social base than had been seen in the pre-war parliamentary party. Finally, in 1949, a document called the Maxwell Fyfe Report – a little misleadingly, as Sir David had rather little to do with the proposals – recommended that candidates should not contribute to election expenses and that the maximum annual subscription of candidates should be £25 and of MPs £50. The Maxwell Fyfe Report thus registered a change that had already taken place; it was not itself the agent of change. Even in 1950, which saw the best post-war intake, a quarter of the parliamentary party were Old Etonians; only in the late sixties did the profile of candidates show much change and only in the eighties did that 'breed of professional politicians', which the reactionary Sir Herbert Williams had feared would be the outcome of the report, begin to appear in large numbers on the Conservative benches.[40]

Foreign Policy and Europe

In 1945 Ernest Bevin had claimed that 'Left understands Left, but the Right does not'.[41] That nonsense was soon forgotten when he got to the Foreign Office. An important element of the consensus was the Attlee Government's pursuit of, not a socialist foreign policy, but a Conservative one. So Conservative was it that when, notwithstanding the large British contribution to the invention of the atomic bomb and contrary to the wartime agreement to continue the sharing of information, America ended nuclear collaboration, the Government decided to build an independent nuclear deterrent. Labour had come a long way since 1934 when Attlee, denying in a vote of censure on the Air Estimates 'the need for increased air armaments', had proclaimed that his party had 'absolutely abandoned any idea of nationalist loyalty'.[42]

No wonder Churchill conceded in 1947 that the Labour Government had 'maintained a continuity' in foreign policy with that of his coalition.[43] Indeed, it was the wartime leader himself who was at first thought to have broken that continuity or bipartisanship in March 1946. In fact, like his pre-war utterances, Churchill's speech at Fulton, Missouri, in which he dramatically pointed to the descent of 'an iron curtain' across the Continent 'from Stettin in the Baltic to Trieste in the Adriatic', was prescient, not extreme. While calling for the creation of an international air force, for 'a special relationship between the British Commonwealth and Empire and the United States', for 'a new unity in Europe', and for the Western democracies and the English-speaking peoples to stand together in defence of freedom against tyranny, Churchill did not believe that war was imminent or that Soviet Russia desired war, only 'the fruits of war'; and he thought another war could be prevented by achieving 'a good understanding of all points with Russia under the general authority of the United Nations Organisation'.[44]

Before long, Churchill's warnings were widely accepted; so much so, he said eight months later, that if he had given them then they would have been 'regarded as a stream of platitudes'.[45] Yet at the time his realism, by destroying illusions about our gallant wartime ally, caused outrage to many. Reactions in the United States were almost wholly hostile, and President Truman distanced himself from the speech he had attended and had in advance privately admired. At home, Attlee and Bevin dissociated themselves from Churchill, and a hundred Labour MPs wanted a vote of censure on the speech. *The Times* maintained its dismal foreign policy record by criticising Churchill for contrasting Western democracy with Communism, suggesting that they had 'much to learn from each other'. Beaverbrook similarly opposed the speech, taking much the same view of Soviet Russia as before the war he had taken of Nazi Germany. Equally predictably, Stalin denounced Churchill as 'a warmonger', likening him to Hitler and his friends.[46] Less to be expected was the disagreement of Eden, who had not been consulted and who ungenerously thought Churchill almost wanted 'a war in order to stage a comeback'. Eden, however, was only critical in private.[47]

Like most people, Britain's post-war leaders frequently misled themselves by viewing the contemporary world and Britain's place in it through spectacles which had fitted them many years ago but which now distorted their vision. They all overestimated Britain's current power and status, Churchill speaking for many of them when he claimed that Britain was 'an equal partner [with the USA] in the English-speaking world', and that 'the foundations of British policy must be an ever closer association with the United States'.[48] They either did not notice, or were surprised, that the United States no longer treated Britain as an equal and, while welcoming British support, had no desire to join with her in 'an ever closer association'.

Nevertheless, none of the British leaders was consistent in his distorted vision. Variously they viewed certain parts of the world with contemporary eyes or even the eye of the future. Thus Attlee and Bevin were contemporary or prescient in their view of India and reasonably contemporary on China; but they were retrograde or reactionary when they looked at Europe or the Middle East, and after the loss of India hopelessly anachronistic in thinking that a new British Empire, almost as powerful as the old, could arise in Africa. In contrast, over India Churchill was, in Eden's words, an 'old Bengal Lancer',[49] and in the Middle East he was a similarly old-fashioned imperialist. Yet over Europe he was far ahead of almost everybody else, viewing it with the eyes of the

41

future. Eden, on the other hand, while sharing Churchill's concern about Mountbatten's undue haste, saw the need for fundamental change in India and initially took a fairly contemporary view of the Middle East, but over Europe he never caught up with the present, sticking obstinately to a past which had proved disastrous. That was probably why Eden, as Macmillan put it, 'stood aloof' from his leader's movement for a United Europe. Another possible cause is that Churchill did not want to commit his probable successor; or perhaps, as both Maxwell Fyfe and Boothby suspected, Eden's exclusion from the British delegation to the Assembly of the Council of Europe at Strasbourg was partly responsible for his hostility to the European movement. Whatever the causes, the consequence was damaging.[50]

Winston Churchill had advocated a United Europe before the war. During it, in an attempt to keep France fighting in 1940, he offered her an 'indissoluble union'; and shortly after El Alamein, on Trafalgar Day 1942, he sent a minute to Anthony Eden in which he looked forward to 'a United States of Europe', adding that 'Europe is our prime care'. After the war, he returned to the subject as early as November 1945 in Brussels, but not until his speeches at Metz and Zurich in July and September 1946 and his article in the American paper *Collier's Magazine* that winter did he bring it to the top of his public agenda.[51]

In recent years attempts have been made to suggest that, while Churchill favoured a United Europe, either he did not intend Britain to be part of that union, or alternatively his support for a United Europe with Britain part of it was limited and tepid compared with his unbounded enthusiasm for the British Empire and the Anglo-American alliance. The former is a natural interpretation of his addresses at Metz and Zurich, but neither is a tenable interpretation of his later speeches and activities. Churchill formed an all-party movement in Britain (and other countries) to foster a United Europe. The suggestion that he did so in order to persuade other countries to unite while keeping his own separate and outside is not credible. Churchill was a British imperialist elsewhere, but not in Europe, and such behaviour would have been an absurd impertinence. Further, his own words leave no doubt that he wanted and expected Britain to be part of a United Europe; to believe the opposite, therefore, necessitates supposing that Churchill did not understand what he was saying – which seems unlikely – or that he was being dishonest, which is equally improbable.

Churchill's frequent use of the word 'we' puts the matter beyond doubt: 'Are we all,' he asked at a United Europe meeting in May 1947, 'through our poverty and our quarrels, for ever to be a burden and a danger to the rest of the world? ... We know where we want to go,' he continued, 'we have now at once to set on foot an organisation in Great Britain to promote the cause of United Europe, and to give this idea the prominence and vitality necessary for it to ... influence the course of national policy.' The United Nations Organisation made provision for regional groupings. The United States and Soviet Russia would form two such regional entities. Then 'there is the British Empire and Commonwealth; and there is Europe, with which Great Britain is profoundly blended. Here are the four main pillars of the world Temple of Peace.'

There were several important bodies, Churchill went on, 'which are working directly for the federation of the European States and for the creation of a Federal constitution for Europe. I hope that may eventually be achieved.' Then he turned to France. 'If European unity is to be made an effective reality,' he said, 'the whole-hearted efforts of Britain and France will be needed from the outset ... They must in fact be founder parties in this movement.'*

After welcoming American support for a United Europe, Churchill turned to the Commonwealth. It was necessary that any policy this island adopted 'towards Europe and in Europe should enjoy the full sympathy and approval of the peoples of the Dominions. 'But why', he asked, 'should we suppose that they will not be with us in this cause? ... If Europe united is to be a living force, Britain will have to play her full part as a member of the European family ... we may be sure that the cause of United Europe, in which the mother country must be a prime mover, will in no way be contrary to the sentiments which join us all together with our Dominions in the august circle of the British Crown.'[52]

In his speech at The Hague a year later, Churchill addressed the question of sovereignty. After pointing out that mutual aid in the economic field and joint military defence had 'inevitably' to be accompanied 'with a parallel policy of closer political unity', Churchill added that it was 'said with truth that this involves some sacrifice or merger of national sovereignty'. But this could be equally regarded 'as the gradual assumption by all the nations concerned of that larger sovereignty which can alone protect their diverse and distinctive customs and characteristics and their national traditions ...' In Amsterdam two days later, after saying 'we have come here from so many lands ... to try to take a step forward together ... towards reviving the old glories of Europe', Churchill expressed the hope of seeing a Europe where 'men of every

---

* To anti-Europeans, this passage presumably means that Churchill intended that France, too, should not be part of the European Union.

country will think as much of being a European as of belonging to their native land ... without losing any of their love and loyalty of their birthplace'.[53]

Churchill thought they could not 'rest upon benevolent platitudes and generalities', but just as he was against the Conservative Party entering into firm policy commitments, he was opposed to the European movement being 'drawn into laboured attempts to draw rigid structures of constitutions'. He did not think Europe in 1948 was 'ripe for either a political federation or a customs union'; yet 'conceptions which are impracticable today may quite possibly be thought obvious and inevitable in a few years time'. Churchill took a similar approach to 'a uniform currency' in Europe. 'As we [had] to build from chaos', this could only 'be achieved by stages'. 'Luckily,' he went on, 'coins have two sides, so that one side can become the national and the other the European superscription.' We do not know what Winston Churchill would have thought now. In 1950 he said that Britain's position as 'the centre of the British Empire and Commonwealth with our fraternal association with the United States' would prevent Britain's 'full membership of a federal system of Europe'. Half a century later, the situation is very different. Britain has no Empire and her relationship with the United States is not quite the same, although there is still no federal system in Europe. Therefore, as Churchill's biographer has said, 'it is sterile to wonder what Churchill's stance on Europe would have been today ... But he was not by nature a sceptical person, he was a visionary.' And that at the time Churchill strongly believed that Britain should take a full part in moving towards a United Europe is not in serious doubt.[54]

The anti-Europeans of the time were better informed than their successors half a century later. They, at least, had no doubt that Churchill intended Britain to be part of United Europe. Sir Herbert Williams, no less, thought Churchill and the other pro-European Conservative leaders were like Colorado beetles undermining Britain's trade, which he fondly expected to be mainly with the Empire.[55] A much more formidable opponent, or at least unfriendly observer, was Anthony Eden. Eden was a good parliamentarian and a masterly diplomatist but, despite his great experience, his judgement on large issues in foreign affairs was suspect – although he had limited knowledge and experience of them, his judgement in home affairs was more reliable. Eden did not think that Britain's destiny lay in Europe, and he shied away from anything so visionary as European unity. The changes that were taking place in Europe were, as his sympathetic biographer concedes, 'a gap in Eden's comprehension that was never to be filled'.

As Sir Robert Rhodes James also says, Eden's 'instinctive prejudices against Europe' were shared by Bevin, Attlee and most of the Labour Government – Maxwell Fyfe harshly but not unfairly later accused Attlee of sharing the general 'mood of smug middle-class isolationist complacency'. Unfortunately, that was not the Government's only trouble. Britain, a Foreign Office Memorandum pointed out in 1945, could only be treated 'as an equal' by 'our two big partners' if she made herself the leader of Western Europe as well as the Commonwealth.[56] Bevin for some time took much the same view, favouring a western bloc or third force, but the Government finally turned against the idea largely because it was fearful of anything that might threaten the Atlantic Alliance. Thus the Labour Government preferred to work with the Americans rather than the Europeans, even though the Americans, pushing for a United Europe, preferred to work with 'Europe' rather than Britain. Indeed, the preamble to the Marshall Plan declared it 'to be the policy of the United States to encourage the unification of Europe'.

The second difficulty was Labour's belief that it was building socialism in Britain and could not jeopardise or dilute that achievement by any sharing of sovereignty with non-socialist neighbours. Labour was prepared to countenance a United Europe only if it was socialist; the concept of European Unity, Labour's National Executive stated, 'might be corrupted in the hands of reaction'. Pointing out that this was on the same level as those who were trying to make a United Communist Europe, Churchill mocked Labour's 'insular socialism'.[57]

In the end, Britain's European neighbours, urged on by the United States, became impatient of Bevin's obstructiveness. The French Foreign Minister, Robert Schuman, who in November 1949 had said that without Britain there could be no Europe, a few months later produced his plan for a supranational authority for coal and steel without consulting Britain – to the vast annoyance of the ailing Bevin, who accused Schuman and the American Secretary of State Dean Acheson of conspiring to keep him in the dark. Despite Bevin's hostility to the Plan, some officials in Whitehall thought Britain should participate. But for the Attlee Government the Schuman Plan was a threat not just to Britain's sovereignty but more importantly to Labour's precious nationalised industries. Nationalism and nationalisation marched together. Hence, even though the French had made clear that there would be 'no commitment except by the signature of a treaty' and the ailing Sir Stafford Cripps favoured Britain negotiating on that basis, the Government churlishly refused even to discuss the Plan.

Acheson was not alone in thinking that thereby 'Britain made her great mistake of the post-war period'. Even Eden thought the decision dangerously misguided, while Churchill complained that Britain's absence 'derange[d] the balance of Europe'. 'The Conservative and Liberal Parties declare', he said, 'that national sovereignty is not inviolable, and that it may be resolutely diminished for the sake of all the men in all the lands finding their way home together.' Churchill thought that the Labour Government's refusal even to participate in discussions of the Schuman Plan was 'a squalid attitude at a time of present stress'.[58] Squalid or not, Labour's refusal set Britain on the wrong road in Europe, a road from which, subsequently, she has seldom deviated.

The Comeback

By 1950 the membership of the Conservative Party had reached some 2,750,000; at the end of 1947 the party had claimed fewer than a million members. With a soaring membership, restored finances, a rebuilt organisation, and a thoroughly researched and appropriate programme, the party was well prepared for the election which Attlee called in February 1950. Attlee may have been forced into an early election by Cripps's high-minded refusal to introduce an election budget. Still, February was an eccentric time of year for the Prime Minister to choose and not one likely to favour his Government. Labour further handicapped itself by including in its manifesto proposals which starkly revealed the absurdity of its nationalisation policy. The industries it now marked down for state ownership might have been picked by a person provided with a list of British industries, a blindfold and a pin, in much the same way as some people choose a racehorse to back in the Derby. The only difference was that all the possible winners on the list had already been selected. Labour's 'shopping list', which included meat wholesaling, water supply, cement and sugar refining together with what was inaccurately called 'mutualisation' of life assurance companies, was, as R. H. S. Crossman later admitted, 'the product of a last-minute haggle between contending factions in the Executive' and was wide open to attack.[59]

Apart from this bonus for the Tories, Labour's programme contained little that was new. The Government fought on its record, stressing full employment, 'fair shares' and the improvements it had brought to welfare. The Conservative manifesto, which was much better written than usual because Churchill had introduced his own literary style, was also cautious. Since in the Conservative view Britain faced an economic crisis, the party could not afford to be profligate in its promises. Nevertheless 'the maintenance of full employment' would be 'the first aim of a Conservative Government', and as soon as 'the prime necessities of life

46

were within the reach of every family and each individual' the existing rationing system would be abolished. The Nuffield Study of the election noted that the Conservative and Labour manifestos overlapped in substance, though not in form, and that their differences were often only in attitude and emphasis.[60]

The election, which, though one of the quietest of modern times, produced a turnout of 84 per cent, was fought under an election law passed in 1948. Its most important innovation was the introduction of postal votes which, because the Conservatives had by far the better organisation, gave the party a considerable advantage. An even greater advantage was conferred on the Opposition by the redistribution of seats, carried through by the Home Secretary, Chuter Ede, with an honesty (not to say altruism) to which the Wilson Government, faced with the same situation twenty years later, did not attempt to aspire. Postal voting and redistribution were worth probably about thirty seats to the Conservatives. Without them, Labour would have had a majority in 1950 that would have been impregnable for a full parliament, and if Attlee had called an early election in 1951 Labour would have won it.[61]

In the event the Conservatives gained eighty-seven seats, the Liberals' total haul was nine, and Labour's majority over all parties fell from 136 to just six and over the Conservatives to seventeen. Labour had in fact done better than the parliamentary arithmetic suggested, winning 46.1 per cent of the total vote, as against 43.5 per cent for the Tories. It was the bias in the electoral system caused by the piling up of massive majorities in mining seats and the 1948 redistribution which reduced their majority to single figures. Later experience showed that a majority of six would probably be sufficient for a few years if not a full parliament, but in 1950 observers were accustomed to the huge majorities of the 1930s and 1940s, and many doubted that Labour could carry on for more than a few months. Apart from a short break in 1945, its leaders had been in office since 1940 and were ill, tired or both.

The Conservatives were cheered by their spectacular recovery and disappointed it had not been quite enough to bring victory. Probably, however, they were lucky to be defeated, because Labour with a small majority, rather than the Conservatives, had to tackle the problems caused by the Korean War, for which Churchill pledged Tory support. Before the election Churchill had indicated that if he lost he would promptly retire. The closeness of the result, however, and the prospect of another chance before long induced him to change his mind and disappoint Anthony Eden. He became more active at Westminster, and the Conservatives stepped up their parliamentary opposition. The party was uncivilised enough to forbid its MPs to pair with Labour members, long debates were held and snap divisions called. Yet the public was unlikely to reward a party that forced a second election immediately after it had lost the previous one, so this skirmishing was something of a phoney war. Not until a year after the election, when the Government had fallen behind the Opposition in the opinion polls for the first time and when all Conservatives were exasperated by the Government's insistence on proceeding with steel nationalisation, did the war become real and the party act in accordance with Bob Boothby's prescription, 'we shall harry the life out of them . . . The only way to get rid of them fairly is to wear them out. We will make them sit up day and night and grind away until they get absolutely hysterical and say "we can't stand any more".' Some, including Maudling, Macleod and Walter Elliot, either did not think such tactics 'fair' or thought them likely to alienate the public. Eden, too, had doubts. Yet the war continued, though it soon slackened because the harriers, who also had to be present, were liable to get almost as 'hysterical' as the harried.[62]

Away from the front line, Conservative activities were on a higher level. If the quantity of new MPs had not been quite sufficient to propel the party into government, their quality was remarkably high. On the invitation of 'Cub' Alport, some of them, dismayed by some lamentable front-bench speeches on home policy, formed a group of nine which included Iain Macleod, Angus Maude, Edward Heath and Enoch Powell. *One Nation* was the title of their first book, published in October 1950, and they duly became known as the One Nation Group. Published by the Conservative Political Centre, with a foreword by Butler who recommended it 'as a healthy piece of constructive work', *One Nation* appeared in time for the Party Conference at Blackpool and sold well.

The authors made clear that the free enterprise system they supported was not *laissez-faire*, 'but what R. A. Butler has described as "private enterprise in the public interest"'. 'The maintenance of full employment', they went on, was 'a first responsibility of government', and they favoured making contracts of employment compulsory. The Korean War had naturally entailed increased spending on defence, thereby creating difficulties for public expenditure elsewhere. Assuming that there could be no additional expenditure on the social services, *One Nation* demanded a more efficient use of resources. Hence food subsidies were attacked for failing to concentrate help on those who most needed it and health service charges were accepted, including charging hospital in-patients for their board. Yet *One Nation* was not an overture to right-wing calls in the eighties and nineties for cuts in the social services. Instead of concealing a wish that the welfare state had never been invented, the authors' words showed genuine pride in its achievement.

They heaped praise on the Beveridge Report. Some stones needed shifting or strengthening here and there, they wrote, but 'the wall of social security has been built at last'. They called on all those engaged in industry 'for a great effort to save the social services'. For the Conservative Party the task was 'to act as a balancing force, to ensure that liberty and order reinforce one another'.[63]

Outside Parliament, the Conservatives stepped up their attack. The chapter on housing in *One Nation*, which was written by Powell, pointed out that in the five years from 1934 to 1938 house-building had averaged 335,000 a year. Nearly all Conservative candidates in the election had given housing a prominent place in their election addresses. Bevan had been in charge of housing as well as health – a combination of tasks which Attlee should not have permitted or imposed and which was also contrary to a promise in *Let Us Face the Future*. Not surprisingly, if Dalton accurately reported his remark that housing ran itself and he 'never spent more than an hour a week' on it, Bevan's housing record did not duplicate his success over health.[64] He rightly insisted on the building of decent houses rather than as many new slums as possible, but he severely restricted private house-building, and he did not get nearly enough of them built. Hence housing was a promising Conservative issue, and at the party's 1950 Conference pressure for a pledge to build 300,000 houses a year became, Butler thought, like an auction. Lord Woolton, having asked if 300,000 was a feasible target, was somewhat reluctantly told that it was. Although he was also warned by Butler that it was an undesirable one since it would 'make it that much more difficult to restore the economy', Woolton announced to the conference in 'beaming surrender, "This is magnificent"'. Had Butler known that he would soon be the Chancellor of the Exchequer to be burdened by this pledge, he would probably have expressed firmer opposition. Yet the promise and the undertaking in the 1951 manifesto to 'give housing a priority second only to national defence' were useful at the forthcoming election.[65]

Away from party politics, the Government's troubles multiplied. The outbreak of the Korean War and the excessive rearmament programme brought Labour additional problems. Controls had to be increased, with all their attendant unpopularity, and Aneurin Bevan's resignation laid bare differences between Right and Left which were to undermine Labour's morale and effectiveness for the next ten years. In Persia in April, the nationalist Dr Mossadeq nationalised the Anglo-Iranian Oil Company and took over its refinery at Abadan. Shinwell, the Defence Minister, and Morrison, the new Foreign Secretary, who in Labour's recent manifesto had been proposing an extension of nationalisation in

Britain, were outraged at Persia following suit. A strong expeditionary force was assembled to teach the Persians a lesson. Luckily the American Secretary of State, Dean Acheson, like John Foster Dulles six years later, was strongly opposed to a British military escapade; Gaitskell took the same view and in the end Attlee decided to abandon Abadan and to evacuate British subjects. The Conservatives denounced what they called 'scuttle' diplomacy,[66] but it was less of a humiliation for Britain than the gunboat variety which came six years later.

In another foretaste of Suez, King Farouk's government in October unilaterally abrogated the Anglo-Egyptian treaty of 1936. Eden stole a march on Morrison by pledging that Britain would protect the Sudan against Egypt, and Churchill was able to make play of the three national disasters: 'Abadan, Sudan and Bevan'. By then another election was well under way. Labour had suffered its usual odd-year economic crisis in September when the balance of payments was in serious trouble. Bevin was dead, Cripps was near death, and Attlee had had enough. Without consulting his Chancellor or his Foreign Secretary, Attlee dissolved Parliament in September, choosing once again the worst possible moment for his party to fight an election.

Labour had nothing new in its manifesto. In the Conservative one which he himself wrote, Churchill included a promise to introduce an Excess Profit Tax in order to head off any allegations that private industry was doing too well out of the new armaments drive. This piece of Churchillian free enterprise, which recalled his support for a similar policy in 1918–19, surprised his colleagues and infuriated Butler, but there was nothing they could do. A longer document, *Britain Strong and Free*, which followed later, contained no such surprises. Conservative rhetoric was more libertarian than in 1950 – the campaign slogan was 'set the people free' – yet the policy had not changed, and the leaders were still cautious. Churchill made a restrained and effective broadcast. Anthony Eden similarly gave little away. Packing his usual complement of clichés more tightly than usual, he told an audience at Birmingham, *The Times* reported, that on the cost of living 'the Conservatives had no patent medicine. He was no conjuror and had no hat to bring a rabbit out of.'[67]

The sensations came from the other side. Having little of their own to offer, Labour fought on smears and fears about the threat that a Tory victory would present to the welfare state and to international peace. Churchill was represented as a warmonger, the *Daily Mirror* asking on polling day: 'Whose finger on the Trigger?' – a particularly misconceived smear since Churchill had, well before the campaign, come out in favour of negotiations with Stalin, and Labour had committed

Britain to the war in Korea. Yet Labour's tactics evidently paid off. Notwithstanding the Government's exhaustion and the widespread resentment of rationing and controls, Labour did much better than expected, being only narrowly defeated and gaining more votes than any party had previously polled.

Once again the Conservatives were indebted to the bias in the electoral system. They gained twenty-six more seats than Labour while polling 200,000 fewer votes, although four large constituencies in Northern Ireland which would have produced enormous Unionist majorities were uncontested. Probably the other crucial factor in the Conservative victory was the sudden drop in the number of Liberal candidates – from 475 in 1950 to 109 in 1951 – of whom only six were successful. The ex-Liberal vote was probably decisive, splitting roughly sixty to forty in the Conservatives' favour.[68] Whatever else the results showed, Labour's support in the poorer areas of the country was still solid.

Conservatism Betrayed?

Throughout the post-war era, some on the Conservative Right have looked back to a golden age when the party worshipped the free market and stigmatised the state. In their eyes, successive Tory leaders have betrayed the true faith, which has been kept alive only by a few brave lovers of freedom in the face of a scornful majority. In the forties the handful of devotees like Sir Waldron Smithers and Sir Herbert Williams, for whom, said Harold Macmillan in 1947, 'time does not merely stand still but, if anything, runs backwards', thought that the golden age lay in the 1930s; as has been seen, they were deluding themselves.[69] Although the governments of that decade did not do enough to guide the economy, the amount of intervention they did permit themselves was a repudiation of *laissez-faire*. To search for the holy grail in the immediate post-war years would obviously be even more fruitless. Yet in the search for traitors or scapegoats the guardians of the faith have had to tread with care, for Winston Churchill bars their way.

As the greatest Conservative leader, and indeed the greatest Briton of the century, Winston Churchill is an icon whom even Conservatives whose attitudes are most at variance with his are usually chary of attacking. Yet if the New Right were consistent, Churchill would occupy a high place in their demonology, for the simple reason that, in the silly language which became common usage in the eighties, Churchill was 'a wet', perhaps the wettest of all senior Conservative politicians. Understandably reluctant though he was to make rigid policy commitments during the war and in the Opposition period, he showed both then and when he returned to Downing Street that he was quintessentially a One-Nation Tory. Unlike the New Right, he believed in inclusion not exclusion. When he invited Patrick Buchan Hepburn officially to become Chief Whip in 1948, he expressed the hope that they would act together 'in a restoration of power of the Conservatives and Tory-progressive forces'.[70] He was always anxious for Liberal co-operation and support and he sought to enlist people of no particular party affiliation. In the social field he was concerned after the war to avoid confrontation or class conflict. He consistently emphasised the Conservatives' honourable history of social reform, taking credit for the fact that much of what the Attlee Government was doing had been hammered out in the days of the coalition government. In short, Churchill gave his imprimatur to the outlook and principles which were the foundation of the policies of every Tory Government up to 1979.

Because of Churchill's status, politicians of the New Right usually confine their attacks on One-Nation Toryism to the period after his resignation. Academics of that ilk are less inhibited. The Conservative Opposition from 1945 to 1951 has been written off as 'one of the least enterprising and admired of modern times'.[71] Even more bizarrely, the Conservative leaders of that time have been condemned as little better than socialists, or at best as socialist appeasers who, by thoughtlessly and fearfully absorbing the socialist atmosphere of the day, opened the door for ever-increasing injections of the deadly virus of socialism. The right-wing view of post-war Toryism has been most cogently articulated by Andrew Roberts:

> Instead of treating it as the freak result it was, an entire generation of Tory politicians was emasculated by the 1945 election result, especially over the issues of nationalization, the growth of the state and trade union reform. They failed to learn the lesson of what an extra two and a half million Conservative voters between the 1945 and the 1951 elections meant, and instead ceded the high ground to the collectivists for a quarter of a century and settled down to manage imperial and commercial decline. This allowed the 'ratchet effect' to pertain throughout the 1950s, 1960s and 1970s, whereby each incoming Tory Government merely preserved the shift to the left made by the previous Labour one.[72]

The trouble with this thesis, even when it is well expressed as here, is that it is factually inaccurate, logically flawed and deeply unhistorical; indeed it is not history but ideology. 1945 was not a 'freak result'. From

1942 onwards the Conservatives had done badly in by-elections, losing a number of safe seats. The opinion polls told the same story. Throughout 1944 the Conservative share of the vote was in the low twenties with Labour always at least ten points ahead.[73] People were surprised by the result of the general election only because in those days they paid little attention to public opinion polls. Moreover the figures in the election itself were not 'freakish', except that as usual with the British electoral system the winners' parliamentary majority was disproportionate to their majority of popular votes, but that cannot be what the right wing mean since few, if any of them, favour electoral reform. In 1945 the Conservatives gained a larger share of the vote than in 1929 which (since both 1931 and 1935 really were freakish on account of the Labour split in 1931) was the last comparable contest as well as being the first election to be fought under universal suffrage. Much of the difference between 1945 and 1929 was caused by the collapse of the Liberal vote and former Liberals, or their descendants, switching to Labour. In 1945 the Conservatives – rightly or wrongly – were no longer seen as the safe party of moderation and sanity.

The reason, apparently, why right-wing writers think 1945 was freakish is that the Conservatives gained two and a half million more votes in 1951. Their logical flaw here is to assume that those two and a half million votes would have been gained even if the Conservative Party had repeated its lamentable performance after 1906 and had moved to the right. Yet had the Conservative leaders in the forties and early fifties adopted something akin to Thatcherism, had the party become, in the words of Anthony Eden after the 1945 election, a 'close corporation for [the] extreme right',[74] the heavy odds are that 1945 would have been repeated at every subsequent election until the party saw reason. In 1936 the Republicans ignored the lesson of Roosevelt's victory in 1932 and their candidate, Alf Landon, carried just two small states. In other words, what made the 1945 result later seem 'freakish' to some was the direct consequence of the post-war party espousing policies which the New Right regard as 'emasculated' and quasi-socialist. Those additional two and a half million votes were won because the Conservative leaders, instead of regarding the voters as mistaken and waiting for them to change (as Labour later tended to do), changed their party to bring it in step with the times and demonstrated that what most voters wanted and valued would be safe with a Conservative Government.

The alleged socialist 'ratchet effect' of the fifties, sixties and seventies is an invention of the New Right. There was no ratchet effect in the fifties. Labour completed its nationalisation of steel in 1950–51, but the Churchill Government took it back into private ownership. The

Wilson Government was not far to the left and did not much extend state ownership except for steel. Admittedly the Heath Government hardly denationalised anything at all, but it could not have subjected steel to yet another upheaval only three years after the previous one, especially as it was being well run by the Conservative peer, Lord Melchett. The Wilson and Callaghan Governments did introduce some socialist measures in the seventies, but the New Right cannot have that in mind because nobody, least of all the New Right, thinks that the incoming Tory Government of 1979 'merely preserved the shift to the left made by the previous Labour one'. So the alleged ratchet effect boils down to the renationalisation of steel, which was certainly a mistake, but one click does not a ratchet make, and the suggestion that Britain moved relentlessly to the left between 1945 and 1979 is fiction.

The New Right have been blinded by their own rhetoric. While denouncing the refusal of earlier Tory Governments to denationalise everything in sight, they have failed to notice that a key element of the post-war consensus or settlement was the preservation of capitalism and private industry. On arriving at the Board of Trade in 1945, Stafford Cripps told his officials that the aim of the Government was to 'create orderly conditions by which private enterprise can make the most effective contribution to the country's economic welfare'. The ideologist of the Old Left, Tony Benn, was far nearer the truth than his fellow ideologues of the New Right when he complained that Labour's 'crushing defeat' in 1979 'followed thirty years of anti-socialist revisionism preached from the top of the Labour Party'.[75]

The New Right's hostility to post-war Conservatism, encapsulated by Mr Roberts, is ahistorical both in particular and in general. He singles out the issues of nationalisation, the growth of the state and trade union reform. Nationalisation has already been looked at. Only steel and road haulage were serious candidates for a return to private ownership, and the Churchill Government duly returned them. Oliver Poole, though keen to denationalise, soon discovered in 1950 that the denationalisation of electricity was 'unworkable and unrealistic'.[76] In any case few outside the far right acclaim the manner in which water, gas and the railways were eventually denationalised, and still fewer admire the way they have since been run.

With trade union reform, the New Right seem to be on stronger ground. Yet it was not just the trade unions which were stuck in the past; so was much of British industry. Some firms had only recently stopped laying off their work-force before a holiday and re-engaging them afterwards to avoid giving them holiday pay; even as late as the summer of 1956 the British Motor Corporation summarily sacked 6,000 workers, paying them only one week's wage in lieu of notice. Further-more, after the war the Tories had the reputation of being the anti-trade union party, and the justified fear that they were going to stir up indus-trial strife by waging war on the TUC would have guaranteed electoral oblivion. In any case the trade unions' behaviour in the post-war years did not suggest that they were conspicuously more in need of reform than other British institutions. Led by the impeccably right-wing trio of Arthur Deakin, Tom Williamson and Will Lawther, they behaved responsibly and for most of the time they secured considerable restraint over wages. Praising the TUC in a speech at Bristol at the end of 1949, Anthony Eden had 'watched the efforts they were making with sincere respect ... if they were successful in their efforts they would further enhance the status of the trade union movement as an essential part of our industrial life'.[77] To the New Right, these are the words of appease-ment, ironically being delivered by an opponent of Chamberlain's foreign policy. To anybody else, Eden was merely acknowledging a fact: there was no wage explosion under the Attlee Government. To import the preoccupation of later times into an age which did not share it is misleading and futile.

The third issue, 'the growth of the state', brings us to the general point. The Conservative politicians of the post-war years had lived through the 1920s and 1930s as well as the war. Having seen the great slump of 1929–31, they knew from experience that the capitalism of those days was not a self-correcting system perpetually ensuring increased pros-perity for all. They also knew that the slump had brought Hitler to power and had led to war. Even before the slump they had seen the ravages of a less regulated capitalism. Because of the great slump, classi-cal *laissez-faire* capitalism had collapsed well before the war, and some-thing different – there were many variants, some of them worse – had succeeded it in most countries.

All the post-war Conservative leaders knew by then what some of them had known all the time, that in the years between the wars many of their fellow countrymen had lived in intolerable conditions. Shortly before his death in 1940, Neville Chamberlain had some families evacu-ated from Birmingham billeted on him. 'I never knew such conditions existed', he wrote to his sister, 'and I am deeply ashamed of my ignor-ance.'[78]* Many others who took in evacuees from the bombed cities had their eyes similarly opened. And thousands of non-political people

---

* A reprise of Disraeli's famous passage in *Sybil* written nearly a century earlier: two nations, the rich and the poor, 'who are as ignorant of each other's habits, thoughts and feelings, as if they were ... inhabitants of different planets'.[79]

who joined the forces also learned much from the men they served with or commanded; in consequence, they were determined that when the war ended the country should not return to the thirties.

The Conservative leaders were similarly determined. They adopted centrist policies which required a larger state not because they had been politically castrated by electoral defeat or because they were solely interested in electoral success but because they genuinely believed in them. (Even in 1940, if, as expected, there had been a general election that year, the Conservatives would probably have proposed much of what was contained in the Beveridge Report.)[80] They thought that the nineteenth-century minimal state – what Harold Macmillan called 'Manchester Liberalism' – had gone for ever and they recognised, in Macmillan's words, 'the truth of the traditional Conservative position that government has its own important part to play in the economic and industrial life of the nation'. Rab Butler later made the same point when he said that people who favoured creating pools of unemployment should be thrown into them and made to swim.[81] Churchill felt much the same.

Post-war Conservatives rejected right-wing free-market policies on their merits. They would have been appalled by the return of mass unemployment and widespread misery in the eighties and nineties, had they lived to see them. Macmillan and Butler did live to see the eighties and disliked what they saw. In short, the idea that the electorate (or the Conservative leaders) could, would or should have countenanced a smaller welfare state and a return to heavy unemployment and beggars on the streets, both of which were effectively banished from 1945 to 1980, is a triumph of ideology over both history and sense. But then, as the expert on Machiavelli, Tommasini, once wrote, 'For a mind accustomed to dogmatic schemes, history ... is as though it did not exist.'[82]

If the New Right are misguided about the past, their bible, Friedrich von Hayek's *The Road to Serfdom* published in 1944, was equally wrong about the future. Just possibly, Hayek did something to influence Churchill's 'Gestapo' broadcast. Certainly his book, contrary to legend, purports to show that central planning would eventually lead to Nazism – Stalinist Communism, like Keynes, is scarcely mentioned.* If Churchill was so influenced (and Hayek was in no doubt that he had been), he soon came to recognise his mistake. When he met Hayek in 1948, he told the free-market sage that 'it would never happen in England'.[84]

---

* Interestingly, in his election address in 1945 the young Iain Macleod warned the electors of the Western Isles that 'Socialism leads to Fascism'.[83]

Undoubtedly it could never have happened under the Attlee Government. Attlee himself bore no resemblance to either Hitler or Stalin, and his Government was closer to Asquith's pre-1914 Liberal administration (of which Churchill had been a prominent member) than to any foreign dictatorship.

Like Asquith's, Attlee's was a reforming Government, though rather more conservative. Harold Macmillan wrote later that it was 'one of the most able governments of modern times'; he thought Attlee, Bevin, Morrison, Dalton and Cripps 'constituted a body of ministers as talented as any in the history of Parliament'.[85] Having had nationalisation foisted on them by a conference rebellion, the Labour leaders carried out that part of the party's programme with ever-decreasing enthusiasm. With few exceptions, the industries Labour nationalised were either clapped out or monopolies, and it ran them in a commercial and capitalist manner. Even when it produced its absurd 'shopping list' in 1950, it did not include the banks, which any seriously socialist government would have done. Attlee justified nationalisation to himself by regarding it as an essential element of a planned economy, yet his Government never developed the will or the machinery to make proper planning possible.

Labour left British institutions much as it found them. 'The new government', the far-left Ralph Miliband complained, 'accepted without any kind of question that it should be served by precisely the same civil servants who had served its predecessors.'[86] It also left alone the universities, and it made no effort to reform the public schools whose intake Churchill had wished to see drastically altered during the war and which any government seriously concerned with equality would surely have attempted. Apart from ineffective gestures, it did nothing to make British industry more modern and efficient. Its foreign policy was conservative, except over Europe where it was reactionary. Over India alone it was radical, and there it was right. The Government was anything but extremist. There was not the slightest danger of it taking the country down the road to serfdom.

Through its extension of social security, its creation of a National Health Service, its Keynesian economics and its objective of full employment, the Attlee Government transformed the life of the working classes, while leaving much else undone. That achievement did not appeal to the middle classes who were as attached to their differentials over the workers as was any skilled trade unionist to his differentials over his unskilled brethren; and Labour, because of its obsession with 'fair shares', did little to assuage middle-class resentment. The disaffection of the middle classes had solid cause. They were heavily taxed and, unlike those of wage earners, their incomes seldom rose with the cost of living. Luckily for the Conservatives, the middle classes (as usual) behaved in a more authentically Marxist way than the working classes in showing far greater class solidarity. While the middle classes became increasingly Conservative, the working classes were more evenly split: about one-third of them voted Conservative, thus providing the party with about half its total vote. To achieve that percentage after five years of Opposition to a not unsuccessful Government was the first of two main Conservative achievements. The second was to offer fierce opposition to the Government while not greatly differing from it. Just as Labour was not Marxist and accepted capitalism, the Conservatives were not *laissez-faire* liberals and accepted a large and active state. There were, said Churchill after the election, 'underlying unities' between the parties 'far greater than our differences'.[87]

The Conservative victory was partly fortuitous – the result of the bias in the electoral system – but it was deserved. Whereas the right-wing extremism of the Conservative Opposition to Campbell-Bannerman's Government after the 1906 defeat had driven the Liberals to the left, the moderation of the Conservative Opposition after 1945 helped to keep the Labour Government near the centre. By its embrace of the post-war world, its repudiation of *laissez-faire* and its avoidance of nostalgia for the nineteenth century, the Tory Party redeemed its shortcomings of the thirties and made itself electable.

Labour was unlucky. Although Britain had won the war, in everyday life there had been disappointingly few tangible signs of victory in the six years since 1945. For that, the Labour Government was only partly to blame; economically, Britain had suffered a heavy defeat in the war. Labour was chiefly at fault for not sufficiently recognising Britain's reduced status. Some of the belated fruits of victory were now to be harvested by the Conservative Party.

CHAPTER
III
─────

Conservatism in One Nation

Max Beaverbrook 'wants the jockey to win', Churchill told his doctor during the election, 'but he hates his horse'.[1] The worries about the horse, fanned by Labour's scares and smears during the campaign, were of course largely confined to opponents of the Conservative Party. Worries about the jockey were prevalent nearer home. Despite his recent victory, Churchill's wife Clementine still thought he should have resigned at the end of the war. Many of his colleagues also thought that, at the age of nearly seventy-seven, he was too old to be returning to office. They were comforted, however, by the thought that he would not be Prime Minister for long; he himself said he would hand over to Anthony Eden after a year.[2]

Shortly after the election Boothby visited Churchill, who wanted him to lead a British delegation to discussions on United Europe, and found the Prime Minister 'very, very old; tragically old'.[3] Churchill's health was indeed frail, as he himself well knew. Fairly deaf, he was more easily tired than before, and although his intellectual powers and energy were still remarkable, they were less than in the past; speeches had become a burden to him. A Treasury civil servant who had been his Private Secretary during the war noticed the change: Churchill had 'lost his tenacity ... and his power of fitting in all the problems one to another'. Also he forgot figures.[4]

Notwithstanding his worries about the much smaller than expected Tory majority, and the uncomfortable knowledge that most voters would have preferred Eden to be leader of the party, Churchill himself had no qualms about returning to Downing Street. He was convinced that his party and country needed his wisdom and experience, especially in international affairs; and he was right. Even with his abilities impaired, he was still head if not shoulders above his colleagues. Hence his age and ill-health did not prevent him leading the most successful British peacetime Government since 1918, any more than in the United States General Eisenhower's seemingly hands-off style, his serious operation, his stroke and his many hours on the golf course in Augusta,

Georgia, prevented him being America's best post-war President.[5]

The jockey's only qualms were about his horse. Before the election Churchill had said he was 'not just going to have the old gang', and after it he swiftly formed, as he had promised in the campaign, a 'broadly based government', in which there were several ministers who were not party politicians or whose party affiliation was only tenuously Conservative – there would have been more, had not Sir John Anderson and the Liberal leader Clement Davies turned down offers of posts.[6] The new Prime Minister saw himself, accurately enough, as the national leader of the British people, not just of the half of it who had voted Conservative. Even if it had not accorded with Churchill's natural instincts, a 'national' approach would have been justified and demanded by the Government's narrow majority, Labour's massive popular vote and the distrust that many still felt for the Conservative Party. In any case Churchill was determined to lead a moderate, centrist Government which would strengthen the post-war settlement and achieve the greatest possible degree of national unity, aims which were reflected not only in the Government's policies but in his ministerial appointments. The key posts went to the moderates, and a number of right-wingers were excluded, although Ralph Assheton was offered (and refused) the Post Office.

In his Cabinet-making, the Prime Minister made one short-lived innovation. Wishing to reduce the size of the Cabinet, the number of Cabinet committees and the ministerial workload – which had virtually killed both Bevin and Cripps – as well as wanting to be surrounded by familiar and trusted faces, Sir Winston appointed some ministers to keep an eye on several departments and co-ordinate their activities. Churchill's co-ordinators were unpopular, partly because they were all in the House of Lords – hence they were called 'overlords' – and partly because they offended the entrenched conservatism of the civil service and the Labour Opposition.

Labour objected to the overlords because they allegedly blurred the responsibility of departmental Ministers to Parliament. In fact there had long been co-ordinating Ministers, although in the past their duties had not been publicly revealed. Furthermore, ministerial responsibility obviously has to be combined with collective responsibility. As Churchill pointed out, major decisions were seldom taken by the departmental Minister; his personal responsibility had to be exercised in harmony with the views of his ministerial colleagues.

The dogma of ministerial responsibility was, and is, deep-rooted. 'The personal responsibility of each Minister to Parliament for matters within his competence', Sir John Anderson had laid down five years earlier, 'is a basic principle of the constitution, a principle as fundamental as the rule of law or the sovereignty of parliament.'[7] As 'Jehovah's' sonorous words suggest, the doctrine of ministerial responsibility to Parliament is important. The trouble is that it is not true. Even in the 1950s it was less a truth than a convenient myth. Admittedly Sir Thomas Dugdale, the Minister of Agriculture, resigned in 1954 because of mistakes by his Ministry with which he himself had had nothing to do, but that was an act of exceptional punctilio. Very few Ministers have ever resigned in such circumstances, and none since Dugdale. When something goes wrong in a department, the doctrine of ministerial responsibility to Parliament means in practice, as opposed to theory, that the departmental Minister is the man who tells Parliament that he was not responsible for the mistake.

Labour's constitutional objection to the overlords was little more than a screen for their real concern that publicity had been given to the overlords' duties and activities in contrast to the then habitual secrecy of Cabinet Committees. 'If the gravamen of the charge against me', Churchill replied to Attlee, 'is that I have not succeeded in hushing it all up as well as [you] did, I can bear that with composure.' The Opposition was indeed, as Lord Salisbury maintained, making a mountain out of a molehill, but they helped to wreck the experiment.[8]

Inevitably Anthony Eden went back to the Foreign Office for the third time, as well as for a day or two becoming Leader of the House for the second time. Most of Churchill's other appointments, however, were far from inevitable. Since the death of Oliver Stanley in 1950, Oliver Lyttelton had looked likely to be the Conservative Chancellor of the Exchequer, but because of his extensive City interests Eden vetoed him. It was feared, too, that 'the House of Commons stuff' might be too much for him. So, after Churchill had extended a probably half-hearted and certainly impracticable invitation to Lord Woolton, he chose Rab Butler for the Treasury. Unlike Lyttelton, Butler excelled in the House of Commons; and he had done more than any other man to rejuvenate the policies of the party. His drawbacks were that he had been an arch-appeaser and was no economist, which might make things difficult for him when arguing against Hugh Gaitskell. Instead of an overlord keeping an eye on him, he had, as it were, an underlord: Churchill imposed on him a Minister of State, Sir Arthur Salter, whom the Prime Minister quaintly called 'the best economist since Jesus Christ'. A more significant constraint on Butler proved to be Lord Cherwell – the 'Prof' – whom Churchill summoned back from Oxford to be, amongst his other duties, a source of independent economic advice.[9]

The fears voiced by the Conservatives during the election about the economy turned out to be justified; the new Government had inherited an economic crisis which the Labour Government had done almost nothing to avert except to make a small reduction in the imports of cheeses.[10] In later years it became customary for a Government after an election to face such a crisis, created either by its opponents or, if it had been in office before the vote, by itself. In 1951, however, this was a new experience. Over lunch at the Athenaeum with the Permanent Secretary of the Treasury and his Private Secretary-to-be, the Chancellor was fed alarming metaphors about blood draining from the system and the prospect of a collapse greater than had been forecast in 1931. The situation did indeed seem critical. Butler circulated a short note in Cabinet, outlining the diminishing reserves and the alarming outlook for the balance of payments, and Churchill took the precaution of ordering a copy to be sent to the Leader of the Opposition to apprise him 'of the financial position as it had been made known to the government when they first took office'.[11]

Butler had to reduce Britain's overseas expenditure. He did so by making cuts in imports of unrationed foodstuffs and raw materials and by halving the foreign travel allowance to £50; he also raised Bank Rate to 2½ per cent. As cheap money had come to be taken for granted – it had been a key element in Neville Chamberlain's policy in the 1930s and had stood at 2 per cent since 1932, being almost an article of faith with the Labour Government – this was deeply unpopular. More cuts in imports had to be made in January, and the foreign travel allowance was halved again. Partly as a result, the Government enjoyed no honeymoon with the electorate. It became unpopular almost immediately, remaining so for the next year. In May the local elections went badly, and Conservative morale was low for most of the Government's first year in office. Sir David Gammans, the Assistant Postmaster General, was not alone in fearing that the voters no longer thought that the party 'had the green fingers of government'.[12] In 1945 Labour had looked set for a long period in office, but lasted just over one term. The Conservatives lasted thirteen years and three terms, but in 1952 they looked unlikely to last more than one. Indeed, if they had adopted a plan cooked up in the Bank of England and the Treasury called 'Robot', they might not have held on for even one term.

Alarmed by the still falling reserves, early in February the Treasury tried to bounce the Government into a drastic change of course. 'Robot' was named after its three chief progenitors: Sir Leslie Rowan, Sir George Bolton and Otto Clarke. Of the three, only Clarke had any pretensions to being an economist; Rowan was a high-class Treasury official, and Bolton was a banker. All three had recently advocated policies directly at variance with the one they were now putting forward. Their new plan had three main elements: the pound was to be allowed to float (or rather sink); it was to be made (partially) convertible into dollars; and most of the sterling balances held in London were to be blocked. Remarkably, at the Commonwealth Conference only a week or so earlier, no hint of any of this had been given to the countries which would be drastically affected by it.[13]

Robot's first two provisions seem reasonable enough today: floating currencies are now common, devaluation sometimes works, as in 1949, 1967 and 1992, and the pound has long been convertible into dollars or into anything else. In 1952, however, the position was wholly different, and for the economic problems of that time Robot was a crude and ill-thought-out scheme. Not surprisingly, virtually every reputable economist who learned of Robot opposed it. Because of the excessive rearmament programme the British economy was already overloaded. Hence devaluation would scarcely have helped our exports; we had little more to export. It would merely have made our imports more expensive, and since they had already been severely cut there was little scope for any spectacular contraction. Our trading position would have been made still worse by the very limited convertibility that was proposed. The British and others would not be allowed to convert their pounds into foreign currency; only non-residents of the sterling area would be free to do so. The Treasury admitted that if foreign countries were short of dollars (and most of them were) they would 'tend to restrict their imports from us, and export as much as they can to us'. Hence the possibility had to be faced that much of our export trade might 'be faced with conditions of great difficulty'.[14]

The third element of Robot was scarcely less damaging. Although Australia and other members of the sterling area were to be allowed to convert 10 per cent of their reserves into dollars, they would hardly take kindly to 90 per cent of their reserves being frozen. As Harold Macmillan commented at the time, this amounted to 'default'. Leaving aside the effect of Robot in Britain, the plan broke the rules of the IMF from which we proposed to borrow money, would probably have killed the newly formed European Payments Union from which we had also just borrowed on a large scale, would have broken up much of the sterling area, and would have infuriated the West Europeans, the Commonwealth and the United States.[15]

Nevertheless, when on 22 February the Chancellor put this crazy plan to Churchill, Woolton, Lyttelton and a few others it was very nearly accepted. The plan's theme of 'freedom' appealed to Churchill, although the freedom was largely spurious, and discussion was not encouraged;

ministers were merely being informed, and immediate agreement was expected. Only Cherwell opposed the proposals, saying he would not be a party to them. In addition, Woolton, usually ready to do Butler down, thought that since the plan affected other countries it should not be accepted until Eden, who was attending a meeting of NATO in Lisbon, had been consulted. Butler collected all the copies of his paper from those who were present, except Cherwell, who refused to give his up. His chief economist, Donald MacDougall, was therefore able to prepare a brilliant document tearing Robot to pieces. Meanwhile a Treasury official flew to Lisbon to brief the Foreign Secretary. Fortunately Sir Edwin Plowden, the Treasury's Chief Planning Officer and an opponent of Robot, was in Lisbon with Eden. Plowden thought the Chancellor had allowed himself to be rattled by the Bank of England, and Eden's private secretary, Evelyn Shuckburgh, thought the plan could only be implemented if the Government called a general election first. The upshot of the discussion was that Eden sent a cautious letter to Churchill suggesting that a lot more thought needed to be given to the matter.[16]

The MacDougall–Cherwell paper to Churchill depicted Robot as 'a reckless leap in the dark involving appalling political as well as economic sacrifices at home and abroad'. The price of food would jump sharply, and unemployment might rise to one million – then an unthinkable figure. Churchill forwarded the paper to Butler saying, 'this is a formidable document'. At two stormy meetings of the Cabinet, Eden attacked the Treasury's proposals on broad social grounds, arguing that any other policy, even a heavy cut in the rearmament programme, would be preferable. In the end Robot's opponents included Churchill, Cherwell, Eden, Maxwell Fyfe, Salisbury and Macmillan. As only Butler, Lyttelton and one or two others were strong supporters, with the remainder being either wobbly or don't-knows, the opponents were both weightier and more numerous. So Robot was rejected. The Treasury – or the less economically literate part of it, since not only Plowden but Robert Hall, Arthur Salter and the Economic Section all strongly opposed Robot – did not accept defeat and tried again in June. But they had missed their moment. As 'Prof's' first biographer put it, Robot was 'essentially a financial *coup d'état* which could only be achieved in an atmosphere of panic, crisis and extreme secrecy'. It would never be accepted in cold blood. So the plan had been not just scotched in February, it had been killed.[17]

Butler, who was an innately cautious and prudent politician, had spent much of the six years in Opposition repudiating the kind of economics and the kind of Conservatism that Robot embodied and implied.

Robot would have caused a sharp rise in the price of food and an even sharper rise in unemployment. Throughout the years 1945–51 Butler and other Conservative leaders had proclaimed that there would be no going back to the thirties. Yet at the first whiff of grapeshot, as it were, Butler espoused a scheme which amongst its myriad disadvantages would have ensured that, as in the thirties, the unemployed and the poorest were the ones who suffered from the Government's economic policy. To adopt Butler's own earlier metaphor, Robot would have put his party back 'in the rough'. At a stroke it would have undone all his efforts and achievements of the last six years. Despite what he said in his memoirs, Butler later admitted that his opponents had been right all along.[18]

The oddity did not stop there. The political risks of Robot were at least as great as the economic ones. Donald MacDougall was told that Butler had privately conceded that it could mean the end of the Tory Party for forty years. Robot was nearly an economic Suez, a disaster which was averted only by the efforts of Cherwell and Eden – unfortunately Butler did not reciprocate at Suez itself – and by Churchill's common sense and willingness to be influenced by 'Prof'. The programme of the Tory Party, the Prime Minister told confidants at Chequers, must be: 'Houses and meat and not being scuppered.' Had he allowed Robot to go ahead, the Tories might well have been scuppered.[19]

Within a few months it was discovered that not only had Robot prescribed the wrong remedies for the crisis but that there had not been a crisis. As was becoming customary, all the Treasury's assumptions and estimates turned out to be mistaken. Not long after a cautious budget in March when Butler raised Bank Rate to 4 per cent and cut food subsidies by 40 per cent, but also cut income tax and increased pensions and welfare benefits to help the worst off, the reserves began to increase rather than drain away. In the autumn Butler was able to tell the Lord Mayor's banquet that the country had gained 'an invaluable breathing space', and he was the star of the Tory Party Conference at Scarborough. By the end of the year the reserves were much higher than anybody in the Treasury had thought possible.[20]

Europe and the United States

If Butler had attempted a drastic break from Labour's economic legacy, Eden's foreign policy all too closely resembled that of Bevin and Morrison. There could never have been, of course, an overlord for foreign affairs: Eden's political position was far too strong and in a few months' time would be stronger still, it was generally believed, when he assumed the premiership. Nevertheless, Churchill's primary concern was foreign policy. Despite his age, he did occupy himself with the whole range of home policy, but throughout his life foreign affairs had been his abiding interest; and in the new age of the atom and (from 1954) the hydrogen bomb they assumed an even greater importance. The great popularity of the younger man altered the previous balance of power between him and the Prime Minister, and Churchill gave him a rather freer hand than in the past when sometimes he had been reduced to being little more than the Prime Minister's factotum. Yet Eden's loyalty to Churchill and his refusal to cabal, in addition to the older man's much stronger personality and character, ensured that the Prime Minister was not far off being an overlord; Eden found his frequent interference maddening.

Anything to do with summits was clearly going to be very much the Prime Minister's business, as well as the Foreign Secretary's. In compensation, Churchill seems to have decided, or agreed, to leave Europe to Eden. Maybe he came to the conclusion that, despite his great speeches on a United Europe, European unity was less important than the restoration of the Anglo-American alliance – which he erroneously thought had been damaged by the Attlee Government – and the securing of some accommodation with Stalin's Russia. Whatever the reason, the division of spoils was damaging, for on Europe Eden was every bit as blinkered and blimpish as Bevin had been, sharing the same delusions of Britain's continued grandeur. In this Eden was at one with most British politicians and most of the British people, who were similarly out of touch with contemporary reality. Only a man with the stature and vision of Churchill could have forced his countrymen to confront it. Unfortunately, Churchill's own vision was now clouded by the general miasma and by his own natural tendency to relive the dramatic days of 1940–45.

Towards the end of his life, Clement Attlee likened Churchill to 'a layer cake. One layer was certainly seventeenth century. The eighteenth century in him is obvious. There was the nineteenth century and a large slice of course of the twentieth century; and another, curious layer which may possibly have been the twenty-first.'[21] In Churchill's last Government the twentieth-century layer was dominant in home affairs; in foreign policy the nineteenth-century and the twentieth-century layers alternated depending on the part of the world he was dealing with, but, unlike in the Opposition years, the twenty-first-century layer had almost entirely disappeared.

The first European issue to face the new Government was the European Defence Community or the Pleven Plan for a European army. Such an army was Churchill's idea. In Strasbourg in August 1950 he had called for 'the immediate creation of a European army under a unified command . . . in which we should bear a worthy and honourable part'. In other words, as Harold Macmillan pointed out, he expected Britain to play 'a leading role not merely cheer from the side lines'.[22]

Unfortunately the European Defence Community would have been very different from the European army envisaged by Churchill at Strasbourg. Churchill did not go into detail, but he was evidently calling for an army composed of national elements, a British, a French and a German division, say, woven together by alliance, common organisation and unified command. In contrast, the plan put forward by René Pleven, the French Prime Minister, but in fact drawn up by Jean Monnet, was the military counterpart of the Schuman Plan, also drawn up by Monnet. Designed to prevent German rearmament, which the Americans wanted, and a German army, which the French and many others still had good reason to fear, it proposed 'a complete merger of men and equipment under a single European political and military authority'. This 'amalgam', in Churchill's words, 'of the European nations divested of all national characteristics and traditions' would not have been an effective fighting force. It was a political solution for a military and political problem. Nevertheless, the Pleven Plan for a European army and British participation in it had been supported when in Opposition by, of all people, the new Foreign Secretary. Anthony Eden had thought it would be 'immensely advantageous' if there could be a German contribution to a European army in which French, Belgian, Dutch and British soldiers served side by side.[23]

On coming into office, Eden purged himself of even the most lukewarm European sentiments as quickly as Bevin had jettisoned his left-can-speak-to-left rhetoric in 1945. Within weeks of the election, the new Conservative Foreign Secretary, ignoring what he had said only nine months before, in Rome rejected out of hand any idea of Britain taking a part in a European army. Eden's contemptuous attitude was all the more gratuitous, since he was well aware that the Cabinet had authorised the new Home Secretary, Sir David Maxwell Fyfe, to make a far less discouraging statement earlier that day to the Council of Europe in Strasbourg.[24]

A few days later Churchill, too, went back on what he had said in Opposition. In a defence debate he gave Attlee and Bevin well-deserved praise for their distinguished part in the establishment of NATO and for embarking on a 'tremendous rearmament programme'; he then stressed the 'broad framework of national agreement' between the parties on defence, while not neglecting to exacerbate the disagreement on defence within the Labour Party. He embarrassed the Labour leadership and infuriated Aneurin Bevan by conceding that apparently 'by accident, perhaps not from the best of motives', Bevan had 'happened to be right' in thinking Labour's rearmament programme too large for the British economy to achieve. Churchill evidently thought that the framework of national agreement before the parties now included the European army. Although he quoted his Strasbourg speech on the subject, he did not, as Attlee noted, quote the passage which had clearly signalled British participation. Britain did not now propose to 'merge in the European army', the Prime Minister said, 'but we are already joined to it'.[25]

On wider European issues also, Sir Winston soon reneged on what he had said in Opposition, but this time only in private. In a Cabinet paper on 'United Europe' he maintained that he had never thought that Britain or the British Commonwealth should become 'an integral part of a European Federation' and claimed that he had never given any support to such an idea, a claim that would be difficult to square with his Albert Hall speech in May 1947.[26] In Opposition he had been careful to avoid both rigid constitutional formulas and distant speculation. His attitude had been both visionary and akin to that of Quintin Hogg, who on the death of his father, Lord Hailsham, had become a reluctant member of the House of Lords and for the time being was effectively out of politics. Winding up for the Opposition on the first day of the debate on the Schuman Plan, Hogg had denied that he was forcing federal union on anyone, expressing willingness to follow the words of Cardinal Newman's hymn 'Lead kindly Light':

> I do not ask to see
> The distant scene; one step enough for me.[27]

Now, probably under Eden's influence, Churchill was reverting to the negativism of Attlee and Bevin for whom one step towards European unity was always one too many.

What Churchill confided to his Cabinet, Anthony Eden voiced abroad. Looking determinedly backwards, the Foreign Secretary told a New York audience that 'Britain's story and her interests lie far beyond the continent of Europe'. Britain's 'family ties' in every corner of the world were Britain's 'life' and made it impossible for her 'to join a federation on the continent of Europe. This is something which we know, in our bones, we cannot do.'[28]

The Tory delegates to the Council of Europe and Strasbourg, angered by Eden's hostility to Europe and by Churchill's apparent change of mind or loss of interest, protested to Churchill, from whom they received an anodyne reply. Other remonstrances were merely passed on to Eden, who paid no attention. The Foreign Office circulated a very negative paper on European integration, which expressed the improbable view that the complete integration of the Schuman Plan countries would not be harmful to the United Kingdom. Harold Macmillan, who as Minister of Housing and Local Government was 'now entirely enveloped in clouds of bricks and mortar', sent Eden a reply which the Foreign Secretary evidently could not be bothered to read. Macmillan took his opposition to Cabinet, but apart from Maxwell Fyfe his colleagues were almost unanimously against him. Writing to Churchill of 'the growing sense of confusion and dismay' of the Tories, who had supported the European movement, and complaining that the opposition of the Foreign Office was 'as strong under your administration as under the previous one', he pointed out that this was 'quite inconsistent' with what Churchill and Eden had said in Opposition. Macmillan contemplated resignation. Both he and Maxwell Fyfe later thought they should have done more, but Eden's prestige was high, the Cabinet was largely excluded from foreign affairs, both men had affection for and loyalty to Churchill, and both were immersed in the important work of their departments. So, understandably, they abandoned Europe to Eden and the Foreign Office.[29]

In February 1952 Macmillan commented in his diary on Churchill's 'strange unwillingness to defend the ideas and ideals which he did so much to promote'. He thought some would attribute this to pure opportunism: Europe had served its purpose while he was in Opposition; now he could forget it. But that, Macmillan believed, was not 'the truth. His mind is now much more obsessed with the practical need of getting some genuine defences into being and with keeping the Americans in the ring. For him, these are the first things which we must pursue first.' Very possibly, too, Churchill was daunted by the prospect of a long and wearing row with Eden, most of his colleagues in Cabinet, the parliamentary party, the civil service and public opinion, if he pursued his European vision. In addition his conduct may have been affected by what his former private secretary regarded as his loss of 'power of fitting in all the problems one to another'. That would accord with Macmillan's view that Churchill's mind tended to concentrate on a single major problem.[30]

The Conservative Government's relapse into the same insularity which its leaders had decried when in Opposition to the Labour administration has often been regarded as another missed opportunity for Britain to have assumed the leadership of Europe. Certainly there was a major difference between what Macmillan called Churchill's 'European conception' and the policy pursued by his Government, but the differences between Eden and Macmillan and the other Tory Europeans were more of tone than of substance. Probably even the policy and attitudes of Macmillan and those who thought like him would not have been far-reaching enough to gain the assent of the continental 'Six'.

Just as the Schuman Plan had been in large part a device to solve the problem of future German industrial dominance in Europe, the plan for a European Defence Community was a device to solve the problem of future German military supremacy. Having seen Europe almost ruined by aggressive nationalism that had caused two world wars, and aware that attempts to keep Germany subdued by force would not work for long, Jean Monnet and other enlightened Europeans had realised that a dose of supra-nationalism was the only way to keep destructive nationalism in check. They saw that the national aims of the countries composing the Six would be best furthered by a pooling of sovereignty in supra-national institutions. Admittedly, as Jean Monnet wrote, Britain had not known the trauma of German occupation and had not been conquered. Therefore 'she felt no need to exorcise the past'. All the same, Britain had suffered much in both world wars, and others besides Winston Churchill, who in Opposition had seen the need for 'some sacrifice or merger of natural sovereignty' and looked forward to 'the gradual assumption by all the nations concerned of that larger sovereignty' which alone could protect their distinctive customs and traditions, should have been able to understand and share the desire of the Six for an injection of supra-nationality into Europe. Yet not even Macmillan, Boothby and the others were prepared to go that far. So, even if the Tory Europeans did not exaggerate the desire of the Six for British leadership in Europe, which they almost certainly did, the chances of agreement between them and the Six of the Schuman Plan in 1951–2 were slender.[31]

Britain looked at the world differently from the Six (other than France), because its leaders and its people thought that the country was still a great power and still very much one of the 'Big Three'. With hindsight, of course, everything seems simple. To statesmen at the time, burdened with overwork and worries, things are more complicated. The British politicians of the post-war era should not be expected to have foreseen the speedy dissolution of the British Empire, but they should at least have noticed what had already happened. India had gone, and the decline of British power had long been staring them in the face, yet for most of the time they averted their glance and carried on as though the decline had not occurred. They behaved as though Britain were still on much the same level as the United States. Even during the war, however, Churchill had known that Britain had ceased to be an equal. In April 1945, after failing to persuade General Eisenhower of the obvious importance of the Western allies taking Berlin, he had told representatives of the Dominions and the War Cabinet that the resources in men and material commanded by the United States 'were vastly superior to our own and they had acquired during this war a new capacity and experience . . .' The British Commonwealth could only 'hold her own', the Prime Minister went on, 'by our superior statecraft and experience, and above all, by the unity of the British Commonwealth of Nations'.[32]

Except in mainly marginal matters, 'the unity of the British Commonwealth of Nations' was now a thing of the past. During the war Britain had been unable to protect her empire in the Far East, and her relations with Australia had sometimes been stormy. After the war Australia and New Zealand were only recognising reality – the decline of British and the rise of American power in the Pacific – when in 1951 they made a defence agreement with the United States which excluded Britain. The Labour Government had taken the Anzus Pact in its stride, but it rankled with Churchill. Although India and Pakistan had been kept in the Commonwealth by the device of enabling republics to be members provided they recognised the British monarch as Head of the Commonwealth, the British Empire and Commonwealth was plainly no longer a unit of power in the way it had been in 1914 and 1939.

Two conclusions followed or should have followed. The first was that only in fantasy could the British Empire and Commonwealth be thought to bring to the United Kingdom an accretion of power sufficient to take her anywhere near parity with the United States and the Soviet Union. The second was that the existence of the Commonwealth was not an adequate, let alone a good, reason for Britain standing aside from moves towards greater unity in Europe, especially as much of the Commonwealth desired greater British involvement in Europe, thinking it would be beneficial to themselves as well as to Britain. When the Conservative MP Anthony Nutting, who became a Foreign Office Minister in 1951, was visiting parts of the Commonwealth in the late 1940s, an Australian leader told him: 'My country is best known in Great Britain for sending over a cricket team every five years [he meant every four years] and an army every twenty-five. If you fellows took a bit more interest in Europe between wars, maybe we wouldn't have to send the army and could concentrate on cricket.'[33]

The Anglo-American alliance and the so-called unity of the English-speaking peoples had more reality but were an almost equal source of delusions. The United States had saved Britain and Western Europe in two world wars although her intervention in the second one had been largely 'involuntary': had not Hitler made the vast and inexplicable mistake of declaring war on her after the Japanese attack on Pearl Harbor, America would probably have confined her military effort to the Far East. And the continuation of American involvement in Europe after the war was a vital British and European interest. Yet the gap between American and British power that Churchill had noted in 1945 widened to a gulf in the post-war years. If Britain was still one of the Big Three, she was at most, as one official wrote, 'Lepidus in the trium- virate with Mark Antony and Augustus'. Only if she was joined with Europe could she have become the equivalent of Mark Antony. That was in fact what the United States wanted, but Britain preferred to be Lepidus on her own. She was happier being a subsidiary partner, or rather a satellite of the United States.[34]

She sought the exclusive favours of her ally rather than enter into a more equal relationship in which those favours would have been shared with France and other European countries. In her obsessive courtship of Washington, Britain often showed a surprising lack of dignity. She flaunted herself as America's greatest love, suggesting in effect that the two countries were joined together in wedlock. And she went on doing so, even though the United States usually spurned her advances, pro- fessing friendship but insisting on keeping the relationship platonic. With all her talk of 'the special relationship', Britain was continually setting herself up as America's chosen partner when, for better or worse, she was always the bridesmaid, never the bride.*

On a visit to the United States shortly before the 1951 election, Eden showed his misperception of the contemporary world by saying in Denver that while the boundaries of British responsibility and influence 'might seem to have shrunk, they had not in fact greatly changed'. Later he advised an audience in Chicago not to underestimate the part 'the Commonwealth and Empire' could play in strengthening the free world; it was upon the United States and the British Commonwealth that 'the chief responsibility for leadership had to fall'. Four months later, on their first post-election visit to Washington, the new Prime Minister and Foreign Secretary had ample opportunity to discover how times had changed since 1945. While finding President Truman nice and cheerful, Eden's Private Secretary found his treatment of 'poor old Winston' occasionally abrupt and wounding. It was impossible, Shuckburgh wrote

---

* From time to time, other powers described Britain's attitude to the relationship in a much less refined way.

in his diary, 'not to be conscious that we are playing second fiddle'.[35]

Shuckburgh's bosses were less clear-sighted. After dinner one night Churchill asked the American Secretary of State, Dean Acheson, if he had not felt that round the table that evening there had been 'gathered the governance of the world'. Such a thought had not struck Acheson. And on his return Eden told the Cabinet he was 'horrified' at the way the Americans had treated us: after listening to what we had to say, they made 'on most issues their own decisions' – as if that were a matter for surprise. More remarkably, Churchill's and Eden's treatment in Washington seems scarcely to have affected their future attitudes and conduct.[36]

Despite Churchill's hope that his wartime friendship with General Eisenhower would serve to re-establish the 'special relationship' when the Republicans won the presidential election of 1952, the new President was clear that, whatever the warmth of his personal relations with Churchill, their official relationship 'had to rest on a different plane'. Noting in his diary that Churchill had 'developed an almost childlike faith' in 'British–American partnership', Eisenhower wished that he would turn over 'the leadership of the British Conservation [sic] party to younger men'. Maybe that was a Freudian slip caused by the President thinking that Churchill and Eden were trying to conserve an ecosystem that no longer existed. At all events Churchill's 1948 conception of Britain's position in the world being based on 'three intersecting circles' – represented by the United States, the British Empire and Europe – was by 1953 a recipe for British muddle and self-deception, helping to foster the illusion of an enormously powerful Britain at the centre of the world stage. The reality was different. The United States welcomed Britain as an ally, but rejected a 'special relationship': we shall deal better with our common problems, the President told Eden, 'if each of us preserves, consciously, an attitude of absolute equality with all other nations'. Moreover, the Americans were hostile to the British Empire and regretted Britain's 'colonial mindset'. The Empire or Commonwealth was a useful grouping of states linked together by history and much else but was incapable of pursuing a common foreign policy. And Britain insisted on remaining outside the inner circle of Europe, even though the United States wanted her to join and lead it.[37]

After a botched operation for gall-stones in April 1953, when the surgeon's knife slipped into the bile duct, Eden's health was undermined and his uncertain temperament became even more mercurial. One of his weaknesses as Foreign Secretary was his tendency to be over-influenced by his personal likes and dislikes. 'Eden's attitude to European unity', Sir Robert Rhodes James has written, 'would have been better justified if his relations with the United States had been more sympathetic.' He did not get on well with Acheson, who rightly, if offensively, told Shuckburgh to 'learn to live in the world as it is', a remark which was directed against Shuckburgh's boss. Eden got on even worse with Acheson's successor, John Foster Dulles, who was Eisenhower's Secretary of State. Another of Eden's weaknesses, as Churchill told him after a row, was that he was 'totally incapable of differentiating great points and small points'. Yet this did not prevent him achieving a series of dazzling foreign policy successes in 1954. His role as peacemaker in Trieste, Austria, Indo-China and the Middle East may have been, as a diplomat has written, largely 'self-selected', but in that role he brought off a series of diplomatic triumphs; over Indo-China, especially, he performed a great, if temporary, service to the world. His part in the formation of the Western European Union was another success, even if a more far-sighted European policy would have achieved a better and earlier result. As an architect of a foreign policy Eden lacked vision, but as an executant of one he was superb; 1954 is rightly considered his *annus mirabilis*. Following Churchill, he became a Knight of the Garter in that year.[38]

Economic and Social Policy

When Eden fell ill in 1953, Churchill took over the Foreign Office, a demonstration that his powers were still massive, even if he did not concern himself with the more mundane aspects of administration. When Churchill himself fell ill, Salisbury took over, and Butler took charge of the Government. After the defeat of Robot – the only time when an overlord at the Treasury might have been helpful – Rab Butler proved himself an excellent Chancellor of the Exchequer. Admittedly he was helped by world conditions. Hayek's prediction in 1944 that 'Conservative Socialism' or any governmental intervention in the economy would set any country unlucky enough to have such a misguided government marching down the road to serfdom turned out to be one of the most inaccurate prophecies ever made. Mindful of the great prewar slump and anxious to provide better conditions for their peoples in the post-war years, all advanced capitalist countries made a 'deliberate attempt to influence the level of effective demand'.[39] Their heretical rejection of *laissez-faire* produced not, as Hayek feared, depression and dictatorship but freedom and growing prosperity. The years between the end of the war and 1973 were the golden age of capitalism. In those years – the Keynesian era – the world economy performed outstandingly well by every criterion. And so by our standards did we. Britain's economic performance between 1945 and 1973 was better than it had been either in the inter-war years or before 1914, and very much better than it has been in the twenty years since. Full employment was combined with only a mild rate of inflation and more growth than for almost a century. Only when the British post-war performance was compared with that of fairly similar economies, and found to be worse than all of them except the United States and Portugal, could gloom replace self-satisfaction; and the early 1950s were too soon for such comparisons to be common.

After Robot's demise Butler, as he said, 'reverted to normal Keynesian economics',[40] and initially his policy differed little from Labour's. More than two years later, when a greater divergence existed between the Conservative and Labour Parties, *The Economist* introduced 'Mr Butskell . . . a composite of the present Chancellor and the previous one' who spoke up for the cause of moderation from both sides of the House.[41] This unexpected example of *Economist* levity proved irresistible to columnists and cartoonists, while doing little to recommend either Butler or Gaitskell to their internal critics. Butler had long been regarded by the Conservative Right, men like Beaverbrook and Bracken, as being little better than a Socialist, while the Bevanites tended to regard Gaitskell as rather worse than a Conservative.

Although Mr Butskell was a brilliant journalistic conceit, it concealed as much truth as it conveyed. Certainly both Gaitskell and Butler favoured Keynesian techniques and sought to maintain full employment. Both were moderates and both had good political manners. Both, too, had considerable respect for each other, but Gaitskell had (in Butler's words) 'unquenchably socialist' convictions and a strong belief in equality; Butler had no such convictions or belief. Moreover, he had in contrast to Gaitskell a belief in monetary policy and much less interest in planning. Butler favoured convertibility; Gaitskell defended exchange controls and the sterling area. They differed, too, on the far greater emphasis that Gaitskell (rightly) gave to the need for Britain to invest more and consume less. A certain amount of agreement between successive Chancellors was nothing new, as we saw of Churchill and Snowden in the twenties. Mr Snowhill or Mr Churchden would have been as apposite as Mr Butskell: unfortunately *The Economist* of that time did not think of it. Curiously, however, it was *The Economist* which on Butler's departure from the Treasury best summed up the differences between the two men: 'The essential achievement of Mr Butler's Chancellorship has been Britain's advance from reliance upon compulsory controls to reliance upon a free market economy.'[42]

The Conservatives came back to office pledged to preserve the welfare state which had been designed by the wartime coalition, and they amply kept their promise. Sir Herbert Williams and Sir Waldron Smithers, who played the organ in his parish church and drank hugely at Westminster, were still in the Commons, but their occasional pleas for a return to the minimal state were echoes from a past to which almost nobody wished to revert. Hence, despite Labour predictions that the National Health Service would be spoiled or ruined by the Tories, spending was not reduced under Churchill, and only minimal charges were added in 1952 to the ones already introduced by the Attlee Government, although even those were highly unpopular.

Churchill's first Minister of Health, Harry Crookshank, was the sort of Conservative front-bencher whose inadequate performance on social matters had led to the formation of the One Nation Group. He would have been a poor Health Minister even if that had been his only job. But he was also Leader of the House, a post for which he was much better suited and in which he soon achieved some note by claiming that when the Government came into office they had found Labour's skeletons hanging like 'candelabra in every office and Department'. Much as Eden had immediately found he could not combine the Leadership of the Commons with the Foreign Office, Crookshank soon found that two hats were too many for the Minister of Health. In March 1952 he made an indifferent speech on the bill imposing the new health charges. Later in the debate the Prime Minister came into the chamber to listen to Aneurin Bevan, then a back-bencher, who accused the Government of wanting 'to dismantle the welfare state' and of taking 'the first long step' towards 'the beginnings of the end of British parliamentary democracy'. Churchill stayed to hear how the next speaker, Iain Macleod, would cope with Bevan's diatribe. After Macleod's opening remarks that he wanted 'to deal closely and with relish with [Bevan's] vulgar, crude and intemperate speech' and that a debate on the NHS without Bevan 'would be like putting on Hamlet with no one in the part of the first gravedigger', the Prime Minister felt no inclination to leave. Instead he asked the Chief Whip who the speaker was and if he was ministerial material. Patrick Buchan Hepburn's reply that Macleod was still quite young did not please Churchill who had been a Cabinet Minister aged thirty-four; and a month later Macleod at the age of thirty-eight became Minister of Health, though outside the Cabinet.[43]

Both for Macleod and the Tory Government, it was an ideal appointment. The son of a doctor, whose interest in health predated his innovative work for the *One Nation* book, Macleod was fully aware that health was a crucial political issue. The young NHS had already transformed the lives of most people, giving them a sense of security they had never enjoyed before. The voters, some two-thirds of whom came from the working classes, were not willing to let go the basic principle of the NHS, that medical care should be free at the point of need. Yet the attitude to the NHS of some Conservative MPs (and some Ministers) could easily be mistaken for hostility; they appeared to regard the health service primarily as a source of financial savings. The Treasury, of course, was also looking for economies. Macleod saw that an inquiry was necessary and might well be helpful. With Butler's help he secured reasonable terms of reference; the membership of the committee under the chairmanship of Macleod's former economics tutor at Cambridge was also encouraging. Bevan predictably interpreted the appointment of the Guillebaud Committee as the prelude to savage cuts. He had misjudged his opponent. If economies could be made without lowering the quality of the NHS, Macleod would make them. Otherwise he would resist them. The existence of the Guillebaud Committee enabled him to ward off the pressure for cuts until it had reported, which was not until after he had left the Ministry. As the economic outlook lightened, Macleod was able in early 1954 to announce an ambitious programme of hospital-building which was desperately needed. On preventive care his record was mixed: he chain-smoked throughout a press conference called to announce a link between smoking and lung cancer, but by a well-publicised visit to the Family Planning Association in North Kensington he brought the important issue of contraception out of the shadows. According to the FPA, his visit did much to dispel 'the clouds of prejudice and hypocrisy' which had prevented proper discussion of the subject.[44]

After the advance of Butler's 1944 Act, these were quiet years in the educational field. In a judgement that demonstrated the patronising attitude some Tories then held towards women in politics, Brendan Bracken dismissed Churchill's third choice for the job – after Clement Davies and Walter Elliot – 'Mother Horsburgh', as a 'disastrous Minister of Education . . . she is a good old girl who doesn't conceal her disbelief in education'. While that was unfair, Florence Horsburgh was not a great success. Admittedly her male colleagues did not make life easy for her. She was kept out of the Cabinet until 1953; the Prime Minister's interest in the subject was tepid; and spending struggled to keep pace with rising demand. Florence Horsburgh was undogmatic, allowing experiments in comprehensive schools 'purely as an educational matter'.[45] Under her regime, fewer than twenty comprehensive schools were approved, in marked contrast to that of the next woman Education Minister: in the early seventies, over three thousand such schools were established. Overcrowded classrooms were still a serious problem when Churchill appointed the far abler David Eccles to succeed Miss Hors-burgh in the 1954 reshuffle, and only after his arrival did educational expenditure per head significantly increase.

Housing was a very different matter. Harold Macmillan had been angered and disappointed when Churchill asked him to 'build the houses for the people', saying to Christopher Soames, if the Prime Minister 'wants to kill me politically, then let him do it, but not this way . . .' Only after consulting his wife, the Head of the Civil Service and the Secretary to the Cabinet did he accept the job. His expectations of anything better had been unrealistic, and even though some of his friends considered the Housing Ministry 'a backwater', no other post could have propelled him so quickly up the political hierarchy.[46]

The party's rash but specific promise to build 300,000 houses a year placed Macmillan in a strong position for the inevitable battles with the Treasury over resources, and Butler anyway knew that housing was very high on Churchill's list of priorities. Despite his initial reservations Macmillan tackled the job with great competence and energy, and in December 1953 he achieved the magic 300,000. More, of course, than the 1950 pledge was at stake: the housing drive chimed in with Conservative aspirations to a 'property-owning democracy', and *One Nation* had linked housing problems to ill health. All the same, some of the massive resources given to building houses would have been better spent on building factories and industrial investment. No other country spent so much on both defence and housing,[47] and Britain's economy would have been stronger had those two fields not pre-empted such a large share of public investment.

Immigration

In February 1955 Ian Gilmour and his wife were invited to a primarily social lunch at 10 Downing Street. Although very deaf to begin with, the Prime Minister became much less so after he had summoned his hearing aid, and he was as far from being ga-ga as anybody else present. After a while he raised the question of the *Spectator*'s attitude to the arrival of immigrants from the West Indies. Gilmour explained his paper's fears that if immigration continued at its current rate there would be an explosion in Brixton or elsewhere; it therefore favoured measures to restrict it. After expressing some measure of approval, Churchill said: 'I think it is the most important subject facing this country, but I can not get any of my ministers to take any notice.'[48]

The problem had originated in June 1948 when the *Empire Windrush*, dubbed a 'little *Mayflower*' in reverse, landed 510 Jamaican passengers and stowaways at Tilbury. A Colonial Office spokesman tactlessly called 'this unorganised rush ... a disaster'. From the Jamaicans' point of view, however, their arrival was well-timed. For the Attlee Government, too full of pride in the Empire to notice that it was already disintegrating, had just passed the British Nationality Act, making the citizens of any UK colony British subjects. The Jamaican influx was therefore legal. Between 1948 and 1950 West Indian immigrants arrived at a rate of some 1,000 a year, a rate which doubled in 1951. After setting up a Cabinet Committee, the Attlee Government decided that to amend their 1948 Act might have disastrous consequences for the Commonwealth, while recognising that legislation to curb immigration might be necessary in the future.[49]

In the first two years of the Conservative Government immigration did not significantly increase, yet at the end of 1952 Churchill drew the Cabinet's attention to 'the difficult social problems' – overcrowding, etc – that were likely to be caused by the Post Office's employment of a large number of colonial workers. As a result the Home Secretary was invited to see if immigration could be prevented, and another committee, this time a civil service one, was set up. When it completed its lengthy deliberations the Committee came to the unremarkable conclusion that immigration could not be curbed without legislation. No action was taken, but the Prime Minister presciently told the Cabinet 'that the rapid improvement in communications was likely to lead to continuing increases in the number of coloured people coming into the country, and their presence here would sooner or later come to be resented by large sections of the British people'. Regrettably, he was right on both counts. New Commonwealth immigration rose to 11,000 in 1954 and to over 40,000 in 1955. The first race riots took place three years later in Notting Hill.[50]

Yet nothing was done. Like the Labour Government, Conservative Ministers thought they were still living in the age of empire. They feared that to curb immigration would disrupt the Commonwealth, even though many Commonwealth countries had placed restrictions on immigration from Britain. With a few exceptions, most Ministers remained complacent, while their supporters were growing restive. All the same, Churchill's evidently reluctant summing-up of the Cabinet discussion in February 1954 held true until the end of his Government. 'It might well be true', he said, 'that the problem has not yet assumed sufficient proportions to enable the government to take adequate counter-measures.' Had he continued in office beyond April 1955, legislation would almost certainly have been introduced far earlier than it was. Ministers' motives were honourable. Their reluctance to abandon 'the doctrine of common citizenship with the United Kingdom and the colonial Empire' was perfectly proper, the *Spectator* commented, 'but doctrines can not always be allowed to take precedence over facts'.[51]

Denationalisation

The Government carried out its commitment to return steel and road haulage to the private sector. Churchill summed up the Government's attitude at the end of November 1953: while they were opposed to the principle, only when they believed that a measure of nationalisation 'was a real hindrance to our island life' had they reversed it; elsewhere they were trying to make a success of public ownership.[52] Surprisingly, road haulage was the more contentious of the two measures, a guillotine being necessary. On steel, Duncan Sandys, the Minister of Supply, wanted a bill which might cause a future Labour Government to leave the industry undisturbed. His preference for a moderate bill, in which he was supported by Butler, Macmillan and Salisbury, and opposed by Woolton and Crookshank, secured Cabinet backing. The Sandys bill transferred the ownership of the industry into private hands while setting up an iron and steel board to supervise it; this was a long way from *laissez-faire*. Even so, the Labour spokesman, George Strauss, who had been opposed to steel nationalisation the first time, oddly found himself promising to nationalise it a second time.

The Churchill Government thus abolished two nationalised corporations; it also created a new one and ended the monopoly of another. Atomic energy was under the Ministry of Supply, where Attlee and the Treasury had decided to leave it despite strong representations from Cherwell. Duncan Sandys took the same view. Eventually, however, the 'Prof', after pointing out that Britain was the only nation to place its atomic undertaking under the control of ordinary government departments, subjecting 'it to the same rule as the collection of customs', won the battle in Cabinet, and the Atomic Energy Authority was set up.[53]

A Committee on the future of broadcasting, chaired by Beveridge, had recommended the continuance of the BBC's monopoly with only one dissenter, the then still obscure Selwyn Lloyd, called 'Mr Celluloid' by Churchill. Yet it was Lloyd's minority report which the Government eventually acted upon. Churchill himself was originally opposed to the monopoly, telling his doctor that the BBC's behaviour had been 'tyrannical'; they had kept him off the air for eleven years before the war. He also thought they were 'honeycombed with socialists – probably even communists'. On the other hand, he told his wife that it was not a subject he felt very strongly about, and later he rebuked Woolton for a Central Office publication which advocated sponsored television; he told the Party Chairman that half the Cabinet was against it and they were trying to stave off this 'stupid and interested agitation'. All the same, back-bench and commercial pressures prevailed over the opposition of Eden, Salisbury and Butler in the Cabinet and others such as Lords Halifax, Radcliffe and Hailsham outside it. The Act was passed in 1954, and what turned out to be the welcome innovation of commercial television began in 1955.[54]

Industrial Relations

For obvious reasons Churchill was anxious to avoid even a mild repetition of the industrial strife of the 1920s – he too had his own belligerent part in the General Strike to live down. The Minister of Labour would therefore be a particularly important post in a Conservative Government. Maxwell Fyfe had seemed destined for it, but during the election campaign he said that a Conservative Government would not legislate on trade union matters 'without a round-table talk to try to reach agreement', an undertaking that nowadays seems highly conciliatory. In 1951 it created a furore, into which Churchill was drawn, a graphic illustration of the then climate of opinion. As Macmillan noted in his diary, Maxwell Fyfe's speeches and writings had anyway thoroughly frightened the unions;[55] so he became Home Secretary, and Sir Walter Monckton went to the Ministry of Labour. A former adviser to Edward VIII and to the Nizam of Hyderabad, Monckton was a clever, charming and emollient man whose legal and negotiating skills had won for the coal owners much larger compensation for their nationalised pits than they had expected or deserved.

'Winston's riding orders to me', Monckton (a keen horseman) later wrote, were 'to do my best to preserve industrial peace' and so disprove Labour's predictions of 'grave industrial troubles' if the Conservatives were elected. Monckton replied that he would seek to do that by trying to do justice 'without worrying about party politics' – which since he had only entered Parliament the previous year he would not find too difficult.[56] Monckton succeeded brilliantly in the task the Prime Minister had set him, gaining the respect of his officials and the trust of the TUC. The trade union leaders of the early 1950s, a very different body of men from the arrogant clique which confronted the Governments of the

1970s, reciprocated Monckton's conciliatory spirit. Strikes were kept down to the minimum. Only in 1954 did the number of man-days lost in strikes rise above two million, the first time that figure had been exceeded since 1948; most of the time lost came from unofficial strikes, of which there were nearly 2,000. Until 1955 there were no major official strikes.[57]

Of course the price for peace was paid in inflationary wage settlements. In consequence Churchill and Monckton have been vilified for their policy of industrial 'appeasement'.[58] Churchill probably did take his anxiety to avoid strikes a little too far: in the railway dispute of 1954–5 even Monckton wanted to stand firm, but the Government gave in; and in 1955 a Gallup poll showed that even most Labour supporters thought the Government should have handled wage claims more firmly.[59] Nevertheless, in giving the highest priority to the avoidance of industrial warfare, Churchill was undoubtedly right on both political and economic grounds. Nothing would have been more damaging to the Conservative Party than the public's realisation that the party could not get on with the unions and that Conservative Government spelled industrial trouble. All the curative work of 1945–51 would have been undone and the party branded as irredeemably committed to class warfare. The Conservatives would soon have been back in the wilderness and would probably have stayed there.

The economic arguments for Churchill's attitude were equally strong. Cherwell scarcely exaggerated when he told the Prime Minister that they had to remember that 'a coal strike lasting even a week would be disastrous; a fortnight would compel us to surrender'.[60] The trade unions were quite powerful enough to cause enormous economic damage and create national chaos if they wished. And as Woolton later wrote, 'strikes for more wages could easily have grown into a strike against the Government's political policies'. Even if that had not occurred, a long strike would probably have caused a run on the pound, necessitating harsh economic measures which would have increased the Government's unpopularity and might before long have led to its fall.[61]

Hence the Government faced a choice of evils. Inflationary wage settlements helped to price British goods out of their export markets and thus slowed the British economy. Between 1953 and 1954, Butler stated in his 1955 Budget speech, output per man rose by two and a half per cent, while wages and salaries rose by about seven and a half per cent; between December 1954 and October 1955, he said in his emergency Budget speech, wages had risen by nine per cent. The Government's compliance in this wage spiral is attributed by today's far Right to a loss of political nerve by Churchill and the Conservative Party: they lacked the political courage to oppose the advance of socialism.[62]

This equation of moral cowardice with opposition to the brand of nineteenth-century liberalism adopted by Conservative right-wingers in the last two decades is improbable; again, it is mere ideology and wholly ahistorical.

In conditions of full employment the balance of power lies with a heavily unionised labour force. Shortly after Churchill had been succeeded by Eden, Walter Elliot, who had been Minister of Health in Chamberlain's pre-war Government and would have been Minister of Education in Churchill's post-war one had he not been out when the Prime Minister telephoned, pointed in Parliament to the power of the unions 'to bring to a dead stop the industrial processes upon which a modern state depends'. He thought a 'new Estate of the Realm' was emerging. 'We can vote', he continued, 'the supply of money without which enterprises of the state can not be conducted; the trade unions can vote the supply of labour without which, equally, the affairs of the state cannot be conducted.'[63] Elliot wanted to see an industrial parliament, as Churchill had advocated a quarter of a century earlier. That was a good idea, but it would not have had an immediate effect. In 1946 the Attlee Government had created a National Joint Advisory Council of employers and trade unions, which had been retained by the incoming Government. Monckton tried to turn it into a body which would have fulfilled some of the functions of an industrial parliament, but the TUC fought shy of anything that might smack of a wages policy.

Some critics wanted the Government to take legislative action against trade unions, such as requiring a secret ballot before a strike could be called. That provision worked well in the 1980s when conditions were quite different. By then the trade unions had comprehensively alienated public opinion; in the fifties, although strikes were unpopular, the unions were still respected. In 1954 a Gallup poll found that only 12 per cent of the public disapproved of the unions; in 1979 that figure had risen to a post-war high of 36 per cent. Even more important, there were some three million unemployed in the eighties; in the fifties there were less than 500,000. Hence the unions were far more powerful. Attlee's remark during the 1955 election that 'today even our opponents cannot put forward something entirely contrary to Labour's point of view' was only mildly boastful; it had a basis of fact.[64]

In any case, strike ballots probably would not have worked. As Iain Macleod, Monckton's successor at the Ministry of Labour, put it both publicly and privately: 'The idea that the workers are less militant than their leaders ... is not my experience, nor is it the experience of any Minister of Labour.'[65]

Above all, of course, there were the problems of unofficial strikes and what to do with those trade unionists who went on strike without a ballot. Put them all in prison? The Government was surely right to rely on what Butler in his 1954 Budget speech called 'voluntary moderation'. That policy had in fact worked well in 1952 and 1953 when rises in wages were small, but then it broke down, leaving what Butler later called 'a gaping hole in our armour'.[66] Yet any other policy could have produced more holes than armour.

Theoretically, of course, the far-sighted option is to push through reforms during tranquil periods when one's opponents are moderate. If only politics could be conducted at that level of abstraction, government would be an easy art. If the Government had legislated against the unions, how long would their leaders have remained moderate? They were already beginning to realise that their restraint and co-operation with the Government had distanced them from their rank and file. For them to support or only moderately oppose legislation which in the climate of the times would have been regarded as ill thought out and almost certainly unworkable, would have undermined their position. So they would have fought the Government. The resulting industrial strife, with or without anti-trade union legislation, might have destroyed the Government at a time when, despite the wage problem, they were enjoying considerable economic success. Monckton and the Conservative Cabinet were men of their time, not of the 1980s. As Roosevelt once said, politicians should try to govern their own generation, not the next one. Churchill's Cabinet did so, and they made a better job of it than later generations of politicians. In the 1950s industrial Butskellism was the least damaging policy. A far better way of fighting inflation than trade union legislation would have been the achievement of faster growth by curbing monopolies, freeing trade, encouraging investment, fostering engineering skills and retraining workers.

The Churchill–Monckton policy enjoyed the support of the whole Cabinet, with only the occasional grumble. The claim that Churchill and his Ministers all lacked the moral courage to fight the trade unions is risible. They did not feel they had to prove their virility and their courage by being aggressive and extreme. They were seeking a united country in an atmosphere of goodwill. Unquestionably their policy bequeathed problems to their successors. But what policy does not? In maintaining good industrial relations and in preserving full employment, the Churchill Government as elsewhere deserves its reputation of having been the best post-war Conservative administration.

Shedding Controls

Three months after coming into office the Government abolished identity cards. That was merely the start of a campaign to free everyday life and the economy by getting rid of unnecessary controls. In October 1951 bacon and ham, cheese, butter and margarine, cooking fats, meat, sugar and chocolate and sweets were still rationed. By July 1954 all rationing had been abolished, thus ending wartime conditions after nine years of peace. Much of the credit for this should go to Churchill, who constantly goaded ministers to do away with rationing of particular commodities. He was anxious to see sweet rationing lifted before the coronation. The Minister of Food demurred, fearing a consequent shortage of sugar. The Prime Minister insisted, and the end of rationing produced not a scarcity of sugar but a glut. Nor did the freeing of food only benefit the well-off, as was alleged by Labour which opposed every derationing order. When eggs were decontrolled, production rose and prices fell. Much the same process was put in train in industry. Controls of raw materials were taken off, and most price curbs were abolished. The number of 'spivs' and 'snoopers' fell sharply as the contraction of the black market restricted the scope of their activities. 'This is the march to freedom on which we are bound,' Butler justifiably claimed. 'Within the limits of law and social justice, our aim is freedom for every man and woman to live their own lives in their own way and not have their lives lived for them by an overweening state.'[67]

Liberating the consumer was made possible by, as well as contributing to, increased prosperity. The growing strength of the economy was the result of both luck and skill. The end of the Korean War and the fall in the price of commodities turned the terms of trade in Britain's favour, but Butler took good advantage of his luck; his handling of the economy was consistently deft. Although his 1952 Budget made no change in the total tax burden, he contrived to make it seem exciting. 'Restriction and austerity are not enough,' he told MPs. 'We want a system which offers us both more realism and more hope.' *The Times* called the Budget 'a triumph'.[68] In 1953 the Chancellor had more scope to promote expansion and was able to cut income tax and purchase tax and to promise the abolition of the Excess Profits Levy which Churchill had inserted into the party's election manifesto.

Apart from introducing a new investment allowance, Butler's 1954 effort was what he called a 'carry on' Budget; Gaitskell called it a 'tiny insignificant' one. At that stage no further stimulation of the economy was necessary or desirable. Things seemed to be going well. There had been, the Chancellor said a month later, 'a year of full employment without inflation'; it was 'the economist's dream – the desirable country so difficult to enter. Perhaps we have found a way.'[69] Butler's inclusion of the word 'perhaps' made his rejoicing at the success of the economy far less hubristic than later Ministers' clamorous boasting of an alleged economic miracle in the eighties; and unlike that of the eighties his optimism was neither preceded nor followed by the nemesis of a damaging slump. Nevertheless Butler, tormented by the fatal illness of his wife, was soon letting the expansion run too fast, and in February 1955, to Churchill's annoyance, he had to raise Bank Rate and reimpose hire-purchase restrictions.

Contrary to the later right-wing orthodoxy, Butler's fault was not to interfere too much but too little. Until 1955, industrial investment was inadequate, and virtually nothing was done to make particular industries more efficient. All the same, the economic record of the Government was one to be envied by all succeeding ones. Apart from the mess they inherited from Labour, the Churchill administration avoided the sort of economic crises that plagued its predecessor and its successors. Butler loosened the economy without endangering social peace. The welfare state was protected and improved. For those blind or conceited enough to believe themselves to be in full possession of the truth and their opponents hopelessly deluded by error, such One Nation centrism seems pusillanimous and even amounting to consorting with the enemy. For those able to distinguish more colours than black and white or red and blue, such an approach seems well-judged and wise. By pursuing it, the Government engineered a contented country; the electorate's response was to say it wanted more of the same.

At the centre of politics throughout Churchill's last premiership lay the question, 'How long will he last?' Despite the initial understanding that he would go after a year, he seemed no nearer retirement when twelve months were up. After he suffered a stroke in June 1953 he probably would have retired, had Anthony Eden not also been ill at that time. He sometimes felt that his powers had been impaired, but after his stroke he was still able to recite, almost word perfect, 350 lines of Longfellow's 'King Robert of Sicily', which he had not read for fifty years. He certainly made an astonishing recovery, enjoying a triumph at the Conservative Party Conference in 1953. As late as June 1954 Hugh Massingham, the leading political commentator of the day, told readers of the *Observer* that the Prime Minister seemed to have acquired an ascendancy over his Cabinet which he had not possessed in 1951. During his last year in office he disturbed his colleagues, especially Eden, by continually changing his mind about the date of his withdrawal. He broke a promise to Eden that he would go in September 1954. He probably should have retired in October. From then on, according to the Secretary to the Cabinet, he was losing his powers of leadership, even though he could still make a great speech, as he did in the Defence debate the following March. Eventually, after his hopes of a summit meeting, which Eden wrongly regarded as his 'lunatic obsession', had once again been dashed, he undertook to leave in April and after a wobble or two he kept his word. Probably the need to put an end to the uncertainty was a better reason for his departure than any decline in his abilities.[70]

In 1953, when both Churchill and Eden were out of action, Butler could perhaps have become Prime Minister had he striven for the job. At all other times Eden, for so long the Crown Prince, was the undoubted successor. Yet Churchill's natural reluctance to leave the stage was strengthened by the doubts he had long harboured of Eden's capacity to be Prime Minister. The night before he resigned he said to Jock Colville: 'I don't believe Anthony can do it.'[71]

Prelude to Suez

Churchill was not alone in his doubts about Anthony. When, a few weeks earlier, he had asked Lord Swinton if he thought that 'Rab' would be a better choice than Eden, Swinton's reply was that anybody would be better, since 'Anthony would be the worst Prime Minister since Lord North'. Boothby told Dalton and others that Eden, Butler and Macmillan were 'not a triumvirate, but a trinity'. He thought the other two would be 'watching Eden [who] may well be pole-axed in eighteen months' time'. That was pretty accurate except that in the end Eden pole-axed himself. Butler, however, who had never been able to take Eden wholly seriously, was not worried by his leader's limitations, which would not matter because he would 'manage him from behind'.[1]

Yet such doubts were confined to political circles. Fortified by his only partially justified reputation as an anti-appeaser before the war, Anthony Eden had long been an extraordinarily popular politician. In 1939 and 1940 he had led the polls as the most desired next Prime Minister, should Neville Chamberlain be ditched. And in August 1945 Gallup found that 31 per cent of voters wanted Eden to lead a post-war Government as against 20 per cent for Churchill and only 4 per cent for Attlee, who was by then Prime Minister. In 1951, too, Eden had achieved a higher rating than Churchill, while at the beginning of 1955 over 80 per cent had thought he was doing a good job as Foreign Secretary. Inevitably, therefore, his accession to Number 10 was widely acclaimed, his approval rating being 73 per cent. In the absence of national papers because of the London press strike, the *Yorkshire Post* assured its readers that 'the prestige and fortunes of Britain remain in safe hands'.[2]

Eden's first major decision accorded more with the doubts than the acclaim. Having lived in the shadow of Churchill for so long, he needed to put his own stamp on the Government. Yet he flinched from a reconstruction of the Cabinet. In addition to ill health, a possible reason for his inaction was that, primed by Rab's old enemy, Woolton, he wanted to shunt Butler from the Treasury. That would have been the centrepiece of the reshuffle, but Butler's wife had died of cancer a few months earlier and Eden, a thoroughly decent man, found it too difficult to move him; he then mistakenly decided not to proceed without his centrepiece.[3] He even botched the only important appointment he could not avoid making. The obvious choice to succeed himself as Foreign Secretary was Lord Salisbury, who had resigned from the Foreign Office with him in 1938 and had then made far the better resignation statement. But evidently thinking that a Foreign Secretary could no longer be in the House of Lords – although since then there have been two distinguished Foreign Secretaries in the Upper House – he appointed Harold Macmillan.

That was a double miscalculation. For one thing, Macmillan was the least likely of all his colleagues to suffer gladly Eden's constant interference in his old department; for another, the Prime Minister was ignoring Churchill's earlier warning of Macmillan's outsize ambition, which he had given in December 1954. At the time Eden had dismissed this as an old man's attempt to divide and rule. Eden had never been close to Butler or Macmillan and did not trust either of them. In apparently seeing Butler as the more likely of the two to 'pole-axe' him, Eden badly misjudged both men.

The other consequential changes were good: Selwyn Lloyd to Defence, Home to Commonwealth Relations, and Maudling, whom the *Spectator*'s political columnist dubbed 'the first dimpled child of Butskellism', to the Ministry of Supply.[4]

Eden was braver in deciding to go to the country even before he had been formally elected leader of the party. The Treasury advised that political uncertainty might set off a speculative movement against sterling; so an early election was desirable. The party argument for 'going quick' seemed to Dalton on the Opposition benches to be 'overwhelming'. Yet Eden hesitated – to the exasperation of his Party Chairman, Lord Woolton, who derided him as a man who could 'not make up his mind, which isn't a very hopeful sign'. In the end, though, Eden accepted the advice, setting 26 May as polling day. Unhappily, the Treasury's advice on the Budget was less good than on the election, and that too was accepted by Butler.[5]

In February, because the balance of payments had deteriorated, the Chancellor had raised Bank Rate to 4½ per cent as well as restoring hire-purchase restrictions. There was a substantial Budget surplus, so on accountancy principles to give half of it away could be justified. On Keynesian principles, however, it could not. The previous year Butler had set off a much-needed investment boom, whose continuance was vastly more important than increased consumption. Unemployment had fallen to 1 per cent, which on any view was over-full employment;

and the economy was plainly overheating. Hence Robert Hall and the economists in the Treasury's economic section were opposed to a tax-cutting Budget. Nevertheless the old guard of Treasury officials hoped that the increased Bank Rate would rein in the economy and gave contrary advice. To his lasting regret, Butler, whose political judgement was still impaired by the death of his wife, sided with the Treasury knights, taking sixpence off income tax, raising personal allowances and reducing purchase tax on Lancashire textiles.[6]

Almost certainly, the Tory Party needed no help from a generous Budget. The lengthy Conservative Manifesto reflected the party leader in home affairs: it was well-meaning, vague and, as *The Times* commented, 'peppered with platitudes'. 'The Conservative way', Eden wrote in one of the best passages of his Personal Statement, 'is to encourage the growth of unity and fellowship in a free and neighbourly society . . .' He believed this could be brought about if we developed 'a property-owning democracy'. For a still predominantly working-class country, that was an 'inspiring' vision, and the capable Minister of Education, Sir David Eccles, may have thought he was contributing to its realisation by proclaiming that 'we are all working class now'. Unfortunately, coming from such an elegantly coiffeured and expensively tailored minister, the announcement seemed condescending and implausible.[7]

The election campaign brought more enjoyment to the Conservatives than to Labour. This time Beaverbrook wanted the horse to win but not the jockey. Eden, however, had a good election, drawing large crowds and being particularly good on television. In contrast, Attlee seemed dated, with four of his Shadow Cabinet over seventy and another five over sixty-five; his party lacked policy and was badly split. Inevitably, therefore, Labour was on the defensive throughout. Unlike 1951, Labour could not boost their vote by smears and fears; the Tory record under Churchill had been too good. Contrary to Labour predictions, there had been no war, and Churchill had proved anything but a warmonger abroad or at home. Full employment had been maintained; and the welfare state had not been cut, but extended and improved. In addition the economy had been managed without a single economic crisis, and most people were better off. On a lower turn-out the Conservatives gained twenty-one seats – the first time since 1841 that a party had improved its position three elections running. The party also won a majority of Scottish seats and, with 49.7 per cent of the total vote, it came nearer than any party since the war to winning a majority of the votes cast.[8]

Although the Conservatives had expected to win even more seats, Eden had every reason to be pleased and confident. The only two blots on his electioneering were his instability and rages behind the scenes when even small things went wrong; and his churlish treatment of his former leader. In compensation for not having heralded a new regime by reconstructing the Government, Eden advertised the new age by treating Churchill as just another parliamentary candidate. Excluded from the national campaign, Churchill was eventually offered a television broadcast, but he had always disliked television and in the end did not do it. The Conservatives' churlish treatment continued when MPs reassembled to take the oath and elect a Speaker. On the former leader's entry into the Chamber, courtesy demanded that he should have been immediately invited to take the oath. Instead he was made to wait while Junior Ministers and Assistant Whips gave themselves precedence over him. In contrast, when it was the turn of the Opposition front bench, Clem Attlee by a courteous gesture invited Sir Winston to take the oath before him. Herbert Morrison patted him affectionately on the back, and Churchill warmly shook his hand. Attlee, Churchill told Moran, 'was very kind to me when I took my seat'.[9]

Once again Eden postponed the reorganisation of his administration. 'In any sphere of action', Churchill had written in the volume of his war memoirs published in 1949, 'there can be no comparison between the position of number one and numbers two, three, or four.' Probably he did not have Eden in his sights then, but six years later Sir Anthony lost little time in demonstrating the truth of that remark. In the year and a half between his resignation in 1938 and the outbreak of war, Eden had displayed his inability to provide leadership, and his pusillanimous conduct in that period probably gave rise to Churchill's doubts about 'Anthony'. Instead of giving his party and country a challenging lead, he had been concerned with getting back into office, sending Neville Chamberlain messages of effusive support. As Harold Nicolson, a would-be follower of Eden, put it at the time, 'Anthony does not wish to defy the Tory Party and is in fact missing every boat with exquisite elegance. We drift and drift and pass the rudder into other hands.' Deprived of Churchill's guidance in home and foreign policy, Eden again drifted when he was Prime Minister but with less elegance.[10]

Anthony Eden's chief and insoluble problem was that he was not Winston Churchill. In his understandable impatience to become Prime Minister, Eden, like many others, had underestimated the difficulties of succeeding a great national leader. The *Spectator* exaggerated a little when it said that with Churchill's departure the Tory Party existed again, yet his mere presence in Downing Street had had a near-magical effect in securing consent for the Government's policies and minimising dissension within the party. During his premiership, Tory MPs voted against the Whip in only ten divisions, and in only two of them were more than three MPs involved. 'The Conservative Party in the House of Commons and in the country', David Butler wrote in the Nuffield Study, 'enjoyed a harmonious existence.' And sadly, when the great conductor left the platform, the harmony departed with him. The reduced fear of 'socialism' caused by two consecutive Tory election victories and the conspicuous taming of the Labour Party, together with the departure of Churchill, made Conservatives much more ready to publicise their discontent.[11]

In 1955 probably even Churchill would have had some difficulty with his party. Strikes in the docks and on the railways had begun during the election campaign. Like the newspaper strike which had ended just before it, they were both inter-union disputes – the first concerned with negotiating rights and the second with differentials. Although fewer than 200,000 workers were involved in the three stoppages, this return to major official strikes damaged the economy and caused much public annoyance. While British trade unions were conservative and generally respected, Eden fairly commented in his memoirs, their 'internal differences goad a tolerant public to exasperation. The British people', he continued, 'resent being penalised for a frontier dispute or battle for authority between unions.'[12]

Industrial relations was one of the first subjects discussed by the Cabinet after the election. Monckton was still opposed to legislation (as was his successor, Iain Macleod) and so were the unions and most of the employers. Eden wanted some action, but the Cabinet decided against legislation for the time being. In July, Lord Nuffield saw the Prime Minister to recommend a secret ballot before a strike and for the election of union officials. Anything that promised to end or diminish unofficial strikes would have been welcomed not only by the public but by most union leaders who thought they were usually fomented by Communists. The trouble, as Eden said on forwarding Nuffield's memorandum to Monckton, was that secret ballots were unlikely to cut unofficial strikes. At that time the union officials were usually a restraining force; it was the union members who were militant. 'You could not fine or imprison large numbers of workers', Eden wrote a few months later, 'for coming out on strike without having voted to do so.' There was no such objection to secret ballots for union elections. But although the Electricians Trades Union was at the time under Communist control, achieved by corruption and other skulduggery, most union leaderships were still moderate, and so the Government did nothing.[13]

The industrial troubles gave Eden a colourable but not a genuine excuse for putting off the reconstruction of the Government. He told

Churchill that he had not time for one, and it might be better to make changes 'just before the summer recess'. The problem was still the difficulty of moving Butler, who added to the mistake of his ill-judged Budget by declining to make a quick departure from the Treasury. Admittedly Eden had now made it more difficult. In May he could have offered Rab the Foreign Office, but in June it was obviously too soon to shift Macmillan. Still, Eden should either have insisted on Butler leaving the Treasury or left him where he was and carried out a major reconstruction elsewhere. His failure to do either gained Eden a deserved reputation for indecisiveness. Worse, it created uncertainty throughout the parliamentary party, as it was realised that even Eden would have to carry out a reshuffle fairly soon. Brilliant back-benchers like Enoch Powell were left without a job – although in Powell's case this was his own fault as he had turned down Churchill's offer of a post in the Welsh Office – and wondering when or if they might get one. Even before Eden's accession there had been a feeling among the 1950 intake that they were being unfairly held back and that too many jobs were going to undeserving public schoolboys, of whom there was still a large number; after the 1955 election, 75 per cent of Tory MPs had been to public school and nearly a quarter to Eton.[14]

Ministers, too, were discontented because of Eden's compulsive meddling with their departments. He was constantly on the telephone to his Ministers; many of them must have come to curse Alexander Graham Bell. Even the usually equable Alec Home became exasperated by the Prime Minister's daily telephonic badgering at the most inconsiderate hours. The wretched Selwyn Lloyd was rung up thirty times in one weekend. Eden would even cancel Foreign Office telegrams which had been approved by Ministers, and sometimes redraft them himself. He knew how annoying this could be, for Neville Chamberlain had done the same to him when he was Foreign Secretary.[15]

Sir Anthony did not make the much-needed ministerial changes 'just before the summer recess' or even during it. In the late summer he told his new press spokesman, William Clark, that international affairs and a looming autumn Budget ruled out an early reshuffle because he could not move Butler and Macmillan. There is seldom an ideal time for a reshuffle. The right thing to do, therefore, is to go ahead and make the changes. Eden wondered if his failure to make them would make people 'think I can't make up my mind'. His fear was justified. At the end of September the *Spectator*'s political columnist, Henry Fairlie, who had warmly welcomed Eden's accession, was writing that his first six months had not been encouraging: 'Sir Anthony Eden has been dithering ... not leading'. His procrastination caused mounting irritation in the Conservative Party. In November, Fairlie mockingly suggested that Sir Winston Churchill should succeed Sir Anthony Eden as Prime Minister.[16]

Butler might have solved Eden's reshuffle problem by leaving the Treasury of his own accord. 'If I had been less scrupulous about the economy,' he enigmatically remarked in his memoirs, 'I would have resigned in May.' He then 'had a very disagreeable summer', being subjected to back-bench complaints about the restrictions he had had to impose in July on credit and capital expenditure; he also had to face a denunciation by Gaitskell that he had 'deliberately deceived the electorate', while his Treasury advisers slowly awoke to the growing danger of inflation which their bad budgetary advice had exacerbated. In September the Prime Minister, recognising his earlier mistake, told Butler that he was unhappy with Macmillan at the Foreign Office, stating frankly that he found it difficult to work with so strong a character. Clearly Eden's only chance of prising Macmillan out of a job he enjoyed was to offer him the Treasury. The Prime Minister told Butler that he thought he had been there long enough, which was true, while explaining to him why he could not go to the Foreign Office: Eden wanted a 'subordinate' there.[17]

Butler had already had to put up with considerable interference from Eden, who laudably did not want the Government to 'appear like the hard-faced men of 1918' but whose economic knowledge was scanty. Yet his meddling intensified. 'I could not get my way,' Butler wrote a few months later, 'and no doubt should have resigned.' Instead he introduced his thoroughly unimaginative 'pots and pans' Budget which increased purchase tax and profits tax and cut capital expenditure. That was his third mistake. Butler's April Budget tax concessions had now been effectively cancelled out and Gaitskell, who was shortly to be elected Leader of the Labour Party, accused him of having 'behaved in a manner unworthy of his high office'. In the subsequent censure debate, both Butler and Eden made good debating speeches, Eden pointing out that Labour had denounced the April Budget as an attack on the poor but now said it had been an electioneering Budget, while clearly it could not have been both. Nevertheless, Butler had been badly wounded.[18]

And so too were the Conservative Party and Government. Central Office discovered that party workers' reaction to the 'pots and pans' Budget was one of 'dismay and discomfort'. Few people, if anybody, had a good word to say for it. The overheating economy and the measures taken to deal with it were enough in themselves to make the Government unpopular. After the effects of the Korean War had worn off, prices had at first risen slowly – by 3 per cent in 1953 and under 2 per cent in 1954. But in 1955 they rose by 4½ per cent while wages rose by 7 per cent. With inflation rising, middle-class exasperation with the unions was bound to extend to the Government. Unlike union members, most of the middle classes were not protected against price rises by an annual increase in their income. And the Government did not seem sufficiently sympathetic to the middle-class predicament. In his July statement the Chancellor did not even mention the word 'inflation'.[19]

Eden, Macmillan and Foreign Policy:
I The Middle East

In 1954, in the face of strong opposition from right-wing back-benchers, Eden had negotiated an agreement with Egypt under which British forces would over the next two years withdraw from their base in the Suez Canal zone. The previous December forty-one Conservative MPs had signed an Early Day Motion rejecting Eden's policy. The explosion of the hydrogen bomb in November 1952 eventually converted Churchill – who had earlier growled that he had not known that Munich was situated on the Nile – to the view that the canal base was now 'obsolescent' and no longer justified its expense. Those on the back benches whom Maudling called the 'blue blood and thunder brigade' did not, however, change their minds. When the treaty was debated in the House and Labour abstained, twenty-eight members of the 'Suez Group', nominally led by Captain Charles Waterhouse and including Julian Amery, Enoch Powell, Lord Hinchinbrooke, Angus Maude and Ralph Assheton, voted against the Government. Eden had been sensible and courageous, and the treaty should have signalled a change in Britain's Middle Eastern policy. Unfortunately he ignored his own signal.[20]

Opposing the treaty, Julian Amery spoke of his 'faith in Britain's imperial mission and destiny without which, in my belief, our people will never be prosperous, or safe or free'. Leaving aside the question of whether it made any sense in 1954 to be still talking about Britain's imperial mission, the odd thing about Amery's profession of faith was that Britain had never had either an empire or a mission in the Middle East, which originally was of importance to her because it was the gateway to India. Since 1918 she had nevertheless enjoyed a remarkable hegemony there – although not one that had been strong enough to prevent an inglorious retreat from Palestine in 1948. The hegemony was remarkable in that it was not based on colonies: except for Aden and Cyprus, Britain had no colonies in the area. Her power was exercised through her control of the foreign policy of countries of varying status, most of whom were nominally independent by 1945. And, leaving internal affairs to the national governments, she did little to improve the condition of their peoples. Paradoxically, however, the absence of colonies evidently made it harder, not easier, for British politicians to abandon what Acheson called their 'colonial mindset'.

After the war most Britons accepted their colonies' wish for constitutional advance, and although they differed over its speed they mostly agreed that it was inevitable. In the Middle East, however, the Arab States were already nominally independent, and many people felt that was as much as they had any right to expect. For their own good, it was thought, they should remain under ultimate British control. Harold Macmillan was pro-Israel and, until the dismissal of Glubb Pasha, Anthony Eden was pro-Arab. But they were at one in not understanding the Middle East and in never recognising the Arab wish to be genuinely independent like other countries and peoples. Hence they thought that Arab nationalism was some unnatural phenomenon whipped up by President Nasser of Egypt to annoy the British, and that without him the Arabs would stay gratefully contented with British hegemony. Both men even talked of 'loyal' Arabs, by which they meant Arabs who put the interests of Great Britain before those of their own country.[21]

At the same time, they did not recognise that the decline of British economic and military power had destroyed the foundation of Britain's hegemony. Either that basic fact had to be recognised and normal relations established with Middle Eastern countries; or it had to be obscured by American backing. As the British Ambassador in Cairo, Sir Humphrey Trevelyan, warned in May 1956, an anti-Nasser campaign was 'quite impossible unless we have not only full American support but active American cooperation in a joint policy'. Unfortunately Eden and Macmillan were as blind to the realities of power in the area as they were to Middle Eastern attitudes. The British, the Prime Minister told the Cabinet in October 1955, 'should not allow themselves to be restricted overmuch by reluctance to act without full American concurrence and support'.[22]

Eden took two initiatives which were in conflict with each other. The public one, which conflicted also with the policy underlying the Anglo-Egyptian agreement, was the Baghdad Pact. The idea of the northern tier of states in the Middle East entering into a pact to contain the USSR originated with John Foster Dulles. None of the Arab States, however, had a joint frontier with the Soviet Union and they were more alarmed by the Israelis than the Russians. Nasser, who was anxious to keep the Arab States non-aligned, was implacably hostile to the plan. Israel, too, was opposed to such a pact; so Dulles abandoned the idea.

Unfortunately Eden did not, even though the pact was much more in line with the attitudes of the 'Suez Group' than with his own previous outlook.[23]

The Anglo-Iraqi treaty of 1932, which provided Britain with air bases and enabled her largely to control Iraq's foreign policy, was due to expire in 1957, and Eden and the pro-British Nuri Es-Sa'id, Iraq's leading statesman, thought it could be more easily perpetuated under the cover of the larger design of the Baghdad Pact. Eden later assured Nehru that Britain had decided upon a new approach, basing her policy on 'the concept of partnership between equal and sovereign states', yet no such approach materialised while he was Prime Minister. Right down to the Iraqi revolution in 1958 the outlook, atmosphere and protocol of the British embassy in Baghdad were more vice-regal than ambassadorial. The Baghdad Pact was contrary to Western interests, as Dulles had seen, for Egypt was by far the most powerful Arab country, and her government was popular whereas Iraq's was not. So in lining up with Iraq against Egypt, Eden was backing an obvious loser.[24]

He was also helping to stultify 'Alpha', his other initiative, which was to seek, this time in conjunction with the United States, a settlement of the Arab–Israel conflict. While Moshe Sharett, Israel's Prime Minister, was in power as well as office, 'the pacifists', as General Burns, the UN Commander, called them, were in the ascendancy in Israel, and the prospects for peace were not unpromising. Although an element in the Israeli Government had tried to wreck the Anglo-Egyptian agreement and to damage US–Egyptian relations by sabotaging Western installations in Cairo – the 'Lavon affair' – the frontier between Israel and Egypt was quiet. When, however, Ben Gurion returned as Israeli Defence Minister in February 1955, the 'militarists' were back in control; and Ben Gurion immediately launched a raid on Gaza which killed thirty-eight Egyptians. Sharett was 'shocked' by what had happened, but could do nothing. Nasser was equally powerless. Israel's military supremacy was overwhelming, and Israeli war planes overflew Cairo at will. Nasser organised *fedayeen* raids in retaliation, while he sought arms. The Americans defaulted on their agreement to supply them, and eventually Nasser made a deal with the Russians. Initially this caused outrage in both the United States and Britain, but both countries soon calmed down, Dulles saying that Egypt could hardly be blamed for buying arms when she felt 'endangered'.[25]

Ben Gurion's Gaza raid was a prelude to aggressive operations on all of Israel's frontiers, culminating in the Israeli occupation of the strategically important demilitarised zone of El Auja in Sinai. Nevertheless Eden, like Dulles, persevered with 'Alpha' and, speaking at the

Guildhall in November, he offered himself as a peacemaker between Israel and the Arabs, implying that the peace should be based on some compromise on Israel's frontiers. Israel rejected the proposal out of hand, while Nasser's Egypt and other Arab states welcomed it – reactions which both Eden and Macmillan later suppressed in their memoirs.[26]

'Alpha' was now probably dead, but Eden made its demise all but certain by vigorously pursuing his other, conflicting policy. He sent General Templer to Amman to bully the young King Hussein and Jordan into the Baghdad Pact. The bullying did not work; it merely provoked disturbances. The Templer mission broke an undertaking to Nasser that no attempt would be made to bring any Arab state other than Iraq into the Pact, and the British Ambassador was instructed to tell Nasser that Templer's mission had not been to press Jordan to join it, a statement which Nasser, who had orchestrated the disturbances, knew to be a lie. Eisenhower, who had warned against trying to pressure Jordan into joining the 'Northern Tier', described the episode as a severe diplomatic defeat for Britain; he had earlier commented that 'the British have never had any sense in the Middle East'.[27]

The débâcle was probably at least as much the fault of Macmillan as of Eden, who had had doubts about the venture. Macmillan told the Cabinet that the Baghdad Pact was the 'grand design' of Britain's Middle East policy with which they should try to solve the dispute between Israel and Egypt. This was cold-war talk taken to its extreme and, not least because both Egypt and Israel were unalterably opposed to the Pact, it was palpably absurd. Eden had for some time been critical of Macmillan's performance at the Foreign Office, complaining that he 'showed little fight' and followed 'Dulles around like an admiring poodle'. Yet on Jordan Macmillan differed from Dulles, and like Eden was probably bent on pleasing the Conservative right wing. Whatever his motives, the Jordan failure cannot have lessened Eden's desire to shift him to the Treasury.[28]

II Europe

After the European Defence Community had been defeated in the French Assembly, Anthony Eden's skilled and energetic diplomacy had repaired the damage done to European defence by extending the Brussels Treaty, which comprised Britain, France and Benelux, to include West Germany and Italy, and by guaranteeing that Britain would keep four divisions and the Tactical Air Force on the Continent, thus establishing the

Western European Union. Although WEU contained a smidgen of supra-nationalism in that Britain undertook not to withdraw her forces 'against the wishes of the majority' of the Brussels Treaty powers, the Foreign Office and Government believed that the death of the EDC spelled the end of supra-nationalism in Europe. That was a serious misjudgement, for 1955 proved to be the year of the *'relance'* spurred on by Belgium and the Netherlands. The Six agreed that at a conference to be held at Messina in June 1955 they would consider the formation of a customs union.[29]

On past form, Harold Macmillan's appointment as Foreign Secretary in April should have given a European tilt to Britain's foreign policy. After all, in 1951, while Eden in response to the disappointment expressed by the Council of Europe and Strasbourg had rather inanely been minuting 'Strasbourg was always a mistake, it is now nearly a calamity', Macmillan had been aghast at Eden's attitude and actions. Yet four years later when the Foreign Ministers of the Six met at Messina, Britain showed no interest. She did not receive an official invitation, but when a senior Quai d'Orsay official telephoned London to sound out the possibility of British attendance, he was told that Messina was 'a devilish awkward place to expect a minister to get to'. So Britain was not represented at Messina, and Macmillan might as well have been still at Housing.[30]

Having reached an agreement at Messina which foreshadowed the Common Market, the Six set up a Committee under M. Spaak to work out the details of a treaty. This time Macmillan did persuade the Cabinet to agree to send a 'representative' to serve on it. Unfortunately this did more harm than good. For one thing, to send a 'representative' rather than an observer raised false hopes among the Six that Britain was seriously interested in the project; for another, the British representative was an official at the Board of Trade, Russell Bretherton, whereas the Six sent 'delegates' who were Foreign Ministers or their equivalents; for a third, the British line was that the Six should do nothing that cut across the work of the Organisation for European Economic Cooperation, an intergovernmental body and one therefore which did not meet the aspirations of the Messina powers. Moreover, as the British had recently emasculated the OEEC by insisting on drastic cuts in its budget, Britain's sudden discovery of its importance was palpably hypocritical. In September Macmillan refused to attend a Ministerial meeting with the Six to review the working of the Spaak Committee, giving the paltry excuse that he was too busy dealing with Cyprus.[31]

The British objective was to sabotage the Messina agreement. As the Permanent Under-Secretary at the Foreign Office, Sir Ivone Kilpatrick, who could usually be relied on to give bad advice, put it, 'Messina is a doubtful, if not actual wrong approach.' The British Ambassador in Paris, Sir Gladwyn Jebb, put the British attitude more pithily: we should 'embrace destructively' the Messina proposals. Eventually, in early November, Bretherton was withdrawn from the Spaak Committee after delivering a memorable funeral oration on the Messina plan:

> The future treaty which you are discussing has no chance of being agreed; if it was agreed, it would have no chance of being ratified; and if it was ratified, it would have no chance of being applied. And if it was applied, it would be totally unacceptable to Britain. You speak of agriculture which we don't like, of power over customs, which we take exception to, and of institutions, which frighten us. *Monsieur Le President, Messieurs, au revoir et bonne chance.*

Rarely can Britain's national arrogance have been so honestly exhibited.[32]

Britain's attempted sabotage of Messina then became more active. Accepting the recommendations of an official committee, Ministers decided to put forward a plan for a free-trade area instead of the Six's Customs Union and to bring pressure on Washington and Bonn to drop their support for Messina. At the same time, the British representative at the OEEC made a gratuitous attack on the Six's proposals on the grounds, among others, that they could not be reconciled with 'a one-world system'. All this was futile and self-defeating, and showed the Six that Britain could not be trusted. Their most pro-British members, the Netherlands and Belgium, were particularly enraged. Even if Eden and Macmillan thought British entry into a Common Market was out of the question, they surely should have seen that the supra-national path pursued by the Six was the correct one since it was the only feasible way of solving the German problem. Macmillan did later recognise that obvious point (as did Eden long after he had retired) but at the time he was blind to it.[33]

'If we had taken a firm line, that we wanted to come in and be a part of this,' Bretherton later said of the Spaak Committee, 'we could have made that body more or less whatever we liked.'[34] The French certainly obtained the concessions that they wanted. The British did not bother to try, discarding Britain's last chance to play a decisive role in shaping the emerging community. Thus, at the end of Harold Macmillan's brief tenure of the Foreign Office, British relations with Western Europe were worse than they had been at its beginning.

The Reshuffle and the Press Attacks

Nevertheless, Macmillan 'did not want to be pushed around' and was reluctant to leave his job. According to his memoirs, the American Secretary of State John Foster Dulles was 'terribly distressed' at losing him and 'wanted to ask the President to call Anthony about it'. Had he and Eisenhower done so, it would have been an American tit-for-tat: for earlier Eden had presumptuously expressed the hope to the President-Elect that he would not make Dulles Secretary of State, advice which, to Eden's surprise, Eisenhower had of course ignored. Even without American pressure, Macmillan exacted a high price for his transfer. He must be, he told Eden, the undisputed head of the home front under the Prime Minister, and while graciously conceding that 'if Rab becomes Leader of the House and Lord Privy Seal that will be fine', he could not agree to Butler being Deputy Prime Minister. Instead of replying that that was a matter for himself to decide, Eden weakly submitted. Butler was, nevertheless, to continue chairing Cabinet meetings when the Prime Minister was away.[35]

Macmillan later admitted that in the light of subsequent events his demands implied that he was 'activated by some degree of personal rivalry with Butler'. Indeed they did. His implausible denial that because of his age – he was older than both Eden and Butler – it had not then occurred to him that he might succeed Eden as Prime Minister is belied by his remark to Woolton at the time that he did not see why he should be ruled out of the succession to the premiership 'in order to ease in Butler'. Meanwhile Butler was easing himself out. Disregarding the advice of Harry Crookshank, Macmillan's oldest friend, that he was committing 'sheer political suicide', Butler committed his fourth mistake, the cardinal blunder of not demanding a major department; he allowed himself to be fobbed off with the Leadership of the House. The new Leader of the Opposition was not alone in noticing that Tory opinion was 'rather veering' towards thinking Macmillan was 'the best of the three'. Be that as it may, Eden had further alienated his two most powerful colleagues without strengthening himself.[36]

When, at least three months after he had decided upon a Cabinet reshuffle, the Prime Minister finally did achieve one just before Christmas, the reconstruction, apart from the moves of Macmillan and Butler, proved a disappointment. Unfortunately Eden could not achieve even an anticlimax without a deal of chaos. He spent some of the day in bed suffering from flu and, probably, stress. Under-Secretaries were ushered into his bedroom. Some of them seemed to have been chosen by chance. Meanwhile the peers in the Government, led by Lord Salisbury, effectively threatened a sit-down strike in the House of Lords unless more of them were brought into the Government. Salisbury resigned and Lords Home and de L'Isle contemplated doing so. Salisbury was then deputed to entice Lord Hailsham into the Government as Paymaster General, but that job, so lucrative in the eighteenth century, was now worth only £2,000 a year; so Hailsham could not afford to take it. Eventually this second 'Bedchamber Crisis', almost as absurd as its predecessor in 1839, was resolved through Eden giving way in time-honoured style to trade union pressure by providing more jobs for peers.[37]

In addition to this outdoor relief for their Lordships, 'that bloody Selwyn Lloyd', as a high Foreign Office official had called him three days before, duly went to the Foreign Office; Walter Monckton succeeded Lloyd at Defence; as had been forecast months earlier, Iain Macleod replaced Monckton as Minister of Labour; Harry Crookshank resigned, Ted Heath became Chief Whip, and two others of the original One Nation Group, Enoch Powell and Robert Carr, achieved junior ministerial office. Eden thus proved better at recognising aspiring talent than handling potential rivals. Macleod's promotion to the Cabinet was a clear gain for the Government; it was probably time for Walter Monckton to move, even though he had recently been praised by Enoch Powell for having handled industrial relations 'so successfully', and had held the post with distinction. Despite its good features, the reshuffle was not well received by the press and did nothing to revive the Prime Minister's waning popularity.[38]

The collapse of confidence in Eden and the Government was like a heavy crash on the Stock Exchange. 'It could be said', Evelyn Shuckburgh noted on 9 December, 'that AE is not doing very well.' A month later such a remark would have been taken as an ironical understatement. The slump was caused by a cumulative feeling that the Government was leaderless and without ideas. Governments should after all make themselves unpopular after an election by doing things which they would not dare do just before one. The Eden Government had made itself unpopular by doing hardly anything at all. Sir Anthony had known for a long time that he was going to succeed Churchill, yet he did not seem to have given any thought to what he would do when the great day came. Disillusionment with Eden's leadership, or lack of it, combined with discontentment over the credit squeeze and inflation to destroy the Government's popularity. The election of Hugh Gaitskell, an old Wykehamist, as Labour leader in place of Attlee increased Eden's difficulties. Although a Conservative MP who ended up in prison, Sir Ian Horobin, joked that politics was now a second-eleven fixture between Eton and Winchester, Labour was considerably strengthened by Gaitskell's arrival.[39]

In the New Year, Eden underwent an even heavier bombardment from the press than he had suffered in the autumn. At the Foreign Office, Eden had got on well with the diplomatic writers but had had very little contact with the political correspondents and had few close friends in Fleet Street – Shuckburgh harshly thought that he had few close friends anywhere. True or not, he certainly had enemies in Fleet Street and at least one personal vendetta to contend with. *The Times* fired the opening salvo on 2 January, claiming that the Government had lost its grip and warning that unless it showed more 'high purpose' it would be driven from office. The next day the *Daily Mail* added 'delay and indecisiveness' to the indictment, but the most punishing attack came from that normally safe Conservative trusty, the *Daily Telegraph*. In an article entitled 'The Firm Smack of Government', it accused Eden of too much 'smoothing and fixing' before complaining that, while one of the Prime Minister's main speaking gestures was to look as though he was going to punch his left hand with his clenched right fist, the punch never landed. Unlike Eden's clenched fist, the *Daily Telegraph*'s punch did land – if not below the belt, at least in the Prime Minister's solar plexus. He let out what Butler called 'a pained and pungent oath'. Naturally the left-wing papers joined in the hunt: 'Eden is a flop,' screamed the *Daily Mirror*. It was almost like bull-baiting. Certainly Harold Macmillan seemed to treat it as a sporting event. 'It will be interesting', he commented, 'to see if Anthony can stay in the saddle.'[40]

Like Macmillan, Rab Butler watched the Prime Minister's travails with detachment; 'I have been very calm,' he said. But, unlike Macmillan, he was indiscreet in public. The papers the following Sunday carried more stories hostile to Eden: the *Observer* told its readers, 'Eden Must Go. Move Grows', while the *People* maintained that Eden was about to retire and would be succeeded by Butler. Questioned about these articles at Heathrow Airport, Butler expressed his 'determination to support the Prime Minister in all his difficulties'. While Eden could have done without that sort of support, it was another of Butler's declarations which won the headlines: Eden is 'the best Prime Minister we have'. No doubt the new Lord Privy Seal was correct in saying that those words were not his but the reporter's; he had merely given his assent to them. Yet they sounded like a typical 'Rabism', and had he felt more warmly to Eden he would probably have been more careful. Nevertheless, unhelpful as Butler had been, the most harm was done by

Eden himself. Reluctantly accepting the – for once – bad advice of his spokesman, William Clark, the Prime Minister issued a denial that he was about to resign. That seemed a demonstration of weakness, and Eden followed it up with a similar misjudgement a week later. In a speech at Bradford, amid some sensible passages on the economy and on the vital importance of education, he launched an attack on 'cantankerous newspapers'. That was, as Rhodes James admits, another 'serious overreaction to the press'.[41]

Prelude to Tragedy

If Anthony Eden's indecisiveness and inability to lead, together with an unpopular economic policy, a hostile press and his overreaction to it, were enough to bring him low, it was his overreaction to events abroad – his alleged field of unique expertise – which finally brought him down. Yet, of course, his home and foreign policies were closely related and interacted on each other. Had Eden been in a stronger position at home and had his health been better, his foreign exploits would have been less excitable and ill-judged.

In January the Prime Minister visited Washington with Selwyn Lloyd. Anthony Nutting thought Lloyd liked acting as 'an office boy', and Lloyd's inability to do anything without Prime Ministerial approval drove Shuckburgh to lament that it became 'daily more apparent that we have no Secretary of State'. Anthony Eden was a natural number two in foreign as well as in home affairs. With Selwyn Lloyd as Foreign Secretary, he was effectively number one and number two – a potentially fatal combination.[42]

Although freed from the presence of Macmillan, Eden's temper on the Atlantic crossing was still uncertain, but at least Selwyn Lloyd, who engagingly admitted that he had 'been over-promoted', could not answer back. Eden's other Middle Eastern policy of seeking an Arab–Israeli peace was still in being. Indeed in December the US and Britain had agreed to help finance the building of the Aswan High Dam, an immense project in which President Nasser had invested much hope and prestige. Yet on the voyage Eden compared Nasser with Mussolini and wanted to place all the emphasis of British policy on the Baghdad Pact. Despite this doomed idea, the American visit was fairly successful. In Washington Eden and Lloyd found Eisenhower and Dulles still strongly in favour of the Messina design and of Britain being part of it. Eden attributed their enthusiasm for European unity to American ignorance and to their great liking for unions and federations. In reality the US assessment was based on a wish to strengthen Europe and on an accurate estimate of British power. Eden's former private secretary, Evelyn Shuckburgh, even decided that Eisenhower had a better grasp of the subjects 'than our man' and envied 'the Americans having Ike and Dulles' to run their foreign affairs. Shuckburgh thought Eden had 'greatly deteriorated: seems to be thinking only of himself'.[43]

The most marked deterioration in Sir Anthony Eden came, however, a month later. His visit to Washington had provided only a brief respite from his troubles at home. Returning with his new Foreign Secretary, the Prime Minister found himself in a row with his old one. Asked earlier to comment on a draft speech by Eden, Macmillan had written to him like a headmaster addressing a rather backward pupil. Criticising the structure of the speech, Macmillan told Eden that he 'would not be wise to attempt an essay on economics'. There were too many experts. And although it related to what he had said about a policy of expansion, his observation that 'the monthly growth of weight of the fine, well-grown bull is better than the temporary blowing up of the frog . . .' was open to misconstruction.[44]

Hostilities reopened while the Prime Minister was returning across the Atlantic. After Eden had expressed an understandable wish for 'one grand Budget' rather than a succession of economic statements as in the previous year, Macmillan, who had found the economic situation 'much worse' than he had feared, responded that he intended to make a statement in February in which he would abolish the bread and milk subsidies and possibly increase Bank Rate. His letter ended with a threat of resignation. Eden, who was strongly opposed to ending the milk and bread subsidies, thought the decision could be put off until the budget. That caused Macmillan to issue another threat of resignation and to follow it up by telling colleagues that if Eden was absolutely determined against the cuts 'he must get another Chancellor'. Eventually a compromise was reached, which gave Macmillan, as he said, 'four-fifths of my demands'.[45]

In a speech the week before his statement, the Chancellor said that between 1946 and 1956 we had turned out 26 per cent more goods and services but had paid ourselves 80 per cent more money for doing so – a short cut to economic suicide. Plainly, stronger medicine was now necessary. Although he very misguidedly suspended the investment allowance which Butler had instituted in 1954, both Macmillan's statement outlining his deflationary measures and the subsequent debate went well. He found the press reaction 'unexpectedly good'. One commentator wrote that nobody doubted 'he is this Government's potential leader, the best Prime Minister we don't have'. Yet, in comprehensively defeating Eden, Macmillan had used up too much ammunition on relatively minor matters. A Minister can credibly threaten to resign on only a very few occasions without his colleagues wishing to see the back of him. Hence on the more important issues of defence expenditure and the Budget, Eden was the winner.[46]

Macmillan was anxious to make savage cuts in defence. We know, he told the Prime Minister in March, 'that it is defence expenditure which has broken our backs. We also know that we get no defence from the defence expenditure.' As he later told the European Press Association, Britain devoted nearly twice as large a share of her resources to defence as the rest of Europe. But Eden was not prepared to cut defence; hence the economy continued to be shackled by vastly excessive defence expenditure. Much less damagingly, Macmillan also lost to Eden on 'a swingeing increase in taxation' that he wished to impose. Eden refused to allow increases in income tax. Instead Macmillan increased profits tax, which was a blunder, and introduced premium bonds. Although he got a good press, his Budget was pretty empty and disappointed many. He should have heeded Eden's preference for 'one grand Budget', not two minor ones.[47]

Elsewhere, the Government's troubles continued to multiply. It suffered a reverse on capital punishment. Support for abolition had been growing: the Evans–Christie cases showed that an innocent man had probably been hanged, Maxwell Fyfe's decision to hang Derek Bentley seemed hard to justify, while Gwilym Lloyd George's incomprehensible decision not to reprieve Ruth Ellis had caused widespread revulsion. Disregarding the advice of the Chief Whip, Edward Heath, who was aware that the Tory ranks now contained a number of abolitionists, the Cabinet decided to propose a motion supporting the continuance of hanging, while allowing a free vote and undertaking to accept the result. As Heath expected, the House duly disregarded the Government's wishes and supported an abolitionist amendment to the Government's motion. Included in the abolitionist majority were forty-eight Tories, while three Cabinet Ministers – Lloyd, Macleod and Heathcoat-Amory – and six other Ministers abstained. Some right-wing Conservatives, notably Powell, Amery and Maude, were abolitionists, but most of the right wing regarded the hangman as indispensable and blamed the Government for another unnecessary shambles.[48]

Greek Cypriot terrorism in Cyprus increased, and calls were made for tough action to stop it. The Government talked of jamming broadcasts from Cyprus, a suggestion which displeased old-fashioned liberals without satisfying the blue blood and thunder brigade. Then on 1 March King Hussein dismissed General Glubb, the commander of the Arab

Legion. Unfortunately Selwyn Lloyd was dining in Cairo that evening with Nasser, and both he and Eden blamed the Egyptian leader not only for the dismissal but also for a deliberate insult in its timing. Nasser had no reason to object to Glubb's dismissal, but in fact knew nothing about it in advance and then thought it was the British who had had him removed. Nonetheless Selwyn Lloyd felt insulted and Eden was enraged. Anthony Nutting persuaded Sir Anthony not to threaten to end our relations with Jordan, but was told that Nasser 'is our enemy and he should be treated as such'. That day Shuckburgh noted that Glubb's dismissal was for A.E. 'a serious blow, and he will be jeered at in the House, which is his main concern. He wants to strike some blow, somewhere to counterbalance.' The Prime Minister and the Foreign Office were indeed violently attacked by the right wing, which attributed Glubb's downfall to our 'scuttle' from Egypt. Eden was again comparing Nasser with Mussolini and considered reoccupying the canal zone. Even learning the truth about Glubb's dismissal did not lessen Eden's enmity to Nasser, which he maintained for the rest of his life. Macmillan, in contrast, tried to restrain Eden and to preserve our relations with Jordan.[49]

In a debate on Jordan the Prime Minister mistakenly insisted on speaking last instead of first, when both he and the House would have been calmer. Making the worst speech of his life, Sir Anthony was shouted down and lost his temper. He did, however, stress the importance of the Tripartite Declaration which bound Britain, France and the United States in any conflict between the Arab States and Israel to take action against the aggressor. To Shuckburgh, Eden seemed 'to be completely disintegrated – petulant, irrelevant, provocative at the same time as being weak'. Nutting took the same view, thinking that from then on Eden completely lost his touch and 'began to behave like an enraged elephant'. A few days later the 'elephant' made his 'counterbalancing blow'. Archbishop Makarios was deported to the Seychelles. This greatly pleased the right-wing and Conservative activists who thought it showed strength when in fact the deportation confirmed Shuckburgh's verdict: petulant, provocative and weak.[50]

By-elections gave the Government no comfort. In February at Hereford the Liberals reduced the Tory majority from 9,400 to 2,150, and in a straight fight with Labour at Taunton, Edward du Cann scraped home by 657 votes. In March, Attlee's old seat at Walthamstow saw a 7.5 per cent swing to Labour – large for that time. 'The middle classes', Central Office told Sir Anthony, 'feel that they have not had a square deal and are looking for somewhere else to go.' If anything, the by-elections understated the Government's unpopularity. By March, its approval rating had fallen since December by 10 points, from 44 to 34 per cent, and James Margach was asking in the *Sunday Times* if Eden was 'the man for the job? Can he stand it? What's wrong with the government?'[51]

Whatever was wrong, the Government continued to drift. The banishment of Archbishop Makarios had been greeted by the right-wing newspapers with hysterical glee, but predictably it proved to be merely the climax of a tale of muddle and procrastination, not the prelude to a peaceful settlement. Terrorism persisted, and negotiations were fruitless in the absence of the Archbishop. The Government's handling of capital punishment – the abolitionist bill passed the Commons but was defeated in the Lords – won it no friends. Middle-class discontent did not subside. At a by-election in Tonbridge in June, a heavy fall in the Conservative vote produced a swing of 8 per cent against the Government and a fall in the Conservative majority from 18,000 to 1,600.

Criticism of the Prime Minister was widespread. Anthony Eden was a good One-Nation Tory, anxious to govern in the national interest, but however sound his instincts, he lacked the knowledge and ability to translate them into effective action; or perhaps, as one of his staff believed, he 'was losing his sense of purpose'. The Prime Minister's declining reputation was all the more remarkable in that it was not even partly caused by a shift of support to anybody else. The absence of a strong rival was reflected by Sir Anthony's irritable remark: 'if they want, they can get rid of me and go back to Winston'.[52] Butler's last unsuccessful months at the Treasury still kept him in the shadows, while Macmillan was thought to be still unproven in high office. Nor was there a large single issue to unite opinion against the Prime Minister. Rather, the leadership coming from Downing Street was simply felt to be inadequate, and a malaise pervaded much of the Conservative Party. Many Tories strongly doubted that Anthony Eden's Government would last a full parliament or be able to win the next general election. Probably only a serious international emergency could enable the Prime Minister to establish his pre-eminence and to rally his party and the country behind him; and there was little sign of such a providential foreign crisis.

CHAPTER V

The Temptation of
Sir Anthony

On 19 July 1956 John Foster Dulles insultingly withdrew the American offer to help Egypt build the Aswan High Dam. Britain followed suit immediately afterwards, although she had no need to do so. A week later, in a demagogic speech, Nasser retaliated by announcing the nationalisation of the Suez Canal Company, an Anglo-French undertaking, based in Paris, which ran the canal. Nasser was provocative in both words and action. After bitter criticism of America and Britain and after pointing out that Egypt had previously received only $3 million a year from the Suez Canal Company, he exulted that with the canal's revenues Egypt would itself be able to finance the building of the Aswan Dam. While he was speaking, the company's offices were taken over by troops, and foreign employees were forbidden to leave their employment on pain of imprisonment – an ill-judged threat which was soon withdrawn. On the other hand, shareholders were promised full compensation.[1]

However offensive its manner, the act of nationalisation was legal. As the Anglo-Egyptian Agreement of 1954 unequivocally stated, 'the Suez Canal . . . is an integral part of Egypt'. All that Nasser had done was to nationalise a foreign-owned company and one, moreover, whose concession would have expired in twelve years' time in any case. Yet the British reacted as though he had stolen the Crown Jewels or blown up Westminster Abbey. 'England', Maynard Keynes had told a friend ten years before, 'is sticky with self-pity and not prepared to accept peacefully and wisely the fact that her position and her resources are *not* what they once were.' Psychoanalysis would show, he thought, that that was the real cause of her reaction to the American loan. In 1956 Britain was again sticky with wounded pride. Whatever had happened elsewhere, and even though her Indian Empire was no more and the Indian army no longer hers, Britain thought that the Middle East was still under her control and its inhabitants should do what they were told. Nasser's action was therefore an intolerable affront to almost everybody. Understandably, the German press, for instance, thought that both Britain and France had had a fit of hysterics over the inevitable shrinkage in their dwindling colonial empires.[2]

Whitehall and the saloon bar were equally outraged. At a dinner four days after Nasser's speech, Harold Macmillan told Robert Murphy, whom President Eisenhower had sent to London to find out what was going on, that he did not expect the Russians to come in, but 'if we should be destroyed by Russian bombs now, that would be better than to be reduced to impotence by the disintegration of our entire position abroad'[3] – eloquence more appropriate to a slightly tipsy soap-box orator at Marble Arch than to a sober Chancellor of the Exchequer in private conclave at 11 Downing Street. Yet Macmillan was unusual only in his bombast. The editor of what was then the *Manchester Guardian*, A. P. Wadsworth, was one of the very few to keep his head. Enoch Powell was another. After opposing the 1954 agreement, he had come to the conclusion that decolonisation was inevitable and the British Empire at an end. Hence he could not now understand what all the fuss was about: 'it was like being in a world where everyone else was a stranger'.[4]

Within a few weeks, much of the country recovered its sanity; unfortunately common sense never returned to 10 or 11 Downing Street. The nationalisation, wrote Anthony Nutting, 'was the challenge for which Eden had been waiting'. Eden's press adviser recorded in his diary that if the Prime Minister did not act 'strongly and effectively he [would] be out'. And Eden's reaction to the news was fierce and apocalyptic. 'The Egyptian has his thumb on our windpipe,' the Prime Minister said. 'He's not going to get away with it.' That continued to be his attitude. Meeting the day after the nationalisation, the Cabinet admitted to itself (but not publicly) that Nasser's actions had not been illegal but decided not to let that affect its decision. Taking it for granted that the Egyptians were incapable of properly managing the canal, it agreed that preferably with the Americans and the French, but if necessary alone, Britain would use force to make Nasser disgorge his gains. The Prime Minister, Murphy observed, 'had not adjusted his thoughts to the altered world status of Great Britain, and he never did'.[5]

Evidently believing that nobody in the United States Government knew any international law, Eden told Eisenhower by telegram that Ministers and the Chiefs of Staff were agreed that Nasser could not be allowed to seize control of the canal 'in defiance of international agreements'; he had therefore instructed the Chiefs of Staff to make a military plan. Unfortunately for him, the State Department told the President that the Egyptians had acted within their rights, while the

American Chief of Naval Operations was certain that taking ships through the Suez Canal was not difficult and the Egyptians would be able to do it comfortably enough. If the British Government ever received such excellent advice, they ignored it.[6]

Even when it became clear that the nationalisation was not illegal, that the plan to grab the canal by force was a military absurdity, that Arab opinion was almost solidly behind Nasser, that world opinion – above all, the United States – was against force, and that its use was likely to have disastrous consequences, Eden and his Cabinet did not change their minds. Doubtless Eden, like his press spokesman, was aware that if his right wing thought Nasser was getting away with it, his Government was probably 'doomed'.[7] His refusal to allow altered circumstances to influence the Cabinet's basic decision indicates that it was less the interests of Britain than the personal feelings and political interests of Ministers that were dictating British policy. Here was the chance to establish that the Government was strong and resolute, and to demonstrate that Eden was not to Churchill as Addington had been to Pitt.

The Egypt Committee – an inner or war cabinet which consisted of Eden, Macmillan, Salisbury, Lloyd, Home and Monckton but excluded Butler who was ill at the time – concluded on 30 July that while our immediate purpose was to place the canal under international control, our ultimate purpose was to bring about the downfall of the present Egyptian government. In Parliament on the same day Eden avowed the first objective but not the second. Nasser responded that the proposed internationalisation of the canal was in fact 'international colonisation', a charge which the conclusions of the Egypt Committee showed to be justified.[8]

However ferocious and unbalanced the Prime Minister was in private – even before the crisis Moran had recorded that the political world was full of Eden's moods at Number 10 and that Churchill thought things could 'not go on like this for long' – in public he preserved the appearance of a statesman. On 2 August reservists were called up, and in a debate in Parliament on the same day, Eden's speech was relatively calm. The Labour peer Lord Stansgate told the House of Lords that he had found 'much more reason, common sense and conviction' in the Prime Minister's words than he had heard from the Labour front bench. Hugh Gaitskell had indeed made a silly speech, telling the House that it was 'all very familiar. It is exactly the same that we encountered from Mussolini and Hitler . . .' Gaitskell did later include some safeguarding sentences about using force only if it was 'consistent with our pledges to the Charter of the UN', but he was deservedly 'a little embarrassed by far too much praise from the Tories', while his speech had made Lord Stansgate's son, the young Tony Benn, 'want to vomit'.[9]

According to Gaitskell, who saw Eden privately before the debate, the Prime Minister assured him that force would be used only if Nasser did something else provocative. If that was true, then the Opposition leader was the first of many people whom Eden deceived over Suez. In any case Gaitskell himself and his Chief Whip warned Eden after the debate that Labour would not support a policy of force. A week later Salisbury noted that Labour was 'steadily sliding away'. The Prime Minister was well aware therefore that if he attacked Egypt without further provocation from President Nasser he would face a bitter battle in Parliament as well as one in the Middle East.[10]

Only if he had been able to launch an attack on Egypt before tempers had cooled could Eden have secured broad public support for military action. But the Chiefs of Staff ruled out a quick strike. The state of the armed services of both Britain and France demanded weeks of preparation before they could be ready to mount an invasion, and while the forces became more ready for war, the British people became less disposed to fight it. A Gallup poll between 16 and 24 August showed only one-third in favour of military action (and only 27 per cent if the US did not support it) and nearly a half against it. Even among Conservative supporters, there was no majority (only 43 per cent) for force. No wonder the former General Eisenhower said he would not have dreamed of committing his country to war with such a division of opinion. Eden was well aware, therefore, that military action would bitterly divide the country and would not even win the support of a majority.[11]

Eden also had difficulties with both wings of the Conservative parliamentary party. Some thirty to forty Tory MPs, led by Sir Lionel Heald, were against the use of force unless it was sanctioned by the United Nations. The party's other wing, which was widely supported by constituency activists, was more outspoken in public. The Suez Group, led by Captain Waterhouse, an ardent appeaser in the 1930s, were itching for a war and would strongly oppose any sensible compromise with Nasser. Absurdly anachronistic though they were, the Suez Group did have a semblance of a case: if Eden's policy was correct now, it had been wrong in 1954; or more plausibly, if Eden had been right in 1954, he was wrong today. At the Party Conference at Llandudno, an amendment in the name of Waterhouse and Maude, much fiercer than the official resolution which only called for 'a just solution', was passed with only one vote against it.[12]

The Cabinet and the Egypt Committee had similarly lost their earlier unanimity. 'I sense', Alec Home told Eden on 22 August, 'that Rab is very unhappy'. The chief Cabinet opponent, however, was Walter Monckton. As Minister of Defence, Monckton was exposed to the views of the service chiefs who were more clear-sighted on the consequences of using force than most Ministers. The First Sea Lord, Mountbatten, told Eden that, because of the heavy Egyptian civilian casualties that would be caused in Port Said, we would be 'plastered round the world as assassins and baby killers'. General Keightley, the Allied Commander-in-Chief, stressed that the invasion had to be launched 'with our moral case unassailable' and the responsibility for the war clearly Nasser's – requirements it was impossible to meet. Later Keightley asked Eden if Britain was going to be better off at the end of the operation, a question which an angry Prime Minister thought inappropriate for a military commander. It was not for mere soldiers to reason why.

Politicians were allowed a little more latitude. At the Egypt Committee on 24 August Monckton made what Home called an 'outburst' which Salisbury found 'both painful and rather disturbing'. All that Monckton had done was accurately to point out the difficulties of what the Government was proposing to do. After it, Home warned Eden that some of their colleagues were 'wavering' about the use of force. The night before Monckton's outburst, indeed, even Selwyn Lloyd had conveyed to Dulles his unhappiness with the military plans.[13]

The Commonwealth and the United States

To a divided country, party and Government, Sir Anthony added a divided Commonwealth and a fractured alliance with the United States. 'For us in Britain,' the Prime Minister told the Conservative Party Conference in October, 'the Commonwealth must always come first.' The nationalisation of the Suez Canal Company had given Eden a great opportunity to prove the genuineness of that sentiment and to display the utility and importance for British foreign policy of those two 'intersecting circles' – the United States and the Commonwealth – which allegedly prevented Britain playing her full part in the third circle, Europe. If he sought an honourable and sensible solution of the problem, Anthony Eden was well placed to secure the co-operation of both India, the key 'non-aligned' state in the Commonwealth, and the United States.[14]

Jawaharlal Nehru, the Indian Prime Minister, liked his British opposite number and admired his role at the 1954 Geneva Conference. In his congratulatory message to Eden when he succeeded Churchill, Nehru assured him of 'not only my personal goodwill but the goodwill of many in India'. Shortly afterwards Nehru confirmed that goodwill by cancelling, at Eden's behest, a decision to buy some Russian military aircraft and buying only British ones. More important, although Nehru had thought the way Dulles had withdrawn the promises of aid for the High Dam insufferably arrogant, he was still more offended by the manner in which Nasser had nationalised the Canal Company. On good terms with Nasser, Nehru used his influence with him to seek an agreement satisfactory to both sides. Yet Eden paid little attention to Indian views or to those of other Commonwealth leaders except Robert Menzies. Instead of using Nehru as a friendly mediator and heeding Indian advice, Sir Anthony merely attempted to gain Indian acquiescence in what he had unilaterally decided upon. The rest of the Commonwealth was similarly expected to conform with Eden's wishes. In the end only Australia and New Zealand supported the British policy. In practice, therefore, as opposed to rhetoric, for Eden the Commonwealth came not first, but nearly last.[15]

Enlisting the help of the United States should have been easier for Eden. The Eisenhower administration had strong reasons for preventing Nasser emerging triumphant from a crisis that Dulles had precipitated. Eden did make far greater efforts to secure American than Indian co-operation, but again on a policy which he had already decided upon. And unlike his relations with Nehru, his relations with Dulles were poor even at the outset of the crisis. They had deteriorated two years before over the Indo-China crisis, which was in many ways a mirror image of Suez. Just as Dulles now urged a peaceful solution to Suez, Eden had then urged a peaceful solution for Indo-China. Indeed, the arguments Eden used in the first crisis convincingly refute the arguments he used in the second.[16]

A ponderous moralist who was devious and doctrinaire – Nehru talked of 'his rather closed head' – John Foster Dulles was in 1942 described by the Permanent Secretary at the Foreign Office as 'the woolliest type of useless pontificating American'.[17] Yet from the two crises he emerged as a far more responsible statesman than Eden. Over Indo-China, Dulles was in the last resort prepared to draw back, to contain his frustrations and to pay attention to the views of his far weaker ally. Two years later Eden was not prepared to draw back, he allowed his frustrations full rein, and eventually, as Eisenhower later said, double-crossed his far more powerful ally. Besides, it was the President, contrary to Eden's belief, not the Secretary of State who decided American policy.

Anthony Eden always resented the common US belief that British and French policy was based on colonialist views. Certainly both Dulles's professed aversion to colonialism and his moralism were hard to take because of his blatant double standards. America still regarded Central America as its own backyard, and the Central Intelligence Agency's overthrow of the Guatemalan regime in 1954 was every bit as colonialist as anything that Britain had done up till then in the Middle East. Eden justifiably contrasted his (understandably reluctant) help to Dulles on that occasion with Dulles's opposition to British policy in the Middle East. Dulles's moralising sat similarly uneasily with his enthusiastic support of the CIA's covert operations which were run by his brother, Allen. Probably Britain's MI6 did plan to assassinate Nasser, or at least to overthrow his regime in such a way as to make his death likely. Yet, had they carried out their plans, Dulles would not have been well placed to take a high moral line. The Chinese believed that the CIA had tried to assassinate Chou En-Lai, their Prime Minister, in 1955. At the last moment Chou changed his travel arrangements , so only his staff were murdered.[18]

All the same, Dulles was correct in thinking that over Suez Britain and France were primarily actuated by colonialist considerations. In his memoirs Eden admits that the chief worry of the French was the effect Nasser's action would have in Algeria, and that the British Government decided that 'failure to keep the canal international would inevitably lead to the loss one by one of all our interests and assets in the Middle East'. So internationalisation was merely colonialism dressed up and made to look respectable. The British, as the US Treasury Secretary George Humphrey put it, 'were simply trying to reverse the trend away from colonisation and turn the clock back fifty years', which could not be done. The real object of Britain and France was not to safeguard freedom of navigation in the canal but, by humiliating Nasser, to protect their interests elsewhere. This made the negotiation of a mutually satisfactory settlement close to impossible.[19]

Nevertheless, both Eisenhower and Dulles believed that if they could delay the Anglo-French use of force, they would prevent it: sooner or later sanity would return to their allies or, even if it did not, they would eventually find they had to enter into a negotiated settlement. Hence the succession of expedients devised by Dulles which infuriated the British Prime Minister. For Eden, who had converted the crisis into a prestige contest between himself and Nasser, the various ploys thought up by Dulles were useless unless they provided an excuse for war. For Dulles, negotiations in the UN and elsewhere were an alternative to force; for Eden, they were an obstacle to it. From at least as early as 3 September, when President Eisenhower told him that American opinion was dead against force, Eden had a choice between working for a peaceful settlement in conjunction with America and going to war without her. Faced with a similar situation over Indo-China, the United States decided to respect the wishes of her ally. Eden decided differently. Even so, Dulles's delaying tactics nearly worked.

France Offers Temptation

Dulles was not the only cause of delay. The military planners of the invasion of Egypt, whose codeword 'Musketeer' was an appropriately archaic emblem for a very old-fashioned operation – Eisenhower called it 'mid-Victorian' – also postponed the invasion. Perhaps because they were mindful of the very flimsy strategic, moral and political grounds for the attack, the planners were more than usually anxious to keep civilian and other casualties to a minimum; they therefore insisted upon a return to the original choice of Port Said as the landing point. In consequence the date for Musketeer had to be put off to 1 October, but even that date could not be met since by then Britain and France were committed to taking their case to the United Nations. The Suez Canal pilots, the absence of whom was expected by the British and French to expose Egypt's inability to run the canal, had been withdrawn, and Britain had arranged for an unusually large number of ships to enter the canal at that time – 'Operation Pile-up'. Nevertheless, the canal authority continued to function efficiently. If Dulles was running short of delaying mechanisms, Britain had run out of pretexts. Under the aegis of the UN Secretary-General, Dag Hammarskjöld, Selwyn Lloyd was negotiating with the Egyptian and French Foreign Ministers and making sufficient progress to make likely an agreement that adequately safe-guarded allied interests in the canal, while failing of course to humiliate Nasser.[20]

At that point Sir Anthony was tempted. On 14 October, the Sunday after the Conservative Party Conference, 'the devil' in the shapes of the French General Maurice Challe and Albert Gazier, the acting Foreign Minister, visited Eden and Nutting at Chequers to suggest that Israel be invited to attack Egypt; Britain and France would then join in. France had been moving ever closer to Israel in the erroneous belief that Nasser was behind the Algerian rebellion, and was supplying her with huge quantities of arms. Attempts were later made to excuse Anglo-French policy on the grounds that it had foiled a concerted Arab attack on Israel. Yet the colourful Israeli Chief of Staff, General Dayan, had declared in 1955 that Israel faced 'no danger at all of an Arab advantage of force for the next eight to ten years'. His briefing meant in Moshe Sharett's words that Israel 'must adopt the method of provocation-and-revenge ... and let us hope for a new war with the Arab countries, so that we may finally get rid of our troubles and acquire our space'. Israel's overwhelming military superiority was not in doubt, and there was no Egyptian or Arab plan to attack her. Immediately after the act of nationalisation Dayan had wanted to attack Egypt, confident that he would reach the canal in a matter of days.[21]

When, early in August, Harold Macmillan, who had enlisted Churchill's support, had advocated the use of the Israelis to bring down Nasser, Eden was 'shocked' and dismissed the idea out of hand. Nuri Es-Sa'id, Britain's able henchman in Iraq (which had had to applaud the nationalisation of the canal company), advised Eden to hit Nasser hard but at all costs to steer clear of the Israelis. Not, probably, that Eden had needed that advice. He knew well that an attack whose main objective was to restore Britain's position in the Arab world would, if carried out with Israel as an ally, damage that position beyond repair. In October, however, Eden listened carefully to his tempters, telling Challe that he would consider the matter and give his answer in two days' time.[22]

Nutting, who was allowed to consult only two Foreign Office officials, produced a report demolishing Challe's idea: the plan suited French interests in Algeria but would be disastrous for British interests in the Middle East. It would imperil British oil installations and pipe lines, endanger the pro-British regimes in the area, disrupt the Commonwealth, offend the United States, wreck Selwyn Lloyd's diplomatic efforts at the United Nations, and put Britain in breach of the Tripartite Declaration.[23] Yet Eden ignored the report. Presumably the devil had argued that only collusion could now provide a pretext for attacking Egypt, and that by it Nasser would be overthrown and Anthony Eden proclaimed a tenacious and daring statesman; and that without a collusive attack Britain would have to agree to the UN compromise which would leave Nasser in control of the canal. Consequently Eden would be left without a victory and with his continued leadership in peril. Whatever the arguments he used, they prevailed. The devil had won. After clandestine journeys and meetings, Britain on 24 October signed the secret Protocol of Sèvres with France and Israel, under which the three countries bound themselves to invade Egypt.[24]

The day after Sèvres, Eden got the Cabinet to agree that, in the event of an expected Israeli attack on Egypt, Britain and France should intervene. Although Eden deceived most of his colleagues about the extent of his collusion – Macmillan and a few others were let into the secret – the Cabinet knew enough to see something was wrong, but

Ministers were either bemused or subservient. Monckton (who having resigned as Minister of Defence had mistakenly agreed to stay in the Cabinet as Paymaster General), Macleod and Heathcoat-Amory were among the doubters. Nobody, however, resigned.[25]

In consequence, when Israel invaded Egypt on 29 October, Britain and France, in accordance with Sèvres, issued an ultimatum ordering Egypt and Israel to cease fighting and withdraw their forces ten miles from the canal. As Israeli troops were at that time nowhere near the canal and Egyptian troops well beyond it, the demand was patently absurd, but it provided a pretext for an Anglo-French invasion. Eden's crazy secret diplomacy involved him and Lloyd in an intricate web of lies. Because they could not admit collusion with Israel, almost everything Eden and his entire Government said in the next few days was false and misleading. They claimed that there had been no time for consultation and that they were merely performing a necessary police action, putting out a forest fire, and separating the combatants. In fact, of course, the alleged policemen were part of the burglary: so far from being firefighters they were arsonists; and instead of separating the combatants they had gone to some trouble to join them together. As for there being no time for consultation, there had in fact been five days but, as deceivers cannot consult those they are about to deceive, no consultation took place with either the Commonwealth or the United States.

Eden's deceit separated him not only from his allies but from the Whitehall machine. He had cut himself off from all sensible advice; in the Foreign Office the Permanent Secretary was almost the only high official admitted to the conspiracy, and his advice did not come into that category. All Britain's top ambassadors, who would have alerted the Government to the folly of what they were doing and told them that they could not go ahead, were kept in the dark.[26] For the same reason the Opposition, too, had to be kept in the dark. Thus Eden committed the supreme blunder of, without warning, taking a divided nation to war on a bogus pretext with only minority support. Inevitably there were riotous scenes in the House of Commons. The Prime Minister was regularly booed when he entered the Chamber, yet, as the *Manchester Guardian* reported, he was not in the least daunted by Labour's insults, 'he held on his way self-possessed, firm and unapologetic'. His differences with the United States, he explained, arose from the canal being of little concern to them while it was a matter of survival for us. The leader of the Opposition lamented in a 'powerful, unrelenting attack on the Government' that Eden had committed us to a 'disastrous folly', which we should regret for years. The folly soon produced its first disaster: as the British Ambassador had earlier warned, the action taken, according to Eden 'in the interests of our own nationals and shipping', caused Nasser to block the canal. As Eden's staff went back to Downing Street with him after the first Commons debate, a cheerful Foreign Office character commented: 'It's rather fun to be at Number Ten the night we smashed the Anglo-American alliance.'[27]

The most important debates, however, took place not at Westminster but across the Atlantic at the United Nations and in the White House. One of the refinements of the Sèvres agreement was that the invasion should take place just before America's presidential election. The importance of the Jewish vote, it was assumed, would prevent Eisenhower from taking firm action against the invaders. The conspirators had misjudged the President. Angry at having been 'double-crossed' by Eden, Eisenhower was resolved to do the right thing, irrespective of any electoral consequences. At that time the United States still had a foreign policy based on the national interest, and not one scarcely worthy of the name derived from the pressures of domestic politics and national minorities. Hence America took the lead at the UN, where the invading states were virtually isolated; the vote on a General Assembly resolution condemning the Anglo-French–Israel action was sixty-three to five. Only Australia and New Zealand supported the delinquent threesome. Eisenhower was determined, too, that Britain should receive no economic help of any kind. When the Syrians blew up the oil pipeline from Iraq to the Mediterranean which carried a quarter of Britain's oil supply, such help was clearly going to be needed.[28]

Another aspect of the 'disastrous folly' was the delay, imposed both by the planners for Musketeer and by the pretence that the Anglo-French intervention was a *bona fide* response to Israel's attack. To preserve appearances, therefore, the allied force had not been able to leave Malta and Algiers before Egypt rejected the Anglo-French ultimatum. Thus, while the RAF bombed Egyptian airfields, and outrage mounted in Britain, the Arab world and the UN, the allied armada was steaming on its six-day voyage to Egypt hindered by the unwelcome accompaniment of the US Sixth Fleet. Landings were eventually made at Port Said where hundreds of Egyptian civilians were killed, and the aggression looked likely to achieve its military, if no other, objective. Eden, however, was a prisoner of his own dishonesty as well as of Britain's economic weakness and the hostility of the great powers. So when both Egypt and Israel had agreed to the cease-fire ordered by the UN, Britain and France's rationale for their intervention required them to do the same. In addition, Britain's currency reserves were falling, although not so fast as a panicky Macmillan claimed, and Eden had received a threatening letter from Bulganin which created fears of Soviet intervention in the Middle East and elsewhere. As the Russians were currently killing thousands of Hungarians in Budapest, they were happy to have the world's attention diverted to the Suez Canal. Hence shortly after the troops had landed, a broken and disconsolate Eden, now a very sick man but outwardly calm and firm, told the Commons that he had agreed to a cease-fire.[29]

Many later claimed that, if he had allowed the action to continue until the allies had reached Suez and occupied the whole canal, their position would have been transformed. That is fantasy. In reality, neither the United States nor Nasser were in any mood to make concessions to those who had broken international law. President Eisenhower, who was overwhelmingly re-elected despite his Middle Eastern difficulties, was determined not to give Britain and France help – 'to let them boil in their own oil, so to speak,' he said – until they agreed to an unconditional withdrawal from Egypt. Hence the only difference made by the allies capturing Suez would have been that they had further to retreat. As Enoch Powell later said, Suez was 'a drama to which there was no intelligent conclusion. So the sooner it was ended, the better.'[30]

The whole episode was by a long way the most senseless foreign adventure ever entered into by a British Prime Minister. Yet the party retained outward unity almost until the end of the fighting. Anthony Nutting, whom Hugh Thomas in his classic account *The Suez Affair* rightly described as 'the one man who conducted himself consistently and with impeccable honour', resigned on 31 October but agreed to postpone the announcement as long as possible. When he heard that Nutting was going to make the traditional resignation statement a week after the cease-fire, Macmillan asked him to tone it down, saying it could easily bring down the Government: 'Why say anything at all? You have already been proved right and we have been proved wrong.' Sir Edward Boyle, the Financial Secretary to the Treasury, also courageously resigned, convinced that the Government had made a gross blunder. On the morning of the day Eden announced the cease-fire, a letter from sixteen Tory MPs hinted at the withdrawal of their support if they were not given assurances that the fighting was about to end. Yet at the first Commons vote after the cease-fire only eight Tories, including Nutting and Boyle as well as Boothby, J. J. Astor and Nigel Nicolson, abstained. Even allowing for the fact that many Tory MPs, perhaps a majority, had not yet realised the dimension of the failure, and also for Gaitskell's ill-judged television attack on Eden which was bound to promote Tory loyalty, the vote was an extraordinary demonstration of party solidarity and discipline.[31]

After the Temptation

Yet no amount of party loyalty could make Suez anything but a calamitous failure. How the British Government could have got itself into quite such a mess is not fully explicable. When Eden had journeyed to the United States at the beginning of the year, he seemed to his former Private Secretary to be 'thin, nervy and in a curious way frivolous'. And when he learned that he was not going to see as much as he would have liked of President Eisenhower (who was recovering from his heart attack and was in fact very generous to Eden with his time), the Prime Minister 'threw a tantrum'.[32] Similarly, the principal impression given by the British Government's policy and actions over Suez is of frivolity; and all the activity – the telephone calls and telegrams, the briefings and plans, the consultations and secret conferences – smacks more of a tantrum than a policy.

British policy was fundamentally frivolous in that it was not based on any proper appraisal of Britain's position in the Middle East or of her interests and how they might be affected by the use of force; nor on any sober appraisal of the effects on the canal of the nationalisation of the Canal Company. If Nasser was going to finance the Aswan High Dam out of canal revenues he had, as Nutting told Eden, to keep the waterway open and satisfy those who used it.[33] The welfare of British subjects in Egypt was virtually ignored. If Nasser fell, no consideration was given to what sort of government would succeed him – Communist, Moslem Brotherhood, Wafdist or none at all. No thought was given to the possibility of reprisals against our oil interests in the Middle East; no attention was paid to the advice of our Ambassador in Cairo, or of other diplomats; nobody took into account the consequences of active American opposition to the adventure; and, although the military plan involving days of delay was obviously impracticable, it was nevertheless adopted. No wonder that when the new First Lord of the Admiralty, Lord Hailsham, was belatedly briefed by the Navy about the military plan, he was told that it was crazy: and no wonder the chief of the carrier force thought that 'the government must have gone raving mad'. No wonder, too, that the Chief of the Air Staff also thought that Eden had 'gone stark raving mad' and that his former Private Secretary thought he had 'gone off his head'.[34]

Many other people doubted the Prime Minister's and the Government's sanity. Eden was never the same man after his serious illness and operations in 1953 but, during 1954, his year of diplomatic success, his attacks of fever did not return. They began again, however, some months before the beginning of the Suez Crisis. All the same, Eden's health seems to have been tolerably good until 5 October when a feverish attack drove his temperature to 105°F. His Press Secretary, who resigned over Suez, thought Eden went mad that day and stayed 'literally mad'. At the very least, his illness and his medicines, it is charitable to assume, affected his judgement.[35]

Nevertheless, his judgement was bad well before October and, as Harold Nicolson's wife put it at the time, 'granted that AE may have lost his wits surely his entire Cabinet can't have?'[36] Monckton, above all, but also Butler, Salisbury, Heathcoat-Amory, Macleod and Buchan Hepburn showed at least some sense, but the same cannot be said of most of the others. Except on a very sinister interpretation of his conduct, Harold Macmillan was no more rational than Eden. At the beginning he was, as has been seen, the most belligerent of Ministers. Early in August, as well as wanting to use the Israelis, Macmillan had put forward a plan to 'destroy Nasser's armies' and march on Cairo. In the following month he told the Cabinet that matters should be brought to a head by the use of force if necessary, in order to restore confidence in sterling. He gave the Cabinet that advice without telling his colleagues that his very distinguished Permanent Secretary, Sir Edward Bridges, had warned him that it was vital for sterling and the economy that we did not go it alone and had maximum support from the United States. Later in September Macmillan gave even more fallacious advice to the Cabinet after a visit to Washington. Suez was barely mentioned when he saw the President, and Macmillan did not question Eisenhower about the likely American response to Britain using force; yet he felt able to assure Eden: 'I know Ike. He will lie doggo.' After the attack had begun and there was talk of oil sanctions, the previously most combative of Ministers, who had taken no precautions to bolster Britain's financial position by drawing funds from the IMF, threw up his arms, saying, 'Oil sanctions! That finishes it.' And at the crucial Cabinet meeting on 6 November he insisted on a cease-fire because of the threat to sterling. Hence Harold Wilson's best remark: Macmillan was 'first in, first out'.[37]

Macmillan's conduct over Suez was so astonishingly inept that, if he was behaving rationally, the sinister interpretation is the only credible one: he was plotting to destroy and replace Eden. If that was his Machiavellian aim, it was completely successful. Much more probably, however, Macmillan was not acting rationally; he genuinely believed his own nonsense. Many others, after all, were almost equally badly smitten. Terrified of being thought 'appeasers', they based their policy on an absurd analogy between 1938 and 1956 and between Nasser and Hitler or Mussolini. Even the normally level-headed Lord Home, who as Commonwealth Secretary should have been urging caution, could commit himself to such a sentiment as 'I am convinced that we are finished if the Middle East goes, and Russia and India and China rule from Africa to the Pacific.'[38]

Macmillan, Home and their colleagues had shared in what the historian of Suez, Keith Kyle, has called the 'emotional spasm'[39] that followed Nasser's act of nationalisation. Some ministers, such as Monckton and Butler, soon recovered; others, particularly Eden and Macmillan, went on reiterating that if we lost 'the oil' we were finished. Just what they expected the Arabs or Nasser to do with the oil they never made clear. As Arab commentators have often said, they could not have drunk it. The wartime commander in the Mediterranean, Admiral Cunningham, who later became Chairman of Anglo-Iranian Petroleum, asked shortly afterwards, 'Why couldn't the fellow understand that the thing to do about oil is to *buy* the stuff, not to fight for it?'[40] Such common sense was alien to nearly all the Egypt Committee and to a majority of the Cabinet, as well as to the Suez Group, much of the Conservative Party and the right-wing press. The British leaders lost their heads at the start and remained in the grip of a collective hysteria which led them to approve or condone collusion and the attack on Egypt. This was followed by a collective amnesia which enabled them to deny or ignore the fact of collusion and the subsequent dishonesty.* Not surprisingly, Michael Foot followed up his 1940 attack on the men of Munich, *Guilty Men*, with an attack on the men of Suez, *Guilty 1956*. But all in all, remembering Keynes's remark about psychoanalysis, a fairer and more charitable verdict would probably be 'guilty but insane'.[42]

The Aftermath

Sanity was slow to return. The weeks following Suez have been called the most humiliating since the early 1780s.[43] Yet the extent of the humiliation was not immediately apparent to Anthony Eden. Like Macmillan, Selwyn Lloyd and some other ministers, he had difficulty in grasping

---

* If the English novel has since the war seemed in decline and its approaching death sometimes proclaimed, the other main branch of British fiction – politicians' autobiographies – has continued to flourish. Over Suez the memoirs of Eden and Macmillan are little more burdened with the truth than the average historical novel, without being as entertaining. Eden and Macmillan do not so much as mention collusion in thier books, while Selwyn Lloyd's trivial discussion of the subject in his memoirs is so mendacious that he would have done better to follow their example.[41]

the enormity of what he had done; on collusion, at least, he believed he could cover his tracks. Having decided in October that the Anglo-American alliance was something that could be turned off like a tap, he took it for granted that when he felt thirsty in November he could turn it on again. President Eisenhower had other ideas. American suspicions of Anglo-French collusion with Israel had been confirmed as early as 1 November, when Pineau spilt the beans to the US Ambassador in Paris; by continuing to deny it, Britain had further embittered the White House. In any case the Americans did not regard the Anglo-American alliance as a British convenience. They were not prepared to restore normal service before the bill had been paid and the damage repaired. Hence, they were determined to be actively unhelpful over sterling and oil, until Britain made an unconditional withdrawal from Egypt. Eden and the bulk of the Conservative Party were taken aback and affronted by American anger at having been double-crossed. When the tap refused to be turned on, they decided to kick the tap. One hundred and thirty Conservative MPs signed a Commons motion censuring the United States for 'gravely endangering the Atlantic Alliance'.[44]

Eden was no nearer reality over the situation in Egypt. He was determined that Britain and France should leave in their own time and take the lead in reopening the canal. Yet Nasser, even less ready than Eisenhower to forgive and forget, refused to allow the countries which had just bombed Egypt's airfields and killed some 2,500 of its citizens to remain on Egyptian soil or take part in the salvage operations to clear the canal. In taking a strong line, Nasser enjoyed the support of virtually the whole United Nations.

The British people had as much reason as Eisenhower and Nasser to be incensed by what had been done in their name, yet at home the Government and the Suez operation gained in popularity. Only after it had proved a dismal failure did the use of military force win the approval of nearly a majority of the country. This was partly due, of course, to patriotic feelings and a great rallying of the Conservatives behind the Prime Minister: 81 per cent of Conservative voters supported the military action. The main reason, however, was that the public had been deceived by the Government, which they believed to be telling the truth about its reasons for launching its attack on Egypt. Like the Chairman of Nigel Nicolson's Conservative Association at Bournemouth, they had 'completely swallowed the PM's specious argument that he has intervened solely to stop Jews killing Arabs'. Although the Secretary of the Cabinet told William Clark that he realised that 'no intelligent men' could support the Government's policy, he was presumably speaking of people who knew something of what had been going on. Those who did not know and had always regarded Anthony Eden as truthful, honest and a man of peace, were not necessarily being unintelligent or gullible in erroneously believing that on this occasion, too, he had still been all of those things.[45]

Conservative MPs are harder to absolve from gullibility. Although some of them were not especially intelligent and so could readily support the Government policy, many of them were quite astute enough to rumble their leader's deception. Nevertheless, an amalgam of party loyalty, fear of their constituency associations, and credulity kept them quiet. Under the remarkable semblance of unity, there was of course considerable turmoil. Yet the strong party cohesion of those days, reinforced by the firm but conciliatory approach of Edward Heath and his Assistant Whips, kept the Conservative Party in one piece.

Since his illness at the beginning of October, the Prime Minister had been kept going by increased doses of drugs and stimulants necessary to counteract the drugs – he had been 'practically living on Benzedrine', he told Gladwyn Jebb. These had induced a superficial calm. There were now 'no rows, no drubbings' at Number 10. But the precarious medical and temperamental balance could not endure. In the middle of November, under the pressure of failure, frustration and sheer exhaustion on top of the drugs and stimulants, Eden's health broke down, and his doctor ordered a period of complete rest, preferably in a warm climate. Astonishingly, the Edens' chosen destination for his convalescence was Ian and Ann Fleming's house in Jamaica, where communications were slow and bad. 'The Captain', Shuckburgh recorded in his diary, 'leaves the sinking ship which he has steered personally onto the rocks.' Poor Rab Butler was left in charge to steer it off the rocks and keep it afloat.[46]

Jamaica did almost more damage than Suez to Eden's standing in the Conservative Party. His departure confirmed his leading colleagues' suspicions (or hopes) that he would not remain Prime Minister for long. They treated his self-imposed Jamaican exile as virtual abdication, and did not even keep him fully informed. The Eisenhower administration had likewise decided that Eden was rightly doomed, but wanted to avoid a Labour Government. Selwyn Lloyd had been sent to the United States in the hope of securing better terms for the British withdrawal from Egypt. He got nowhere. To the distress of our Ambassador in Washington, the President could not find time to see the British Foreign Secretary, although on that day he managed to see the Prime Minister of Ceylon, the Foreign Minister of Venezuela and a popular singer.[47]

George Humphrey, the Treasury Secretary, thought Butler the strongest man to succeed Eden, while Eisenhower favoured Harold Macmillan as 'a straight, fine man'. The American Ambassador in London, Winthrop Aldrich, a charming and sociable banker who, though sometimes derided on the cocktail circuit as 'a man with open flies and a closed mind', was a more capable and assiduous diplomat than he seemed. In close touch with both Macmillan and Butler and presumably prompted by them, Aldrich told the President that the Tories would need a 'fig leaf' to withdraw from Suez and still remain in power. Eisenhower authorised him to say that, once withdrawal had been announced but not before, the administration thought it could 'furnish a lot of fig leaves'.[48]

An announcement of unconditional withdrawal from Suez would be a humiliating admission of defeat, which the Cabinet realised would be highly distasteful to much of the Tory Party and the far-away Prime Minister as well as disillusioning to public opinion. All the same, the growing economic crisis forced Harold Macmillan to the conclusion that capitulation to the American demand was inescapable. Butler was more reluctant to cave in, but on 28 November Macmillan persuaded the Cabinet to accept his view. Flying home for the Cabinet meeting, Selwyn Lloyd decided to resign because of the failure of his American mission. He was talked out of it, probably by Macmillan; his reward was to be given the unenviable task of justifying the Cabinet's decision to withdraw from Egypt to Parliament and the country. Deprived by the United States of any fig leaves adequate to cover their shame, the Government decided to brazen it out by saying that we were withdrawing because our action had successfully achieved its objectives. 'We sympathise with the Right Honourable and learned gentleman', said Bevan for the Labour Party, 'in having to sound the bugle of advance to cover his retreat.' Yet however absurd the Government's argument and however 'disagreeable' the debate for poor Selwyn Lloyd, only fifteen right-wing MPs abstained in the division three days later.[49]

Eden later told Lloyd that 'we all should have resigned' at the end of November. In his Jamaican retreat he was being treated almost as though he had already resigned. He objected to what he regarded as the ignominious terms of withdrawal, but was barely consulted. 'I know', Butler condescendingly telegraphed to him, 'how difficult it must be for you to form a judgement on all that has gone on since you left.' Eden, who probably thought it would have been easier to do so if he had been kept fully informed, cannot have been greatly cheered by learning from Butler that there were 'many who would like to see you back, including members of the Cabinet'. He wanted to return early but was dissuaded by his PPS. His greatest humiliation was reserved for when he did come home. The statement which he wished to make denouncing 'the Moscow–Cairo Axis' and the United States, the Soviet Union, China and the United Nations was firmly vetoed; he had to read out some anodyne remarks prepared by his colleagues.[50]

If that episode had left Eden in any doubt about the decline of his authority, his reappearance in the House of Commons on 17 December should have dispelled it. When he entered the chamber, only two MPs stood up to cheer him. His reception was distinctly half-hearted though less embarrassingly so than is usually claimed; it was suitable not for the Conquering Hero, but for the Prodigal Son. In the country he still was more popular than his party or Government, but in the House he had lost the confidence even of the solid centre. He had forfeited their respect because in their eyes he had simply run away.[51]

Some MPs were worried, too, about the widespread rumours of collusion between Britain, France and Israel. In a letter to *The Times* on 18 December, Attlee pressed Eden for a 'clear statement' on the subject. That evening in the course of an unconvincing display at the 1922 Committee – he was not able to answer a simple question about the Tripartite Declaration – the Prime Minister was equivocal on collusion. Clearly he was going to have to say something about it in public. Three days later he told Parliament: 'I want . . . to say it quite bluntly to the House that there was no foreknowledge that Israel would attack Egypt – there was not.' Thus Eden's House of Commons career ended, sadly, with a lie.[52]

Having lost the confidence of his colleagues and of many backbenchers Eden could not have lasted long, even though most of the Cabinet, including Butler, would probably have preferred him to go only after a decent interval. His health, however, rather than his lost political authority, precipitated his speedy exit. Early in the New Year three doctors were insistent that Eden's continuance in office for even a short period would endanger his life; so after a farewell Cabinet on 9 January the Prime Minister drove to Buckingham Palace and submitted his resignation to the Queen.

In the 1930s Eden's political career was presciently summed up by Britain's two great wartime leaders. When Eden became Foreign Secretary, Winston Churchill said, 'I expect the greatness of his office will find him out.' It did, but not while he held the office to which Churchill was referring. It found him out only when he assumed the premiership to which, ironically, Churchill had done so much to elevate him. And when Eden resigned in 1938, Lloyd George said, 'Eden has today paid a big cheque into the bank on which he can draw in future.' That, too, was prophetic. From then on, Eden drew on that cheque. And only in 1955–6 did he become critically overdrawn.[53]

The Actor Manager

After kissing hands on his appointment as Prime Minister, Harold Macmillan told the Queen that the new Government might not last longer than six weeks. Although made 'half in joke', his warning was also 'half in earnest'. It was certainly more serious than his later claim that the premiership was then a 'not very alluring post'; at the time he had thought it sufficiently alluring to make every effort to attain it without, however, being too blatant. Hence his summons to the palace was a surprise to most people. Almost the entire press thought the obvious successor to Eden was Butler, as did Rab himself, who had spent the evening Eden resigned pondering what he should say in his first broadcast to the nation as Prime Minister.[1]

In reality, Butler's chances had faded in the aftermath of Suez. During Eden's Jamaican convalescence, he had run the Government as competently as he had done when Churchill was incapacitated. Yet as acting head of the Government he was saddled with what he called 'the odious duty of withdrawing the troops'. While Selwyn Lloyd thought that in Eden's absence he had been 'splendidly supported' by Butler, Rab gained little credit for limiting the damage he had not caused. Instead, the salvage man was blamed for the wreckage. Butler's equivocations over the Suez operation itself were also held against him. Although his deviousness over Suez had been as nothing compared with the duplicity of Eden and some of his colleagues, his lack of enthusiasm for the use of force had offended the party's large pro-Suez element (many of whom disliked him anyway), and his failure to prevent it had disappointed the antis. He had ended up pleasing no one. By contrast, Macmillan, whose record on Suez was far worse – he later admitted that it was 'a very bad episode' in his life – had pleased the gunboat-minded by his initial fire-eating and then disarmed the opponents of force by his sudden switch to favouring a cease-fire. Unlike Butler, Macmillan was thought at least to know his own mind, even if he changed it.[2]

Butler had made matters worse for himself by being, even by his standards, inordinately indiscreet. While in public he robustly defended

Suez, he said very different things in private, being almost suicidally imprudent to right-wing MPs at a dinner of the oddly named Progress Trust. To recover from, or bury, the Suez disaster the Conservatives needed not only guile but panache, a quality which Butler notably lacked. His damaged arm, his sad irregular features, and his clothes, deemed by Channon to be 'truly tragic', left him with a charisma deficit which he should have partially offset by making flamboyant speeches to give heart to his dispirited party.[3]

Such oratory was especially needed at a meeting of the 1922 Committee after Butler had had to tell the Commons that Britain would co-operate with the UN in Egypt – a concession highly distasteful to many Conservative MPs. Yet, when Butler and Macmillan addressed the meeting, Butler contented himself with a drab account of events. This did something to calm the fractious back-benchers, who had been led up to the top of the hill by Eden and were now being led down again by Butler, but nothing for his own leadership prospects. That was not a trick Macmillan, who was then asked by Butler to add a word or two about oil, was going to miss. 'With all the skill', as Enoch Powell put it, 'of the old actor manager', the Chancellor of the Exchequer gave a bravura display for thirty-five minutes during which he not only upstaged the man who was supposed to be the principal actor but by his theatrical arm-waving nearly knocked him out of his seat. Powell thought the performance 'verged upon the disgusting', but it brought the house down. Finally, Butler had not mounted a leadership campaign. Perhaps he was too busy; perhaps he thought it was unnecessary because he was bound to win; or, more probably, he thought Eden would be able to hold on until Easter or even the summer, so that a campaign would be premature. Again, that was not a mistake made by Harold Macmillan, who had come to the conclusion that Eden would soon have to go, and acted accordingly, courting, Butler claimed, the younger Cabinet Ministers. Probably only three members of the Cabinet sided with Butler. Churchill liked Butler more personally but gave his backing to Macmillan, as did the Chief Whip, the Chairman of the Party, and the Chairman of the 1922 Committee. Eden gave no formal advice but indicated that he preferred Butler.[4]

The choice of Macmillan was widely seen as a victory for the Right over the Left. But in so far as those words had any meaning when applied to the Tory Party of that time, Macmillan was if anything probably slightly to the left of Butler. In any case there was no right-wing candidate anywhere in sight; whatever the result, therefore, continuance of the One-Nation policies pursued by Churchill and Eden was not in doubt. Speaking at the party meeting which officially chose him to be leader, Macmillan dismissed 'silly talk about the Left and the Right', stressing that under his leadership the Conservatives would never be 'a Party of any class or sectional interest'. Certainly he did not appoint a right-wing Cabinet. The most spectacular promotion was that of Peter Thorneycroft, who had had a good and liberal record at the Board of Trade, to the Treasury. The most surprising retention was that of Selwyn Lloyd at the Foreign Office, for which Butler was the obvious candidate. Lloyd, who had retained the confidence of the Suez Group but not of our allies, plainly should have been moved, as even he himself evidently believed. He was not moved because the Prime Minister wanted to avoid appointing Butler and to run foreign affairs himself. Macmillan tried to make his manoeuvre less obvious by claiming in his memoirs that Butler had asked to be Home Secretary, when in fact Butler had reluctantly accepted that post after having been refused the Foreign Office.[5]

A week after his appointment, Macmillan delivered the broadcast that Butler had expected to make. The speech was so strewn with clichés that it might have been written by, or for, Anthony Eden, by then on a voyage to New Zealand to recover his health. Macmillan's address contained a lot about greatness – 'Britain has been great, is great and will stay great, provided we close our ranks and get on with the job' – and character – 'As for courage and character, I know the British people have this in full measure' – and much more in the same vein. While such banalities could be defended as necessary post-Suez therapy for a bruised and bewildered country, the hyperbole of the one passage which Macmillan later thought to be 'perhaps worth recalling' was less excusable since it was seriously meant. 'A lot of people', the Prime Minister told his viewers, 'are worried about relations with the United States. The life of the free world depends upon the partnership between us.' Macmillan claimed that we would not be 'satellites' of the Americans, but so large was the disparity in power between the two countries that we could be nothing else.[6]

Two months earlier President Eisenhower had thought that for the British one of the blessings in disguise of Suez was that it might impel 'them to accept the Common Market'. Dulles, too, thought that irritation with the US would advance 'the momentous step of European union'. Konrad Adenauer took a similar view. He told Guy Mollet that as France, Britain and Germany could never be powers comparable to the USA and the USSR, the only way they could play a decisive role in the world was 'to unite to make Europe. England is not ripe for it,' Adenaueur went on, 'but the affair of Suez will help to prepare her spirits for it.' Suez had indeed amply confirmed that Britain was now a European, not a world power. Yet what was clear to the American

President and Secretary of State, the West German Chancellor and a great many other people was not apparent to the British Prime Minister and his Cabinet. Harold Macmillan thought only of restoring relations with the United States. So, like a naughty but only half-repentant child, Britain ran back to nurse.[7]

Under the guidance of Anthony Eden, the presumed expert on foreign affairs, Britain not only suffered humiliation in the Middle East but decided not to take part in Europe's economic integration, a decision judged by a former British Ambassador in Washington to have been 'a far more fatal error than Suez'.[8] After Britain had walked out of the Spaak Committee in November 1955, Whitehall, prodded by Macmillan, had embarked upon a desultory hunt for a European policy. Unfortunately, over Europe Harold Macmillan was little more effective at the Treasury than at the Foreign Office. Eventually, in July, the so-called Plan G was produced which envisaged a free-trade area between Britain and the Six.

Plan G demonstrated that Britain's now habitual over-confidence in her dealings with the Six had not deserted her. The Government proposed to retain the right in this free-trade area to reimpose trade restrictions if necessary 'to protect sterling'. More importantly, foodstuffs were to be excluded 'in the interests of home agriculture policy and . . . the Commonwealth', which, Roy Jenkins pointed out, the Messina powers 'would not swallow'. Plan G was therefore unlikely to have any great attraction for the Six. In any case, owing to the need to consult British industry and the Commonwealth, as well as the distractions of Suez, the Government did not bring Plan G before the House of Commons until November, by which time, as Harold Macmillan later admitted, 'there was a certain unreality about the discussions . . .' In the meantime the Six, having at Venice in May 1956 decided to draw up a treaty for an economic community, had pressed on with the drafting; and after Suez France was able to secure satisfactory arrangements for her colonies.[9]

Paradoxically, Britain would probably have taken a more European course had the previously anti-European Eden stayed in Downing Street. After Suez, Eden's unjustified resentment against the United States led him, as Dulles expected, to look more favourably on the Six. Suggesting that one of the lessons of Suez might be 'to work more closely with Europe', Eden noted shortly before his resignation that 'the timing and conviction of our approach' would probably determine Europe's reaction to our overtures. And at the last meeting of Eden's Cabinet the Foreign Secretary's theme was that, because of differences with the United States, Britain should try 'to make Europe less dependent upon

America' by pooling its resources 'with our European allies' to make Europe a nuclear power comparable with the two superpowers. Selwyn Lloyd did not, as he said, 'get much sympathy from his colleagues'.[10]

Eden's reputedly more pro-European successor had no such far-sighted ideas. He was looking across the Atlantic, where he had the great advantage of his wartime friendship with President Eisenhower. Delighted by the President's suggestion of a meeting in March in Bermuda, Macmillan was afraid that France might try to turn it into a tripartite affair. He need not have worried. Unlike Macmillan, Mollet had drawn the correct lesson from Suez and was concentrating on Europe. In Bermuda, Eisenhower and Dulles found Macmillan and Lloyd still so 'obsessed' with getting rid of Nasser that it was difficult to talk 'constructively' with them about the Middle East, but the Americans were tolerant and, even though Dulles later told Adenauer that Bermuda had been a failure and that 'the British had no foreign policy and were finished', the meeting did not go too badly. Macmillan was justified in claiming that things were back 'on the old footing' with Eisenhower, and his restoration of good relations with the United States was a considerable achievement. Yet while he was in Bermuda the Six signed the Treaty of Rome, an event that seemingly passed by the British Prime Minister. The sad truth was that Macmillan had no need to choose between the United States and Europe. He could have had both. The US wanted Britain to join the Common Market.[11]

Rather woundingly, the editor of *Punch*, Malcolm Muggeridge, thought Harold Macmillan had about him a faint whiff of 'mothballs', and when Macmillan began a speech in the House with the words 'Mr Speaker, all my life I have been . . .' the future Labour Chief Whip Bob Mellish tellingly shouted 'an actor'. Yet the new Prime Minister's slightly faded Edwardian image and his apparent unflappability suited the hour. Macmillan had expressed a common view when he had said the Government might be out in a few weeks. Lord Hailsham, who had entered the Cabinet as Minister of Education, told his colleagues that it was their duty to clear up 'the mess we have made' at Suez but they would be lucky if 'we were not skittled out by July'. Hence a display of calm (however studied) and confidence (however inwardly lacking) were badly needed as a partial salve to what in February Powell called 'the deep Suez wound'.[12]

Suez caused more acrimony among friends, families and institutions than any issue since Munich. So divisive was it that even the staid Athenaeum, the Pall Mall refuge of bishops and civil servants, was affected; the club, in which tempers were rarely inflamed by more than a glass or two of dryish sherry and controversy was as likely to arise over the dating of St John's Gospel as over the diplomacy of Sir Anthony Eden, was reported to have banned discussion of the subject on its premises.[13] No doubt the Conservative Party wished it could do the same.

The party's tradition of tolerance had kept it in one piece during the crisis, but only just. And its unity was still tenuous. The new Prime Minister's healing skills held it together. By bringing into the Government Edward Boyle from the Left and his son-in-law Julian Amery from the Right, Macmillan demonstrated his ecumenical attitude and his desire for differences over Suez to be forgiven, if not forgotten. Most of the party, though not the constituency associations of Nigel Nicolson and other opponents of the Suez adventure, followed his lead and showed similar forbearance.

After Eden, almost any Prime Minister would have seemed calm and decisive, but at least some of Macmillan's sang-froid was genuine and his own. Once he had told his Ministers what he expected, he kept off the telephone, although like Churchill he frequently sent them written minutes. Even more important, he set out to dominate the House of Commons and succeeded. In those days, what happened in the House was before long reflected in the country and the press. A Prime Minister who was a commanding figure in Parliament would soon be seen in the constituencies, therefore, as the strong leader of an effective Government. Macmillan's growing confidence was scarcely dented by some poor by-elections. The results were no worse than before Suez, and despite its great opportunity Labour was still in the doldrums.

A potential setback to the Conservative recovery was Lord Salisbury's resignation at the end of March over the release of Archbishop Makarios from the Seychelles. To his credit, Salisbury was the first Conservative Cabinet Minister to resign because of a disagreement on policy since Duff Cooper in 1938. But over the years he had had too many 'resigning moods' and this time, to the astonishment of many including, probably, Salisbury himself, he found his resignation accepted. Macmillan's aide, John Wyndham, thought the Prime Minister accepted it because he did not expect to be in office much longer and wanted to show who was the boss. Certainly Macmillan seemed to be taking a considerable risk because Salisbury had been an influential figure, and some thought his departure the first sign of a disintegrating Government.[14]

Yet there were two good reasons for letting him go. The first was that Salisbury was plainly wrong on the issue. The deportation of Makarios in March 1956 had had less to do with solving the Cyprus problem than with appeasing the right-wing opponents of Anthony Eden. A year on, the banishment had proved ineffective as well as ill-conceived, and if Macmillan's description of the Government's change of policy as 'a generous act of statesmanship' was over-laudatory the change was certainly a step in the right direction. The second was that if Salisbury, having threatened resignation over Cyprus, had won his point, he was likely to do the same over the reopening of the Suez Canal, and that would be far more dangerous since then he would enjoy strong party support. To let him go was therefore sound tactics. In the event, Salisbury's resignation caused only a brief tremor, and he largely disappeared from public view.[15]

In April Macmillan was still vainly hoping 'for enough pressure on Nasser to bring him down'. As there was never any possibility of that happening, the Government in the following month had to accept the loss of face and, by removing the ban on the use of the canal by UK shipping, acknowledge that Nasser had won. A two-day debate followed, beginning on the 15th. Petrol rationing was finally abolished on the first morning – a typical Macmillan coincidence – and, as the Prime Minister happily recorded, news that the H-bomb had been successfully tested preoccupied the papers on the 16th. Macmillan's opening speech on the first day was poor, but his winding-up on the second day was a triumph. With only fourteen Conservative MPs abstaining, the Government had a majority of forty-nine. When the figures were announced, 'the whole Tory party', Macmillan recorded, 'stood up and cheered me. At the Speaker's chair I turned and bowed.' The Prime Minister was greatly touched by this embarrassing display, thinking that it showed that the British 'rather like a gallant failure' like the retreat from Mons. Leaving aside that there was nothing 'gallant' about Suez, Tory MPs were surely exhibiting by their cheers not their British affection for failure but their relief that the Suez crisis was behind them. By then the opinion polls were registering a consistent Labour lead of around 10 per cent, but after the May vote Macmillan himself was confident that the Government could run its full term. And rather than the six weeks he had mentioned to the Queen, he lasted six years.[16]

The Suez controversy even disappeared from party politics, scarcely figuring in the 1959 general election. Yet it had longer-term effects. Just before the invasion, Oliver Poole, the Chairman of the Party, had feared that the Conservatives had lost the 'liberal vote' (by which he meant the intellectual or opinion-formers' vote) for a long time, perhaps for ever. Iain Macleod later came to the same (probably correct) conclusion. Certainly that support was lacking throughout the sixties.[17]

The Treasury Ministers

Whatever the long-term political fall-out of Suez, its economic effects were immediate. A new weaker Government could not risk widespread industrial unrest which might well lead to a collapse of sterling. In the autumn of 1955 the President of the TUC, Charles Geddes, had concluded that it was 'useless to disregard the warning that wage demands are threatening the economic structure of the nation'. Unfortunately the old guard of the TUC was changing. Jock Tiffin, Arthur Deakin's successor at the TGWU, died at the end of the year, and the union fell under the leadership of the left-wing Frank Cousins. At the TUC Conference in 1956 Cousins struck a very different note from Geddes the year before and carried the Congress with him. It passed overwhelmingly a resolution effectively rejecting out of hand appeals for wage restraint, Cousins declaring that 'in a period of freedom for all, we are part of the all'.[18]

Although the unions were less militant than expected at the beginning of 1957, by March the Government faced a battle on three fronts – in the shipyards, in the engineering industry and on the railways. The Prime Minister feared there might be something approaching a General Strike. A difficulty for the Government was that in the different pre-Suez circumstances it had urged a policy of wage restraint on the employers, who thought that was still the Government's position. The unions also believed, as Iain Macleod told Harold Macmillan, that 'the employers are acting under our instructions, and have said that the real fight is against the Government'; the industrial scene was indeed 'full of politics'. In reality, however, both sides of industry misunderstood the Government's current attitude: because of its own weakness, it now favoured a far weaker stance. 'In the long run and for the common good,' the Prime Minister said at Leicester in March, putting a philosophical gloss on the Government's retreat, 'the umpire is better than the duel.' So the employers settled. The Government had sold out, noted the Chief Economic Adviser, Robert Hall, 'because they had been such fools over Suez'. Further strikes, some of them pushed by Cousins, followed in the summer. The settlements were too high, and more work days were lost in strikes in 1957 than in any year since 1926, but the pound and the Government survived.[19]

Industrial unrest did not prevent Peter Thorneycroft from producing a cautious rather than a severe Budget. Because of Butler's post-election measures and Macmillan's strict Budget, growth in the calendar year 1956 had been only 1.1 per cent, while inflation had risen to 4.9 per cent. Yet the Chancellor saw 'some grounds for cheerfulness . . . Expansion must be the theme.'[20] He was able to cut taxes (including surtax) while increasing the Government's surplus above the line and leaving only a very modest overall deficit. Thorneycroft's task had been made easier by the change in defence strategy which had been announced by Duncan Sandys in a White Paper in February. Henceforth Britain was to rely more on the nuclear deterrent, thereby allowing substantial cuts in spending on conventional forces. Conscription was to end in 1960. Even after the cuts, however, Britain was still going to spend a far higher proportion of her income on defence than her European allies.

Harold Macmillan was usually a shrewd, indeed cynical, judge of character, yet in making his Treasury appointments he had been naïve, if not downright careless. His Treasury team was, politically, an exceptionally strong one, with the abnormal feature that in some ways its captain was the weakest player. In the Commons Peter Thorneycroft was a good debater, but at the Treasury he badly missed Sir Frank Lee, his Permanent Secretary at the Board of Trade and (with Bridges and Brook) one of the outstanding civil servants of the day; Lee did not move to the Treasury until 1961.

Macmillan had brought Sir Roger Makins from the Foreign Office to be Permanent Secretary at the Treasury because he thought Treasury officials arrogant. If so, the arrival of Makins was unlikely to be a humbling influence, since according to Lee, his successor, he regarded the Chancellor of the day as his spaniel. In any case Thorneycroft did not hit it off with Makins whom Nigel Birch (and probably Thorneycroft, too) wrongly considered to be 'hopeless'. The Chancellor and his lieutenants had peculiar relations with the official Treasury and scarcely used the very few economists in the building. In return, the Treasury economists had a low view of the economic knowledge and competence of their political masters.[21]

Recommending Enoch Powell to Butler for a ministerial job in 1954, Iain Macleod had said, 'his ability of course is not in doubt, only his judgement'.* Powell's intellectual equipment was undoubtedly formidable, and as Financial Secretary to the Treasury he now devoted it to bringing Government policy into line with the principles of Gladstonian

---

* Since then, Powell had gone some way to strengthening that doubt by writing (with Angus Maude) *A Short History of Britain* up to 1950 which, while containing seven lines on Sir William Beveridge, and mentioning *inter alia* King Arthur, Anne of Cleves, Captain Boycott, King Canute, Joe Chamberlain, Lord Randolph Churchill, Ethelred the Unready, John of Gaunt, Bonar Law, Llewelyn the Great, Lord North and Woodrow Wilson, avoided all mention of Sir Winston Churchill. Fortunately for Powell, it was not a work that Macmillan would have read.[22]

finance. Sir Robert Hall soon came to regard him as 'a very queer man indeed, fanatically holding principles of economy and austerity which he does not understand in the least'.[23]

The third member of Thorneycroft's team, Nigel Birch, is usually but wrongly regarded as the Lepidus of the triumvirate. As Secretary of State for Air in the Eden Government, he had, in common with Walter Monckton, been exposed to the wisdom of the armed forces over Suez and had written five letters of resignation but never sent them. His chief interest, however, lay in economic affairs where he was far more right-wing – he had made his name attacking Dalton and the Labour Government – and had therefore gratefully accepted a technical demotion to become Economic Secretary at the Treasury. A clever man who was convinced the Government would lose the next election, he was a good and witty speaker – usually without notes – and a forceful character whom officials found 'personally congenial'. Both Birch and Powell had a contemptuous dislike for the Prime Minister.[24]

By the end of May the Chancellor's Budget-day cheerfulness had changed to alarm. The Governor of the Bank was worried about the future of sterling, while by July the Prime Minister was similarly concerned about the future. His famous 'Never had it so good' speech was later misquoted and censured as a vulgar celebration of triumphalist materialism, when it was in fact a warning of hard times ahead unless something was done to curb wage increases and inflation. 'Can prices be steadied', Macmillan asked, 'while at the same time we maintain full employment in an expanding economy? Can we control inflation? This is the problem of our time.' The right answer to those questions, though Macmillan did not give it, was probably, 'No, unless we define full employment as three per cent unemployed instead of the usual one or two per cent.'* Unlike later commentators, the audience of 200 at Bedford absorbed the sombre tenor of the speech. They were 'slow to respond', said the Central Office report, 'and there was no great enthusiasm'.[26]

At the time of Macmillan's Bedford speech, the man Sir Samuel Brittan has called 'Thorneycroft I' was still at the Treasury. This Chancellor was in favour of an incomes policy, which was rejected by the Cabinet.

---

* In a Cabinet paper in September, Peter Thorneycroft advocated policies whose 'success would probably be reflected in an increase in the level of unemployment to around 3 per cent. This would be forgiven us. A collapse of the pound would not.'[25] Economically, the Chancellor was almost certainly right; he was on weaker ground in thinking that it would have been politically acceptable. When unemployment reached 2.8 per cent in January 1959, there was an outcry. Running the economy with 3 per cent unemployment in the fifties would probably have been electoral suicide.

The Government did, however, set up an Independent Council on Prices, Productivity and Incomes, which was before long shunned by the trade unions. At the end of July Peter Thorneycroft was still open-minded enough to tell the House: 'There is clearly no simple act of policy which is a remedy for inflation. If there had been it would have been discovered a long time ago.'[27]

Enoch Powell was determined to cut Government spending because he had come to believe that the size of that expenditure was the crucial factor in determining the rate of inflation and the rate of economic progress. He combined this belief with a dash of monetarism, which was enjoying a temporary revival. Macleod referred disparagingly to his friend's adoption of free-market economics as 'Enochery', and yet monetarist rhetoric was used to embroider what was in essence a policy of old-fashioned deflation. All this was congenial to Nigel Birch, who had been successful in the City before the war and retained many of the City attitudes of that time. Evidently Thorneycroft's two lieutenants then persuaded the Chancellor, transforming Thorneycroft I into Thorneycroft II.[28]

In fact, as a Treasury minute pointed out in July, Government spending was not out of control; it had been 'stable if not actually reduced' in real terms between 1954–5 and 1957–8. Yet in August Macmillan endorsed Thorneycroft's demand that Government spending in the next financial year should be no higher than the estimated expenditure for the current year, which would entail a substantial cut. The Treasury Ministers did not have to wait long for another opportunity to apply their deflationary prescription. A run on the pound began in August, not primarily caused by the fear of British inflation, but by the devaluation of the French franc and by rumours of a general realignment of currencies. Probably the best course would have been to let the pound float. The balance of payments was favourable, and almost none of the conditions which had ruled out 'Robot' in 1952 was still operative. But the opportunity was lost; instead, Thorneycroft proposed a rise in Bank Rate to 7 per cent, the highest level since 1921, a cut in public investment, and a restriction on bank lending. The Prime Minister initially jibbed at the rise in Bank Rate, but after a night's sleep he swallowed the whole package, to his subsequent regret.[29]

Macmillan had good cause to rue the package which was arguably the worst available. It shirked, in Keith Middlemas's words, 'a direct assault on consumption at the price of debilitating industry and undermining managerial confidence in Government'. Industrial costs were raised, as was the cost of servicing the national debt, while public investment was cut. To safeguard the pound at a level which was probably already too high, the Chancellor had forced Britain into a recession, christened by Nicholas Davenport 'The Thorneycroft Slump'. Whatever the cost to the economy, the serious overkill did at least halt the run on the reserves. In attempted justification, the Chancellor told the Cabinet that 'it was essential that the supply of money should be restricted . . .' However, some Treasury officials thought that Thorneycroft confused Government expenditure with the quantity of money. In any case, before his September measures the money supply had for several years been falling rapidly as a proportion of GNP. Only in the following twelve months did it increase. The September measures were not even well received in the City.[30]

After press reports of 'inspired' selling of gilts in advance of the Bank Rate announcement, the Shadow Chancellor, Harold Wilson, demanded an investigation into an alleged leak of highly sensitive information. When the Government turned down his request, Wilson used parliamentary privilege to impute the probity of not only Peter Thorneycroft but also Oliver Poole 'with his vast City interests'. Poole, who on Hailsham's appointment as Conservative Party Chairman the previous August had stepped down to Deputy Chairman, naturally insisted that his name be cleared. Accordingly, Macmillan set up a Tribunal of Inquiry under Lord Justice Parker. Appearing before the Tribunal, Wilson was unable to substantiate his disreputable smears, and the Tribunal found there was 'no justification' for Wilson's ridiculous allegations against the Treasury Ministers and 'not a shred of evidence' against Oliver Poole. Characteristically, Wilson did not apologise – he was, Macmillan told Peter Carrington in Australia, 'a mean little creature'. Instead in the parliamentary debate in February on the Tribunal's Report, after Butler had powerfully condemned 'the political weapon of the smear', Wilson pleased Labour MPs with a vastly long and mendacious defence of his McCarthyism. It was a foretaste of his discreditable behaviour in the Profumo affair five years later.[31]

The Treasury trio still had some painful blows in store for the British economy. In December the provisional departmental bids for spending in 1958–9 were £276 million above the original estimates for 1957–8. They included £150 million which the Government had long been committed to spending on bringing many old people into the National Insurance Scheme. Even ignoring the special circumstances of the £150 million, the sought-for increase was proportionately no greater than that of 1954, and senior Treasury officials were not alarmed. Powell, in contrast, urged drastic cuts in the welfare state. The Chancellor demanded that £153 million be lopped off the 1958–9 estimates and intimated that he was considering resignation. He and Powell wanted to save £65 million by removing the family allowance for the second child. The Minister of Pensions, John Boyd-Carpenter, who had not been consulted and was strongly in favour of family allowances, attended the Cabinet meeting. The Cabinet was almost unanimously opposed to cutting family allowances – Boyd-Carpenter would have resigned if they had been removed – but cuts amounting to over £100 million were identified. After the Chancellor had threatened resignation, the Prime Minister asked him if he would stay if he got economies totalling £113 million. Thorneycroft looked uncomfortable and said he wanted time to consider.[32]

Many Cabinet Ministers had already been alienated by Thorneycroft's hectoring rudeness. Iain Macleod accused him of 'Hitler tactics'. Treasury officials were similarly unhappy. Hall thought Thorneycroft's 'bad error of judgement' was 'based in the end on a sort of *laissez-faire* morality' and reported that the Permanent Secretary suspected that he 'was being egged on by Birch and Powell, who in their different ways are both rather mad'. At a dinner with the Prime Minister between Cabinet meetings, Macleod also thought that Thorneycroft was 'obsessed and dominated by Powell', while Butler more surprisingly was shocked by the Treasury's irresponsibility in asking the Cabinet to make great changes of policy at short notice without preparation – had he borne 'Robot' in mind, he would have remembered that that was an old Treasury custom.[33]

The Chancellor had said that he wanted '£30 million certain from welfare', to which Boyd-Carpenter had replied that he did not see why 'welfare' should be singled out. In summing up, the Prime Minister came down firmly on the One-Nation side. 'Disinflation,' he said, 'if enforced to the point at which it created a stagnant economy or provoked a new outbreak of industrial unrest, would defeat its own ends.' Abolishing the family allowance for the second child 'was neither politically nor socially desirable. It would be contrary to the traditions of the Conservative Party,' and other cuts in welfare services would provoke fresh wage claims. The next day all three Treasury Ministers resigned, the Chancellor sending a truculent letter, which Macmillan thought was 'calculated, if unanswered, to do the maximum injury to sterling'.[34]

While the Treasury trio were determined to go if they could not claim a victory, they probably did not expect their resignations to be accepted, hoping to force at least a partial climbdown by Macmillan and the rest of the Cabinet; they probably also hoped to compel the Prime Minister to postpone his tour of the Commonwealth which was due to begin the following day. The night before the resignations, however, Macmillan had foreseen a 'complete disintegration of the Cabinet' leading to a general election and a Labour administration. That danger would have been all the greater had he delayed his departure and negotiated with the Treasury trio. Accordingly he made the well-respected Derick Heathcoat-Amory Chancellor and set off for India. At Heathrow, with well-prepared but admirable insouciance, he told the press that he had thought it best 'to settle up with these little local difficulties and then to turn to the wider vision of the Commonwealth'.[35]

In his recommendation of Powell for a job in 1954, Macleod had dismissed fears that he was likely to resign 'over a minor issue'. Now Powell had not only done just that, he had taken two other Ministers with him. Or had he and they resigned, as they claimed, on a major issue of principle? In later years Harold Macmillan was denounced by right-wingers as the father of inflation – though even allowing for 'lags' in economics, the 'lag' here was surely too long for a paternity suit to succeed. Correspondingly, the resigning Ministers were worshipped as proto-Thatcherites, martyrs to the cause of monetarism and fighting inflation, who had been sacrificed and betrayed by a cynical Prime Minister, intent only on buying votes to win the next general election. One particularly devout hymnist of monetarism even writes of Thorney-croft's later 'apotheosis' and heads his chapter, 'Peter Thorneycroft: a Chancellor Betrayed', without revealing, however, any trace of betrayal in the chapter itself.[36]

Arguably indeed, if there was treachery anywhere, the resigners betrayed the Prime Minister who had given spectacular promotion to Thorneycroft and had invited Birch and Powell to serve in the depart-ment which most attracted them. And as was pointed out long ago by the right-wing sage, Peter Utley, who admired Powell and wrote the first book on him, 'the Conservative Party was at the time in an extremely poor state ... and the authority of its leader was far from being firmly established. The simultaneous resignation of the three minis-ters at such a time was predicted by many to be a mortal blow.' Many such people thought Thorneycroft would soon be Prime Minister; others thought, as the Prime Minister had feared, that the Government would disintegrate and the next Prime Minister would be Hugh Gaitskell.[37]

As Utley also conceded, 'the resignation issue was extremely narrowly defined'.[38] It amounted to a difference of only £50 million, which even in those days was a fairly small sum. Any great issue of principle is difficult to discern. That the wishes of the Treasury team must always prevail? That the Prime Minister must always support his Chancellor of the Exchequer, however wrong-headed the latter may be? That public expenditure should never be allowed to rise whatever the circumstances? None of these is promising, and there appear to be no others. Furthermore, the later right-wing allegations had all been refuted in advance by events and by the actions of Thorneycroft and Powell. So far from inflation accelerating as a result of the Prime Minister and the Cabinet refusing to swallow all of the medicine prescribed by the Treasury triumvirate, inflation declined. In the calendar year 1959 it was almost zero, the lowest it has been since the war. In January 1958, therefore, the British economy did not require further deflation. Wage inflation had abated, and the economy was growing only slowly. Britain's greatest handicap both at home and abroad was its slow rate of growth (stemming partly from a poor record of industrial investment), which Thorneycroft's measures were better designed to aggravate than cure.

The electoral argument is no more plausible. In January 1958 the current Parliament had nearly two and a half years to run. Had the Prime Minister and the Cabinet so wished, they could have tossed the Treasury Ministers the £50 million additional cut in expenditure they demanded and then reflated later. They had plenty of time to do both. Finally, in 1960 the Macmillan Government, judged by the criteria the Treasury trio had adopted in 1958, should have been more objectionable to such strict guardians of public finance than it had been two years previously. Yet Thorneycroft and Powell rejoined it and served without demur.* Indeed, as Minister of Health, Powell proved an enthusiastic dispenser of public money. So, if a great matter of principle existed in 1958 and again in the seventies and eighties, between 1960 and 1963 it mysteriously disappeared.

Interviewed by Macmillan's biographer, Alistair Horne, in 1980, by which time he could already see some of the results of monetarism in practice, Peter Thorneycroft was less sure than Birch and Powell that they had been right. He thought it was questionable whether they were 'right to resign ... we probably made our stand too early'. That seems a fair conclusion.[39]

After his regrettable resignation letter, Thorneycroft conducted himself impeccably. His resignation speech in the House was restrained and impressive. He was on strong ground in stressing that for twelve years we had 'been trying to do more than our resources could manage' – seeking to be a nuclear power, maintaining a welfare state at a high level, repaying massive debt abroad, and 'seeking to conduct a great

---

* Nigel Birch, who was not invited back into the Government, was far from being a prophet of Thatcherism. In his fine little 1949 book *The Conservative Party* – surprisingly not mentioned in Powell's brilliant essay on him in the *DNB* – he wrote *inter alia* that society was 'a living body – not a mere convenience', that Conservatism distrusts 'the plenary inspiration of the *Zeitgeist*', and that Conservatives refuse 'to worship fashionable idols'.

international banking business'. The problem, he said, was not whether we should cut Bank Rate or physical controls, since neither worked very well; it was that we were spending too much money because of trying to do too much. If all this was not a reversion to 'Thorneycroft I', it was a move to 'Thorneycroft 1½'.[40]

Whatever he may have thought before he resigned, Thorneycroft was not the man to lead a rebellion against the Government, nor was the party in any condition to rebel. Much as Anthony Eden's fight against appeasement after he had resigned in 1938 took the form of playing five sets of tennis a day in the South of France, Peter Thorneycroft's fight against inflation twenty years later took the form of a long cruise to Australia and New Zealand.

A Turning Point

Within three weeks of losing his Treasury Ministers, Macmillan almost lost his Minister of Labour as well. Iain Macleod contemplated resignation not because he opposed the Government's policy of wage restraint, but because his Chief Industrial Conciliator at the Ministry had with his permission offered the London Transport Executive and the General Workers Union a Committee of Investigation to help settle their dispute over the claim of 50,000 militant London bus workers for a rise of twenty-five shillings a week. The Cabinet had then accepted the Treasury view and overruled Macleod. Since Macleod had to repudiate his Industrial Commissioner, he asked his Labour opposite number if he should resign; Alf Robens advised him to stay.[41]

The Cabinet's decision made a bus strike certain. Neither Macleod nor Frank Cousins, the left-wing leader of the TGWU, would have chosen that political battleground – Macleod owing to his earlier consent to an inquiry, Cousins because he knew that the busmen's militancy was far greater than their industrial muscle. Both men realised that if left by themselves the busmen would lose. Everything depended, therefore, on whether the dispute would be spread by Cousins or quarantined by Macleod. Here Macleod had the advantage; he and Macmillan were able to head off a national railway strike by getting the Cabinet to agree to an offer of 3 per cent. Cousins was disliked by his fellow union chieftains. Vic Feather, a future General Secretary of the TUC, privately thought that Cousins had no 'integrity' and was 'eaten up with vanity', adding that Bevan, after lunching with him three times, could not face doing so again because Cousins was 'intellectually bankrupt'. So averse to him were the TUC leaders that they privately urged Macleod to stand firm, thinking it was time for Cousins's pride to have a fall. This was a startling demonstration of confidence in One-Nation Tory government, and Macleod obliged. Because of Cousins, the busmen lacked support, and after an eight-week strike, which caused much inconvenience to the public and the loss of 1,600,000 working days, they returned to work. The Government had won a clear victory. In consequence the next three years were free of pay-policy crises.[42]

Earlier the Prime Minister had been worried that the departed Treasury Ministers might cause trouble in the party over the Government's handling of the dispute, and possibly even topple him. The Chief Whip had warned, he confided to his diary, that 'Peter Thorneycroft together with Birch and Powell are ready to pounce' and on another occasion he thought Thorneycroft might be able 'to do on me tit for tat (like Palmerston on Johnny Russell) . . .' Such fears were exaggerated, if not groundless. In any case, Macleod won the political as well as the industrial battle. After Gaitskell had imprudently attacked the Government's handling of the disputes, Labour put down a motion of censure on Macleod. That motion rebounded as such motions often do. Expressing his 'scorn and contempt for the part that the Leader of the Opposition [had] played', Macleod enjoyed a triumph almost as great as his reply to Bevan six years before.[43]

Gaitskell realised that Labour had 'lost a lot by supporting' an unpopular strike; and to Harold Macmillan, Edward Boyle and many Conservatives the bus strike seemed a turning point in the party's fortunes. When he became Chairman of the Party the previous September, Hailsham had found it in a 'complete spirit of disarray', a disarray which was then exacerbated by the rise in Bank Rate. The Gloucester by-election that month heralded the first of the post-war Liberal revivals. On a high poll, the Tory vote was halved, and the Liberals, who had not contested the general election, won 20 per cent of the vote. The September Gallup poll showed Labour on 52, the Conservatives on 33 per cent, an unprecedented lead at that time, and the following month the Prime Minister's approval rating was down to 30 per cent, having been 50 in January.

Hailsham and his deputy, Oliver Poole, were an ideal combination. Hailsham was the right man to rally the party – an inspirational orator with a flair for publicity, as well as being one of the cleverest men in politics – while Poole was a masterly administrator and a shrewd judge of the party's needs and moods.[44]

The new Party Chairman made an immediate impact on the party at the Brighton conference in October. Firstly he delivered at the CPC meeting a fine exposition of Tory philosophy, *Toryism and the Future*.

Secondly he went every day for an early morning swim in the Channel, to the delight of the press corps. And thirdly, at the close of the conference, instead of following the normal procedure of just presenting the bell used by the Conference Chairman to her to keep as a memento, he rang it louder and louder, swinging it round his head and shouting that he was ringing it for victory and proclaiming that it tolled for the defeat of the Labour Party at the next election. The party rank and file loved it and stood up laughing and cheering. The only person not best pleased was the Prime Minister who found his leader's speech that afternoon upstaged and driven from the front pages of the Sunday papers by the exploits of his bell-ringing Chairman. 'You must be gratified by the reception you have had,' he grudgingly wrote to Hailsham.[45]

Despite the Rent Act of 1957, which brought in the staged decontrol of rents – an unpopular but necessary measure which mainly affected the middle classes – Conservative fortunes improved in the autumn, a recovery which was aborted by the January 1958 resignations. By May the party's poll rating was down to 34 per cent, having been 40 in January, and in the interval three by-elections were lost. At Rochdale, the Liberals had a particularly strong candidate in Ludovic Kennedy, who did not win the seat but pushed the Conservative contender into a bad third place. Although a Tory defeat had been expected, the Prime Minister found the result a 'tremendous shock', and the Party Chairman offered his resignation, which was not accepted. Rochdale was the first televised by-election. In the mid-fifties television coverage of politics was absurdly circumscribed. The so-called 'fourteen-day rule', which banned discussion on television of any subject due to be debated in Parliament during the next fortnight, had only recently been rescinded by the *force majeure* of the Suez crisis. Now the Attorney-General, the sometimes buffoonish Sir Reginald Manningham-Buller, tried to scare off television coverage of the by-election, but ITN, which had employed Kennedy as a newscaster, ignored him.[46]

The party's position looked so grim after Rochdale that the Steering Committee even considered offering the Liberals an electoral pact, something which was not considered again until 1974. Home and Heath were its principal supporters, and Macleod, backed by Hailsham, its main opponent. The idea was dropped. At Kelvingrove, Glasgow, in March the Conservative loss of support in a straight fight with Labour was small, but enough to lose the seat. Then at the end of the month the Liberal Mark Bonham Carter won Torrington in Devon by 219 votes. Though from a famous Liberal family – the Asquiths – Bonham Carter had been disposed to become a Tory candidate, and in 1956 the preliminaries had been completed with Oliver Poole. Then, understandably, Suez drove him back to the Liberals. He was a considerable loss for the Conservatives.[47]

The Budget followed ten days after Torrington. The former Minister of Agriculture and new Chancellor, Derick Heathcoat-Amory, proved a more than adequate 'Goschen' to Thorneycroft's 'Lord Randolph Churchill'. The *Economic Survey* declared 'the economic climate [to be] less inflationary than for several years' and forecast a substantial balance of payments surplus. That turned out to be correct. 1958 was a year of recession. Growth was only 0.4 per cent, the lowest of any year since the war until 1974, and by the year's end unemployment was over 600,000. Yet Heathcoat-Amory's Budget was probably about as cautious as one from Thorneycroft II would have been. 'We are not yet strong enough to give more than a minor stimulus,' he told the Commons, and he made only a few cuts in purchase tax, increased the capital allowances for industry and rationalised the profits tax. Macmillan called it a 'good, but humble little package'. Despite widespread disappointment with the Budget, 62 per cent thought it was fair – the highest figure yet recorded for a Budget – and it evidently did not inhibit the beginning of yet another Conservative recovery.[48]

If the County Council elections were poor in April, the borough elections in May were better. The Prime Minister's own ratings also sharply improved. In May he gave a polished performance in a television interview with the American Ed Murrow, who had done much to awaken the United States to the reality of the war by his broadcasts during the blitz – 'This – is London.' Macmillan's opponents contributed to his growing ascendancy. In the Commons, Bevan satirically dubbed the Prime Minister 'Mr MacWonder', whereupon Jo Grimond, the Liberal leader, muttered to his new recruit Mark Bonham Carter, 'What a bloody silly thing to say.' The left-wing cartoonist Vicky later made a similar mistake with his cartoons of 'Supermac'. Attacks that were intended to knock the Prime Minister's standing had the effect of boosting it. By October his approval rating had risen to 57 per cent, twenty points higher than in May. The summer by-elections – five on the same day in June – produced no shocks. Torrington turned out to be the last by-election defeat of the Parliament.[49]

International troubles favoured the Conservatives. Lebanon was near civil war, because of the endeavours of its President to rig the constitution to allow himself a second term. In Iraq in July 1958, as a delayed consequence of Suez, the government was overthrown and the pro-British Nuri Es-Sa'id was murdered. In most of the Third World Macmillan eventually learned the lessons of Suez, but in the Middle East he never recovered from his Suez hangover. Consequently he thought that these events were a rerun of 1956, with the crucial difference that the Americans would this time be on our side. Selwyn Lloyd had the same idea, telling Hammarskjöld that he hoped to involve America in a Middle East adventure to prove that we had been 'right about Suez and the United States wrong'. Macmillan hoped for a Suez-type Anglo-American operation which would have involved invading Syria and Iraq as well as sending troops to Lebanon and Jordan. Luckily Eisenhower had no intention of taking part in such madness, and the British had reluctantly to accept the American view.[50]

The only Anglo-American reaction, therefore, was to send American marines to the Lebanon and British soldiers to Jordan, though what either of them were supposed to be doing there was not altogether clear. Suez enthusiasts welcomed the action, claiming that it showed Eden had been justified, thereby demonstrating their inability to see the obvious distinction between a police action (i.e. sending troops to a country at the request of its government) and an aggressive action (i.e. invading a country in order *inter alia* to overthrow its government).* The Anglo-American interventions in 1958 were clearly police actions, even if they had less in common with Superintendent Maigret than with Inspector Clouseau. Nevertheless the American and British Governments looked impressively decisive, and Labour made the elementary mistake of opposing the British but not the American intervention, allowing the Prime Minister to ask in the House, 'If it is not right to vote against America, why is it right to vote against Britain?'[52]

The bus dispute was not the only strike in the summer. Miners struck because they were not being allowed to work sufficiently long hours to keep up with their hire-purchase payments. Dockers followed suit over an issue which had nothing whatever to do with the docks: a new regulation had raised the speed limit on lorries from 20 to 30 m.p.h. These were not the only nonsensical strikes. Between 1945 and 1955 the number of strikes doubled, and between 1950 and 1960 they again doubled, from 1,300 to over 2,800; 90 per cent of them were unofficial. Vic Feather privately thought Britain had more wild-cat strikes than other countries because 'every man in this country is his own trade union'. He therefore thought it impossible, however desirable, to legislate to strengthen the power of the unions over their members or that of the TUC over the unions. Others had a different diagnosis. The rise

---

* Macmillan's account of the crisis in his memoirs is another masterpiece of fiction. He suppressed all mention of his hopes for a large-scale invasion, ludicrously calling the American despatch of troops to Lebanon 'a recantation – an act of penitence – unparalleled in history'.[51]

of shop stewards had reduced the power of the trade-union barons, which led to a new group solidarity – and more strikes. Alternatively, many trade unionists were more ready than before to be led by the nose by Communists or other militants or malcontents. Whatever the causes, the many silly strikes were a symptom of industrial sickness.[53]

More strikes made the unions more unpopular, especially among Conservative supporters, many of whom called for something to be done. In June the Inns of Court Conservative and Unionist Association published *A Giant's Strength*, which called for unofficial strikes to be made illegal and an industrial tribunal to be set up, to which any industrial dispute would have to be referred before it developed into a strike. As the authors realised, the latter proposal raised the question of a wages policy, a problem which they did not tackle.

To most of the trade-union bosses, a wage policy was anathema. Unlike the militant shop stewards and men like Frank Cousins, they were aware, as a White Paper had hinted in 1956, that full employment could not be maintained indefinitely without wage restraint. Yet in the fifties (and later) almost the last bastion of *laissez-faire* was the trade unions. While usually favouring planning and control of most other things, they were firmly opposed to any government interference with trade-union free collective bargaining. That would have been more defensible had the trade-union structure been less hopelessly old-fashioned. Like much of British industry, it was a living relic of the nineteenth century. The United States had 138 trade unions, West Germany, whose trade unions had been set up by Britain after the war, had twelve, and Britain had 651.[54] The Ford Motor Company at Dagenham had to negotiate with twenty-two trade unions, almost double the total number of unions in Germany. Such a structure cried out for reform, but the TUC had very little power over its members, and nobody else could do the job.

The Government was equally unready to legislate against strikes. Macleod sent a message to warn the authors of *A Giant's Strength* that the more publicity their pamphlet received, the more political damage it would do. The problem of how to enforce a trade-union law against strikes when unofficial strikers broke it had not been solved. Furthermore, the Government was still relying on the moderate trade-union leaders to restrain their members and was unlikely to promise legislation against men who had just given them vital help in defeating Cousins and the busmen. Finally, as Macleod pointed out in a paper he wrote on the Rochdale by-election result, the Conservatives needed the votes of three million trade unionists and their families if there was to be a Conservative Government.[55]

Strikes were economically damaging and a source of anger and frustration to many Conservative activists, but electorally they were more of a liability to Labour than to the Government. The Conservative recovery continued for the rest of the year. By August the party had drawn level with Labour, and by October it was four points ahead. Remarkably, this was more in spite of the economy than because of it. Probably any overload of the economy had been removed by the end of 1957. Hence Heathcoat-Amory's Budget had been too cautious and prolonged the recession. Production had been virtually stagnant since 1955: growth was 1.1 per cent in 1956, 1.8 in 1957 and only 0.4 in 1958. In the summer and autumn the Chancellor took various steps to relax policy such as reducing Bank Rate, ending the credit squeeze and removing restrictions on hire purchase. Nevertheless, unemployment continued to rise, and in January it reached 628,000, or 2.8 per cent, the highest it had been since the war, apart from the 1947 coal crisis. Assuming that the trend would continue, Labour chose to debate unemployment on the day the February figures were announced. Once again their tactics misfired. Macleod was able to tell jubilant Tory and dismayed Labour MPs that unemployment had declined by a virtually unprecedented 58,000. 'I have no doubt the Opposition will improve,' he told the House. 'The first seven years in opposition are always the most difficult', adding that he could not help it if 'every time the Opposition are asked to name their weapons they pick boomerangs'.[56]

Macleod was right about the Opposition. Although Labour's poll ratings improved in the New Year, their leaders had been aware at least since the autumn of an impending election disaster. Labour had failed to come to terms with the higher living standards of many of its erstwhile supporters and floating voters. While Labour of course took pride in the achievements of the Attlee Government, the party failed to adjust to the changes wrought by full employment and the welfare state. Its appeal seemed stuck in an earlier age. Social change was against it. There were over a million more white-collar workers in 1959 than in 1951, and half a million fewer manual workers. Since roughly three-quarters of the middle class voted Conservative and slightly less than two-thirds of the (twice as large) working class voted Labour, this was a boost to the Conservatives. Yet Labour had little excuse for being so ineffective an Opposition. The party was still divided, facing both ways on nationalisation. Gaitskell would probably have made an outstandingly good Prime Minister, but he did not shine in Opposition. He never achieved high poll ratings. He was down to 32 per cent in September 1958 and, although he had risen to 48 per cent by April, he was still twelve points behind Harold Macmillan.[57]

Whatever the deficiencies of Labour as an Opposition, Macmillan was taking no chances of letting them become a Government. Unemployment always brought back to him memories of Stockton-on-Tees before the war, and for some time he had been bombarding the Treasury with pleas for less caution. Yet when the pound was made fully convertible for non-residents at the end of 1958, another opportunity to let it float was lost. The previous summer the Chancellor had feared accusations of bringing in another 1955 election Budget and for a long time he was a very tentative expansionist. Yet January's unemployment figures were alarming, and not only his colleagues but Treasury officials thought further expansion was necessary. The balance of payments was healthily in surplus, and in the last financial year inflation had been zero. So in his Budget Amory responded with a range of tax cuts, including 9d. off income tax – the Economic Secretary, Anthony Barber, had favoured a shilling off. In addition, the investment allowances suspended by Macmillan were restored, and the levy on beer was reduced by 2d. Unfortunately, Treasury officials and ministers all underestimated the expansionary effects of what had been done in the summer and autumn. Had this very open-handed Budget been introduced a year earlier, its generosity would have been beneficial. In 1959, coming on top of an expansion already in progress, it was too much too late, and set off an unsustainable boom.[58]

The 1959 Election

The election battleground strongly favoured the Government. With Suez forgotten, the economy was the dominant issue. In the eight years the Conservatives had been in Government the average real pay for industrial workers had risen by over 20 per cent. This increased wealth was beginning to blur traditional class loyalties, and the Conservative campaign slogan, 'Life's Better under the Conservatives. Don't let Labour Ruin it', exploited both the growing prosperity and the mounting sense of it. Even in March Macleod had been able to boast that British unemployment was the lowest in the 'league table' of Western Europe, and since then it had fallen substantially.[59] Production rose by 6 per cent in 1959, and prices were stable. Consumer confidence was high: outstanding hire-purchase credit rose by more than a third between 1958 and 1959. As a result of the 1959 Budget, the basic rate of income tax had fallen from 47.5 per cent in 1951 to 38.75 per cent (7s. 9d. in the pound) at the time of the election.

Anthony Eden was not prepared to give Macmillan a personal

endorsement, although he could not refuse to endorse the Conservative Party. President Eisenhower was more co-operative. Visiting Washington in March, Macmillan had annoyed the President by what Dulles called his 'outrageous' publicity-seeking, but Dulles and Eisenhower were prepared to be generous because they did not 'want to see Bevan win the election'. In July the Prime Minister succeeded, presumably for the same reason, in persuading the President to include Britain in his world tour – he had earlier managed to persuade himself that if Eisenhower did not come it would be an unforgivable 'insult to the Queen and the whole nation'. The President was given a hero's welcome by massive crowds in the streets; sitting beside him in an open car, Macmillan gained ideal pre-election exposure. The Prime Minister even inveigled President Eisenhower into making a joint television appearance with him from Downing Street in which sugary references were made to their being old friends and to 'the special relationship'. Their somewhat embarrassed and certainly embarrassing conversation provided excellent Conservative propaganda, and was accurately labelled the first of the campaign broadcasts.[60]

Yet, with the Government apparently holding all the aces, a few days into the campaign Labour began to think they could win; more out of the ordinary, some well-placed Conservatives held the same opinion. Gaitskell and Labour were fighting a sparkling campaign which impressed that shrewd judge of elections, Oliver Poole. 'You know, we are losing this election,' he told Hailsham, who agreed with his deputy. Since much of the Conservative counter-attack was directed against the financial unsoundness of Labour's policy, Labour's leaders were faced with the perennial difficulty of explaining where they would find the necessary resources to pay for the improved social services they were promising. The usual answer was the one Wilson gave on television: 'They are going to be paid for not out of increased taxation but out of increased production.' A few days later, prompted by a rumour that the Tories were about to produce a scare that Labour would increase income tax by 2s. 6d. in the pound, Gaitskell went further than Wilson, promising that there would be 'no increase in the standard or other forms of income tax'. As soon as he heard the news, Hailsham told a meeting in Doncaster that 'The Lord hath delivered them into our hands.' Macmillan found Gaitskell's pledge 'queer for an ex-Chancellor' and asked him to extend it to other taxes. Then a journalist found an old hand-out at Labour's headquarters promising a reduction in purchase tax, which the Secretary of the Labour Party, Morgan Philips, foolishly told him was another Labour commitment. These promises robbed Labour's spending plans and Gaitskell himself of credibility, and the momentum that Labour had seemed to generate was checked and then reversed.[61]

Whether Gaitskell's speech was a decisive blunder or, as is more probable, the Government would have won anyway, the Conservatives gained an overall majority of 100 seats, winning 49.4 per cent of the popular vote. That was an extraordinary achievement. In early 1957 even a narrow victory had appeared out of the question. The Conservative Party and Government had seemed stricken, and the precedents were discouraging. Noting in a Cabinet paper in September 1957 that it had been very rare for the same party to win even two elections running, Macmillan had added, 'and to win three is almost a miracle'. Yet now it had been done and by a handsome margin.[62]

Most of the credit for the Tory triumph went to the Prime Minister, who made a much-praised final election broadcast, although Hailsham thought, quite rightly, that a good deal of it should go to him. From Macmillan, at least, it was not forthcoming. The Prime Minister wrote him 'a reasonably polite letter of thanks' before demoting him. Hailsham's exile to the gulag of the Ministry of Science was not punishment for misdemeanours at Central Office or for being a possible Prime Ministerial rival – he was still safely anchored in the House of Lords – but arose, as Hailsham later discovered, from Macmillan's misunderstanding of the role he had played in a divorce case concerning a relation of the Prime Minister.* When Macmillan realised his mistake, he made belated amends for what his victim regarded as 'his almost Borgia-like behaviour'.[63]

In 1959 Harold Macmillan had no cause to be wary of possible rivals. Two-thirds of the electorate thought he was doing a good job. That figure rose to 72 per cent in January 1961, before dropping to 35 per cent in March 1963. Macmillan's average popularity during his tenure in Downing Street was only just below that of Churchill and Eden and considerably above that of every subsequent Prime Minister. In performance, too, he was probably the third best premier since the war; Churchill was easily the best, Attlee was a distant second, and Macmillan a similarly distant third. A complicated character, he was courageous, immensely intelligent, hard-working, extraordinarily well-read, witty and humorous, often far-sighted, a man of broad social sympathies, but also vulnerable, inhibited, crafty and surprisingly insecure. When John Boyd-Carpenter asked him to dinner before they both spoke in Boyd-Carpenter's constituency, Macmillan refused because he would never eat

---

* Hailsham had been asked to swear an affidavit that a child, whom he had seen while staying with friends for a weekend, had appeared happy and well looked after. He could not have honourably refused.

before a speech. Sometimes he would throw up before Prime Minister's Questions in the House. So, what Hailsham called the Prime Minister's 'unflappability' was, as Boyd-Carpenter wrote, the result of 'great efforts of will and self-control'.[64]

Yet Macmillan so courted publicity that even Woolton, himself no devotee of the back room, criticised his excessive showmanship. During his visit to Moscow in early 1959, he wore an eye-catching white fur hat, a publicity stunt which pleased the British press but which might have back-fired: luckily his hosts did not realise that it was a relic of Finland's resistance to the Soviet Union in 1940. With his publicity-seeking went a streak of vulgarity. For all his love of nineteenth-century literature – he was reading *Pride and Prejudice* when he received the summons to the Palace to become Prime Minister – Jane Austen would not have admired his best-known phrases : 'Never had it so good' was a colloquial follow-up to his 'There ain't gonna be no war', with which as Foreign Secretary he stole the headlines after the Geneva conference in July 1955.* Yet while he could be ruthless, as Hailsham found, he could also be kind, and he was generous to young journalists with his time and his whisky.[66]

---

* Macmillan did not even get his Geneva vulgarism right. What he in fact said was: 'There ain't gonna be any war'.[65]

Seeking a Role

Economic prosperity had won the election, but both before and after it Harold Macmillan was at least equally preoccupied with foreign and colonial affairs. Dean Acheson's observation to the West Point cadets in 1962 that 'Britain has lost an empire and has not yet found a role' is justly celebrated. His next sentence was equally to the point. 'The attempt to play a separate power role – that is a role apart from Europe, a role based on a "special relationship" with the United States, a role based on being the head of a "Commonwealth" which has no political structure, or unity, or strength and enjoys a fragile and precarious economic relationship – this role is about played out.' Although both of Acheson's sentences were the simple truth, they further wounded Britain's already battered pride and created a storm in the press. While thinking that Britain 'ought to be strong enough to laugh off this kind of thing', the Prime Minister compared Acheson's 'error', rather oddly, with those of Philip of Spain and Louis XIV. He also let off steam in his diary, bursting out that Acheson was 'always a conceited ass'. Acheson may have been conceited; he certainly was not an ass. Macmillan's anger probably stemmed from Acheson's failure to recognise his attempt to forge a new role for Britain and in equal measure from the knowledge that in doing so he had started too late and was proceeding too slowly.[1]

Between 1945 and 1964 the overseas population governed by Britain fell from 500 million to fewer than 15 million. Most of that decline was the result of the independence of India and Pakistan, and under the first two Conservative Colonial Secretaries, Oliver Lyttelton and Alan Lennox-Boyd, the pace of the movement towards independence for Britain's African colonies varied between slow and imperceptible. By the time of the 1959 election, out of eighteen colonies only Sudan and Ghana had achieved independence, while Nigeria was close to doing so. The very much quicker pace after the election was mainly owing to two events earlier in the year.

After many months of sporadic if minor violence, the disturbances in

Nyasaland had become more serious, at least twenty Africans being killed. Nyasaland contained only 8,000 white settlers, and the African population of over two and a half million feared that the country's propulsion into a Federation with North and South Rhodesia in 1953 had been a device to perpetuate European domination. A few days after the deaths, the Governor declared a state of emergency and 1,300 people, including Dr Hastings Banda and other leaders of the African National Congress Party, were arrested; allegedly they were plotting to massacre Europeans and their African rivals. Ironically, the arrests were made in the same week as Archbishop Makarios's triumphant return to Cyprus after his arrest and deportation on similar charges. The Government seemed slow to learn. A Commission of Enquiry was set up under a High Court Judge, Sir Patrick Devlin; and among the three other members was Sir Edgar Williams, formerly Montgomery's Chief of Intelligence in the Eighth Army and then Warden of Rhodes House.

The Commission's Report was erroneously sent to the Colonial Office before publication, whereupon the Government persuaded Devlin to change it. Even its sanitised version, however, was hostile to what had been done, finding that Nyasaland was 'no doubt temporarily – a police state'. The Prime Minister was horrified, attributing the report's unfavourable tone to Devlin being Irish and a lapsed Roman Catholic as well as being disappointed at not having been made Lord Chief Justice; others attributed it to Sir Patrick being a radical. In fact Devlin, an outstanding judge, probably should have been Lord Chief Justice and, as the former Tory MP, Christopher Hollis, pointed out, he was a Conservative, having helped Hollis in his constituency. Indeed, Hollis went on, had he not preferred to stay at the bar, he would have had a safe Conservative seat, in which case he would no doubt have become a Law Officer and the Government would have been spared the services of Sir Reginald Manningham-Buller.[2]

The Government unwisely rejected the Devlin Report and on the day of its publication brought out an answer allegedly from the Governor of Nyasaland, but in fact written by Ministers. In the ensuing parliamentary debate Manningham-Buller opened for the Government. A few years before he had led the prosecution of Dr Bodkin Adams for the alleged murder of old ladies at Eastbourne and had seen his case demolished not only by the defence but by the trial judge, one Sir Patrick Devlin. Whether or not his ignominious showing in that case influenced the Attorney-General, he made a deplorable speech, attacking Devlin and the Commission. Although the Government had a comfortable majority, the more reliable judgement of Sir Edgar Williams on the whole business was that it was 'a disgraceful episode'.[3]

The Hola affair in Kenya ran concurrently with the Nyasaland diffi-culty. On 3 March, after a riot in a Mau Mau detention camp, eleven detainees had been clubbed to death. Although an inquiry exonerated the Colonial Secretary, he was anxious to resign over both Hola and Nyasaland. However, after the Prime Minister had polled every Minister in Cabinet and all had opposed his resignation, Alan Lennox-Boyd agreed to stay until the election. Earlier Macmillan had recorded in his diary, 'we are in a real jam'. Still, the Government managed to ride out the crisis, though not before Enoch Powell had made probably his great-est speech.[4]

Powell, who had rejoined the One-Nation Group in June, was speak-ing not only for himself but for the group, most of whose members were clustered around him in the chamber to give support. As an ex-minister, he could expect to be called fairly early on and he stood up each time another speaker finished, but first the Deputy Speaker and later another deputy looked fixedly away from him and called somebody else. Consequently Powell, the last back-bench speaker, did not begin his speech until 1.15 a.m., so that popular newspaper reporting of his speech was truncated. One of the earlier speakers had suggested that we need not worry too much about the eleven African deaths because the men were 'sub-human', which at least gave Powell the opportunity to demonstrate that he was far from being a racist. He dismissed that idea as 'a fearful doctrine' and, in a powerful speech, stressed that Parliament was responsible for everything that was done in its name. 'We can not,' he said, 'we dare not, in Africa of all places, fall below our highest standards in the acceptance of responsibility.' Despite his intervention, Powell remained on good terms with Lennox-Boyd, and though under subsequent Conservative administrations such a speech would have ended all hope of preferment, under Macmillan's it did not.[5]

Some civil servants in the Cabinet Office had earlier seen that the Government's policy of gradualism did not produce stability, yet it was not until Hola and Nyasaland that the Prime Minister saw its dangers. At the Cabinet meeting to discuss Hola, the two ministers most outraged at what had happened there were Hailsham and Macleod. With Hail-sham out of the running, the obvious choice for a Prime Minister who wanted a more liberal Colonial Secretary was Iain Macleod.[6]

Offering him the Colonial Office after the election, Macmillan said, 'Iain, I've got the worst job of all for you.' Macleod was interested in colonial affairs – his brother farmed in Kenya – and he turned out to have a great liking for Britain's colonial and ex-colonial subjects. The Colonial Office was the job he most wanted, yet in one respect it was indeed 'the worst job of all', for although he was a great Colonial

Secretary, the job fatally damaged his prospects for eventually winning the Conservative leadership.[7]

In the end Macleod probably moved faster than even Macmillan expected or wanted. Yet the Prime Minister himself told the South African Parliament in February 1960: 'The wind of change is blowing through this continent, and, whether we like it or not, this growth of national consciousness is a political fact.' Macmillan's famous sentence was no exaggeration at a time when even de Gaulle had decided that France must leave Algeria. Unfortunately the French President was well ahead of the Conservative right-wing. Men like Lord Salisbury, who was reliving the days of his grandfather, thought the Africans did not 'want power' but wanted to be governed by Britain. Answering Salisbury after he had left office, Macleod agreed that there had been 'a deliberate speeding up of the movement towards independence' when he became Colonial Secretary, adding that in his view 'any other policy would have led to terrible bloodshed in Africa'. By putting Britain's East African colonies on the fast track to independence – not, he wrote, 'as fast as the Congo and not as slow as Algeria' – Macleod avoided bloodshed in Africa at the cost of wounding his career. By conciliating African nationalism, he inflamed nationalism within his own party and earned the unforgiving enmity of its right wing. Salisbury made a personal attack on him in the Lords, calling him 'too clever by half', an allegation that was not even true of Macleod's African policy, let alone of the man himself. But the jibe stuck.[8]

Salisbury and right-wing back-benchers were not Macleod's only problem. He had difficulty, too, with some Cabinet colleagues. He clashed with Alec Home, the Commonwealth Relations Secretary, whose views on Africa were closer to Salisbury's than to Macleod's; the two men did not trust each other. Home nearly resigned, while Macleod himself came close to doing so on at least three occasions. According to Macmillan's diary, Macleod's threatened resignations were 'a daily event', but he also recorded that 'Macleod, with many faults, has been persistent, imaginative and ingenious'. In January 1961, reckoning that he had 15 per cent of Tory back-benchers against him and that if the percentage rose much higher he would have to go, he thought he would 'very likely be out before the end of the year'. And so he was, but he was replaced by Reginald Maudling, who, Macmillan was disappointed to discover, was 'quite as progressive' and in some respects *plus royaliste que le roi*. In November the Monday Club, named after 'Black Monday', the day of Macmillan's 'Wind of Change' speech, was formed to oppose Government policy in Africa and to promote true Conservatism in other fields. Joined by ten MPs and Salisbury as patron, the sect became increasingly disreputable over the years. By the time the party lost office in 1964, Southern Rhodesia was the only problem still remaining in Africa. For that, the credit was due to Macmillan, Macleod and Maudling.[9]

Europe

The Macmillan Government found it easier to get out of Africa than into Europe. Negotiations on the British proposal of a free-trade area with the Six proceeded slowly. Maudling, who was put in charge of the negotiations in August 1957, had a first-class brain and a congenial personality, but he was insular in outlook, was still wedded to the Commonwealth, and except in conviviality had little in common with his continental opposite-numbers. In any case, the Six were more interested in completing their own arrangements than helping out Britain. Maudling's chief difficulty, however, was that Britain, as she usually did in European affairs, was overplaying her hand. In proposing a merely industrial free-trade area which excluded agriculture and allowed Britain to maintain her Commonwealth preferences, Britain was seeking, as Maudling conceded, an arrangement which 'naturally seemed to France and Italy . . . a very unfair bargain'. The continental economies were performing better than the British: in 1958 Germany overtook Britain as an exporter of manufactured goods. Yet despite all the evidence, the British Government continued to think that the Six needed Britain more than Britain needed the Six. It soon learned better. The negotiations were probably always a lost cause but, when de Gaulle came to power in May 1958, they were certainly doomed. In November the French Minister of Information Jacques Soustelle announced that the sort of free-trade area the British desired was 'not possible'. Sir David Eccles, who had made a tactless anti-German speech the year before, hinted that if the French did not co-operate they might regret it. France rightly regarded that as an impotent threat, and the negotiations were over.[10]

Britain then formed a European Free Trade Area with Denmark, Norway, Sweden, Switzerland, Austria and Portugal – another misjudgement. The British objective in forming EFTA, as it was called, was to strengthen our hand against the Six. It did not. Nor did it bring economic advantage to Britain. As Britain had higher tariffs than her partners, the free-trade area opened British markets to them while, as they all had small populations, no corresponding benefit flowed to Britain. British trade grew faster with the EEC than with its free-trade-area partners. Even the Americans, whom the British were always so anxious to please, disliked EFTA. They favoured the Common Market because it was an attempt to unify Europe. EFTA had no such advantage; in their eyes it was merely divisive. Nor did EFTA help the Prime Minister to improve relations with France or West Germany. Adenauer was angered by Macmillan's visit to Moscow in February 1959, when Khrushchev was making belligerent noises about West Berlin. Macmillan came to think that Adenauer was 'half crazy', while the German Chancellor with more justification thought Britain was 'like a rich man who had lost all his property but does not realise it'.[11]

Events abroad and at home, however, aroused the Government if not the country to see the necessity of change. The first Eisenhower–Khrushchev meeting at Camp David in September 1959 established that the US President could meet the Russian leader at the summit without being shepherded up the hill by the British Prime Minister, and the failure of the Four Power Summit in Paris in May 1960, which drove Harold Macmillan 'almost to despair', exhibited Britain's limited importance at a summit even when she was invited. Britain was not the partner of the US but her subordinate. Very possibly, too, Eisenhower indicated to Macmillan that American–British relations would be damaged if Britain did not join the EEC. And the Commonwealth looked an increasingly shaky foundation for Britain's trade and international standing. International developments were not the only factors turning the Prime Minister's thoughts towards the Six. The relative failure of EFTA, Britain's economic difficulties, the change of heart by the chief employers' organisation on the need for British entry into the EEC, the promotion of Sir Frank Lee, the only top civil servant who had favoured joining the Common Market in the mid-fifties, to be Permanent Secretary at the Treasury, and above all the obvious success of the EEC all contributed. As Macmillan admitted to the Australian Prime Minister, we had not joined the Six because 'we thought they would not succeed and we have been proved wrong'.[12]

The Government's conversion, in which the Prime Minister was the major force, was rapid. At the end of 1959 Maudling, the new President of the Board of Trade, had told the House of Commons that, as signing the Treaty of Rome would circumscribe Britain's relations with the Commonwealth, he could 'think of no more retrograde step economically or politically'. Little more than six months later, the Cabinet agreed that it would be desirable to seek membership of the EEC, though on special terms which would protect the Commonwealth. A Government motion calling for 'political and economic unity' in Europe was passed in the Commons by 215 to 4, with Labour abstaining. The next step took longer. British agriculture, the Conservative Party, and the Commonwealth had first to be softened up. In the Cabinet reshuffle in July, pro-Europeans were placed in the key posts: Edward Heath became Lord Privy Seal and number two at the Foreign Office; Duncan Sandys became Commonwealth Secretary, and Christopher Soames Minister of Agriculture. Within three months Soames was able to tell Macmillan that so far as agriculture was concerned we could go ahead and join the EEC. The pro-European Peter Thorneycroft also returned to the Cabinet as Minister of Aviation, while a year later the sceptical Maudling was moved to the Colonial Office.[13]

Nevertheless, not until 22 July 1961 did the Cabinet reach what Macmillan called a *'unanimous* decision in principle' to apply to enter the Common Market, a decision which he announced to the House of Commons on the 31st. This important shift did not entail an additional determination to abandon being a US satellite. During his visit to Washington in May to meet the new American President, Kennedy, the Prime Minister had sought presidential approval for Britain's application. That was graciously given, and the following day Macmillan told George Ball, the US Under-Secretary of State, 'Yesterday was one of the greatest days of my life'.[14]

That excitement was not reflected in his announcement in Parliament. Harold Macmillan has often been accused of downplaying the political aspect of Britain's application. In fact he said on 31 July, 'This is a political issue as well as an economic issue. Although the Treaty of Rome is concerned with economic matters it has an important political objective, namely to promote unity and stability in Europe.' That seems pretty clear. All the same, the Prime Minister's statement was limp and half-hearted. As it was announcing a decision not to join the EEC but merely one to ask for official negotiations with the Six, to see if we could get good enough terms to enable us to accede to the Treaty of Rome, Churchillian oratory would have been out of place. Even so, 'the plunge', as the *Guardian* commented, was being taken by a 'shivering Government'; it had made 'a depressing start', which diminished the chances of successful negotiations.[15]

Edward Heath, who was in charge of Britain's application and brilliantly conducted the detailed negotiations, sounded a far better note in his introductory statement in Paris, yet the talks dragged on for over a year. The delay before the application was made and the protracted nature of the negotiations, which began with Britain pitching her demands far too high, were probably fatal, for all the time President de Gaulle was becoming stronger in his own country. Although Chancellor Adenauer expressed doubts to Ball whether Harold Macmillan was 'ready to get on the European bus', the rest of the German government were enthusiastic supporters of British entry, as were four other members of the Six. France was the only obvious opponent, her President fearing that Britain's close relations with America and her links with the Commonwealth would make her an awkward addition to the Community.[16]

Opposition in the Conservative Party and the Commonwealth slowed the negotiations, and public support declined – before the application was made, two-thirds of voters could not correctly say whether Britain was in the EEC or EFTA. The Cabinet remained solid. At one time the Prime Minister feared that a Minister, probably Rab Butler, who represented an agricultural constituency, might play Disraeli to his Peel. That was never a likely role for Butler, who instead took what he called 'a staunch decision to back the Common Market' and was made chairman of the Cabinet Committee overseeing the negotiations, partly to placate him and partly to reassure the National Farmers Union. Although only 4 per cent of the working population was engaged in agriculture, the NFU, which Christopher Soames found an 'infernal nuisance', influenced about eighty Tory MPs. In the parliamentary party as a whole, about forty to fifty MPs were opposed to entry. As the Government was not formally committed to join the Community until it knew the terms, it felt it could not campaign whole-heartedly for entry for fear of encouraging the Six to stiffen them. That analysis was probably faulty: a more enthusiastic approach would have shortened the negotiating period and might have led to more concessions.[17]

Together with seeking a new international role for Britain, the Government sought 'modernisation' at home. In December 1960 Dr Richard Beeching had been appointed Chairman of the British Transport Commission. Beeching's background in ICI was an unusual training for a transport expert; he was also an opponent of nationalisation on principle. In February 1963 Beeching produced *The Reshaping of the British Railways* – a report which advocated the closure of over 2,000 stations at a likely cost of 70,000 jobs. The social implications of the report were not restricted to the job losses; the vitality of thousands of rural communities was threatened, and Beeching failed to take adequate account of the movement of population from urban centres to the suburbs and the new towns. Sir Burke Trend, the Secretary to the Cabinet, advised Macmillan to commission a 'complementary study . . . on the problems of roads and road transport', excellent advice which was ignored. So were the serious social consequences of the report, and the massively unpopular Beeching proposals were implemented. As a result, Britain's railway network had been cut by 50 per cent by 1975. Beeching was only the beginning of over thirty wasted years of Conservative transport policy.[18]

Rab at the Home Office

Butler proved an excellent reforming Home Secretary. He was stuck with the Government's Homicide Bill, since it was already on its way through Parliament, and he deftly put it on the statute book. The bill, which introduced degrees of murder, was difficult to defend, but it had been made necessary by the disagreement between Lords and Commons over capital punishment. While he was at the Home Office, Butler became a convinced abolitionist, though that did not cause him, when considering whether or not to grant a reprieve, to err on the side of leniency. Even at the time, many thought his decision to allow the hanging of James Hanratty a serious misjudgement.[19]

Elsewhere the Prime Minister allowed him 'a completely free hand' with his reforms, a liberality probably made all the easier by Macmillan's awareness that they would make the Home Secretary a target of right-wing abuse. When Home Secretary, Churchill had laid down that 'the mood and temper of the public with regard to the punishment of crimes and criminals is one of the unfailing tests of the civilisation of any country'. Butler took Churchill's dictum as his text and, undeterred by signs that many on the right of his party would fail that test, he embarked on a comprehensive plan of penal reform. Pointing out that after examining all the available evidence the Cadogan Committee had concluded that flogging was not a deterrent, he refused to reintroduce corporal punishment. The new MP for Finchley, Margaret Thatcher, felt strongly, however, that 'the fashionable tendencies in penal policy' – the Cadogan Committee had in fact reported in 1938 – 'should be sharply reversed' and voted to bring back the birch or the cane for violent young offenders, the only time in her Commons career that she voted against the party line. It was then, as Butler wrote, that he had his main controversy with elements in the Conservative Party, 'Colonel Blimps of both sexes – and the female of the species was more deadly, politically, than the male'. The annual outing of the hangers and floggers at the Conservative Party Conference in full cry against the Home Secretary was not a spectacle for the squeamish. Butler routed his opponents with a brilliant speech at Brighton in 1961, yet his stand was, as he said, held against him by many members of the party.[20]

Much of the legislation for which the Home Office was responsible, Butler told a CPC meeting in 1959, was still 'laced in Victorian corsetry'.

After the Wolfenden Committee had recommended the effective removal of prostitutes from the streets and the legalisation of homosexual acts between consenting adults in private, one of his junior ministers, David Renton, told the Home Secretary that, while he would be happy to help with legislation over prostitution, his conscience – he presumably meant his prejudices – would not permit him to help remove the criminal sanctions against homosexuality. As Butler soon found that much of the parliamentary party suffered from the same 'conscience', he could enact only the first part of the Committee's recommendations. Elsewhere, however, he could loosen the Victorian corsets without exciting the deeper emotions of the Conservative Right.* The law on charities was reformed, and licensing hours and the law on obscene publications were both liberalised. In addition, by the introduction of betting shops, Butler's Betting and Gaming Act for the first time enabled the poorer classes to place a bet without breaking the law. Unfortunately, MPs were so determined to make betting for such people as joyless an activity as possible that not until Ian Gilmour's private member's bill in 1983 legalised the provision of reasonable amenities did betting shops stop resembling what Butler called 'undertakers' premises'. Nonetheless, Butler's Act was a valuable reform.[21]

Butler's modernising social legislation was broadly supported by the left wing of the party and by centrist and liberal opinion in the country; it was opposed or merely tolerated by right-wingers. Over immigration, the Home Secretary was supported by the right (though many of them would have liked him to go further) and opposed by those who were usually his allies. The Eden Government had come close to restricting immigration in 1955, but drew back after opposition and a threat of resignation from the Colonial Secretary, Alan Lennox-Boyd. After race riots in Notting Hill, Dudley and Nottingham in September 1958, Macmillan minuted that it was time to consider legislation again. However, the judiciary dealt severely with the rioters, and once again the Government took no further action. Surprisingly, immigration was scarcely an issue at the 1959 election, although at North Kensington one of the candidates, Sir Oswald Mosley, argued for mass repatriation at Government expense. In Birmingham, also, some Conservative candidates more temperately raised it; Enoch Powell did not.[22]

Almost equally surprisingly, immigration was not seriously discussed by the 1922 Committee until December 1960. By the following year legislation, long overdue, had become inescapable. Immigration from

---

* Years later, Butler reminisced happily about having removed more prostitutes from the streets than Gladstone had ever dreamed of.

the West Indies, Africa and the Indian subcontinent had grown from 21,000 in 1959 to 58,000 in 1960 and 136,000 in 1961. If spread evenly round the country, these immigrants could have been fairly easily absorbed. But as they were concentrated in a few areas, they inevitably gave rise to racial tension, even though most of them were valuable additions to the country. Both Butler himself and Iain Macleod, by then Leader of the House, who together piloted the Immigration Bill through the Commons, found the legislation distasteful. 'I detest the necessity for it,' Macleod told the House, but necessary he believed it to be. In answer to the charge that the Government was acting with undue haste, Macleod answered that 'we have taken years to decide it', which was all too true. The bill was bitterly attacked by *The Times* and the serious press and savaged by Gaitskell and the Labour Party. Gaitskell called it 'this miserable, shameful, shabby bill', and denouncing Butler and Macleod for failing to stop it by threatening resignation, called them 'hypocrites'. If Gaitskell remembered that the Attlee Government had recognised that such legislation might be necessary in the future, the hypocrisy was his. Most probably he did not, and his indignation was genuine. In any case, after his premature death Labour abandoned opposition to restricting immigration; and the Wilson Government introduced controls which were stricter than those of Butler.[23]

Economic Troubles

Even well before the election Heathcoat-Amory had begun to worry that he had done too much in his Budget and was warning Downing Street that consumer spending was 'overheating' the economy because of a 'too reflationary' policy. Butler, too, had 'the smell' of expansion going too far. The Treasury remained complacent, however, and Hall told the Chancellor that there was very little resemblance between 1955 and 1959. Amory was still more worried in December, but Hall, who later conceded that Amory had been 'ahead of everyone else in the Treasury' in wanting restrictive measures as early as Christmas, remained sanguine until February. Even then the Prime Minister thought that after the previous year's Budget and the election 'a deflationary Budget would either be very foolish or very dishonest'. He favoured 'a standstill' one. Amory and his advisers sent him a strong reply, arguing that to act now was the best chance of making really extreme measures unnecessary in a few months' time. Nevertheless, Macmillan won the battle if not the argument, and the Budget, wrote Hall, 'was in the right direction but not nearly far enough'. The profits tax was raised, but purchase tax was not, although it should have been the other way round. In consequence more had to be done in the summer. Luckily the Labour Opposition could not make much capital out of the Government's difficulties since at the time they had complained that the 1959 Budget did not do enough to expand the economy.[24]

After the election Amory had told the Prime Minister of his wish 'to exchange the fierce conflict of national politics for the comparative calm of business and philanthropy'. Macmillan had persuaded him to stay on for one more Budget, but when in July Amory insisted on leaving, Macmillan, too, thought it was time for him to go.[25]

Twice already a Prime Minister's wish to keep Butler away from the Foreign Office had damaged the Government. In 1955 Eden did not want Butler to be Foreign Secretary because he wanted to have a 'subordinate'. When forming his Government in 1957, Macmillan had left Selwyn Lloyd at the Foreign Office for the same reasons. On this third occasion, Prime Ministerial determination to prevent Butler becoming Foreign Secretary did not damage foreign policy. Although Lord Home's appointment was greeted with some incredulity, he proved a competent Foreign Secretary. The harm was done at the Treasury, where Selwyn Lloyd modestly admitted that he knew 'nothing about the job'. He was indeed way out of his depth, whereas Eccles or Maudling would have been well within theirs. If Macmillan had been willing to make Butler Foreign Secretary, Lloyd could have gone to the Home Office and would almost certainly have been an excellent Home Secretary. Only when he became Leader of the House in 1963 and, later, Speaker, were the attractions of Lloyd's personality and his talents as a conciliator fully revealed.[26]

For some time businessmen had been resentful of the harm done to their companies by 'stop–go', and Lloyd's appointment as Chancellor virtually coincided with similar thoughts and feelings at last permeating the Treasury. Having realised that Britain's economy was still laggard, officials had become more concerned with the long-term problems of growth; they had been convinced that new measures were needed to close the gap between the growth of wages and the growth of productivity. Robert Hall had come to two conclusions. The first was that workers and managers did not work hard enough, which was, he thought, 'the basic trouble'. The second was that the Government and the Treasury had 'really run the economy too fast' for the last decade. If there was little the Treasury could do to cure the basic trouble, it could remedy or at least alleviate the second one by running the economy at a slightly higher rate of unemployment to curb strikes and wage increases. Many officials thought that 3 per cent – the figure earlier favoured by Beveridge and later by Thorneycroft – would be about right. Action was all the more necessary because the pound was becoming overvalued and most of our competitors did not have a similar problem. As they were growing faster, they could better absorb wage increases, and Germany for example had a rational trade-union structure and a strong fear of inflation derived from her experiences in the 1920s, while in France the trade unions were weak and divided.[27]

By July 1961 the Prime Minister, who had been to some degree also his own Chancellor of the Exchequer and Foreign Secretary, was exhausted and 'seriously contemplated resignation'. At least since his own time at the Treasury, he had blamed inflation on excessive wage increases. In his memoirs he described 'some of our wounds as self-inflicted', citing 'the desire to consume [starting] to outrun the willingness to produce'. But neither when he was Prime Minister nor in his memoirs did he appreciate that the wages difficulty was in a sense a wound inflicted by himself. In the absence of faster growth, wage inflation could be curtailed only by unemployment or an effective incomes policy. In his diary Macmillan railed at 'the utter irresponsibility of labour' (wildcat strikes) in some industries and its 'hopeless conservatism' (restrictive practices) in others. Yet because of his knowledge of the misery of unemployment on Teesside before the war, he refused to contemplate the use of even 3 per cent unemployment – a figure that would have been regarded as impossibly low by his successors in the eighties and nineties – as a weapon against inflation, and would not even allow the matter to come before the Cabinet. His attitude was creditably humanitarian, but unless others co-operated – and the unions did not – he was carrying his One Nation Conservatism to self-defeating lengths. In consequence his Government had to introduce a crude and vastly unpopular pay policy.[28]

When he became Chancellor, Selwyn Lloyd had jocularly asked the Chief Economic Adviser how soon the country was going bust, yet nothing dramatic occurred for a year. Lloyd's first Budget was slightly deflationary, but while he feared that 'the cost-inflationary process' would speed up, adding that it was 'a menace' which it was impossible to exaggerate, the only action he took was likely to aggravate that menace. At the Prime Minister's urging he substantially raised the threshold for the start of surtax, which was fully justified, but at a time of rapidly rising wages it should have been accompanied, as Frank Lee and other officials argued, by a proper capital gains tax. Instead the Chancellor raised profits tax and promised an inadequate short-term capital gains one.[29]

After a revaluation of the German Mark, the UK's reserves began to fall, and in July the central bankers demanded action. The economy was already off the boil, and the pound was overvalued; hence floating would almost certainly have been the best remedy. But that would have annoyed the United States – 'the special relationship' was a totem, and the pound was another totem. Even Harold Macmillan thought it had become a symbol, so that devaluation would be politically damaging. The only alternative was to damage the economy; hence, as in September 1957, a much too deflationary package was assembled. On 25 July Lloyd announced that consumer taxes would be raised by 10 per cent, Government spending and bank advances curbed, and Bank Rate increased to 7 per cent, measures which ensured a near-stagnating economy for nearly two years. In addition he announced 'a pay pause'.[30]

As well as his deflationary package, which followed a familiar pattern, Lloyd proposed in July the foundation of a National Development Council. This was an attempt to get away from Treasury short-termism and stop–go. (At the same time the Plowden Committee set up by Amory recommended that public spending should be planned not annually but over a five-year period.) What became the National Economic Development Council was to be a tripartite body, representing Government, management and unions, and containing independent members, to discuss ways of improving Britain's economic performance. One such way was by planning. The Federation of British Industry had become converts to planning. Many had noticed that growth in France had been rapid and that the French had had a succession of four-year plans, and they thought, wrote Donald MacDougal, Neddy's first Economic Director, 'that there might be some connection between the two'. The Council had its first meeting in March 1962. Most of its members arrived puffing because the lift had broken down, a failure which was taken by some to symbolise the state of the British economy.[31]

When making the original announcement, Lloyd said that 'the controversial matter of planning now arises. I am not frightened of the word.' Some were frightened at the time, however, and many more later. As an interference with sacred market forces, the very idea of planning offends the New Right. According to that body of opinion, therefore, July 1961 was the month in which the Conservative Party forsook sound policies, straying into a nightmarish labyrinth of planning, bureaucracy and 'corporatism', which became a scare word for the New Right. In fact, Neddy had highly respectable Tory antecedents. Winston Churchill and Harold Macmillan had envisaged a similar body in the 1930s, as had the *Industrial Charter* and Leo Amery in the 1940s.[32]

Neddy was not based on an abstract socialist or neo-corporatist blueprint, but was inspired by the highly successful French Commissariat-General au Plan. Yet it could never emulate its French prototype because it reflected 'the profoundly differing conceptions of government and administration in the two countries'. Consequently the NEDC lacked the impressive bureaucratic resources enjoyed by its French opposite number. According to a Fabian Society report in 1964, the Government's planning was only assisted by 'about the same number of senior economists and statisticians as are employed by a big progressive firm'; the civil service was not augmented by experts as it had been during the Second World War.[33]

Thus the usefulness of the NEDC was necessarily limited. But for twenty years it did valuable work, and the Conservative manifesto of October 1974 promised that a future Conservative Government would strengthen it. In the 1980s and 1990s, however, the NEDC fell into desuetude because Conservative Chancellors of the Exchequer felt themselves to be in possession of all relevant knowledge which provided them with infallible guidance for policies that were undoubtedly correct. Outside help and advice were therefore superfluous and, during Norman Lamont's ill-fated Chancellorship, Neddy was killed off.

In the early sixties the Government, in Margaret Thatcher's view, was 'beginning to lose touch with the instincts and aspirations of ordinary Conservative-minded people'.* She thinks that was particularly so of its management of the economy, but also of 'issues as different as trade unions and immigration, law and order and aid to the Third World'. Norman Tebbit thinks that Macmillan suffered from 'lack of purpose or direction (except that of staying in office)' and like President Kennedy 'had no real principles'. Although superficially different, Lady Thatcher's and Lord Tebbit's criticisms are essentially the same. Decoded, both 'out of touch' and 'lacking real principles' mean that Macmillan was not right-wing and 'not one of us'.[34]

The Tebbit–Thatcher criticisms also exemplify two great differences between the Conservative Governments of Churchill, Eden, Macmillan, Douglas-Home and Heath, and those from 1979 to 1997. Right-wing critics of the earlier Toryism often confuse principles with ideology, and in particular with the doctrine of nineteenth-century or Manchester liberalism. Because the earlier Tories had no doctrine or ideology, the New Right think they had no principles. The nearest the post-war Tory Governments – and indeed all their pre-war and nineteenth-century predecessors – had to a doctrine was an anti-doctrine; they believed that all political theories were at best inadequate, at worst false. That was the party's great strength and the only sensible basis for a Conservative

---

* Harold Macmillan was nevertheless sufficiently in touch to give Mrs Thatcher her first Government post in the Ministry of Pensions and National Insurance.

Party. When everything else is changing, it is futile to think political institutions, political arrangements, and political ideas should stay the same. Conservative principles and the Conservative Party have changed in line with everything else. So, in every age, Conservatives have to do what Disraeli erroneously believed Bolingbroke to have done: 'eradicate from Toryism all those absurd and odious doctrines which Toryism had adventitiously adopted'. Hence scepticism and empiricism are, or should be, the foundations of Conservatism; and dogma, ideology and 'absurd doctrines' are excrescences to be avoided or eradicated.[35]

The second great difference between the pre- and post-1979 Conservative Governments was their attitude to the party's activists in the constituencies. The earlier Tory Governments worked to maintain the loyalty of their party workers, but they would have scorned the idea, had it ever occurred to them, that they should evolve their policies to fit the prejudices of Conservative activists. The contrast between the two approaches is most clearly seen in the penal policies of Rab Butler and Michael Howard. Butler based his proposals on the best evidence available to him from experts, research and experience, whereas Howard ignored the views of those in the Home Office who were closely acquainted with the facts, preferring the advice or at least the applause of the Conservative Party Conference and the editors of tabloid newspapers.

In the fifties and sixties the Conservative activists were far more representative of the electorate than they were in the eighties and nineties. There were far more of them, and they were of all ages – in the nineties the average age of a Conservative Party worker was 62.[36] And as the number of activists shrank, they became increasingly sectarian in their views. Yet even in the earlier period the party workers were not only unrepresentative of the country, they were not even representative of Conservative voters. Although they were not extremists or fanatics, their intensity of opinion – which made them activists in the first place – necessarily made them unrepresentative of ordinary voters. As Hailsham wrote, 'party activists always tend to be more jealous for party faith and party orthodoxy than those who are responsible for policies in Government', and they wrongly identify their views with public opinion. Unlike in most other countries, a winning British party takes over the whole executive power, but it becomes the Government of the whole country, not just of its party voters, and still less of its party activists. Hence, while the views of the activists must be taken into account, pleasing them should not have the highest priority. That is especially true of a One-Nation Tory Government. For such a Government, the party activists are little more than a useful ammunition train. The

Government has to see that the train does not blow itself or the Government up, but the Government, not the train, decides how the ammunition is used. Hence the frequent misgivings of right-wing activists and the confusion evident in the Thatcher–Tebbit criticisms.[37]

In any case Selwyn Lloyd's economic policies, above all his pay pause, were unwelcome not just to 'Conservative-minded voters'; they were deeply disliked by almost everyone. Lloyd's April 1961 Budget had made him the most unpopular Chancellor since the war, a record he retained for twenty years. His July measures, which were thought likely to succeed by only 29 per cent of the public, brought a further decline in his popularity and that of the Prime Minister. The pay pause put Labour ahead of the Government in the polls for the first time since the general election, and they remained ahead for the rest of the 1959 Parliament.[38]

A clutch of by-election disasters followed. At that time Governments had not fully grasped that the only sure way to avoid losing by-elections is not to hold them. Orpington, Blackpool North and (in June) Middlesbrough West were all self-inflicted wounds arising not from the deaths of the sitting members but from their elevation to the judicial bench or the House of Lords. Central Office soon realised that because of its social mix Orpington was likely to be tricky. To add to the problem the Tory candidate, Peter Goldman, was not good on the doorstep but was clearly Cabinet material, while the Liberal candidate was the converse. The party hierarchy therefore decided to break with custom and hold the easier contest at Blackpool North on Wednesday 13 March so as to give a confident lead to the voters in Orpington the following day. Although Blackpool was duly held, the Conservative vote halved and the Tory majority fell by 15,000 to 953. The lead given by Blackpool, therefore, was in the wrong direction; and on a turn-out of 80 per cent and a swing of 27 per cent Orpington saw a Conservative majority of 15,000 turned into a Liberal majority of 8,000.[39]

No wonder that when the Prime Minister and the Party Chairman addressed the Conservative Central Council the next day, *The Times* thought they did so in 'the spirit of Verdun'. A few days later the NOP national survey put the Liberals slightly ahead of Labour with the Conservatives in third place. Harold Macmillan thought the Liberal revival was partly 'a *Poujadiste* movement', a 'revolt of the middle class or lower middle class who resent the vastly improved conditions of the working classes and are envious of the apparent prosperity and luxury of the rich . . .' After an opinion-poll survey at Orpington, Iain Macleod, who had succeeded Butler as Chairman of the Party and Leader of the House in October 1961, was able to provide him with a more precise analysis: the leading factor in the defeat 'was the dislike of the pay policy and general dislike of the Government which I suspect more than anything else is also connected with this'. Macleod concluded by expressing the hope that the following week Selwyn Lloyd's Budget and his speech would demonstrate that there was light at the end of the tunnel and emphasise that the Government's object was a policy of growth.[40]

The Chancellor did nothing of the sort. Lloyd and his advisers might be admired for ignoring the electoral plight of the Conservative Party and Government if they had not also overlooked the state of the real economy. In a singularly uninspiring Budget speech, Lloyd gave no grounds for optimism. A Cabinet revolt had forced him to promise the abolition of the Schedule A tax on residential property. Otherwise, with political and economic obtuseness, he made the most notable feature of his Budget a tax on ice-cream and sweets, which was naturally derided as a lollipop tax. More damagingly, Lloyd based his Budget on the judgement that demand was rising, when it was already falling. Instead of stimulating an economic recovery, therefore, the Budget stimulated the rise in unemployment that had been going on since the previous July as well as a fall in much-needed investment. The pay pause, which, however much it damaged the Conservative Party had benefited the economy, ended in March and was followed by a more flexible 'guiding light'. But Macmillan, who was eager for expansion, thought Lloyd was slow to develop a workable incomes policy, and the stand-still Budget did nothing to lessen his impatience with his Chancellor.[41]

At the end of April, while Macmillan was visiting the United States, the Party Chairman sent him a personal and confidential minute pointing out that in the seven by-elections in the preceding two months the Conservative percentage of the vote had fallen by over 21 per cent, and the Budget would not improve the situation. Economic policy was the most important factor. 'Our supporters feel that our policy is one of restraint when they are in fact in a mood, rightly or wrongly, for expansionist policies . . . for myself, I believe that the issue of nurses' pay has done an immense amount of harm. It is really very difficult to project the image that "Conservatives care" in the face of this.'[42]

In later years Enoch Powell came to be regarded by the historian of the social services as 'one of the great Ministers of Health'. This is largely because he entered into the spirit of state planning with his usual dedication, launching a far-reaching and expensive hospital plan which envisaged the building of many new hospitals and the renovation of old ones. That was a considerable achievement. At the time, however, he was regarded as the hair-shirt scourge of the NHS, who behaved more like the Financial Secretary to the Treasury he had formerly been than a Minister of Health. Certainly his increases in health charges and in insurance contributions did much to reunite and revive the Labour Opposition after its prolonged quarrel over Gaitskell's unsuccessful attempt to abolish Clause 4 of Labour's constitution. Powell was later renowned for his opposition to Commonwealth immigration and to incomes policies. Yet when he was Minister of Health, in addition to his far-reaching hospital-building programme, many West Indian nurses were imported for the NHS, and he supported Lloyd's pay pause with fanatical intensity, suggesting that the nurses be offered only a 2½ per cent increase; even the Treasury were prepared to let them have three times as much – which in the end was what they got. Powell's unavailing stand was deeply unpopular not merely with the nurses themselves but with the country. Indeed it was the most reviled feature of the pay policy – hence Macleod's anxious remarks about it to Macmillan.[43]

Shortly after the Budget the Chancellor had begun to realise that once again the Treasury had got it wrong, and he relaxed hire-purchase controls in June. Otherwise he remained dour and resistant to appeals for a more imaginative approach. Had the by-election results improved, he might have survived a little longer. But Middlesbrough West was lost and the safe seat of Derbyshire West was only narrowly held; by July, Macmillan, Butler and Macleod had all come to the conclusion that he must go. On 11 July Macleod intimated to the Prime Minister that in the by-election later that week in Leicester North East, where the Liberals had not even fielded a candidate in 1959, the Conservatives would come a bad third; if Macmillan was contemplating ministerial changes, the Party Chairman believed they should be made 'before we rise for the recess'.[44]

Macleod thought the Prime Minister was going to do the deed the following week, but an indiscretion by Butler to Lord Rothermere produced a front-page splash by Walter Terry in the *Daily Mail* which persuaded the Prime Minister to act immediately. Lloyd was brutally dispatched without the offer of another job. With the help of Nigel Birch, he wrote a stiff letter of resignation, insisting that his policies had been 'right and had had a considerable measure of success'. Like Thorneycroft's resignation letter, this was published and Birch himself wrote an even sharper two-sentence letter to *The Times*, attacking the Prime Minister.[45]

When Macmillan further learned that Lloyd's friend John Hare, the Minister of Labour, was contemplating resignation, he evidently panicked. In order to make Lloyd's dismissal look less brutal, he decided to sack six other ministers as well, which, done equally abruptly, merely made matters worse.

Individually the departures of Mills (Without Portfolio), Watkinson (Defence), Maclay (Scotland) and Hill (Housing) would have created little stir; in conjunction with the dismissal of Kilmuir, the Lord Chancellor, and Eccles they created a sensation. Kilmuir was no great loss, but he was still respected and was an old European ally of the Prime Minister, while Eccles had been a very successful Minister of Education, possibly the best between 1945 and 1997. Macmillan offered him a return to the Board of Trade, which Eccles refused, indicating that he would accept only the Treasury. He was gaffe-prone in his speeches but was probably the best Chancellor available, and Butler thought Macmillan wrong to let him go. Like Hill and Kilmuir, Eccles resented the manner as much as the fact of his dismissal, telling his friends that he had been 'sacked with less notice than a housemaid'.[46]

Macmillan's Last Year

The botched 'Night of the Long Knives', as it was called, did Macmillan enormous harm. The dismissal of one-third of his Cabinet showed weakness, not strength. The allegedly 'unflappable' Prime Minister had been shown to be very flappable indeed. Greater love hath no man, said the Liberal Jeremy Thorpe, than to give up his friends for his life. Amidst the carnage, the replacements were less noticed, but they were of a high calibre: Maudling to the Treasury, Edward Boyle to Education, and Keith Joseph to Housing. Thorneycroft was transferred to Defence, and Powell entered the Cabinet. Thus, with Macmillan himself, Butler, Hailsham, Macleod, Heath, Maudling, Powell, Joseph and Boyle, this was the most intellectually distinguished Conservative Cabinet of the century.

The less intellectually distinguished but hitherto competent Henry Brooke became Home Secretary in succession to Rab Butler. This change was another of Macmillan's misjudgements during the Cabinet massacre. In October 1961, when Iain Macleod was moved from the Colonial Office and offered the Chairmanship of the Party, he had insisted on being Leader of the House as well. Thus Butler had lost two of his three posts, leaving him only with the Home Office. In March 1962 Macmillan, tired of the squabbling between the Colonial and Commonwealth Offices, formed a new Central African Department and asked Butler to take charge of it. Butler had agreed, characteristically adding his new department to the old one. Now he had lost the Home Office and was left with his Central African responsibilities plus the honorific title of 'First Secretary of State'. Throughout his premiership Harold

Macmillan showed a surprising ability to heap burdens onto Butler and then to strip him of them again almost at will. Less surprisingly, the good-natured Butler accepted both the accumulation of offices and their divestment like the great public servant he was.

Brooke was a poor and unpopular substitute for Butler. Yet the Government gained in Africa. At the Victoria Falls Conference in July 1963 Butler achieved the seemingly impossible feat of an orderly dissolution of the Central African Federation without conceding full independence to Southern Rhodesia. In demanding the Leadership of the House in addition to the Party Chairmanship, Macleod had mistreated his old patron, Butler, as well as saddling himself with two offices that were doubtfully compatible: as Leader of the Commons he had to be conciliatory to the other parties in Parliament, while as Party Chairman he had to attack them in the country.

Macleod was unlucky enough to be at Central Office when the party was losing elections, for which, unfairly, he was given much of the blame. Yet both then and later he was a unique inspiration to the young, bringing into the Tory Party many who without him would not have considered becoming Conservatives. He was even the hero of the young John Major. In Macleod there was an element of romanticism or poetry, which as much as the liberalism of his political views attracted the young and uncommitted. As Minister of Labour he tried to improve relations in industry by persuading employers to treat their employees as responsible individuals, and he had favoured the introduction of a code of practice setting out the rights of workers, contracts of service, and redundancy payments: all these were later achieved. He had no time for the backwoodsmen of both sides of industry, 'those coelacanths' as he called them. He did not think strikes and restrictive practices could be abolished by law, but with the support of Butler and Heath he favoured the inclusion of a proposal to set up an inquiry into the trade unions in the 1959 election manifesto though in the final version it was dropped. At the Colonial Office he had extended the notion of One Nation to that of One World, telling the 1961 Party Conference in his last great speech as Colonial Secretary: '. . . I believe quite simply in the brotherhood of man – men of all races, of all colours, of all creeds.'[47]

As Party Chairman at the next year's Party Conference, he again emphasised his One-Nation beliefs. Disraeli's remark that 'the Tory Party is a national party, or it is nothing' was for Macleod more than a cliché. He never allowed himself to forget that to win an election you needed to get thirteen million and one people to vote for you, as against your opponents' thirteen million. That meant that a party's policy had to be much more than an invocation of past dogmas. You had to learn from the voters as well as try to lead them. Breadth of appeal was vital. For him, winning elections by being a national party was only part of the Conservative Party's task. If the country was one nation, this was not an inevitable development. The one nation had to be preserved and constantly recreated. The Tory Party had to devote all its energies to that task and not fall back into contemplating the glories of days gone by.

In the early sixties Macleod was worried that people no longer believed that 'Conservatives care' and thought the party was too concerned with the interests of the very rich. Accordingly he told the faithful at Llandudno that 'the people of this country think that the society we have created is not sufficiently just . . . they are puzzled by the fact that still in this twentieth century the child of a skilled manual worker has only one chance in a hundred of going to the university, while the child of a professional man has thirty-four chances'. They were also puzzled that over 40 per cent of the country still earned £10 a week or less. As there was certainly no cry for equality, he went on, 'we should oppose the word equality with the word justice'. For Macleod 'the just society' was one 'which can confidently invite the men and women who compose it to make their own way in the world, because no reasonable opportunity is denied to them. You can not ask men to stand on their own feet if you give them no ground to stand on.'[48] At the time of this *credo* Britain had no beggars in the streets and no underclass. Thirty years later when she had both and was far more unjust a society, the One Nation strand of Conservatism had so withered that no Conservative leader was capable of such a perception.

At Llandudno there was a shout from the floor, 'stop dawdling, Maudling'. The new Chancellor had a 'close accord' with Harold Macmillan on economic policy, but on the Prime Minister's advice he was sensibly cautious in reversing the policies of his predecessor. Selwyn Lloyd had been held in high regard by international bankers, and an immediate dash for growth might have endangered the pound. In the end Maudling probably deferred changing course even longer than Lloyd would have done. In consequence, unemployment continued to mount; its rise was accelerated by the worst winter weather for nearly a century.[49]

During the Cuban Missile Crisis, shortly after the Party Conference, the Prime Minister provided a sympathetic audience for President Kennedy on the telephone. Macmillan thought the whole episode 'like a battle, and we in Admiralty House felt as if we were in the battle HQ'. He gave Kennedy useful reassurance, but probably had little or no influence on events.[50] Certainly the crisis had no helpful electoral effect in Britain. At five by-elections in November the Government lost two seats – Glasgow Woodside and Dorset South, where a prominent local Conservative standing as an anti-Common Market candidate helped defeat Angus Maude – and only avoided losing a third, Central Norfolk, by 220 votes after a recount.

By now the Government had begun to reflate, Maudling having announced a cut in purchase tax at the beginning of November. He also gave special help to areas of high unemployment. In January he reduced Bank Rate, but unemployment had mounted to 3.5 per cent by February. (By then it had reached 7 per cent in the north-east, where the Prime Minister's political career had begun; after the 'estrangement' between him and Hailsham had been ended when Macmillan was apprised of his misconception, he responded to the north-east's problems by giving Hailsham special responsibilities for the area.) A generous Budget was plainly necessary. Apart from the need to reduce unemployment, the Budget's chief objective was to restrain wage demands and gain trade-union support for an incomes policy. Maudling's tax cuts were therefore aimed at the less well-off and were the equivalent for many workers of a 2 per cent wage increase. In consequence he won the unique – for a Tory – accolade of having his Budget praised by the TUC Economic Committee. Although open-handed, Maudling's Budget went only a little further than the recommendations of Treasury officials and less far than the Prime Minister had suggested and many commentators would have wished.[51]

The Veto

Macmillan had an anxious few days at the Commonwealth Conference in London early in September. He persuaded the conference to agree that Britain's application to join the EEC should continue, but most of the leading countries were clearly apprehensive for the future of their trade if it succeeded. Shortly afterwards, Hugh Gaitskell came off the fence. In a speech on the Common Market at the Labour Party Confer-ence, which embarrassed his friends and would have come more appro-priately from Harold Wilson, he fiercely opposed entry. Dwelling on the gallantry of the Canadians at Vimy Ridge in 1917 and the Anzacs at Gallipoli, he said membership would 'end a thousand years of history' (which at least demonstrated that the political implications of entry had not been concealed from him). All this delighted the Labour Left, and Gaitskell even had a reconciliation with Frank Cousins.[52]

In defiance of British industry, which strongly supported British entry, Gaitskell seemed chiefly worried about British trade with the Commonwealth and the end of Commonwealth preferences, which had already been substantially eroded. His absurdly retrograde speech may have given rise to Dean Acheson's remarks at West Point quoted above, but it united his party. At the same time, as over Suez, Gaitskell also united the Conservative Party. The Conservative Party Conference was now practically unanimous in favour of entry. The very few opponents were ill received, and only about fifty of the 4,000 delegates voted against. Butler gave a crushing retort to the Leader of the Opposition. 'For them a thousand years of history. For us the future.'[53]

Probably by then the European issue was already academic. Gaitskell could have saved his breath and safeguarded his reputation. As early as May the British Ambassador in Paris had come to the conclusion that President de Gaulle did 'not want the Brussels negotiations to succeed'. At Rambouillet in December, Macmillan's meeting with de Gaulle became what he called 'a wrangle'. The President suggested that the arrangements of the Treaty of Rome 'might be too rigid for the United Kingdom', implying that Britain was not ready for Europe. Moreover, at present France could say 'No' to the other five members. If Britain and the Scandinavian countries joined, things would be different. In other words, French leadership of the EEC would be endangered. Macmillan said this was 'a most serious statement', understandably adding that 'if that was really the French view it ought to have been made clear at the start'.[54]

Nevertheless, the Prime Minister made himself believe that de Gaulle's attitude would be softened if he could persuade President Kennedy, whom he was about to meet at Nassau, to assist France over nuclear weapons. As long ago as Christmas 1960 Macmillan had thought that American help with France's *Force de Frappe*, which was central to de Gaulle's ambitions for the restoration of France's greatness, was the key to winning de Gaulle's support for British membership. Unfortunately Kennedy himself and many of his advisers were markedly unenthusiastic about the British deterrent, let alone a French one. In July 1962 Robert McNamara, the American Defence Secretary, with both Britain and France in mind, said publicly that 'limited nuclear capabilities, operating independently' were 'dangerous, expensive, prone to obsolescence and lacking in credibility as a deterrent', suggesting further that any new independent nuclear force would encourage proliferation. Such attacks, the British Ambassador in Washington reasonably told Macmillan, were likely to make de Gaulle even more determined to persist with his 'present nuclear policy', while the Americans thought the British deterrent had a similar effect on the French President. Many of Kennedy's advisers were strong supporters of a united Europe and British entry, not appreciating that those aims would be frustrated by their nuclear objectives. Only in July 1963 did the Kennedy administration come up with the idea of providing the French with vital nuclear information in order to persuade de Gaulle to sign a test-ban treaty. Had such an offer been put forward six months earlier, Macmillan wryly commented, it might have made the crucial difference to Britain's Common Market negotiations.[55]

How far the British nuclear deterrent was genuinely 'independent' was a moot point. Macmillan thought it was; his Private Secretary was less sure, telling him it was 'doubtful whether we could in fact use our deterrent independently'. Independent or not, the British nuclear arsenal probably did have some deterrent value, and to scrap it unilaterally was plainly unthinkable. Yet its future was threatened late in 1962. Two years earlier, in exchange for Britain allowing the US a base on the Clyde for their nuclear submarines, President Eisenhower had agreed to sell her America's airborne Skybolt missile to which British nuclear warheads would be fitted. Hence indications from McNamara that Skybolt was proving a failure and would probably be cancelled caused consternation in London. At Nassau, Macmillan after bitter argument eventually persuaded Kennedy to let Britain have the far superior Polaris missile.[56]

Had Britain been kept out of the EEC and also been left without a delivery system for her nuclear weapons, the Government's position would have been desperate – many Tory back-benchers had made it clear that they were not prepared to tolerate Britain's loss of her nuclear status. Yet if de Gaulle was not already determined to veto the British application, the Nassau agreement finally decided him. After Macmillan's urging, Kennedy had agreed to give France the option to buy Polaris on 'similar' terms to Britain. Unfortunately de Gaulle was the last man to be grateful for crumbs which fell from a rich man's table. Besides, because France, unlike Britain, could not make the nuclear warheads for the Polaris missile, Kennedy's offer was of little value to the French. In de Gaulle's eyes, Nassau merely demonstrated Britain's American, rather than European, orientation; his veto followed shortly afterwards.[57]

That de Gaulle was making a mistake similar to Britain's in the previous decade – grossly overestimating the power of his country – was small consolation. Even less of a consolation was the fact that at least some of de Gaulle's fears about Britain in Europe later turned out to be justified. (Had we entered in 1963, they probably would not have been.) Unlike the leaders of the French Fourth Republic, Macmillan had not properly learned the true lesson of Suez: that individual European countries were no longer world powers. His fatal mistake had been to turn almost exclusively to the United States when he became Prime Minister. Had he turned, instead, to Europe, de Gaulle and the Fifth Republic would not have been able to thwart him.

The veto was a shattering blow to the Government. 'You know,' Butler later told Wedgwood Benn, 'the Common Market breakdown was a much bigger shock for us than you chaps realised.' If so, the Labour 'chaps' must have been at the very least remarkably insensitive, if not also blind and deaf. At Westminster, Tory disappointment and dismay were palpable. Entry into the EEC was not merely the Government's main foreign policy objective, it was also the core of its election strategy.

'Europe was to be our *deus ex machina*,' Michael Fraser later told the authors of the Nuffield Study. 'It was to create a new contemporary political argument with insular socialism; dish the Liberals by stealing their clothes; give us something *new* after 12–13 years; act as the catalyst of modernisation; give us a new place in the international sun. It was Macmillan's ace, and de Gaulle trumped it. The Conservatives never really recovered.'[58]

A Fit of Morality

Bitter blow as the Common Market failure was, the Conservatives probably would have recovered from it but for a series of unpredictable events.

Several incidents between 1961 and 1963, which involved national security or were alleged to have done so, cumulatively did great damage to the Government and to Harold Macmillan. Early in 1961 the 'Portland Spy Ring' was exposed with the help of the CIA and a Soviet defector, and its members sent to prison. Then the spy George Blake, whose treachery had caused many deaths behind the Iron Curtain, was arrested. Unfortunately, instead of giving credit to the Government and the security services for his detection, the press heaped blame on them for his espionage. Consequently, when Lord Carrington, the First Lord of the Admiralty, told the Prime Minister that they had caught another spy, John Vassall, his reaction was, 'Oh, that's terrible. That's very bad news', before explaining that, while of course he wanted spies detected, 'when we find a spy . . . there's trouble, more trouble than if we don't!' The catching of this spy brought Macmillan even more trouble than he could have expected. Vassall, a homosexual, had been in the private office of Carrington's Junior Minister, Tam Galbraith, and, on a postcard that Galbraith had sent him beginning 'My dear Vassall', the gutter press erected a mountain of smear and innuendo, implying that the Minister had known that Vassall was a spy but had kept quiet about it because he was his lover. Such was the pressure on Galbraith and his family that he offered his resignation. Macmillan accepted it, an action which he subsequently regretted and which had injurious repercussions. Carrington was also smeared, the *Daily Express* alleging that he had deliberately concealed from the Prime Minister the presence of a spy in the Admiralty.[59]

A Committee of Inquiry under Lord Radcliffe was set up. While it was still hearing evidence, Kim Philby, tipped off in Beirut by the Russians that the British had discovered unassailable evidence against him, fled to Moscow. The Radcliffe Tribunal found that Carrington and Galbraith had been merely the victims of press hysteria and malice, and they were completely exonerated. Fleet Street, not Westminster or Whitehall, were the culprits. Of the 250 press reports on the matter that Radcliffe had examined in detail, it found that not one was justified; all were false. Some journalists were frank about their 'sources'. The *Daily Express*'s Percy Hoskin admitted that his sources for an article which claimed 'new disclosures' about another spy were reports that he had taken unacknowledged from other newspapers. Some of his colleagues were less candid, and two reporters were sent to prison for refusing to reveal their 'sources'. They were hailed by Fleet Street as martyrs to the freedom of the press but, as the Tribunal made clear, their reports had been 'fiction'. Evidently they did not reveal their sources because they were either derisory or non-existent. In addition, as was pointed out in the parliamentary debate on Vassall, libertarian arguments are not necessarily on the side of refusing disclosure. If Senator McCarthy had been compelled to reveal his 'sources', McCarthyism would soon have been scotched with immediate benefit to the freedom of the American press.[60]

The so-called popular press was shown not only to have fallen below even its own subterranean standards but to be deeply unpopular. That the public sided with the Government deepened the newspapers' humiliation and sense of grievance. Macmillan had won his battle with the press, but at heavy cost. From now on, he and his Government could expect no quarter from Fleet Street. The only surprising feature of the next 'security' scare, therefore, about which rumours had long been rife, was that the Leader of the Opposition and the Labour Party joined the popular press in the gutter of innuendo and McCarthyism.

Late at night on 22–3 March, George Wigg, R. H. S. Crossman, and other Labour MPs used parliamentary privilege to repeat the rumours that the War Secretary, John Profumo, had had an affair with Christine Keeler, a girl who had at the same time been involved with Yevgeny Ivanov, an attaché at the Soviet Embassy, and that he had interfered with the course of justice by spiriting her out of the country to prevent her appearing as a witness in a criminal trial. Shortly after he had taken sleeping pills, Profumo, an energetic and capable minister, was woken and questioned at the Commons by five colleagues. The still groggy Minister denied the allegations, as he had earlier done when questioned by the Law Officers,* and agreed to make a personal statement, a sentence of which claimed that there had been 'no impropriety whatso-ever' with Miss Keeler. When he learned the next morning of what was proposed, Butler wisely urged delay. But Macmillan disastrously insisted that the statement should go ahead. Early in June, Profumo admitted his lie and resigned. The Prime Minister was bitterly attacked for alleged negligence over security and for accepting Profumo's original denial; had it not been for his unfortunate experience over Tam Galbraith, he probably would not have done so.[62]

Mr Profumo was of course inexcusably wrong to have told a lie in his personal statement. All the same, of all the lies that have been told in the House of Commons both before 1963 – most notably over Suez – and since, his was surely one of the most trifling. Indeed the whole Profumo imbroglio was utterly trivial, and had Hugh Gaitskell still been alive, it would probably never have emerged. George Brown, now Labour's deputy leader, thought the party 'ought to keep out of this'. But, as he had shown over the Bank Rate Tribunal, Harold Wilson did not possess that sort of sensitivity or scruple. Even though the Profumo case had little more substance than the Vassall scandal, it came close to bringing down the Government.[63]

Wilson and the Labour Party claimed not to be concerned with morals – oh no, of course not – but solely with Britain's security. Because Ivanov had been involved with Christine Keeler at the same time as Jack Profumo, it followed, said Labour, that Profumo had been a security risk. In the parliamentary debate after Profumo's confession Wilson accused the Prime Minister of gambling with the nation's security, alleg-ing that there had been a 'degree of security risk that no Prime Minister could tolerate for a moment after the facts were conveyed to him'. Not content with that, the Leader of the Opposition stated no less than four

---

* As early as February, Profumo had given his version of events to Redmayne, the Chief Whip, in the presence of Tim Bligh, the Prime Minister's Private Secretary, and asked if he should resign. Probably every other Conservative Whip this century would have said, 'Yes, and come back into the Government when all this has blown over.' With his usual lack of judgement, Martin Redmayne said 'No'.[61]

181

times that we should never know if there had been an actual security leak, a peculiarly absurd and disreputable smear. Wilson's speech, however dishonest, was undeniably effective. Macmillan's reply was the opposite: it was honest but ineffective, and his admission that 'I do not live among young people much myself' strengthened the conviction of many that it was time for a change. At the end of the debate, during which Nigel Birch joined in the hunt, declaring that until the Prime Minister departed there would be 'never glad confident morning again', twenty-seven (mostly obscure) Conservative MPs abstained, a number which would have been even higher had not the Whips suggested to waverers that Harold Macmillan would soon be resigning. Probably most of the parliamentary party believed his resignation could not be long delayed.[64]

A visitor from America, who had been a close observer of the McCarthy era, deemed Wilson's performance 'the pure milk of McCarthyism'. Senator McCarthy, wrote Antony West, had been 'the great artist in the use of the unchecked fact', and it was 'this game' that Wilson, Wigg, 'that industrious garbage-collector', Crossman, Tom Driberg and others were now playing. Pointing out that the leadership of both American parties had refused to follow Senator McCarthy, West added that 'the United States, in its occasional collapses into political squalor, has never exhibited anything so despicable as the spectacle of Mr Harold Wilson leading his entire following away from serious matters to snuffle and jostle round the dirty linen from Miss Christine Keeler's various beds in the hope of finding some easy way to power'.[65]

In fact Wilson's conduct was even more despicable than Antony West could then have known. On 29 March, a few days after Mr Profumo's personal statement, George Wigg, Wilson's chief adviser on the case, had sent him two documents. The first, 'An Appreciation of the Keeler Case', began: 'In my opinion Profumo was never, at any time, a security risk. The Intelligence Services were aware of his meetings with Ivanov and with [sic] his subsequent meetings with Christine Keeler.' The rest of the appreciation was a laboriously detailed account of the sniffing around by the 'industrious garbage-collector' and, in view of his opening paragraph, wholly uninteresting. As that paragraph made clear that there was no genuine 'security' aspect of the affair, that should have been the end of the matter. All that properly was left of the Profumo affair was the Minister's denial of 'impropriety'. And as that lie concerned only a minor personal peccadillo, and as the Leader of the Opposition was himself hardly a shining embodiment of truth, it would have been scarcely worth pursuing. However, the knowledge that the security issue was bogus was no more a stumbling block to Wilson than to Wigg, his smearmaster-general. Wigg had thoughtfully sent Wilson a second document. This was exactly the same as the first except that it carefully omitted the key opening paragraph, and on 9 April Wilson duly sent this misleading document on to the Prime Minister. Had the first of those two documents come to light at the time, Wilson would have been unmasked as a dishonourable hypocrite and the whole Labour campaign about alleged risks to national security exposed as one of the sleaziest episodes of post-war politics.*

At the annual 1922 Committee lunch held at the Savoy in early April the Prime Minister had told MPs that he intended to lead the party at the next election, an announcement which was greeted with enthusiasm. At the same time the party's and Macmillan's own poll ratings had improved. But in June the position had drastically changed. Labour took a twenty-point lead and only 23 per cent of voters thought Macmillan should stay as Prime Minister. The Chairman of the 1922 Committee, John Morrison, started talking of a Government 'formed by a new man', and the Chief Whip and Oliver Poole asked Butler if he would be willing to serve in a new Government. Macmillan's PPS told him that four junior ministers, among them Margaret Thatcher, were 'not in full support'. Macmillan himself contemplated resignation before the next election.[66]

While gossip multiplied, the Tory Party was infected by the rumours spread by the deeply hostile press. As Macmillan later put it, all and sundry were charged 'with every kind of depravity'. Only the dullest ministers, it seemed, had not indulged in sexual orgies of some sort and had their cupboards unfurnished with skeletons. The Conservative Party panicked, and the Prime Minister scarcely exaggerated when he wrote in his diary that 'a kind of Titus Oates atmosphere' prevailed; to check the flood of rumour and innuendo, he asked Lord Denning to undertake a judicial inquiry. Reporting in September, Denning stated the obvious truth that 'scandalous information about well-known people [had] become a marketable commodity', but on this occasion he found what had been marketed was untrue. Some of the rumours he found to be 'preposterous'; all of them were without foundation.[67]

In his report Lord Denning also said that Mr Profumo's admission of his lie had so shaken 'the confidence of the people of this country' that they were ready to believe remarks that they would normally have scouted. That is very doubtful. The hysteria and insatiable appetite for

---

* It came to light a few years later in the course of an action that Wigg brought against the *Spectator* for alleged libel in Antony West's article, when it was revealed – almost certainly by mistake – by Wigg's solicitor, Lord Goodman. On discovering their mistake, the plaintiff and his solicitors became anxious to settle the case out of court – which it was, without payment of damages.

salacious tittle-tattle which were so evident in London were largely a metropolitan phenomenon. Away from Fleet Street and Westminster, most people adopted a fairly understanding attitude, seeing the Profumo affair in its correct (very small) proportions. In the Tory Party in the constituencies, the general reaction was that the Prime Minister was being unfairly traduced and deserted by unreliable, disloyal MPs. As a later member for Winchester once memorably said, 'the Conservative party never panics except in a crisis', and the crisis was soon over. Not only did the Tory parliamentary party recover from one of what Baldwin used to call its 'rages', but public opinion also soon swung some way back to the Government. In August Gallup showed the Government's approval rating higher than it had been since November, while NOP showed the Conservatives only about six points behind Labour as opposed to eighteen or twenty.[68]

Well before Lord Denning reported, the Prime Minister had notched up a notable international achievement; in Moscow the USA, USSR and Britain had initialled a treaty imposing a partial ban on nuclear tests. As another sign of Hailsham's rehabilitation, Macmillan had chosen him to be the British representative. 'A very able man, Lord Hailsham,' Khrushchev told the British Ambassador, 'I understand that he is going to be promoted as a result of what he is doing here.' On 25 July the Prime Minister was able to tell Parliament that the negotiations were successfully concluded. All the Conservatives and many of the Opposition stood up to acclaim him. It was, Macmillan recorded, 'like the greatest of my parliamentary successes'. Earlier on that day the Prime Minister's end-of-session speech was well received by the 1922 Committee; he himself even thought it 'a triumphant vote of confidence'. Over the Moscow treaty Britain had not merely followed in America's wake. Macmillan's influence on the successful outcome is not in doubt. He managed to persuade President Kennedy to accept the British view rather than that of his own advisers.[69]

Pondering his future in the recess, the Prime Minister was surprised by his own 'vacillation'. Often he thought he could not lead the party in another election. His successor could not be 'a pedestrian politician', for the party needed 'a man with vision and moral strength – Hailsham not Maudling'. Macmillan added in his diary that he had sent 'H to Moscow on purpose' to test him out. 'He did *very* well.' In his autobiography Macmillan says he 'favoured either Hailsham or Macleod, preferably the former, for I felt that these two were the men of real genius in the party, who were the true inheritors of Tory radicalism, which I had preached all my life'. Nevertheless, it seems unlikely that at that time he seriously considered Macleod.[70]

In line with these ruminations, the Prime Minister came in September to 'an irreversible decision' to tell the Party Conference that there would be no election that year and he would renounce the leadership in time to let his successor play himself in. The Queen was told, and then the irreversible decision was reversed. The words of the song that Macmillan had used to describe Gaitskell at the Llandudno Conference, 'She wouldn't say "yes", and she wouldn't say "no"', which *Private Eye* set to music, now applied to him. All the Prime Minister's confidants were now right-wingers. Apart from his family, Macmillan took advice from Home, Dilhorne, Sandys, Morrison and Redmayne, while Butler, Macleod and Maudling were not in the inner ring. Macmillan seldom saw even his designated successor, Hailsham. The closest adviser in this right-wing coterie was Alec Home, who consistently favoured Macmillan going at a time of his own choosing but certainly before the next election. Up to the Monday before the Blackpool Conference, however, Macmillan continued to waver. He was then told by his Private Secretary that the Cabinet was rallying to him and that Duncan Sandys 'was very strong for me going on', while 'Alec Home was balanced . . .' So he finally decided to stay and fight the election. The Queen was informed. Yet already he was in great pain from prostate trouble. He could not go to Blackpool, and the medical advice, which turned out to be bad, was that he should leave office as soon as his successor had been chosen.[71]

CHAPTER VIII

The War of the
Macmillan Succession

The 1963 Conservative Party Conference at Blackpool has been described as 'a bear garden' and as the place where the Conservative Party had 'a nervous breakdown in public'. Butler thought that great 'harm was done to the Conservative Party' at Blackpool and 'dignity was altogether lost'. This distaste for the 1963 Conference stems from the belief that the struggle for the succession to Harold Macmillan should not have taken place in front of the children – that is to say, the constituency representatives at the conference – but should have been waged behind closed doors in London.[1]

In fact the public row – the coincidence of Macmillan's retirement with the Party Conference, and the manoeuvring, the electioneering and the arguments at Blackpool – made the Conservative Party more interesting than it had been for years. After it, the standing of the party and the Government in the polls did not fall; it rose, if only slightly. But those who liked the result of the leadership struggle did not like the row, and those who liked the row did not like the result. So Blackpool got a bad name. Yet whatever was discreditable in the war of succession did not take place in public in Blackpool but in private in London.[2]

Many of the key moves in the leadership struggle had been made well before the Party Conference. At the end of July, Parliament passed an Act which enabled an hereditary peer to resign his peerage and stand for membership of the House of Commons. So far as the future leadership of the party was concerned, the Peerage Act affected only two peers, Lords Home and Hailsham, neither of whom had had anything to do with the House of Lords revolt which produced the crucial amendment. This allowed established peers to disclaim their peerage immediately instead of at the end of the current Parliament. Many months before, at a meeting suggested by Home, he and Hailsham had agreed that to avoid harming the Upper House they would not both leave it. Also before the amendment had been passed, Harold Macmillan had in June told

Hailsham that if he resigned the leadership before the election he wished Hailsham to be his successor. Khrushchev's aside about Hailsham in Moscow was therefore near the mark.[3]

Macmillan had also told Hailsham that Alec Home had been his first choice, but that Home had not been enthusiastic and anyway lacked the steel and the economic expertise to cope with Harold Wilson. So the Prime Minister had come to the conclusion that Quintin, not Alec, was the right man. Others, particularly those who themselves had no economic expertise, took a different view. The Chairman and Vice-Chairmen of the 1922 Committee, Major John Morrison, Sir Charles Mott-Radcliffe and Sir Harry Legge Bourke, decided in June to encourage Home to run. These three 'knights of the shires' were good, solid citizens, hangers and floggers, who deplored what had been done in Africa and thought the Government had moved far too far to the left at home. Typical of the old Conservative Right, they were part of the ballast of the party, and like a ship's ballast they should not have been allowed anywhere near the bridge. Yet they felt they should have a prominent part in choosing the captain – which was roughly the equivalent of three left-wing trade-union bosses taking it upon themselves to choose the leader of the Labour Party.[4]

In any case the leaders of 'the 1922' believed in Major Morrison's words that 'we can't go wrong with a shooting gent', and Morrison himself was deputed to approach Alec Home. This he did early in July and, after demurring, Home said 'I will see my doctor'. Later, at Blackpool, the *New York Times* correspondent said that 'anybody who had seen a reluctant candidate in America would agree that Alec Home . . . appeared to fit the part to perfection'. The distinguishing feature of a reluctant candidate is that his candidacy is more real than his reluctance. Such an assessment is of course at variance with the general view of Home's character. Alec Home was indeed an upright man and probably the nicest leading politician in Britain since the war. Yet as a rule it is safer to judge a man's character by his actions than to judge his actions by what is assumed to be his character. And Home's actions from June to October 1963 leave little room for doubt that he wanted the leadership and went out of his way to get it. Had his reluctance been genuine, he would not have capitulated to John Morrison. He need not have gone so far as General Sherman,* but he could easily have said that he was not a candidate and should be ruled out of consideration. He did nothing of the sort.[5]

---

* When urged to accept the Republican nomination for the Presidency in 1884, Sherman replied, 'If nominated, I will not accept; if elected, I will not serve.'

To their credit, however, neither of the peers who were candidates took any public action in the summer to further their cause. Two of the potential candidates from the Commons were less reticent or loyal. In January 1962 the Prime Minister had told Butler that if he went before the election 'all falls to you', but by the summer of 1963 that was a (relatively) long time ago and evidently no longer relevant. When Macmillan made him his heir, Hailsham said, 'What about Rab? Surely he's the obvious successor?' 'On no account,' replied the Prime Minister. 'Rab simply doesn't have it in him to be Prime Minister.' At much the same time, after asking Butler if he would join a new Government, John Morrison had brutally added, 'the chaps won't have you'. Morrison was in Butler's words 'old-world', and of course wholly out of sympathy with his policies and outlook. But on this occasion, at least, he did not misrepresent the many back-benchers who wanted the leadership to move to another generation, even if he himself wanted to stick with the older one – Alec Home.[6]

In June that wish had created a groundswell of support, or what seemed to be one, for Reggie Maudling. Some polls of MPs in the *Daily Telegraph* showed the Chancellor of the Exchequer well ahead of his rivals. They were probably unreliable, but Maudling evidently believed them. Uncharacteristically, he visited Butler to discuss their mutual prospects, asking to stay at the Treasury if Butler got the job, and saying that if he himself got it there was 'no one he would wish more to have by him' than Rab Butler, Delphic as ever, intimated that all this was premature. Maudling even made his candidacy public, telling a Conservative fête in Cambridgeshire that the party had to get 'with it' and that they had not gained the allegiance of young voters 'because we have not yet found a way of talking to them in language they understand or in terms of the ideals they cherish'. Butler, too, cautiously threw his hat into the ring, or at least waved it, saying on *Panorama* that he was 'pretty well aware that people want us to give a fresh impression of vigour and decision before the next election'.[7]

Of the two other possible candidates, Iain Macleod made a strong speech in favour of Macmillan carrying on, and Edward Heath kept quiet, but paid a significant visit to John Morrison in Scotland. Morrison told him about his interview with Home, and from then on Heath was firmly in the Home camp. Morrison's proselytising would have been pointless, of course, if he had not been convinced that Home was a candidate. Both Macleod and Heath doubtless thought they would have a better chance themselves in later years, but whereas Heath, who got on well with Home at the Foreign Office, was happy to envisage a short

Home interlude before taking over himself, Macleod, who had differed drastically from Home over Africa, would be better placed to succeed if Macmillan stayed on at Number 10.[8]

Though in great pain, Harold Macmillan bravely presided at the pre-Blackpool Cabinet meeting on 8 October. After two hours of Cabinet business, he announced his plan to remain in office and fight the election, before withdrawing to allow freer talk in his absence. Everybody agreed to back him, except 'Aristides' (Enoch Powell) who thought he should resign. During the brief discussion before most of the Cabinet left for Blackpool, the Lord Chancellor, Dilhorne (previously Manningham-Buller), said that if ill-health made it impossible for the Prime Minister to continue, he would be able to help in discussions about a successor, as he was not a candidate. Astonishingly, Home then said that he, too, would be able to assist, since in no circumstances was he a candidate. In his autobiography Home tried to explain away his declaration as 'merely a statement revealing that at that time the question of my succession to Macmillan had simply not crossed my mind', an assertion in the best traditions of political-autobiographical fiction. Not only had it crossed his mind, it had been encouragingly discussed with the Chairman of the '1922'. According to Home's biographer, he had been considering his possible candidacy on and off for ten months; Richard Thorpe therefore regards his pledge in Cabinet that he was not a runner as 'a crucial tactical error'. But if it was an error, it was a moral one. Tactically it was a masterstroke, deceiving all his colleagues who, like Macmillan, clearly knew nothing of his conversation with Major Morrison. And it raises the question of how disinterested was Home's earlier advice to Macmillan to leave office before the election.[9]

Later that day the Prime Minister's doctors decided that an operation was unavoidable, and in the evening Downing Street announced that he would not be coming to the conference. At Blackpool it was immediately assumed that his premiership was drawing to a close. The next day Hailsham had incomparably the best reception in the conference hall; and in a speech at Morecambe he said, 'Harold, get well quick . . . And when you come back we will hand back to you a Government and a party in good order . . .' Developments in London, however, had made that message redundant. Alec Home had sent Macmillan a note of the Cabinet discussion in which he said he had told the Cabinet that he and others had emphasised the difficulties Macmillan would face if he carried on. Home's biographer thinks that the pain Macmillan was suffering and Home's account of the feelings of the Cabinet made him determined to resign. And he stuck to that decision, even though his personal physician, Sir John Richardson, who had been away at the beginning of the week, told him that his condition was less serious than he believed and that he would quite soon recover.[10]

Butler believed at the time and afterwards that Macmillan's later statement of his intention to resign had been extracted from him by Lord Home, writing that he himself 'would not have asked a wounded and sick man to make such a declaration at such a febrile time'. Butler was right. Overnight Macmillan had drafted a letter to Butler telling him that he was going to resign but did not intend to announce his decision at that stage, and asking him to decide with other ministers how to proceed with the Party Conference and make arrangements for the succession. The next morning, when Maurice Macmillan saw his father, before Home did, the Prime Minister had no intention of making a public pronouncement about his intended resignation. Home changed all that. Instead of a private letter from Macmillan to Butler, a letter to Home in his capacity as President of the National Union to read out at the conference was decided upon. That in itself was remarkable, since the announcement of the Prime Minister's prospective retirement should either have been in a statement from Downing Street or made in Blackpool by the acting head of the Government, Rab Butler.[11]

The key sentence of the letter expressed Macmillan's hope that it would 'soon be possible for the customary processes of consultation to be carried out within the party about its future leadership'.[12] Having the announcement made at the conference obviously aided the chances of the two peers, Home and Hailsham, who would have an opportunity to shine in front of the faithful; had it been made a few days later in London, the candidates in the Commons would have had the advantage.

On the Thursday Iain Macleod brought the conference to its feet, no mean achievement at ten in the morning in the days before standing ovations had become part of the conference ritual. He ended with the stirring words: 'And will we win? Yes of course we shall ... Let the faint hearts go their ways. Whoever they be, there is no room for them in our party. We are better without them' – which were later used against him. Yet that was not the main event of the day in the conference hall. Giving the ill Prime Minister no chance to sleep on his new decision and possibly change his mind again, Alec Home hastened to Blackpool and read Macmillan's retirement letter to the expectant delegates.[13]

Following that announcement, Hailsham, who, unlike other contenders, had made no move while there was any chance of Macmillan continuing in office, decided to disclaim his title. In addition, Julian Amery had seen his father-in-law in hospital and been told 'to go to Blackpool and get Quintin elected'. Maurice Macmillan had the same instructions. So that evening seemed the right time to strike. Hailsham's speech to the annual CPC meeting was nothing like so good as his effort in 1957; it was too long, and the theatre was too hot – the Hailsham camp reckoned Rab had turned on the radiators. Hailsham came out strongly and repetitively against what he regrettably called 'pre-mărītăl intercourse', but replying to the vote of thanks he made his disclaimer beautifully, with dignified restraint.[14]

Nevertheless his declaration produced pandemonium. Even the platform party – including Martin Redmayne, to his obvious discomfiture – had to stand up and cheer with everyone else. Of those on the platform, who included Keith Joseph and Bill Deedes, only Peter Thorneycroft looked supportive.[15]

The general enthusiasm culminated in the singing of 'For he's a jolly good fellow'. All this was considered dreadfully vulgar by many at Blackpool and elsewhere. Some journalists likened the occasion to a Nuremberg rally, to which it bore not the remotest resemblance. It was more like a football match, an event which, like a Nuremberg rally, such journalists had probably never attended. Butler's description of Hailsham being 'surrounded by hysterical and weeping women on the lines of a Hitler campaign' was similarly extravagant. In fact the only possible resemblance of Blackpool to the Nazi era was that much of the anti-Hailsham propaganda was almost as inaccurate as that of the late Dr Goebbels. It was said that Hailsham had been histrionic and that there had been emotion and hysteria at the meeting. The charge of being histrionic is an odd one to level at a politician – Churchill, Roosevelt and de Gaulle were all histrionic. The ability to excite emotion in an audience is one of the tests of a leader, and a political party is held together more by emotion than by intellectual assent to a series of dubious dogmas or propositions. And anyway Hailsham had been dull rather than histrionic, and there was no hysteria at the CPC meeting. Later in the evening Hailsham was tumultuously received at the Young Conservatives Ball, and that, too, was held against him.[16]

Home later claimed that, when in reaction to Hailsham's disclaimer a number of Conservatives told him that he ought to consider coming forward as 'a potential Prime Minister, it was the last thing which I had anticipated, and the last thing which I sought'. Again that was pure fiction. As soon as Home arrived in Blackpool it was clear to most people that he was running hard. Oddly, those who took longest to recognise that obvious fact were his colleagues and potential rivals. When Hailsham was warned by Dennis Walters and Ian Gilmour of Home's candidacy, he refused to believe it, saying 'Alec has told me he is not a candidate, and we have agreed that we could not both leave the Lords simultaneously'. Iain Macleod's reaction to the rumours was similar. 'Don't be bloody ridiculous,' he told his PPS. 'That's absolutely cuckoo. Alec told us in Cabinet he wasn't a runner.'[17]

After Home had relayed to the conference Macmillan's decision to resign, he told Hailsham that he had his support, but later claimed that he did not then know that Hailsham, was about 'to throw his claim to the leadership in the ring'. In a later conversation Home informed Hailsham that he was 'under strong pressure to throw his [own] hat in the ring', whereupon Hailsham, according to his account, reminded him of their previous agreement that they would not both leave the Lords. He also told Home that as he had no experience of home affairs he would not be a good choice as PM and would not last long. Undeterred, Home gave a television interview to Robin Day that evening (Thursday). During it, he so carefully refrained from discouraging support for himself, while being cleverly disparaging about his rivals, that afterwards Maudling turned to Day and said, 'well, Alec is obviously going to run'. That interview was given well before the anti-Hailsham bandwagon had been set in motion.[18]

By Friday, four candidates were clearly in the field: Butler, Hailsham, Home and Maudling. The press believed the struggle between Butler and Hailsham to be one between Left and Right. This was no better founded than the similar misconception about Butler and Macmillan in 1957. Hailsham was highly partisan against Labour but was no more a right-winger then than he had been in the forties; nor of course was Maudling. The only right-wing candidate was Home, who was speaking on foreign policy to the conference on Friday morning. When Hailsham arrived, the delegates started cheering as soon as he entered the hall, so he sat down among them to stop the cheering and to avoid stealing Home's thunder, but that too was held against him: it was said that he was playing to the gallery when, in fact, he was playing against it. Home made a good if not outstanding speech, which was very well received, and gained a standing ovation. Saying at the beginning of his speech, 'I am offering a prize to any newspaperman this morning who can find a clue in my speech that this is Lord Home's bid for the leadership', he deftly directed the conference's attention to his candidacy while feigning not to; understandably, somebody on the platform whispered, 'Alec, you're lying.'[19]

The summer boom for Reggie Maudling, which even then was slightly artificial, had weakened 'for some reason which I [Maudling] could not quite discern', but he was still in with a chance. All depended on his conference speech on the Friday. Moving the economic motion, Peter Walker, a strong Hailshamite, resisted the temptation to say that Maudling was so good at the Treasury it was vital that he stay there. Walker's self-denial made no difference, however, because after three minutes of Maudling's speech it was obvious that he *would* be staying there. His text was fine but, disregarding Macleod's advice, he spoke much too fast in the wrong tone of voice and quickly lost his audience. Jim Prior and other supporters had hoped 'to engineer a standing ovation', but it could not be done. As Maudling himself recognised, his delivery wrecked his speech, and from then on he was virtually written off as a serious contender. 'How could Reggie do it?' asked Macleod, practically in tears.[20]

In the bar of the conference hotel Nigel Birch, although he had earlier pledged his support in writing to Maudling, was drumming up support for Home. He claimed that Hailsham was 'now madder than ever' and cited his behaviour at his CPC speech which Birch had not seen. It was pointed out to him that Hailsham had in fact done it very well, a view which was confirmed by another right-wing MP who had been there, Colonel Lancaster. All the same, Hailsham had laid himself open to some justified criticism that morning. His wife had been advised not to bring their baby daughter to Blackpool but had not been able to find anybody to look after her; so Kate came to Blackpool too. Hailsham, urged on by the press, made the blunder of feeding his daughter in the foyer of the hotel, which was denounced as a vulgar electioneering gimmick. In fact the Hailshams had no sitting-room, and the incident, which happened because of inefficiency and lack of organisation, was obviously not a bid for votes. Yet it did Hailsham untold harm. Even those who realised that he had not brought the baby to Blackpool as an electioneering aid blamed him for not having employed a nanny. Randolph Churchill, anxious to support Macmillan's candidate, also offended many of the stuffier big-wigs by his noisy and less than sober support of Quintin Hailsham. Unfortunately he had arrived from the United States with a large supply of 'Q' badges which he insisted on attaching to people who had no wish to wear any badge, let alone a 'Q' one. When the rest of the Hailsham camp tried to keep away from him, he shouted at them that they were 'wet'.[21]

Nigel Birch was only one of the right-wingers who were supporting Home. As has been seen, John Morrison – whom Hailsham had taken to calling James James Morrison Morrison Weatherby George Dupree[22] – with the right-wing officers of the 1922 Committee, had plumped for him in June. So, effectively, had the Chief Whip, Martin Redmayne, who like Morrison was now working hard for his cause. Home was promoted as the compromise candidate between Butler and Hailsham, which was curious, because first Quintin's and Rab's political opinions were very similar, and secondly, as there was no formal voting mechanism, there could never be a deadlock that would require a 'compromise' candidate.

Rab Butler, who, ostentatiously and probably misguidedly, kept himself aloof from all that was going on in Blackpool, had successfully put forward his claim to make the leader's speech in place of Macmillan on the Saturday. On the previous day the story went round that it was impossible to get on the train on Saturday morning – so many representatives were anxious to leave before Rab's afternoon rally. On Saturday morning Hailsham was rapturously acclaimed by the delegates, though the chairman, Mrs Shepherd, managed to cut off the applause by shrieking through the microphone that they must get on and smiling one of her most devotional smiles.[23]

Also on the Saturday morning, the Executive of the 1922 Committee met at Blackpool. Mott-Radcliffe and one of the secretaries, Philip Goodhart, were absent but Redmayne and the Chief Whip in the Lords were in attendance. Two of those present supported Maudling and two supported Hailsham. All the rest heavily favoured Home. As the Committee's historians put it, the Executive agreed to a form of consultation which favoured Home. MPs were to be asked not only for their first preference but also their second and whether they were particularly opposed to any of the candidates. Further, the consultations were to be carried out by the Whips who knew that both their chief and '"the back-bench cabinet" had plumped decisively for Lord Home'.[24]

The Homes and the Butlers lunched together before the final rally. Alec Home announced that he was going to see his doctor for a medical the following week. When Butler asked him why, Home explained it was because he had been approached about being the party's leader. Both Rab and his wife were 'amazed' by this intelligence, having thought that Home had ruled himself out when he avowed in Cabinet that in no instance would he be a candidate.[25]

There was worse to come. At the rally Home read out a long letter from Macmillan about the Conservative Party, brilliant in its way, but better read individually than listened to in a mass meeting. In his introductory remarks Home made a snide reference to Hailsham's bathing activities, although at this conference he had been nowhere near the sea. In his speech Home also said, 'we choose a leader not for what he does or does not do at the Party Conference, but because the leader we choose is in every respect a whole man who in all circumstances is fit to lead the nation'. As Home was then, if not the actual front-runner, one of the three front-runners, this was a strange pronouncement and one that would have been sharply criticised if it had been made by any of the other candidates. Even, however, without the aid of Macmillan and Home, Butler's speech would have flopped. Like Maudling's, his text was good, but he eschewed all the oratorical arts, and the applause was more dutiful than whole-hearted.[26]

London

Act Two of the drama was set in London, and although still in hospital Macmillan was its actor manager. 'Sick as he was,' his biographer writes, 'Macmillan was still going to hold all the strings in his hand until the very last minute' and, strangely, the leadership contenders allowed him to do so. In consequence, instead of being the leading actors, they became mere extras, if not puppets. From his sick-bed, Macmillan drafted a minute proposing that 'soundings' of the Cabinet should be undertaken by the Lord Chancellor (Dilhorne), of other Ministers and back-benchers by the Chief Whip (Redmayne), of the Tory peers by Lord St Aldwyn, and of Lord Chelmer and Mrs Shepherd (representing the National Union) by Lord Poole. All those making the soundings were Home supporters except Oliver Poole, who backed Hailsham. Butler and the Cabinet were sufficiently trusting or negligent to accept the minute without a dissenting voice – a grave misjudgement by all the leadership contenders (except of course Home) and most of the rest of the Cabinet. Maybe the Cabinet thought the consultations would take some time and the issue would come back to them. In the event, as Macmillan intended, they were completed in the next two days, and the Cabinet had effectively abdicated in favour of Macmillan and his choice.[27]

After Blackpool, the joint Chairman of the Party, Iain Macleod, was unwontedly inactive. That was mainly because he was deemed to be a possible candidate and therefore excluded from the soundings. More surprisingly, Macleod deemed himself to be a candidate, even if very much an outsider. On Monday 14 October he told Randolph Churchill to keep an eye on the back of the field for a dark horse named Macleod, and the next day he told a Hailsham supporter and others that he thought the odds against him were about 15 to 2, although to anybody else they seemed about 100 to 1.[28]

In January 1964, Iain Macleod reviewed in the *Spectator* Churchill's book on the leadership struggle, which he regarded as 'the trailer for the screenplay' of Macmillan's memoirs and which had indeed been written with Macmillan's active co-operation. In his article Macleod claimed that from the beginning to the end of his premiership Macmillan

had been 'determined that Butler, although incomparably the best qualified of the contenders, should not succeed him', and that the succession
had been determined by what amounted to a conspiracy by a 'magic
circle', comprising Macmillan himself, Dilhorne, Redmayne, Morrison
and a few others. Although confirmed publicly by Powell (and later by
Butler), Macleod's account seemed at the time to be over-drawn; in the
light of later knowledge it is much more convincing.[29]

Exactly when Macmillan switched peers in midstream, as Nigel Birch
put it, is not known, since he did not bother to inform Hailsham or
even his own clan that he had done so, but it was probably on Monday
the 14th or Tuesday the 15th. On Monday he saw Dilhorne and
Redmayne, who gave him a colourful account of Hailsham in Blackpool,
alleging that he had paraded the baby and the baby food. Macmillan
was all the more impressed by what he was told since he believed that
both Dilhorne and Redmayne were in principle 'Hoggites'. Dilhorne
had originally supported Hailsham when he thought Home had ruled
himself out but then quickly switched, while Redmayne had favoured
Home since June and had always been strongly opposed to Hailsham.
All the same, that night Macmillan felt that Hogg 'with all his absurdities
and posturing and emotions' represented what he and others had 'tried
to represent from 1924 onwards. Those who clamour for Butler and
Home are really *not* so much shocked by Hogg's attitudes as his *honesty*.
He belongs both to this strange modern age of space and science *and*
to the great past – of classical learning and Christian life. That is what
they instinctively dislike.'[30]

Even if Macmillan had not decided on Monday to nobble his original
horse and mount the alternative peer, his meeting with Home on Tues-
day would have ensured his switch. Whereas Hailsham said nothing to
Macmillan about Home that he had not already told him to his face,
Home at his meeting with the Prime Minister sank his knife deep into
Hailsham's back. Even before the meeting Home had conveyed to the
Prime Minister's private secretary, Tim Bligh, to be passed on to Macmillan, his 'alarm at Hailsham's behaviour'. Home 'now believes', wrote
Bligh, that 'the person concerned was actually mad at the time'. To
suggest your rival is insane is going pretty far even for a 'reluctant
candidate'; all the more so, since what Home was saying about Hailsham
was by no stretch of the imagination true, as anybody who saw him in
action can testify. Home further thought, Bligh reported, that Hailsham
'was regarded as right-wing and would therefore lose some votes on the
Left', which was also pretty rich, as Home was well to the right of
Hailsham and would lose many more votes on the Left. After all this,
it is no surprise that Bligh told the Prime Minister that 'Lord Home

would be prepared to undertake the task if he was asked by the Prime Minister to do so in order to prevent the Party collapsing.' Even that was not enough for Home. He told Macmillan that the British Ambassador in Washington had telephoned in 'a great state to say that if Lord Hailsham was made Prime Minister this would be a tremendous blow to Anglo-American relations and would in fact end the special relationship'. Nothing that had been done at Blackpool by Hailsham or anybody else descended to this level of farce.[31]

Macmillan thought Hailsham had done '*very* well' in Moscow. The British Ambassador there had found him 'very entertaining', and Khrushchev, as has been seen, thought him 'a very able man'. But apparently Harriman and the rest of the American team in Moscow had found him too entertaining, too 'able a man', and insufficiently submissive and deferential to them. Even if they were right, which is highly improbable, the idea that their views should have any relevance to the British leadership contest passes all understanding. After all, with honourable exceptions, the Americans have not been notably successful in choosing their own Presidents, yet here they were, trying to choose – or at least have a veto on – the British Prime Minister. And neither Home nor (apparently) Macmillan even thought it odd. This was the clearest demonstration that the so-called 'special relationship' was one between an American sun and a British satellite.[32]

In his first draft of a memorandum dictated on the 15th, Macmillan noted that 'Lord Home is clearly a man who represents the old governing class at its best and those who take a normally impartial view of English history know how good that can be. He is not ambitious in the sense of wanting to scheme for power, although not foolish enough to resist honour when it comes to him.' There was a good deal more in the same strain, all of which may or may not have been true, but it scarcely addressed the main question: was Alec Home a suitable man to lead the Tory Party and govern the country in 1963? At that stage the Prime Minister, in the light of the findings he had been given, noted that 'the party in the country wants Hogg; the parliamentary party wants Maudling or Butler; the Cabinet wants Butler. The last 10 days have not altered this fundamental fact.' The next three were only to appear to do so.[33]

When a war over voting rights looked likely in South Africa, the American humorist 'Mr Dooley' gave President Kruger some sagacious advice based on much American experience. He told Kruger to give the Uitlanders all the votes they wanted, but to count them himself.[34] That was the procedure now followed in Britain by Macmillan, Dilhorne, Redmayne and others. In consequence Macmillan got, if not the candidate he had first supported, certainly the one he (and they) wanted. On Thursday those counting the votes had completed their figures. Redmayne and Morrison told Macmillan that, of over 300 MPs canvassed, Home had won 87 first choices, Butler 86, Hailsham 65, Maudling 48, Macleod 12 and Heath 10. Furthermore, Home had the most second preferences and the fewest enemies. In addition, Redmayne regarded the quality of Hailsham's backing as 'comparatively unimpressive', whereas Home was backed by more senior and experienced MPs; like Morrison, Redmayne was impressed by the quality of the never-has-beens on the 1922 Executive who backed Home.[35]

How much creative accountancy was required to produce Redmayne's figures is not exactly known, but certainly a good deal. Selwyn Lloyd, who was shown the lists by the Chief Whip, told Peter Walker that Hailsham had the most first preferences. Redmayne took the trouble to send a cable to Aidan Crawley, a Home supporter, in Johannesburg, yet MPs who were more easily available in London, but were less likely to produce the right answer, were not approached. In any case the Whips were not counting votes so much as assessing them and trying to get the answer they wanted. Jim Prior had little doubt that he was put down as a Home supporter, although Maudling was his first choice and Butler his second and he had merely said that Home 'would be possible'. Willie Whitelaw, who soon afterwards succeeded Redmayne as Chief Whip, was asked what he thought at the time was 'rather an extraordinary question' and what he later considered to be 'a totally irregular one'. 'If Alec Home was available would you be prepared to support him?' When Freddy Erroll, the President of the Board of Trade, told the Chief Whip on the Wednesday that he thought the succession should go to Maudling, Redmayne told him he was too late: 'it's all arranged – it's going to Alec Home'. That put it pretty well, although an even better word would have been 'fixed'.[36]

Dilhorne's accountancy was still more creative than Redmayne's. When many years later Enoch Powell was shown Dilhorne's record of the Cabinet's votes, he thought it was either a forgery or the result of Dilhorne's failing to hear what was said. Dilhorne's figures, though, were too weird to have been produced by any self-respecting forger, and even a deaf mute could scarcely have contrived them. The Lord Chancellor claimed that 10 members of the Cabinet had voted for Home, 3 for Butler, 4 for Maudling and 2 for Hailsham. Knowing only that Dilhorne had reported a Cabinet majority for Home and unaware of his detailed figures, Macleod wrote in his *Spectator* article that Dilhorne's findings had reached 'true absurdity'. He knew of eleven Cabinet Ministers who had not supported Home and of only two who had. Even if the remaining half-dozen were all for Home, the Lord Chancellor's figures were 'impossible'.[37]

Dilhorne's findings were even more impossible than Macleod then realised. In his list of Home's supporters Dilhorne included not only Macleod himself but Edward Boyle, which conclusively dismisses the Lord Chancellor as a reliable witness or judge. Highly improbable though it is, Macleod might just conceivably have voted tactically for Home in order to keep out Hailsham; it is inconceivable that Boyle would have done so. In addition if, for whatever reason, Macleod had voted for Home, how could he have subsequently refused to serve in Home's Government? And how could he have been so foolhardy as to attack Dilhorne's figures in his *Spectator* article? Dilhorne could then have blown him out of the water by revealing that Macleod had been part of the Cabinet's majority for Home. The Lord Chancellor's silence strongly suggests that he knew his figures to be phoney.[38]*

There is at least one other major absurdity in the Lord Chancellor's record. According to Dilhorne, Hailsham told him 'that he was by no means certain he would serve if R. A. Butler was chosen'. In fact Hailsham told his entourage at Blackpool, 'Rab is my favourite candidate: if I had not stood, I don't think he would have got it. He would have missed it again. I don't think I have done him any harm. He may get it now.' Hailsham's preference for Rab over his other rivals was confirmed by his attitude and conduct the following week in London. Early in the week he tried to meet Butler but was rebuffed, and later on he agreed to serve under Butler to stop Home.[40]

As a result of the refined researches of Redmayne and Dilhorne and of his own preference, Macmillan decided to recommend Home as the man the Queen should summon to the palace. Almost inevitably a decision reached by such dubious methods caused a row when the news of it prematurely leaked on the Thursday evening. Maudling, Macleod, Powell, Erroll and Aldington (the party's Deputy Chairman) assembled at Powell's home. 'We all thought a mistake was being made,' wrote Maudling, and having summoned Redmayne, they asked him to report their dissent and their support for Butler. Macleod and Powell telephoned Home to tell him of their opposition to his becoming Premier. From his home in Putney, Hailsham, who had heard from Peter Thorneycroft that Macleod thought the choice of Home calamitous, tele-

---

* When in early 1964 Enoch Powell supported Macleod's view of Cabinet opinion in his *Spectator* article, Tim Bligh, now Home's Private Secretary, complained, and Powell went to see him at Number 10. Bligh had the papers in front of him, and when Enoch maintained that there had been a majority for Butler in the Cabinet, Bligh looked at the top paper and said: 'Yes, I can see how that could be.'[39]

phoned Powell. 'Aristides,' he said, 'Themistocles here. This is a calamity
. . . It will be disastrous for the country as well as the party . . .' Aristides
agreed. Hailsham then rang Home to tell him calmly, if brutally, the
same thing. He also telephoned Maudling who did not show much sign
of fight. Finally he telephoned Butler, an exchange which differed from
the other conversations because Quintin kept on repeating aloud what
Rab had just said, in the same way that barristers sometimes repeat the
answer of a witness when they are particularly contemptuous of it. 'Oh
you were just dozing off, were you, dear Rab?' 'You will take note of
what I have said and possibly act on it.' Finally Quintin said, 'You must
don your armour, my dear Rab, and fight.' Regaining his armchair with
difficulty (he had hurt his leg), Hailsham observed that everyone was
running true to form. 'Aristides was open and definite, Reggie thought
it "not a very good idea", and Rab was "taking note of my remarks".'[41]

The next day, too, everyone ran true to form. When he learned of
the strength of the opposition to him in the Cabinet and realised the
damage that might be done to the party, Alec Home characteristically
wanted to withdraw. That the anointing of the proclaimed compromise
candidate, behind whom all the Cabinet and the party could allegedly
unite, had created a furore among senior ministers, virtually none of
whom wanted him and many of whom were on the brink of refusing
to serve under him, was indeed an absurd situation. Nevertheless Macmillan was not going to let Butler gain the crown in the last act, and
he urged Home not to withdraw. In his diary Macmillan found the
coming together of 'all the unsuccessful candidates . . . somewhat distasteful'. He thought that there 'was something rather eighteenth century
about this (Fox–North coalition perhaps)', a notably inapt comparison.
Apart from anything else, there was almost no difference on issues
between Butler, Hailsham, Maudling and Macleod: and as to the eighteenth century, Macmillan's own behaviour was rather sixteenth century
(Machiavelli, perhaps).[42]

Another Machiavellian feature of Macmillan's course of action was
that, in the words of the Queen's biographer, he 'bounced' the Queen
into choosing Home. After visiting Macmillan in hospital, the Queen
sent for Home, not appointing him Prime Minister but asking him to
form a Government. Even at that stage Butler need not have been beaten.
Had he 'stood firm', as he later agreed with John Boyd-Carpenter, he
would have been Prime Minister. Home could not have formed a
Government without Butler, and without Hailsham, Maudling,
Macleod, Boyle and Powell, all of whom would have refused to serve
if Butler had given a lead. And if they had refused office, other Ministers
who privately agreed with them would have done the same. Home

would have had to return to the palace to tell the Queen that he had failed to form an administration. In a passage in his diary which he wisely did not reproduce in his memoirs, Macmillan wrote that if Home withdrew, 'Butler would fail to form a Government; even if given another chance (for the Queen might then send for Wilson), no one else would succeed. We should have a Wilson Government or a dissolution.' That is wildly implausible. Of the outgoing Cabinet only Sandys and Home himself might possibly have refused to serve under Butler, and with such a powerful phalanx at the top, the rest of the party – even Redmayne, Mott-Radcliffe and James James Morrison Morrison Weatherby George Dupree – would certainly have rallied round.[43]

Powell later spoke graphically of having handed Butler 'a loaded revolver and told him that all he had to do was to pull the trigger'. Butler's wife was also urging him to fight. But his heart was not in it and after reserving his position he became Foreign Secretary – at last. In the end only Macleod and Powell refused to serve. 'One does not expect', Macleod said, 'to have many people with one in the last ditch.'[44]

Home naturally resented Powell and Macleod's refusal to join his Government, and certainly one of the reasons they gave – that by Home's selection the Tories were admitting they could not find a leader among 365 Tory MPs – was insubstantial. That of course was why it was used: it was the only one that could be given in public without doing irreparable damage to Home and the party. In any case, while Macleod and Powell's refusal was mistaken, it was largely Home's own fault. Had he been more open about his candidacy in Cabinet and elsewhere, they could hardly have declined office.* The real differences between him and them were over policy; Africa was one. Powell was said to have asked: 'How can I possibly serve under a man whose views on Africa are positively Portuguese?' Macleod felt the same, while Home 'had always thought' Macleod as Colonial Secretary 'to be the wrong man in the wrong place'. Macleod also opposed Home because he thought he knew little about domestic policy and had no views on it. In the end, though, both Powell and Macleod believed, as Macleod put it in the *Spectator*, that if he 'felt strongly enough to tell Lord Home that I thought it wrong for him to accept an invitation to form an administration I could not honourably serve with him in that administration'. The two last-ditchers there-fore honourably jeopardised their political careers, making themselves vastly unpopular not only with Home but throughout the Conservative Party.[45]

Home was in many ways a very popular choice in the Conservative

---

* But of course if he had been more open, he probably would not have got the job.

Party. He was after all an extraordinarily likeable man who had almost no enemies. Yet in choosing him the Conservative Party was pleasing itself rather than protecting its future. It was as if an army had chosen a very popular officer from the reserve to be its Commander-in-Chief, even though it knew he was unlikely ever to win a major battle. One of the arguments most used by the Hailsham camp was that their man would win the election. This view was shared by people as diverse as Field Marshal Montgomery, who may not have known much about politics but knew a good deal about winning battles, and Lord Carrington – as well as by Harold Wilson, who on the Wednesday told the Labour MP Desmond Donnelly that he was praying the Tories would chose Home or Butler and that the two he feared were Hailsham and Macleod. Of course the Butler and Maudling camps also thought that their men, too, would win the election. Even Home, after all, who as Butler told him 'spoilt the image of modernisation', nearly won, though handicapped by the absence of Macleod and Powell. Probably, therefore, any of the other candidates would have secured the Conservative Party another term of office.[46]

Hence it was not the row at Blackpool which damaged the Tory Party but the result. Had Butler or Hailsham gained the succession and gone on to win the 1964 election, we should have been spared the Wilson years. A fourth election defeat in a row would surely have split Labour. The party realignment that nearly occurred in the 1980s, or the modernisation of the Labour Party that eventually took place in the 1990s, would have been completed in the sixties. Labour would not subsequently have moved to the left, nor the Conservatives to the right, and British politics would not have taken the direction which Harold Macmillan later deplored.

In his farewell message to the Conservative Party, read out by Home on the last day at Blackpool, Macmillan wrote:

Since 1945 I have lived to see the Party of our dreams come into being . . . I have seen our policies develop into that pragmatic and sensible compromise between the extremes of collectivism and individualism for which the Party has always stood in its great periods. I have seen it bring to the people of our own country a degree of comfort and well-being, as well as opportunities for living the good life . . . Thus, the silent, Conservative revolution has come about . . . The Conservative Party has always had the *faith* to honour the things that history has taught us to cherish and revere. But it has also had the *courage* to grasp what is new and fresh . . . Today we need this double inspiration if we are to ensure that the responsibili-

ties are met and the opportunities seized. Let each and every one
of you resolve to prove equal to the challenge . . .[47]

Regrettably, Harold Macmillan himself did not prove equal to that
challenge. The chief charge against him is not that he switched his
runners or manipulated the procedure but that he did everything in his
power to stop Rab Butler. Once he had come to believe – which may
have been correct – that there was too much opposition to Hailsham
for him to win, he should have either stopped controlling events or
switched to Butler. Like Quintin Hailsham, Reggie Maudling and Macmillan himself, Butler was squarely in the One-Nation tradition of Conservatism, and Alec Home, though far from a rabid right-winger, was
not. By going along with those whom Iain Macleod called 'the stupid
men' in the party, Macmillan dealt a near-fatal blow to One-Nation
Toryism. 'The Tory Party', Macleod wrote in January 1964, 'for the
first [but not the last] time since Bonar Law is being led from the right
of centre.'[48]

Later, Alec Home himself came to believe it might have been better
if Butler had got the job, since anybody else was seen as a somewhat
'unnatural' successor. Macmillan, too, had painful second thoughts.
'Hogg was far the best – the only one of genius –' he told a friend in
1965, 'but he destroyed himself at that unlucky Blackpool . . . Alec did
his best – with courage and dignity. But he could not impress himself
on Parlt. or people enough for a P.M.' In the eighties, Macmillan admitted that it would perhaps have been better if Butler had succeeded him:
'then we could have won the 1964 election'. By then, Macmillan could
not fail to recognise the harm he had inadvertently done to the Conservative Party. By barring Butler's way, he had helped to turn the 'Party of
our dreams' into one more like his nightmare: to Macmillan's regret
much of the party's leadership had not only repudiated 'the pragmatic
and sensible compromise between the extremes of collectivism and individualism', it had stigmatised the Governments of Macmillan himself
and of other Tory Prime Ministers as misguided collaborators with the
socialist enemy. Both the Conservative Party and the country had paid
a high price for Macmillan's insistence, in 1963, on holding 'all the
strings in his hand until the very last minute'.[49]

CHAPTER
IX
───────

Home and Heath

If the choice of Home was something of a disaster for the Conservative Party, it was not a disaster for the nation. Home proved to be a far better Prime Minister than many had expected. Before the new Premier could properly get down to work as party and national leader, however, he had to change his name and enter the House of Commons. The fourteenth Earl of Home became Sir Alec Douglas-Home and, after a creditable by-election campaign in which he made seventy-two speeches, MP for Kinross and West Perth. (Lord Hailsham was similarly metamorphosed into Mr Quintin Hogg, MP for St Marylebone.) Home's by-election delayed the reassembly of Parliament, a postponement which Wilson later termed an 'impertinence'[1] but which was clearly necessary. When Parliament did at last meet, the Prime Minister's opening speech displayed his inability to command his audience, a defect which was equally glaring in the general election a year later.

Well before then, his light-hearted but unfortunate admission, in an interview with the *Observer* the previous year, that he was dependent on a box of matches for his understanding of economic documents, had been pounced on by a gleeful Opposition. Wilson derided him as the 'matchsticks Premier'. So to Alec Home's image as a man who was out of date and out of his depth, was added the general impression that he was a 'man who knew nothing about domestic affairs'. If the impression was only partly justified, it was shared by many of his colleagues and ex-colleagues. As has been seen, Iain Macleod and Quintin Hogg certainly held that belief; and in January Rab Butler told a journalist that the Prime Minister was 'an amiable enough creature [but] I'm afraid he doesn't, you know, understand economics or even education at all'. Nor, evidently, did he understand publicity. With him as party leader, the detrimental 'grouse-moor' image was more convincingly fastened onto the Tory Party. On several weekends Home was photographed going out shooting clad in a surgical collar which made him look conspicuously non-Prime-Ministerial. Not until the middle of January did he realise that shooting was bad for his image.[2]

Nevertheless, on foreign affairs Sir Alec was fully at home. After paying a fine tribute to the assassinated President Kennedy, he crossed the Atlantic to attend the funeral. He was preceded by an anguished appeal from the Foreign Office for an appointment with the new President, Lyndon Johnson; 'it might look odd if he came to Washington and did not have any time with the President at all'. The FO need not have worried. While, with Macmillan and Adenauer no longer in office, de Gaulle stole the show, there was no danger of Alec Home being shunned like Selwyn Lloyd in 1956.[3]*

Their next meeting, in Washington in February, did not go well. Johnson, who had been a successful Majority Leader of the Senate, using a unique blend of cajolery and threats to keep Democratic Senators in submission, thought he could do the same with the British Prime Minister. He tried to induce Home to cancel the sale of Leyland buses to Cuba, a contract to which the Eisenhower administration had not objected. Having firmly resisted Johnson's pressure, the Prime Minister then further angered the President by light-heartedly saying in an after-dinner speech at the White House: 'Occasionally we may, perhaps, send buses to Cuba, but never will anything interfere fundamentally with the friendship and delight which we feel in the company of a great ally and partner.' Johnson thought the buses were no laughing matter, and his idea of a great partner was one which did what it was told. When he saw Rab Butler two months later he was still annoyed. Fingering a wad of dollar bills, he suggested to Butler that the British Government should cancel the contract and send the bill to his Texas ranch and he would pay it. The President's boorish behaviour was not the happiest demonstration of the so-called 'special relationship', but it gave Butler much sardonic pleasure.[5]

The Home Front

Back in London, Douglas-Home had trouble with the two refuseniks. In January Iain Macleod, reviewing Randolph Churchill's book in the *Spectator* and provoked not only by Churchill's tendentious account

---

* This was not their first meeting. In November 1960 the Vice-President-elect had paid a surprise visit to London. Harold Macmillan cancelled a weekend trip to see him, and Alec Home gave a large dinner in his honour at the Foreign Secretary's official residence. Before ten o'clock Johnson left, saying he was tired and had a heavy schedule the next day. The British guests who had hoped to hear of the incoming administration's plans and to talk to the future Vice-President were disappointed but understanding. The next day their disappointment turned to annoyance when they discovered that Johnson had left not to go to bed but to spend four hours in a Park Lane night-club.[4]

but also by a speech by Martin Redmayne defending his actions, reopened the wound of the leadership struggle. Henry Brooke, the Home Secretary, cut Macleod at a party, many MPs and activists were enraged, and Macleod kept away from the Commons for a month. As David Watt wrote, also in the *Spectator*, the article seemed to the party 'a monstrous treason' when what was needed were 'touching protestations of loyalty'. Surprisingly the Chief Whip was relaxed and friendly throughout, and kept the recriminations within limits.

Harold Macmillan thought Macleod's article suited the press, 'most of which loves to attack Eton and the aristocracy', because it touched off 'the "inverted snobbery" emotion which is very strong today'. No doubt that was true, but Macmillan ignored the ordinary snobbery on the other side, exemplified by John Morrison's faith in 'shooting gents', Nigel Birch's obscure remark about Alec Home 'having eaten the Queen's salt', and his own eulogy of Home in his memorandum to the Queen. Macleod's article was written in a hurry, and some phrases would have been altered had Macleod known how they would be interpreted, but the phrase which caused most Conservative anger – 'the magic circle of old Etonians' – was a misquotation, the result of telescoping two phrases more than a column apart.[6]

Enoch Powell publicly confirmed the accuracy of Macleod's 'narrative on all matters within my knowledge' and endorsed his 'general assessment' of what had happened. Otherwise his contributions to Conservative disunity, while of much greater importance in the long term, created less discord at the time. Powell now expressed opposition to any form of Government intervention in the economy. Since the economic policy of the Government of which he had recently been a member did not alter under the new Prime Minister and involved a good deal of Government interference with market forces, Powell's new stance required opposition to much of the Government's activities which he variously described as 'hocus-pocus' and as nonsense well beyond that normally permitted to politicians. In three articles in *The Times** in April, in addition to cogently deriding the Commonwealth, he argued that the Conservative Party should espouse a capitalism as dogmatic, rigid and complete as the socialism extreme left-wingers had tried to foist on Labour. For the Conservative Party suddenly to don the clothes of the nineteenth-century Liberal Party seemed to many Tory MPs a particularly undesirable form

---

* Surprisingly, they were only signed 'A Conservative'. Powell never confirmed or denied that he had written them, but his authorship was in no more doubt at the time than Sir Walter Scott's of the Waverley novels. 'I find it difficult to accept', said the Lord Chancellor, the ineffable Dilhorne, 'that the gentleman who wrote this . . . can really claim to be a Conservative.'

of political transvestism. Reacting to Powell's criticism of regional policy, Quintin Hogg said that he seemed to be becoming 'a sort of Mao-Tse-Tung of Toryism'. Even those who agreed with Powell's speeches thought they were politically inopportune.[7]

Sir Alec could fairly blame Macleod and Powell for sowing dissension when party unity was imperative. Yet he had largely himself to blame for the longest and most debilitating battle in the party: the abolition of Resale Price Maintenance (RPM), the system which allowed manufacturers to stipulate the price at which their goods were sold by retailers, thus preventing department stores and supermarkets from offering goods at a lower price than corner shops. The abolition of RPM was Sir Alec's Poll Tax. Unlike the Poll Tax, the RPM bill was a desirable measure, but like the Poll Tax it was electoral poison. Earlier Cabinets, including Macmillan's, had shied away from enacting it because of the trouble it would cause in the parliamentary party and in the country. Clearly it was a measure to be introduced in the first year of a Parliament; to enact it in the last year was electoral madness. Some 450,000 small shopkeepers were affected by it, nearly all of them Conservative supporters. Not only that; they were also important opinion-formers. To alienate them unnecessarily just before a general election showed astonishing political ineptitude. RPM scarcely figured in the election because the other parties, who favoured its abolition, were silently grateful for the Government's generosity in supplying them with so many votes.[8]

Had Macmillan still been Prime Minister, RPM would have remained in the pending file at the Board of Trade. The Queen's Speech had already been decided upon, and RPM was not included. Nor would any of the other major leadership contenders have dreamed of touching the subject in 1963–4. Butler, Hailsham and Maudling all thought it politically foolish, as did Macleod. Admittedly two private members' bills were due to be debated; the Government would therefore have had to take a position on them, yet the subject could easily have been kicked into touch until the next Parliament.

Very probably Heath, as President of the Board of Trade, had decided the election was already lost, and he wanted to have one important modernising measure to his credit before he left office. Even the apostle of *laissez-faire*, Enoch Powell, had doubts about abolishing RPM, thinking it should not be enacted on its own and fully appreciating the strength of the opposition to it – had he and Macleod still been in the Cabinet, they would surely have stopped it. Even without them, the new and well-liked Leader of the House, Selwyn Lloyd, Hailsham, Maudling, Butler and Redmayne, nearly defeated Heath. But after a three-hour discussion and making some concessions, Heath, supported by Boyle,

Joseph and others, above all the Prime Minister, though he had 'many reservations' and, later, regrets, gained Cabinet approval for his bill. Perhaps the least bad argument for abolishing RPM in 1964 was that as a modernising measure it would do something to offset the image of a non-modern Prime Minister and a 'grouse-moor' party. Unfortunately, the remedy was as damaging as the illness.[9]

RPM caused even more trouble in the parliamentary party than in the Cabinet. At an unusually long and unusually crowded meeting of the 1922 Committee on 23 January 'there was almost unanimous criticism of the Government's proposals on the ground of timing', the minutes recorded, adding that 'members appeared almost equally divided on the merits'. In the next few months the Committee spent more time on RPM than on any other issue in the previous decade. On the second reading of the bill, twenty-one Conservatives voted against the Government and about twenty-five others abstained – a large number in the days when Tory MPs seldom took their opposition as far as the division lobbies. And on one amendment at the committee stage the Government scraped through by one vote. Even then, their troubles were not over. On 15 April, the Chairman of the 1922, John Morrison, wrote to the PM to tell him that unless Ted Heath made more concessions there would soon be 'another very dicey win or a defeat', adding, 'I thought I ought to put it in writing before he, Ted Heath, succeeds in breaking us up entirely which, though I sincerely trust I am wrong, is in my opinion quite likely.'[10]

Many Tory MPs thought the Government would be better occupied in legislating against the restrictive practices of trade unions than those of small shopkeepers. A trade-union measure would have been popular, too, with the party in the constituencies, which for some time had been pressing for action against unofficial strikes. It would also have been less damaging electorally than RPM and, especially in the light of the decision of the TUC Conference to oppose wage restraint in any form, fully justifiable. Furthermore, the House of Lords' decision in July in *Rookes* v. *Barnard*, which appeared to deprive the unions of immunities they thought they had long possessed, gave the Government the occasion to act. In February even the One Nation Group put down an Early Day Motion asking for a Royal Commission on the trade unions, and in July it asked for a Government statement on trade-union law and practice before the election. The Government did not provide even that.[11]

Both the long-running RPM battle and the state of the economy were central to the debate on the best date for the general election. Maudling's opposite number, James Callaghan, had complained that his 1963 Budget had been 'too cautious', a complaint that had been echoed by the two brightest economists on the Labour back-benches, Roy Jenkins and Anthony Crosland. But before long it was clear that the economy was booming. The Chancellor had recognised from the start that his policies carried two dangers: cost inflation and a balance of payments deficit. Both materialised. The theory behind Maudling's dash for growth was that his 1963 Budget and other measures would create a virtuous circle whereby increased spending, caused by tax reductions, would lead to increased investment, which would lead to an expansion of exports. This strategy has been likened to a First World War plan for an attack – the 'assumption that willingness to incur heavy losses was sufficient to ensure success'. In fact the strategy created a vicious circle: increased spending led to wage claims and a flood of imports. A better way to achieve a virtuous circle would have been first to increase investment so that when people had more money in their pockets British goods were available for them to spend it on. Yet Maudling was by no means the last Chancellor to launch a First World War attack in the attempt to procure faster growth and halt Britain's relative economic decline.[12]

Because of the economic uncertainty, Maudling wanted an early election. By February the National Economic Development Office had decided that deflation would soon be inevitable, and in that month the Chancellor raised Bank Rate. RPM prevented a March election. In his April Budget, Maudling raised taxes by £110 million (not negligible compared with the tax reduction of £269 million the year before), having before the Budget pressed for an election in June.[13]

In his memoirs, Reggie Maudling was generous about Alec Douglas-Home, claiming that the only argument he had with him when he was Prime Minister was over the timing of the election. At the time, however, he was contemptuous, regarding the Prime Minister as useless and even implying to Iain Macleod that he regretted not having stayed out of the Government with him and Enoch Powell. In favouring June for the election, the Chancellor was supported, Macleod pointed out, by 'the younger men' in the Cabinet, the Government and the back-benches. In the middle of March the One-Nation Group was practically unanimous in favour of June on the grounds that it would be wrong to hang on until the last minute and, more importantly, that October would be bad for sterling.[14]

A fortnight later Harold Macmillan, who privately complained that RPM was 'a very boring business', wrote to the Prime Minister that 'the Party in Parliament has been thoroughly upset by RPM [which] reacts on the constituencies'. Since the bill could not be carried till the end of May, he continued, 'this confusion [would] injuriously affect a

June election'. A more powerful argument was the Central Office one that an election would be lost in June but might be won in the autumn; consequently Sir Alec announced in April that there would be no election before October. Although that decision may seem to have been justified by the Government coming so close to victory, in overriding his Chancellor's pleas for June the Prime Minister neglected the national interest for electoral gain. In any case 1964 turned out to be only the first instalment of defeat; the second followed in 1966. Wilson thus ended up with a bigger majority and one more year in power than he would have enjoyed had Douglas-Home accepted Maudling's advice. So both the country and the Tory Party would have benefited from a summer election and the consequent avoidance of the 1964–6 interregnum.[15]

In the House of Commons the Prime Minister was so modest, friendly and open with his back-benchers that he won over even those who thought he was the wrong man for his office.[16] His dignity and decency also helped him with the electorate, especially as his performances on television improved without ever becoming good. Yet his poll ratings were always well behind those of Harold Wilson. They marched in step with those of the Government, and he consistently ran much further behind Wilson, who admittedly was an unusually popular and effective Opposition Leader, than did the Conservatives behind Labour. As expected, therefore, the Conservative Prime Minister was not an electoral asset. Moreover, Sir Alec was particularly ill-suited to fight the main issue of the party battle: the modernisation of Britain. In the contest with Wilson and Labour over which would best modernise Britain, Douglas-Home and the Conservative Party seemed like a horse-drawn plough competing with one pulled by a tractor.

Indeed the Prime Minister's cast of mind had a certain amount in common with the age of the horse. As the Conservative Research Department found him a difficult man to brief or write speeches for, its Chairman, Michael Fraser, asked him to distil his political philosophy onto a few sheets of paper. In response Douglas-Home produced what he called his 'confession', which talked of a 'half-educated' electorate; 'countrymen who living close to nature have a sixth sense of what is possible or impossible'; Britain having to be 'in the First XI and among the top batsmen'; not leading from behind or from the middle but in front; being 'prepared to scrap and build again; and I like going fast but on the rails'. Fraser was himself a keen racegoer, but the document can have made him little wiser; presumably it confirmed his earlier forebodings when he learned that Home was going to become Prime Minister.[17]

All the same, Sir Alec had no chance to turn his right-wing inclinations into policy, and anyway had insufficient knowledge to impose his views. Thus on the day of the publication in October 1963 of the Robbins Report recommending a massive expansion of higher education, the new Prime Minister went on television to announce that the Government accepted it. Expansion was badly needed – Kingsley Amis's objection that 'more means worse' was neat but irrelevant – but a little right-wing caution, or indeed ordinary caution, particularly over the assumption that enough science students could be found to fill the new scientific establishments, would not have come amiss.[18]

The 1964 Election

In April the Conservatives had sustained a crushing defeat in the first elections for the Greater London Council, which they had set up and which, regrettably, a later Conservative Government abolished. But in May, although a very marginal seat in Scotland was lost, Charles Morrison held the far from safe seat of Devizes. The opinion polls also began to record a slow improvement. What later came to be called 'the feel-good factor' was working in the Government's favour. By the time of the election, the Conservatives could respond to the charge that they had presided over 'thirteen wasted years' by producing impressive statistics on living standards. Since 1951, the number of cars had risen by three and a half million; more than half of all householders now enjoyed the convenience of a washing machine, while the proportion with refrigerators had leaped from 5 to 37 per cent. Of these householders, 44 per cent were now owner-occupiers – up by 7 per cent since the year of the last election.[19]

On 30 August Reggie Maudling told Iain Macleod that he thought the economy would 'just stand up' till the election. Earlier, because of the delayed election and the deteriorating balance of payments, he had asked the Treasury to propose emergency plans for whichever party formed the Government after the election. These included import quotas, an import surcharge and almost certainly, though Maudling later denied it, floating the pound or devaluation.[20]

By 15 September, when the Prime Minister announced the election would be on 15 October, the Conservatives had narrowed the gap to 3 per cent. The Conservative manifesto, *Prosperity with a Purpose*, issued three days later, was intended to show that the party had not run out of momentum despite its long period in office. The document promised an inquiry into the trade unions and legislation to enhance the powers of the Monopolies Commission. *Prosperity with a Purpose* did not deviate from One-Nation Toryism. 'Under Conservatism,' it proudly stated, 'the value of social security benefits has outpaced both prices and average earnings', and it pledged that 'those receiving such benefits [would] continue to share in the higher standards produced by an expanding economy'.[21]

Prosperity with a Purpose was the high spot of the Tory election campaign, most of the rest of which was ill-planned and mismanaged. Maudling was given the task of handling the press and presiding over the morning press conference, while Heath was put in charge of television. Because he had done some good interviews during the Common Market negotiations, Heath was apparently thought to be a good television performer. Yet in a party political broadcast in May he had flopped so badly that even a Tory back-bencher (Gilmour) on the programme, who was said to have sounded 'like a man in a TV commercial about indigestion', was judged to have been better than him. The roles of Maudling and Heath should have been exchanged. Heath remained poor on television, whereas his drive and aggression would have been right for the press conferences. Conversely Maudling with his friendly manner would have been right for television, but was too relaxed to set the right tone of the campaign at the morning press conferences.[22]

Even in 1959, when they had started off plainly ahead, the Conservatives had had to abandon a quiet campaign. Yet in 1964, when they began plainly behind and obviously had to fight for votes, contrary to Poole's advice they again started quietly. Maudling sat on the issue where Labour was most vulnerable – the cost of its programme, which Home had earlier called 'a menu without prices' – for so long that when he did use it there was no time for it to make an impact. Hence Labour was not thrown onto the defensive and had little explaining to do.[23]

Many thought Alec Home was not up to the job of Prime Minister, too amateurish and old-fashioned to modernise the country and too out of touch with home affairs. Instead of combating that view, his campaign seemed better designed to confirm it. After starting the election badly on the BBC's *Election Forum* by referring to old-age pensions as 'donations', he embarked on an exhausting nationwide whistle-stop tour; he was his usual engaging self but seemed far away from the thick of the election. 'The voters', the BBC's political correspondent astutely discovered, 'are playing a key role in the election' – unlike, he might have added, Sir Alec Douglas-Home, who scarcely got onto the stage, and when he did was liable to be hooted off it. Seldom during an election, the authors of the Nuffield Study concluded, had a Prime Minister's words attracted less attention.[24]

That was partly Alec Home's own fault and partly that of his campaign's organisers. Out on the stump, he seldom said anything sufficiently newsworthy to capture the headlines. Conservative Central Office scheduled him to make only five set-piece speeches. The last of these, at Birmingham Bull-Ring, the organisers failed to make an all-ticket affair. The Prime Minister was therefore howled down not by heckling but by systematic bellowing of 'Tories out' and 'We want Wilson'. Home battled on for an hour but could make no impression on the mob and was unfairly worsted. He himself thought the Bull-Ring non-speech was the turning point of the campaign, as did the Party Chairman, Lord Blakenham. Even if it was, it need not have been, for there was a full week to go before polling day. Yet astonishingly neither Blakenham nor Home decided to lay on another large set-piece speech to efface the unfortunate impression left on TV viewers by the Bull-Ring affair. Home's final television appeal did not improve matters. He was seldom effective on television and spent too much time on nuclear weapons.[25]

Home's remark about 'donations' was far from the only gaffe of the campaign. Among others, Quintin Hogg spoiled an entertaining press conference by arguing that the Liberals were 'insignificant and meaningless' and that anybody who voted Labour was 'stark, staring bonkers'. Worse was the interview which Rab Butler, whose job Home had already secretly promised to Christopher Soames, gave to George Gale of the *Daily Express* on the train to Darlington. Butler, who thought the interview was off the record, told Gale that the election was very close, 'but things might start slipping in the last few days', unfortunately adding the remark, 'they won't slip towards us'. For good measure Butler also told Gale: 'Alec has done very well. Possibly he has spent too much time outside London . . . He's a bit bored with Ted [Heath].' No more than with Eden in 1956 was that the sort of support that Home wanted from Butler.[26]

'Donations' (from the City and industry) was the proper word for over 80 per cent of the income of Conservative Central Office. In 1964 they were higher than ever before, and Central Office spent more than double what it had spent in 1959.[27] Yet massive advertising could not offset the mistakes of the campaign or the Conservatives' two greatest handicaps: thirteen years in office, and the fact that as a leader to modernise the country Alec Home seemed palpably outclassed by Harold Wilson. All the same, Home came very close to winning. The final score showed Labour with 317 seats, the Conservatives with 304 and the Liberals with nine.

The Achievement

Harold Macmillan's mishandling of the succession severely impaired his legacy to the Conservative Party, yet the Macmillan–Home years achieved much for the country. The greatest achievement was the pre-dominantly peaceful divestment of most of what remained of the Empire and the large step taken towards turning Empire into Commonwealth. Arguably, of course, the Africans paid the price for this British states-manship. Yet, if decolonisation has often proved disastrous for Africa, the experience of those colonies which had to fight for independence does not suggest that attempts by the imperial powers to retain control of their colonial possessions ultimately produced a better result. The subsequent history of Algeria, Zaïre, Angola and Mozambique has not been enviable. Hence Iain Macleod's claim that 'of course there were risks in moving quickly, but the risks of moving slowly were far greater',[28] has not been contradicted by events. In Africa the Macmillan Government was quick to recognise the inevitable, and its swift with-drawal in good order from Africa was a notable feat.

Macmillan was too slow to recognise the inevitable in Europe and so could not claim a comparable success. The Prime Minister's own over-concentration on Anglo-American relations, combined with the forces of inertia, illusion and Little-Englandism, ensured that the British appli-cation to join the Common Market was too late and insufficiently whole-hearted to succeed. All the same, the Government was right to make the attempt: it paved the way for Edward Heath's successful venture a decade later.

The Macmillan Government succeeded in substantially reducing Britain's inflated expenditure on defence, though it remained excessive. Conscription was ended, and between 1957 and 1964 armed-services manpower was cut by 40 per cent. An effective nuclear deterrent was produced and maintained, although the extent of its independence remained open to question. The establishment of a unified Ministry of Defence contained inter-service rivalry within limits, without however eliminating it. Our armed forces were modernised. Had British industry and the British economy been as efficient and as well run as the armed services, the British economic problem would have soon been solved.

'Stop–go' did much damage to the economy and to the Tory Govern-ment. Yet the 'stops' were very mild affairs compared to those of the eighties and nineties. Indeed, unlike their later successors they were not actual 'stops'. The economy never stopped growing. The slowest growth rate was 0.4 per cent in 1958, and the next slowest 1.3 per cent in 1962. Between 1959 and 1964 growth averaged 3.8 per cent a year, unprecedentedly high by British standards, and investment in manufacturing industry rose by 26 per cent. Wage inflation remained fairly moderate until towards the end of the 1960s. In the years 1959–64 unemployment averaged a mere 1.8 per cent, yet Britain's inflation rate averaged only 3 per cent.[29] To see Macmillan and his Government as the parents of inflation is, therefore, historically false. The fruits of this economic progress were widely spread. The wage rates of manual workers were in real terms nearly 20 per cent higher in 1964 than in 1959. Indeed, as the Tory manifesto fairly claimed, 'in the thirteen years of Conservative government the living standards of the British people have improved more than in the whole of the previous half-century'.[30] Why then did the Conservatives lose?

In addition to the factors already mentioned – choosing the wrong leader, the absence of Powell and Macleod, and abolishing RPM – the climate of opinion had changed to their disadvantage. In the early sixties, Penguin published a flurry of books on the theme of 'What's wrong with Britain?' The impression given was that the intellectual community believed Conservative misrule to be at the root of the British malaise. Suez and boredom with the same party continuing to govern had much to do with that feeling. By contrast, Labour was held to be in tune with the new public mood which had been expressed by Harold Wilson's 'white heat' of technology speech at the 1963 Labour Conference. A more probable cause of the Labour victory was the belief that Labour could now be trusted to build on Conservative achievements and that it was time for a change from a backward-looking Conservative Party. The Conservatives lost many votes to the Liberals – many more than they would have done under any other leader. Labour's percentage share of the vote was only 0.3 per cent higher than five years earlier, while the Liberal share nearly doubled to 11 per cent, and the Conservative vote fell by 6 per cent.

Opposition

Home was characteristically gracious and dignified in defeat. He was also exhausted. Three weeks after the election he still looked as though he had not been to bed for months. Privately, he thought the result was better than if it had been the other way round, which was probably true but coming from him showed admirable detachment: had it been the other way round he would, after all, have still been in Downing

Street. He brought Powell and Macleod back into the fold. Macleod found him rather pathetic, trying to work out his Shadow Cabinet as though with matches but this time with little bits of paper. In public, too, Home did not seem cut out for Opposition. Had Labour won a working majority, he would probably have retired, but with Wilson's tiny majority making an early election certain, he was trapped. Even so, despite his popularity with the parliamentary party and a particularly good speech on the Address, speculation about his successor did not take long to start.[31]

If Alec Home did not look like a Leader of the Opposition, the new Prime Minister still behaved like one. The latest balance of payments figures appeared on the day of the election, and it became a key element in Harold Wilson's political tactics to make them seem as bad as possible, in order to denounce Conservative economic policy as having been disastrously incompetent and irresponsible. That might have been justifiable and sensible, had Wilson's outrage been combined with an immediate decision to devalue the pound. But it was not. The crucial decision was taken by Wilson, James Callaghan, the new Chancellor of the Exchequer, and George Brown, cumbersomely entitled First Secretary of State and Secretary of State for Economic Affairs, on the Saturday after the election. Earlier Callaghan and Brown had had a meeting with three civil servants: Donald MacDougall and two Treasury knights. Everybody in the room was asked if he favoured devaluation – MacDougall was the only one to do so. At the later, decisive meeting all three ministers were opposed to it. For Wilson, as earlier for Macmillan, the pound was a status symbol, and he was fearful of Labour being branded as the party of devaluation. MacDougall thought the three politicians were against devaluation for the following reasons: Wilson, in addition to the political risks, because his adviser, Thomas Balogh, had persuaded him that 'socialist' policies would solve the balance of payments problem; Callaghan, because he had promised the US Secretary of the Treasury that he would not; and Brown, because he thought devaluation would be an act hostile to the working class.[32]

Which of those reasons was the least compelling is difficult to decide, but seldom can a crucial decision have been made for worse ones. The former US Assistant Secretary of State George Ball has argued that one of the great disadvantages of 'the special relationship' was that for her own convenience the US Government often assisted Britain to avoid taking a decision needed to improve the long-term health of her economy.[33] This was one of those occasions. An immediate devaluation would have been blamed on the Conservatives and, more important, it was the right policy. The pound was overvalued by 10 to 15 per cent, and the alternative to devaluation was prolonged deflation – and eventual devaluation. This fatal mistake on Labour's first Saturday in office debilitated the six years of Labour Government, while in the short term the decision to magnify the gravity of the economic situation vastly exacerbated the Government's difficulties.

Wilson made as much as possible of a projected balance of payments deficit of £800 million. That figure – it turned out to be £750 million – was reached by adding together the capital and current accounts. Nearly half of the £750 million, as Maudling pointed out, was 'invested in mines, factories and oil wells overseas: new, income-producing assets bringing strength to Britain'. There were, as Wilson admitted on 23 November, 'reserves and borrowings more than adequate to meet' the trade gap, yet his deeply ingrained opposition habit of mind and his compulsion to attack his opponents destroyed overseas confidence and produced a savage sterling crisis. In July Wilson had promised a first 'hundred days of dynamic action'. Instead, his hundred days produced a sharp rise in Bank Rate, an increase in income tax, a new corporation tax, large international borrowing, an increase in mortgage rates and the breaking of nine international trading agreements – all without consulting our trading partners.[34]

Following Butler's acceptance of Wilson's offer of the Mastership of Trinity College, Cambridge, and a peerage, Home shuffled his Shadow Cabinet, transferring Maudling, at his own request, to foreign affairs and making Heath Shadow Chancellor. As a controversial Finance Bill would clearly follow Callaghan's first spring Budget, Maudling had made a serious tactical error; he gave Heath the chance to further his leadership prospects by leading a fierce fight against Callaghan's proposals. Heath had already seemed more addicted to political opposition than his rival, accepting only one City directorship while Maudling accumulated thirteen.[35] In any event, before there could be a new leader the rules had to be changed. As the 'magic circle' could not be permitted an encore, Home readily accepted the need to replace the old antiquated procedure.

Agreement was reached in February. The Chairman of the 1922 Committee would organise a vote of all the party's MPs; the winning candidate would require an overall majority and a lead of over 15 per cent. If these targets were not reached on a first ballot, nominations would be reopened; on the second ballot, a candidate would be elected if he or she received a simple overall majority. If not, the three candidates receiving the highest number of votes would go into a third and final ballot. Each voter would indicate his or her first and second preferences, and a candidate would at last secure a majority. As soon as the new procedure was in place, Alec Home should probably have used it to resign and stand again. Tory MPs were not agreed on a successor, and he would almost certainly have received a resounding vote of confidence. Unwisely, he declined to ask for one.[36]

On that most testing occasion for the Leader of the Opposition, the immediate answer to the Budget, Sir Alec made an excellent speech. Heath then gained new admirers for his organisational skills and the aggression which he and his team displayed in the fight against the Finance Bill, subjecting the House to a number of all-night sessions and inflicting three defeats on the Government. Although some of Heath's supporters agitated for a change at the top, the continuing possibility of a snap election provided strong protection for Home's continued leadership. In addition the Macleod camp mainly wanted him to stay, knowing that their man would have no chance in an early contest. Maudling, too, wanted Home to remain. Accordingly, Home announced on 26 June that he would continue as leader. Yet Wilson's virtually simultaneous announcement that there would be no election that year, which removed the chief barrier against another leadership struggle, immediately put that continuance in doubt.

Almost certainly Home could have clung on, had he really wanted to do so. The Conservatives had, after all, recently gained over 500 seats in the local elections. But, as he told James Margach, he did not think it made sense to 'go bashing ahead against a Government's policies' which might be right, just to make his back-benchers happy. Then, on a visit to the office of NOP, he was shown a poll which disclosed that not only did twice as many people think Harold Wilson was 'pleasant' as thought he was, but also that more people thought Wilson was 'straight' and 'sincere' – that was enough to make any man despair. In addition, an article in the *Sunday Times* by William Rees Mogg called 'The Right Moment to Change', which was rich in cricketing metaphors, evidently influenced his decision.[37]

More important, probably, were events in the parliamentary party. As Home wrote in his autobiography, 'there was a movement to displace me from the leadership. Ted Heath took no part in it . . . but it was there and it was unsettling.' On 5 July, on the initiative of a strong Heathite, the Executive of the 1922 Committee debated the leadership question. The eventual decision was that Home should stay, but the vote, which was kept secret, was nine to eight, and even that margin was achieved only by the casting vote of the Chairman. Evidently the older MPs were for Home, and the younger ones against him. Whatever the clinching factor, Home understandably decided he had had enough and announced his resignation on 22 July. The Conservative Party thus got it wrong again. Home should not have got the job, but neither should he have been pushed out of it. Despite his majority of two, Wilson was highly unlikely to be forced into an election. He would call one at the time of his own choosing when he was virtually certain to win. The party would have done better to go down to honourable defeat with Home than to impose that burden on a new leader.[38]

Iain Macleod immediately announced that he was not a candidate. A straight fight between Heath and Maudling would have been a rerun of Macmillan v. Butler with no right-wing candidate. Although Heath is sometimes said to have been the right-wing candidate in 1965, his campaign was run by Peter Walker, assisted by Charles Morrison and others, all of whom were on the left of the party, while Maudling's campaign was run by Patrick Wall, Tony Lambton and William Clark, all of whom were on the right of the party. Furthermore, Macleod and most of those closest to him voted for Heath. Another apparent resemblance to 1957 was that the Heath campaign like Macmillan's had been discreetly in operation for some time, while Maudling's like Butler's had not. Maudling had had something of a row with Home about the timing of his departure, Patrick Wall complaining of it at the meeting of 'the 1922', and the Maudlingites were certainly less well prepared than the Heathites. Yet, unlike Butler's in 1956–7, the Maudling campaign had already been much more active than most people realised.[39]

The chief difference from 1957 was the intervention of a right-wing candidate – Enoch Powell. He had no chance of winning but was evidently anxious to put down a marker for the future.* Powell had continued his free-market crusade from inside the Shadow Cabinet and was gaining adherents, but they were not ready to see him as a potential leader. His free-market thinking even failed to attract the support of Margaret Thatcher, who was persuaded by Keith Joseph to vote for Edward Heath. Hence Powell's candidacy was an error: his meagre fifteen votes made him seem less influential in the party than he was.[40]

Peter Walker ran the Heath campaign far better than anybody ran Maudling's. The Maudling team was naïve enough to believe MPs' expressions of support; consequently it was complacent. Much of the press came out for Heath, but, as Churchill once remarked, Members of Parliament do 'not take their opinions from the newspapers'. Fortunately for Heath, they do not take them from the public either.

---

* Putting down such a marker is usually mocked by the future. Geoffrey Howe, Jim Prior and John Peyton all put down markers in 1975. Like Enoch Powell, none of them took part in the next leadership election.

Polls in the *Express* and the *Mail* put Maudling well ahead. Walker's final estimate of Heath's support was just under 160 votes. He won 150 which, as Maudling won 133, meant that he had not quite cleared the 15 per cent hurdle erected by the new rules. Maudling, however, despite being 'intensely' shaken by 'this rejection', soon rang up Heath to concede, to congratulate him and to offer to serve.[41]

Edward Heath made few changes in the Shadow Cabinet. Maudling became Deputy Leader; Home, Shadow Foreign Secretary; and Macleod, Shadow Chancellor. The only other important change was the promotion of Powell from Transport to Defence. During the leadership contest Quintin Hogg had summed up the difference between the two principal candidates: with Heath we should have to fasten our seat-belts because the flight would be bumpy, whereas with Maudling we should have a much quieter time but might just go on taxiing around the airport without ever taking off. Before long, a number of MPs began to wonder whether a bit more taxiing down the runway might have been preferable. Heath had won support because he was thought to be the man most likely to unsettle the Prime Minister. Even Richard Crossman, who believed Maudling would have been 'a far better, wiser leader', thought Heath would be 'the more formidable'. That soon looked doubtful. Admittedly in the Prime Minister–Leader of the Opposition tournament, because it is easier and more conclusive to give a telling answer than to ask a telling question, the advantage lies heavily with the Prime Minister. But certainly, in the opening rounds after the leadership election, Wilson easily worsted Heath, who could never match his opponent's verbal dexterity.[42]

As Crossman also noted, the two men had much in common. They shared similar backgrounds, were the same age (forty-nine), and were seen as representative of a new technocratic era. Both, too, were dedicated to politics although, unlike Wilson, Heath had serious outside interests in music and sailing. Temperamentally, however, they were very different. Unlike his predecessor Hugh Gaitskell, Wilson preferred compromise to combat within his own party, whereas Heath had shown over RPM that at least on some occasions he preferred combat to compromise. Heath abhorred Wilson's addiction to gimmicks, which was particularly indulged while Labour had a tiny majority; they were useful for diverting attention from the Government's troubles.[43]

Around this time Heath seems to have undergone something of a personality change, or maybe there always had been two Heaths. Gone at any rate was the genial, humane and successful Chief Whip of the 1950s, and in his place, in public, was a brusque and dour Leader of the Party. Although Henry Kissinger was right in thinking that Heath's 'renowned aloofness was more apparent than real', it was very apparent to his back-benchers – and not only to them. Reggie Maudling denied the 'consistent rumours of arguments between Ted and myself'. Yet their relations were not intimate. 'We seldom if ever had a meal alone together,' Maudling recalled, even though they were Leader and Deputy Leader.[44]

When he became leader, Heath inherited the results of a policy review which, as Chairman of the Advisory Committee on Policy, he had overseen under Home. In 1964–5 the Conservative Party, said its then Chairman, 'reformed under fire'. John Blakenham meant that because of the certainty of an early election the party had to do things at speed rather than in style. Yet the election threat did not inhibit attempts at detailed policy-making. As one of the brightest lights in the Conservative Research Department, James Douglas, told Michael Fraser, 'too many people are doing too many things too superficially'. From 1964 to 1970 the party went to the other (and wrong) extreme from Churchill's, and in Opposition it accumulated an excess baggage of policy for which it later had to pay.[45]

The policy studies were collected and published in time for the 1965 Party Conference. Unlike his predecessors who had merely descended from on high to deliver a speech at the leader's rally at its end, Heath was present throughout the conference. *Putting Britain Right Ahead* – the final word was added at the last minute because Maudling feared that people might ask who had put Britain wrong – made few promises but contained many policy proposals. The Conservatives intended to increase incentives by cutting taxation, when circumstances allowed, and to reform the trade unions. If the document had a theme, it was to make Britain more efficient so that she would be fit to prosper in Europe. Nothing was said about a prices and incomes policy. This was partly because of differences in the Shadow Cabinet – Maudling was strongly for one, Powell and Joseph against – and partly because the Wilson Government's adoption of an incomes policy had made the question more difficult.[46]

Oppositions can and do choose particular issues on which to fight. But because Governments act while Oppositions can only talk and because people generally vote against a Government rather than for an Opposition, the actions and the stance of a Government have been the predominant influence in determining the site of the political battle. In the nineties the Labour Opposition was able to occupy the centre ground only because the Conservative Government had long since left it. In the sixties the Conservative Opposition had much more difficulty in occupying the centre ground because the Labour Government was firmly encamped there. The Wilson administration was even less 'socialist' than the Attlee Government had been.

Iain Macleod thought it was possible to argue that on trade unions and immigration *Putting Britain Right Ahead* represented a move to the right, and on Europe and the social services 'a victory for the left'. The terms 'right' and 'left', he added, had very little meaning inside the Tory Party; but while that may have been so in the past it became less true during the sixties as a segment of the party became increasingly ideological.[47]

When taxed with the omission of the incomes policy from *Putting Britain Right Ahead*, Heath replied that there was more to an incomes policy than just the setting of a norm; the whole section on employment amounted to an incomes policy. That explanation was true in one important sense: an incomes policy was unlikely to work for long, if at all, in the absence of other measures. In any case the omission was only temporary. After a public disagreement between Maudling and Powell, the Shadow Cabinet came down on Maudling's side, and the 1966 election manifesto maintained that 'our new economic programme [would] make a prices and incomes policy really effective'. *Putting Britain Right Ahead* was a series of policy proposals rather than a thoroughgoing philosophical review, because the party divide between the pro-free-market Conservatives led by Powell and the pragmatists led by Maudling put an agreed and coherent philosophical document out of the question.[48]

Another deep division in the Tory Party which, no less unfairly, made Heath seem ineffective, was over Southern Rhodesia. Heath's reaction to the Declaration of Independence by the Southern Rhodesian Government in November 1965 was, and remained, far better-judged and more far-sighted than that of Wilson – who grandiloquently boasted of ending the rebellion in 'weeks rather than months', unnecessarily involved the United Nations in the problem, and mistakenly refused to talk to the Rhodesian leader, Ian Smith. As usual, the Wilson Government combined strong words with weak actions. Yet, because of Tory divisions, Wilson was able to make party capital over the issue, accusing the Conservatives of supporting the Rhodesian rebels. In a vote in December on the imposition of oil sanctions, fifty right-wing Conservatives voted against them, thirty-one left-wingers voted with the Government, and the rest followed the Shadow Cabinet in abstaining. In 1946 the party had similarly split three ways over the US loan. Yet unlike Churchill, Ted Heath, who had never been Prime Minister, was not immune to charges of weak and ineffective leadership. His popularity went on falling; his Gallup rating, which had been fifty after he became leader, was down to 40 by February, scarcely higher than Douglas-Home's a year earlier.

The Rhodesian crisis and *Putting Britain Right Ahead* caused a minor eruption against the leadership by Angus Maude. A clever man and a good speaker, Maude had been unlucky not to achieve office in the Conservative Governments of the fifties; exasperated by his exclusion, he left politics to edit the *Sydney Morning Herald*. When that venture did not prosper either, Maude returned to British politics only to be defeated in the South Dorset by-election in 1962 by the intervention of an anti-Common Market candidate. No doubt soured by these experiences, he eventually returned to Westminster as Member for Stratford-upon-Avon in 1964, later becoming a front-bench spokesman on Commonwealth affairs. Having fired a sighting shot in the *Sunday Telegraph*, Maude took careful aim at the Tory leadership in January 1966 in an article in the *Spectator* called 'Winter of Tory Discontent'. Beginning with the assertions that the Conservative Party had 'completely lost effective political initiative', had worried its supporters in the country, and had become to the electorate 'a meaningless irrelevance', Maude suggested that Edward Heath, unlike previous Conservative leaders, was unwilling to discuss what the people wanted and to impart a needful change of direction. 'For Tories simply to talk like technocrats', Maude wrote in an obvious strike at Heath, 'will get us nowhere.' The Tories needed to differentiate their policy clearly from Labour and to 'stop pussyfooting' about the trade unions, direct taxation and the social services.[49]

As Sir Gerald Nabarro, temporarily out of the Commons and himself a truculent critic of his party in the past, pointed out, Maude simply ignored the deep party divisions on prices and incomes, Rhodesia and other matters. Heath had been put in an impossible position. If he left Maude where he was, he would appear a weak leader. If he sacked him, he would look intolerant and dictatorial. After some hesitation, he decided intolerance was the lesser evil, thus making another important enemy in the party. And a decade later that enemy had the last laugh when, during Margaret Thatcher's successful leadership challenge, Maude largely wrote her important article for the *Daily Telegraph* attacking Heath's record.[50]

'The current Tory malaise', as Nigel Lawson, Iain Macleod's successor as editor of the paper, wrote in the *Spectator* in early 1966, had 'nothing to do with Mr Heath'. Its true cause was that

the party no longer has an *idée force* in which it can believe and on which it can crusade. The Empire has gone, and the Commonwealth is no substitute. Old-fashioned liberalism (individual liberty, free trade, laissez-faire and the market economy) needs too many qualifications today to pass as an *idée force* for anybody except Mr Powell. Europe, perhaps alone, could still be an *idée force* for the Conservatives, as Mr Heath well recognises; but the time for that is yet to come.[51]

It probably would have come in the 1970s, had the 1974 election result been different. As it was, the party remained without an *idée force* until the late seventies when it adopted the old-fashioned liberalism which Mr Lawson had decried and which, ironically, despite his part as a speechwriter and adviser to Ted Heath up to 1975, he himself then fashionably espoused.

A fortnight after Maude's article, Labour won the marginal seat of Hull North after Barbara Castle promised to build a bridge over the River Humber – as has been well said, 'the intervention was hardly more necessary than the bridge itself'. If repeated in a general election, the 3.8 per cent swing there would give Labour a working majority, and after some hesitation the Prime Minister decided to go to the polls on 31 March.[52]

Had the Government been in office for longer, the Tories would have had a good chance. For all Wilson's talk in Opposition of 'white heat' and radical action, his Government was devoid of both. He dwelt on 'the thirteen wasted years', yet did little to remedy whatever he thought had been wrong with them; he had talked much about modernisation, but made Frank Cousins, the trade-union dinosaur, the Minister of Technology. The new Department of Economic Affairs was supposed to break the Treasury's monopoly over economic matters; on paper that was an excellent idea, but it remained on paper. The Treasury knights might not be skilful at running the economy, but in defending their own power and position their skills were unrivalled. The new Ministry had no chance against them, and the little hope that it might have had disappeared when devaluation was ruled out. That decision had also doomed George Brown's much-vaunted National Plan long before it was unveiled. Instead of expanding at the unrealistic 4 per cent rate put forward in the Plan, the growth rate had sharply declined to 2.5 per cent, and instead of a successful incomes policy, which in practice consisted merely of loud exhortation from Brown, inflation was appreciably higher than it had been in 1964. To describe Labour's unfortunate combination of stagnation and inflation, the new Shadow Chancellor coined the word 'stagflation', a word which was to see much service in subsequent years.[53]

All in all, the Wilson Government had little to boast of, but it had survived; and that was enough. For the election was fought not on Labour's current performance, but on the past; and not on Labour's recent past but on that of the Conservatives. The Conservative manifesto, *Action Not Words*, maintained that 'the Labour Government has had its opportunities and has failed'. Conceding that it was easy enough to say, 'Give them another chance', it claimed that to do so 'would be taking an immense chance with everybody's future'. On Labour's performance to date that was fair comment. The trouble was that most people did think that Labour had not had a fair chance and tended to blame not Labour but the Conservatives for what had gone wrong. Wilson's exaggeration of the economic crisis he had inherited had done much damage to the British economy, but it had brought the Labour Government a large political dividend.[54]

The other Conservative problem was similarly insoluble, for, however good their current policies, they had no answer to the question, 'Why did you not operate them during your thirteen years in office?' *Action Not Words* was surprisingly well received by the press, perhaps because it was so conveniently short. While Labour's manifesto was 10,000 words, the Conservatives needed only 3,000 for theirs. Yet brevity was almost its only virtue. When it was discussed at a planning meeting, Douglas-Home sensibly suggested that 'ideas' should also be included. Certainly it contained none. The manifesto read less like a political document than a Commander-in-Chief's staccato orders for a massive offensive on all conceivable fronts. Most paragraphs were one or two lines long and, if the document did not manage to accommodate a single idea, Ian Macleod calculated that it included no fewer than 131 'distinct specific promises'. For all the impact they had, the party might just as well have promised nothing at all.[55]

The Conservative pledges in *Action Not Words* enabled James Callaghan to turn one of the Tories' most trusty weapons against them, asking them how they would find the money to pay for all their promises, which included lower taxation.[56] Yet Labour did not need extra ammunition. There was never any possibility of the Government losing; by polling day the odds against a Conservative victory had stretched to twenty to one. Labour gained 6 per cent more of the vote than the Conservatives, whose vote fell by nearly 600,000 even though the Liberal share of the vote also dropped. Peter Thorneycroft and Christopher Soames were among those who lost their seats. Wilson returned to Downing Street with a majority of ninety-six over all other parties.

Heath had trailed much further behind Wilson than his party behind Labour, but he had fought a good campaign and, like Gaitskell's in

1959, his reputation was enhanced by defeat. In any case his warnings about the economy were soon vindicated by events. More than most electoral victories, Labour's in 1966 was gained on a false prospectus. Just before the campaign began, Callaghan assured the Commons that he saw 'no reason for severe increases in taxation this year', and during it Wilson painted a glowing picture of the future. Yet as soon as the election was safely won, optimism was abandoned and Callaghan announced severe increases in taxation. In his book on the Labour Government, Wilson denied that the change was for 'electoral reasons'. Callaghan's appreciation on both occasions, according to Wilson, was 'strictly based on Treasury advice [and was] an honest non-political assessment'. Even if the first assertion is true, both Wilson and Callaghan were fully aware how fallible Treasury advice had recently been. The second assertion is implausible. With the exception of Stafford Cripps, no Chancellor since the war would have been capable of making a 'non-political assessment' a few weeks before a general election, and certainly not one in a Government led by Harold Wilson.[57]

Whatever the reason for the Government's reassuring economic optimism during the election, its switch to pessimism necessitating a deflationary Budget in May was not enough to restore confidence. A sterling crisis followed in July, which was the moment to undo the mistake of 1964 and devalue the pound. Devaluation accompanied by some deflation would have been the right policy, but only six Cabinet Ministers – including Brown, Jenkins and Crosland – favoured it; so the Cabinet opted for deflation alone. Taxes were raised, expenditure cut and a six-month wage freeze imposed.[58]

Ted Heath could justifiably claim that he had been proved right, but neither he nor his party gained any immediate advantage from the July measures. Heath needed electoral, or at least opinion poll, success to abate his unpopularity in the parliamentary party and to give him more authority to resolve policy differences. In what the Army used to call 'man management', the wartime colonel and successful Chief Whip showed himself as a leader to be deplorably defective. To back-benchers he did not know well, he was often distant or even rude, sometimes not even recognising them or realising they were MPs. What was readily forgiven Churchill in his late seventies was not forgiven Heath. Yet no offsetting electoral popularity was visible. By February 1967 Heath's poll ratings had fallen to the then unprecedentedly low figure of 24 per cent. In the same month, despite the Government's failures, the Opposition was eleven points behind it.[59]

In 1966 the Wilson Government adopted the Tory policy of attempting to enter the EEC. Even if Wilson's discovery of Europe was, as Hugh Cudlipp of the pro-Europe *Daily Mirror* put it, a gigantic attempt 'to distract attention from Rhodesia and the economic mess at home', it was still an important shift. For all the Conservative denunciations of Labour for being 'doctrinaire' and 'socialist', the Wilson Government, with the single exception of its renationalisation of steel, was neither. It was merely incompetent. Yet to keep their troops happy and to conceal from them that they were faced with a centrist Government, the Opposition front bench attacked (with the exception of Wilson's attempt to join the Common Market, which it creditably supported), every measure the Government introduced, especially its attempts to make its incomes policy effective. A number of Tory MPs resented going into the division lobby night after night to vote against measures which they considered in the circumstances to be inescapable, but the bulk of the party was happy to think they were fighting 'socialism'.[60]

Only in March 1967, when the full impact of the July measures was at last felt, did the electorate come to the aid of Edward Heath. Even then, his own ratings stayed abysmally low; yet the Conservatives won the Glasgow Pollock by-election and in April moved ahead of the Government in the polls, remaining there until 1970. The big cities were not then no-go areas for the party, and in the local elections the Conservatives took control of Bradford, Leeds, Liverpool, Manchester and Newcastle, and almost annihilated Labour in London, winning eighty-two of the 100 seats on the GLC. In the autumn two more by-election gains were made at Cambridge and Walthamstow West – the latter on a swing of 18.4 per cent.

Then in November Wilson was forced to admit defeat and devalue the pound from $2.80 to $2.40. The Opposition was fully entitled to criticise the Government for its economic failings which had made devaluation inevitable. Unfortunately Heath went much further, treating devaluation as a moral and patriotic issue, and as being wrong in principle, when it was almost the first sensible economic decision that the Government had taken.[61]

Heath had been elected because his supporters thought he would be a tougher and more aggressive Opposition leader than Maudling. Yet he never relished the role of carping critic of a Prime Minister who ignored the usual rules of engagement. Even less congenial than attacking Labour was the next major challenge that faced him: a long, drawn-out and deeply injurious row which erupted within his own party.

CHAPTER
X

The Powellite Challenge

James Callaghan, correctly, resigned over devaluation and went to the Home Office. He was succeeded by Roy Jenkins, who after some initial fumbling ensured the success of devaluation and turned out to be one of the three best Chancellors in the half-century since the war – the other two being Butler and Clarke. Jenkins was also a great reforming Home Secretary. During the six years of the Labour Government much of the 'Victorian corsetry' of our social legislation was unlaced and destroyed.[1]

These social reforms are particularly associated with Jenkins, although the abolition of capital punishment and the reform of the divorce laws took place before and after his tenure as Home Secretary. Much as Butler when Home Secretary had helped Jenkins's Obscene Publication Bill reach the statute book, Jenkins now assisted private members' bills, which legalised homosexuality and abortion under certain circumstances, to become law. Most Tories favoured less governmental interference with the economy while opposing a similar liberalism on moral issues. Most Labour MPs favoured the opposite, and since there were more of them than there were Tories and since some Tories agreed with them, the bills went through.

Many Conservative supporters in the constituencies would have welcomed a Tory move to restore capital punishment, but Heath, Macleod and Joseph, like Powell, voted in favour of permanent abolition in December 1969. Indeed, to their credit, the Opposition accepted all of Labour's social reforms including those on race relations, sexual equality, censorship, and civil rights. The reforms of the sixties produced what their enemies called 'the permissive society' and what Jenkins called 'the civilised society' – it was both. Then and later, the reforms were attacked by right-wing newspapers and politicians who looked more leniently at 'permissive', though scarcely 'civilised', practices in financial and economic affairs. Yet few if any of the politicians who castigated 'the permissive society' ever said which of the reforms they wished to repeal, and even after eighteen years of Thatcherite rule all of them were still on the statute book. Except for capital punishment, for which right-wing Tories and most of the public continued to hanker, they enjoyed considerable and growing popular support.

Jenkins's economic regime at the Treasury was anything but permissive; its necessary strictness was highly unpopular. Consequently the Conservative by-election successes continued; and until the middle of 1969 the Opposition was usually more than twenty points ahead in the public opinion polls. That naturally lifted Conservative morale. Yet the improvement in the party's fortunes was soon overshadowed by a row created by Enoch Powell. One of Edward Heath's fundamental objectives was entry into Europe. Hence a reason for Powell being a good choice for the Shadow Defence job was his enthusiasm for European unity. In April 1965 the One-Nation Group had published a pamphlet called *One Europe*. Like other One-Nation members of the Shadow Cabinet, Powell, who had voted for entry into the EEC in 1961 and was to do so again in 1967, did not sign the pamphlet, but he not only strongly agreed with its content, he wrote about a quarter of it himself. The rest was largely written by his disciple Nicholas Ridley, who shortly afterwards was his chief backer in the leadership election.[2]

One Europe would today be denounced by the Europhobic press as 'federalist'. After ridiculing the 'sovereignty' argument – pointing out that 'no country can be an economic island today' and that Britain had already lost much 'sovereignty' to such organisations as IMF, GATT, NATO and UNO – it urged Britain not to be frightened of political union. By joining in the political working of the Community, we could 'wield our influence on its policies as a whole'. And 'political integration', *One Europe* maintained, 'must go hand in hand with economic or military combination'; it came down, too, in favour of a European nuclear deterrent and even a common foreign policy.[3]

A wartime brigadier, Powell had clear and often far-sighted views on military combinations and other matters. Once he had belatedly realised that the loss of India had transformed Britain's position in the world, Powell shed every vestige of his imperial ideas and drew the logical conclusion: Britain was now a European power and should deploy her armed forces in accordance with this new reality. Since she no longer had an empire, her continued maintenance of military outposts all over the world was an absurdity as well as an expense which she could not afford. Before long, all British parties came to share Powell's insight, but only because of the pressure of events, and not in the years 1965–7. At that time Powell had few supporters in the parliamentary party, being closer to Labour's left wing than to most of his colleagues or to the Labour Government.[4]

In 1965 Powell believed that the party leader's views on defence were similar to his own. For that reason he asked for the Shadow Defence job; presumably he was right, or Heath would not have given it to him. Certainly such ideas well accorded with Heath's views on Europe and on the need to strengthen the British economy. On the other hand, the party's foreign affairs and defence establishment and the great majority of its MPs were 'East of Suez' men. This came as no surprise to Enoch Powell. At a One-Nation dinner in May 1964 attended by only three other members, Powell, who had just come from a meeting of the party's Foreign Affairs Committee where everybody present had been jingoistic on Aden except himself, had remarked that the Conservative Party's capacity for being wrong for the eighth time in exactly the same way as in the previous seven without noticing always amazed him. At other One-Nation dinners in 1965–6 Powell more than once emphasised his belief that on defence Ted Heath agreed with him. At the 1965 Party Conference Powell spoke in favour of concentrating Britain's defence effort in Europe, effectively questioning her world-wide role. This was directly contrary to the views of most of his audience, but such was the power of his oratory that he won an enthusiastic standing ovation.[5]

Powell was also something of a party heretic on nuclear weapons and even more so on Vietnam. Like his colleagues, he accepted that Britain's independent nuclear deterrent was essential for her security, but unlike them he believed that nuclear weapons only deterred a nuclear attack. Hence nuclear weapons were no substitute for conventional ones, and Britain should, therefore, build up her conventional forces to aid the defence of Europe. Powell's scepticism about the value of nuclear weapons annoyed his colleagues, and Heath vetoed a CPC pamphlet by him. Yet here too, Powell, however inconveniently, was largely right.[6]

In opposing the Vietnam War, Powell was in a much smaller minority in the party. Two back-benchers later wrote a letter to *The Times* saying it was a war the Americans could not win, but they were almost alone. During the 1966 election Vietnam caused a public difference between Powell and the leadership. According to Powell, he was told by Central Office that Heath wished him to comment on the rumour that the US was pressing Britain to send troops to Vietnam. He therefore did so, with the additional comment that under Labour Britain had 'behaved, perfectly clearly and perfectly recognisably, as an American satellite'. Once again Powell was right. The American and British Governments, we now know, had made a secret agreement, under which the US propped up the pound in return for Britain not devaluing or withdrawing from east of Suez. In Ben Pimlott's words, Britain was 'the United States' hired help'. Unfortunately Heath, recently back from Vietnam, strongly supported the American intervention there and believed it would be successful. Accordingly, Central Office issued a statement disowning Powell.[7]

Whatever its cause, the incident did not help Powell–Heath relations. These had already been soured by what Powell regarded as Heath's resiling from support of Powell's defence views, although the balance of opinion against Powell in the Shadow Cabinet and elsewhere in the party gave Heath little alternative. In any case, as Powell's biographer Rob Shepherd suggests, the estrangement over defence between Powell and Heath was probably a prime cause of the break between them in 1968.[8]

Immediately after the election, 'words not action', Powell told the City of London Young Conservatives, best described the role of the party, adding that some of the words would be 'harsh, fierce, destructive ... aimed in defiance and contempt at men and policies we detest'.[9] Predictably, Powell's contempt and defiance were not confined to the policies of the Labour Government. He almost equally detested some of the policies of his own party. Despite his defence responsibilities, the main thrust of the Powellite crusade was still towards economics where his *laissez-faire* doctrines had in Maudling, Boyle and others some formidable opponents.

Heath and Macleod had to try to bridge the gap. Spurning Powellite dogma, they clung to the 'sensible and pragmatic compromise between the extremes of collectivism and individualism' extolled by Macmillan in his Blackpool letter. This inevitably gave Heath an aura of weakness, picturesquely described by Richard Crossman who at that time saw Powell as the coming man:

> The titular leader sits nervously strumming on his piano in Albany, while our latter-day Savonarola rampages round the country summoning devout congregations of the faithful to reject as heretics those Conservative leaders [who] in his view have departed from the straight and narrow path of nineteenth-century *laissez-faire*.

Crossman foreshadowed much post-1975 right-wing propaganda, when the heresy-hunting was extended from Heath and Maudling to all the post-war Conservative leaders.[10]

When transport spokesman, Powell had advocated the denationalisation of the airlines. In his speech after the 1966 election he told the Young Conservatives that believers in free enterprise had to 'liberate themselves from the ratchet of nationalisation which seems always to advance and never retreat'. This was probably the first mention of the imaginary ratchet which was to figure so prominently in right-wing speeches in the next decade.[11]

Later, Powell's follower Nicholas Ridley persuaded the policy group of which he was chairman to come out in favour of a radical programme of denationalisation. The report was very weak on the financial implications of such a policy, which would anyway have been electorally damaging, if not suicidal. Moreover, the party already had too much policy. Accordingly Heath and the Shadow Cabinet buried it. Ted Heath has been much criticised by the New Right for his negative attitude to the subject. Such criticism demonstrates the danger of reading history backwards. When the Ridley report was considered by the Economic Policy Group, the Shadow Minister of Power said that 'coal alone was a commodity which it might be realistic to see as sold in competition with other products. All the other power industries, however, were public utilities . . . This in fact meant that they were bound to be monopolies and would have to remain public enterprises.' The Shadow Minister was Margaret Thatcher.[12]

Nevertheless, Powell thought he was winning the battle for the free market within the Conservative Party. 'It's only Reggie Maudling who's the problem,' he told Crossman after debating with him at the Cambridge Union, 'and Reggie is so busy with his business affairs that he's hardly ever with us. If it was not for him,' Powell continued, 'I think Iain Macleod would go along with us.' Powell did not think much of Macleod as an economist: 'You really ought to take an interest in economics,' he would say. Others did not think much of Powell as an economist. Basing his judgement on a collection of Powell's speeches, Samuel Brittan wrote that Powell seems 'to have read no economics'. A decade earlier Robert Hall had said much the same of Powell in his diary. At that time Harold Macmillan thought Powell (and Birch) brought to their study of economic problems an inappropriate 'degree of fanaticism'. Certainly in the sixties Enoch Powell, even in private, argued the *laissez-faire* case with an uncritical passion which bordered on the fanatical.[13]

Iain Macleod's attitude was at the other extreme from bigotry; on economics he was agnostic, if not atheistic. He was not an economist and had no wish to become one. He was opposed to Powell's 'ivory tower economics' and avoided large theoretical pronouncements, partly because they were likely to be wrong and partly because he wanted to hold the party together, not split it with dogma. Macleod's natural ability, eye for essentials, command of the Commons, power of invective, skill at marshalling his team, as well as his hatred of unemployment at a time of almost continuous economic trouble for the Government, made him an outstandingly effective Opposition spokesman. He was also a good spotter of talent. Before she had had much chance to shine, Macleod decided that he must have Margaret Thatcher as his deputy. Not long afterwards, having heard his deputy in particularly effective action, he told Angus Maude that it was no longer absurd to think that 'there might one day be a woman Prime Minister'.[14]

As Macleod once said, he enjoyed travelling with Enoch but preferred to leave the train before it ran into the buffers. Almost certainly, there-fore, Powell was wrong in thinking that, but for Maudling, Macleod would have gone along with him. In any case, in March 1968 Macleod and Robert Carr, the Shadow Employment Minister, belatedly recom-mended to the Shadow Cabinet that the party should cease to vote against every Government order that sought to implement its incomes policy. Macleod was opposed to a compulsory incomes policy but argued that in Government the party would need one for the public sector and for trying to influence 'key wage negotiations'. That view was accepted, and the decision was the last Shadow Cabinet tussle with Powell on that subject. Before the end of the year Macleod attacked Powell as a 'pedlar of panaceas', but he was not talking about economics.[15]

Foaming Tiber

In 1961 Enoch Powell had pressed for stricter controls on immigration than those that were later embodied in the 1962 Act. Yet when his lips were unsealed by his return to the back-benches in autumn 1963, they scarcely moved on immigration. His only pronouncement on the subject was more in accordance with his free-market principles than his later view on Commonwealth immigration. 'The immigrants who have come already . . . *are* part of the community,' he wrote in June 1964. 'Money is colour-blind, and economic forces will help the work of integration which must be done if a homogeneous community, local and national, is to be restored.' During the election he told the local press that, locally, immigration was the 'biggest issue', emphasising that control of it was essential. He thought that the numbers being admitted were excessive, and as there was 'an inescapable obligation of humanity to permit the wives and young children of immigrants already here to join them', new admissions should be further reduced. In line with this humanitarian stance, Powell kept well clear of the racialist campaign that was being waged in nearby Smethwick.[16]

After the election, Powell hardened his line. So did the party, but not as much as he did. Powell now urged that Commonwealth immigrants should be treated like those from foreign countries, which meant that they would lose the right to bring in their families: he also suggested that many immigrants who were unhappy here should be encouraged 'to return home'. Yet there was nothing offensive in Powell's speeches on this important issue – especially important in his constituency, Wolverhampton. He was not exploiting the racial issue for political gain. Indeed, while he had space in his 1966 election address to make a strong plea for the removal of barriers between Britain and Europe, he mentioned immigration only in passing.[17]

In 1967–8, because of the actions of the Kenyan government, Britain faced an influx of Kenyan Asians. Duncan Sandys and Powell called for tough controls. These speeches influenced both the Kenyan Asians – by stimulating their immigration – and the British Government, who decided to curb it. In his speech at Walsall in February, Powell for the first time on this issue used emotive language, which produced complaints about his tone from Quintin Hogg, the Shadow Home Secretary, and Iain Macleod in Shadow Cabinet. His speech also brought 800 letters in his support, and Callaghan introduced legislation to deprive Kenyan Asians of their right of entry. In the *Spectator* Auberon Waugh stigmatised his bill as 'one of the more immoral pieces of legislation to have emerged from any British Parliament'; it was certainly a clear breach of a promise that Britain had earlier given. Although the Shadow Cabinet supported the legislation, Macleod and fourteen Tory MPs from the right and the left of the party joined thirty-five Labour MPs and the Liberals in voting against it.[18]

In April the Shadow Cabinet had to decide its attitude to Callaghan's new Race Relations Bill. His opposite number, Hogg, who was a moderate, objected to parts of the bill but had come to the conclusion that some such legislation was necessary. Macleod, Joseph, Boyle and Carr were all anxious not to vote against the bill; so were many backbenchers. Eventually, to preserve the unity of the Shadow Cabinet and the party, and to avoid an all-out battle with the Government, a reasoned amendment with only a two-line whip was decided upon. Heath asked each member of the Shadow Cabinet if he had any comment. Powell, who according to Hogg had 'a face like a sphinx' and remained silent throughout the discussion, had none. He was a member of the subcommittee set up to draft the amendment, and confirmed to Hogg that he accepted the very mild wording that had been agreed. If the wording had been less anodyne, or if the decision had been to vote against the bill, a number of back-benchers who abstained would have voted for the bill.[19]

Powell gave no inkling to Hogg or to any of his colleagues that in three days' time he was going to make an explosive speech on the subject. Yet he told a friend that his speech 'would go up like a rocket and would stay up'; so he was fully aware of the importance of what he was about to say in Birmingham. That famous speech was propelled upwards or downwards not by any dramatic new proposals but by its sensational language, its heavy racialist tone and its grubby use of (apparently inaccurate) 'hearsay' anecdotes. Not only was Powell's language apocalyptic, his figures were wrong and his logic was twisted. What was discriminatory, according to him, was not racial discrimination but the legislation that tried to stop it. 'The kindest thing', he maintained, that could be said of those who supported such legislation – who in various degrees included his colleagues, Heath, Hogg, Joseph, Boyle and Carr – was 'that they know not what they do'. Powell ended with his famous quotation from Virgil: 'As I look ahead, I am filled with foreboding. Like the Roman, I seem to see "the River Tiber foaming with much blood".'[20]

In The Times William Rees-Mogg's leading article termed the speech 'disgraceful' because it was 'calculated to inflame hatred between the races'. This was 'the first time that a serious British politician [had] appealed to racial hatred, in this direct way, in our post-war history'. That was true, for, as we have seen in earlier chapters, British politicians, other than Churchill, had stayed at the opposite extreme and been consistently and lamentably short-sighted over immigration. They allowed it to take place without the British people feeling they had been consulted, and the failure of politicians of all parties (including Powell) to respond to popular fears and resentment had done much to diminish public faith in British institutions. Yet by the time Enoch Powell made immigration his leading issue, Britain was well on the way to becoming a multi-racial society; hence he had a duty to treat the issue responsibly and not, as Hogg chided him, to go about flicking cigarette ash over gunpowder.[21]

The Birmingham speech evoked an unparalleled public response. Powell received over 100,000 letters, nearly all of them favourable. Eight hundred dockers marched to Westminster in his support; so did some Smithfield porters, and the Kenyan High Commissioner was insulted because he was black. Similar marches were seen in Wolverhampton and elsewhere. More predictably, the Monday Club and the National Front gave Powell their backing. But if Powell's speech went up 'like a rocket' and stayed up, Powell himself soon thudded to earth and stayed down.

Like Rees-Mogg, Powell's colleagues were outraged by the racialist feel of his speech, and they had another cause for anger: the way he had treated them. Powell claimed that it had been unnecessary to give them warning of his speech because it was in line with party policy. That was sophistry. Some of his colleagues had already complained of the far less aggressive phrasing of his speech at Walsall, and Powell's command of English and his careful use of inflammatory language eliminated any possibility that he did not know his words would cause a sensation. He was similarly aware that his Birmingham speech jarred with the reasoned amendment, which was to be debated three days after his speech and to which he had given his *imprimatur* only three days before it. As well as telling Whitelaw, the Chief Whip, what he proposed to say, Powell's minimum obligation was to clear his words with Hogg, who had responsibility for race relations; yet when presented with the opportunity to inform Hogg of his speech, Powell went out of his way not to take it. He did not even send his speech to Central Office for circulation to the press, which would of course have given the Chairman of the Party notice of what was about to happen.[22]

Appalled by what Powell had said, Ted Heath decided to sack him. He would in any case have had no option. Margaret Thatcher 'strongly sympathised with the gravamen' of Powell's argument and favoured no action. But Hogg, Macleod, Boyle, Carr and others would have resigned if Powell had stayed. Heath told Powell that he was dismissing him because he considered his speech 'to have been racialist in tone and liable to exacerbate racial tension'. Powell was not a racist, yet he had made a racialist speech. He was an honourable man, yet he had behaved dishonourably to his colleagues – so much so that Whitelaw decided that he could never trust him again.[23]

Powell's earlier relative quiescence on immigration suggests that it was not the issue itself, but some combination of ambition, frustration and lack of judgement that drove him to behave in an atypical way. Maybe Powell was temperamentally and intellectually unsuited to British collegiate government (or shadow government) and could not for long bear its restraints. Earlier in April he had told the *Sunday Times* that he deliberately included a startling assertion in every speech to attract enough attention to give him 'a power base' in the party, so that 'Ted Heath can never sack me from the Shadow Cabinet'. That hubris duly led to nemesis. The only doubt was whether in the long run the nemesis would be his or Heath's.[24]

Whatever the cause of his behaviour, its results were to make Enoch Powell the best-known, most popular politician in Britain and to wreck his political career. The public sided with Powell; the parliamentary party did not. Yet Powell's popularity outside Parliament was a standing reproach to Heath, whose own approval rating had dropped below thirty. Before the conference in 1968, Heath moved the party's policy towards Powell by favouring tighter controls on immigration, and Powell extended his challenge to industrial policy, while Wilson enjoyed himself at Labour's conference by treating Powell, not Heath, as the Conservative leader. At the Tory conference Powell chose to speak on immigration and was tumultuously applauded. Fortunately Hogg, the platform speaker, was, apart from Macleod, the only orator in the party on a par with Powell. In a fine speech he won over the conference, recommending to Powell the Greek tag 'Mêden Agan' – 'moderation in all things'.[25]

Unhappily, Enoch Powell was a moderate in nothing, least of all on immigration. Speaking at Eastbourne a month after the conference, he went even further. Contradicting what he had said the previous year, he ruled out assimilation. 'The West Indian or Indian' did not, he claimed, 'by being born in England, become an Englishman'. He was a West Indian or an Indian still. If there were more than a tiny minority of them, the nation would suffer. Once more he sought to buttress his argument, such as it was, with dubious anecdotes, which did not even convince the *News of the World*. Sir Edward Boyle suggested that Powell was likely to produce a quite unnecessary race-relations crisis: of the two possible mistakes – the first being to assert there wasn't a problem – the second, which was for Britain to talk itself into a crisis by prophecies of inevitable doom, was the greater danger, largely because of 'the baleful genius of one politician who has made himself, whether we like it or not, a household name'.[26]

The immigration row was one of the causes of Boyle's retirement from the front bench. A Birmingham MP but very much on the left of the party and one of the straightest and most brilliant men in politics, Boyle had been under continuous attack because of his support for comprehensive education and his liberal stand on immigration and race relations. Although a close friend of Edward Heath, Boyle realised that party pressure would probably prevent him from becoming Education Secretary, and accepted an invitation to become Vice-Chancellor of Leeds University. Boyle's decision was an immense loss to the Tory Party, though the full extent of it was not seen until a year later. He was succeeded by Margaret Thatcher, which represented a sharp 'tilt to the right' but which, ironically, did not slow the stampede to comprehensive schooling; it may even have speeded it up. In the field of education the verdict of the social historian Rodney Lowe is that the conviction politician was not Margaret Thatcher but Edward Boyle.[27]

Soon after Powell's departure from the Shadow Cabinet, Alec Home, who largely agreed with him on immigration, was betting that in a matter of months Powell would come out against the Common Market. Home was right. With all three parties now in favour of entry, Europe was another issue on which Powell could strike an individual and populist note – the Common Market was then unpopular – and one which chimed with his now dominant theme of English nationalism. The reason he gave for his U-turn was blatantly self-serving. He ascribed his conversion to the sovereignty issue. Yet that issue had been there all the time from 1961 to 1967 when he had supported British entry. If it had changed at all, it had changed in a direction which undermined Powell's very flimsy case. As a result of 'the Luxembourg Compromise' of 1966 insisted on by General de Gaulle, every member state retained a national veto whenever it considered an issue to be of overriding national importance. Powell could hardly admit, however, even to himself, that the real reason for his apostasy from Europe was his quarrel with the Conservative leadership.[28]

Enoch Powell regarded himself as a Tory, and Harold Macmillan and other Conservatives with whom he disagreed as Whigs. He got it the wrong way round. His dogmatic *laissez-faire* approach was, as Iain Macleod pointed out, 'a Whig rather than a Tory doctrine'. Powell was that unusual combination: a Whig demagogue.[29]

In Place of Strife

Powell was one of the very few in the Conservative Party who doubted the need or justification for trade-union reform. This was partly because he feared it might evolve into an incomes policy and, more fundamentally, because of his doctrinaire certainty that trade unions were incapable of raising the price of labour, since that was determined by the iron laws of economics. Even if that had been true, his view left out of the account the economic damage caused by strikes and restrictive practices. Though not, of course, for Powell's reasons, the issue of trade-union reform was to lead to one of the two crucial mistakes the Tory Party made during its years in Opposition.[30]

Ever since *Putting Britain Right Ahead*, trade-union reform had been high on the Conservative agenda. The party's proposals had been carefully – too carefully – worked out and were published in April 1968 in *Fair Deal at Work*; they were then included in the party's mid-term manifesto – *Make Life Better* – which was issued later that year. Both Keith Joseph and Robert Carr, his successor as shadow spokesman, were moderates, who avoided such provocations as attacking the political levy and sought a balanced package which gave trade unions new rights as well as imposing new duties and restrictions. A new legal framework, complete with a new industrial court, was proposed. Agreements between trade unions and employers were to be legally binding, and trade unions could no longer be protected from civil proceedings if they struck in breach of such an agreement. Certain other strikes, such as 'sympathy' ones or to enforce a closed shop, were also to lose immunity.

The Royal Commission on Trade Unions under Lord Donovan, which had been set up in 1965, reported later in 1968. It produced an excellent analysis of the chaotic condition of British industrial relations but no remedy worth the name. Essentially it endorsed the status quo. Only a cogent reservation by Andrew Shonfield addressed the problem of how to create order out of chaos; and the problem had become increasingly urgent. For devaluation had not ended the difficulties of the Labour Government. Roy Jenkins had indeed halted the continued growth of public spending since 1964 and had drastically increased taxes. Public and private consumption were both cut to release resources for increased exports. Unfortunately, just as the Government established control of consumption, it lost control of wages and prices.[31]

The wage explosion of 1968 was not confined to Britain, but that was no great help to the Government. The new union militancy among the most powerful trade-union leaders came on top of a sharp growth in unofficial strikes. These grew from nearly 1,400 in 1966 to nearly 2,000 in 1969 and 3,750 in 1970. The number of days lost in strikes was three times higher in 1970 than it had been in the years 1964–7. Bravely, the new First Secretary of State, Barbara Castle, and Harold Wilson decided to act. The Government's White Paper *In Place of Strife* was partly based on *Fair Deal at Work*. It did not go as far as Conservative policy, but it contained two crucial proposals: the Government should have the power when a strike was threatened to impose a cooling-off period of twenty-eight days and also the power to order the union or unions involved to hold a strike ballot. These sensible proposals naturally infuriated the unions. After the war the major union leaders realised that full employment had radically altered the balance of industrial power in their favour but that they had to wield their new strength with restraint if they were not to jeopardise their great prize and provoke an irresistible reaction against excessive trade-union power. By the late sixties the union leaders were no longer capable of that prudent perception; still less so, of course, were the militants on the shop floor.[32]

Not only the trade unions were vehemently opposed to *In Place of Strife*; a large section of the Labour Party also revolted against it, as did some members of the Cabinet led by James Callaghan. A decade later

Callaghan's Government was destroyed by irresponsible trade-union power. Ted Heath did not vote against *In Place of Strife*, yet his Government, too, was destroyed by that same power; almost certainly it would not have been, had he supported the Labour proposals. Jim Prior, who was then Heath's PPS and later Mrs Thatcher's first Employment Secretary, afterwards wrote of the Opposition's 'major tactical error. We should have realised that the prize of a united approach would have done wonders for the country and still left the Labour Party seething with discontent. I believe', Prior concluded, 'that Ted and Iain Macleod should have spotted our opportunity and supported the Castle proposals.'[33]

It was indeed a lost opportunity. The Opposition's line should have been that, while Labour's new approach was insufficient and would have to be augmented by the Conservatives after the election, the Government's proposals were infinitely better than the current anarchy and would therefore have full Conservative backing. Unfortunately, the Opposition's policy had been worked out so carefully and for so long that it had become for Conservatives the *sine qua non* of progress and made everything else seem defective. They therefore dismissed *In Place of Strife* as 'a ragbag of odds and ends' which were 'hastily contrived and obviously inadequate', and did not support the Government. Consequently, despite his assertion that the Trade Union Bill was 'essential to the Government's continuance in office', Wilson duly capitulated to the trade-union chieftains, getting a fairly worthless undertaking from the TUC to make his surrender seem less abject. The Conservatives had insisted on sticking to their own proposals in the deluded belief that, once they had gained 'a mandate' from the electorate, the over-mighty unions would not dare to oppose them. In reality, as Robert Carr later reflected, the unions' victory over a Labour Government made it much more likely that they would 'fight even harder and believe they could win against a Tory Government'.[34]

Selsdon Man

Even before the wave of strikes in 1969, trade unions and strikes were both unpopular. Public sympathies were generally against strikers by 60 per cent to 15, while 64 per cent against 25 thought the unions had too much power. Yet the Government's failure to enact trade-union reform probably helped to make it less unpopular, for the wages explosion continued; this made its beneficiaries feel better, while the economy was not yet suffering from it. The trade figures improved and the balance of payments was in surplus. The enormous lead the Conservatives had enjoyed in the polls for more than two years shrank. They were still ahead, and in December they won the Wellingborough by-election with nearly a 10 per cent swing, but victory in the general election no longer looked assured. Moreover, the Labour Government had made victory easier for itself by shameless gerrymandering. In sharp contrast to Chuter Ede's conduct before the 1950 election, James Callaghan announced that the Government would ignore the recommendations of the Boundary Commission. At the time this was widely thought to deprive the Opposition of about twenty seats; in the event it probably only made a difference of ten.[35]

At least financially the Conservatives were well placed for the election. Labour's failures had helped the party's fund-raising; an appeal headed by Lord Carrington was launched in 1968, and easily hit its target of £2 million.[36] Policy reviews had been in progress almost continuously since 1966. The main problem for the party was that, except for nationalising steel, Labour had inconsiderately declined to provide distinctively socialist policies for the Opposition to attack; indeed, in its attempt to replace incomes policy with trade-union reform, the Government had adopted exactly the same strategy which had been heralded as a Tory move to the right in 1966.[37]

According to the Nuffield Study of the 1970 general election, the Shadow Cabinet 'compensated for rejecting the views of *laissez-faire* radicals by using their language'. That was only partly true; in September 1969, for instance, Heath made it clear in Dundee that the Conservatives would 'refuse to condemn large parts of the kingdom to slow decline and decay, to dereliction and to persistent unemployment, in pursuit of old-fangled nineteenth-century doctrines of *laissez-faire*'. As Iain Macleod had said in a fine speech at the 1966 Party Conference, 'We are not all pace-setters, we are not all competitors . . . so competition needs compassion.' The *One Nation* ideal, the second draft of *Make Life Better* suggested, 'was a free society in which men and women are free to make the most of their individual talents', adding in an advance refutation of one of Mrs Thatcher's most famous remarks, 'but it is a society – not a collection of individuals: a society in which the young are cared for as well as the old, the backward as well as the pace-setters, the deprived as well as the high flyers'. That One-Nation approach was safe with Heath; yet the media's assumption that some right-wing remarks represented the party's true intentions was largely the leadership's own fault.[38]

In January 1970 the Shadow Cabinet gathered at Selsdon Park Hotel in Surrey to co-ordinate the policy proposals of individual spokesmen.

In fact very little happened there, and the meeting would long since have been forgotten but for a clever taunt from Harold Wilson. As the party's 'Adjutant', Michael Fraser, later complained, the Shadow Cabinet was remarkably reluctant throughout the years of Opposition to discuss any policy for dealing with inflation. That was certainly so at Selsdon. The subject was the last item on the agenda and was never reached – largely by design to avoid a clash between the free-marketeers and Maudling and Walker. The failure to hammer out an agreed policy to curb inflation was the second great Conservative failure of the Opposition years and almost as important as the party's refusal to support *In Place of Strife*. Heath had forgotten that he was to brief the lobby correspondents until he was told they had arrived, and as there was virtually nothing to tell them the briefing presented a problem. Iain Macleod solved it by saying, 'It's quite easy, Ted. Just tell them we believe in law and order, that always goes down well.' If anything, it went down too well. The Sunday and Monday press suggested a sharp swerve to the right. The Conservatives were looking like a Government-in-waiting 'but', *The Economist* thought, 'not a visibly compassionate one'.[39]

Heath made a bad mistake in sounding inflexible before the election and in the manifesto. This was a tactical decision partly to satisfy potential right-wing critics within the party but mainly to present a contrast to the palpably unprincipled Wilson. However, as Enoch Powell rightly guessed, the Selsdon conference did not mark a shift to the right. Yet Wilson was depressed by Selsdon, which he thought had been a great success – the Conservatives' private polls suggested he was right. Unaware, of course, of Macleod's remark, Wilson was particularly worried that the Tories might make law and order one of their main themes. In consequence he launched a bitter attack on them for being hard-faced and right-wing, coining the phrase 'Selsdon Man' to create the impression that Heath and his colleagues had adopted policies which should appeal only to cave-dwellers.[40]

Selsdon Park seemed to help Heath's confidence, which had been growing since the beginning of the year when he had returned from Australia having won the Sydney–Hobart yacht race. Crossman noted his increased confidence and his 'new standing'. On the face of it, though, Heath had less to be confident about. In March a by-election in Ayrshire South produced only a 3 per cent swing. The Conservatives' poll lead also narrowed, and in April, for the first time since February 1967, a poll reported a Labour lead. Although he could do nothing to curb wage inflation, Roy Jenkins, almost alone among post-war Chancellors, did not try to bribe the voters with an election Budget. Even so, Gallup showed Labour five points ahead in April, and the Conservatives lost 350 seats in the local elections. 'All this casts a gloom,' recorded Douglas Hurd, then Ted Heath's political secretary.[41]

Wilson called an election on 18 June. The Conservative programme was much the same as in 1966, although an obdurate tone pervaded the manifesto; a compulsory incomes policy was rejected as unthinkable. Iain Macleod, who had earlier been gloomy, was one of the few leading Tories who believed the party would win, thinking that 'Ted would have a breakthrough. His honesty will come over.' Macleod may well have been right. Harold Wilson fought a presidential and conservative campaign, telling an audience in Cardiff of 'a feeling of national liberation, of a loosening of restriction on personal initiative, of a freedom of individual choice, combined with a national system of order and stability which makes us the envy of the civilised world'. Except that Heath would have said that those things were what he wanted and did not yet exist, the words were more appropriate to a Conservative leader. As Crossman remarked in his diary, Wilson was running the election in a 'Macmillan-like way', yet, as Crossman also noted, Wilson, unlike Macmillan, had given the voters 'three years of hell and high taxes'.[42]

Otherwise Wilson did little except move around, expecting to be admired, and confident that he had made the right decision. Theoretically the Prime Minister's power to choose the date of a general election gives the governing party an immense advantage. In practice, his privilege is often double-edged, as Clement Attlee had twice demonstrated. Wilson could have waited some time to see if his party's apparent recovery was firmly based, but instead of doing so he became confident that in June he would coast to victory and to another spell in Downing Street.

His complacency seemed justified by the polls and the press. On the eve of the campaign Marplan found that 67 per cent of voters expected Labour to win; in January that figure had been 27 per cent. In response, the bookmakers had pushed the Conservatives out to 6 to 1; at one moment Labour became 20 to 1 on, and at times it was impossible to place a bet on the Government. Five days before polling day, NOP showed the Conservatives 12.4 per cent behind. On 14 June, the *Sunday Times* claimed that only 'a miraculous turn-around in public opinion' could save the Tories from defeat. Yet Heath retained his optimism. Even when Central Office sent him to do a walkabout in Norwich on early closing day, he was cheerful and buoyant. Macleod, too, was still confident of victory. Other Conservative leaders were not. Believing defeat to be inevitable, some of them thought the only way to prevent Enoch Powell taking over the party was to bring back Alec Home. As in 1963, Home initially demurred, but it was arranged that the day after the election Whitelaw and Maudling would meet at Home's house in Scotland to assess the situation.[43]

Only one poll during the election predicted a Conservative victory; on polling day ORC put the Tories ahead by 1 per cent and then only after a good deal of (legitimate) doctoring of the figures. Unlike the pollsters, the voters gave the Conservatives a 3 per cent lead with a swing of 4.7 per cent; the Conservatives gained seventy-seven seats and an overall majority of thirty. The pollsters also felt that Enoch Powell had crucially aided the Tories, although his impact is less evident in the actual voting figures. But then, as Powell himself said, 'it is not possible to attribute specific causes to electoral movements local and general'. Yet Powell's stand on immigration probably influenced many voters and, just possibly, made the crucial difference between a Conservative majority of thirty-one and a Labour one of about ten. If so, it was not intentional. Powell evidently shared the common belief that Heath would lose. That suited him well, provided that he could not be blamed for the defeat.[44]

The pollsters' débâcle over the result produced the theory of a late swing to the Tories. There was much talk of Wilson's march to victory having been halted by England squandering a 2–0 lead in the World Cup quarter-final in Mexico, and even more decisively by last-minute trade figures showing a balance of payments deficit. The late swing, however, never took place. Many Conservative candidates, such as Jim Prior and Robert Carr, were convinced they were well ahead right from the start. Peter Walker, Charles Morrison, Dennis Walters and Ian Gilmour rang each other up every few days, and all agreed that there was a noticeable swing to the Conservatives from the beginning of the campaign and that it was not increasing. Detailed canvassing returns for Banbury told the same story, as did many constituency, as opposed to national, opinion polls. Oliver Poole and Ted Leather, the Vice-Chairman of the Party, took the same view.[45]

Late swing or not, the Conservatives won. So Ted Heath became Prime Minister, and neither Alec Home nor Enoch Powell became Leader of the Opposition. Instead, Home became Foreign Secretary and Powell remained a back-bencher; and on Friday the 19th Willie Whitelaw, instead of driving over the border to see Home in Scotland, flew down to London to help the new Prime Minister choose his Government.

CHAPTER XI

Heath's Rough Ride

The quality of the refreshments provided for Heath's and Whitelaw's late Friday-night session in Downing Street – beer and pork pies – confirmed for Whitelaw that the standards of public life had declined in the Wilson years. Luckily their discussions were not difficult. Nearly all the Shadow Cabinet were appointed to the Ministries they had been shadowing, and Whitelaw himself, who had been an outstanding Chief Whip, became Leader of the House. Exceptionally, Sir Keith Joseph, whose recent series of speeches on competition and free enterprise had led to him being unfairly called 'Selsdon Man incarnate' – unfairly, because Joseph envisaged a strong role for Government intervention in industry as helper of last resort – went to Social Security instead of Industry. The Foreign Office and the Home Office presented a problem only because there were three strong candidates for them. Maudling had been Foreign Affairs spokesman, but as a former Foreign Secretary and Prime Minister, Douglas-Home had the better claim. So Maudling became Home Secretary, displacing Hogg who had been shadowing the Home Office. Hogg therefore agreed to return to the Lords, from which he had escaped only seven years before, to become Lord Chancellor, largely abandoning involvement in party politics. At the time this seemed a good arrangement, even though it deprived the Government of one of its two best debaters in the House of Commons.[1]

Before the election, the new Chancellor of the Exchequer, Iain Macleod, was aware that he had been pushed too far in the non-interventionist direction and that this would have to be redressed in office. Certainly, despite an almost unique public-sector surplus and a favourable balance of payments, the state of the economy – which was suffering another severe bout of what he had earlier christened 'stag-flation' – did not argue for benign neglect. Prices were rising at 5 per cent, wages were rising at 14 or 15 per cent, growth was low at 1.5 per cent, a rash of strikes was spreading, and unemployment was at the then high level of 2.5 per cent. Macleod was therefore justified in saying that, in view of the level of unemployment – 'the worst since 1947' –

and the highest rate of wage increases for twenty years, 'nobody could conceivably claim that it is a happy heritage that we have taken over'.

Sadly, apart from telling Parliament that the Government had a duty to use their influence 'firmly and openly on the side of non-inflationary [pay] settlements' in the public sector, Macleod had no chance to show how he would have dealt with his stagflationary heritage. In acute pain while he read that speech, which he considered the worst he had ever made, he was rushed to hospital at the end of the debate. Although an operation seemed successful and he returned to 11 Downing Street, he died of a heart attack on 20 July. Macleod was an irreparable loss to the Government. Maudling was distracted by Northern Ireland, all too passive on many matters outside his departmental interest (though a superb Chairman of Cabinet Committees – in the Rab Butler class), and before long to leave the Government altogether; Home lacked knowledge of domestic affairs and was fully engaged at the Foreign Office; and Hogg was out of action in the Lords. Heath and Macleod were, therefore, the two people on whom the fortunes of the Government depended. Macleod had been the only man fully able to stand up to Heath and the only man of comparable stature on whom the Prime Minister could lean.[2]

The loss of the second most important man in the Government would have been a bitter blow at any time; in 1970 it was calamitous. Only ten years before in his great address to both Houses of Parliament in Westminster Hall, General de Gaulle had paid tribute to British institutions: 'At the worst moments', he asked, 'who ever contested the legitimacy or the authority of the state? . . . Sure of yourselves . . . you put in practice in freedom a well-founded and stable political system . . . Thus without closely correlated constitutional texts but by virtue of undeniable general consent you find the means of assuring always the best results from democracy.' On 18 June 1969, a fortnight after Harold Wilson had memorably told the boss of the engineering union, Scanlon, to 'get your tanks off my lawn, Hughie', the Prime Minister had, by abandoning *In Place of Strife*, surrendered his lawn to 'Hughie' and the other TUC chieftains. At least until then, the General's generous tribute had seemed justified. Since the seventeenth century Britain had been remarkably successful in organising political consent. Indeed, to use Bagehot's terms, British Government had often been better at 'gaining authority' than 'using' it. Now that was beginning to change. The political system was soon not to seem 'well-founded and stable', and 'the legitimacy or authority' of the state was about to be tested. Unlike many Prime Ministers, Edward Heath was much better at using authority –

taking decisions – than gaining it. Had Iain Macleod survived, he would have supplied what the Prime Minister lacked. Macleod would probably have improved the quality of the Government's decisions; he would certainly have transformed its ability to gain consent for its policies.[3]

Shortly after Macleod's death, Heath further curtailed the Government's future capacity to gain consent. In 1964, in an attempt to appear 'Kennedyesque', Wilson had launched his Government into a 'hundred days' of mainly futile if not damaging activity. To be as unlike Wilson as possible, Heath sent his Ministers off on a summer holiday after the Queen's Speech had been debated. The holidays were not necessary. The adrenalin produced by the taste of power after years without it is far more restorative to mind and body than any amount of sunshine or sightseeing. And the holiday exodus, combined with the virtual cessation of ministerial activity so soon after an election campaign in which the Tories had stressed the gravity of the country's situation, gave the impression that the Government was drifting, and that Ministers were detached from national concerns and insufficiently dedicated to their political duties. Heath was so determined to point the contrast with Wilson, who had continually popped up on the television screen, that he made matters worse by not once appearing on television in his first hundred days. Cartoons in the press showed enquirers at the door of Number 10 asking if anybody lived there. By taking a holiday from politics, the Prime Minister and his Government deprived themselves of a honeymoon with the electorate. By October the Government had lost its lead in the polls, and although the Opposition was, and remained, in a sorry condition, Labour was well ahead in January and stayed ahead until January 1974.

Macleod was irreplaceable at the Treasury. The best successor would have been Edward Boyle, but he was not available. The next best substitute would probably have been Keith Joseph. Although eyebrows had been raised at some of his pre-election speeches, Joseph was not until 1974, in his words, 'converted to Conservatism', by which in fact he meant nineteenth-century Liberalism.[4] In his heathen state, he was still, as his record at Social Security clearly showed, a good One-Nation Tory, and Joseph Mark I would probably have been an excellent Chancellor. But having kept Joseph away from Industry, Heath was not tempted then to risk him at the Treasury, which accordingly went to Anthony Barber, an expert in tax law. Barber had been an efficient Party Chairman and had been rewarded after the election with what, in view of the Government's primary objective of entering the EEC, was the key job of handling the European negotiations. The new Chancellor was a popular, able man and a very adequate parliamentarian, but he was not a heavyweight and could not last even one round with the Prime Minister.

Two high-spending ministers that Barber had little more success controlling were Keith Joseph at Social Security and Margaret Thatcher, who was at Education. Mrs Thatcher opened her Cabinet career by picking a row with her officials over putting out without consultation a circular which reversed Labour's policy on comprehensive schools. Like Douglas-Home's announcement, also made in July, that Britain would resume the sale of arms to South Africa, Mrs Thatcher's circular was unavailing. She was unable to withstand the tide towards comprehensive schools; during her time at Education a record number of grammar schools was closed, and the proportion of children in comprehensive schools was almost doubled.[5]

After the reshuffle Geoffrey Rippon was moved from the Ministry of Technology to replace Barber as chief negotiator with Europe; in turn, John Davies was catapulted from a month-long career as a back-bencher, first to replace Rippon and later to head what soon became the Department of Trade and Industry (DTI). Davies had been Managing Director of Shell and, more recently, Director-General of the Confederation of British Industry (CBI). Yet the right-wing Republican Senator from Ohio, Robert Taft, had said of the phalanx of businessmen in President Eisenhower's Cabinet, 'I don't know of any reason why success in business should mean success in public service.' Davies's appointment, which was savagely criticised by Enoch Powell, abundantly confirmed Taft's doubts. The choice of Davies for any Cabinet post at that time would have been a mistake, but to send him to the DTI was particularly ill-judged because that department was in the front line of most of the big controversies of Heath's premiership. In Peter Walker, Heath had a much better candidate with business experience for the DTI, but he was initially sent to the Ministry of Housing and Local Government.[6]

Davies soon demonstrated the disadvantage of inexperience. At the Blackpool conference that autumn he promised 'not to bolster up or bale out companies when I can see no end to the process of propping them up', and shortly afterwards he told the Commons that 'the essential need of the country was to gear its policies to the great majority of people who are not lame ducks and who do not need a hand . . .' Both speeches were more nuanced than their more outspoken passages indicated, but that did not lessen the embarrassment they were soon to cause.[7]

Davies was never in the Prime Minister's inner circle. Heath was closest to Whitelaw (Lord President), Prior (Agriculture) and Carrington (Defence). His Cabinet was exceptionally harmonious and, far from dictating Cabinet decisions, Heath usually allowed others to lead the discussion. Despite the grave problems facing the Government, there were no serious disagreements in Cabinet, and leaks to the press were rare. No Cabinet Minister resigned for political reasons, and none was sacked from the Cabinet. Yet, after a presidential-type election campaign, the Prime Minister's personal dominance was inevitably emphasised by the media, and his public pronouncements had a displeasing flavour of inflexible direction from the top – another element of contrast with the pliable Wilson.[8]

At the Party Conference, Heath made a radical speech unveiling his 'quiet revolution', a phrase originally used by Iain Macleod in 1965. The party, he told the conference, had been 'returned to office to change the course of history of this nation – nothing less'. Individuals were to be encouraged 'more and more to take their own decisions, to stand on their own feet, to accept responsibility for themselves and for their families'. Inflation was identified as the greatest threat to Britain's future (although no trace was revealed of a policy to fight it), and Heath warned that companies which granted excessive wage increases would not be rescued from the consequences of their irresponsibility. The nation's problems were so deep-rooted that nothing short of a revolution was needed; the Government's task was 'to win the hearts and minds of our people' and permanently change the nation's outlook. This transformation of Britain would take more than one Parliament to complete; he prophesied that the Conservatives would still be conducting the revolution 'way into the 1980s'.[9]

Yet Heath's apparently abrasive radicalism was firmly rooted in his One-Nation convictions. At the end of his first parliamentary speech as Prime Minister, he had looked back to his 'first work' as a back-bencher, the One Nation publication of 1950. One Nation, he told the House, was 'a concept' which went 'far wider than social and economic spheres', covering also 'our industrial relations, the young people and those who have now retired', as well as the spheres of race and religion. 'I firmly believe', he concluded, that the great task of the administration is 'to create unity in our country . . . to create within freedom in Britain one nation'.[10]

Heath hoped that the promise of purposeful government at a time of crisis would evoke a similar response from his audience. Yet the abrasive or divisive language of his speeches, like that of the manifesto, was at variance with the content of the policies he aimed to pursue. Heath was not a natural communicator, and his instinctive reluctance to temper his harsh words with honeyed reassurance and encouragement had been strengthened by the erroneous idea that the general election had been won by his last-minute appeals to reason. However admirable, his refusal to modify his style was a grave political mistake which invited personal disaster should his plans for Britain go wrong.

When Parliament re-assembled after the 1970 conference season, the first stages of Heath's 'revolution' were implemented. A reorganisation of Government departments heralded by a White Paper created new 'super-ministries'; Trade and Industry and the rather misleadingly-named Department of the Environment were brought into that category to join Health and Social Security, which Wilson had set up in 1968. According to the White Paper, Government would attempt less but perform better in its proper sphere; the Cabinet had already been cut to eighteen from Wilson's twenty-one, and the number of junior ministers had also been reduced. The quality of advice available to ministers was to be enhanced by the formation of a Central Policy Review Staff (CPRS) under the colourful Labour supporter Lord Rothschild. This body, recruited largely from the universities, was designed to rise above the boundaries between departments and, by providing long-term advice for the Cabinet, to counteract the temptation to choose the expedient short-term option. Decisions, it was hoped, would thus be based on better information, and the system of Programme Analysis Review (PAR) was implemented to assess their results. These innovations were far from exciting, but they were prosaically useful and they demonstrated that Heath's reformism embraced institutions as well as policies and attitudes.

Anthony Barber's mini-Budget before the end of October was similarly unspectacular. Since 1968 the trade unions had become increasingly militant; in addition to a multitude of strikes, hourly wages were now rising twice as fast as in the second half of 1969. But as the Government's policy to deal with inflation amounted to little more than the hope that good sense would prevail, the Chancellor could do nothing about wage inflation except refrain from increasing aggregate demand. In 1964 public expenditure had been 44 per cent of GDP; by 1970 the proportion was over 50 per cent. Taxes had also appreciably risen, and the larger sums that wage-earners found themselves paying to the state – between 1967 and 1970 the threshold for paying income tax at the standard rate was lowered by almost a third – were an important cause of trade-union militancy. Hence to reduce public spending and taxes was sensible and necessary.[11]

Barber did not promise a drastic reversal of current trends, but ministers responded to his call for savings. Cuts in public expenditure were planned to realise almost £1 billion by 1974; National Health charges were increased (and admission to museums and art galleries was no longer to be free), several grants were phased out and, most contro-versially of all, free school milk was to be abolished for over-sevens. Margaret Thatcher had been expected to find her department's share of the savings by winding up the newly founded Open University, which for some reason Macleod had disliked. Choosing school milk instead was an early sign of political courage which did little to help her image with the electorate; she did, however, have the unstinting support of the Prime Minister throughout. Amid the abuse, 'Thatcher, milk-snatcher', that was lavished on the Education Secretary, which 'hurt and upset' her, few people remembered that only two years earlier the Labour Government had scrapped free milk in all secondary schools; it had also repeatedly delayed raising the school-leaving age, which Mrs Thatcher achieved two years later. Nevertheless, the cuts in school milk and the projected charges for admission to museums, neither of which raised much money, reinforced the hard-faced image suggested by the Government's rhetoric.[12]

Barber used the savings to cut income tax by 6d. to 7s. 6d. in the pound, below the level it had been when he was Economic Secretary in the Macmillan Government. He also reduced the rate of corporation tax and, as promised in the manifesto, Selective Employment Tax, which discriminated against service industries, was to be scrapped by the end of 1973; in the meantime, its rate was halved. Finally, the Government used this early opportunity to dismantle some of the interventionist machinery set up by Labour; the Industrial Reorganisation Corporation and Prices and Incomes Board were abolished, while regional grants were to be replaced with tax allowances. The decision reflected the Cabinet's conviction that much public expenditure was simply wasted, and that some forms of state intervention could be obstructive rather than helpful. By the end of the 1960s almost £1 billion per year was being awarded to private industry, with no noticeable effect on morale or performance.[13]

None of this benefited the poor. Shortly before the election, the Child Poverty Action Group had published a memorandum arguing that the poor had got poorer under Labour, an indictment to which Crossman, on the radio on 27 January, had pleaded largely guilty, and during the election campaign Heath and Macleod had powerfully taken up the theme. Keith Joseph had therefore an even greater than normal induce-ment to help the lot of the poor, especially as the manifesto had promised to 'give priority to those most in need . . . the children in families below the poverty line'. He had discovered, he told Parliament in a command-ing speech opening the debate, that to raise family allowances would not help 'about one-third' of working families living below supplementary level who had only one child. Accordingly, he introduced the Family Income Supplement which gave a subsidy to low-wage-earners with families. This, like most means-tested benefits, or, as in this case, 'income-tested' benefits, had the disadvantage of relatively low take up, and it enlarged 'the poverty trap' – many poor people were 'trapped' because when they earned more they lost their welfare benefits and so were hardly better off. FIS was therefore vilified by the Left, while being denounced on ideological grounds by the Right. In an ill-informed speech, Enoch Powell attacked it for resembling 'Speenhamland' – the system introduced by Berkshire Magistrates in 1794 to augment out of the rates the wages of starving agricultural labourers. Keith Joseph had already answered this criticism earlier in the debate, pointing out the many differences between his scheme and 'Speenhamland'. He need not, however, have been worried by the comparison since the Speenhamland system had been a much-needed remedy for serious evils. Joseph's FIS was a similarly fine acknowledgement that humanitarian considerations and ideals should not be trampled on by economic dogma; and although he declared it to be only 'a temporary, first-aid measure' it lasted until 1988.[14]

Reflating the Economy

At the end of 1970 wage settlements were 11 per cent higher than the year before, the highest rate since 1919. In January 1971 the rate rose to 13.5 per cent, and in February Lord Wilberforce's Court of Enquiry ended the dangerous electricity workers' dispute with the excessive award of pay rises of 15 and 18 per cent. Yet in January and February more working days were lost in strikes and go-slows than in the whole of 1970. At the same time unemployment was still rising fast. Much of the increase was secular. The rapid rise in wages since 1968 had made British labour uncompetitive, something that was not fully appreciated at the time. In any case, the Government was determined to do every-thing it possibly could to reduce unemployment.[15]

Accordingly, in his first full Budget in March 1971, Barber cut taxes again. His decision to carry through Iain Macleod's policy of removing the distinction between earned and unearned income effectively reduced the highest rate of tax from 90 to 75 per cent. In addition to announcing the introduction of Value Added Tax in place of purchase tax and Selective Employment Tax from 1973, Barber embarked on a series of ambitious reforms to simplify the system. He also increased old-age pensions and child allowances, yet the overall effect of the Budget was more beneficial to the wealthy than the poor. Although taxation was too high, Barber's largesse to higher-tax payers, like Selwyn Lloyd's in 1961, did not sit well with the calls for restraint that were constantly preached at wage-earners. The shape of the Budget reflected the Government's belief that the country's economic performance had been held back by the lack of proper 'incentives' for individual effort; once these were restored, the whole of society would feel the benefit. This was a sanguine view, but at least it had not been disproved when the Heath Government took office in 1970, and the press echoed the warm reception which Barber received from Conservative MPs.[16]

The Budget measures, the Government believed, would be sufficient to regenerate the economy, but it was disappointed by the response. Despite the popularity of the Chancellor and his Budget, the voters were growing restive too. In the May elections the Conservatives had lost nearly 2,000 local councillors, and Labour overturned a majority of over 10,000 in the Bromsgrove by-election – its only by-election gain in the 1970 Parliament. Barber's Budget had been based on an over-optimistic assessment of likely growth, and in July he announced new measures to reflate the economy, including a hefty cut in purchase tax, the abolition of hire-purchase controls and public works programmes for the hardest-hit regions. This reflation, which doubled the cuts in taxation that Barber had announced in March, was a response to a post-Budget Treasury forecast that without them unemployment would be higher in 1972 than had been thought likely at the time of his Budget. It was also the Government's side of a bargain with the CBI which in return promised to limit price increases to 5 per cent over the next twelve months and to encourage its members to support British entry into the EEC. Yet while the July measures could be defended on these grounds, they were ill-judged and excessive. Their likely inflationary effect was enhanced by the ending of restrictions on bank lending fore-shadowed by the Bank of England's document *Competition and Credit Control* – 'all competition and no control', its critics complained. Donald MacDougall, the Chief Economic Adviser to the Treasury, thought the scheme 'inherently inflationary', and it set off a credit boom. Unfortunately most of the credit went into property, not productive industry. The money supply increased, yet in Sir Alec Cairncross's judgement the dominant causes of the inflation of 1973–4 were rising import prices followed by rising labour costs, and the expansion in bank credit was 'a natural consequence of rising prices rather than their cause'.[17]

The Industrial Relations Act

The Heath Government tried to do too much. Entry into Europe, the reform of industrial relations, the transformation of local government, the thoroughgoing reform of the taxation system, the rationalisation of housing subsidies and, during the last eighteen months, the imposition of comprehensive control of prices and incomes, were too big a meal for one Parliament, even for one which ran its full term, and the 1970 Parliament lasted only three and a half years. Even if all those measures had been perfectly conceived, which in the nature of things they were not, the British people's appetite for radical reform would have been satiated.

One measure that merited early enactment, both because of the urgency of the issue and because the party had long been committed to it, was trade-union reform. Unfortunately the Industrial Relations Act was the least perfectly conceived of all the Government reforms and the least perfectly executed. The Conservatives did not create the almost unprecedented trade-union militancy of the early seventies, which, though worse in Britain than in nearly every other country, was an international phenomenon.[18] Nothing like it had been seen since the years just before and just after the First World War. Well before 1970, as has been seen, 'Hughie' Scanlon and other trade-union bosses had mobilised their tanks, and many militants had even less respect for the legitimate processes of democratic government than Scanlon and Jack Jones. A likely dock strike, the causes of which had nothing to do with the new Government, had to be considered at its first Cabinet meeting; when it started less than a month after the general election, it necessitated the declaration of a State of Emergency, the first of five during the Heath years.

To change the law before many other such disputes occurred seemed sensible and necessary. Another reason for speed was the crucial position the reform of industrial relations occupied in the Government's counter-inflation policy. Indeed it was almost the only element in that policy. The Government did evolve what it called an 'N minus one' policy (the norm minus one) under which each wage claim in the public sector was to be settled at 1 per cent less than the previous one. This was more an ambition than a policy and a needless provocation to trade-union leaders who did not relish being seen to have done less well than their predecessors. Yet after Lord Wilberforce's award to the electricity workers seemed to have wrecked N–1, an unsuccessful strike by the postal workers, who like the busmen in 1958 had the power to inconvenience the public but not to wreck the economy, resurrected it; and it more or less worked for a while at the cost of many long drawn-out stoppages. Still, only by introducing a law to reduce trade-union power, it was thought, could excessive wage claims be prevented and restrictive practices diminished.[19]

If speed was important, the Government, as Jim Prior later wrote, should have abandoned its own proposals and simply enacted those contained in *In Place of Strife*. Although the union bosses would still have howled, even Harold Wilson and Barbara Castle could hardly have gone to war against their own proposals. Once again, however, the Conservatives were too wedded to their own over-complicated and unrealistic plans to pull off such a brilliant political coup. In addition, they were curiously unaware of the dangers of what they were seeking to do. They had a naïve belief in the power of the ballot box, considering that they had a 'mandate' for trade-union reform, which would be sufficient to secure success. Yet even Margaret Thatcher, who was opposed, then as later, to consensus politics, had in 1968 been wary of a so-called mandate. 'I myself doubt', she said in her CPC lecture, 'whether the voters really are endorsing each and every particular when they return a Government to power.' She was undoubtedly right. The doctrine of the mandate is highly implausible. Nobody can be certain whether a majority has voted primarily against one party's record or for the proposals of the other party. And even if the majority is assumed to have looked forward rather than back, plainly not all of it knew, let alone approved, of all the planks in that party's platform.[20]

Of course everybody should in the end accept laws passed by democratically elected governments, but equally the presence of an item in its election manifesto does not give a Government a completely free hand to do what it likes on this issue. Even if we have what in the later seventies Lord Hailsham called an 'elective dictatorship', that dictatorship is not absolved from all constraints once it has been elected. According to Robert Carr, the Employment Secretary who had shadowed the department before the election, his study group had done 'their homework very thoroughly indeed', having had people 'from both sides of industry – [including] a leading official of the TUC in his private capacity'. Even though most of the homework had been done by Geoffrey Howe and other lawyers who had no experience of industrial relations, Robert Carr, an intelligent moderate and one of the few members of the Government who fully understood industry and industrial relations, evidently thought that consultation had been adequate, for when he met the General Council of the TUC in October 1970, he told them that 'the eight central pillars' of his proposals were not negotiable. Consequently the TUC refused to discuss them, saying correctly that this was a 'wilful denial' of what had been 'accorded to the TUC by every Government for at least the past thirty years'. The Government's behaviour was all the more unaccountable in that, like Carr, Heath was anything but a union-basher. Indeed, Jack Jones, the leader of the Transport Union, who formed a left-wing axis with Scanlon, later wrote that Heath 'gained more personal respect from union leaders' than Wilson or Callaghan. Vic Feather and other trade unionists held the same view, although at the time they acted as though they thought the opposite.[21]

The Government's refusal of proper consultation was a disastrous error for at least three reasons, any one of which should have led it to take the opposite course. First, its refusal united virtually all trade unions against the Government's proposals. Second, it gave Mrs Castle a feeble pretext for attacking a measure which resembled *In Place of Strife*. Labour was entering its most disreputable years since the thirties; Wilson and Castle would very probably, therefore, have opposed the measure anyway, but it was rash to provide them with an excuse for doing so. Third, the Government's proposals were so deeply flawed that they would have greatly benefited from full consultation with both the TUC and the CBI. They contrived to antagonise the unions, without pleasing the employers.[22]

The bill, which became law in August 1971 but was not fully operational until March 1972, required unions to register with a new National Industrial Relations Court. This body was to police a tighter definition of legal strikes and could order unions to pay compensation if they broke the new rules. It was given authority to impose a 'cooling-off' period – although experience of America's Taft–Hartley Act, which was an important inspiration of the Conservative proposals, had shown cooling-off periods to be largely useless if not damaging – and, if that failed to produce a settlement, to order a secret ballot of union members. Some concessions were offered to encourage unions to register under the Act: better legal recognition, a conciliation service, and improved training and worker participation. In addition the closed shop was not completely outlawed, and employees were offered extra protection against unfair dismissal.

This immensely elaborate Act was absurdly over-legalistic. As Andrew Shonfield, the only member of the Donovan Commission who had gone to the root of the matter, wrote in *The Times*, the Government was trying 'to restrict the scope for industrial action much too severely', apparently not understanding that trade unions were 'in the last resort

256

fighting organisations'. Indeed the Government's legislative stance would have been an appropriate method for dealing with a bunch of Friendly Societies. Like *In Place of Strife*, the Government's Act sought both to strengthen the trade-union leaders against their own members and to weaken them against the employers and the Government. Both objectives were highly desirable, but they were to some extent contradictory and required different approaches. Thus, while to give unions greater power over their militants would reduce industrial anarchy and might appeal to most of the union leaders, it would clearly require the fullest consultation with the latter, who should be treated as allies or at least not as enemies. On the other hand, the objective of reducing the trade unions' legal immunities and powers was bound to engender trade-union animosity; hence the bill needed to be so carefully drafted that the TUC had no means of evading or frustrating its main provisions.[23]

Instead, the Act was drafted to facilitate its own defeat. The first large loophole it helpfully provided for its trade-union opponents was to make agreements between unions and employers legally enforceable only if both sides agreed. The Government had foreseen that, if the unions were given the option of making their agreements not legally enforceable, they would exercise it, and the employers would not object – 'most of them would choose the peaceful way out'. Even so, the Government thought that the party's frequent reiteration of its belief in 'free' collective bargaining required it to offer that option, although, if the Government really did still 'believe' in free collective bargaining, it should not have been introducing the Industrial Relations Act. In any case its Act provided the crucial loophole and, sensing that the Act would fail, the CBI recommended that its members should rely on voluntary agreements with the unions. Legislation which sought to make agreements between trade unions and employers legally binding, while effectively ensuring that no such agreements were ever made, might be thought sufficiently self-defeating, but just in case the unions were too obtuse to notice the weapon they had been given, the Act presented them with another one.[24]

Rather than making the Act apply to all trade unions which had been listed as such on the day of the general election, the Act promised that only unions which registered would enjoy its benefits – that is to say, those powers and immunities which the Act left to trade unions, as well as various tax advantages. Yet trade unions could decline to register under the Act, which meant that they could treat it as though it did not exist. This was fully legal, and although it left them open to legal penalties as a result of strike action, it was, as Carr subsequently admitted, 'a damnably effective tactic' which nullified the Act. The danger that unions might decide not to register had also been foreseen but discounted on the grounds that it would be clearly in their long-term interests to do so. Here again, though, if the unions had shown themselves capable of acting in their long-term enlightened self-interest during the previous ten years, no Industrial Relations Act would have been required.[25]

In March 1971 the TUC stunned the Government by 'advising' its members not to register. When the bill became law, the advice was changed to a positive instruction; more than thirty unions were suspended from the TUC for obeying the Government, and twenty were eventually expelled. Because of its cardinal flaws the Industrial Relations Act dashed the high hopes that had been placed in it. The Government's economic strategy depended on the curbing of union extremism – more sensible pay settlements would reduce inflation and avoid an unacceptable rise in unemployment – and its rhetoric during and after the election had left it no other way of doing so. Ideally, the Act might have worked as a background threat which was very rarely used, but in practice it stood as a provocation to a militancy already swollen by the Wilson years. Eleven million working days were lost through strikes in 1970; in 1972 this figure climbed to almost twenty-four million. Those union leaders who regarded the strike as a political weapon were pleased by this trend; the moderates saw no alternative but to join in the orchestrated defiance.[26]

One bizarre aspect of the struggle over industrial relations was that, while the unions fought as if the Government was engaged in an all-out class war, the Tory Right were criticising it for being too soft. Before it even published the bill, the Government had announced a rescue package for Rolls-Royce, which was facing ruin over a £150 million contract to supply aero-engines to the American company Lockheed. Nationalisation of the aero-engine section seemed the only way to rescue one of the most prestigious names in British industry. Not even Margaret Thatcher could find fault with this decision in hindsight, yet the timing of the crisis fitted neatly with subsequent right-wing allegations of a 'U-turn' by Heath. By an irony typical of these years, the decision to take over part of a major manufacturer coincided almost exactly with the Government's modest programme of denationalisation, which returned the Cook's travel agency and a few pubs in the Carlisle area to the private sector. Although not threatened with denationalisation, the chairmen of the nationalised industries were uneasy under Heath, protesting that their commercial policies were being decided by a Government concerned above all to keep prices under control.[27]

The Government was faced with a more difficult decision over Upper Clyde Shipbuilders, a rickety consortium put together by the Labour Government in 1968, which in Opposition Nicholas Ridley had marked down for 'butchery'. Despite refusing further credits for UCS in October 1970, John Davies renewed them in February 1971, but the threat of closure did not produce a more disciplined work-force or a more efficient management. Subsequently, however, following Davies's decision that UCS should be liquidated, the work-force under the then Communist Jimmy Reid began a disciplined work-in. The rise of unemployment to over the one million mark in 1972 and a warning from the Chief Constable of Glasgow, where unemployment was exceptionally high, that he could not guarantee the maintenance of public order if the yards were closed, induced the Government to give in, injecting further public funds and saving 4,000 jobs. UCS was the lamest of ducks, and Margaret Thatcher later thought it a 'memorably inglorious episode' in which 'the Government's resolve' had been found 'wanting'. But in the circumstances Davies and the Government were well-advised to prefer eating their words to risking even less palatable activities.[28]

Joining the EEC

After their election defeat in 1964 Home and the Shadow Cabinet had remained firmly committed to entering the EEC. The 1966 election manifesto promised that the Conservatives would 'seize the first favourable opportunity of becoming a member of the Community'. And when Wilson, not the Conservatives, decided to attempt entry, the Opposition issued a three-line whip to support the Government, giving Wilson a majority of over 400. Yet in the 1970 election manifesto this unequivocal pledge to gain entry was reduced solely to a commitment to negotiate – 'no more, no less' – and the potential drawbacks of membership were discussed along with the advantages. Apart from the need to avoid giving our prospective partners the impression that Britain would join whatever the cost, domestic considerations prompted a cautious form of words. Between the two elections, the Labour Government had failed in its bid to overcome de Gaulle's opposition to British entry, Powell had done a right about-turn on Europe, and in April 1970 a Gallup poll found that only 19 per cent favoured entry into the EEC. At this stage over half of the electorate even rejected the idea of any talks with the Six.[29]

Iain Macleod and other supporters of entry urged Heath to call for a national referendum on the terms of entry. The idea might have got into the manifesto, but Heath and Douglas-Home were opposed. Heath's objection, whether based on constitutional grounds or fear that the real issues would be obscured by partisan point-scoring, led him to miss an opportunity. The promise of a referendum would have strength-ened his position against Wilson and against the Conservative anti-Marketeers. Ironically, in view of his opposition to the idea, Heath was later accused of breaking an implicit undertaking to hold one. On 5 May, before the election date had been announced, he had told the British Chamber of Commerce in Paris that he did not believe that Parliament would approve a settlement which was unfair; nor, he added, would it be in the interests of the Community for its enlargement to 'take place except with the full-hearted consent of the Parliaments and peoples of the new member countries'. The phrase 'full-hearted consent', as Douglas Hurd later commented, 'fell victim to Mr Wilson's talent for distortion'. The sentence did not mean that Heath was suggesting a referendum; it clearly meant that Britain's consent would be gained, or not, by a decision taken by a majority in Parliament. At that time, of course, all three British parties were in favour of entry. At that stage, too, Wilson was similarly opposed to a referendum, telling Benn that he could not have 'a plebiscite'. Yet, as so often, Heath had used words which could later be thrown back against him.[30]

The negotiations opened on 30 June, the date fixed by the Labour Government, but made slow progress. The community did, however, assure the British negotiators that if after entry 'unacceptable situations arose, the very survival of the community would demand that the insti-tutions find equitable solutions' – an undertaking which proved impor-tant ten years later in the negotiations over the British contribution to the Community Budget. As before, France, where Gaullist influence remained strong, raised most of the difficulties. By the spring of 1971 a stalling or a breakdown of the negotiations seemed possible. All depended on the outcome of a meeting between Edward Heath and the French President. In the twelve hours of talks on 19 and 20 May – most of them between the two men alone with their interpreters – Heath convinced Pompidou that unlike Wilson he was a genuine European. 'The spirit of our talks', the French President said at a joint press confer-ence, 'enables me to think that the negotiations will be successful.'[31]

The negotiations were concluded at dawn on 23 June when Geoffrey Rippon reached an agreement to safeguard New Zealand dairy products. By securing a relatively good deal for New Zealand, Britain made the terms stiffer for herself. Nevertheless the French had made concessions, and a new formula on sugar was acceptable to the Commonwealth sugar producers; only fishing was left till later.

A White Paper on the agreement, published in early July, ended with the words: 'Every historic choice involves challenge as well as opportu-nity. Her Majesty's Government are convinced that the right decision for us is to accept the challenge, seize the opportunity and join the European Community.' On the same day a brochure explaining the terms was issued, and the Prime Minister gave a televised address. A majority of the country was still opposed to entry, although around 80 per cent accepted that it was inevitable. The White Paper necessarily left imprecise the extent of the economic benefits that entry would bring, since that depended on how British industry responded to the challenge of membership. It denied that there would be 'erosions of essential national sovereignty'; instead there would be 'a sharing and an enlarging of individual national sovereignty' in the EEC.[32]

Understandably, the White Paper made a reference to Harold Wilson's arguments for entry in 1967, when he had said, 'we won't take no for an answer'. This was an optimistic attempt to shame the Labour leader into supporting Heath's agreement just as Heath had supported Wilson's attempt in 1967. That was, of course, too much to expect. Ever the politician, never the statesman, Wilson was determined to oppose entry 'on Tory terms'. 'If the leader of the Labour Party', David Watt had written in the *Financial Times* in May, 'starts to discover a sudden burst of indignation on behalf of Caribbean sugar producers, Scottish fishermen and New Zealand farmers, many of us will be quietly sick.' During the next three years Harold Wilson was to induce widespread queasiness as he successively divested himself of all the major policies he had pursued as Prime Minister. His sole concern was the unity of the Labour Party under his leadership; the national interest was a trifling matter to be neglected in the pursuit of party advantage.[33]

Wilson was not the only Labour politician to upset the squeamish. In May 1971 James Callaghan had preceded him. Callaghan, who less than a year before had been a prominent member of a Government seeking entry into the EEC, announced that membership would threaten the 'language of Chaucer'. Whether or not he expected cohorts of distraught Chaucer-speakers to join the Labour Party, disappointingly he did not reveal how this menace would be enforced. There was nothing obscure about Denis Healey's position. The genial Healey managed to rat and re-rat in the space of four months. At the end of May he became a pro-Common Market convert; by the autumn, he had reverted to his earlier opposition, donning Benn's populism to enquire whether membership of the EEC would 'put an extra pat of butter on the plate of the ordinary man and woman in Britain?'[34]

Luckily many members of Wilson's party took a more exalted view of their duty than did their leader. George Thomson, whom Wilson had picked as his Common Market negotiator, said the Tory terms were ones which he 'would have recommended a Labour Cabinet to accept'.

George Brown also declared the terms 'acceptable' and 'fair'. So, more importantly, did the party's deputy leader, Roy Jenkins, who told the parliamentary Labour Party that if we lost the opportunity of entry now it would 'be gone for at least a decade and probably a lifetime'.[35]

Although both the major parties were deeply divided, the party conferences went well for their respective leaderships. At Labour's, the National Executive defeated by one million votes a left-wing proposal to withdraw from the Community, and the leadership's weasel policy of opposing 'the Tory terms', moved by Callaghan, gained a five to one majority. At the Tory conference in Brighton, Enoch Powell, washing out of his mind his earlier strong support for British entry, emulated Hugh Gaitskell with talk of a 'thousand years' of British independence, saying that he would not consent to British 'sovereignty being abolished or transformed'. Referring to Powell's previous strong support for British entry, Geoffrey Rippon had said, 'people may change their minds, but they should be humble about it'. Not so Powell, who had all the arrogant certainty of the convert. He was well answered by Alec Douglas-Home, and the conference voted eight to one for entry. The difficulties of the party leaderships were not at the seaside, however, but at Westminster.[36]

The successful conclusion of the negotiations had increased public support for entry – in July the pros drew level, or slightly ahead of the antis. But the temporary change in public opinion did not influence the Conservative MPs who were against the Common Market. In 1970 forty-four MPs had signed an Early Day Motion opposing British entry, and a year later the number of Conservative opponents approached sixty – more than enough to defeat the Government unless Labour MPs came to its aid. In these circumstances the Chief Whip, Francis Pym, recommended a free vote. His argument was that the Conservative antis felt so strongly that their numbers in the 'No' lobby would not be significantly diminished by a three-line whip and would certainly be higher than the Government's majority, while the granting of a free vote by the Government would encourage the Labour Party to follow suit and allow the Labour pro-Europeans to come into the Government lobby. Pym's argument was backed by a letter to the Prime Minister from Bill Rodgers, the organiser of the Labour Marketeers, urging a free vote since that would produce the biggest majority. Heath, Maudling and other senior ministers were initially opposed to the idea, understandably thinking that the Government should use its majority to approve the terms that had been agreed with the Six. Nevertheless Pym persevered, winning Whitelaw round, and shortly before the six-day debate, which began on Trafalgar Day, 21 October, the Prime Minister accepted the advice of his Chief Whip and authorised a free vote.[37]

Labour did not, however, follow suit. Either because Wilson deliberately broke a promise to Roy Jenkins, or more probably because he was overruled by Tony Benn (who had terminated his pro-Europe phase and was in many ways a mirror-image of Powell) and other members of the Shadow Cabinet, Labour imposed a three-line whip, and the front-bench Labour pro-Europeans – Jenkins, Thomson and Lever – were gagged. After Heath in the final speech had said that no Prime Minister had 'stood at this box in times of peace and asked the House to take a positive decision of such importance', the House voted. Thirty-nine Conservatives took advantage of the free vote to join the Labour Party in the 'No' lobby, while Roy Jenkins and sixty-seven Labour MPs, sustained by the knowledge that they were supporting Labour's former policy and that Heath's terms were at least as good as Wilson would have achieved, defied their party's three-line whip and went into the Government lobby, giving Heath a majority of 112. After two hours of celebration, the Prime Minister returned to Downing Street with a few close friends who listened to him playing Bach's First Prelude and Fugue for the 'Well-Tempered Clavier'.[38]

The majority of the Labour Party was not well-tempered. In the Commons chamber the Left were at their ugliest, and physical violence against the Labour Europeans looked likely. In the end the assaults stayed verbal, somebody shouting 'Fascist bastard!' at Roy Jenkins. Even without such nasty scenes, Labour's Europeans would have had to end their open co-operation with the Government. For the passage of the European Communities Bill, the Government was ostensibly on its own. This time evoking Pétain at Verdun, Powell declared, 'the bill will not pass'. The majority on second reading was only eight, and later once fell to four. But the Labour Marketeers were not prepared to let the success of their rebellion be nullified by subsequent votes. Christopher Mayhew, who joined the Liberals in 1974, and some elderly Labour MPs, who were not seeking re-election, remained in touch with the Government to ensure that enough of them were always absent to allow narrow Government victories. In consequence the Government won all of the 104 votes, and the bill passed the Commons unamended. That was a triumph for Pym as well as Heath.[39]

On Europe, as on other matters, Labour moved to the left, and Wilson followed his party. After Wilson and enough members of the Shadow Cabinet had changed their minds, or at least their votes, to give a narrow majority for the Benn scheme for a referendum on Europe, Roy Jenkins decided that he had had enough. He, Thomson and Lever resigned from the Shadow Cabinet, and Rodgers, Taverne, Owen and Mabon resigned from their junior jobs. This seemed a tactical error which strengthened Wilson's position. Certainly the Leader of the Opposition appeared well satisfied with Jenkins's resignation. In the lavatory of the Government lobby in the House of Commons,* contentedly puffing a large cigar, Wilson proclaimed, 'No man is indispensable, you know.' His audience, trapped in the next-door stall vainly trying to evade the worst of the cigar fumes, could only murmur assent.[41]

Napoleon, who demanded luck above all from his marshals and generals, would not have employed Ted Heath. On election night, as the victor made his way through the crowds outside Central Office, he had a cigarette painfully stubbed out on his neck by a Labour supporter. In January 1972 as he signed the Treaty of Accession in Brussels – Wilson declined to attend the ceremony, but George Brown had the courtesy to accept – a woman protesting against (of all things) the redevelopment of Covent Garden threw ink over him. The Europhobes have been throwing ink ever since, but Heath has continued to defy them. As Douglas Hurd rightly said, 'Heath believed passionately that realism should prevail if facts were reasonably presented.' That was a surprisingly optimistic attitude for a Tory statesman and is presumably one reason why he has been judged a clumsy politician in the modern age of cynicism. Heath's supporters might wish that he had adopted some of the showmanship of his mentor Macmillan on the European issue – with a touch more flair, his policies in every field would have been better received. Even with that, Heath would still have been almost unique among recent political leaders: a Prime Minister who was undone by an overdose of integrity.[42]

Both then and later, the Europhobes claimed that Heath and the Government had misled the Conservative Party and the country about the political implications of joining the EEC. The allegation was as false about 1970–73 as it was about Harold Macmillan's earlier application. There was no concealment. Like Macmillan, Heath made it clear from the start that joining Europe was a political venture, which was why Powell had so violently attacked it at the Brighton conference. The Government's White Paper was fairly widely read, and a short version of it was delivered to every household in the country. Nor was there any camouflage in the party's literature. A leaflet published by Central Office, *Sovereignty and the Common Market*, squarely set out the pos-

---

* For some reason Wilson preferred to use this lavatory, where he was more likely to meet Conservative than Labour MPs. From July 1973 onwards, he had some significant meetings there with Powell who was considering defecting from the Conservative Party. 'There were half a dozen meetings with Wilson in the loo,' Powell said later.[40]

ition. After pointing out that, because many decisions were governed by 'outside influences' and 'international obligations', Britain already did 'not have complete freedom of action', the leaflet said:

> If Britain joins, certain important decisions will become a joint responsibility instead of just a British one. But as an equal partner we would have an equal say in influencing those decisions ... For this reason it is misleading to talk of Britain 'surrendering' sovereignty. As others would influence our future, we should influence theirs ... Common Market membership would mean that Britain and her partners would exercise sovereignty in a new and larger dimension.

And in a CPC pamphlet, published in June 1971, *Our European Destiny*, Alec Douglas-Home wrote that on two counts he was

> in full agreement with the most vocal opponent [Enoch Powell] of our entry into Europe. The first is that our application is a step of the utmost political significance, and the second is that there is a danger of its being overlooked in the public debate on the economic issues.

Sir Alec thought much of the controversy about entry was over the economic effects because these concerned the public most. But 'if anyone had the stamina', Sir Alec continued, 'to read a year of speeches ... by ministers ... he would find that they constantly return to this theme' of the political case for entry. He thought it 'misleading to talk about sacrificing and surrendering sovereignty'. After all, we shared sovereignty in NATO. Although it might seem 'paradoxical', he thought 'the only way to preserve our independence [was] to join a large grouping'. Only the most frustrated conspiracy theorist could find in either of these publications any intention to hide the political implications of entry from the British people or the Conservative Party. Despite the Right's attempt to rewrite history, the Government's campaign to join the EEC was free from concealment and chicanery.

The 1972 Miners' Strike

Britain's prospective entry into the European Community was one of the main factors determining the future course of the Government's economic policy. On his visits round the country the Prime Minister had seen abandoned factories in the old industrial areas, as employers exercised their preference for expanding in places far away from existing, out-of-date plant. He was, however, convinced that the old industrial conurbations could not be written off and that economic recovery required a transformation not only of them but over the whole country. He thought British industry needed to be modernised on a scale that the defeated countries of Europe had achieved after the war with the help of Marshall Aid.

The second main factor was the seemingly unending rise in unemployment. A generation that has grown accustomed to unemployment being two or three million on the official figures – the real total being often much higher – may find it difficult to understand the general anger and dismay in 1971 at the failure of the Government's economic measures to prevent unemployment rising to the one million mark. That dismay was not confined to a man like Heath who had been schooled by Harold Macmillan in the horrors of unemployment in Stockton-on-Tees before the war; it was widespread. In November, Barber put the reduction of unemployment at the head of the Government's objectives, and virtually everybody agreed that it had got its priorities right. All the same, unemployment was clearly going to rise above one million fairly early in the New Year.

Both entry into the EEC and the compulsion to lower unemployment pointed to the need for expansion. The third major factor – a miners' strike – pointed to the need for an incomes policy. The leadership's short-sighted ruling out of such a policy in the 1970 manifesto demonstrated its misplaced faith in its proposals for the reform of industrial relations. These, it was assumed, would restore rationality to pay bargaining and thus halt the inflationary push of excessive wage settlements. While the necessary legislation was being prepared, the Government, as has been seen, had operated an informal incomes policy for the public sector, attempting to hold wage increases below the level of inflation to set an example for other employers. For most of 1971 this policy enjoyed a qualified success largely because of the rise in unemployment. In December, however, the National Union of Mineworkers narrowly voted for a strike to press a pay claim of 47 per cent.

During the previous decade the mining work-force had fallen by more than half, from 700,000 to under 300,000, and the miners' place in the earnings league had also declined. Under the firm but benevolent rule of Lord (Alf) Robens, Chairman of the National Coal Board, these adjustments had been peacefully achieved. They may, however, have been too precipitous, and anyway Robens had left in 1971, succeeded by Derek Ezra, an able technocrat with no political experience and few of Robens's political skills. In July there had been a sign of an imminent eruption when the union's conference decided to reduce the majority necessary to authorise strike action. This was a timely decision for the union's militants; under the old rules they would have lost the vote in December.[43]

Nevertheless, the Government was lamentably ill-prepared for a strike. The miners' union was widely regarded as an extinct volcano, and the Department of Employment grossly underestimated the miners' resolve to regain their former position. The department was also remiss in not having taken note of a new and effective weapon employed in a dispute in Yorkshire in 1969 by a young militant from Barnsley, Arthur Scargill: flying pickets, which could be bussed around the country to blockade ports and power stations. Finally, the department was out of touch with opinion in the coalfields, believing that the moderation of the miners' leader, Joe Gormley, was shared by other officials, many of whom were in fact both militant trade unionists and, like Scargill, political extremists eager to fight the class war. Consequently, no precautions had been taken to avoid a serious strike, and no plans had been made to defeat it. Although coal stocks were low, the department was not even particularly perturbed by the onset of the strike, believing that after letting off steam for a week or two the miners would settle for a reasonable sum.[44]

All those calculations were wrong. The miners were united behind the strike, and nobody evinced any inclination to compromise. The police had no answer to Scargill's flying pickets. His well-planned campaign culminated in a mass demonstration at Saltley Coke Depot in Birmingham where there were, it was wrongly believed, large stocks of coal. The Chief Constable of Birmingham regarded the action of the pickets who were blockading Saltley as 'illegal and tantamount to intimidation'. That was putting it mildly, but he assured Maudling, the Home Secretary, that only over his dead body would the miners succeed in closing it. Shortly afterwards, however, with more than 10,000 pickets outside the gates and only a few policemen to control their intimidation, the Chief Constable decided that there might be other dead bodies if he did not close the depot. He therefore abandoned the struggle. To colleagues who wondered why Maudling had not used troops to support the police, the Home Secretary replied that, if they had gone in, 'should they have had their rifles loaded or unloaded?'[45]

The implication of Maudling's question was correct. While neither the Government nor the police distinguished themselves, Scargill's army of flying pickets and 'the class war' he revelled in – 'we wished to paralyse the nation's economy', he later said – could only have been beaten by an unacceptable degree of force. In any case the miners had won. Even before its defeat at Saltley, the Government had had to declare another State of Emergency. People were asked to heat only one room in the house. Much of industry had to work a shorter week, and nearly a million workers were laid off. In Whitehall there were fears of a total black-out and of riots and sewage in the streets. The generous Lord Wilberforce had again to be called upon. His speedy report conceded, as *The Times* said, 'almost all the miners' case and most of the money they demanded'. Even that was not enough. So strong was the miners' position that at a meeting at Downing Street with Heath, Barber and Carr, the leaders of the NUM were able to wring further concessions from the Government before graciously agreeing a return to work.[46]

Even at the end of the strike the miners enjoyed much public sympathy. The Government's case was further weakened because MPs had tactfully awarded themselves a 28 per cent pay increase, more than doubling the Queen's Civil List at the same time. Against this background, Scargill's tactics could not easily be presented as a major threat to the British system of Government, even though he exulted on television that Saltley 'was living proof that the working class had only to flex its muscles and it could bring Governments, employers, society, to a complete standstill'. Made overconfident by his victory, 'Britain's Lenin', as Jimmy Reid later called him, discovered a dozen years later that a flexing of muscles was not necessarily enough to bring the country to a standstill or to save his union from decimation and future impotence.[47]

In a broadcast the Prime Minister stressed the absurdity of a class war: 'there could not be any "we" or "they". There was only "us" – all of us. If the Government is defeated, then the country is defeated.' The Government was ready to sit down with the employers and unions. 'We must find a more sensible way to settle our differences.' Although Heath was dignified and sensible, his belief in reason led him to ignore a fundamental flaw in his approach. Many trade unionists, Scargill among them, did not want a more sensible way of settling differences, because they did not want those differences settled except on their own terms; they preferred the maximum amount of disruption in the misplaced confidence that however much damage they caused they would come out on top in the end.[48]

As the Government's first objective was to bring down unemployment by expanding the economy, deflation and rising unemployment could obviously not be used to fight wage inflation. The only alternative weapon was an official incomes policy, something which Heath in more optimistic times had ruled out. Maudling, on the other hand, had never thought much of the Government's N–1 efforts and had always favoured an incomes policy. Well before the miners' strike, in the autumn of 1971, he had written a memorandum on the subject for the Cabinet, which at Heath's request he did not circulate. In his memorandum Maudling pointed out the defects of other solutions: 'To restrict the volume of money only means in modern conditions that, while the socially powerful continue to expand their incomes, more and more of the less powerful lose their jobs altogether while the economy stagnates and investment collapses.' Maudling concluded that in modern circumstances a capitalist economy had to be prepared 'to accept a far greater degree of systematic control over the level of incomes and prices than we have ever contemplated before'. The logic of Maulding's argument was shortly to be made inescapable not only by the miners' strike but also by the evolution of the Government's economic policy. Yet before Barber could open his 1972 Budget, the Government was faced with yet another crisis in which Maudling played a central role.[49]

Northern Ireland

Shortly before Lord Wilberforce produced his report on the miners' strike, William Rees-Mogg in a leading article in *The Times* contended that the Home Secretary should not have been expected to act as Chairman of the Emergency Committee while he was also 'the Minister responsible for Northern Ireland'. Probably, indeed, Reginald Maudling should never have been the Minister responsible for Northern Ireland. One of the major disadvantages of Quintin Hogg not going to the Home Office in 1970 was that he was not the Minister in charge of Northern Ireland. Coming from an Ulster family, Hogg understood its complexity and was aware of the intense prejudices of most people in the country. Maudling did not have that knowledge and was too rational a man to understand or sympathise with the people of the province. His remark that the best that could be hoped for was 'an acceptable level of violence' was ill-judged. As a friend told him, his addiction to logic was an obstacle to him making progress there. Amid all his multifarious problems and duties as Home Secretary – immigration, law and order, rising social protest – Maudling lacked the time and the temperament to master the problems of Northern Ireland – if indeed such a thing was possible.[50]

In 1970 the main problem facing British soldiers in Northern Ireland was rioting between the two communities on the streets. The Army combated the rioting with skill, good humour and restraint, although curfews and other necessary measures further alienated the nationalist community. It was not sufficiently alienated, however, for the Provisional IRA, which decided that terrorism would be a quicker way of getting rid of the British. After the murder of three very young off-duty Scottish soldiers on 10 March, violence intensified. The Northern Ireland Government, believing that stronger measures were necessary, pressed for the introduction of internment – imprisonment without trial. That was not the view of the Army. On their frequent visits to Northern Ireland, Defence Ministers always asked soldiers of all ranks whether the politicians were stopping them doing things which might cut down terrorism, and they invariably received the answer 'no'. Senior officers thought internment would merely exacerbate the situation.[51]

Nevertheless Brian Faulkner, the Northern Irish Prime Minister, and the loyalist community were sure that internment was justified by the level of violence and would help to bring it down. On a visit to London, despite military advice to the contrary, he converted Maudling and Heath. The frequent complaints that Maudling was lazy were nearly always ill-founded; he only seemed so, because his mind worked so quickly that he was able to despatch business in much less time than was needed by his slower-witted colleagues. Yet over internment the Ministry of Defence thought the Home Office had been far too casual. Certainly the results were disastrous. Internment had sometimes worked in the past, but it was unlikely to do so unless the Republic also introduced it, and in 1971 there was no chance of Dublin following suit. That the North would resort to internment had been rumoured for some time; consequently many of the IRA leaders took refuge in the South. That was not the fault of the Home Office. Yet the minimum requirement of internment, if the policy was to have any prospect of succeeding, was that the right people should be interned. And it was here, in the view of the Ministry of Defence, that the Home Office should have been more assiduous in checking the information it was acting on.[52]

Whoever was to blame, over 300 men were rounded up and put behind bars on 9 August 1971. As nearly all of them were Catholics and many of them were either innocent or had long been inactive, the chief beneficiaries were the IRA. Maudling conceded that 'the resentment in the Catholic community was extreme' and that internment had made the political situation 'far more dangerous', but claimed that 'the security situation had been improved'. If that was so, it was because far more soldiers had been sent to the province. Yet it was hard to detect any improvement. Instead, the casualty figures suggested a marked deterioration. Twenty-five people were killed in 1970, 173 in 1971 and 474 in 1972; and of the 173 who died in 1971, all but twenty-eight were killed after the introduction of internment.[53]

The blunder of internment was followed by the disaster of 'Bloody Sunday'. After an illegal march by civil-rights activists in Londonderry on 30 January 1972, stones were thrown at soldiers, and the Parachute Regiment was ordered to disperse the stone-throwers. They thought they were being fired on (although recent evidence suggests that the firing came from another unit of the British Army working under cover) and they ended up killing thirteen unarmed civilians. An inquiry by Lord Widgery, the Lord Chief Justice, largely exonerated the paratroops, but the incident has never been fully explained. In any case it gave a new impetus to terrorism, greatly increasing the number of atrocities. 21,000 soldiers were now in the province, and the 'estrangement between the two communities', Maudling told his colleagues, was 'virtually complete'; the system of Government had broken down. Having so many of its soldiers on duty in Northern Ireland, the British Government decided that security in the province must be entirely in its hands. Accordingly, Direct Rule from London was imposed, and Whitelaw became the first Secretary of State for Northern Ireland, a post in which he excelled. The Stormont Government and parliament were abolished. Right though it was, that decision led to the breaking of the alliance between the Conservative Party and the Ulster Unionists. As a result, the Conservatives and their supporters won fewer seats than Labour in the 1974 election. And so, two years after the ending of Stormont, the Heath Government itself was brought to an end.[54]

CHAPTER XII

Undermining One-Nation[1]

Northern Ireland on the brink of civil war was the gravest and most important problem confronting the Heath Government. But it was only one of several crises that were consuming ministers' energies: the continual risk of defeat in the series of close votes on the European Communities Bill; the rise of unemployment to over 1 million in January; a motion of no confidence in February which was defeated by a mere eight votes; and a six-week miners' strike. The first two months of 1972 were, in John Campbell's judgement, 'the most dreadful short period of concentrated stress ever endured by a British Government in peacetime'.[1]

The quality of Anthony Barber's 1972 Budget, which was opened three days before the imposition of Direct Rule, may have been affected by this concatenation of crises. Certainly it was itself a potent source of a later crisis. To bring down unemployment and to re-equip industry to meet the challenge of increased competition within the EEC, Barber (although the guiding hand was the Prime Minister's) had put together a massively reflationary Budget. Industry was allowed free depreciation on new plant and machinery. Taxation was reduced, while pensions and benefits were raised. At the same time public expenditure was even more drastically increased. The PSBR estimate for 1972–3 was nearly trebled. The Budget's measures were intended to accelerate the rate of growth to 5 per cent a year before slowing down. For the Government to embark on such a dash for growth was, in the light of previous experience, remarkable. The Prime Minister hoped to break out of the stop–go cycle once and for all. 'This time,' he told the NEDC in September 1973, 'we are determined to sail through the whirlpool.' While that may be correct nautical practice, yachtsmen do not usually create their own whirlpool before deciding to sail through it.[2]

Such a hectic expansion would have been unwise at any point, but this one was particularly ill-timed. As the other leading industrial countries were also expanding, commodity prices rose by 10 per cent in the first quarter of 1972 and were to double in two years. Furthermore, without an incomes policy, such an expansion was bound to fuel wage inflation. And finally the removal of credit restrictions in 1971 had already fuelled a credit boom, which had not found its way into industry owing to the poor rate of return, but into property and hotel building.[3]

Even more remarkable than Barber's reckless policy was the support it enjoyed. Tory back-benchers gave the Chancellor a standing ovation; the Leader of the Opposition praised him. Nobody in the Cabinet objected. Keith Joseph and Margaret Thatcher, two of the Budget's greatest beneficiaries and, later, two of its sternest critics, greatly increased the spending of their departments. Joseph increased the proportion of GNP devoted to social expenditure from 23.4 per cent to 27.3 per cent. Mrs Thatcher was not far behind: her fine White Paper, *Education, a Framework for Expansion*, published in December 1972, envisaged a rise in spending in real terms of 50 per cent over the next decade. The Chief Economic Adviser, Donald MacDougall, who had earlier warned that it was dangerous to try to bring down unemployment so quickly, was worried by the increased public expenditure, most of which would come on stream at the top of the boom just when it was least wanted; but he was almost alone. The top civil servants favoured expansion. Even the Governor of the Bank, who was not in the inner circle, had said earlier that unemployment was 'much too high'. The National Institute doubted if Barber had done enough to ensure the required growth. *The Times*, too, which was soon to become a citadel of rigid Friedmanite monetarism, did not mention inflation in its leading article on the Budget and was 'by no means certain' that the Chancellor had done enough 'on either economic or social grounds'.[4]

In his Budget speech the Chancellor had said that it was 'neither necessary nor desirable to distort domestic economies . . . to maintain unrealistic exchange rates . . .' Three months later an exchange crisis forced Barber to act on his own hint. The pound, which in December 1971 had been fixed at the Smithsonian Conference at what was even then the too high rate of $2.60 to the pound, was allowed to float. Because of recent high wage settlements and industrial unrest, it floated down. This aided exports, but as world commodity prices steadily rose, it also aided inflation.[5]

The U-Turns

On the evening of Budget Day, the Government published a White Paper heralding an Industry Bill which had been devised by Heath mainly in consultation with Sir William Armstrong, the Head of the Home Civil Service, and other officials. This was partly because the ministerial team at the DTI included the right-wing free-marketeers Nicholas Ridley and Fred Corfield. They had to be excluded from the planning of the Act, and by the end of March they had been despatched. As well as providing 100 per cent capital allowances for industry, the bill set up machinery which bore a suspicious resemblance to institutions swept away in the early days of the Government. The new Industrial Development Executive (IDE) might be under direct ministerial control, unlike Labour's IRC, but the new brand of alphabet soup could not disguise the similarity of the basic ingredients. Despite strong initial opposition from the Prime Minister, Peter Walker (who replaced Davies at the DTI in November) used the Act to launch ambitious investment programmes in the steel and coal industries, and aid was directed towards high-technology enterprises such as the computer firm ICL. As Walker wrote, 'in a frantic phase, the DTI attempted to rationalise and modernise British industry'. That was all to the good, but while the investment programmes were admirable in themselves, they increased the strain on an already overloaded economy.[6]

In an interview conducted during the bill's progress through Parliament, Heath admitted candidly that 'We have got a tremendous problem in communication as a Government.' That was an understatement but, despite the lack of warning of this abrupt change of policy, the Government's back-benchers took it calmly. The bill gained a second reading without a division, the right-wing Jock Bruce-Gardyne having failed to find a seconder to force one. Nevertheless the attitude of many back-benchers was thought to be 'one of acquiescence rather than support'. What was frequently described later as Heath's adoption of socialism was not attacked at the time. Not even Enoch Powell or Nicholas Ridley said a word in opposition. So uncontentious was the bill that there was not even a debate on the third reading, let alone a vote.[7]

The Cabinet was similarly acquiescent. Margaret Thatcher wrote in her memoirs that 'Keith and I and probably others were extremely unhappy.' Nevertheless their unhappiness did not translate into serious opposition in Cabinet. Only later did she wonder if she should have resigned. The best explanation she could then give, in her memoirs, for not having done so was that 'those of us who disliked what was happening had not yet either fully analysed the situation or worked out an alternative approach'.[8]

Talks with the unions and (separately) with the employers on pay and prices started before the Budget. Those with the unions were bedevilled by troubles caused by the Industrial Relations Act. In April the Government won from the NIRC (National Industrial Relations Court) an order for a fortnight's cooling-off period before a national railway work-to-rule. When that made no difference, the new Employ-ment Secretary, Maurice Macmillan, acting on Geoffrey Howe's advice, applied for and obtained a court order for a ballot on the offer to the union that was on the table. The vote was three to one in favour of resumed strike action. Howe, the Solicitor General and chief author of the Industrial Relations Act, later admitted his misjudgement, generously conceding that if Robert Carr had still been the Employment Secretary the error would probably have been avoided. A very nice man, Mac-millan had been an excellent Minister at the Treasury, but sending him to Employment was almost as eccentric as sending John Davies to Industry. An involuntary teetotaller was the last man to deal successfully with the union leaders.[9]

Almost immediately afterwards came a much greater setback, for which judges not politicians were to blame. Some Liverpool dockers blacked and picketed the new container terminals and the lorries that used them. One of the firms hit by the dockers' action, Heaton's, took the Transport Union to the NIRC, which ordered the dockers to stop their action. The TGWU, which did not recognise the court and therefore paid no attention, was fined £55,000 and faced the sequestration of its assets if it did not pay. With the TUC's permission the TGWU then paid the fine and appealed against the decision of the NIRC. In an astonishing judgement, Lord Denning and the Court of Appeal ruled that unions could not be held responsible for infringements of the new law by individual members. On hearing the news, Robert Carr and Geoffrey Howe, his co-author of the Act, 'both felt we might as well jump off Westminster Bridge that morning'. Although Denning had long been the outstanding judge on the bench, the Appeal Court's judgement was blatantly wrong, if not mischievous. (Howe later speculated that the higher judges may have felt a touch of 'jealousy' of 'the crisp clarity of Mr Justice Donaldson's written judgements' in the NIRC.) Yet, mis-taken as it was, Denning's judgement highlighted the Act's flaw over registration and its poor drafting. The House of Lords soon reversed Denning's decision and restored Donaldson's judgement, but by then the damage had been done.[10]

Denning's ruling had left the NIRC no alternative but to press charges against individuals, and three London shop stewards were warned they faced imprisonment for contempt of court. This gave the unions a wel-come cause for indignation – 35,000 dockers were already on strike. While the prospective incarceration of the shop stewards was a disaster for the Government, it was also a reverse for the TGWU leader, Jack Jones. Denning, too, was uneasy at what had happened. 'We were influ-enced', he later said, 'perhaps by the state of the country, by the realisation that there would be a general strike which would paralyse the whole nation . . .' Accordingly, at Denning's suggestion, a previously unknown figure, the Official Solicitor, was cast as the good fairy to help spirit the imprisoned shop stewards away from the threat of Pentonville. He appeared in the Court of Appeal on the dockers' behalf and, on the spurious grounds that the NIRC had acted upon insufficient evidence, Denning and his fellow judges stopped the warrants for the men's arrest. Deprived of the chance to share immortality with the Tolpuddle Martyrs (with whom, idiotically, they were compared by Tony Benn), one of the men protested that the decision to keep him out of gaol was 'a bloody liberty'.[11]

In another dockers' case the NIRC, acting in accordance with Denning's judgement, ordered the imprisonment of five more pickets. They were arrested by a bad fairy, the Tipstaff, who conveyed them to Pentonville. Sympathetic strikes and mass demonstrations outside the prison were organised in support of the 'Pentonville Five', who attracted massive public backing. However reprehensible their actions – and what the dockers had been doing was indefensible – most people firmly believed that in Britain strikers should not be sent to prison. On 26 July the TUC called for a one-day general strike at the end of the month which, unlike 1926, would have been a general strike for a political not an industrial purpose.[12]

Before that, fortunately, the House of Lords had overturned Denning's judgement, and the Pentonville Five were released, though still in contempt of court. The dockers remained on strike, however, and the Government was forced to declare another State of Emergency. By their behaviour over the years the dockers had driven trade and work away from the traditional ports to the new container ports. Now, to induce them to return to work, they were guaranteed pay in jobs which they had destroyed or were about to destroy – not a happy example of the Government's modernisation of Britain.[13]

Denning's fallacious judgement, followed by the legal flummery of the Official Solicitor and the Tipstaff, had now effectively killed the Industrial Relations Act. Its underlying principles continued to enjoy public support, but its unhappy history did not enhance the Government's reputation for competence. Although the unions could rejoice at their apparent victory now, a decade and a half later they turned out to be the main victims of their own campaign.[14]

In their talks with the Government the unions not surprisingly pressed for the abandonment of the Act. Equally unsurprisingly the Government would not agree. Yet, after the CBI and the unions had discussed the idea of a new conciliatory body, Heath told the unions that the Government hoped that the Act 'would only be used as a matter of last resort'; and the unions did not press for its formal repeal. The Government's object in the talks was to lower the level of wage claims. Wage restraint had been made all the more necessary by the recent Budget and the Government's aim of 5 per cent growth. Inside the Cabinet, Reginald Maudling pressed for a statutory prices and incomes policy, but he was forced out of office in July because of his peripheral connection with the corrupt architect, John Poulson. Heath authorised the preparation of a bill as a contingency plan, but like the majority of his Cabinet he still preferred a voluntary solution. By September he was offering a deal which linked restrictions to a continuation of the ambitious growth strategy. The package also included an element of social justice, with help for pensioners and the lower paid. There was, as Heath's judicious biographer has written, 'near universal support for Heath's approach in 1972 . . . and little confidence that the country could be saved from the abyss by any other means'.[15]

Had the trade-union leaders been the reasonable men Ted Heath assumed them to be, they would have accepted his package. They had long claimed a share in Government, yet now when they were given the chance they 'found it easier', in Keith Middlemas's words, 'to have the terms imposed by government than to persuade their own members to accept what the majority of them regarded as necessary'. Some of the union leaders, still in the tradition of their predecessors in the fifties and early sixties who had operated in conditions of full employment without grossly exploiting their bargaining position, did want to accept. Others, intent on exercising all the power at their disposal, maintained, like earlier over-mighty subjects in British history, an unswerving allegiance to their own short-term interest. In the fifties and sixties, George Brown said in April 1972, the leaders of the unions had been 'genuine social democrats', but that was no longer so. Now there was 'a different kind of leadership, with a different interest', a change which Heath did not properly take into account. Hence his continuing optimism that the TUC would in time see reason and accept his generous terms.[16]

Heath also underrated the close links between the TUC and the Labour Party. The Prime Minister was probably misled by his good personal relations with a number of the union leaders. He got on well with Vic Feather, the General Secretary of the TUC. Like some other union leaders, Feather was a genuine social democrat, but he was a prisoner of more militant spirits on his council. Even such non-social democrats as Jack Jones and Hugh Scanlon later testified to the efforts of Heath to offer 'an attractive package to work people', Jones writing that the Prime Minister had 'revealed the human face of Toryism'. But, at the time, he and Scanlon were too confident of their continuing strength to respond to his lead.[17]

And the unions were indeed strong. The British trade unions were the most politically powerful in the world. Cecil King even considered them to be 'stronger than the Government'. So did some trade unionists, and on 28 September the TUC General Council, thinking they could get more out of the Prime Minister, rejected the Government's proposals 'as unacceptable'. On television that night Heath appealed to people 'to think rationally' and 'to think of the nation as a whole'. Society could 'only beat rising prices if it acted together as one nation'. But the One-Nation concept was even less appealing to the union bosses than to the Conservative Right. Heath continued the talks, still unrealistically hoping that reason would prevail, a hope which was scotched at tripartite talks at Chequers on 16 October and later in Downing Street. Jones and Scanlon would not budge from their position that prices should be legally controlled while wages were left free, a proposition so obviously absurd that further discussion was futile, and on 2 November the talks were at last broken off.[18]

Four days later Heath told the House that the Government had 'come to the conclusion that we have no alternative but to bring in statutory measures' to control prices and incomes. Harold Wilson's reaction was muted, but Enoch Powell, in Hurd's words, 'hissing balefully from behind', asked the Prime Minister if 'in introducing a compulsory control of wages and prices, in contravention of the deepest commitment of this party [he had] taken leave of his senses?' In fact Powell, not Heath, was suffering a rupture from reality. In the early years of the Thatcher Government it was often claimed that there was 'no alternative' to the Government's policy when there clearly was. Under the Heath Government that claim was seldom made, though in 1972 it was more true. Both the Prime Minister and the Chancellor of the Exchequer were badly at fault over the 1972 Budget, but Powell's implicit belief that rising wage claims could be prevented by a massive dose of deflation (euphemistically called 'controlling the money supply') was in the circumstances of 1972 mere moonshine. Deflation works by creating heavy unemployment, which the unions would not have passively accepted; and such key unions as the miners' and the electricity workers' had demonstrated their power to cause havoc and disruption. Even von Hayek, a much more expert exponent of free-market economics than Enoch Powell, had formed the view that 'the only hope of escape from the vicious circle would seem to be to persuade the trade unions in general to agree to an alternative method of wage determination . . .' Yet Powell preferred to stick to being a 'pedlar of panaceas'.[19]

The lack of an alternative was confirmed by the absence of Cabinet opposition to statutory controls. Neither Keith Joseph nor Margaret Thatcher raised any objection, and nobody mentioned that the policy they had now adopted had been ruled out in the party's election manifesto. Geoffrey Howe went even further, entering the Cabinet, under Peter Walker at the DTI, as 'the nation's comprehensive price controller'. The parliamentary party was only slightly less unanimous in its support. Powell alone voted against the bill, which imposed a ninety-day freeze on prices and industry, while Biffen, Bruce-Gardyne and Neil Marten abstained. The overwhelming majority of Conservative MPs agreed with the new policy; even Angus Maude had spoken in support of a prices and incomes policy at the Party Conference.[20]

The Party Chairman, Lord Carrington, sent a long letter to every Conservative constituency chairman explaining why the Government had resorted to incomes policy, but approval within the parliamentary party was already echoed at the grass roots and in the press. Ministers could point to concrete evidence to back this popular support; although Labour's statutory policy had ended in tears a few years earlier, a similar package was now working well for President Nixon in the United States. In the following month the Government held off Labour in the closely fought Uxbridge by-election, but in the normally safe Conservative seat, Sutton and Cheam, it was defeated by the Liberals (who had earlier seized Rochdale from Labour). In July 1973, moreover, the Liberals took Ripon and the Isle of Ely from the Conservatives, and during the year the party won more votes than either the Government or the Labour Party. The recurrent post-war Conservative nightmare of a sustained Liberal revival was added to Heath's many problems.[21]

The unions declined to take part in negotiations on the next phase of the incomes policy to succeed the freeze of Stage I. At a press conference at Lancaster House in the middle of January, Heath unveiled Stage II which established a Pay Board and a Price Commission – bodies which differed very little from Labour's Prices and Income Board, culled by the Government in 1970. To replace the freeze, a new norm was set which permitted pay increases of £1 per week plus 4 per cent. Once again, low-paid workers would do best; those on the highest salaries were restricted to yearly increases of £250. The TUC refused to co-operate with either the Pay Board or the Price Commission, but after a few short strikes, the most serious of which was by the gasworkers, Stage II like Stage I was generally observed. A summons by the TUC for 'a day of national protest and stoppage' on 1 May was answered by only some 1,600,000 workers; and the miners rejected their leaders' call for a strike.[22]

279

The Government was determined to persist with its target of 5 per cent growth. Accordingly, Barber's March Budget was what he called 'broadly neutral', which meant that it made no adjustments to the wildly reflationary course he had set the year before. Such adjustments had been made all the more necessary by the commodity price boom which sharply raised the price of imports. Only two months later, therefore, Barber had to take action and cut public expenditure for 1974–5 in a package which also reduced the current year's spending. This implicit acceptance that the growth policy had gone too far was a bitter blow to the Government; even so, it was insufficient to stop the economy overheating. By October, the Government faced a balance of payments crisis as the cost of imports soared and the price of industrial raw materials rose in response to the new pressure of demand. Even the revival in exports after the flotation of the pound could not compensate for the leap in import costs. The deficit on the current account for 1973 turned out to be £1 billion – almost as large as the 1971 surplus.[23]

In a paper to Heath's Steering Committee in February, Michael Fraser had warned that while most people were reluctantly prepared to accept a statutory authority 'as a temporary expedient to deal with a critical situation', few people would be prepared in the long term to accept such a 'prodigious extension of the power of the state'. Fraser envisaged a new body to deal with the problem of pay relativities, but nothing was done. Probably Heath's best course, both economically and electorally, would have been to announce then a strict Stage III, which would have taken him over the next election, to be followed by a gradual liberalisation.[24]

But the Prime Minister's urge for negotiations with the TUC got the better of him, and further talks began in April. Heath was misjudging the TUC and his own party. Labour had partly recovered from its three years of in-fighting, and its agreements with the TUC made it unlikely that the Prime Minister could persuade the union leaders to reach an agreement with him. At the same time Heath, who had long been impatient with industrialists for absorbing the extra tax incentives offered by the Government without increased investment, and who in a different connection was shortly to 'condemn the unpleasant and unacceptable face of capitalism', annoyed many of his colleagues and the CBI by his further overtures and prospective concessions to the TUC.[25]

The negotiations broke down as they were bound to do, and Stage III was announced in October. Under it, wages could rise by either £2.25 or 7 per cent; the upper limit on rises was now relaxed to £350. In addition, the Government tried to ease worries about inflation by devising a system of 'threshold' payments, which would be triggered automatically as prices rose. There would also be a flat £10 Christmas bonus for pensioners. The package was well designed, but the Government's incomes policy had now lasted for a year, and public support for it was falling. A year before, *The Economist* found, 75 per cent had favoured a lowering of union pay claims; now over half thought the unions were justified in seeking more money. Still, other things being equal, the policy might just have held, but as usual for the Heath Government 'other things' were not.[26]

What Gore Vidal calls 'the serene corruption of American politics', allied to the intrigues of Henry Kissinger, had frustrated the plan of the US Secretary of State, William Rogers, for a fair settlement of the Arab–Israeli conflict. Kissinger wanted a more pro-Israeli stance and Rogers's job. Hence it was only a matter of time before Egypt and Syria launched a war to regain their land occupied by Israel since 1967. Heath, Home and other European leaders were well aware of the dangers but, as always, Kissinger, who had in 1973 got Rogers's job, thought he knew best. It was not 'physically possible for the Arabs', Alec Douglas-Home told the Conservative Party Conference after the war had begun, 'to go on gazing indefinitely across cease-fire lines at their own lands without the eruption of war'. The Europeans were 'genuinely concerned', Kissinger later conceded with good reason, 'that our failure to press a settlement on Israel had produced war, that we had in effect put European interests at stake for reason of American domestic politics'. As the war was indeed largely the fault of Kissinger and the US, Heath was under no obligation to help Kissinger make the Middle East mess even worse. Like the other European powers (except the Netherlands) therefore, he did not allow the Americans to fly arms to Israel from British airfields. Nonetheless that could not exempt Britain from the quadrupling of the price of oil imposed by Saudi Arabia and other oil producers in response to America's behaviour.[27]

Unlike all America's other European allies, Heath did not dissociate Britain from the United States' gratuitous bombing of Vietnam in 1972. 'What you did', Nixon later told him, 'didn't go unnoticed.' All the same, Kissinger wrote in his memoirs, 'we were witnessing a revolution in British foreign policy'. It was hardly that; Douglas-Home merely told Kissinger that there was not much point in Britain unflinchingly supporting America when there was underlying disagreement. Heath was certainly not anti-American, but his commitment to Europe made him determined not to repeat Macmillan's mistake of appearing to be America's surrogate in Europe. Hence, according to Kissinger, the

United States 'faced in Heath the curiosity of a more benign British version of de Gaulle'. Almost uniquely among recent British Prime Ministers – Conservative or Labour – Heath did not fawn on the White House; sensibly avoiding the phrase 'the special relationship', he merely talked of the 'natural relationship'.[28]

The Yom Kippur war was a disaster for the world, bringing 'the golden age of capitalism' to a close. More immediately, it was disastrous for the Heath Government. That, however, was not yet evident at the Conservative Party Conference at Blackpool which virtually coincided with the beginning of the war and the announcement of Stage III. In his last speech to the party as leader, Heath recited the achievements of the Government in accordance with the party's election manifesto, ending with a confident assertion, soon to be proved ill-founded, that 'as a nation we are beginning to remember how to work together as we do at all the great moments in our history'. The Prime Minister's speech was well received, but the most memorable piece of oratory at the conference was Tony Barber's criticism of Powell. In a speech at Stockport in June, Powell had hinted that because of Europe he would support Labour at the next election. In response Heath had, with accuracy as well as asperity, called Powell 'a bitter and backward-looking man'. And Barber received great applause from the conference when he attacked Powell for having displayed 'all the moral conceit and intellectual arrogance that are the hallmarks of the fanatic'.[29]

Nevertheless, the Arab–Israeli war forced Barber to move some way towards Powell; since the shortage of oil and the quadrupling of its price removed any remaining credibility from the Government's strategy of fast growth, some measure of deflation was now inescapable. At least equally damaging for the Government, the oil crisis drastically increased the bargaining power of the NUM. Despite the large wage rise won by their strike in 1972, the take-home pay of the miners had not kept up with that of other workers, and in July the union's congress had agreed to press a claim for rises ranging from 22 to 47 per cent to regain their place at the head of the wages league. Naturally determined to avoid another defeat by the unions, Heath, together with Sir William Armstrong, had a secret meeting with Joe Gormley in Downing Street. An informal agreement was reached that the miners would settle provided special arrangements were made for them under Stage III. But, as is the danger of informal agreements, there was a misunderstanding about its exact terms, and anyway all three men overestimated Gormley's ability to carry his union with him. Gormley was not even the most powerful figure in the NUM; Lawrence Daley, the General Secretary, was more influential. Hence the Government would have been better off if the meeting had never occurred. Without the confidence it gave that the miners would settle under Stage III, Heath might well have seen, as soon as the extent of the oil crisis was known, the need to treat the miners as a special case and take them out of Stage III.[30]

Unlike the Prime Minister, the Coal Board had learned nothing from 1972. Admittedly, it did not know of the Downing Street meeting, but that did not excuse its ineptitude in making its maximum offer at the very start of the negotiations, thereby depriving Gormley of any opportunity to claim credit for prising concessions out of the NCB. The NUM rejected the Coal Board's offer and on 17 November began a ban on overtime. Partly because of the ban and partly because of the oil shortage, the Government declared a State of Emergency the next day. Heat and lighting restrictions were imposed, and television broadcasts had to end at 10.30 p.m. Also in November, after the balance of payments figures revealed the worst ever trade gap, Barber raised Bank Rate to 13 per cent and announced a credit squeeze. When Heath learned, at an abortive meeting with the NUM leaders at Number 10, that by 18 to 5 the executive had defeated Gormley's proposal to submit the Coal Board's revised offer to a ballot of its members, he brought Whitelaw back from Northern Ireland to succeed Maurice Macmillan at Employment.[31]

Heath's agreement with Gormley had involved paying the miners extra for 'unsocial hours', but the Government extended that proviso to all shift-workers, thus removing the unique position of the NUM and making the concession worthless for Gormley. The only other possibility of a deal – Gormley's idea that the miners should be paid extra for waiting and bathing time – was intentionally sabotaged by Wilson who put it forward as his own idea. Although the Communist-dominated rail drivers' union ASLEF began an overtime ban in December, 4,000,000 workers had by then settled under Stage III, and more were set to follow. There was therefore little scope for Whitelaw's undoubted negotiating skills. To allow the miners blatantly to flout Stage III would put those settlements at risk as well as infuriating the CBI and the Conservative Party.[32]

Barber cut public expenditure; Heath imposed a three-day week to take effect from December, and the first cuts in electricity supplies were made. Despite the Government's difficulties, there were signs that the nation was rallying behind it. A *Times*/ITN poll gave the Conservatives a five-point lead over Labour, and for only the second time since the general election the Gallup poll gave Heath a higher approval rating than Wilson. Heath also beat Wilson to be one of the most admired men of 1973; but except for Prince Philip the company was not quite what he would have chosen. The other three most admired men were Nixon, Kissinger and Enoch Powell.[33]

The February 1974 Election

Even before the miners' crisis had worsened, and long before the Government's improvement in the polls, the far-sighted Director of the Conservative Research Department, James Douglas, was recommending an election in December. Nigel Lawson, who joined the CRD in November, was another strong advocate of an early election. Douglas Hurd took the same view and, while Employment Secretary, Maurice Macmillan had been convinced that the miners' strike could not be settled without an election. These views, which were conveyed to the Prime Minister, had no visible effect. Heath remained non-committal, absorbed in his efforts to persuade the miners to settle within Stage III.[34]

The Chairman and Deputy Chairman of the Party, Carrington and Prior, however, strongly favoured a general election in January or early February; they thought an election was the only way out of the miners' dispute and would at that time be won. A Conservative Government, which had just won a second election and had the prospect of five years in power, would be far stronger than one nearing the end of its term. In addition, an election would strengthen the hand of the moderates in the NUM and the TUC. The Prime Minister was unconvinced, because he feared an election would be divisive. Whitelaw and Pym, who had both given Heath much good advice over the years, were also opposed to an early appeal to the electorate.[35]

Whitelaw did not want an election because he felt he had just been brought back from Northern Ireland 'to help in settling a dispute, not in precipitating a general election'. Pym did not want an election because he thought one unnecessary and because he had just gone to Northern Ireland (in succession to Whitelaw); the enlightened Sunningdale Agreement had been reached a few days after his appointment. The agreement set up an all-party power-sharing Executive for Northern Ireland and also a Council of Ireland in which the Dublin government would participate.[36]

Had the Heath Government lasted, the Sunningdale Agreement might well have survived. But the power-sharing Executive was a lot to ask the Unionists to swallow, and they should not have been asked also to accept the additional provocation of a Council of Ireland. Heath was at fault in pressing it, as was the Unionist leader at the talks, Brian Faulkner, in acceding to it. The nationalists were astonished to win such a concession. In any case, the Ulster Unionist Council repudiated the agreement and their traditional alliance with the Conservative Party was severed. Nevertheless, the power-sharing Executive of Unionists and Nationalists was set up on 1 January, but clearly needed time to take root; hence Pym's opposition to an election.[37]

While all the reasons of Heath, Whitelaw and Pym for resisting an early election were creditable, none of them fully addressed the main issues, which were: was it possible to avoid a general election? And if not, would the Government be more likely to win an early or a later one? The answer to the second question was clear. As Gilmour told Whitelaw, when asked for his views outside the Cabinet room on 17 January, '"We should go for 7 February, since we cannot keep the British people geared up for action for any length of time, and if we delay, 'the quiet life syndrome' will soon take over and we shall be scuppered."'[38]

At the beginning of January the answer to the first question was still open. Indeed, shortly afterwards, the Government was presented with an opportunity to avoid an election. At an NEDC meeting on 9 January, the TUC leaders said that if the Government sanctioned an exceptional settlement for the miners, they undertook to see that no other union would treat it as a precedent for a similar settlement for them. Barber, who had had no warning of the offer, did not reject it out of hand but was less forthcoming than Geoffrey Howe advised. When he reported his reaction to the Cabinet, nobody criticised him. Heath, Whitelaw and the other senior ministers considered it later, but made no response. With hindsight, the Government made a decisive misjudgement.[39]

The TUC leaders may or may not have been sincere. They might or might not have been able to restrain other unions from following the miners in defying Stage III. But whatever their sincerity and whatever their power, the Government should still have accepted their offer. No other union except the electricity workers was as capable of disrupting the country as the miners; so no other strike would have caused such difficulty. And if another union had called a major strike after the TUC's undertaking, the Government would have been in a stronger position electorally to go to the country. Tory MPs would have been angered and disappointed by a surrender to the miners, but in such circumstances they would surely have accepted it.[40]

Having spurned that opportunity, the Government should have called an election on 7 February. Most of the Cabinet, including certainly Walker, Howe and Windlesham, as well as Carrington and Prior, wanted an election. So did all the party's area agents. In addition to all the other pleas for an early election that had been made to Heath, his communications group – men from the media and public relations such as Geoffrey Tucker and Jim Garrett – had all separately and unanimously at a dinner at Chequers advised him to dissolve parliament immediately or not at all. Unfortunately, in accordance with his usual luck in those years, Heath was unwell as well as exhausted. 'Many people noticed', his biographer records, 'that he had become very slow, overweight, physically and mentally ponderous.' Evidently 'he was already suffering from a thyroid deficiency which was not diagnosed until 1975'. This made him uncharacteristically indecisive.[41]

The latest day for an announcement of a 7 February election was 17 January, and once again the Prime Minister's power of dissolution proved a two-edged sword. Had the decision been one for the Cabinet, a 7 February election would have been announced. But at Cabinet on the morning of 17 January the discussion was 'totally unreal since we went round and round the subject without mentioning an election. Eventually toward the end Peter Carrington got exasperated and started talking about an election, but Ted speedily steered off the topic. Upshot: no discussion of an election, and therefore no election on February 7th.' All the Labour MPs, Jim Prior told the Prime Minister later that day, had been telling him in the tea room that the Government had 'let them off the hook'. 'They're throwing their hats in the air – they haven't been in that kind of mood for weeks.' Conservative MPs were correspondingly bewildered and depressed by Heath's failure to seize the opportunity.[42]

Nobody can be sure about the result of an election which did not take place, but almost certainly the Government would have won on 7 February. The Conservatives' pollsters thought the party would win. During the campaign there would have only been a miners' overtime ban, not a strike; the three-day week during which production fell remarkably little – an alarming comment on the normal efficiency of the British economy – was still a novelty, if an unwelcome one, and something of what, had he been Prime Minister, Harold Wilson would have called the Dunkirk Spirit prevailed. In the nature of things, that could not last. Before long, people just wanted a 'quiet life' and a return to normality.[43]

In politics, as in war, apparently minor events and decisions often have crucial effects, and almost certainly Heath's indecisiveness on 17 January and earlier cost him his premiership as well as having other far-reaching consequences. A week later, the NUM executive called for a strike ballot. The result was published on 4 February: 81 per cent of miners supported the call for a strike. Three days later Heath announced that an election would be held on 28 February. 'Times are hard,' he said on television, 'we are all in the same boat, and if you sink us now we will all drown.'[44]

The party manifesto *Firm Action for a Fair Britain* promised a new look at industrial relations but could not admit that the existing Conservative legislation had been a failure. During the campaign Tory support seems to have grown among working-class voters while declining among middle-class ones because of defections to the Liberals. The representatives of industry did little to help the Government; massive profits for the banks were announced day after day during the campaign, and shortly before polling day the Director-General of the CBI called for the repeal of the Industrial Relations Act, apparently unaware that the BBC was recording his speech.[45]

Enoch Powell's blows were more calculated and should not have surprised the Tory hierarchy. At the end of November, when Heath defended Stage III, Powell had said of him that 'One cannot but entertain fears for the mental and emotional stability of a head of Government to whom such language can appear rational.' Others thought it was Powell's stability that was in doubt. Commenting on his outburst, the political editor of *The Times*, David Wood, believed Powell to be 'set on a sustained, embittered and personalized strategy of destroying his party leadership'. In accordance with Wood's assessment, Powell wrote letters on 7 February to his constituency chairman, his agent, and the press that he would not be seeking re-election because the election would be 'essentially fraudulent'. Many of his supporters, who had worked with him for twenty-five years, learned of his decision from the newspapers. Powell gave Wilson rather better notice of his intentions, keeping in touch with him throughout the campaign, so that timing and tactics could be correlated. 'Such', said Powell, 'was the nature of the alliance.'[46]

Powell waited for a fortnight before delivering another savage attack on Heath in a speech in Birmingham. Although he did not use the actual words either then or in a speech two days later, his message was clear: Vote Labour. As Labour was offering the country a massive extension of public ownership and trade-union power, that was odd advice from the apostle of free enterprise. Powell attempted to justify it by the European issue, claiming that 'the whole story of Britain and the Common Market to date has been one long epic of deception'. As we have seen, that claim was itself a deception, and in any case Labour was not promising to take Britain out of the EEC; only to 'renegotiate' the terms of entry. Maybe Powell, as Wilson's biographer has suggested, had taken 'Labour's "re-negotiation" stance more seriously that it deserved' or, more probably, in his determination to 'destroy his party leadership', he found Europe was the best available weapon. No wonder that even

287

his devoted pupil, Nicholas Ridley, thought that on the EEC Powell was 'an opportunist'.[47]*

Another intervention, two days before Powell's last speech, was perhaps even more damaging. A briefing by the Deputy Chairman of the Pay Board suggested that a disastrous mistake had been made in the calculation of the miners' pay, which instead of being above the national average was in fact 8 per cent below it. This sensational news, indicating that the crisis and the three-day week were quite unnecessary and the result of a Government blunder, was immediately seized upon by Wilson and Labour. Because Heath, Whitelaw and Barber could not be reached for comment, the allegation went unrefuted in the national press for twenty-four hours, galvanising Labour's campaign while striking a chill into the Conservatives. And the delayed denial never killed the deeply damaging original canard. Although the Nuffield Study exonerated the Pay Board official, a known Labour supporter, of any malicious intent, many were unconvinced.[49]

Notwithstanding clear evidence that the Liberals were doing strikingly well, the pollsters, the press and the bookmakers all expected the Conservatives to win. At least they correctly forecast which party would win the most votes. Despite the Conservative share of the vote having dropped by a record 8.6 per cent since 1970, with 37.8 per cent they secured more votes than Labour, while the Liberal share rose from 7.5 per cent to nearly 20 per cent. Yet the Liberals won only fourteen seats, and Labour with 301 gained four more than the Conservatives. But for Heath's statesmanlike efforts to settle the Irish problem, the Conservatives would have been ahead: the Sunningdale Agreement had deprived Heath of the support of ten Ulster Unionists.[50]

At a Cabinet meeting the next day, Heath told his colleagues that he and all those he had consulted were in favour of holding on to try to reach an agreement with the Liberals. At that time it looked as if the Conservatives would be only one seat behind Labour. Only later did Labour beat Plaid Cymru at Carmarthen by three votes, and the Liberals beat the Conservatives at Bodmin by nine votes, while the next day the Scottish Nationalists won Argyll from the Conservatives. To attempt a deal with the Liberals seemed at the time, therefore, legitimate and sensible. Margaret Thatcher afterwards wrote that she 'was conscious that this horse-trading would make [the party] look ridiculous' and a 'bad loser'; at the time, however, only Keith Joseph seemed uneasy about

---

* Very few people took Labour's 'renegotiations' stance seriously. Wilson would be remembered, Jeremy Thorpe said immediately after the first 1974 election, as the man 'who nearly got us in and nearly got us out'.[48]

the Government hanging on. In any case no deal was possible, since Jeremy Thorpe could not carry his party into an alliance with the Tories. So, after the weekend, Heath tendered the resignation of his Government.[51]

A surfeit of right-wing obloquy, together with the final misfortunes which destroyed the Heath Government, have obscured the substantial achievements of 1970–74. Overwhelmingly the most important, of course, was Britain's entry into the EEC, but the Government carried out what the Nuffield Study called 'a notably high proportion' of its specific manifesto commitments. Barber's tax reforms, the changes in the Whitehall machine and Peter Walker's encouragement of council-house sales would be better remembered were it not for the three-day week and the power cuts. Although Labour councils obstructed Walker's policy, 7 per cent of council stock was sold between 1972 and 1974. This was only part of Walker's plans for housing, which culminated in the Housing Finance Act passed before he left Environment for the DTI in 1972. This replaced the haphazard system of local subsidies with a uniform scheme of rent rebates for both private tenants and those who continued to rent their council houses. In private, Richard Crossman told Walker that the Act would be 'the most socialist measure to be introduced in housing'; in public, Anthony Crosland denounced it as 'reactionary and socially divisive'. In reality, it was a further application of One-Nation principles, designed to focus state assistance on those who needed it most rather than continuing with a system under which affluent tenants often paid no more for their housing than their unemployed neighbours. As such, the reform introduced a means test, and eleven Labour councillors in Derbyshire were surcharged for their refusal to implement the Act.[52]

Given the furore caused by Powell in 1968, the Government's decision to permit Asians expelled from Uganda by Idi Amin to settle in Britain was also commendable. Under pressure from the right, the Government had promised 'no further large-scale permanent immigration' in its manifesto, and introduced an Immigration Act in 1971, which was designed to restrict the number of 'New' Commonwealth entrants. These fell from 44,000 in 1971 to 32,000 two years later. But the feelings stirred up by Powell could not be so easily quietened and, when Amin acted in 1972, the suggestion that nearly 60,000 Asians might be allowed to settle in Britain evoked a violent public response. Whatever the Government decided on this issue, it would have been in difficulty because the words of the 1970 manifesto clashed with an implied promise of refuge to the Asians that had been given when Uganda became independent. As Hurd wrote, 'the mistake was to be so absolute' when writing the manifesto. Heath's idea of asking other countries to help worked well; eventually less than half of the expelled Asians came to live in Britain. Even so, they caused a row at the Executive of the National Union and many defections from constituency parties. In this area, Layton-Henry judges, Heath's policies were 'courageous and consistent. He acted as a national statesman and not merely as the leader of a political party.'[53]

Ted Heath's fatal tendency – fatal for him – to act as a national statesman, subordinating the interests of his party to those of the country, has deeply affronted right-wing critics. In this he strongly resembled Peel and was utterly different from his successors as Conservative leader. Most of the other contrasts, however, that are drawn between him and Margaret Thatcher once again have more to do with ideology than history. Even the electoral contrast – Mrs Thatcher's three victories out of three, Heath's three defeats out of four – is not what it seems. No Conservative leader could have won in 1966, and very few, if any, could have won the second election in 1974, while in only one of her victories, 1983, was Margaret Thatcher a clear electoral asset to her party.

The other comparisons between the two leaders similarly ignore the differences between the 1970s and the 1980s. One of the best illustrations of the change of circumstances is the behaviour of Margaret Thatcher herself and of Keith Joseph during the Heath administration. If Heath's Government 'failed the nation', as Mrs Thatcher claimed in her campaign to succeed him, they were part of the failure. They were members of the Cabinet, after all, when the reviled 'U-turns' were conducted. 'I think that Ted Heath's position', Keith Joseph told Anthony Seldon with characteristic honesty shortly before his death, 'was extremely understandable. After all, I never lifted my head and protested in all his years as Prime Minister.' That was equally true of Margaret Thatcher.[54]

Conditions in the early 1970s bore little resemblance to those a decade later. The claim that Heath won the 1970 election on a Thatcherite agenda and then funked carrying it out is a convenient myth for his enemies. In 1970 inflation was identified as the most urgent problem for the next Government. Nobody realised that Heath had 'inherited', as Robert Skidelsky has observed, 'not just the Wilson, but more importantly, the Nixon stop' of 1969–70. When, therefore, unemployment inexorably rose, memories of the 1930s induced Heath to change tack. This was the natural response of any One-Nation Tory; even Mrs Thatcher regularly referred to the memories of enforced idleness in the years up to 1979, and the Saatchi Brothers' famous advertisement before the 1979 election exploited memories of the dole queues.[55]

Both the Labour Party and the trade unions were far stronger in the early seventies than they were after 1979. The union excesses during the Heath years and, still more, during 'the Winter of Discontent', paved the way for the Thatcher Governments. The economic conditions and the climate of ideas similarly changed. Heath had no North Sea oil and faced inflationary conditions which were international, not just British. The very high unemployment of the eighties and nineties would not have been tolerated in the early seventies. Margaret Thatcher had different world conditions to contend with and a massive windfall of North Sea oil to pay for unemployment. Between the seventies and the eighties, also, Britain was steadily becoming a different country. The old working class was declining both in numbers and in strength, and working-class communities were becoming less homogenous. The old heavy industries were declining; white-collar employment was growing and prosperous suburbs were spreading. Leaving aside, for the time being, the question of how well 'Thatcherism' worked in the eighties, it could not even have been tried in the early seventies. Hence to attack Ted Heath for not having behaved like Margaret Thatcher is little more sensible than to say that the First World War could have been won more cheaply by using the methods of the Second.

CHAPTER XIII

In the Steps of St Francis

As in 1964, the close election result ruled out an immediate change of leader. Ted Heath had in any case no intention of resigning. Nor did he intend to change the policies he had pursued in office, while the few changes he made in the Shadow Cabinet mostly stemmed from Barber's long-standing decision to quit politics. In making Robert Carr Shadow Chancellor, Heath had once more overlooked the claims of Keith Joseph for a leading role in the making of economic policy.

Being passed over a second time may have sharpened Joseph's reappraisal of the political scene. As Social Security Secretary, he had offended against free-market dogma as badly as most – during the election campaign he rehearsed a familiar claim that he had been responsible for exceeding Labour's spending by 30 per cent per year over a corresponding period. But soon after the election he set off on a remarkably quick journey to Damascus. 'It was only in April 1974', he later confided, 'that I was converted to Conservatism. I had thought that I was a Conservative but I now see that I was not one at all.' Joseph had already helped to set up the Centre of Policy Studies, a think-tank designed to complement the work of the Institute of Economic Affairs which had been feeding him ideas for several years. The IEA was more interested in propagating free-market doctrine than dabbling in party politics; the CPS was going to do both. Fittingly, it was headed by a real convert – Alfred Sherman, who was a former Communist. In such company, Joseph could feel that his own past sins were paltry. For reassurance, he recruited his fellow former sinner, Margaret Thatcher, to be a vice-president.[1]

Bolstered by his new allies, Joseph began to develop a critique of post-war Conservative policy which at any other time since 1945 would have destroyed his chances of leading the party. Conservative Government had been in office for seventeen out of those twenty-nine years; nevertheless, Joseph adopted the Powellite notion of a 'ratchet effect' which now threatened to destroy British freedom. Whatever their original intentions, Governments from both main parties, Joseph's argument ran, had so extended the scope of the state that Hayek's nightmare of *The Road to Serfdom* was now about to come true. All this was fantasy, but it was increasingly accepted and it did not conflict with the more respectable contemporary idea that Government had become over-loaded. Having, according to Margaret Thatcher, introduced 'the most radical form of socialism ever contemplated by an elected British Government', Edward Heath fell into a special category of guilt. Norman Tebbit, who had been elected to the Commons in 1970, thought Heath had won power on a right-wing manifesto without understanding it. If so, he was not the only one; Mrs Thatcher herself later explained that she had failed to develop 'a coherent framework of ideas' before joining the Government. In fact, as we have seen, the 1970 manifesto bore only a very superficial resemblance to the ideological programme favoured by the hard right. But once Heath had lost power, the truth about his record was soon replaced by myth.[2]

Back in Opposition

After forming a minority Government on 4 March, Harold Wilson had to appear as moderate and businesslike as possible before choosing the right moment for another election. That involved, of course, ditching virtually all of his party's election manifesto. Heath's task was more difficult; the minority Government had to be harried enough to satisfy restless back-benchers but not so much as to precipitate an immediate election or alienate the voters.

Tacking and weaving were never among Ted Heath's talents, and he made his situation even more difficult by misunderstanding the constitutional position, even though it had been patiently explained to him. Over the opposition of Hailsham, Carrington and Gilmour, Maurice Macmillan succeeded in persuading a majority of the Shadow Cabinet and the party leader that the vote on the address was the one chance the party had to turn Wilson out without precipitating an election. This was so obviously wrong that it was hard to understand how anybody could accept it. No Prime Minister had been refused a dissolution for over 150 years, and the Queen would undoubtedly have given Wilson one, even if Heath could have shown that he enjoyed the whole-hearted support of the Liberals and the Ulstermen – which was anyway impossible. Furthermore, in such circumstances an election would have produced a stunning victory for Wilson.[3]

Undeterred, the Opposition tabled an amendment deploring Labour's intention of abandoning Stage III of the prices and incomes policy. That infuriated about forty right-wing Conservative back-benchers who were itching to see the end of Stage III. Luckily Michael Foot saved the Shadow Cabinet's face by announcing that Stage III would continue for the time being. Otherwise Heath would have faced either a disastrous election or a large-scale back-bench rebellion. The pity was that he had begun the debate on the Queen's address with a good and funny speech, which had easily outshone Wilson's dull and uninformative reply. Yet the unnecessary shambles over the amendment was a miserable start to a period of Opposition. And party morale was not improved when Heath spurned the chance to appease some of his back-bench critics with a generous sprinkling of knighthoods.[4]

The election results left no room for doubt of the Conservatives' need to reclaim the million votes lost to the Liberals if they were to win again. A few Tories, including Nigel Lawson and Gilmour, thought the best way to do so was to attempt a limited electoral pact with the Liberals, which was pretty clearly the only possible way of winning. Heath made polite noises in response to their suggestions, and Carrington seemed in favour. But the professionals at Central Office were strongly opposed to the idea and effectively killed it. Nevertheless something had to be done, and during the summer Heath accepted advice to appeal to the Liberal voters by playing on the theme of national unity. This strategy appeared to work. Labour's lead narrowed in July; ORC even put the Tories ahead.[5]

Unfortunately Keith Joseph struck a discordant note at the beginning of September. Joseph's Preston speech, which was largely written by Sherman and was the first fruit of Joseph's 'conversion', suggested that the Conservatives could not achieve party, let alone national, unity. In his first great blast of monetarism Joseph maintained that inflation was caused by Government and could only be conquered by controlling the money supply which would mean a temporary increase in employment. The speech, which coincided with an opinion poll giving the Conservatives a two-point lead, was an obvious gift to Harold Wilson; for that reason a number of Joseph's colleagues begged him not to make it. His insistence on going ahead suggested that he wanted Labour to win the election. Otherwise, there was no point in making such a speech just before an election instead of after it.[6]

Less than a fortnight after the Preston speech, the Prime Minister announced that the election would be held on 10 October. Because of a leak by trade unionists at the firm which printed it, the Tory manifesto, *Putting Britain First*, had already been published. It was based on the theme of national unity. 'The Nation's crisis', it proclaimed, 'should transcend party differences.' While the party's objective was to gain a clear majority, 'the Conservative Party, free from dogma and free from dependence upon any single interest' would use their majority 'to unite the nation'. After the election there would be consultation with the other party leaders, and people from 'outside the ranks of our party' would be invited 'to join with us in overcoming Britain's difficulties'.[7]

These sentiments made the heavily partisan Margaret Thatcher 'deeply uneasy', but she was the star Conservative performer during the campaign. Under pressure from Heath and the Conservative Research Department, she agreed that the party should promise to abolish the rates and to reduce the mortgage interest rate, a proposal which horrified Nigel Lawson. Mrs Thatcher was herself none too happy about these policies, but she propounded them with great skill and did a superb election broadcast on the subject.[8]

On economic policy the manifesto was ecumenical, promising rigorous control of 'public spending and the money supply', while at the same time stressing the need for 'restraint in prices and incomes'. The manifesto was well received by the press, but the electorate had no great enthusiasm for politics. A public opinion poll in September found 79 per cent of people 'unhappy with the way things are going'. The Conservatives' aim was to avoid a repetition of 1966, when Labour had followed up an inconclusive election by winning a large majority. The Tory objective was achieved. Labour won a million more votes than the Conservatives but gained an overall majority of only three. Given the tactical advantage of the Government, the Opposition had done well, but in politics there are no prizes for gallant losers.[9]

Heath had put up a courageous fight, made more difficult by the personal blow he suffered in September when his yacht *Morning Cloud III* sank with two of its crew, one of whom was his godson. Yet he had not made full use of the popular theme of national unity. And despite the urging of some of his friends and closest advisers, he had refused to say that, if he proved an obstacle to national unity, he would be prepared to step down from the Conservative leadership. Such obstinacy was unreasonable, because the gesture would have cost him nothing. If he won, nobody would ask him to leave and, if he lost, he would have to leave anyway. That mistake was followed by a far graver one: Heath's failure to resign immediately after the election. Two defeats in a year had made his position untenable, and a quiet departure would have ensured both a dignified exit and a congenial One-Nation successor. At that stage Whitelaw would surely have been elected. At the very least Heath should have submitted himself for re-election, but although plotting against him was already widespread he stubbornly did nothing.[10]

Admittedly Heath was the best man for the job, and he could point to continuing support in the constituencies. That, however, reflected traditional backing for incumbent leaders rather than full-hearted enthusiasm, and outward loyalty concealed discontent in the suburbs which led in 1975 to an explosion of middle-class pressure groups. In Parliament, a senior back-bencher demonstrated the intensity of the party's hostility when he told Norman Fowler that Heath should stay on as leader because he 'has not suffered enough'.[11]

In one respect, the new procedure for selecting the leader favoured Heath; if the old 'customary processes' had still been in place, he might well have been pushed out after the second defeat. Now there was irresistible pressure to change the new system, so that the leader could be challenged even when he thought that there was no vacancy. Accordingly a committee, which was set up under Lord Home in November, soon recommended that a challenger should need only two nominations to force a contest at the beginning of every parliamentary year.

Obviously Heath would be challenged: the question was, by whom? With Enoch Powell out of the way (having become an Ulster Unionist MP in October), another long-standing enemy, Edward du Cann, was expected to stand. Du Cann's exclusion from Heath's Cabinet had given him plenty of time to attract a dissident following, and in November 1972 he had been elected Chairman of the 1922 Committee. Although he was totally unsuitable for the leadership, he would probably have won on the first ballot. Eventually, though, he decided not to run for reasons which had little to do with his incapacity for the job. With the crown in sight, Keith Joseph aroused new controversy with a speech in the Powellite Midlands, which implied that the poor were breeding too fast. The resulting outcry forced his withdrawal. Other names were mentioned, but in the end only one former Cabinet Minister stood against Heath. When Joseph told Margaret Thatcher that he could not stand, she replied that if he was not going to, she would. Heath's reported reaction was dismissive, yet his position looked more vulnerable after she had launched a successful attack on the Chancellor, Denis Healey (a formidable Commons performer himself), in January's debate on the Finance Bill. On the other hand, at the close of nominations on 30 January, Heath's supporters were encouraged by the emergence of the right-wing Hugh Fraser as a third candidate.[12]

The Peasants' Revolt

If Fraser's intrusion presented some right-wingers with an unwelcome puzzle, the situation was much more complicated for some moderates who wanted to be rid of Heath but did not want Thatcher. William Whitelaw was unable to put himself forward while his leader remained in the field, but Whitelaw could run in the second ballot if an inconclusive result led to Heath's withdrawal. The problem for those moderates was how to bring about such an outcome. Mrs Thatcher was the obvious vehicle for protest votes, but if she received too many, the contest might never reach a second round. On the other hand, if Heath fell short of an overall majority but was comfortably ahead, the ultra-loyal Whitelaw would not be able to stand.

In the event, the anti-Heath moderates went astray in their calculations, and far too many of them plumped for Mrs Thatcher. Their error was abetted by the shrewd management of Airey Neave, who was understandably eager to take revenge for Heath's remark over a decade earlier that a heart-attack had 'finished' him. Neave (not noted as a right-winger) had originally supported du Cann; when his favourite refused to enter the stalls he decided to back Thatcher as the most likely candidate to topple Heath. A Colditz escapee, Neave skilfully enlisted pessimism as a principal weapon: he and his assistants spread the word to waverers that Heath might well secure a decisive vote in the first ballot. Remarkably the Heath camp played into his hands by spreading the same story. In consequence, a number of Whitelaw's supporters were panicked into voting for Mrs Thatcher despite their distaste for her well-known right-wing prejudices; as Julian Critchley later put it, 'she seemed to share the views so often expressed by party workers, and what was worse, to be prepared to articulate them'. Heath did not help his own case. He gave the impression of resenting the contest and, while his opponent spent as much time as possible in the Commons tea-rooms, the leader held a series of dinners which did not endear him to potential supporters.[13]

The result announced on 4 February showed that Thatcher had beaten Heath by 130 to 119; as Mrs Thatcher later put it, Fraser had only succeeded in winning 'right-wing misogynist votes' – sixteen in total. Her defeat of Heath set the challenger's band-wagon rolling. The only possible means of stopping it was for Whitelaw to be Mrs Thatcher's sole opponent. Yet Geoffrey Howe, John Peyton and Jim Prior joined Whitelaw in contesting the second ballot with her. Whitelaw, Carr and

Gilmour tried at a meeting to stop some of the other candidates standing, but to no avail. Margaret Thatcher was worried by Howe's intrusion, but he only added three right-wing 'misogynists' to Hugh Fraser's tally when the votes were cast on 11 February. Whitelaw trailed Thatcher by 146 to 79; Prior dead-heated with Howe on nineteen votes, while only eleven MPs backed Peyton.[14]

The usual verdict that the outcome of this 'Peasants' Revolt' was an accident is only partly true. The result, as Lawson said, was 'more a rejection of Ted – on personal and political grounds alike – than a positive endorsement' of the winner; and she would not have won but for the misdirected votes of some Whitelaw supporters, who were 'too clever by half'. Yet Margaret Thatcher fought an excellent campaign. Her public alliance with Joseph was an asset rather than a hindrance; it created the impression that she must be a 'thinker', though she made none of the gaffes which had made Joseph seem an impracticable leader. Moderates, who were upset by her allegation in a *Daily Telegraph* article that the Heath Government had 'failed the people' and that the Conservative Party was apparently riddled with socialists, could only console themselves with the hope that her extremism would evaporate in office.[15]

After she had won, Mrs Thatcher commiserated with her defeated opponents, expressing the hope that 'we shall soon be back working together as colleagues for the things in which we all believe'. That hope was widely shared; most MPs were anxious for the whole party to rally behind the new leader in opposition to a weak Labour administration. As one of the defeated candidates later put it, 'We were united in believing that there had to be a shift from taxing earnings to taxing spending; that public expenditure must be brought under control; and that every effort had to be made to free the economy and individuals from the burden of statutory and bureaucratic controls.'[16]

Despite this broad agreement, Mrs Thatcher had run against Heath's record, and few senior figures had supported her in either round of the election. This complicated the construction of her Shadow Cabinet, the most difficult problem being Heath himself. During the leadership campaign Mrs Thatcher had promised to offer him a Shadow Cabinet post, but after her victory she hoped that he would refuse and in fact knew that he would do so. Her visit to Heath's recently bombed Wilton Street home in a friend's Mini was therefore an exercise in public relations. As such, it was not well received by Ted Heath, who had been advised by friends to stay out of the Shadow Cabinet. After a very brief interview, the ex-Prime Minister's PPS, Timothy Kitson, took Mrs Thatcher upstairs to avoid a quick, undignified re-emergence to the assembled reporters. Her supporters quickly planted the idea that Heath's refusal to co-operate with this gratuitous ploy meant that he had 'sulked'; thus making it easy for them to claim that Heath's later criticisms were inspired by pique not principle.[17]

Mrs Thatcher behaved better to Heath's supporters. Peter Walker, who had been a firm opponent of Keith Joseph's monetarist ideas, was asked to stand down because the leader wanted to 'get some young people in'; as Walker was the youngest member of the Shadow Cabinet, that made him laugh. There were no places either for Paul Channon, Peter Thomas and Nicholas Scott. Otherwise Mrs Thatcher was magnanimous. Of Heath's close allies, Whitelaw became Deputy Leader; Prior, Employment spokesman; and Carrington remained Leader in the Lords. Other members of the new Shadow Cabinet known to lack sympathy for Mrs Thatcher's views were Heseltine (Industry), Pym (Agriculture), Raison (Environment) and Gilmour (Home Office). More surprisingly, Reginald Maudling was given Foreign Affairs. This was partly to bring back a big name and partly to exclude Robert Carr, her old boss in the Shadow Treasury team, who would not have accepted anything less.[18]

The new leader told a friend that she would show her true intentions in a reshuffle before the next election. But in one area at least she had already shown them. Although she had strong views on most issues, her keenest interest was in the economy. Here she already knew the answers, and her Shadow Chancellor would have to be equally enlightened. She was talked out of appointing Sir Keith Joseph, who quickly proved the wisdom of this advice with a peculiar speech on the 1975 Budget, sharply satirised by Denis Healey. Nevertheless, Geoffrey Howe was a reasonable substitute. Mrs Thatcher disapproved of his commitment to discussions between Government, unions and employers, and as early as 1969 Howe had expressed private concern that although Mrs Thatcher's 'economic prejudices' were 'sound' she was 'inclined to be rather too dogmatic for my liking'. But Howe had attended meetings of the right-wing think-tanks for many years, and her choice enabled her to hint that she bore no grudge against her fellow candidates in the leadership contest. Meanwhile Joseph was given third place in the party hierarchy; without a specific portfolio, he enjoyed a licence to conduct policy research wherever his celebrated intellect led him, while his personal warmth continued to collide with his addiction to right-wing dogma.[19]

The new leader was also keen to 'get some control' of the party machine. Demonstrating an uncharacteristic sense of history, she brought in Peter Thorneycroft to replace Whitelaw as Party Chairman; another 'martyr' from the past, Angus Maude, was put in charge of the

Conservative Research Department. Two elections within a year had strained the party's finances, and Thorneycroft was soon making what he called 'some pretty drastic economies'. The most controversial change had nothing to do with the need to save money; the much-admired Director-General of the Party Organisation, Michael Wolff, was abruptly dismissed. An angry Jim Prior confronted Mrs Thatcher over this decision, and was wrongly told it was Peter Thorneycroft's.[20]

The Right-Wing Approach

For the first two months of her leadership Mrs Thatcher enjoyed con-siderable popular approval, but soon the public began to share the misgivings of some of her senior colleagues. In April 1975 her rating dropped by 15 per cent, and during the summer she trailed Wilson by around ten points in the Gallup poll. While the Prime Minister had jettisoned the socialist lumber picked up while his party was out of office, he had kept his promise to buy off the unions. The miners had been awarded twice the sum offered by Heath, and the Industrial Relations Act was repealed; Heath's statutory incomes policy was aban-doned in favour of a voluntary 'Social Contract' which Wilson described as 'the boldest experiment in civilised government' ever seen. In reality it was neither bold nor successful; by April 1975, wage increases were up by 10 per cent even though official unemployment was again to top one million before the end of the year. The Government began to cut spending and raise taxes to keep the PSBR under control: Denis Healey's 1975 Budget increased the basic rate of income tax to 35 per cent and introduced a 25 per cent VAT rate for 'luxuries'. Before Wilson resigned in March 1976 he had lost faith in his bold experiment and moved closer to another attempt at a statutory policy on prices and incomes.[21]

Wilson had told the Queen that he intended to resign around his sixtieth birthday; his health was declining, and he was increasingly obsessed by real or imaginary plots against him. Wilson's voluntary departure surprised the public, many taking it as a sign that not even he could see a way to manoeuvre through the economic crisis; the announcement had been postponed for a few days because his birthday coincided with a dramatic slump in the value of sterling.[22]

By the end of 1976 the situation had been transformed by the Govern-ment's negotiations with the International Monetary Fund for support on the currency exchanges. Even before the deal was agreed in December, the Cabinet had decided after prolonged argument to make further deep cuts in the public spending which had kept the unions sweet. Inflation had actually peaked before the fund was called in, and the Treasury's dire PSBR forecast was an overestimate. Within a year the Bank of England was intervening to limit the rise in sterling. All the same, for the Government the cost of restoring international confidence in the pound was a collapse in Labour's domestic reputation. Although as late as September the two main parties were almost level in the polls, the November Gallup survey put the Conservatives 21 per cent ahead, and the Government was defeated in by-elections at Walsall North and Workington.

At the Labour conference in late September, the party's new leader, Jim Callaghan, tried to impress the markets with a rational defence of the Government's new economic approach. In a speech heavily influenced by his monetarist son-in-law, Peter Jay, he attacked the idea 'that you could spend your way out of a recession and increase employment by cutting taxes and boosting Government spending'. This effort to divert public criticism from Callaghan to Keynes was scarcely fair. Certainly the consequences of the oil shock called for a revision of Keynes's work. But the Jay–Callaghan thesis ignored the fact that by trying to keep at least some of its reckless electoral promises Labour had spent itself *into* a recession – a course of action which Keynes would have deplored. While Callaghan's unpopular 'conversion' to monetarism was tactical, the new squeeze on Government spending most benefited the party leader who would have pursued the same policy out of conviction.[23]

Against this background, *The Right Approach* (published for the 1976 Conservative conference) appeared tame to right-wingers in the party. The document, sub-titled 'a statement of Conservative aims', represented a compromise between Right and Left. Although Keith Joseph was involved in the drafting, his theory of a 'ratchet effect' was toned down, and previous Conservative administrations were congratulated for at least trying 'to turn the tide'. 'A steady and disciplined monetary policy' was identified as important, but not as the only way to tackle inflation. A future Conservative Government would reduce union power, but it would maintain the role of the NEDC as a meaningful forum for economic discussion. A carefully-worded section on incomes policy argued that it would be unwise to rule this out, but that at best it could only be a temporary solution to Britain's problems. Tax cuts and council-house sales were promised, but although the record of state-owned industry was savaged, the commitment to denationalisation was heavily qualified. Overall, *The Right Approach* echoed most of the policy statements released by the Conservative Party since the war. It was, Keith Middlemas has written, a 'relatively vague and uncontentious document'. For Mrs Thatcher, it was 'a fudge – but temporarily palatable'.[24]

By the following October Mrs Thatcher had lost her taste for fudge. When the committee which produced *The Right Approach* followed it up with a similar document, *The Right Approach to the Economy*, the leader ensured that this one went out under the names of its individual authors (Howe, Joseph, Prior, Maude and David Howell) rather than as an official Shadow Cabinet publication. The Right was far happier with 'Stepping Stones', a report on trade unions written by an informal group of Mrs Thatcher's advisers at the end of 1977. This was strongly opposed by Jim Prior, who objected that a strident campaign against the unions would reunite the Labour movement and possibly reverse its growing unpopularity. No wonder Mrs Thatcher later admitted that 'we were not a particularly successful Opposition in the ordinary sense of the word. Differences kept on emerging between us . . .' Only thirty-one Conservative MPs (10.5 per cent of the total) failed to cast a vote against the party line in this parliament.[25]

A New Style of Leadership

The first big issue in Mrs Thatcher's probationary period was the referendum on EEC membership held on 5 June 1975. 'For a number of reasons,' she later reflected, 'I would have preferred a challenge on some other topic.' One of those reasons was the difficulty of trying to look enthusiastic about her predecessor's greatest achievement. Heath took a far more active role as a vice-president of the 'Britain in Europe' campaign. As he toured the country delivering speeches to enthusiastic crowds, his relish for politics returned. The pro-EEC campaign gave an opportunity for moderates in all parties to see that a government of national unity really could have worked. By contrast, the anti-Market campaign was dominated by politicians who shared Mrs Thatcher's distaste for consensus politics, and whose crusading zeal alienated the voters. While 'Britain in Europe' received well over £1 million in donations, the antis managed to raise the sum of £8,629.81, although they were also given free assistance by some trade unions. Almost two-thirds of the electorate turned out, and of these a similar proportion voted 'yes'. After a full debate of the issue, this ought to have been conclusive; on the day after the poll Rees-Mogg's leader in the pre-Murdoch *Times* rejoiced that 'Europe will now be the context of our political and economic life for this generation.'[26]

To compensate for her low profile during the referendum campaign, Mrs Thatcher won plenty of publicity with her ventures into diplomacy.

In November 1976 she sacked Maudling on the grounds that he had not made enough speeches. Differences on a range of policies were the true reason; Mrs Thatcher grudgingly admitted that when the ex-Chancellor 'put his mind to it', he 'actually had the grasp of economics to give his arguments weight'. That was putting it mildly. Maudling knew much more economics than anybody else in the Shadow Cabinet, and in the House of Commons Smoking Room enjoyed demolishing monetarist arguments. In addition, he was 'totally opposed' to the Shadow Cabinet's tendency to move further to the right, and he did not think that the Opposition should seek to make party capital out of foreign affairs, which was not at all the view of his leader. Finally, as he said, 'there was a considerable difference of temperament' between him and her. Once, after some minor event in South-east Asia, Mrs Thatcher said brightly in the Steering Committee, 'What do we think of Vietnam, Reggie?' 'We think', replied Reggie, 'that Vietnam is a long way away.' That was tactless, but as Maudling was one of the very few heavyweights in the Shadow Cabinet it was profligate to dismiss him.[27]

In any case the new leader had already started to make pronouncements without consulting her Foreign Affairs spokesman. Her supporters were delighted by her anti-Soviet rhetoric, and after a speech in Kensington a journalist on the *Red Star*, the Soviet army newspaper, gave her an unexpected boost when he dubbed her 'The Iron Lady'. As she rightly said, this put her on 'a pedestal' as the Soviet Union's strongest European opponent.[28]

Maudling's departure was soon followed by that of Alick Buchanan-Smith, the Scottish Affairs spokesman. When Labour's Scottish and Welsh devolution bill reached its second reading in December 1976, Mrs Thatcher, who had for some time wanted to abandon the Conservative commitment to a directly elected Scottish Assembly, forced a decision to oppose it on a three-line whip. Buchanan-Smith asked permission at least to abstain rather than cast his vote against a policy based on principles which he had advocated in public, but his leader turned down this compromise. Buchanan-Smith duly resigned, accompanied by Malcolm Rifkind; both were among the five Conservatives who voted with Labour, along with the front-bencher Hamish Gray, whom Mrs Thatcher decided not to punish. Ted Heath abstained with twenty-six others. Buchanan-Smith was replaced by Teddy Taylor, who had earlier been a supporter of devolution but was now a fervent opponent. Fortunately for Mrs Thatcher, the Labour Party was equally divided and clutched once again at the device of a referendum to solve its internal difficulties. Ironically its own bungling over devolution later triggered the election which brought Mrs Thatcher to power.[29]

If devolution caused the most serious Conservative rebellion during these years, the Opposition leader's worst breach of political etiquette concerned the issue of race. Mrs Thatcher's ideas on this subject were already well known within the party. She had deplored the sacking of Enoch Powell in 1968, and in 1976 had tried to impose another whipped vote against Labour's Race Relations Bill. She also opposed any official involvement by the Conservative Party in a Joint Committee Against Racialism. In a television interview of January 1978, without any previous consultation with her deputy and Home Affairs spokesman Willie Whitelaw, Mrs Thatcher made her feelings public, declaring that 'people are really rather afraid that this country might be rather swamped by people with a different culture'; she went on to agree that the Conservatives would welcome defectors from the National Front. Whitelaw was furious, for some days contemplating resignation. Eventually he decided to continue, but his careful bridge-building with immigrant communities had been wrecked. Even in retirement, Lady Thatcher was baffled by the uproar caused at the time by her remarks, believing that they reflected views which were 'all but universally accepted' in the 1990s.[30]

By 1979 those who had regretted Mrs Thatcher's election as party leader were increasingly anxious. Her economic views were unappetising for One Nation Conservatives, and on many issues she had pushed policy to the right by making commitments in public instead of debating them with her colleagues. In normal times the flight from the political middle ground would have led to defeat, as it had done in 1964 for the US Republican Party. The 1970s in Britain were, however, abnormal; when in Opposition, Labour had fled much further from the middle ground and yet had won in February 1974 despite a manifesto pledge to take a controlling interest in virtually the whole of British industry. Faced with a Government which was both weak and incompetent, few Conservatives wanted to rock the party boat, and moderates could hope that the leader would be transformed by the experience of power – a hope given substance by her behaviour in the Heath Government.[31]

The Winter of Discontent

Mrs Thatcher's musings on immigration coincided with, or more probably caused, a temporary increase in the Conservatives' poll lead, but by November 1978 Labour was again five points ahead and more than half the electorate approved of Callaghan compared to a third who favoured Mrs Thatcher. A £67,000 Saatchi and Saatchi advertising campaign in the summer, which included a brilliant poster with the caption

'Labour isn't Working', had caused a stir in the press but little movement in the polls. Divisions within the party were exposed to the public at the Party Conference, where Heath rebuked the leadership for having moved to a flat rejection of incomes policy. Although party managers had arranged that he spoke while the BBC was broadcasting *Play School*, he later gave a series of television interviews to ensure his point was registered. While the Right had hoped that Heath would have lapsed into a non-person after his defeat, both he and his line on incomes policy were popular; as a potential Prime Minister the public preferred him to Mrs Thatcher by 55 per cent to 33 per cent.[32]

Jim Callaghan was expected to call an October election but decided on further delay when Labour's own pollsters suggested that at best an autumn contest would put him back at Number 10 at the head of another minority Government. This was yet another example of a Prime Minister's disastrous failure to use his power of dissolution to his party's advantage. If he had consulted the mood of his trade-union allies rather than that of the public, he might have made a better decision. As, however, the Government's new version of prices and incomes policy had produced rising living standards, with both inflation and unemployment apparently under control, Callaghan chose to press on into 1979.

In July the Government had announced a limit of 5 per cent on pay increases. The policy was rejected by the TUC and the Labour Party Conference; workers began to rebel against it on the shop floor. After the start of a lorry drivers' dispute in January, the weary Prime Minister tried to deflect questions when returning sun-tanned from a Caribbean summit. *The Sun*'s invented headline – 'Crisis? What Crisis?' – quickly took the place in the public mind of what Callaghan had actually said – his denial 'that other people in the world would share the view that there is mounting chaos'. By the end of the month one and a half million workers had taken part in a 'day of action'; hospital staff and even undertakers joined the strikes, providing the imagery which was still helping the Conservatives in 1997. February's Gallup poll put the Opposition 20 per cent ahead.[33]

Most of the disputes were quickly settled, and the Government renewed its vows with the unions on Valentine's Day 1979. Unfortunately for Labour, however, before the Government could regain its popularity, it was struck down in the House of Commons. For two years Callaghan had relied on minority party backing for survival, but once the Lib-Lab pact had broken down his future was in the hands of the various nationalists. On 8 March the referendum vote in favour of devolution for Scotland fell short of the criteria inserted into the legislation by a Labour back-bench revolt, and the Welsh delivered a clear negative. On a vote of confidence on 28 March the Government was defeated by 311–310. For the first time in over half a century, an administration had been forced to call an election by a defeat in the Commons. Whether 'unsuccessful' or otherwise, the Opposition now held all the cards. According to the February Gallup poll, nearly two-thirds of the voters expected the Conservatives to win the next election, and Mrs Thatcher now led Callaghan by 15 per cent. The assassination of Airey Neave by the INLA two days after the confidence vote was a terrible personal blow to the leader and a sad loss to the party; nevertheless, Mrs Thatcher's dignified reaction showed the public that her 'Iron Lady' image was based on more than rhetoric.

A New Kind of Mandate?

By April 1979, even though party policy had moved to the right, Mrs Thatcher had managed only a slight shift in the balance of her Shadow Cabinet. Keith Joseph had added Industry to his role of philosopher-at-large, and John Biffen accepted responsibility for small businesses. John Nott, another impeccable right-winger, was now spokesman for trade. But the front-bench majority was still centrist, and even the Right could see the value of a cautious approach, to avoid frightening the electorate. To counter the Prime Minister's claims that voting for her party would be 'too big a gamble for the country to take', Mrs Thatcher argued that the Conservative manifesto represented 'a broad framework for the recovery of our country, based not on dogma, but on reason, on common sense'. The 'five tasks' identified in the document comprised familiar priorities of post-war Conservatism, although the emphasis on controlling inflation was stronger than usual and 'proper monetary discipline' was now described as 'essential' in the undertaking. With this exception, the 1979 manifesto was more moderate in content than that of 1970, and the tone was more conciliatory. Unlike 1970, however, when Edward Heath had exaggerated the differences between himself and the 'unprincipled' Harold Wilson, Conservative right-wingers were now wisely anxious to conceal their real views from the voters to ensure that the election was fought on the Government's undistinguished record.[34]

Challenged to a televised debate by Callaghan, Mrs Thatcher wanted to accept but was talked out of it lest she should come over as 'hectoring and aggressive'. Her first major campaigning speech was delayed for two weeks, and when it was delivered her impatience showed. In Cardiff, the Prime Minister's home territory, Mrs Thatcher announced that she was 'a conviction politician' and compared herself with the Old Testament prophets. When she said, 'This is my faith and vision. This is what I passionately believe,' she was evidently not referring to the careful compromises enshrined in the manifesto. Fortunately she avoided spelling out her ideas in detail, and the Saatchi brothers were on hand to counteract the harsh rhetoric by cajoling her into such stunts as a fifteen minutes' embrace with a calf in Suffolk. She drew the line, however, at appearing together with Edward Heath, astonishing her team with her explosive response to Peter Thorneycroft's suggestion.[35]

The policies the Conservatives put forward, particularly on taxation and law and order, were popular, and the winter of discontent crippled Labour; one in three trade unionists voted Conservative. The election result gave the Conservatives an overall majority of forty-three, with 44 per cent of the vote – a significant recovery from October 1974, although as recently as 1970 the party had won 46.4 per cent of the votes. The swing between the main parties was the highest since 1945, as was the 7 per cent Conservative lead over Labour; 1979 saw Labour's worst performance since 1935. In the days before the election Callaghan told his adviser Bernard Donoughue that there had been a 'sea-change' in the outlook of voters. If so, it had taken place since the previous autumn, and its cause was the winter of discontent. In other words it was Jim Callaghan's fault and not the result of a deep movement of opinion. Since 1974, Labour Government had been a hand-to-mouth affair, and the main reason for its original victory – the idea that it would avoid conflict with the unions – had been thoroughly discredited.[36]

Yet the new Prime Minister was one of those who agreed with Callaghan's analysis. For her, the outcome was a vindication of the philosophy which party managers had urged her to tone down; it was 'a new kind of mandate for change'. In fact, however, the Conservative Party had won more despite than because of her. By the end of the campaign, she was nineteen points behind James Callaghan, and polls suggested that the party would have fared far better under Ted Heath. Nevertheless, the new Prime Minister had no doubts and, standing on the steps of Number 10, she intoned a prayer of St Francis of Assisi, 'Where there is discord, may we bring harmony.' Coming from her, that was, Jim Prior said, 'the most awful humbug'. Appropriately, the prayer was equally spurious; it was a nineteenth-century pastiche of St Francis.[37]

The First Term

Margaret Thatcher had recently affirmed her intention of having a 'conviction Cabinet' composed only of people who wanted to go in the direction she wanted. As a result, Nicholas Ridley and his friends always 'found it inexplicable' that Mrs Thatcher appointed to her first Cabinet so many people who did not share her views. He thought it was in many respects Willie Whitelaw's Cabinet. That seems unlikely. Mrs Thatcher presumably decided that it would be less dangerous to include in her Cabinet political opponents than leave them out, particularly as she did not intend to use the Cabinet in the usual way. Whatever the reasons, all the Shadow Cabinet survived except John Peyton, while Peter Walker was brought back to be the Minister of Agriculture.*

Ridley himself was bitterly disappointed at getting only a junior job at the Foreign Office. Yet Mrs Thatcher did not hide her real opinion of the moderates she had appointed, telling Prior, who had gone to Employment, that he must accept either Leon Brittan or Patrick Mayhew as his deputy because she was determined 'to have *someone* with backbone' in the department. Thus the new Prime Minister already identified agreement with her own policies and attitudes with the possession of backbone, and disagreement with spinelessness. This was a curious confusion. To agree with her required no spine at all, whereas to disagree did require a modicum of backbone.[39]

Except for Prior, Mrs Thatcher's allies monopolised the key economic departments. Despite repeated battering from Denis Healey, Geoffrey Howe became Chancellor of the Exchequer, with John Biffen as Chief Secretary, Nigel Lawson as Financial Secretary and Lord Cockfield in the Lords. This team had to work quickly since the unexpected dissolution had prevented Healey from producing a full Budget. Keith Joseph was installed at the Department of Industry. The right-wing element was reinforced by Nott at Trade and Maude as Paymaster-General. The lower ranks of the Government were well stocked with candidates for future promotion; apart from Ridley, Cecil Parkinson, John Moore and

---

* But Edward Heath was not. On the Saturday morning, the new Prime Minister, who had heard Gilmour say on television on election night that Heath should be in the Government, possibly as Foreign Secretary, told him sharply, when offering him a Cabinet job in the Foreign Office, that Ted Heath was not going to be Foreign Secretary or in the Cabinet. Instead Mrs Thatcher foolishly made him a written offer of the Embassy in Washington, which he naturally refused.[38]

Norman Tebbit became junior ministers in 1979. Yet the very able Kenneth Clarke was given a post in the Department of Transport rather than remaining Joseph's deputy at Industry as he had expected; because of his moderate views, he had to wait six years before his next upwards step.[40]

The Monetarist Experiment

The economic ministers, including the First Lord of the Treasury (Margaret Thatcher), were all fervent believers in monetarism; and as the outstanding feature of the Government's economic policy in its early years was the subjection of the British economy to this doctrine, a brief consideration of the theory is unavoidable. Its central idea was that the economy is a place where individual agents barter supplies and demands for goods and services (including their own labour) and money. If appropriate relative prices can be found, the story goes, all markets will clear simultaneously; this implies, among other things, that there will be no unemployment, since the demand for labour will always match supply if the real wage is right, i.e. low enough. Any attempt to reduce unemployment below this market-clearing rate by increasing the stock of money, or by deficit spending, will fail, only causing inflation; it may, in the short run, create 'unreal' jobs while people are being fooled by 'money illusion' into supposing that the real wage on offer is higher than it actually is. But reality will eventually catch up with them, and in the inflation which has meanwhile been created, unemployment will become higher than it would have been if the expansionary policy had never been attempted.

Astonishingly, this crazy, if coherent, vision which, as Maudling said, was 'totally divorced from reality', was uncritically accepted by the economic ministers and many others.[41] Unfortunately it carried very strong implications for policy. Sustained growth of the economy could never be achieved, the doctrine taught, through the expansion of aggregate demand, as had mistakenly been believed for twenty-five prosperous and reasonably stable years after the war. And by the same token, no amount of restrictive fiscal policy could increase unemployment other than temporarily. The only way to achieve sustained full employment was to remove all obstacles to the proper functioning of market processes and to create a stable non-inflationary environment by keeping the 'money supply' under strict control. The way to increase the growth rate was to provide incentives for hard work and entrepreneurial endeavour as well as disincentives to shirkers. Inflation was purely a monetary phenomenon which could be prevented by, and only by, maintaining proper control of the money supply.

For a period this doctrine held not only the Government but nearly the whole press and academic world in thrall. Unfortunately, when the Government tried to put theory into practice, they found that it was literally impossible to control the growth of the money supply. Even more unfortunately, the attempt to control it, because of the tight fiscal and monetary policy this was thought to require, caused an unprecedented collapse in output together with a rise in unemployment to unheard-of levels. In addition, the alleged link between monetary growth and inflation was broken in a way which the monetarist prophet Milton Friedman and his followers had maintained was scientifically impossible. When the inflation rate did eventually fall, this followed a period of exceptionally rapid growth in the money stock.[40]

Monetarism in Action

The need for swift budgetary action allowed Geoffrey Howe to set the tone for the Government's first term within six weeks of the election. 'Monetarism is not enough,' Keith Joseph had warned in Opposition. 'We must also have substantial cuts in tax and public spending and bold incentives and encouragements to the wealth creators.' Howe followed this prescription. The top rate of income tax was reduced from 83 per cent to 60 per cent, and the highest rates for investment income were slashed. The basic rate was more modestly chiselled by 3 per cent to 30 per cent, and tax allowances raised by more than inflation. To pay for all this, Howe raised VAT from 8 to 15 per cent. On the face of it, this was a dubious move by an inflation-hating Government, since it had the direct effect of raising prices by 3.5 per cent. Yet Treasury Ministers were not disturbed by this, since monetarist doctrine laid down that such things as VAT increases could not cause inflation; only an increase in the money supply could do that. Price controls on nationalised industries were also lifted, and the Government honourably fulfilled one rash election promise by funding the Clegg Commission's proposals on public-sector pay. Treasury Ministers were confident that cuts in public expenditure, together with a 2 per cent hike in Bank Rate to 14 per cent, would bring prices under control. In fact, inflation, which had stood at 10.3 per cent in May 1979, had doubled to 21.9 per cent a year later. Wynne Godley and the Cambridge Economic Policy Group correctly predicted the Government's first Budget would cause a disastrous recession.[43]

The Conservative leadership had been warning of a shift from direct to indirect taxation at least since the time of *The Right Approach*, but Howe had denied any plan to double VAT during the election campaign. The Chancellor also took what Nigel Lawson described as the 'politically brave' decision to relate future pension increases to the rate of inflation rather than earnings. This meant that pensioners would soon become considerably poorer, and there had been no mention of it in the manifesto. Direct taxation was certainly too high and needed to be reduced, yet the VAT increase hit the poor disproportionately hard, while the income-tax changes unashamedly rewarded the rich. The argument about incentives was trotted out to justify the tax cuts, although the experience of the Heath Government had cast doubt on this psychological assumption. As John Biffen recognised, many businessmen could be expected simply to work shorter hours for the same money.[44]

Meanwhile, higher interest rates helped those with savings but were a blow to industrial investment and raised costs for mortgage holders. A further 3 per cent rise in November pushed sterling higher in spite of the abolition of exchange controls announced by Howe in October. With inflation still steep, a Government which blamed the unions for pricing British goods out of international markets was showing that two could play at that game; at the same time, cheaper imports made it harder for British industry to compete at home. World demand was already shrinking due to a new threefold oil price rise after the Khomeini revolution in Iran. Before the election, Mrs Thatcher had attacked the Labour Government for missing 'a golden opportunity' to use North Sea oil as 'the booster pumping fresh energies through the arteries of our great industries'. That was even before Britain had become a net exporter of oil. Now, combined with wrong-headed Government policies, the oil was helping to give 'our great industries' heart failure. By the end of 1980, sterling had soared to $2.50 and DM5; output had fallen by nearly 6 per cent, manufacturing output by 15 per cent, and in September unemployment exceeded two million for the first time since the 1930s.[45]

Obviously the monetarists in the Government had not intended such massive destruction, yet they had caused much the biggest slump since 1929–31. In his 1980 Budget, even Geoffrey Howe was forced to reflect on what he chose to describe as 'a significant slowdown in growth'. With the expansion of demand ruled out, the Right clutched at the only answer which could be squared with its economic dogma. Despite the higher interest rates and the spending cuts, Treasury Ministers decided, the money supply had not been brought under control after all. Everything would be rectified by the Medium-Term Financial Strategy, which (in Mrs Thatcher's phrase) 'burst on an astonished world' in this second Budget. In truth there was nothing astonishing about this alleged strategy which set out targets of declining ranges of monetary growth. The real cause for astonishment would have been the hitting of the targets; only in one year did the Government come near to doing so. In the meantime its search for spending cuts led it to contradict the language of its election manifesto; while the manifesto had rightly praised Child Benefit, Howe's 1980 budget raised it by less than the inflation rate. Other benefits were cut by 5 per cent, and prescription charges raised by £1.[46]

By the time of the 1980 Conservative conference, Mrs Thatcher was worried that the public was showing only 'limited understanding of what we were trying to do'. She used the occasion to swipe once again at the Heath Government: 'You turn if you want to. The lady's not for turning.' The speech typified the new logic which prevailed in Downing Street. Edward Heath had responded to events, then lost two elections. Therefore the new-model Conservative Party should ignore events. If a policy was unpopular, then public 'understanding' had to be improved. Yet, if the public had understood the dangers which full-blown monetarism presented to the British economy, James Callaghan could have called an election in autumn 1978 and secured a working majority. By December, only 18 per cent of the public expected the Conservatives to win the next election; more than two-thirds thought that Labour would return to office.[47]

The Government's policy dismayed even its traditional allies. At the 1980 CBI conference, Sir Terence Beckett gave notice that he wanted a 'bare-knuckle fight' with the Government over the exchange-rate, but the crisis which made the employers temporarily bold also left them powerless. Although a shake-up had been necessary in 1979, Britain lost nearly a quarter of its manufacturing capacity between the election and the first half of 1981; production fell by 17 per cent. Anxious to erase the stain on Conservative honour caused by Heath's supposed generosity to 'lame ducks', the party's new leaders had sauntered out with shotguns and butchered a quarter of the flock, regardless of the health of the birds.[48]

Evidence had by now accumulated to prove that the monetarist slaughter had been performed in the name of a false god. An all-party Treasury Committee report published in February 1981 concluded that there was 'no direct causal link' between the money supply and inflation, and doubters on the Government benches were stirring. In November 1980 Howe had been defeated in Cabinet over public spending. The qualities extolled in the election manifesto, reason and common sense, required the Chancellor to change course in his 1981 Budget; he only moved faster in the wrong direction. The ideologue John Hoskyns, the head of the Downing Street Policy Unit, pleaded with Howe to 'give the country a *real shock* which would be good for the authority and credibility of the Government', and the Chancellor obliged. In the Budget he compensated for the public-spending defeat by freezing income-tax allowances, thus further reducing demand at a time when the economy needed stimulation. An increase in employee National Insurance contributions would also come into effect in April. Howe had at least realised that high interest rates were strangling the economy, and these were cut back to 12 per cent. In his alarm over public borrowing (which already compared favourably with that of most Western nations), Howe even imposed a windfall tax on the banks designed to raise £400 million. The PSBR for 1981–2 turned out to be £2 billion less than forecast – exactly the yield from the frozen tax allowances. This Budget really did 'burst on an astonished world'; 364 economists signed a letter of protest in *The Times*, and Howe set a new record by winning an approval rating of only 24 per cent.[49]

All the discussions before the 1981 Budget were confined to a Treasury team which, in Jim Prior's harsh phrase, contained no one with 'any experience of running a whelk stall, let alone a decent-sized company'. In fact, even the Prime Minister was reportedly 'not amused' by the Budget, but accepted that the tax increases were necessary in order to allow a reduction of interest rates; these only needed cutting because Howe has raised them too much in the first place. There was another row in Cabinet, and three Ministers discussed the possibility of resigning. Geoffrey Howe believes that this came to nothing because the dissidents feared 'being identified, exposed and crushed as a hostile cabal'. Their position, as Howe now generously concedes, was not unlike the one he and Nigel Lawson found themselves in seven years later. In any case they decided, probably wrongly, not to resign as they had learned of the Budget too late to stop it. After his Budget speech, Howe's reception by back-benchers would have ended the career of any Minister who enjoyed less than total support from the Prime Minister. But, as he noted later, there was a sufficient 'hard core of loyalty' among both Ministers and back-benchers to pull him through the crisis.[50]

The depth of party discontent prevented Mrs Thatcher from crushing the 'hostile cabal' immediately after the Budget. In July the Prime Minister found herself isolated, with only Howe, Joseph and Leon Brittan (the new Chief Secretary at the Treasury) in support, over a plan to cut spending by a further £5 billion. On this occasion, even Biffen and Nott joined the critics. Plainly, some of Mrs Thatcher's opponents had to be removed before the conference season. The September sackings included Soames, Gilmour and Carlisle; Norman St-John Stevas had been ejected in January, when Biffen was moved to Trade. The Party Chairman had turned out to be more like Thorneycroft I than the hoped-for Mark II version; after several critical briefings to the press he also was dropped, to be replaced by the vigorous Cecil Parkinson, who was promoted to the Cabinet. Jim Prior was moved to Northern Ireland, although he remained a lone figure on the Economic Strategy committee. This downsizing of the moderate element within the Cabinet did not make the monetarist case any sounder, but the Prime Minister seemed to think that, if the contradictory voices were banished from her counsels, awkward facts would also disappear.[51]

The Cabinet row in July almost coincided with the serious rioting in Liverpool and Southall. This followed April's disturbances in Brixton, and led to outbreaks in Manchester and other inner-city areas of the north and midlands. Such things had happened before in Britain, but in the democratic era the scale of disorder was without precedent. As Lord Scarman's inquiry later found, racial feelings and resentment of the police contributed to the trouble; there were a few 'copy-cat' incidents, and in some places the usual drunken activities of a Saturday night were inflated into riots by an unhelpful media. Yet the main cause of the riots was undoubtedly the large number of youths in urban areas with nothing to do and with no obvious reason to respect the norms and property of a society from which they were excluded. At Selsdon Park in 1970 even Keith Joseph had acknowledged that unemployment causes crime. In 1981 Mrs Thatcher's initial private response was to express sympathy for the shopkeepers whose premises had been looted; later she praised the policy and denied any link between the violence and unemployment, a contention which would have been more convincing had people run amok in Leamington Spa or Tunbridge Wells.[52]

By the time of the 1981 Party Conference the Government was faced with an unprecedented combination of economic malaise, social discontent and party disunity. At a fringe meeting, John Biffen reflected the apprehension of many Conservatives by suggesting that the party might be heading for an electoral disaster on the scale of 1906 or 1945. Mrs Thatcher's claim that 'there would be no question of sticking doggedly to so-called dogma' provided very limited reassurance. While a group of young Conservative MPs called for 'an emphasis on construction rather than destruction' in Government policy, Michael Heseltine was permitted to announce a special programme to help the inner cities. This high-profile initiative was a temporary swerve under pressure, not a U-turn or even a change of gear. By December Mrs Thatcher had emulated the feat of her Chancellor, receiving the lowest popularity rating of anyone to hold her position. But if the British tradition of orderly protest might be breaking down, the Conservative Party's loyalty to an incumbent leader was not so easily shaken. The moment passed, the Prime Minister survived, and the experiment proceeded.[53]

Industrial Relations

In September 1981 Christopher Soames had been sacked for being proved right against Prime Ministerial wishes. He had proposed a sensible pay deal for the civil service in April, which most of the Cabinet supported, but the Prime Minister would not agree. The result was a lengthy and expensive strike (costing £1.5 billion in uncollected taxes) which was eventually settled at precisely the figure suggested by Soames. This unhappy incident took place soon after the Prime Minister had decided to cancel a programme of pit closures in the face of a threatened miners' strike. In Opposition, Mrs Thatcher had promised further support for nationalised industries provided that work practices changed, and the Government went on finding resources for BL and British Steel. Although the ultimate aim of this generosity was to sell them to the private sector and much of the money was used to finance redundancies, to right-wing Ministers the policy seemed a strange contradiction of the ruling philosophy, which particularly disturbed Keith Joseph. After recommending that BL should receive a £1 billion subsidy in December 1980, he changed his mind and attacked his own policy in a Cabinet committee. In the September reshuffle he was moved at his own request to Education.[54]

The costly civil-service strike and the dispute over pit closures were uncomfortable reminders of trade-union power. Conservatives were agreed that the unions must be tamed. The problem was how to do so; *In Place of Strife* and the Industrial Relations Act were inauspicious precedents, and since then the Labour Government had further entrenched the closed shop. Jim Prior adopted a gradualist approach despite opposition from the Prime Minister. His 1980 Employment Act curtailed the main abuses such as the closed shop and secondary picketing; it also provided Government funding for secret ballots and union elections. Prior's successor at Employment, the former trade unionist Norman Tebbit, had likened Prior to Pétain and Laval but soon realised the advantages of a piecemeal approach. Another Act in 1982 eroded union legal immunities and further undermined the closed shop without abolishing it. Rising unemployment did much to ensure the success of

Prior's policy. Between 1979 and 1983 TUC membership dropped from over twelve to below ten million, and in the same period the number of workers in stoppages dropped from 4.6 million to 574,000. TU reform was popular; as in 1979, almost a third of trade unionists voted Conservative in 1983. In the different climate of the early 1980s, the unions failed in their bid to bring the country to a halt with a national 'day of action', and the Government's 'hands-off' approach to disputes helped to defeat a strike by railwaymen in July 1982.[55]

Jim Prior's union reforms benefited the country but did not reconcile the Prime Minister to a moderate who disliked her economic policy. By replacing him with Tebbit, Mrs Thatcher ensured that the successful reforms would be associated in future with the right wing of the party which had originally called for sterner measures; in Opposition, Dr Rhodes Boyson had demanded that strikes in the public sector should be banned. Tebbit in practice followed Prior, not Boyson, but he introduced a new style of rhetoric which dominated the headlines; at the 1981 conference in response to a speech which connected rioting with unemployment, Tebbit recalled his father who had 'got on his bike and looked for work' in the 1930s.[56]

Tebbit's populism contributed to the growing polarisation of British politics. Labour's inglorious record in Government made an angry inquest within the party inevitable. The Left was already convinced that the Callaghan Government had failed because it had not been socialist enough, and Mrs Thatcher's disdain for the post-war settlement provided further cause for an ideological spasm. Labour's moderates were dismayed by the party's sprint away from the middle ground, just when the Conservatives had abandoned it to them. In January 1981, after a special conference had chosen a bizarre electoral system for choosing the Labour leader, Roy Jenkins, David Owen, Shirley Williams and William Rogers set up the Social Democratic Party. In the autumn of 1981, the new party moved into first place in the polls and stayed there for six months; it seemed to have broken the mould of the two-party system. On the basis of by-election results like Crosby and Glasgow Hillhead (won by Shirley Williams and Roy Jenkins respectively), the SDP looked set to introduce an entirely new mould with its Liberal allies; at the time of the 1981 Conservative conference, a relatively unknown Liberal had caused a major upset at Croydon. Unfortunately for the 'Gang of Four', the SDP's roots were too shallow to survive when events turned against it; although several were tempted, only one Conservative MP, Christopher Brocklebank-Fowler, decided to join. The result was a split opposition which helped to give Mrs Thatcher a landslide victory in 1983 despite a small fall in support.[57]

The Falklands Conflict

Ever since the election, Lord Carrington and Foreign Office Ministers had seen the danger of an Argentine invasion of the Falkland Islands and known such an invasion could not be successfully resisted without a massive increase in troops and equipment. Since there was no possibility of such an increase – indeed Mrs Thatcher was looking for defence cuts – they favoured a compromise, but their colleagues did not. The Prime Minister was displeased when her ally Nicholas Ridley told her, after a visit to the Falklands, that like the rest of the Foreign Office he thought that sovereignty over the islands should be ceded to Argentina, which would then lease them back to Britain. This sensible solution, which would have depended on the consent of the islanders, was crushed by a cross-party Commons assault. With negotiations stalled, the new Defence Secretary, John Nott, supported by the Prime Minister, announced that HMS *Endurance* – Britain's only naval presence in the area – would be withdrawn to save money. Foreign Office Ministers, usually regarded by Mrs Thatcher as appeasers, strongly objected, knowing that such a conspicuous and unnecessary withdrawal would be interpreted by Buenos Aires as readiness to surrender. They were overruled. Yet when the Argentinian junta duly invaded on 2 April 1982, Carrington, not Mrs Thatcher or Nott, was treated as the culprit. Shortly after a sulphurous meeting with the 1922 Committee, he honourably resigned.[58]

On the day after Carrington's resignation, an NOP poll found that 60 per cent believed Mrs Thatcher was responsible for the invasion. She was certainly more so than he was. The Prime Minister merits censure for having combined verbal intransigence with weakness in action – the prospective withdrawal of HMS *Endurance* which, as her biographer put it, was the result of 'the financial dogmatism of the Medium-Term Financial Strategy' – in the lead-up to the invasion. Yet her conduct of the seventy-four-day war – including the unavoidable decision to attack the *General Belgrano* – was exemplary. Argentina was an aggressor, and the rights of the islanders had to be defended. Some of the later recriminations, which included Denis Healey's allegation that Mrs Thatcher 'gloried in slaughter', were no more justified than the Government's own attacks on the allegedly insufficient patriotism of the BBC and the Archbishop of Canterbury. These distasteful quarrels showed that the brief moment of shared national concern was no antidote to the poisonous atmosphere of British politics after 1979.[59]

The 'Falklands factor' played a major role in the 1983 election victory (not least in distracting media attention from the SDP), but the Conservative manifesto presented the war as just one of a long list of foreign-affairs successes. Early in Mrs Thatcher's premiership the long-running problem of Rhodesia was finally settled, and Britain received a considerable rebate on its contributions to the EEC budget. The Prime Minister was widely praised in both these instances; the praise was justified in that she did not prevent either agreement. Had she been allowed, however, to follow her own inclinations on Rhodesia, there would have been no settlement. On Europe, the Conservative manifesto had complained that the 'frequently obstructive and malevolent attitude of Labour Ministers had weakened the Community as a whole and Britain's bargaining power within it'; once in office, Mrs Thatcher apparently concluded that such an attitude strengthened Britain's bargaining power. Arguably her shrill demands were the perfect foil to the more traditional tactics of Foreign Office Ministers and officials, but in fact they made a solution more difficult. Mrs Thatcher's description in 1977 of the Conservatives as 'the European Party in the British Parliament' was not something she thought of repeating after 1979.[60]

Beginnings of Recovery

Even before the Falklands crisis, the fortunes of the Conservative Party had started to mend. In the spring of 1982 inflation was at last falling. Labour had abdicated as an alternative Government, and the SDP was not 'interest-based' and lacked a social constituency. An Opposition divided into two major parties, one of which was even more extreme than the Government, helped to rescue the beleaguered Conservatives. In March 1982, the month that Jenkins won Hillhead, MORI found that support for the Tories had risen to 34 per cent from a miserable 27 per cent in December 1981. After the Falklands, Mrs Thatcher's personal rating soared to 59 per cent. By October, the Conservatives led Labour by 13 per cent; the new alliance between the Liberals and the SDP languished at around 20 per cent in the polls. The pre-Falklands Conservative revival began despite the unemployment figures exceeding three million in January 1982, and continuing to rise until 1986. In 1976 Mrs Thatcher had declared that the Conservatives would have been 'drummed out of office if we'd had this level of unemployment'. At that time the level in question was 1.3 million; after she had been in power for four years, about the same number had been out of work for more than a year.[61]

Yet, for those still in work, living standards were beginning to rise, and less than half of the jobless attributed their plight to the Government. In 1982 a House of Lords Committee found that unemployment was costing the taxpayer over £15 billion a year. Yet many taxpayers either accepted the Government's contention that proper job creation should be left to the free market or heeded its argument that unemployment in the 1980s caused far less suffering that it did in the 1930s – a position which ignored both the demoralising effect of losing one's job and the misery experienced by those who had just enough to live on but were excluded from the general rise in living standards. Repeated changes to the methods of counting unemployment demonstrated that Government could at least do something to reduce the monthly figures; during the election campaign, the removal of many older claimants from the register produced an entirely artificial fall of 121,000.[62]

'When inflation fell, as the Chancellor had intended, the wets had lost the intellectual battle,' was the verdict of one Thatcherite academic. Like everybody else, of course, One-Nation Conservatives knew that inflation could be brought down if the economy was squeezed sufficiently hard, especially at a time when world commodity prices were falling. The 'wet' case was that, in obedience to an erroneous dogma, the monetarist clique in charge of the economic ministries had caused needless carnage to the economy and the social fabric of the nation. Despite Britain's possession of North Sea oil, the recession was deeper and more prolonged here than in countries which were dependent on imported fuel. That hardly looked like an intellectual victory.[63]

The 'intellectual' victory that the right wing claimed over 'the 364 economists' was also spurious. In their letter to *The Times* after the 1981 Budget, mentioned earlier, the economists maintained that 'present policies would deepen the recession' and that 'the time has come to reject monetarist policies'. This letter has been much used in attempts to vindicate the Government policy of that time on the grounds that 'ironically' the economy started to turn up immediately after the letter was published and continued rising for the next seven years. As it happens, however, no recovery worth the name started in the spring of 1981. Growth was well below that of productive potential until the end of 1982, while unemployment rose another three-quarters of a million.[64]

Although ministerial memoirs and other defences of the monetarist period usually underplay it, the documents of the time put it beyond doubt that controlling the money supply was the central aim of Government policy – to the point where both fiscal and monetary policy was to be entirely subordinated to that end. Accordingly, the Government in the 1981 Budget set declining targets for the growth of M3: 6–10 per cent in 1981–2, 5–9 per cent in 1982–3 and 4–8 per cent in 1983–4. And when the 364 economists said that 'present policies would deepen the recession', they clearly took 'present policies' to be what the Government was saying its policies actually were. In the event, the money supply targets were egregiously exceeded: M3 grew by 13 per cent in 1981–2 and at an average rate of 11 per cent in the three years to 1983–4 – much higher than the top of the range which had been laid down. And that continued in subsequent years. M3 rose by 18 per cent in 1985–6. So, largely by mistake, the Government followed the economists' advice and abandoned monetarism.[65]

The 1982 Budget was broadly neutral. From then on, however, the erstwhile hairshirt monetarists, who had scoffed at previous Conservative booms, embarked on one themselves. The Government's failure to meet its money-supply targets largely resulted from its progressive removal of all controls over credit. In consequence the rise in output, when it came, was not the kind of growth which had been promised, based on supply side measures which would allow market forces to work; it was a boom of just the wrong, unsustainable kind, based on consumption and inflated property values. The importance of the abolition of controls over consumer credit in July 1982 was quickly recognised by one of the 364, Godley, who, in August 1982, described the move as 'a most hazardous gesture' which would add enormously to demand. But the hazards were not generally noticed and, however ill-judged, a consumer boom was at least an improvement on the dogmatic and disastrous monetarist experiment which had preceded it. For a time, economically, it brought some 'Franciscan' harmony, where monetarism had brought only discord.[66]

CHAPTER
XIV

The 'Economic Miracle', or From Slump to Slump

The beginning of a consumer boom was a prime example of 'electoral Keynesianism'. Unlike many of her predecessors, Mrs Thatcher did not choose the wrong date for an election. Only when the encouraging polls were confirmed by a strong Conservative performance in the May 1983 local government elections did she pick 9 June as the date. The party's manifesto was another cautious document; its most notable feature was its promise to extend the denationalisation programme, which had begun with the sale of shares in British Aerospace, Cable and Wireless and the National Freight Corporation and which the Government had been slow to realise could reduce the PSBR, 'roll back the frontiers of the state', reward the City of London and enable it to be the champion of 'popular capitalism'. Council-house sales were to be given further encouragement in a second Conservative term; the policy, pushed hard by Peter Walker in Opposition, had produced an additional 500,000 home-owners by 1983. Even this, however, was marred by free-market dogma; although private building slumped during the recession, the Government's housing budget was slashed and councils were forced to put most of the receipts from sales towards the repayment of debt.[1]

On taxation and spending the manifesto was appropriately sheepish. Credit was naturally taken for the cuts in income tax, but the rise since 1979 of 5 per cent in the proportion of GDP taken in all forms of taxation was quietly ignored. Similarly, the Government made a virtue of its failure to achieve an overall reduction in public expenditure, boasting of its generous welfare spending and its fulfilment of pledges on the police and armed forces. The social security budget had been inflated massively by the threefold rise in unemployment, and demographic change required increased spending on the National Health Service. Another reason for performance falling so far short of the party's original undertakings on cutting public expenditure was the leadership's belief in its own rhetoric about the spendthrift socialism of the Labour

Government; in fact, Labour ministers had been forced against their will to hack at public spending well before 1979. Mrs Thatcher was irritated by the welfare state, telling one of her ministers that she thought Britain would have to return to soup kitchens. But, for the first term, at least, this kind of reform remained a dream for the hard Right.[2]

The chief uncertainty of the 1983 general election was whether Labour or the SDP/Liberal Alliance would be second. The Falklands factor, the divided Opposition, and Labour's manifesto, which made the party even more unelectable than it had previously seemed, made heavy contributions to the eventual landslide. Any good tidings for the Conservatives did not lack messengers: an estimated 75 per cent of the adult population read a Government-supporting daily newspaper in 1983. A redistribution of seats by the Boundary Commission earned the Conservatives approximately thirty seats. In addition, the economic disaster which befell Britain between 1979 and 1983 was unlike those which destroyed the Governments of Heath and Callaghan. No amount of propaganda could camouflage power-cuts and the three-day week, or uncollected rubbish and picket-lines at hospital gates. In 1974 and 1979 these symptoms of failure were visible to the overwhelming majority of voters. The damage caused by Government policy in 1979–81 was more lasting and serious. Yet only the unemployed and their families had suffered it directly; and, to symbolise the new Two-Nations philosophy which presided in Downing Street, the geographical distribution of poverty made it literally invisible to most people.

The devastation inflicted on manufacturing industry was similarly not apparent to many consumers who, in the mini-boom which preceded the election, were able to choose from a plentiful variety of foreign goods. And manifesto claims that unemployment had resulted from a world recession and the necessary slimming down of British industry contained just enough truth to satisfy many people. Thus the Government was re-elected with an overall majority of 144 on 42.4 per cent of the vote. This was a smaller percentage than Douglas-Home had received when he lost in 1964, and less than half of those who voted Conservative claimed that they had done so for positive reasons. But in seats it was enough to give Mrs Thatcher the largest winning margin since 1945.[3]

In August 1980 J. K. Galbraith wrote that Britain had 'volunteered to be the Friedmanite guinea pig'. More truly she had been conscripted, but Galbraith was right in thinking that the body politic would survive. The phlegmatic guinea pig had refused to bite while the experiment was conducted, and had now even preferred the existing scientist-in-chief to the eager researchers of Left and Centre in the 1983 general election.[4]

Even experiments, however, which advance human knowledge rarely leave the guinea pig unscathed. The benefits of wider home-ownership and union reform were considerable, but were offset by the dramatic rise in unemployment and the unprecedented damage to manufacturing industry. The psychological benefits of the right-wing project were also dubious. Victory in the Falklands War had certainly helped morale. There were few signs, however, that tax reductions for the rich had transformed Britain into an entrepreneurial powerhouse, or that Margaret Thatcher's individualist rhetoric had inspired the kind of rational, thrifty conduct which she had admired in her father.

Young people in some areas responded to the end of secure employment prospects by preparing themselves for long-term dependence on the dole – precisely the reaction which the Government wanted to avoid, but one which, on right-wing premises, was the 'rational' thing to do when there were no jobs. Older people, who had grown up under Governments which secured full employment, now had to readjust their thinking or leave the work-force for good. Mrs Thatcher blamed the welfare state for its 'perverse encouragement of idleness and cheating', yet her Government had done more to foster these regrettable traits than any previous administration. In what had already become Two-Nations Britain, many communities, particularly in some inner cities, regarded dependency not as a stigma but as a settled way of life. In more fortunate areas where jobs were still available, the stigma remained; so the Two-Nations economy was mirrored by divided attitudes in different parts of the country.[5]

Although Margaret Thatcher thought the 1983 manifesto lacked a 'crusading spirit' to inspire the Government, she took the Conservative victory as a signal to ride into battle. In an unguarded moment during the election campaign the Foreign Secretary, Francis Pym, had remarked that 'landslides on the whole don't produce successful Governments'. They do, however, allow Prime Ministers a relatively free hand with Cabinet appointments, and Pym, who had been out of favour since resisting spending cuts during his earlier spell at the Ministry of Defence, was sacked two days after the poll. Peter Walker (now at Energy) and Jim Prior (still at Northern Ireland) stayed in office, but Mrs Thatcher was unlikely to allow the One-Nation minority much influence when she had overridden the views of more than half the Cabinet.[6]

The post-election reshuffle included some notable promotions. Nigel Lawson and Leon Brittan, now respectively Chancellor and Home Secretary, had only held Cabinet rank for two years. Cecil Parkinson, who had joined the Cabinet as late as April 1982, was the original choice to replace Pym at the Foreign Office. Having told the Prime Minister of problems in his private life, he had to be content with Trade and Industry while Howe got the Foreign Office.

Believing that her problem was having 'too few revolutionaries' in her Cabinet, the Prime Minister used the reshuffle 'to recruit some', although she did not find Nicholas Ridley a place until October. With a new consignment of back-bench believers, the parliamentary party was also beginning to conform to her wishes. The 1983 victory produced 101 new Conservative MPs, including the subsequent ministers Michael Howard, Michael Forsythe and Peter Lilley. Of the newcomers, only 25 per cent had attended both public school and Oxbridge, as opposed to 42 per cent of the whole parliamentary party. Even so, the recruits were not necessarily representative of the electorate in either their social standing or their views. 'They're mostly hard-nosed businessmen,' one older member lamented, but many of them were professionals, such as lawyers and accountants. There were still none of the great 'captains of industry' with whom the party had once been associated. John Major, a middle-ranking bank official first elected in 1979, was therefore much more representative of the parliamentary Conservative Party than Jim Prior, who became Chairman of GEC after leaving office in 1984.[7]

Despite the advent of George Walden, an independent-minded *émigré* from the Foreign Office, the new intake was likely to support right-wing policies in the lobbies whatever they might think in private. A study of the 1983 newcomers concluded that 'apart from a couple of exceptions the next generation of Mrs Thatcher's troops may hold roughly similar views to the old Tory squires they are replacing'. That was doubtful; in any case very few 'old Tory squires' had sat in the 1979–83 Parliament; the most distinguished of them now became leader of the House of Lords as Viscount Whitelaw, whom the Prime Minister had found 'indispensable' in Cabinet.[8]

The Miners' Strike

In spite, or because, of her comfortable majority, Mrs Thatcher encountered parliamentary turbulence before her second term was over. The 1984–5 session alone saw twenty-one revolts of various sizes on eleven separate issues, and in April 1986 the American bombing raid on Libya coincided with a rebellion by more than seventy MPs against a Shops Bill which sought to legalise Sunday opening. Plans to sell Austin Rover and Leyland trucks to Ford and General Motors had to be scrapped; the wages councils which Churchill had established to set minimum wage rates in some low-pay industries, were not abolished, contrary to Lawson's wishes; nevertheless protection was removed from young workers. The most serious challenge, however, came from 'out-of-doors'. Although the country had voted decisively against full-blooded socialism at the election, Arthur Scargill, who professed to favour proportional representation, was determined to reverse that outcome by means which were anything but proportional.[9]

In 1981 Scargill had interpreted his own election as leader of the National Union of Mineworkers as a mandate to bring down the Government. At first he was thwarted, as the Government backed away from confrontation and poured subsidies down the pits. After the election the Government gave him his opportunity. Ian McGregor, who had improved productivity at British Steel by halving its work-force, was appointed Chairman of the National Coal Board, to wreak a similar transformation. The Board's announcement in March 1984, without having consulted the NUM, of the closure of Cortonwood pit in Yorkshire brought the Yorkshire miners out on strike. Over the past few months the Board had spent more than £1 million on Cortonwood and had promised that the pit would stay open until 1989 despite the losses it made. Although the Government had promised there would be no compulsory redundancies and had offered generous terms for voluntary redundancy, this sudden U-turn was an egregious public-relations blunder, threatening to uncork sympathy for the miners which persisted despite the events of 1973–4.[10]

Fortunately for the present Government, it enjoyed three assets which Heath had lacked. The most important of these was Mr Scargill himself. He had played a crucial role in previous strikes: this time there was no Joe Gormley to restrain him. Like Lenin, Scargill was too excited to delay his revolutionary attempt until the moment prescribed in the textbooks. But unlike Lenin, who conducted a successful Marxist coup in Russia without waiting for the preliminary bourgeois revolution, in Britain Scargill could not make his bid for power effective while coal stocks were plentiful and summer was approaching. Having picked the wrong time for his strike, Scargill defied his union's rules by refusing to hold a national ballot; he did so because, as several area votes showed, he would certainly have lost it. Scargill's conduct persuaded most other trade unions to restrict their class solidarity to verbal support, and the bourgeois lackeys of the Labour Party (now led by Neil Kinnock) did even less; Kinnock refused to turn up at a picket-line until January, by which time the strike was beginning to crumble.[11]

The Government owed its other advantages to Mrs Thatcher. Even before coming to office she had anticipated a strike, and the high level of coal stocks reflected a deliberate policy. Her other shrewd move was the choice of Peter Walker as Energy Secretary in place of Nigel Lawson. In his new capacity of Chancellor, Lawson provoked uproar in the Commons by describing resistance to the strike as 'a worthwhile investment for the nation'. Ill-phrased as it was, his claim was true even though the 'investment' in question eventually totalled £3 billion, including an estimated £140 million for police overtime. Remembering the skilful guerrilla tactics employed by Scargill in previous strikes, Walker rightly opposed using the new union legislation against the NUM. Along with the fact that the new Minister was a well-known critic of the party's neo-liberals, this created the impression that the Government was holding aloof from the dispute. The illusion was remarkably successful, even surviving the Prime Minister's likening of the battle against the strikers to the Falklands conflict. Mrs Thatcher was a stout supporter of Walker in his stand, although many of her usual Cabinet allies were keen to try out the new laws against Scargill.[12]

The miners' strike did resemble the Falklands in that it was an unnecessary and tragic conflict which eventually produced the best outcome. The Government's defeat of the miners secured its union reforms and represented a victory for constitutional action in a year which also saw the IRA's attempt to assassinate the Cabinet in the Grand Hotel at Brighton. Yet the nightly images of bloody picket-line clashes between police and strikers did little to enhance the nation's sense of well-being; they were especially disturbing not only because of the extent of the violence but because most of the miners were trying to preserve their communities, not to swell their pay-packets like the men of 1974, or to bring about the rule of Chairman Scargill.

The closure of 'uneconomic' pits could now proceed. Of course, most of these were in places like South Wales and north-east England where unemployment was already high; and the Government's failure, despite Walker's urging, to take more active steps to reduce high unemployment in those areas confirmed the widespread impression that it was unconcerned about the existence of Two Nations. By trying to turn his revolutionary fantasies into reality, Scargill wrecked his union as well as damaging the national economy and the coal industry. While the NUM was finished as a threat to the state, picket-line violence was not yet over; the spring of 1986 saw fierce battles outside the Wapping plant of News International, owned by the Government's favourite newspaper magnate, Rupert Murdoch. Like Scargill, the print unions had long been riding for a fall and, as with the miners' strike, this dispute ended with a decisive defeat for the union side to the considerable benefit of the newspaper industry.[13]

Well before the miners' strike, the Government had shown that it was not content to let the trade-union issue rest with its prudent legislation of 1979–83. In January 1984, trade unions were banned from the Government Communications Headquarters at Cheltenham; in an extraordinary move, members were asked to exchange their rights for £1,000 a head. GCHQ had been affected by the civil-service strike of 1981; action against the unions there was delayed partly because the Government was reluctant to admit the existence of this listening post. Publicity surrounding the 1983 trial of Geoffrey Prime, a GCHQ employee who had spied for the Soviet Union, removed the veil, allowing the Government to proceed, although its addiction to secrecy prevented it from consulting the unions over a decision which had been contemplated for nearly three years. The ban was widely seen as a second repayment on the debt which Mrs Thatcher owed to President Reagan for his assistance during the Falklands War. The first had been extracted in October 1983, when US forces invaded the Commonwealth island of Grenada after only token and belated consultations with London; in April 1986 the Reagan administration received a third instalment when in another display of its trigger-happiness – its attack on Tripoli – it was allowed to use British bases.[14]

The Government combined its attack on the unions with furthering the interests of the Conservative Party. The 1984 Trade Union Reform Act introduced some valuable changes, including secret ballots for the election of officials. It also required, however, that a union should vote every five years on the renewal of its affiliation to the Labour Party. The legislation's aim was thwarted, however, by union members overwhelmingly supporting continued links with the Opposition; two unions even chose this moment to contribute to Labour's funds for the first time.[15]

Unlike Geoffrey Howe, the new Chancellor was well versed in economics. Nigel Lawson had once been an enthusiastic Keynesian and an adviser to Edward Heath; as one of his aides later remarked, 'Nigel has been in favour of most things at one time or another.'[16] His legacy from Howe was mixed. Although GDP rose by a very respectable 3.8 per cent during 1983, unemployment had climbed above 10 per cent and, despite record productivity gains, manufacturing output was still some 15 per cent below what it had been in 1979. As a result, the increased spending power of those in work sucked in more imports. Between 1981 and 1984 imports of manufactured goods increased by more than a third; without North Sea oil the overall trade deficit for these years would have been £5 billion. Inflation had fallen below 5 per cent, but it was still higher in Britain than in Japan, Germany and the USA. An awkward part of his inheritance had been bequeathed by Lawson to himself; the 'astonishing' Medium-Term Financial Strategy, which had been his brain-child, was still nominally in place. Yet not even Lawson's verbal wizardry could produce a correlation between the inflation rate and the money supply, however defined. Nevertheless, the Chancellor continued to toast the healthy offspring until, in his Mansion House speech of October 1985, he conceded that he had been nurturing the wrong baby. From now on, the Government would focus on sterling M0, which measured notes and coins in circulation, rather than the broader M3. In reality, as the *Financial Times* noted, the speech was a death certificate for the MTFS.[17]

As the Government had failed to control the money supply, Lawson had had to abate his monetarism. The exchange-rate largely took its place. This was a shift towards economic realism which, if adopted prudently from the start, would have spared industry a great deal of pain between 1979 and 1981. While the attention of the Government and the financial world was still fixed on sterling M3, unfavourable statistics in November 1984 (later revised) had triggered off a run on the pound which had almost brought it to parity with the dollar by the following February. Any cheer that this might have given to exporters was obliterated by a compensating interest rate rise of 4.5 per cent to 14 per cent. The deteriorating balance of payments made the currency vulnerable. More manufacturing capacity was needed to remedy the weakness; unfortunately, Lawson's self-imposed dogmatic shackles prevented him from doing much to encourage investment. While the consumer-driven recovery had started in 1982–3, manufacturing investment only revived in 1987 – in good time for the next recession.[18]

Sterling faced another crisis in autumn 1986. The pound, such a symbol of national virility in the Government's early years, lost 16 per cent of its value between the fourth quarters of 1985 and 1986. Of more concern, however, to consumers than a fluctuating exchange-rate and ill-behaved monetary aggregates was the growth of real incomes – around 20 per cent between 1983 and 1987 – and a prolonged period of inflation below 5 per cent. In 1986, too, the Government's unemployment figures at last began to fall from an official peak of 3.3 million; the Budget of that year reduced the basic rate of income tax to 29 per cent, and in November Lawson increased public spending for the next two years by over £10 billion, showing particular generosity to the National Health Service.[19]

By ignoring his 'expansionist critics', the Chancellor claimed in his 1987 Budget speech, he had ensured that the British economy was now in an 'unprecedentedly favourable position'. The basic rate of income tax was lowered by another 2 per cent and excise duties were frozen. In the prevailing mood, where MORI found economic optimists out-numbering pessimists by 17 per cent, any concerns that the Chancellor had been too bountiful could be dismissed as the familiar groans of professional kill-joys. While the drastic tax cuts of the Reagan adminis-tration had only produced a yawning budget deficit, Lawson managed to repay £4 billion of Britain's debt in 1987–8. Backed by the 'feel-good factor' produced by Lawson's Budget, the Conservative 1987 manifesto boasted that 'for the first time in a generation this country looks forward to an era of real prosperity and fulfilment'.[20]

All the same, Lawson was behaving just like the 'expansionist critics' he derided. Higher real incomes, coupled with the removal of lending restrictions, had enticed financial institutions and consumers into a *folie à deux*, a wild financial spree and credit explosion which the Govern-ment made no attempt to control. Lawson had the fortitude to thwart Mrs Thatcher's perennial desire to raise mortgage tax relief – which he wanted to abolish altogether – but house prices had already shot upwards again, most notably in the south of England. While the number of homeless families more than doubled between 1978 and 1989, others were treating property as a source of profit rather than shelter. In a deregulated mortgage market which allowed borrowers to take out loans out of all proportion to their assets, mortgage debt soared from £42.1 billion in 1979 to £298 billion by 1988. The last thing needed in such dizzy times was even a mildly expansionist Budget, yet not until after the election did the nation discover that Lawson's management of a boom was no improvement on Howe's response to a recession.[21]

Privatisation

A crucial reason for the encouraging PSBR figures during these years was the Government's privatisation programme. Yet the Government's claim that privatisation improved the public finances was misleading, if not fraudulent. The trick was to treat all privatisation proceeds, whether they took the form of sales of shares or of council houses, as though they were the equivalent of tax receipts, which they are not. The sale of existing assets does not withdraw purchasing power from the econ-omy; while it does reduce public debt, it reduces publicly owned assets by a roughly equivalent amount, so that there is little change in the total net worth of the public sector and correspondingly little difference either to the net wealth or the disposable income of the private sector. If anything, indeed, the privatisation programme during the eighties had an adverse effect on public finances because the assets were generally sold at prices significantly below their market value.[22]

Accordingly the real benefits of privatisation derived from any improvements in the way the industries were run. Nearly all the privatised industries were certainly better run, although ironically the Government itself cast some doubt on its deeply held belief that private is always better than public by improving the performance of the nationalised concerns. Productivity in the Post Office increased faster than in the privatised British Telecom. By 1989 the state-owned industries were making an overall profit for the taxpayer – and this after some of the most attractive assets had joined the private sector.[23]

'In advance of every significant privatization,' Nigel Lawson noted in his memoirs, 'public opinion was invariably hostile to the idea and there was no way it could be won round except by the Government going ahead and doing it.' He must have been thinking of the later privatisations such as water and electricity, on which the public has still not been 'won round'. By contrast, the earlier sales were popular from the start. The Telecom issue of November 1984 was over-subscribed four times, with 2.3 billion applicants; by the end of the first week of trading, the share price had almost doubled. Despite the temptation to grab a quick profit, the proportion of shareholders rose from 7 to 21 per cent of the adult population between 1979 and 1993.[24]

Between 1983 and 1987, fifteen major companies returned to the private sector, including British Gas, British Airways and Rolls-Royce, which had been profitable ever since its aero-engine division was nationalised by the Heath Government. While the rhetoric of popular capitalism was backed by concrete evidence of wider ownership, critics had a point when they deplored the expensive advertising associated with each sale as disguised party propaganda. A stronger criticism is that public assets were sold too cheaply. The persistent undervaluation of the shares sold to the public encouraged what might be called casino capitalism, were it not that the Government was giving money away, which a casino never does. Nevertheless, the sales conducted by the second Thatcher Government strengthened the economy.

The real problems arose after the 1987 election, when the remaining candidates for sale fell into three categories: natural monopolies, truly crippled ducks like nuclear power, or absurd nurseries of free enterprise like prisons. The 1983 manifesto rightly stressed that 'merely to replace state monopolies by private ones would be to waste an historic opportunity'. But as the hype surrounding the policy increased, Mrs Thatcher decided that the 'historic opportunity' was too good to fritter away by waiting for 'the ideal circumstances for privatization which might take years to achieve'. In practice, however, the Prime Minister rightly balked at some of the most outlandish suggestions, which her successor did not.[25]

The Westland Affair

The 1983 victory seemed to remove any remaining doubts about Mrs Thatcher's survival as Conservative leader. Despite occasional crises, the Gallup polls of this Parliament showed that even if she was unpopular her approval rating was invariably higher than that of her Government. Idle speculation turned to the identity of a successor who would probably have to wait even longer than Anthony Eden. Cecil Parkinson was the first anointed, but after the 1983 conference he was forced to resign from the Cabinet because of continuing repercussions from his affair with Sara Keays. His replacement at Trade and Industry, Norman Tebbit, had many admirers on the party's right wing, but this sentiment was not shared by the Prime Minister who briefly transferred her affections to John Moore. Conservative moderates increasingly pinned their hopes on Michael Heseltine, who continued to win applause at party conferences despite his enthusiasm for economic intervention and closer co-operation with Europe. After the 1983 election he moved from Environment to Defence, where his combative performance over the siting of US Cruise missiles at Greenham Common did no harm to his prospects of further promotion.

The Westland affair of January 1986 both threatened Mrs Thatcher's continued tenure of Downing Street and removed Heseltine from the Cabinet. Heseltine was promoting a European bid for the ailing Westland Helicopters, while Leon Brittan (recently demoted from the Home Office to the DTI), supported by Mrs Thatcher, favoured an American bid for Westland. After the Defence Secretary had annoyed the Prime Minister and her staff by publishing a provocative and, in their view, inaccurate letter to the European Consortium, Downing Street saw the chance to settle the matter by some sharp practice. The Solicitor General was to be asked for a written opinion. Althought it is a firm constitutional rule that advice from the Law Officers is always kept confidential, the only point of this manoeuvre was to leak the opinion; a private remonstrance to Heseltine would have served no purpose. The Solicitor General's (mistaken) claim that there had been 'material inaccuracies' in Heseltine's letter was then selectively leaked to the Press Association. The leak created uproar, Heseltine being called a 'liar' by the gutter press.[26]

At the next Cabinet meeting, Mrs Thatcher ruled that all future ministerial statements on the subject must be cleared with the Cabinet Office, whereupon Heseltine, who had been enraged by the leak, gathered his papers and left the Cabinet. Almost equally angered by the leak, the Law Officers demanded an inquiry, which Mrs Thatcher had to concede.[27]

Although the inquiry under the Cabinet Secretary, Sir Robert Armstrong, was predictably inconclusive, the main culprits were clearly in Downing Street. The Government tried to hang the whole blame on Colette Bowe, an official within Leon Brittan's DTI, but this unprecedented exposure of a civil servant to media attention only produced the impression that Ms Bowe was an honest and prudent employee who would never have acted without full clearance from Downing Street. After the 1987 election John Biffen dubbed the Prime Minister's Press Secretary, Bernard Ingham, 'the sewer, not the sewage'; by January 1986 he was already known to be a reliable conveyance for the Prime Minister's thoughts. These were made clear enough in the House of Commons on 23 January, when Mrs Thatcher declared that making the 'inaccuracies' in Heseltine's letter 'known publicly' was 'a matter of duty'. How this could have been done without leaking a confidential letter from a law officer remained a mystery.[28]

Mrs Thatcher feared she might be toppled by the Westland saga and, if Neil Kinnock had not fluffed his opportunity by making a rambling speech in the House of Commons instead of asking a few pointed and unanswerable questions, she probably would have been. Once again, therefore, the sacrificial victim was one of her Ministers. On 23 January, Brittan, who despite his intelligence had never gained a parliamentary following and was widely regarded as Mrs Thatcher's creation, was savaged by the 1922 Committee in one of its ugliest moods. He loyally resigned the next day, and although the real blame lay in Downing Street he did not spill the beans. Had Brittan 'made public all he knew', Lawson later wrote, 'she could not possibly have survived'.[29]

The 1983 general election had shown that Governments can survive mass unemployment. Westland showed that they can also survive constitutional scandal. Mrs Thatcher's approval rating briefly revisited pre-Falklands depths, but by the end of the year it was back where it had been before the rumpus. In the 1987 general election Westland was not an issue. Yet Geoffrey Howe considered that it marked a turning point for the administration, and after January 1986 the Conservative Party began a new phase in its journey away from reality. Ministers and back-benchers were coming to believe that they had created a constituency of contented or complacent voters who would keep the Conservative Party in power regardless of complaints about the plight of the unemployed or the conduct of the Government – or, for that matter, the behaviour of back-bench MPs. Already one veteran parliamentarian had been contemptuous of the 1983 Conservative intake: 'They may be a clever lot – everyone says they are – but they're not my idea of gentlemen . . . they behave as badly as the other side.' Two of the most damaging scandals to affect the Major Government, 'cash for questions' and 'arms for Iraq', had their roots around the time of the Westland crisis.[30]

The 1987 Election

The Westland fiasco entailed a Government reshuffle which brought Paul Channon (son of the diarist 'Chips') to the DTI, while the Secretary of State for Scotland, George Younger, had replaced Heseltine at Defence. Other notable substitutions also changed the team between 1983 and 1987. Jim Prior left the pitch voluntarily in September 1984; Keith Joseph, whose plans to reduce state assistance to university students had provoked uproar from Conservative back-benchers, retired in May 1985. Some of the changes represented clear gains, but were only made for want of less-qualified alternatives. Douglas Hurd (Northern Ireland and then Home Secretary) and Kenneth Clarke (Paymaster General) had been held back by their association with the previous management; their belated promotion to Cabinet rank reflected more the shortage of employable right-wingers than a new mood of reconciliation in Downing Street. The same was true of Malcolm Rifkind, who replaced Younger at the Scottish Office. Mrs Thatcher thought that Rifkind's 'judgement was erratic and his behaviour unpredictable': during the 1970s he had been 'erratic' enough to stay loyal to the Conservative policy on devolution. But Rifkind at least was a Scottish Tory MP – a rare enough animal on the Government benches even before the 1987 general election, which more than halved the party's representation in Scotland to ten MPs. Former sinners like Rifkind might accommodate themselves to the new regime, but they could never be wholly trusted. The Prime Minister had come to think that 'the Left seemed to be best at presentation, the Right at getting the job done'. The businessman Lord (David) Young seemed to combine these attributes and was unswervingly loyal, so he was given the sensitive job of Employment Secretary although he 'did not claim to understand politics'.[31]

To add to her difficulties in Cabinet-building, Mrs Thatcher had already discovered that addiction to right-wing policies was no guarantee of lasting friendship. Some of her early backstage admirers, such as

John Hoskyns and Alfred Sherman, quickly fell away. After the American invasion of Grenada, those born-again zealots, Rupert Murdoch and Paul Johnson, expressed concern that the Prime Minister was losing her grip; in these cases, at least, the tiff was only temporary. After the usual Conservative losses in mid-term local elections in May 1986, John Biffen called publicly for a 'balanced ticket'. For that crime, he was labelled only a 'semi-detached' Minister by the unchastened Bernard Ingham and was never forgiven by the Prime Minister.[32]

The sensible Anglo-Irish Agreement of November 1985 had cost Mrs Thatcher the devoted services of her PPS, Ian Gow; it also inspired the Thatcherite forefather, Enoch Powell, to accuse her of treachery. At this stage, extreme Unionism apparently had more hold over the Conservative Party than Europhobia; Mrs Thatcher's almost simultaneous agreement to the Single European Act, which extended the range of decisions which could be taken on a majority vote in the Council of Ministers and included a reaffirmation of European Union as an ultimate goal for the Community, caused little fuss. In the subsequent Commons vote, even the Europhobe William Cash supported the move. But during the election campaign, tensions between Mrs Thatcher and the Party Chairman, Norman Tebbit, came to a head. Tebbit was unconvinced that the Prime Minister should be presented as the party's greatest electoral asset; Lord Young had no doubts on that score (or any other). Consequently he soon replaced Tebbit as her preferred strategist, even though he had never fought for a parliamentary seat.[33]

These family problems might help to explain why Mrs Thatcher 'wobbled' during the 1987 campaign, even though there was never a chance that the Conservatives would lose. The mid-term by-election performance had been poor – as late as May 1986, the SDP Liberal Alliance took Ryedale, after similar victories at Portsmouth South and Brecon and Radnor – but the Government had far too much ammunition for the Opposition parties, and plenty of knighted Fleet Street editors were anxious to fire it. Labour's unilateralist defence policy was ridiculed as inviting a Soviet invasion, and the Alliance also fell into disarray over nuclear weapons. Nigel Lawson, relishing his brief period as the electoral talisman of the Conservative Party, costed with the help of civil servants Labour's public expenditure plans at £34 billion above the Government's existing targets. Even though the Soviet Union was supposed to be desperate for a Labour victory which would allow it to annex Britain without resistance, Mrs Thatcher was warmly received there on a pre-election visit. At the same time, Kinnock and Denis Healey had a meeting with Ronald Reagan in Washington which looked more like a tense encounter between two hostile powers. The President thought Healey was the British Ambassador, having earlier mistaken General Colin Powell for the janitor.[34]

Despite Mrs Thatcher's worries and some effective broadcasts by Labour, the Conservatives entered the campaign with an average poll lead of 11.5 per cent and ended with a similar winning margin. They won 42 per cent of the vote, while Labour only crawled up to 31 per cent – an increase of three points since 1983. The Alliance fell a similar distance, to 23 per cent. For the third election in a row, the Conservative proportion of the vote had dropped, though only slightly. The party won an overall majority of 101 – less than before. The party was still outpolling Labour in every social category but the very poorest; among the apparently crucial 'C2s' the lead was 42–35 per cent. The Conservative manifesto (*The Next Moves Forward*) indicated that the Government had certainly not run out of ideas, whether its intended moves were to be forward or back. In its third term it promised to extend privatisation to water and electricity (though not to health, on which the Prime Minister satisfied herself with a sly reference to the value of 'enterprise in the public sector'); to cut the basic rate of income tax (when prudent) to 25 per cent; to establish a core National Curriculum in schools; to force local authorities to 'contract out' many of their services; and to replace the system of local rates with 'a fairer Community Charge' which 'should encourage people to take a greater interest in the policies of their local council and getting value for money'.[35]

The 'Community Charge' was a gift to the Opposition, but Labour was too obtuse to accept it, probably because local government was seen as a bad issue for the party. Whatever was happening to make Labour slightly more electable at a national level was undermined by tabloid stories (sometimes accurate) of 'loony left' councils throwing away ratepayers' money on bizarre projects in aid of minority groups. Although nearly half of new Conservative MPs in 1983 and 1987 had at one time been councillors, local government had few friends within the New Model Conservative Party. With one or two notorious exceptions, even Tory-controlled councils were regarded as alien obstructions similar to the trade unions. In its contempt for local democracy and resentment of any power but its own, the Government had already removed the power of local authorities to decide the level of their taxation through the Rates Act of 1984; their spending had in fact been brought under control in the late 1970s and fell as a proportion of GDP between 1979 and 1983. The 'rate-capping' legislation was intended to appease the clamour of middle-class residents and to satisfy the Treasury's lust for further economies.[36]

The Government proceeded to abolish the Greater London Council despite a rebellion on the back-benches and in the Lords. After an effective campaign run by the GLC's charismatic left-wing leader, Ken Livingstone, only a fifth of voters approved of abolition. Embarrassingly, the three Environment Secretaries involved in the decision – Tom King, Patrick Jenkin and Kenneth Baker – had all at one time expressed strong support for the GLC. The dash for central control by an administration which boasted of curbing the 'over-mighty' state was to cause it a deal of trouble after 1987. Like most voters, the Government had forgotten the traditional Conservative attitude to local government; this had been enshrined in the 1949 policy document *The Right Road for Britain*, which had promised to 'Give confidence and responsibility to local government and stop meddlesome State interference with it'.[37]

In her Foreword to her party's manifesto, Margaret Thatcher had made a striking claim: 'Together we are building One Nation of free, prosperous and responsible families and people. A Conservative dream is at last becoming a reality.' The lack of reality in those sentences is probably explained by her later remark to a speechwriter that she did not know what 'One-Nation' meant. Her Government was in the same state of knowledge. For certainly the second Thatcher administration had done nothing to heal the divisions caused by the first. Increasingly isolated from all but her hand-picked admirers, the Prime Minister continued to ignore any evidence of failure – perhaps, as her aides carefully selected the press reports which reached her, she never saw any. Much later, Ingham confirmed that she relied on her cleaner and hairdresser to remain 'in touch with what ordinary people were thinking'.[38]

They probably gave her a better sense of public feeling than Conservative MPs; more than half of those elected in 1987 had first entered Parliament after Mrs Thatcher became leader, and were unlikely to confide doubts even if they harboured any. An academic study of new Conservative MPs unearthed only one who could be classified as even 'damp'. The parliamentary position after the general election was very satisfactory for the Government but, outside Westminster and Mrs Thatcher's entourage, the public wanted an end to 'the revolution'. In 1979 there had been an equal demand for tax cuts and better services; now the majority for improved services over tax cuts was 55 per cent. That Britain had 'recovered her confidence and self-respect' under Conservative rule had become an article of faith. Yet a Gallup poll in 1985 found that only 18 per cent of voters felt more pride in their country than they had five years earlier; 42 per cent felt less. The extent of decline in Conservative Party membership was unclear at this time, but a recruitment drive in 1988, launched by the Party Chairman, Peter Brooke, gave a worrying signal. Before 1979 there had been plenty of high-profile 'conversions' to Mrs Thatcher's way of thinking; now the supply had dried up. She had enjoyed eight years in which to transform attitudes and turn the country around; clearly her revolution still had a long way to go as she prepared for her third term.[39]

'The Miracle' Exposed

The discrepancy between public attitudes and voting behaviour in 1987 suggested that the public's doubts would remain a secret between themselves and the pollsters so long as they felt better off under the Tories. Nigel Lawson was given great credit for the victory, although Mrs Thatcher's feelings towards him were less favourable. Lawson had decided as early as 1981 that economic stability could only be secured by Britain's membership of the ERM, but when he raised the issue during 1985 the Prime Minister imposed her personal veto. The combative Chancellor decided to pursue his policy by other means. Interest-rate policy would be determined by Lawson's desire to 'shadow' the Deutschmark – preventing the exchange value of the pound from moving outside a range of 2.8 to 3 Deutschmarks. In this way, Britain would be anchored to the strongest economy in Europe – one which really had experienced something like an 'economic miracle'.[40]

For several reasons, Lawson's actions were likely to infuriate the Prime Minister. Even having a view about the best exchange-rate for the pound was an offence against free-market dogma. The implication that the British economy was subservient to West Germany was still more unpalatable to Mrs Thatcher, whose original ill-feeling towards Europe had abated for a period but had now returned. Finally, Lawson's behaviour conjured up the threat of a new Michael Heseltine, defying her authority at will but too powerful to confront directly. According to the courtier Nicholas Ridley, Chancellors, like other Cabinet Ministers, only exist to help the Prime Minister, who is First Lord of the Treasury; they 'have no status or independent positions'. If a servant had started to bark orders of his own, he would have to be handed his cards.[41]

In November 1987 the First Lord delivered a public rebuke to the hired help, telling the *Financial Times* that there was no exchange-rate target. On 4 December Lawson replied by cutting interest rates, in order to keep the pound below the dreaded DM3 ceiling. This was the third interest-rate cut since the 'Black Monday' stock-market crash of October, and came when the Bank of England was already fretting about inflationary pressures in the economy. The obvious signs of an unsustainable boom dictated a cautious, even deflationary, Budget in the coming spring, but Lawson had convinced himself that the economy was 'stronger than at any time since the war'; he had even come to believe that Britain was indeed 'experiencing an economic miracle'. Hence it would be safe to produce a spectacular package like that of 1981. If Geoffrey Howe could defy common sense by cutting demand in a deep recession, his successor could emulate him by increasing it in a runaway boom. On 15 March 1988 Lawson lowered the top rate of income tax to 40 per cent (from a previous maximum of 60 per cent); he also claimed to have fulfilled a manifesto pledge by cutting the basic rate to 25 per cent. In fact the actual promise had been to do this when it was prudent.[42]

Alex Salmond of the Scottish Nationalist Party was suspended from the House for shouting that the Budget was 'an obscenity'; this showed unusual foresight, because his outburst happened before Lawson announced the top-rate cuts – even Margaret Thatcher would have preferred a top rate of 50 per cent. The left-wing Labour MP Dave Nellist caused such an uproar afterwards that the whole House was adjourned for ten minutes. At least the Chancellor took belated action to calm the frenzied housing market, restricting mortgage interest relief to £30,000 per household instead of £30,000 per person; even so, the bill to the taxpayer for this middle-class handout was £7 billion in 1989, and delaying the change until August provoked a last-minute scramble among house-buyers. Lawson later claimed that the Budget was neutral and could point to the repayment of another sizeable chunk of public debt, but the inevitable effects of the cuts in direct taxation were to increase domestic consumption at a time when demand needed to be reined back – and to trumpet the fact that this Thatcher Government, like the previous two, was the rich man's friend. Forty per cent of the tax-cuts (which totalled around £6 billion) went to the top 5 per cent of earners; at the same time, the social security budget was slashed to make amends for the Chancellor's pre-election spending binge. For the second year in a row, Child Benefit was frozen, and in September sixteen- and seventeen-year-olds lost their automatic entitlement to supplementary benefit.[43]

The 1988 Budget was received with great pleasure on the Conservative benches. Mrs Thatcher approved of the measures more than the man. Her instinctive dislike for the exchange-rate policy was being fostered by her economic adviser, the unrepentant monetarist Sir Alan Walters; she demanded changes to the section of Lawson's speech which dealt with sterling. The Budget was preceded by an increase in interest rates which soon forced the pound above DM3. This may have confirmed the Prime Minister's view that 'you can't buck the market', but it was hardly a triumph for British exporters. During 1988, exports rose by only 0.7 per cent, while imports soared by over 13 per cent; the balance of payments deficit for 1989 was a record £19 billion. By the summer of 1989 a Government which crowed about conquering inflation was presiding over a rate of 8.3 per cent; the belated improvement in industrial investment was choked off by a rise in interest rates to 14 per cent.[44]

In his 1989 Budget speech Lawson trotted out the official explanation that the disaster arose from an overreaction to fears of a global slump after the stock-market crash of 1987, but only the infatuated fell for this or for Lawson's renewed claims about the 'unprecedented strength of the British economy'. Like Howe in 1980, he admitted that there might be 'some slowdown in real growth over the following year'. In fact GDP barely grew at all in 1989, and from the middle of 1990 Britain suffered a second recession almost as bad as the first. The Thatcherites who had always been so scornful of the Heath Government's boom had produced a more irresponsible one of their own. The only miraculous feature of the Government's economic policy was that anybody still believed there had been an economic miracle. Instead of eradicating the depressing post-war cycle of stop–go, the Thatcher Governments had produced a new and more violent cycle of bust–boom–bust.[45]

The European Menace

While Mrs Thatcher wrestled with her new enemy next door, she was also having trouble with more familiar foes across the Channel. Many of her admirers see her signature of the Single European Act in December 1985 as the greatest (or only) blemish on her record. At that time her enthusiasm for the free market overcame her attachment to a narrow definition of national sovereignty, but she soon regretted her decision. Believing in action rather than words, she was convinced that foreigners believed the opposite, and was dismayed that the President of the European Commission since 1984, Jacques Delors, was serious about closer union. In September 1988 Delors put himself beyond the Thatcherite pale by expounding his visions to the Labour Party Conference – and winning a standing ovation. Less than a fortnight later the Prime Minister spoke up for England in her famous Bruges speech. In what Sir Michael Butler, one of her former advisers, called 'perhaps the most misleading manifesto of the decade', Mrs Thatcher warned of a European superstate which would undo the successful Conservative assault on overmighty government at home. The long-suffering Geoffrey Howe, who throughout his tenure was an excellent Foreign Secretary, had suggested the Bruges visit as a fitting occasion for a constructive speech; he later noted correctly that the delivered text 'veered between caricature and misunderstanding'. Europhobic back-benchers were not expected to be able to learn the realities of European institutions, but when a veteran attender of European Councils began to fulminate against the power of Brussels bureaucrats, the reaction of our partners varied between incredulity and contempt.[46]

The European issue had been fairly quiet for some years: Bruges condemned the Conservative Party to a decade of turbulence during which the right wing managed an even greater output of nonsense than they had achieved in the monetarist period. The bug spread to the party's advisers, who for the 1989 European Parliament elections devised the slogan 'If you don't vote Conservative next Thursday, you'll live on a diet of Brussels'. This was a winning phrase – for the Labour Party, which took thirteen seats from the Conservatives. The Conservatives won only 34 per cent of the vote – up to that time, their worst performance of the century at a national election. Perhaps the vegetables featured in the Conservative posters helped the Green vote. That party did so well in the elections that the Prime Minister was scared into making some concerned noises about the environment.[47]

Immediately after the election – Mrs Thatcher's first defeat in a nationwide contest – the Prime Minister accompanied Howe and Lawson to the European Council at Madrid. The Chancellor and Foreign Secretary both decided that Mrs Thatcher had changed. Howe thought she had come to believe that 'her interests were axiomatically those of Britain. Any criticism of her was an unpatriotic act', while Lawson sensed a change after William Whitelaw retired from the Government following a stroke in December 1987. In fact it was they who had changed; she remained much the same. She had always needed to have her own way, and she had always needed enemies. Towards the end of the eighties she had more or less run out of these. The only enemies now available were card-carrying Thatcherites, and Lawson and Howe were first in the line of fire. Both of them had become less inclined always to let the Prime Minister have her way, and both had modified their views. In the later eighties Lawson deplored Mrs Thatcher's 'truculent chauvinism' in Europe, whereas in the early eighties he had shared it. Howe, too, had become much more pro-European at the Foreign Office than he had been at the Treasury. In addition, neither of them any longer shared what Lawson called her 'unconstructed parochial monetarism'; and both of them wanted Britain to join the Exchange Rate Mechanism (ERM), to which she was still strongly opposed both on monetarist and anti-European grounds.[48]

Before Madrid, in what Mrs Thatcher later called an 'ambush', Lawson and Howe by a joint threat of resignation had prised out of the Prime Minister a statement of intent to join the ERM under certain conditions. Although she refused to name a date and made clear her opposition to the rest of the Delors plan for European Monetary Union, this was a serious defeat for Mrs Thatcher. In July she struck back. While Howe was reflecting on the sad changes in the Prime Minister, she had been finding plenty of alteration in him; his alleged 'insatiable appetite for compromise' had grown steadily worse in the Foreign Office. So he was replaced by the new court favourite, John Major. As compensation, Howe was offered a bundle of offices recently vacated by Whitelaw, and the Leadership of the House of Commons. After some hesitation, during which a letter of resignation was drafted, Howe accepted, provided that his titles included that of 'Deputy Prime Minister'. This arrangement was not likely to last; during their interview, Mrs Thatcher acknowledged that he would never fill the confidential role which Whitelaw had enjoyed, and Bernard Ingham removed any chance of amity by rubbishing the 'Deputy' title. It also emerged that Howe had originally been offered the Home Office, without the present occupant, Douglas Hurd, having been informed.[49]

None of this was likely to make the 1989 Party Conference a happy occasion. To switch attention from unpopular new policy ideas, such as the proposal to introduce an 'internal market' into the NHS, the new Party Chairman, Kenneth Baker, came up with the slogan of 'The Right Team'. Unfortunately, before the 1990 conference, as Lawson later noted, a third of 'The Right Team' were no longer in it; the faithful Young had already departed. With Howe now 'semi-detached', Lawson was Mrs Thatcher's primary target. The Chancellor was received well by the conference, surprisingly so as even the *Daily Mail* had now spotted the failure of his policies, labelling him 'This Bankrupt Chancellor'. This was an early sign that Lawson had been identified by the Prime Minister's friends in the press as the scapegoat for the sinking economy. Yet during the conference outward appearances were just preserved.[50]

As soon as it was over, the forced smiles of the warring couple were removed by the *Financial Times*'s printing of Alan Walters's opinion that the ERM was 'half-baked'. This was an old quotation, but it reflected the current thinking of both Walters and his pupil. The markets were understandably confused by the conflicting messages, and Lawson's patience gave out. Matters were going badly enough for him without this background noise; the trade deficit for the first three quarters of 1989, John Smith pointed out in the House, had already exceeded his Budget forecast for the whole year. Lawson told the Prime Minister that unless Walters was removed, he would resign. Mrs Thatcher belatedly informed Geoffrey Howe that she had been unable to appease Lawson 'in spite of intensive efforts'; yet they were not intensive enough to include an offer to sack her part-time, unelected adviser. That was the obvious solution, for if Walters had been removed, he could still have given advice informally. Yet Mrs Thatcher had to prevail. The authority of the First Lord of the Treasury was at stake; she therefore preferred to lose Lawson than sack Walters. Lawson was replaced by the versatile Major. Nicholas Ridley was the first choice but, as Mrs Thatcher delicately put it, his 'scorn for presentational niceties' ruled him out. Now that the damage had been done, Walters resigned.[51]

The Poll Tax

Despite the wholesale changes already inflicted on it, local government remained the preferred outlet for the Cabinet's hyper-activity. The third Thatcher Government carried out its manifesto pledge to attack the role of elected representatives in the education system. The Inner London Education Authority was abolished in Kenneth Baker's 'Great' Education Reform Bill of 1988 (scornfully nicknamed GERBIL), which also gave schools the right to opt out of local authority control with the usual bribes thrown in. This gargantuan exercise in law-making, which eventually ran to 238 clauses, also abolished tenure for university teaching posts and scheduled the promised National Curriculum for 1992. Under another Act of 1988, council tenants unable to take advantage of the increasingly generous 'right to buy' schemes were encouraged to enlist with housing associations instead of their old Town Hall landlords. In the following year Nicholas Ridley (now at Environment) instructed councils to put out their services for 'competitive tendering', a clever two-pronged attack on local budgets and the remaining power of trade unionists in council employment. After back-bench pressure, this Local Government Act also included a clause which barred councils from promoting homosexuality.[52]

These measures added up to an unprecedented assault on the local autonomy which had always been prized by the Tory Party. Yet the Government intended to tighten still further the grip of the central state. In 1974 Mrs Thatcher had been persuaded to promise abolition of the rates, and she had exempted this pledge from her general determination to entomb the Heath years because it offered the chance of helping those she regarded as 'our people'. By her third term, however, the Prime Minister had forgotten the accompanying 1974 pledge to relate the replacement tax to the ability to pay. In 1981 Michael Heseltine had published a Green Paper which rehearsed possible alterations without enthusiasm. One of them was a form of 'poll tax' to fall on persons rather than property. Heseltine was less enthusiastic about this than the other options; according to one account, the review group broke into laughter when it was suggested. Still, the idea continued to be kicked around Whitehall and right-wing bodies like the Adam Smith Institute. After an outcry in February 1985 against the revaluation of Scottish rates, Mrs Thatcher called a meeting at Chequers where she decided to plump for the new tax, and another Green Paper was published in January 1986. Shortly afterwards a Gallup poll found that more than half of voters approved of the idea, although signs of unease in the country grew as the full implications were absorbed.

The Poll Tax epitomised Margaret Thatcher's personal rule. Apart from Walker and Lawson, the Cabinet was supine, and initially the great bulk of the parliamentary party was innocently obedient. Later, a number of Conservative MPs did vote in favour of the 'Mates Amendment' which sought to fulfil the old commitment to fairness, the Government's majority falling to twenty-five. In the Lords, however, a mass migration from the backwoods to Westminster ensured the bill's easy passage. Party Whips told Mrs Thatcher that over a hundred MPs had serious doubts on the subject. Lawson himself thought that the public could only be 'won round' by implementing unpopular policies and waiting for them to gain approval; the 1987 Party Conference applied this doctrine to the Poll Tax, forcing the Government to bring it in at once instead of introducing it in phases as originally intended. As a result Lawson was pestered for repeated injections of public money to subsidise a charge which he had always regarded as 'dreadful'; before the 1988 Budget Nicholas Ridley even asked the Chancellor to sacrifice his ambitious tax-cutting plans in order to reduce local bills. By that time 70 per cent of the public were opposed to the Poll Tax.[53]

Subconsciously at least, the Government seemed to recognise that there was no rational defence for the Poll Tax by giving it the Orwellian name of 'the Community Charge'. Yet, at the time, right-wing ideologues saw it as a master-stroke of statecraft. If it redistributed money from the poor to the rich, this was not a departure from Thatcherite practice. Ridley was alleged to have asked his local newspaper, 'Why shouldn't the duke and the dustman pay the same?' Few right-wingers were as honest as Ridley, but to them the tax would bring electoral as well as material gains. When rational average earners were exposed to the real cost of local services, the Right believed, they would vote for the party which charged them the least. According to Government propaganda, Labour councils invariably charged more because they were Labour, not because they were normally found in inner-city areas, and they escaped punishment from voters only because those liable for rates were outnumbered in the local electorate. On this view, the Poll Tax would turn the entire local government map blue, which would save the Government the trouble of abolishing it. The Junior Environment Minister, Michael Portillo, boasted at the 1990 conference that the tax was 'the most potent weapon ever put in the hands of ordinary voters to defeat incompetent and malign Labour councils'.[54]

Months before Portillo's speech, almost everyone else had realised that the Poll Tax was better described as the most potent weapon Labour had yet been given. In March 1990 the Conservatives lost Mid-Staffordshire on a then unprecedented 22 per cent swing to Labour. Unemployment had begun to rise again, and the Government had so many reasons for unpopularity that the precise effect of the new tax was difficult to gauge. The Trafalgar Square demonstration at the end of the month gave a clearer indication. This large gathering was exploited by fringe troublemakers and ended in a riot covering almost the same areas as the Poll Tax disturbances of 1381. Before repressing the rebellious peasants in that year, Richard II had given at least an approximation of a One-Nation speech; not so Mrs Thatcher, whose first instinct was to denounce the 'hooligans' who had caused the riot. The grievance which had inspired the demonstration was too widely shared, however, for this formula to work as well as it had done in 1981, or after violent outbreaks in Handsworth and Tottenham in autumn 1985.

By this time Mrs Thatcher had noticed that Ridley's 'scorn for presentational niceties' was as serious a drawback at Environment as it would have been at the Treasury. He was replaced by the emollient Chris Patten, but not even he could make the charge seem equitable. The May local elections brought resounding defeat for the Conservatives, although the party did well in the London Boroughs of Wandsworth and Westminster, which had set negligible taxes. This convinced Mrs Thatcher that the Poll Tax would work, given time; in any case, she was not going to perform a U-turn on it. The Poll Tax had become as much a matter of personal authority as her free choice of economic advisers. If they wanted to get rid of the Poll Tax, worried Conservative MPs would have to get rid of the Prime Minister too.[55]

The End of an Error?

If Conservative MPs had the will to eject the leader who had led them to three successive election victories, they certainly had the means. Party rules permitted an annual election provided that a challenger secured a proposer and seconder. In November 1989 the pro-European back-bencher Sir Anthony Meyer had stood against Mrs Thatcher as a principled protest rather than a serious bid for the leadership. His bold move cost him the support of his constituency party, but in the vote sixty MPs refused to back the Prime Minister – an outcome which was laughed off by Mrs Thatcher's 'hallelujah chorus' of a press but carried a clear warning for the future.[56] As the opportunity for a new challenge in 1990 drew closer, the situation looked much more favourable for a coup. July saw a personal blow to Mrs Thatcher when Ridley was forced out of the Government for disclosing his intemperate views on Germany to the *Spectator*. Since the previous Christmas there had been two more ministerial departures, which significantly were both voluntary retirements from 'The Right Team'. Norman Fowler decided to spend more time with his family in January, while Peter Walker left in May after three successful years as Secretary of State for Wales.

According to the MORI polls, the Prime Minister remained more popular than her party, but this was of little help when throughout 1990 her average disapproval rating was 70 per cent. In October the danger of a horde of MPs being dragged to defeat on her coat-tails was underlined when the Liberal Democrats overturned a Conservative majority of 17,000 in the Eastbourne by-election, caused by the IRA's callous assassination of Ian Gow. Even before this, Mrs Thatcher's agreement to Britain joining the ERM had indicated her weakening position, but she remained defiant. On her return from the Rome EC Summit at the end of the month, she repeated her rejection of monetary union in the sort of language which had greatly embarrassed Nigel Lawson. This was a miserable initiation for her new Foreign Secretary, Douglas Hurd, and the final straw for his predecessor but one. Geoffrey Howe at last resigned on 31 October. The Thatcher revolution had finally devoured one of its parents.[57]

Howe's departure should have been less troublesome to Mrs Thatcher than Lawson's. Since his ejection from the Foreign Office, the influence of the new Deputy Prime Minister had been diminished. Also he was unlikely to say anything as incendiary as Lawson's remark in his resignation speech that a Prime Minister should 'appoint Ministers he or she trusts and then leave them to carry out the policy'. Such expectations were confounded by Howe's lethal resignation statement, especially its concluding words, 'The time has come for others to consider their response to the tragic conflict of loyalties with which I have myself wrestled for perhaps too long.' A number of MPs immediately thought and said that the Prime Minister had been holed below the water-line. At least she seemed certain to face a serious leadership challenge – if not from Howe himself, then from someone else who could not be dismissed as a 'stalking horse'. Michael Heseltine might have stood anyway, but when the Prime Minister's acolytes began to taunt him – 'put up or shut up' – they virtually made the decision for him.[58]

The parliamentary Conservative Party has been described as 'the most sophisticated electorate in the world', an accolade it scarcely deserves. It is little, if at all, more sophisticated than the British electorate. Anybody who has seen the ballot papers of MPs knows that they are capable of spoiling them in much the same way as do some of their constituents who customarily write in green ink. In any case, on this occasion, unlike 1975, there was no need for sophistication since few if any voters were looking forward to a second ballot in which other candidates could take part. They were voting for or against Margaret Thatcher and Michael Heseltine.[59]

After the election, the hard Right set up a groan about Mrs Thatcher's poor campaign team, her absence abroad on the evil day, and the 'unfair' rules which denied her an outright victory on the first ballot by four votes despite outpolling Heseltine 204–152. They pointed out the raucous support which Mrs Thatcher still enjoyed in the shrinking constituency parties, even though the right wing had ignored the staunch loyalty of the grass-roots membership to Edward Heath fifteen years earlier. In fact the Prime Minister's minimal contribution to the campaign and her decision to attend the Paris Summit were both conscious decisions intended to play down the seriousness of Heseltine's challenge. Unlike Heath in 1975, Mrs Thatcher had not actually been beaten in the first ballot. She was therefore determined to 'fight on'. The trouble was that she was almost certain to lose outright in the second ballot. Few if any MPs who had voted for Heseltine on the first ballot were going to switch to her, while a number of those who had reluctantly supported her were likely to join Heseltine's bandwagon.[60]

After telling the Queen that she was going to stand in the second ballot, Mrs Thatcher decided on the odd procedure of seeing her Cabinet one by one. Kenneth Clarke, the first Minister to appear, bluntly informed her that she 'would lose big'. Others were more tactful, but their predictions were similar. Having made the situation as awkward as possible for her Cabinet, Mrs Thatcher was 'grieved' by what she called the 'weasel words whereby they had transmuted their betrayal into frank advice and concern for my fate'. Just why an honest estimate that she was going to lose should constitute betrayal, she does not explain. But as usual the ability to tell her what she did not want to hear was in her eyes a sign of cowardice. Nevertheless, she had to bow to the traitors, and resigned.[61]

Her own courage was as high as ever. Even though she had had to withdraw, she could still 'fight on' in other ways. None of her opponents could deny that her final performance at the dispatch box was a triumph of will, and no doubt some of those who had brought her down felt some regrets as she dominated the House. As Tony Benn noted, she drew strength for this last performance from an ideological fervour which was still unsatisfied.[62]

Thatcherites prided themselves on their economic expertise. Through monetarism and strength of character, they were going to bring unprecedented stability and non-inflationary growth to the British economy. Alas! However good their intentions, they forthwith subjected the British economy to a period of unprecedented instability. In the first two years of the Thatcher Government fiscal and monetary policy caused total output to fall absolutely by 6 per cent; a credit boom caused it to rise 22 per cent in the five years between 1984 and 1989, but the 'bust' which followed led to another drop of 3.5 per cent between 1990 and 1992. Inflation was just 10.5 per cent when Mrs Thatcher came to power, rose to 22 per cent a year later, fell to 3.5 per cent in 1983 but rose again to 10.5 per cent in the second half of 1990 before falling back again. Not surprisingly, in a survey of economic stability of the fourteen largest industrial countries Britain ranked two from bottom.[63]

Much has been made of other international comparisons which show that Britain's growth performance since 1979 deteriorated less than that of other countries.[64] But the fact that the growth rates of other countries have (roughly speaking) come down to ours is a poor basis for claiming a positive degree of success. The blunt fact is that, despite North Sea oil, growth during Mrs Thatcher's period of office averaged 1.9 per cent a year, which is much less than during any period of the same length before she came to power. Inflation, by which such great store had been set, was also the same when Mrs Thatcher left as it had been when she arrived, but the unemployment record was dreadful. Unemployment was 1.1 million when Mrs Thatcher came to power and 1.7 million when she left, having been well over three million by the official count.

The social fabric also suffered. In at least two crucial respects the 1979–90 Governments pursued policies which were the antithesis of the One-Nation approach. Everybody knew that inflation could be subdued by creating unemployment, but the necessary measures, as Denis Healey said in 1976, 'would produce riots on the streets, an immediate fall in living standards and unemployment of three million'. Healey's prophecy was only inaccurate in one respect: living standards did not need to fall for everyone during a slump. The Government's extra Two-Nation twist to the familiar deflationary spiral was to effect a redistribution of wealth from the poor to the rich in the name of 'incentives'. Under Mrs Thatcher, the standard of living for the top 10 per cent rose by 60 per cent in real terms; for the poorest 10 per cent, it either stood still or even fell by 14 per cent.

Another Two-Nations twist by the Government was to launch regular attacks against the so-called 'dependency culture' at the same time as its policies were making more people 'dependent'. The number of people relying on the main means-tested benefits increased from about 4.4 million in 1979 to almost seven million in 1990. Ministers tried to make the unemployed ashamed of their situation.[65]

Whenever the Government chose a section of society for hanging, they first gave it a bad name. In the case of the trade unions this was hardly necessary; during the winter of discontent the unions thrust their own heads into the noose. That campaign, however, was only the beginning. Under the Thatcher Governments, the BBC, schoolteachers, the universities, the Church, local authorities, social workers, health professionals, lawyers and those with a conscientious objection to nuclear warfare were less treated as valuable public bodies or public servants, than scorned as if they did not properly belong in the new Britain. To make amends for Mr Heath's remarks about 'the unacceptable face of capitalism', almost the only group in society exempted from the right-wing anathema was the City. The consistent Two-Nations approach of the Thatcher Government was, together with its abysmal record of economic management – two miserable slumps and one crazy boom – a prime cause of the disaster the Conservative Party suffered seven years after Margaret Thatcher's fall.[66]

Although people now remember right-wing propaganda better than actual events, Britain was certainly approaching ungovernability in 1979. Major reforms were urgently needed. The Thatcher Government made Britain governable again and effected the necessary reforms – especially the trade-union ones. Yet a non-ideological One-Nation Tory Government would have achieved no less. And if it had told the people that it aimed to bring harmony out of discord, it would have meant what it said.

CHAPTER
XV

Drifting with Dogma

The field for the succession was a strong one. Of the three candidates, Douglas Hurd looked the best Prime Minister available, and Michael Heseltine the most charismatic party leader; John Major seemed the least prime ministerial and the candidate least endowed with the attributes of leadership, lacking both the achievements and the abilities of his rivals. Yet he easily beat them. Why? One obvious answer is that he was emphatically Mrs Thatcher's preferred choice whom she had earlier appointed to two of the great offices of state: Foreign Secretary and Chancellor of the Exchequer. Yet that explanation only raises further questions: why had she appointed him to those offices, and why was he the man she chose to succeed her?

John Major had always been seen as affable and competent, but he had shown no signs of exceptional brilliance. As a Junior Minister at the DSS, Major had in 1986 helped guide Norman Fowler's ambitious pension reforms through the Commons. Although Labour MPs (and pensions experts) spotted the deep and preventable flaws in the pensions proposals and accurately predicted the damage they would cause, Ministers ignored them, and many people who were persuaded to buy private pensions duly suffered. Fortunately for Major, the disastrous results of the legislation only became apparent after he had reached Downing Street. He had joined the Cabinet after the 1987 election, when he was made Chief Secretary to the Treasury at Nigel Lawson's request; Mrs Thatcher had wanted to make him Chief Whip, a job in which he would have excelled.[1]

Major's promotion to the Foreign Office in place of Geoffrey Howe was regarded as one of Mrs Thatcher's more eccentric changes. Howe himself was initially kept in the dark about his successor; when one of his advisers guessed his identity, the immediate reaction was 'it can't be'. The response cannot have been very different in the country; a survey in *The Economist* found that only 2 per cent of the population had heard of the rising star, the member for Huntingdon since 1979. Apart from some travelling when he was a banker, nothing in Major's career suggested he was a suitable candidate for the Foreign Office; his own reported view was that 'Douglas Hurd was the obvious choice', and when offered the post he asked the Prime Minister if she was sure that it was a good idea.[2]

Lady Thatcher's memoirs state that she wanted to give him broader ministerial experience in case he proved worthy of succeeding her; his inexperience of foreign affairs was no great handicap in her eyes and his unfamiliarity with the Foreign Office a positive advantage. Unfortunately her hopes that Major would benefit from his experience as Foreign Secretary proved unfounded. His only epiphany was a visit to a Commonwealth summit at Kuala Lumpur with the Prime Minister. Not for the last time, Major found his country in a minority of one, this time negotiating with, or rather against, all other countries in the Commonwealth over the sanctions against South Africa which Mrs Thatcher loathed. He did it quite well until the Prime Minister wrecked his conciliatory efforts by issuing a supplementary *communiqué* of her own, which Major had naïvely not realised would infuriate the entire Commonwealth.[3]

His uneasiness at the Foreign Office was no bar to further promotion; and the next round of ministerial musical chairs, precipitated by Lawson's resignation, put him in the Chancellor's seat, back in the more congenial surroundings of the Treasury. In some minor respects, Major's period as Chancellor resembled Harold Macmillan's. While Macmillan had managed to steal some helpful headlines with his premium bonds, Major introduced Tax Exempt Special Savings Accounts (TESSAs) in what was the first televised Budget. Unlike Macmillan, however, Major had risen rapidly and was regarded as the Prime Minister's poodle when he replaced the fractious Lawson. By the time of the leadership election he had slipped the leash to the extent of joining with Douglas Hurd to persuade Mrs Thatcher to sanction UK membership of the ERM. To secure membership of the ERM had been a long-term Treasury goal under Lawson, and if Major caught Mrs Thatcher while her position was at its weakest, he had succeeded where Lawson had failed. Yet the Prime Minister and Chancellor of the Exchequer took Britain into the mechanism with the pound at a rate so excessively high that it was bound to be both damaging and unsustainable. Few in the party realised that at the time, however; nor did Labour, which foolishly supported the Government's decision.[4]

John Major's ministerial record of achievement was not sufficiently glittering, therefore, to account for either his spectacular promotions by Margaret Thatcher or his easy success in the leadership election. The explanation must be sought elsewhere. The clue was provided by his friend Robert Atkins in a television programme not long after Major had become Prime Minister. Atkins, who was then MP for South Ribble and Minister for Sport, told of a holiday a few years before that he and John Major spent journeying along English canals. On their barge they discussed Major's chances of ever becoming Prime Minister; eventually they decided that his prospects would be good provided he never took a strong line on any issue, thus leading right-wing Conservative MPs to think he was on the Right and left-wing ones that he was on the Left. This was not just a holiday *jeu d'esprit*. Major acted on what he and Atkins had decided. Years later, Andrew Marr recalled in the *Independent* how in a seaside hotel he had 'bumped into one of the most Pro-European Tory MPs' and later had 'had a drink with a fiercely Euro-sceptic right-winger'. Both had been impressed by the little-known Chief Secretary to the Treasury, John Major. 'Why? Because he had given both of them the impression that he agreed 100 per cent with their views.'[5]

As we know, Major's tactic was brilliantly successful. Margaret Thatcher and the Right were convinced that he was 'one of us', while many of the Tory Left and Centre were convinced that he was one of them. His two rivals could not hope to match that remarkable accomplishment. They were anything but chameleons, and neither could expect an endorsement from Mrs Thatcher: Michael Heseltine for obvious reasons, and Douglas Hurd because of his old association with Ted Heath. Hurd had been a good Northern Irish Secretary during the negotiations leading to the Anglo-Irish Agreement and then a civilised and generally successful Home Secretary before confirming Major's view that he was the best man for the Foreign Office. Even if his character had not prevented him from trying to prove to Thatcherites that he was really a closet right-winger, his record would have made the claim hard to credit. Michael Heseltine had always enjoyed some right-wing support, but his challenge to Mrs Thatcher ruled out his doing any productive foraging for additional votes from the Right.

The two previous Conservative Prime Ministers, who had won the leadership through election in 1965 and 1975, had been the offspring of a carpenter and a grocer. These cases proved that the party was able to recognise proven merit regardless of its origins. In 1990 by contrast, Douglas Hurd's merits were obscured by his origins. Having been to Eton, even on a scholarship, was apparently now an insuperable barrier to becoming Prime Minister. When asked about the 'rarefied' atmosphere of his background, Hurd understandably replied, 'I was brought up on a farm . . . This is inverted snobbery.' Hurd had a talented team of supporters, including Kenneth Clarke and Chris Patten, but other natural Hurd supporters, who had voted for Heseltine on the first ballot, thought they could not switch horses for the second.[6]

The other candidates had no problems with their origins. Michael Heseltine had often mused that he who wields the dagger seldom wears the crown. Had Margaret Thatcher stood on the second ballot, he would almost certainly have disproved that adage. But once Mrs Thatcher stood down, it came into force. Having achieved their aim of getting rid of the Prime Minister, some MPs could safely assuage their feelings of guilt by murdering the prime assassin. When faced with a choice between two men whose hands were not stained with blood, they and those who had voted for Mrs Thatcher on the first ballot chose John Major, largely because they thought he agreed with them, partly because he was her chosen heir and partly because, according to the polls, he would be the most popular leader.[7]

The final outcome technically fell short of an outright victory; Major secured 185 votes when the winning line was 187. Hurd received 56 votes, while Heseltine's support had shrunk to 131. Clearly a further ballot would have been pointless, and both the losers immediately and gracefully conceded. Had John Major's diligence in agreeing with every Conservative politician he happened to be listening to been merely a successful, if scarcely noble, method of winning the leadership, it would still have brought him future trouble. But it went deeper than that, for it was the outward manifestation of Major's lack of strong political views, a deficiency that was later to cause far worse trouble.

Margaret Thatcher was the first to be disillusioned by Major's election tactics, though mistakenly so. After hearing the election result, she had told him 'it's everything I've dreamt of . . . the future is assured'. Her ecstasy presumably reflected her joy at Heseltine's defeat; whatever its source, it did not last. Three weeks later she was complaining that the new Government had 'embarked on a course of great danger'; they wanted 'to undo many of the things we have accomplished'. Worse still, 'all the wrong people are rejoicing'. This sad turn of events may have stemmed from Major's decision to give Heseltine the Department of the Environment, where he could defuse the Poll Tax issue on the lines proposed during his campaign. Maybe Mrs Thatcher did not notice that the job of sinking her 'flagship' kept the interventionist minister away from Industry, which remained in the immobile hands of Peter Lilley.[8]

Michael Howard, still at Employment, was similarly disinclined to take Keynesian measures to reduce unemployment. Major was not strong enough to carry out a purge of Thatcher supporters, even if he had wanted to, and only Cecil Parkinson and David Waddington left the Government. The most important change was Norman Lamont's promotion from Chief Secretary to Chancellor as a reward for his help during the leadership campaign. Thatcherite die-hards were hostile to Chris Patten, who now became Party Chairman, but Mrs Thatcher had trusted him with the presentation of the Poll Tax. Another Hurd supporter, Kenneth Clarke, had pushed through market-inspired reforms in health and education. So, if the shape of the first Major Cabinet was any indication, the rejoicing of the 'wrong people' was clearly premature. Mrs Thatcher's subsequent assertion, in March 1991, that she had detected 'a tendency to try to undermine what I have achieved and to go back to giving more power to government' was doubly wrong: Major was not trying to undermine what she had achieved, and she herself had given a great deal of power to government.[9]

If Anthony Eden's insoluble problem had been that he was not Winston Churchill, John Major's inescapable asset was that he was not Margaret Thatcher. Consequently one thing changed immediately Major took office: the Government became much more popular. Labour's average poll lead had narrowed during 1990, but in December the Conservatives went ahead for the first time since May of the previous year. Major's own rating soared in January 1991, as the Gulf War moved towards a successful conclusion. For that Margaret Thatcher deserves much of the credit. She had already pledged support to Kuwait, which Iraq had invaded the previous 2 August, and 33,000 British troops had been sent to the Gulf as part of Operation Desert Shield before Major took over. Although America was clearly the dominant partner in the anti-Iraqi coalition, Major successfully passed his first serious leadership test, quickly establishing a warm relationship with the US President George Bush, who had had none of Reagan's ideological affinity with Mrs Thatcher.[10]

After the defeat of Saddam Hussein's forces at the end of February, attention returned to the problem of the so-called Community Charge. The flagship might be earmarked for the scrapyard, but it was still expensive for its designers. The Conservative recovery in the polls was not sustained in the Ribble Valley by-election in March, which the Liberal Democrats took on a 25 per cent swing. Lamont's first Budget increased VAT by 2.5 per cent, in order to wipe £140 off every Poll Tax bill, and two days later Heseltine announced that the ill-fated levy would be replaced by a Council Tax. Critics bemoaned the complexity of Heseltine's compromise, which in effect restored the rates, bringing back house prices as the chief factor just as the 1980s boom was collapsing. The Government's opinion-poll rating also fell, but in May they lost Monmouth on only half the swing registered at Ribble Valley.[11]

By the time of the 1992 general election, the net political effect of the

Poll Tax was probably neutral – if not positive for the Conservatives. Some 700,000 people had failed to put themselves on the electoral register in the mistaken belief that this would help them avoid the tax; few of these are likely to have been enthusiastic Tories. Even though most of the 'guilty men' remained in office, the public seemed happy to regard the whole fiasco, whose total cost was a scarcely credible £20 billion, as the product of the defunct Thatcher regime. That nothing had been done to erase the other policy mistakes of the 1980s – or to halt the momentum towards new doses of dogma in most fields – was expertly obscured by the blizzard of publicity surrounding the end of the Poll Tax. Mrs Thatcher was not the only one to confuse this single revision with the end of her legacy.[12]

The Major Government managed to pull off a similar success over the state of the economy. In April 1992 only 4 per cent of respondents blamed it for the recession; the remainder divided the blame between Mrs Thatcher and the rest of the world. When Major moved from 11 to 10 Downing Street he took some awkward figures with him. Inflation peaked at over 10 per cent in October, and unemployment had begun to rise again after falling to 1.6 million in the spring. As usual, manufacturing industry was suffering most. In 1979 employment in services had been less than double that in manufacturing; by the end of 1990 the ratio was three to one. By 1991, manufacturing output was only 6 per cent higher than it had been when the Conservatives took power twelve years earlier; manufacturing investment was 11 per cent lower, and in 1991 48,000 companies went out of business. This time, though, the geographical impact of recession was a little more even; during 1991 the fastest increase in unemployment was registered in the south-east. Just as this region had seen the worst excesses of the housing boom, now the inevitable consequences hit it hardest. In the whole country, more than 75,000 houses were repossessed in 1991 – five times the number in 1989 – and a further 250,000 people were more than six months behind with their mortgage payments.[13]

When Chancellor, Major had coined the genial phrase 'if the policy isn't hurting, it isn't working'. Whether or not the policy was now working, it was certainly hurting. Major's Government did not quite match the economic sado-masochism of the early Thatcher years, yet it determinedly ignored the lessons of that heroic monetarist period. Although public expenditure increased dramatically, this mainly reflected the relentless growth of official unemployment – which kept on rising until January 1993 when it peaked at 2,992,000 – and the decline of Government revenues. In addition there were other increases – electoral Keynesianism – to help win the election, but nothing to reduce unemployment. In real terms, the cost to the Exchequer of unemployment had almost tripled since 1979. In 1991, according to government statistics, 13.5 million people had an income below half the national average; the figure in 1979 had been 5 million. As in the early 1980s, the Government thought soaring unemployment was (in Norman Lamont's characteristic phrase) 'a price well worth paying' in the war against inflation, and anyway free-market dogma demanded that no direct action be taken to limit this price – even though 'natural' Conservative voters were now paying it along with the rest.[14]

With the UK in the ERM and the Europhobic Mrs Thatcher out of office, Britain seemed poised at last to play a more positive role in the European Community. This impression was reinforced in January 1991 when the Employment Secretary, Michael Howard, told the European Commissioner for Social Affairs that Britain could accept half the Commission's proposed directives, and it was confirmed in March when Major, visiting Bonn, declared that during his premiership Britain would be 'at the very heart of Europe'. To the Europhobes within the party this seemed an alarming deviation from the old regime's approach which decreed that Britain should only be at the heart of every quarrel. Their fears should have been calmed a month later, however, when Britain raised objections to a draft treaty on European Union.

Major had come under pressure from the so-called Eurosceptics in the Cabinet – Kenneth Baker, Howard and Peter Lilley – while the former Prime Minister stirred up anti-European feelings on the backbenches. Forgetting her previous stance on a referendum, Margaret Thatcher now demanded one on any move towards a single currency. At the European Council meeting held at Maastricht in December 1991, Major secured two opt-outs: one from monetary union, and another from the proposed Social Chapter. The latter gave particular pleasure to the Right, who no doubt regarded Lord Shaftesbury's Factory Acts and other nineteenth-century social legislation as illegitimate interferences with the free market. Major himself crassly claimed to have won 'game, set and match' at Maastricht. Even during the 1997 election campaign the Prime Minister sought to remind the public of these alleged personal triumphs. In fact, Jacques Delors had offered him the economic opt-out in the summer of 1991; with the odds on a Labour victory in 1992, European officials felt that they could tolerate the antics of the British Conservative Government.[15]

The Election and Black Wednesday

Having rejected the idea of doing anything to reduce unemployment, the Government's only weapons against recession were interest rates and incantation. By October 1989 interest rates had risen to 15 per cent to puncture the unsustainable boom; a year later, when Britain joined the ERM, Major, at Mrs Thatcher's insistence, cut them to 14 per cent, and by the time of the election they had been whittled down to 10.5 per cent. Otherwise the Government's only resource was Dr Pangloss; his most notable appearance was at the October 1991 Party Conference when Norman Lamont claimed to have spotted the 'green shoots' of recovery. During the 1992 election campaign John Major prophesied that the economy would start to move as soon as his Government was re-elected. Although these remarks were no more firmly based than Jim Callaghan's similarly confident and misleading reassurances during the 1966 election, they were given credence because the Conservatives still enjoyed a reputation for economic competence; more precisely, they were seen as less incompetent than Labour. Between November 1991 and January 1992 the party's opinion-poll lead on inflation and prices jumped by 14 per cent.

In an attempt to close this gap, the Shadow Chancellor, John Smith, was unwise enough to produce an alternative Budget which was predictably ridiculed by the Government. 'Labour's tax bombshell' was designed to fall on only the higher earners, who stood to lose less than they had been awarded in the 1988 Budget alone. Yet its tax increases began far too low down the income scale to be politically wise and enabled the Conservatives to argue that they proved Labour to be still seething with Bennery. With the help of Treasury officials, Labour's spending proposals were imaginatively costed at £37.5 billion, which could only be funded by substantial tax rises for everyone. By contrast, the real Budget announced by Lamont in March was politically clever and economically irresponsible. Because of the recession, the Government's finances had sharply deteriorated. Cuts in taxation were therefore inappropriate, yet Lamont cut the rate of income tax on the first £2,000 to just 20 per cent. Added to earlier measures which eased the repayment of mortgages, and Major's promises of economic recovery, this was sufficient to persuade enough voters that the Government should be allowed to get on with the job. Major's assertion during the campaign that the Government had 'no plans and no need' to impose VAT on domestic fuel was believed; the Conservative Campaign Guide protested against Labour's 'unfounded and irresponsible smears' on this subject.[16]

When Major asked the Queen to dissolve Parliament for an election on 9 April, Labour were three points ahead in the opinion polls. The usual explanation of the final result – a Conservative majority of twenty-one seats with only 41.9 per cent of the vote – is that Labour threw away the election by mishandling the taxation issue and indulging in a premature and distasteful victory celebration at Sheffield. Labour also botched its appeal over health; the party's spin-doctors sparked off the 'War of Jennifer's Ear', fought over the political allegiances of a little girl's family, instead of campaigning on the widespread public fears of 'creeping privatisation' which had been provoked by the appearance of 'fund-holding' GPs and hospital trusts stuffed with Conservative businessmen. John Major's admirers claimed that his decision to tour the country with a soap-box swung the contest at the last minute, while Rupert Murdoch's *Sun* gloated about its campaign of vilification against Neil Kinnock. No doubt all these factors contributed something to the outcome but, as in 1970, the result was a surprise only because commentators were misled by erroneous opinion polls. 'In reality,' Ivor Crewe has concluded, 'the Conservatives were ahead throughout the campaign, and probably in the run-up to it.'[17]

For the Conservatives to win their fourth successive general election at the bottom of a deep recession was a remarkable achievement (although the dire economic situation may have decided many voters to 'cling to nurse' rather than risk a Labour Government), and it was a personal triumph for John Major. In his campaign for the leadership, Major had promised to build a country 'at ease with itself'; and shortly after the election another Cabinet Minister told a journalist that he was 'looking forward to some peace and quiet'. Major's remark clearly implied, first, that under Margaret Thatcher Britain had not been 'at ease with itself' and, second, that he would alter course to make it so. In the event, except for abolishing the Poll Tax, he did nothing of the sort. His election victory had now given him a second chance to do so and to bring 'some peace and quiet'. But perhaps because he did not himself have strong political convictions, Major could not see that the country was ready for different treatment; it did not want any more Thatcherite medicine rammed down its throat. Or maybe Major, like Macbeth after the murder of Duncan and Banquo, decided that 'returning' would be more 'tedious' than continuing with his current habits.[18]

That proved harder than he expected. Whatever the merits of Major's stance at Maastricht, his performance had been hailed by party managers as striking a perfect balance between the competing Conservative factions. Even so, the Europhobes were unimpressed. If much of his popularity with the electorate stemmed from his not being Mrs Thatcher, to the Conservative ultras at Westminster that was a rank and unforgivable offence. The displaced leader gladly stoked their resentment, even though the Single European Act, which she had signed in 1986, was a far more 'federalist' measure than the Treaty of Maastricht.

Having left Major a damnable legacy – the Poll Tax, a mismanaged economy, a recession and bad relations with our European partners – the least Mrs Thatcher owed him was silent support. Whatever may be thought of Ted Heath's treatment of his successor, he always acted alone; he never caballed against her. The same could not be said of Margaret Thatcher. Not even confining her private attacks on Major to Europe, she censured him for allegedly 'spending like a socialist'. The election campaign forced a temporary cease-fire, but Major's victory soon brought a resumption of hostilities. After winning his own mandate, the Prime Minister looked capable of shutting his ears to the hectoring 'back-seat driver' and her fellow navigators. Instead of trying to keep Major on the right road, the belligerent ultras seemed more intent on crashing the car regardless of casualties. The 1992 Queen's Speech announced plans to ratify the Maastricht Treaty, and the monarch herself addressed the European Parliament; Mrs Thatcher responded with a speech of outrage at The Hague. Twenty-two Conservatives voted against the second reading of the Maastricht Bill. They were only the advance guard; encouraged by a negative vote in the Danish referendum of early June, eighty-four Conservative MPs signed a motion complaining about developments in Europe.[19]

In July the UK started its six-month presidency of the EU, which inevitably drew the growing disarray on the Government's benches to the attention of foreign-exchange dealers. The markets already knew that sterling had joined the ERM at the wrong rate, and Britain's economic difficulties were heightened by high German interest rates, the result of botched economic measures after the Berlin Wall was demolished. Following the German example would deepen the British recession; ignoring it would send sterling below its ERM threshold. Nevertheless, the Prime Minister was bullish about the British economy, suggesting that it would soar above Germany's. Less surprisingly, if equally rashly, Major placed continued membership of the ERM at the centre of the Government's economic strategy.

Luckily, a way out was available. As the pound was not alone in its troubles, a co-ordinated realignment of European currencies against the Deutschmark was the obvious solution. Astonishingly, Norman Lamont rejected this compromise at a meeting of finance ministers which met under his chairmanship at Bath. Instead of using his position to search for a workable consensus, the Chancellor tried to bully the Bundesbank President Helmut Schlesinger into cutting German rates. This return to the diplomatic techniques of the *ancien régime* showed Lamont's ignorance of decision-making both in Europe and the Bundesbank; Schlesinger could not have made a decision alone even if he had wanted to. Lamont achieved nothing except to incur the hostility of Schlesinger, and had shown that like his leader he was over-promoted; Chief Secretary to the Treasury should have been his ceiling.[20]

The failure of the Bath meeting increased pressure on the weakest European currencies, the pound and the Italian lira. Major and Lamont reaffirmed their commitment to the exchange-rate mechanism. At a Cabinet meeting Major praised Lamont and ruled out devaluation; nobody objected. Then on 10 September he gratuitously dug himself deeper into the hole. In a speech to a CBI dinner Major assured his audience that the Government would not be 'driven off their virtuous pursuit of low inflation by market problems or political pressures', as previous governments had been. 'The soft option,' he continued 'the devaluer's option, the inflationary option, would be a betrayal of our future.' In any case, devaluation would not work. It would bring 'rising import prices, rising inflation and a long-term deterioration in Britain's competitiveness which would offset any short-term gain'. Fortunately almost none of this was true. For some time it had been clear to many people outside Downing Street and the Treasury that the over-valued pound was doing inordinate damage to the economy. Yet here was a Prime Minister promising to preserve that sorry state of affairs and dogmatically laying down that the obvious remedy of adjusting the pound to its proper value would not work.[21]

The weekend after Major's speech, the Italians devalued and the Germans agreed to a small reduction in interest rates. A number of Treasury officials, realising that the lira's devaluation would make sterling the main target of the currency speculators, made a belated attempt to convince the Bundesbank that the pound was at the right parity with the Deutschmark. Unsurprisingly, the Bundesbank was not convinced; while it was prepared to fulfil its obligations to sterling, it was not prepared to do anything extra to try to prevent what it regarded as inevitable. Tuesday 25 September saw sterling, despite heavy intervention by the Bank of England, near to its lowest permitted level in the ERM, and that evening Schlesinger made some unguarded remarks suggesting there should have been 'a more complete realignment' of currencies. On Wednesday morning interest rates were raised from 10 to 12 per cent; by then, the Bank had spent $10 billion in its vain

defence of the pound. At a lunch-time meeting, Major and senior ministers decided on a further rise in interest rates to 15 per cent, although
the increase was not to take place till the next day. In fact the battle
was already lost, and that evening Lamont announced the suspension
of Britain's membership of the ERM. The Government's defeat cost the
taxpayer between £3 billion and £4 billion; the cost to the Government
was more crippling. Not only its 'economic policy lay in ruins', Philip
Stephens judged, but 'Major's political reputation was in shreds, his
party torn asunder'.[22]

Major needed to do two things to revive his political reputation and
the fortunes of his Government. The first was to secure the resignation
of Norman Lamont. For a Government to suffer such a humiliation
without offering the ritual sacrifice of the Minister immediately responsible was, or should have been, unthinkable. After all, Jim Callaghan
had done the decent thing and resigned after the devaluation of 1967;
clearly Lamont should have done the same. Yet Major evidently feared
that the disappearance of Lamont would have the same effect on himself
as the devaluation of the lira had had on sterling: without Lamont to
attract hostility, he would become the main target of criticism. So, for
the time being, Lamont stayed on, a flagrant emblem of failure and of
constitutional impropriety.

The second thing needed was what Major had failed to do after the
election: stop the Conservatives from being the most right-wing governing party in Western Europe, with an outlook more akin to the
Republicans in the United States than to the Christian Democrats in
Europe, and revert to the traditional centrist policies of the Tory Party.[23]
The lost opportunity in May was now, after Black Wednesday, a necessity. A basic ingredient of Major's electoral success had been the voters'
acceptance of the Conservatives' relative economic competence, an
acceptance which, in view of the record since 1979, demonstrated the
electorate's lowered expectations. Yet, however low these had become,
the voters were shocked by the conspicuous incompetence shown over
Britain's exit from the ERM. Belief in the Government's economic skills
had been a dam that restrained the voters' animosity against the Conservatives on other matters. Hence, once that dam had been burst, dislike
of the Conservative Government became untrammelled – in October a
poll found only 16 per cent satisfied with a Prime Minister who just six
months earlier had been an electoral asset. The only hope of holding
that dislike within bounds, and then reducing it, was for Major to bring
his party and his Government into line with public opinion; and that
entailed a belated return to One-Nation principles.

Opinion surveys had for some time showed that the voters had never been converted to Thatcherism. Despite the incessant bombardment of right-wing propaganda, the voters had remained centrist. They voted Conservative only because they had no alternative, thinking Labour was not yet fit to govern. In opinion, indeed, though not in voting, the electorate moved left, not right, during the Thatcher years. Hence the Conservative Party could only afford the luxury of an unpopular ideological approach and unpopular ideological policies while Labour remained unelectable.[24] That insight should have been all the more obvious to Major because of the popular vote in the last four general elections. Although the Conservatives had twice gained enormous majorities in the House of Commons, they had never won even 44 per cent of the popular vote. Once, therefore, the Labour Party was seen to be electable again – which was as soon as Neil Kinnock, who had been made an electoral liability by press campaigns against him, had been succeeded by John Smith – the Conservatives were likely to be in electoral trouble, even if they managed to hold on to much of the popular support they had enjoyed since 1979.

Such a perception should certainly not have been beyond the understanding of a man who claimed Iain Macleod as his political hero. In 1962, as we saw earlier, Iain Macleod told the Party Conference that 'the people of this country' did not think the society that the Conservatives had created was 'sufficiently just'. Yet it was by any standards much more just than that created by the Conservatives since 1979. The 1980s had been – not only in Britain but also in the United States and in other countries – one of the most right-wing decades of the century. Some of what had then been done in Britain was necessary and valuable, but heavily regressive taxation, neglect of the poor, an ideological devotion to the market and excessive dedication to business and financial interests were deeply unappealing to many voters. Hence a return to Tory One-Nation principles was long overdue.[25]

One-Nation Toryism is not, of course, a rigid creed whose original tenets have been ossified into binding dogma. Like everything else, it has to move with the times. But however loosely One-Nation Toryism is envisaged or interpreted, the Conservative Governments since 1979 had come nowhere near it. John Major now had the chance to move his Government in that direction. He would not have had to recant or admit previous error; he merely had to adapt his rhetoric and his policies. In doing so he would have encountered opposition from within the parliamentary party which again contained the sort of 'hard-faced men' disliked by Stanley Baldwin. But Major had already had difficulties with them and was bound to go on doing so whatever he did. He should therefore have overridden them and at long last, in defiance of Lady

Thatcher, given 'all the wrong people' some cause for 'rejoicing'.

He did not do so; he made not the smallest attempt to lead his party and Government into the One-Nation tradition. Probably the thought never occurred to him. How far he himself was from One-Nation ideas and from Iain Macleod was shown by his outburst on beggars. In Macleod's day, of course, there were no beggars on the streets; Macleod would have been appalled by their return to London and the big cities and would have taken steps to relieve them. John Major merely denounced them, a position made no more respectable by Tony Blair and New Labour taking much the same line.[26]* Thus Major kept to the Thatcherite path; in many ways, indeed, his Government became even more right-wing than hers. In consequence he and his Government were doomed.[28]

Their only conceivable chance – short of the Labour Party once more destroying itself – was a well-timed economic recovery which might induce voter amnesia and deliver them yet another electoral victory. Norman Lamont later claimed to have sung in his bath the night Britain was forced out of the ERM. To boast of singing after presiding over such an ignominious defeat was a display of insensitivity fully consistent with Lamont's failure to resign. Yet the cheerful song, which rang out from his bathroom that evening, was a much more accurate forecast of the course of the British economy than Major's anti-devaluation speech on 10 September. Devaluation in a deep recession has effects opposite to those foreseen by Major; and in 1992, instead of leading to higher inflation, it brought it lower. Indeed in May 1993 the inflation rate fell to 1.3 per cent, the lowest for nearly thirty years. The same month saw the fourth consecutive fall in the official unemployment figures. Ironically, these welcome developments almost coincided with the belated sacking of Lamont. After breaking the Government's election promise by imposing VAT on domestic fuel in his March Budget, which (rightly) increased taxes by £6.7 billion, Lamont had managed to displace Howe as the most unpopular Chancellor since the war. For Major the final straw came when, during the Newbury by-election campaign, his former campaign assistant glibly boasted that he had no regrets about Black Wednesday. Newbury saw a 28 per cent swing against the Government, and on the same day, 6 May, the Conservatives lost nearly 500 seats in local-government elections.

---

*. This attitude was not even in accordance with Victorian values. John Ruskin's directions on the treatment of beggars were: 'Put a sou into every beggar's box who asks it there – it is none of your business whether they should be there or not, nor whether they deserve the sou – be sure only whether you yourself deserve to have it to give; and give it politely, and not as if it burnt your fingers.'[27]

Lamont's sacking came too late for Major to gain credit from it. Nor, much more importantly, did the economic recovery restore his popularity. Since what had happened was so diametrically opposed to what he had tried to achieve and, so far as he was concerned, had come about entirely by mistake, the voters understandably withheld their gratitude from the Prime Minister and his Government.

While the removal of Lamont did not help Major with the electorate, it increased his difficulties with the parliamentary party over the ratification of the Maastricht Treaty. The resignation statement of the disgruntled ex-Chancellor, who showed himself to be suffering from advanced Europhobia, added to the impression that the Government was helplessly drifting. In July 1993 Major suffered a Commons defeat over the Social Chapter, which Labour supported out of conviction and the Conservative Europhobes out of a desire to defeat or embarrass the Government. The defeat was reversed by a vote of confidence the following day, and the treaty was finally ratified twenty months after Major had returned in triumph from Maastricht. The Prime Minister had showed grim determination during the prolonged guerrilla war, but his temper had been severely tested. Soon after the confidence debate, he was reported to have called three Europhobic Cabinet Ministers 'bastards'; the only surprise was that he had said three when there were at least four. Before July was over, the Conservatives lost Christchurch to the Liberal Democrats on an unprecedented post-war swing of over 35 per cent. August brought some relief with the parliamentary recess and a general collapse of the ERM. At least Major could enjoy a rest and find time to plan a conference speech which would re-unite his party around the theme of 'Back to Basics'.

The Moral Maze

The original intention of 'Back to Basics' was to provide a unifying theme for the Government's legislative programme. In such fields as education and criminal justice the Conservatives would act to restore traditional British respect for institutions and the rule of law. If delivered with sufficient clarity, that message might only have made people wonder why a Conservative Prime Minister found it necessary to launch such a campaign after his party had been in power for fourteen years. Unfortunately Major's words invited other, more damaging, interpretations. Throughout the twentieth century Britain has been unlucky in its newspaper proprietors and never more so than after the arrival of Rupert Murdoch – or rather, his newspapers, since he himself soon went off to the US. And Major and his advisers badly miscalculated the damage that his speech would allow the tabloids to inflict on his Government. In consequence 'Back to Basics' was in folly comparable to the Prime Minister's anti-devaluation tirade a year earlier.

While the Government lurched towards Black Wednesday, the tabloid press had been enjoying itself with stories about the married Heritage Secretary, David Mellor, and an actress. Mellor was a close friend of the Prime Minister, who correctly defended him for two months before new revelations forced Mellor out of office. As a former inhabitant of the Whips' Office and therefore someone who was familiar with the habits of many of his colleagues, Major should have been fully aware that any suggestion of a moral crusade would rebound on the Government. The Prime Minister protested that the slogan had nothing at all to do with private morality, but family respect and responsibility had figured prominently in his conference speech, and Britain's tabloid editors were bound to seize the opportunity to pry into the private lives of Conservative MPs.

The Government was already being hounded by Lord Justice Scott's inquiry into the sale of arms to Iraq, which made this a particularly inappropriate time for the Prime Minister to deliver a sermon on public standards. Furthermore, the recently departed Education Secretary, John Patten, had emphasised sexual morality as one area in which schools could perform better, and ministerial attacks on single mothers at the previous Party Conference had been used by the right-wing press as an excuse for pages of moral speculation. A law of privacy, combined with a freedom of information Act, would have done much to improve the situation, but the Government was too frightened of the press to risk anything of that sort. Hence Major would have been wise to follow Harold Macmillan's advice and leave sermons and morality to the Archbishops.[29]

Major had escaped blame for the recession and the Poll Tax, but he could not achieve a hat-trick with 'Back to Basics'. Having himself led the party to victory in 1992, he could no longer pass off society's problems as a hangover from the old regime. To an audience of Conservative activists, the permissive 1960s could be made to seem a convincing scapegoat for alleged national decadence, but the party faithful were, less than ever before, a representative sample of public opinion. Recruitment had always been more difficult while the party was in office and unable to trade on the unpopularity of a Labour Government, but the current malaise was unprecedented. While membership was around 1.5 million in the seventies, a careful independent survey in the early 1990s suggested that this figure had been halved and that the average age of the activists was now sixty-two; on the current trend, membership would be down to 400,000 at the end of the 'Conservative Century'. The Conservative Party was dying on its feet, or in its wheelchairs.[30]

Because the party was doing so much dubious fundraising abroad, the need to raise money at home by gaining new party members was lessened, and more than a decade of right-wing policies had provoked a mood of public apathy, in which Conservative MPs were most likely to attract enthusiastic interest when they were caught out in sharp practices or unorthodox leisure activities. By the end of January 1994 three members of the Government had resigned for a range of misdemeanours, and Major himself had given unconvincing testimony to the Scott inquiry. The Conservative-run Westminster Council was under investigation for allegedly turning the remarkable success of council-house sales into a vote-rigging strategy. In the following month the MP Stephen Milligan was found dead in women's stockings.

The Government could not complain that the 'Back to Basics' fiasco was distracting the media from better news elsewhere. The public sector borrowing requirement was expected to reach £50 billion in 1993–4. In November 1993 Lamont's replacement, Kenneth Clarke (assisted by the right-wing Chief Secretary Michael Portillo), had celebrated the first full autumn Budget by cutting benefits and raising taxes by £1.75 billion, although by halving the contingency reserve Clarke was able to cushion the recent VAT increases. Yet the Chancellor's skilful presentation could not disguise the fact that an allegedly tax-cutting Government had brought about the biggest tax increase in modern times; the two 1993 Budgets raised the tax burden by 3 per cent of GDP. Hence the Conservatives duly suffered miserable defeats in local and European elections, receiving respectively 27 per cent and 28 per cent of the national vote; they also lost the Eastleigh by-election brought on by Milligan's death.[31]

Office without Power

In June 1993 Michael Heseltine suffered a serious heart attack. Since switching from Environment to the Presidency of the Board of Trade, he had disappointed admirers who hoped that he would turn his interventionist rhetoric into action. His announcement of thirty-one more pit closures in October 1992 had revived public sympathy for the miners and provoked one of the Government's many back-bench revolts. In the month before his illness struck, he published a White Paper which confirmed the hands-off industrial philosophy of the Thatcher Governments. Nevertheless, anxious MPs had not forgotten the high poll ratings he had enjoyed during the 1990 leadership contest, and he and Kenneth Clarke were the two most colourful figures in a drab Government. Even some Europhobes were prepared to consider Heseltine as a caretaker leader, especially when his plan to privatise the Post Office made him seem more Thatcherite than Thatcher; this was one of the pieces of family silver which the ex-leader had declined to sell.

In May 1994 the former Chief Whip Sir Timothy Renton predicted that the Conservatives would soon split into two parties. Under the old conditions some senior party dignitaries might have tactfully intimated to John Major that it was time to make way for an older successor. In such circumstances Heseltine would have been the ideal person, had not the Labour leader John Smith been killed by a massive heart attack in May. Smith had recovered from one serious heart attack to succeed Neil Kinnock after the 1992 election. Heseltine seemed to have regained most of his old vigour – but so had Smith, who had given a typically witty speech on the night before his death. Any substitute for John Major would have to be chosen soon, to give him time to establish himself before the election. Heseltine had not been back on the front bench for long enough to prove that his recovery was complete, and before the end of 1994 new questions about his political judgement were raised when back-bench pressure forced him to shelve his plan to privatise the Post Office.[32]

Other than Heseltine, no candidate could gain even the superficial allegiance of the bulk of Conservative MPs. Within the Conservative Party since the election there had been, over Europe, what John Major called 'an artificial frenzy'. Back in 1963 Iain Macleod had warned Harold Macmillan of the 'danger that the latent xenophobia and jingoism of the parliamentary party' would rise to the surface. By 1994 that xenophobia, which now took the form of Europhobia and was whipped up by Britain's foreign-owned newspapers and Lady Thatcher, was not latent but rampant. A survey of the parliamentary party in 1994 found that 59 per cent of Conservative MPs believed membership of the EU to have brought more drawbacks than advantages; 32 per cent disagreed with them, and only 9 per cent remained truly 'sceptical'. The party was deeply unpopular, and many MPs blamed its divisions and its unpopularity on Major's indecisiveness. Yet plotters had to recognise that a firmer lead from anybody else might cause even deeper divisions.[33]

That was particularly true of Michael Portillo, regarded by the Right as Mrs Thatcher's true heir. Portillo might once have been a devoted admirer of Harold Wilson, but as yet he had shown none of his old idol's trimming abilities; although he went on to help devise the Council Tax, he had clung to the wreckage of the Poll Tax with Mrs Thatcher and Nicholas Ridley while everybody else was taking to the boats. Wilson's leadership chances had been enhanced by his having resigned with Bevan, but Portillo, who made embarrassingly dreadful anti-European speeches at party conferences, had entangled himself too deeply with the Europhobes to be acceptable to the remaining moderates within the party. Kenneth Clarke would have been highly acceptable to those moderates but anathema to the party's growing body of extremists. The new Chancellor had stuck to the traditional Tory position on Europe which the Right now saw as the hallmark of a fanatic. Clarke had implemented reforms at Health and Education which not even Rupert Murdoch could have called 'socialist' – indeed, when Mrs Thatcher wavered in her support for the Health reforms, he had stood firm. Yet Clarke's sense of fun and his obvious humanity did not endear him to the humourless faction on the Right. As Chancellor, moreover, he was hampered by the legacy of Lamont, and was forced to introduce new tax increases of his own when the 1994 Budget provoked a back-bench rebellion over the introduction of the full 17.5 per cent VAT rate on fuel. Another possible candidate, Chris Patten, who had given the Right their best moment of the 1992 election when he lost his seat in Bath, had exiled himself by accepting the Governorship of Hong Kong.[34]

Ever Wider Disunion

The lack of a suitable candidate, together with party disunity, thus prevented a leadership challenge. The opinion polls remained abysmal, deteriorating even further when Tony Blair took the vacant Labour Party leadership. The only thing impressive about the Government was its unpopularity. In July 1995, Gallup found that 13 per cent approved of its record; 76 per cent disapproved. By January 1996 its ratings had improved. As many as 16 per cent approved of its record, and only 73 per cent did not. This massive public distaste had many causes, most of which were justified. The chief of them were its palpable incompetence and inadequate leadership, higher taxes, Conservative disunity and the Government's extremism. Major and other Ministers did not seem to realise how right-wing they were. This was because the Conservative Party now contained so many people even more besotted with Victorian economics than the Cabinet that they gave Ministers the illusion that they were in some way moderate and centrist. This illusion was fed by the even more right-wing Conservative newspapers. Major should have emulated Baldwin and taken on the right-wing press. In doing so, he would have aligned himself with public opinion. But that would have demanded a depth of political commitment and knowledge which Major did not possess. So he continued to take on the public without being sufficiently aligned with the right-wing press to win their ungrudging support.

Thus Major waded ever deeper into the Thatcherite bog. His Government, consolidating Britain's unhealthy position on the extreme right wing of Western Europe, maintained the Thatcherite contempt for public service and hostility to the state. In the grip of fundamentalist dogma, in 1993 it even abolished the wages councils, which was the very antithesis of One-Nation politics. Wages councils had been set up by Winston Churchill to protect the lowest paid. Their abolition was fully in line with the Thatcher Government's equally retrograde withdrawal – unique in the developed world – of all employment protection from the young in 1986; but reducing the pay of the lowest paid seemed a curious way for the Government to further its declared ambition of creating a classless society.

Still enslaved to privatisation, in 1993 the Major Government also authorised the sell-off of British Rail, a move which Mrs Thatcher had prevented Cecil Parkinson from even mentioning at the 1990 Party Conference. While Nigel Lawson had wanted to abolish the NEDC, which admittedly served little useful purpose under the Conservatives because they ignored it, Mrs Thatcher had failed to show the necessary 'radicalism and courage'. The Major Government stepped in where she had faltered and the NEDC was abolished in June 1992. As a close colleague, Ian Lang, justifiably put it, Major was 'more Thatcherite than the lady herself'.[35]

Protecting the Constitution

Major's view of constitutional issues was at least as Thatcherite as that of 'the lady herself'. His attacks from his soapbox on Labour's plans for Scottish devolution had done much, he believed, to win the 1992 election. Improbable though that opinion was, he cast himself as the protector of the constitution. His adoption of this role was made easier by his not having read such writers as Simon Jenkins, Andrew Marr and Ferdinand Mount, and being unaware of the damage done to the constitution and the country's institutions by Conservative Governments since 1979. One of the perpetual themes of Thatcherism was the need to 'roll back the frontiers of the state' and to 'cut back the powers of Government'. In theory that was what the Thatcher Governments were doing; in fact Mrs Thatcher's administration did more to amass and centralise power than any peacetime British Government this century. And Major's administration blindly continued that process.[36]

Lenin's slogan in 1917, 'all power to the Soviets', was a precursor of Thatcherite practice: 'all power to Westminster'; and, as Parliament is only formally sovereign, 'Westminster' in this context meant Whitehall and Downing Street. So while allegedly rolling back the frontiers of the state, the Government extended the tentacles of Whitehall further and further into almost every facet of British public life. So far was the process of centralisation taken that in 1991 the Major Government almost abolished local government altogether, which would have come near to justifying Rousseau's jibe that the people of England were only free once every five years during a parliamentary election. All this was of course directly contrary to the Tory tradition, exemplified not only by Disraeli but by that paragon of the Right, the third Marquis of Salisbury.[37]

Local government's powers were either removed or handed over to an unelected 'quangocracy'. In the nineteenth century, Gladstone and other reformers had greatly reduced patronage. Now the patronage state was recreated. Elected politicians were replaced by people appointed by the Government. These 'new magistrates', as they were sardonically dubbed, amounted to some 63,000 people who were responsible in 1992 for the spending of some £35 billion of public money. These beneficiaries of patronage usually had to be persons 'with business experience'; that was code for Conservative supporters. One hapless Junior Minister, Baroness Denton, admitted she could not 'remember knowingly appointing a Labour supporter'.[38]

Although, for Tories, Britain's intermediate institutions have always been an important element in the constitution, Thatcherism was hostile to that pluralist tradition. As Norman Tebbit explicitly said of local government, the idea that it should provide a check and balance to Westminster was 'an entirely new and quite false constitutional theory' – in fact it was a well-established and quite true constitutional theory. Local government was far from being the only such institution to suffer. The universities, the Church and the television authorities were among those attacked, as were the professions, a vital element in a modern civilised state. Parliament itself was not immune. Although, as we saw earlier, Margaret Thatcher had been sensibly sceptical about the doctrine of the mandate in 1968, that doctrine was ruthlessly employed in the 1980s to force the Government's proposals onto the statute book, the committee and report stages of Government bills becoming, in Ferdinand Mount's words, 'a mockery'.[39]

Nevertheless John Major regarded himself and his Government as the defenders of the constitution. While other Western European countries were making themselves less centralised, Major was firmly opposed to the idea of a Scottish parliament. Both a Royal Commission and the Conservative Party had favoured devolution in the 1970s – in 1976 William Whitelaw, Margaret Thatcher's deputy, had 'restated our commitment to a directly elected assembly in Scotland'. Yet Major characterised Scottish devolution variously as 'a folly' and 'teenage madness'. By doing so he stirred up resentment against Scotland in England while offending the majority of Scots who wanted more control of their own affairs. Major was thus arguing for 'subsidiarity' in the European Union while at the same time ruling it out in Britain. This was fully in accordance with 'all power to Westminster', but like the Government's economic and social outlook it was directly contrary to One-Nation Toryism.[40]

Turning and Fighting

By May 1994, if not before, both Labour and the Liberal Democrats seemed to be getting nearer to the ideals of One-Nation Toryism than the Government. That development heralded electoral disaster for the Conservative Party. Short of the Government changing course and suddenly becoming moderate, the only possible means of avoiding such a disaster was the slow economic recovery over which the Government found itself presiding and which might offset Conservative unpopularity. Yet the polls did not offer much hope that even economic recovery could greatly help the Government. Both in June 1995 and February 1996 Gallup showed that twice as many people thought Labour would handle the economy better than the Conservatives would.[41]

Meanwhile the Europhobes' 'artificial frenzy' over Europe had infected John Major. His utterances on the subject emulated the hostile insularity of Lady Thatcher and so, after an interval, did his actions. In March 1994 Major announced that when the European Union was enlarged he would oppose any alteration in the voting machinery of the Council of Ministers. This would make the taking of decisions even more difficult and would go some way towards making the Community like the early Polish Diet, whose requirement of unanimity had made it impotent. Major's position was indefensible, and after an ultimatum from our partners the Prime Minister had to make a humiliating climbdown. In July, out of pique, he retaliated by vetoing our partners' unanimous choice of the next President of the Commission, the Belgian Prime Minister, M. Dehaene. The Prime Minister's excuse for his veto was that Dehaene was too 'federalist', an assessment which caused merriment in Brussels. In consequence Major ended up with Jacques Santer as the next President of the Commission, a man who was on any view much more 'federalist' than Dehaene.[42]

John Major's two unhappy strikes at Brussels did not appease his party's Europhobes at Westminster. By showing that he caved in so easily to their pressure, he stimulated them into pressing him harder. After defying the Government Whip in a vote on the European Budget in November 1994, eight MPs had the Whip withdrawn. A ninth decided to share their martyrdom. A number of political careers have survived near-ostracism from the Conservative Party, but few have actually benefited from what is meant to be severe punishment. The 'Whipless ones', who with two exceptions had formerly been deservedly obscure, now became prominent, their new status making them the toast of the die-hard circuit. Eventually the Government had to beg them to end their martyrdom and return to the fold.

By the summer of 1995 Major realised that something had to be done. A leadership challenge looked certain in the autumn. On 13 June Major was heckled at a packed meeting of the 'Fresh Start' Europhobe group. This coincided with the publication of Lady Thatcher's second volume of memoirs, which well portrayed her early years but predictably strayed onto present discontents. In an eccentric, ghost-written political testament which spoiled an otherwise good book, Margaret Thatcher maintained that her policy on Europe had been 'entirely reversed' by the Major Government. Short of withdrawing completely or declaring war, her successor could scarcely have done more to continue her record of making trouble in Europe. Yet Lady Thatcher and the other Europhobes thought that everything Major did was wrong by definition. In a series of interviews promoting her book, its author attacked Major and the Government. Incredibly, she attributed the Government's unpopularity to its not having 'been Conservative enough', by which she meant insufficiently right-wing. Even more implausibly, she claimed that the Government had 'hit at everything I believed in'.[43]

If John Major had still had doubts about the need for action, Lady Thatcher's book and her extravagant advertising of it would have removed them. To his credit, Major turned and fought, calling a press conference on 22 June in the garden of Number 10 to announce his resignation; at the same time the extra telephone lines which had proved invaluable during the 1990 campaign were being installed at his headquarters. This pre-emptive strike made Major confident enough to tell his critics to 'put up or shut up', even though Bernard Ingham's use of that phrase in 1990 provided an unhappy precedent. Norman Lamont's willingness to stand was indicated by an article in *The Times*, rehearsing the familiar Europhobic case against his old friend. Lamont was not, however, the ideal standard-bearer for the Right, since his flamboyant personality might distract attention from what they regarded as the real issue: Britain's supposed servitude to Germany. Fortunately for Major, he faced in the end a quite different challenge from someone widely suspected of having no personality at all.[44]

John Redwood had become Secretary of State for Wales in May 1993. His connection with Wales was not close, but few suitable Tories had any roots in the principality. For Redwood the campaign was a great success. He had the courage to 'put up' while Portillo, the previous favourite of the Right, skulked in a tent which, like Major's head-quarters, was amply provided with telephone lines – just in case. Redwood's policies were less than convincing; he wanted to stay in Europe while pursuing a line which would make continued membership impossible, and he demanded dramatic cuts in a Budget which had already been attacked by many right-wing shears; at the same time he promised to retain the royal yacht.[45]

After the first Redwood press conference, journalists made fun of his campaign team – a predictable group of malcontents with badly co-ordinated battle dress. This set the tone for coverage of the election, which ignored the serious points. At a time when Tony Blair was increasing Labour's already considerable popularity by removing any trace of ideological baggage from its policies, a sizeable group of Tory MPs had decided that the only way to attract voters was to make their party even more ideological. Much of the inspiration behind this remarkable assessment came from the United States, where Newt Gingrich's Republicans had won the 1994 Congressional elections on a programme which would have shaken even President Hoover. Although Redwood later paid him homage in Washington, Gingrich turned out to be a very transitory victor.

The leadership election result showed that a large section of the Conservative Party had lost all contact with reality and that Redwood had saved the Prime Minister. Major won by 218 to eighty-nine with twenty-two abstentions or spoiled papers. Downing Street quickly acclaimed this as a marvellous endorsement, pointing out that the Prime Minister had received more votes than Mrs Thatcher had managed in 1990 from a larger electorate. The comparison was of course spurious. Over one-third of the parliamentary party had refused to support Major. Had a complete nonentity polled the number of votes given to Redwood, even Major's spin-doctors could not have hailed the result as a victory. Yet, almost certainly, Redwood gained few, if any more votes than a nonentity would have received. So by making Major's victory seem considerable against a former Cabinet Minister, Redwood had salvaged the Prime Minister.

The immediate danger was over, but the Europhobes were not going to keep quiet. The chances of Britain pursuing a sensible policy in Europe after the election were not improved when early in the campaign Douglas Hurd, who, with Heseltine and Clarke, was one of the three most respected men in the Government, announced his resignation. Most of the right-wing papers had supported Redwood, using the leadership election to give Major experience of the treatment previously lavished on Neil Kinnock. In 1990 the public had been induced to think that it had a new Government when only the leader had been changed; now the majority of the party hoped that a similar illusion could be created without even changing its leader. That, however, was an illusion too far.

Not Drifting but Drowning

Major's claim that Iain Macleod was his political hero, and his call for a 'classless society', whatever he meant by it, were rhetorical flourishes. In practice, his Government did nothing to halt the trend towards growing inequality which had disfigured the 1980s or to help the least well-off. Unsurprisingly, the public were better judges of the Government's activities than either Lady Thatcher and the hard Right or the Government itself. In November 1995 an opinion poll found two-thirds of voters thinking that under Major's leadership Britain was becoming still further distanced from the One-Nation ideal and was now even less united than it had been when Mrs Thatcher left office. That was an accurate assessment. The nearest that Major had come to reviving One-Nation politics was again a piece of rhetoric; the name chosen for his most publicised policy initiative, 'The Citizen's Charter'. The Conservative charters of the late 1940s had pointed the way towards co-operation between Government and industry; the 1990s model merely demanded better services from low-paid public sector workers who were now to be identified by name badges.

Understandably, Tony Blair had launched an open bid for the One-Nation mantle that the Conservative Party had cast off; his success was certified by the poll's finding that over 40 per cent of the electorate thought he would make the best Prime Minister, compared with less than 20 per cent who plumped for Major. Blair's success was facilitated by the loosening of the ties between both the main parties and their respective sectional interests, but, whereas Blair was working hard to reduce the influence of the trade unions, businesses were deserting the Conservatives of their own free will. In March 1993 the party announced that it had an overdraft of £19 million. With respectable sources of funds disappearing, Conservative managers looked abroad for financial help; the publicity surrounding these unsavoury ventures caused even deeper disillusionment both with and within the party, whose decline continued.[46]

Sleaze and the Nolan Committee

The November 1995 poll appeared soon after the Party Conference, where Major had once again appealed for unity. The appeal fell flat. The headlines were dominated by the defection to Labour of Alan Howarth, MP for Stratford-upon-Avon, almost the only Conservative MP in the 1992 Parliament to make One-Nation-type speeches, and by a particularly cheap jingoistic speech by Michael Portillo, now the Defence Secretary, who managed to dredge an attack on Europe out of the subject of military cap-badges. His remarks disgusted senior officers in all three services. Before long, Howarth had been followed out of the party by Emma Nicholson, who decamped to the Liberal Democrats, and Peter Thurnham. Both MPs cited the Nolan Report on parliamentary standards as their 'breaking point'.

The increasing number of semi-professional Conservative MPs, the development feared in the 1940s by Sir Herbert Williams, who would have found the Conservatism of the 1980s and 1990s otherwise congenial, produced a lot of back-benchers who had had no career except politics before entering Parliament. They were therefore short of money and sought ways of supplementing their parliamentary salaries; unfortunately some of them hit on methods which fell below even the relaxed standards of the day. Briefly reviving its old tradition of investigative journalism, the *Sunday Times* exposed two Conservative MPs who accepted £1,000 each for asking questions in the House of Commons.[47]

In 1989 one of them, Graham Riddick, had chosen the subject of 'lawlessness' for an adjournment debate in the House. After blaming, in his sermon, the decay of society on Churchmen and the Labour Party, he pronounced that 'it is we, along with those who influence us, who must develop and improve our standards of behaviour and our self-discipline'.[48] 'If one gives people more responsibility,' this pillar of rectitude continued, 'they act in a more responsible manner.' Whether or not that is generally the case, it did not seem to be true of Conservative

MPs. The continued revelation of the sleazy conduct of a number of them, together with the manifest failure of the Government and Parliament to control it, had forced Major in October 1994 to set up a Committee on Standards in Public Life under the chairmanship of Lord Nolan. The committee's first report found no evidence of systematic abuse of public office but made some important proposals to prevent MPs acting as paid lobbyists and to require them to disclose their pay and interests.

In May 1995 John Major had promised to accept in full Nolan's proposals to tighten the regulations on MPs' earnings. This decision greatly unsettled many on the right, so despite his victory over Redwood, Major beat his usual retreat and entrusted the task of watering down the legislation to a Select Committee. Allegedly the issue was to be decided on a free vote, but those MPs like Nicholson who continued to support the original proposals came under pressure. Critics of Nolan argued that sitting on company boards gave Conservative MPs an invaluable glimpse of life outside the Commons chamber. Although such experiences would have been better achieved before entering Parliament, certainly all too few of them had had many glimpses of life outside politics. Not that the boards they mainly sat on could do much to remedy that defect, since they tended to be of organisations which lobbied Whitehall and Westminster on behalf of major companies. So, unlike the men with hard faces in Baldwin's day, who made money as businessmen, their present-day successors were people who merely hoped to make money out of businessmen.[49]

The take-up by Conservative MPs of so many profitable consultancies was the parliamentary equivalent of Conservatives outside Parliament enriching themselves out of the quango state. The Government had thousands of appointments to make every year, and the rewards could be high – the banker Sir Brian Shaw earned £150,000 for 36 days' work on the Port of London Authority – and by definition principled opponents of Government policy had excluded themselves from these lucrative careers. But even Sir Brian's salary was meagre compared to the pickings enjoyed by the executives of the privatised utilities, who seldom made news except when they dismissed their staff while increasing their own pay and emoluments. The contrast between the Government's tolerance of the 'fat cats'' greed and plunder and its hostility to welfare scroungers and beggars strengthened many people's aversion to the modern Conservative Party.[50]

That aversion was not diminished by the long-awaited Scott Report into the sale of arms to Iraq, which revealed that Ministers had misled the House – one had written a total of sixteen inaccurate letters to MPs.

But under John Major this was not considered to be a resigning matter, even though innocent businessmen had been prosecuted for following the Government's secretly changed guidelines. Senior Conservatives, including Lord Howe, lined up to discredit the report before it appeared, and Labour's spokesman Robin Cook was given no time to prepare for the debate when it did; even so, the Government only survived by one vote.

Other Ministers (notably the Home Secretary, Michael Howard) hid behind a baffling distinction between 'policy' and 'operational' matters to escape the blame when things went wrong. Now that the Government was rapidly 'hiving off' departmental business into semi-autonomous agencies, this was a useful distinction for Ministers in trouble. The Government, Cook justly pointed out during the Scott debate, was 'fond of lecturing the rest of the nation on its need to accept responsibility ... yet, when it comes to themselves, suddenly, not a single minister can be found to accept responsibility for what went wrong'. And much went on going wrong. Although Major was unlucky in that many of the scandals were hangovers from the last reign, he was excessively tolerant of misconduct in high places. When Junior Ministers such as Tim Smith and Neil Hamilton were forced to resign over serious allegations of corruption, they seemed resentful that only they had been singled out for punishment.[51]

Nearing the End

Many of the record number of Tories who stood down in 1997 were moderates; the Right had less reason to leave. The 1995 leadership election had not slowed the party's lurch in their direction. While his successful Chancellor, Kenneth Clarke, struggled to keep the party within the bounds of common sense, Major promised a referendum in the next Parliament if the Cabinet approved the introduction of a single European currency. From a stronger leader this would have seemed a good decision on a matter of undoubted constitutional importance, but by this stage most of Major's actions were judged to be yet more concessions to the right wing. This appeasement reached its apogee in May 1996, two months after the Health Secretary Stephen Dorrell had told the House of Commons about a possible link between mad-cow disease (BSE) and the fatal human version, Creutzfeldt-Jakob's disease.

In the 1980s the Thatcher Government's elevation of profit above all else and its dislike of Government regulations had led to Britain, unlike her European partners, taking inadequate measures to control BSE. This had two consequences: in 1996 Britain had some 180,000 mad cows, nearly twenty times the rest of the combined EU; and many countries, including the United States, Canada, Australia, Kuwait and Hong Kong, had for some years banned the import of British beef. The British Government must have known that Dorrell's announcement would lead to further restrictions, yet when the European Union placed a world-wide ban on the export of British beef, the Government and the press were outraged. Cheered on by his back-benchers, Major denounced 'a clear disregard by some of our partners of reason, common sense and Britain's national interests', and declared that Britain would block EU business until the ban was lifted. Not for the first time, it was Major who was disregarding reason, common sense and Britain's national interests to ingratiate himself with the Europhobic Right. Not surprisingly, our partners thought Britain had gone mad. Major's action was both unlawful and self-defeating. The blocking of business entailed Britain sometimes obstructing developments which she had long wanted and from which she would benefit. The rest of the Union were too disgusted with Major and the British Government to save them from their own folly; all that Major gained from the Florence Summit in June was a face-saving formula. Nobody doubted that he had suffered a heavy and well-deserved defeat in this 'beef war'.[52]

The whole episode lent credence to the criticism early in 1996 of Mrs Thatcher's former Cabinet Minister, Lord Young, who said, 'The trouble with John Major is that he doesn't believe in anything or look more than forty-eight hours ahead.' The Prime Minister's abortive boycott only stimulated the Little-Englandism of right-wing Conservatives who, while denouncing the 'unelected bureaucrats of Brussels', applauded the influence of the unelected billionaire, Sir James Goldsmith. Goldsmith had decided to buy himself into British politics à l'Americaine, although American billionaires, who believe their wealth entitles them to run the country, do at least live there and pay American taxes. Goldsmith was seldom in Britain and probably paid no more British taxation than Rupert Murdoch. Undeterred, Sir James launched his anti-European Referendum Party to wring more concessions from John Major.[53]

Like the foreign newspaper magnates, Conrad Black and Rupert Murdoch, Goldsmith had good reason for hostility to the European Union. They were all extreme right-wingers who were far closer to the views of the US Republican Party than to those of mainstream European parties. Moreover, Murdoch and Black (like Goldsmith in the past) ran multinational empires. They were too powerful to have much to fear from any 'nation state'. The European Union, on the other hand, might well tame them.

Ordinary British Conservatives had no such sensible rationale for their Little-Englandism and Europhobia. The choice before Britain had long been plain. It had been well put as long ago as 1970 by, of all people, the then Anthony Wedgwood Benn. 'Of course,' said Benn, 'we can stay out and stand alone, but we will still find that European, American and Russian decisions will set the framework within which we would have to exercise our formal parliamentary sovereignty.'[54] That was still true. Either Britain, by helping the European Union to be one of the major powers in the world, could retain considerable control over her own destiny, or she could cling to formal sovereignty, while in reality becoming an American satellite and enjoying the international influence equivalent to a county council.

Former Tory empiricism and rationality on Europe and internal politics had long been replaced by ideology. Indeed, like some crazed American religious cult, the Conservative parliamentary party seemed intent on mass suicide. Unlike such cults, however, its leader was not intent on persuading his followers to commit suicide; he was merely unable to talk them out of it. And even the most suicidally inclined wished to postpone the ceremony for as long as possible. By the autumn of 1996 the Government had no purpose in life but to try to wrong-foot the Opposition and occasionally clear up after itself: the Queen's Speech of October 1996 included the fifth Criminal Justice Act in six years, the consequence of Michael Howard's penal policy being largely determined by the Conservative Party Conference. After six years in office, Major was presiding over a nation profoundly ill at ease with itself; despite the great improvement in industrial relations, over three-quarters of voters believed that a class struggle was under way in Britain. The continuing and well-conducted economic recovery had made the Government no more popular; yet Ministers, oblivious of the public's deep-rooted contempt for the Government, went on hoping that something would turn up.[55]

Alec Douglas-Home, who like Major had become leader because he seemed the safest candidate, had put off the 1964 election until the autumn with damaging effects on the economy. But he had a large majority in the House of Commons, had only become Prime Minister a year earlier, and had been fully able to govern. To most people, therefore, his postponement of the election seemed justifiable. John Major had been Prime Minister for six years, had no overall majority and was palpably unable to govern. Hence his decision to hang on to office until the last possible moment did not seem justifiable; it plainly had nothing to do with the national interest. His parliamentary party had become a rabble, and so far from considering the national interest,

his Europhobes were scarcely capable of considering their party's interest. They put faction well before party, with the country trailing far
behind. So the party's disunity persisted.

In the circumstances Kenneth Clarke's last Budget was as good as
could be reasonably expected. Taking one penny off income tax was as
little as the Chancellor could get away with without provoking yet
another almighty row in the parliamentary party. While a large cut in
taxes, as advocated by the Right, would not have restored the Government to public favour, a very small one did not help at all. On electoral,
as well as on other grounds, Major should have dissolved Parliament
in the autumn of 1996.

John Major could not claim as an excuse for continuing to limp on
in office that he was at least postponing the installation of a dangerously
left-wing socialist Government. Tony Blair's 'New Labour' Party had
moved so far to the right that it was in danger of leaving One-Nation
principles to the left of it. Arguably Labour's rightwards march provided
a justification for the right-wing stance of the Conservative Government,
suggesting that the voters, too, had at last moved to the right in pursuit
of the Conservatives. Certainly the country did not want any drastic
political change – except in personnel, it never does. And certainly it
did not want a socialist Government – with the possible exception of
1945 it never has. Most of Blair's dumping of past Labour policy was
long overdue but, in going so far to the right, he was less bringing his
party into line with the voters than responding to the wishes of the
newspaper proprietors. Having seen what Murdoch and the others had
done to Neil Kinnock, he was understandably anxious to avoid the same
fate.

The British tabloid press is nastier and less scrupulous than almost
any other. Even so, New Labour's fear of it was excessive. Yet Blair's
wooing of Murdoch, Rothermere and other press controllers was clever
electoral politics, going far to neutralise the right-wing newspapers while
remained to the left of Major's high and dry Conservatism. No doubt
Blair's tactics caused a few abstentions on the Left, but most voters had
only one aim – to get rid of the Conservatives – and New Labour
was the only army that could defeat the Government. Furthermore, by
removing all but minor differences between Labour and the Liberal
Democrats, Blair facilitated tactical voting by both parties.

When Major did at last call the election, he tarnished still further
his Government's reputation by announcing that Parliament was to be
prorogued two weeks before it was dissolved. Since the only effect of the
unnecessary prorogation was to prevent the publication of Sir Gordon
Downey's Report on the allegations of sleaze made against a number

of MPs, nearly all of whom were Conservatives, the general assumption was that that was its cause. As a result, the first two weeks of the campaign were almost entirely concerned with sleaze, an issue which could only do the Government harm.

Even when sleaze lost its place on the front pages and other subjects gained an airing, the campaign remained sterile. Knowing they were well ahead, Labour took no risks and fought a wholly defensive campaign. The Conservative Party managers did not know whether to talk up their own proposals or just attack Labour. The inevitable result was that they did not do either very well, but a mainly negative campaign was sensible, as some of their policy proposals managed to be both misguided and unpopular.

Rail privatisation had not quite proved to be a 'Poll Tax on wheels' that the late Robert Adley MP had predicted, but with much adverse publicity surrounding South West Trains, which had cancelled numerous services because they had sacked too many drivers, London voters were unimpressed by a promise to privatise the Underground. The continuing scandal over the 1980s pensions reforms, for which thousands had not yet been compensated, was an unpromising background for the unveiling of an even more ambitious scheme for the twenty-first century; and promises to reduce further and eventually abolish Inheritance Tax meant little to pensioners who feared losing everything in retirement. The initiative passed to Labour's spin-doctors who gleefully imitated recent Conservative tactics by costing the party's manifesto at £15.5 billion.[56]

John Major had now become a card-carrying Eurosceptic, but his conversion was too belated to be convincing, and anyway for the voters Europe was not an important issue in the election. Major also started talking about One-Nation and helping the have-nots. His denunciations of the allegedly 'job-destroying social chapter and minimum wage' chimed better with the first than the second conversion. The Social Chapter had not destroyed a single job in Europe, and most other countries, including the United States, have a minimum wage. Major's stated intention of helping the have-nots and serving 'the many, not the few' was too much at variance with the last eighteen years to be serviceable. Nothing was said about sleaze in high places, but the manifesto contained proposals to 'crack down further on benefit cheats'; it was in no doubt that 'social security fraud must be stamped out'.[57]

None of that was going to win many votes. The only strong card the Conservatives had was the economic recovery – perhaps the best-managed since the war, which was primarily due to Kenneth Clarke. But because Clarke was the leading pro-European in the Cabinet and therefore the chief target for the animosity of the Europhobes, he was kept off the centre of the stage. That self-defeating decision prevented the Government making proper use of their best issue.

Towards the end of the campaign, Clarke complained that the election was being dominated by too many millionaires. As usual the newspaper proprietors were conspicuous. Unusually, they permitted or ordered their various publications to take different editorial lines. Thus Murdoch's *Sun* backed Labour, his *Sunday Times* the Conservatives, and, absurdly, his *Times* the Eurosceptics of all parties. Lord Rothermere's *Evening Standard* came out for Labour, while the day before the election his *Daily Mail*, which had become as Europhobic as our foreign-owned press, published a leading article on its front page, superimposed on a Union Jack, claiming that the election 'could undo 1000 years of our nation's history'.* This must have been deeply embarrassing for Rothermere, a tax exile in Paris; after Blair's victory he announced, presumably as a penance, that he would sit on the Labour benches on his infrequent visits to the House of Lords and Britain.

Aside from the newspaper proprietors, Paul Sykes, a Yorkshire millionaire and the only one of the election band, as Clarke pointed out, who was normally resident in this country, announced that he would give £2,000 to every Conservative Constituency Association whose candidate undertook to vote against a single currency. Not merely questions, it soon became evident, could now be bought, but also views and future votes. The haste with which associations rushed to grab Paul Sykes's proffered £2,000 demonstrated yet again how many Conservatives had lost all sense of political propriety. Mr Sykes agreed to pay out some £400,000.

Compared with the outlay of Sir James Goldsmith on his Referendum Party, that was chicken feed. Sir James was prepared to spend £20 million on his expensive new toy. Goldsmith and the Conservative candidates who rushed to publicise their Europhobic sentiments in order to ward off the threat of a Referendum Party candidate standing in their constituencies were seemingly unaware of the history of third-party contenders in the USA and elsewhere. Such parties tend to take their support almost equally from both the main parties. Unless they poll an enormous vote, therefore, they have little or no effect on the electoral results. That was the fate of Goldsmith's Referendum Party. It did not affect the result in a single constituency with the possible exception of Harwich.[58]

---

* The Editor of the *Daily Mail* did not explain what had happened 1,000 years ago to merit dating 'our nation's history' from the reign of Ethelred the Unready. The Union of England and Scotland is less than three hundred years old.

The Conservative Party's unconvincing manifesto, its tired attacks on Labour, its continuing disunity – even in the middle of the campaign, two Junior Ministers broke ranks on Europe – and its failure to convince his constituency party that Neil Hamilton should not stand as a Conservative candidate, similarly made little difference. The voters had had enough of what they saw as the arrogance, complacency, sleaze, right-wing ideology and incompetence of the Conservatives. Most of them had made up their minds long before the campaign belatedly began. Except for one rogue ICM poll in the *Guardian*, the opinion polls showed Labour so far ahead that many people assumed they must be wrong. Yet they were approximately correct, and the voters duly inflicted on the Conservatives their worst defeat since 1832. Labour gained only some 43 per cent of the vote, a similar proportion to that won by the Conservatives in elections in 1979, although crucially most of the Liberal Democrat voters in 1997 were much nearer to Labour than to the Conservatives, whereas in earlier elections they had been preponderantly against the winners. In at least one respect, indeed, 1997 was worse than 1832. The Conservatives, having lost every seat in both Scotland and Wales, became in the worst sense a 'One-Nation' party – of England.

The Rise and Fall of One-Nation

Remarkably, some Conservatives, William Waldegrave among them, saw the Conservatives' defeat not as 'a rejection but an endorsement of what Mrs Thatcher and Mr Major achieved'. A Conservative loss of 182 seats and a Labour overall majority of 176 may seem a curious endorsement of Conservative achievements, yet Tony Blair's right-wing platform in the 1997 election can certainly be regarded as a demonstration of his and Labour's conversion to neo-Liberalism or Thatcherism. But it can also be viewed as a reversion to genuine Old Labour. Labour's crucial mistake in the twentieth century was to adopt its 1918 constitution, thus becoming an avowedly socialist party; combined with the British electoral system, to which, astonishingly, it has remained addicted, this resulted in its being electorally one of the least successful major political parties in Western Europe. Had it aimed to be a left-wing radical party in the tradition of Tom Paine, it would have had a far more prosperous electoral career. Yet Labour did try to mitigate its mistake. While it often made loud socialist noises when in Opposition, in Government it was rarely if ever socialist in practice.[59]

There was nothing socialist about the two MacDonald Governments;

there was little that was socialist in the activities of the Attlee Governments, although many regarded the state capitalism of the nationalised
industries as monuments to socialism, which in a sense they were. Much
the same applied to the two Wilson Governments and the single Callaghan one. Tony Blair chiefly differed from his predecessors by disappointing socialists before instead of after forming a government.*

Blair and Gordon Brown differed from MacDonald and Snowden
in eschewing even the traditional incantations of socialism, but they
resembled them in their devotion to orthodox economics and their
acceptance of a largely Conservative framework. The great contrast
between the nineties and the inter-war years lay in the Conservatives,
not in Labour. 'The wholesome decency' of Baldwin and Chamberlain,
Peter Clarke has written, gave 'Britain the most civilized form of right-
wing domination in Europe'. That claim could not be made for the
right-wing domination of 1979 to 1997.[61]

Although the inter-war Conservative Governments of Baldwin and
Chamberlain made plenty of mistakes, they never became infected by
ideology – Baldwin even thought that socialism and capitalism did not
really exist. They could therefore remain broadly in line with events and
with public opinion. The Conservative Governments of 1979–97 had
no such self-control. They were fervently ideological and triumphalist.
Hence they made little attempt to conceal the favours they bestowed
on the rich, while piling taxes on the poor. The Conservative Party
seemed intent on enriching itself as well as its supporters. It looked
corrupt, avaricious and divided. As William Hague said during the subsequent leadership election, the words people associated with the Conservative Party were 'sleaze', 'greed' and 'division'. That could never
have been said of the Baldwin and Chamberlain Governments.[62]

The differences between 1945 and 1997 are similarly great. Most
obviously, 1997 was a far heavier defeat. In 1945 the Conservatives
managed to win nearly 40 per cent of the vote; the tally half a century
later was only 31 per cent. Since in that other great Conservative disaster,
1906, when the Conservatives got 43 per cent, the previous lowest vote
that a defeated Conservative Government won this century was 38 per

---

* Margaret Thatcher, of course, thought Britain had seen a great deal of socialism since
the war. 'No theory of government', said the first chapter of her memoirs 'was ever given
a fairer test or a more prolonged experiment' [than democratic socialism]. 'Yet it was a
miserable failure.' Admittedly, that introductory chapter sounded less like her than most
of the rest of the book, yet her ghost-writers were evidently faithful reflectors of her
views. Not only was the Labour Party always socialist, she believed; so, even as late as
1990, were elements in the Conservative Party. Michael Heseltine's challenge to her
leadership had to be defeated, she told Simon Jenkins, because 'he will bring back
socialism'.

cent in 1929. Again, in 1945, the revulsion against the Conservatives was the result of the failings of earlier Conservative politicians in the 1930s, for which the Conservative leadership in 1945 was not responsible. For their defeat in 1997, however, Conservative Ministers had nobody to blame but themselves. Even greater was the contrast between the party leadership after the elections of 1945 and 1997. In 1945 the Conservatives had a great war leader and a number of popular and talented colleagues. In 1997 they had William Hague, who was unknown; and the senior colleagues he had chosen – Michael Howard, Peter Lilley, Brian Mawhinney and Cecil Parkinson – had at least one thing in common: none of them was popular.

After the 1945 election, as we saw earlier, the Tories refused to move to the right and soon took steps to begin the party's recovery. After the 1997 election the parliamentary party seemed incapable of understanding the causes of the disaster and therefore intent on continuing along the way which had brought it about. Because ideology still governed their heads, MPs, though not the party as a whole, rejected the only candidate, Kenneth Clarke, who was clearly qualified to be their leader. That was one demonstration of how far the Conservative Party had declined since 1945. Another demonstration was a remark of Michael Howard, one of the right-wing candidates for the leadership and the one in favour of whom William Hague briefly agreed to abandon his own candidacy. During the leadership campaign Howard, who may have been the worst Home Secretary in the two centuries the office has been in existence and who was later made Shadow Foreign Secretary by Hague, said that 'Tories should not believe in "One-Nation" policies but in "One British nation" policies'. Auberon Waugh thought Howard's remark 'nasty, fatuous and wrong'; and if it meant anything, it meant that the Conservative Party should abandon social reform and embrace a strident and damaging nationalism.[63]

Of course the Conservatism of the eighties and nineties had borne no relation to One-Nation Toryism; indeed the Conservative Governments of 1979–97 had not even pursued One-British-Nation policies, but One-South-east-England policies. Such attitudes will probably be even less appropriate in the coming decades, when the worship of the market is likely to be on the wane. Right-wing neo-Liberalism probably reached its peak in the eighties and early nineties when the globalisation of the world economy was taken to justify every right-wing excess. But once the social damage – not to mention the economic damage – caused by the uncontrolled self-interest of individuals and companies has become clear to all but the blindest, the balance will have to be redressed; and that development seems bound to help the Labour Party.

Electorally, the Conservative Party was uniquely successful from 1979 to 1992. But two of the factors which produced the run of success – Labour's lurch to the left and the rise of a significant third party – helped in the 1980s to disguise how widely their policies were resented. Uniquely in the post-war period, that resentment turned in the 1990s into hatred among a sizeable proportion of the public. Thanks to One-Nation policies, Winston Churchill was able in the early fifties to enjoy his successful Indian summer. In 1997 his creed was as popular as ever with the public but it had been abandoned by the party he led with such distinction. In consequence, the Conservatives looked set to embark on their Wilderness Years.[64]

Notes

Introduction

1. Disraeli, *Sybil*, Book II, Chapter v; Butler, Foreword to *One Nation*, p. 7
2. Butler and Kavanagh, *The British General Election of 1992*, pp. 29–30; Margaret Thatcher in *The Times*, 12 January 1996; *Rowntree Inquiry into Income and Wealth 1995*, I, p. 6; *The Times*, 24 February 1997; *Daily Telegraph*, 3 November 1995
3. Robbins, *Political Economy, Past and Present*, p. 108; Hume, *Of Commerce, in Essays, Moral, Political and Literary*, p. 271
4. 'Has the Electorate Become Thatcherite?' in Skidelsky (ed.), *Thatcherism*, pp. 25–49

Chapter I: Prologue

1. S. Orwell and Angus (eds), *The Collected Essays, Journalism and Letters of George Orwell*, I, pp. 296–7; Avon, *The Reckoning*, pp. 33, 57–8; Churchill, *The Gathering Storm*, pp. 258–9; Gilbert V, pp. 1012–5, 1038–9, 1043–4; Nicolson, *People and Parliament*, pp. 60–1
2. Orwell and Angus (eds), *III*, p. 431; Rhodes James (ed.), *Chips*, p. 497; Bullock, *Ernest Bevin, II*, p. 389; Pimlott, *Hugh Dalton*, p. 410; Avon, *The Reckoning*, p. 522; Rhodes James, *Anthony Eden*, p. 296; Christianson, *Headlines All My Life*, pp. 144–5, 241
3. Hollis, *Along the Road to Frome*, p. 185; Maudling, *Memoirs*, p. 38
4. Personal knowledge
5. Churchill, *Europe Unite*, p. 114
6. Churchill, *Europe Unite*, pp. 114, 88
7. Somervell, *Stanley Baldwin*, pp. 29–30; Boardman, *The Glory of Parliament*, p. 48
8. Carlton, *Anthony Eden*, p. 27
9. Schumpeter, *Capitalism, Socialism and Democracy*, p. 366
10. Clayton, *The Rise and Decline of Socialism in Great Britain 1884–1924*, p. VII
11. Snowden, *An Autobiography, II*, p. 647; Miliband, *Parliamentary Socialism*, p. 155

12. Templewood, *Nine Troubled Years*, p. 37; Macleod, *Neville Chamberlain*, pp. 161–2
13. Churchill, *Europe Unite*, p. 115
14. Addison, *The Road to 1945*, p. 33
15. Amery, *My Political Life III*, p. 29; Cross, *Philip Snowdon*, p. 66; Marquand, *Ramsay MacDonald*, pp. 484–7, 520–1, 537–8, 547–50
16. Miliband, p. 162; Foot, *Aneurin Bevan*, p. 138
17. Addison, *Churchill on the Home Front*, p. 304; Keynes, *Essays in Persuasion*, p. 161
18. Hayek, *The Road to Serfdom*, p. 9; Macmillan, *The Middle Way*, p. 198; Macleod, *Neville Chamberlain*, p. 146
19. Feiling, *The Life of Neville Chamberlain*, p. 229; Addison, *Churchill on the Home Front*, p. 306; Stewart, *Keynes and After*, p. 78
20. Addison, p. 308; Clarke, *Hope and Glory*, pp. 180–1; Timmins, *The Five Giants*, p. 29
21. Whiteside, *Bad Times*, pp. 80–5
22. Rhodes James, *Bob Boothby*, p. 87; Boothby, *The New Economy*, p. 157
23. Simon Haxey, *Tory MP*, pp. 25–6; Roberts, *Eminent Churchillians*, p. 145; HC July 1, 1942, c. 228
24. Carlton, *Anthony Eden*, pp. 45–8, 124; Dilks (ed.), *The Diaries of Sir Alexander Cadogan*, p. 415; Dutton, *Anthony Eden*, pp. 35, 47, 66–7, 81
25. Avon, *The Reckoning*, p. 445; Colville, *The Fringes of Power*, pp. 79, 74
26. Avon, *The Reckoning*, p. 21; Taylor, *The Origins of the Second World War*, p. 174; Strang, *Home and Abroad*, p. 147; Rhodes James, *Anthony Eden*, p. 208
27. J. Harvey (ed.), *The Diplomatic Diaries of Oliver Harvey 1937–1940*, p. 47; Ramsden, *That will Depend on who writes the history: Winston Churchill as his own historian*, pp. 18–19
28. Rhodes James, p. 187
29. Macleod, *Neville Chamberlain*, p. 212
30. Rhodes James, pp. 186–8; Charmley, *Chamberlain and the Lost Peace*, pp. 40–51
31. Rhodes James, p. 190
32. Feiling, *The Life of Neville Chamberlain*, p. 372
33. Macleod, pp. 255–6; Charmley, pp. 131–42
34. Rhodes James (ed.), pp. 213, 217; Churchill, *Into Battle*, pp. 42, 51
35. Howard, *RAB, The Life of R. A. Butler*, pp. 77–8; Feiling, *Neville Chamberlain*, p. 359; Colville, p. 84; Swinton, *Sixty Years of Power*, p. 120; Charmley, pp. 148, 155; Rhodes James (ed.), p. 220; Cowles, *Looking for Trouble*, pp. 180, 197
36. Eden, pp. 37–8
37. Lamb, *The Drift to War*, p. 283; Roberts, *The Holy Fox*, p. 141; HC 15 March 1939, col. 435–9, 460

38. Charmley, pp. 164–7; Rhodes James (ed.), p. 230; Malcolm Thompson, *Lloyd George*, p. 445
39. *HC*, 1 September 1939, col. 130; Watt, pp. 539–42, 567, 574–89; Charmley, pp. 207, 197–8; Roberts, pp. 171–4; Lamb, pp. 335–40
40. Watt, p. 601; *HC*, 3 September 1939, cols. 291–2
41. Boothby, *I Fight to Live*, p. 247
42. J. B. Morton, *A Bonfire of Weeds*, p. 40
43. Duff Cooper, *Old Men Forget*, pp. 255–6
44. Wheeler-Bennet, *John Anderson*, pp. 185–6, 271
45. Chisholm and Davie, *Beaverbrook*, pp. 370–3
46. Barnes and Nicolson (eds.), *Empire at Bay*, p. 777; Ramsden, p. 30
47. Eden, Diary, 12 July 1943, quoted in Charmley, *A History of Conservative Politics 1900–1996*, p. 110
48. Grigg, *Prejudice and Judgement*, p. 177
49. Booth, p. 156; Cripps and others, *Problems of a Socialist Government*, pp. 23, 39
50. Dalton, *The Fateful Years*, p. 42
51. Cripps and others, pp. 186, 204–5, 208
52. Watson, *Politics and Literature*, pp. 47–70; *Daily Herald*, 14 March 1937, in Swinton, *Sixty Years of Power*, p. 123
53. Addison, *The Road to 1945*, p. 126
54. Hennessy, *Never Again*, p. 50
55. Addison, *The Road to 1945*, p. 214
56. Bullock, *Ernest Bevin, II,* p. 225; Harris, *William Beveridge*, pp. 376, 421
57. Harris, p. 420
58. Addison, *The Road to 1945*, p. 168; Bullock, *II,* p. 228
59. Williams, *A Prime Minister Remembers*, p. 57
60. Churchill, *The Hinge of Fate*, p. 861
61. Moggridge, *Maynard Keynes*, pp. 706, 709; Barnett, *The Audit of War*, p. 47; Harris, pp. 429–35
62. Barnes and Nicholson (eds.), p. 848; Hailsham, *A Sparrow's Flight*, pp. 209–10; Timmins, p. 95; Middleman and Barnes, *Stanley Baldwin*, p. 435
63. Churchill, *Onwards to Victory*, pp. 33–45
64. Timmins, *The Five Giants*, pp. 92, 110, 111–2, 161
65. Moggridge, *Maynard Keynes*, p. 714
66. Churchill, *The Dawn of Liberation*, pp. 262–3
67. Addison, *The Road to 1945*, p. 182; Churchill, *Victory*, p. 195
68. Hayek, p. 134
69. Vierek, *Conservatism Revisited*, pp. 1, 114
70. Gilbert, *Never Despair*, p. 35
71. Craig (ed.), *British General Election Manifestos 1910–1974*, p. 127
72. Woolton, *Memoirs*, p. 335; Craig (ed.), p. 113; Churchill, *Victory*, pp. 202–3

73. McCallum and Readman, *The British General Election of 1945*, pp. 47–61; Craig (ed.), pp. 113–23
74. Avon, *The Reckoning*, p. 545; Churchill, *Victory*, pp. 188–9.
75. Boardman, *The Glory of Parliament*, p. 148
76. Mary Soames, *Clementine Churchill*, p. 382
77. Gilbert, *Never Despair*, p. 47
78. Soames, p. 388

Chapter II: 1945–51 'The Road to Serfdom'?

1. Rhodes James (ed.), *Chips*, p. 499; Chandos, *Memoirs*, p. 329; Rhodes James, *Boothby*, p. 333
2. Ehrman, *The Younger Pitt, III*, p. 109
3. Cairncross, *Years of Recovery*, p. 6
4. Hancock and Gowing, *British War Economy*, p. 546
5. Cairncross, pp. 7–8, 90
6. See Morgan, *The People's Peace*, p. 10
7. Cairncross, pp. 499–501, 18–23
8. Morgan, p. 22; Shinwell, *Conflict without Malice*, pp. 172–3, 176
9. Churchill, *Victory*, p. 237
10. Hennessy, *Never Again*, p. 200
11. Morgan, p. 29
12. Kelf-Cohen, *Nationalisation in Britain*, pp. 28–9
13. Mercer, in Jones and Kandah (eds.), *The Myth of Consensus*, p. 150
14. Hanson, *Parliament and Public Ownership*, p. 38
15. Cairncross, p. 354
16. Morgan, p. 69
17. Morgan, p. 86; Williams, *Hugh Gaitskell*, p. 157
18. M. Gilmar; Curson, p. 363; Clarke, p. 233
19. Stuart, *Within the Fringe*, pp. 145–7; Carlton, *Anthony Eden*, p. 267
20. *The Diaries of Evelyn Waugh*, pp. 629–30
21. Churchill, *Victory*, p. 238; Churchill, *The Sinews of Peace*, p. 53
22. Churchill, *Europe Unite*, pp. 26–7; Churchill, *The Sinews of Peace*, p. 59
23. Butler, *The Art of the Possible*, p. 135
24. Hoffman, *The Conservative Party in Opposition, 1945–51*, p. 140
25. Butler, p. 140
26. Butler, *The Art of the Possible*, pp. 145–9; Churchill, *Europe Unite*, p. 99; Maudling, *Memoirs*, pp. 45–6; Ramsden, *The Age of Churchill and Eden, 1940–1957*, pp. 150–8
27. Hogg, *The Case for Conservatism*, p. 51–3; *The Industrial Charter*, pp. 10, 3, 16
28. Thatcher, *The Path to Power*, p. 50; Rhodes James, *Anthony Eden*, pp. 325–6; Ramsden, *The Making of Conservative Party Policy*, p. 134
29. Churchill, *Europe Unite*, pp. 343–5

30. 8 June 1949, Carlton, p. 282
31. Macmillan, *Tides of Fortune*, p. 167
32. Cairncross, p. 18
33. Churchill, *Triumph and Tragedy*, p. 509
34. 2 April 1946, Gilbert, *Never Despair*, p. 515
35. Shinwell, *Conflict Without Malice*, pp. 185–6; Foot, *Aneurin Bevan 1945–1960*, pp. 58–9, 235–8; Ramsden, *The Age of Churchill and Eden, 1945–57*, p. 165
36. Churchill, *Triumph and Tragedy*, pp. 467–8; Ramsden, *Age*, pp. 49, 73
37. Ramsden, *Age*, p. 235
38. Harrison, *Trade Unions and the Labour Party since 1945*, p. 36
39. Cooper, *Old Men Forget*, pp. 138; Davies, p. 107; Hogg, *The Purpose of Parliament*, p. 38; Ramsden, *Age*, p. 13
40. Ramsden, *Age*, p. 133
41. Bullock, *Ernest Bevin, II*, p. 384
42. Somervell, *Stanley Baldwin*, pp. 42–3
43. Churchill, *Europe Unite*, p. 226
44. Churchill, *The Sinews of Peace*, pp. 93–105
45. Churchill, *Europe Unite*, p. 143
46. Gilbert, pp. 203–4, 212
47. Carlton, *Anthony Eden*, pp. 264–6; Dutton, p. 320
48. *Collier's Weekly*, 4 January 47; *Europe Unite*, p. 117
49. Rhodes James, p. 321
50. Macmillan, *Tides of Europe*, pp. 156–7; Kilmuir, *Political Adventure*, p. 177
51. Churchill, *The Hinge of Fate*, p. 504; Churchill, *The Sinews of Peace*, pp. 44, 171–5, 198–202
52. *Europe Unite*, pp. 77–85
53. *Europe Unite*, pp. 310–21
54. *Europe Unite*, pp. 316, 465; Churchill, *The Highroad of the Future*, in *Colliers Magazine*, 4 January 1947; HC, 26 June 1950, cols 2158, 2156; Sir Martin Gilbert in *The Times*, 7 October 1996
55. Ramsden, *The Age of Churchill and Eden, 1940–1957*, pp. 195–6
56. Rhodes James, *Anthony Eden*, pp. 320–1; Kilmuir, *Political Adventure*, p. 186; Young, *Britain and European Unity 1945–1922*, p. 7
57. Quoted in Macmillan, *Tides of Fortune*, p. 160; *Europe Unite*, p. 231; HC 27 June 1950, col 2144
58. Lamb, *The Failure of the Eden Government*, pp. 60–1; Acheson, *Present at the Creation*, p. 385; HC 26 June 1950, cols 1907–24, 2144, 2146, 2148, 2152
59. Shepherd: *Iain Macleod*, pp. 57, 554; *Daily Mirror* August 6, 1957
60. Craig (ed.), *British General Election Manifestos 1900–1974*, pp. 142, 144, 152; Nicholas, *The British General Election of 1950*, pp. 118–9
61. Ramsden, *Age*, pp. 212–4
62. D. Butler, *The British General Election of 1951*, pp. 13–4

63. One Nation; Shepherd, *Iain Macleod*, pp. 61–6; Shepherd, *Enoch Powell*, pp. 83–7
64. Dalton, *High Tide and After*, p. 358
65. Butler, *The Art of the Possible*, p. 155; Ramsden, *Making*, p. 159; Timmins, pp. 192–3
66. Shuckburgh, *Descent to Suez*, p. 17
67. Addison, *Churchill on the Home Front*, pp. 197, 209–10; Carlton, p. 292
68. Butler, *The British General Election of 1951*, pp. 270–2
69. Macmillan, *III*, p. 306
70. Ramsden, *Age*, p. 184
71. Carlton, *Eden*, p. 292–3
72. Roberts, *Eminent Churchillians*, pp. 253–4; Charmley, *A History of Conservative Politics*, p. 126
73. Ramsden, pp. 67–9
74. Rhodes James, *Anthony Eden*, p. 310
75. Jones and Kandiah (eds.), pp. 139, 147, 153; Benn, *Arguments for Democracy*, pp. 212–3; Charmley, pp. 135–7
76. Ramsden, *Making*, pp. 133–4
77. Carlton, pp. 293–5
78. Davies, p. 305
79. Disraeli, *Sybil*, Bk II, Ch. 5
80. Ramsden: Making pp. 91–2, 138
81. Butler, *The Art of the Possible*, p. 61
82. Whitfield, *Machiavelli*, p. 7
83. Shepherd, *Iain Macleod*, p. 39
84. Addison, *Churchill on the Home Front*, p. 383
85. Macmillan: Tides of Fortune, pp. 59, 64
86. Miliband, *The State in Capitalist Society*, p. 101
87. D. Butler, *The British General Election of 1951*, p. 60

Chapter III: Conservatism in One Nation
1. Moran, *Churchill, The Fight For Survival*, p. 348
2. Soames, *Clementine Churchill*, pp. 429, 448; Colville, p. 632
3. Nicolson, *Diaries and Letters 1945–62*, p. 212
4. Moran, pp. 349–54; Gilbert, pp. 633–4
5. cf. Medlicott, *Contemporary England 1914–1964*, p. 522
6. Moran, p. 344; Hennessy and Seldon (eds), p. 68
7. Anderson, *The Machinery of Government*, pp. 3–4
8. Daalder, *Cabinet Reform in Britain 1914–1963*, pp. 110–20; Hennessy and Seldon (eds), p. 69
9. Seldon, *Churchill's Indian Summer*, pp. 154–6; Chandos, *Memoirs*, pp. 342–4; Butler, *The Art of the Possible*, p. 156
10. Maudling in the *Spectator*: 13 May 1955; cf. Williams, *Hugh Gaitskell*, p. 188
11. R. Butler, pp. 156–7

12. Morgan, p. 113
13. Cairncross, *Years of Recovery*, pp. 237, 244–5, 270; MacDougall, *Don and Mandarin*, pp. 85–6, 90–1; Seldon, pp. 171–2
14. MacDougall, pp. 90–3; Cairncross; pp. 248, 269–70; Brittan, *Steering the Economy*, pp. 199–200
15. Cairncross, pp. 247, 251–3, 259–60, 269; MacDougall, pp. 91–4; Macmillan, *Tides of Fortune*, p. 382
16. MacDougall, pp. 89–90; Seldon, pp. 172–3; Cairncross, pp. 249–50; Howard, p. 187; Shuckburgh, *Descent to Suez*, pp. 36–8
17. Morgan, pp. 120–2; Dutton, *Anthony Eden*, 267; MacDougall, pp. 98–9; Birkenhead, *The Prof in Two Worlds*, p. 289
18. Addison, *Churchill on the Home Front*, pp. 397, 412; MacDougall, p. 91; Cairncross, p. 270
19. MacDougall, pp. 90–6; Birkenhead, *The Prof in Two Worlds*, p. 285; Colville, p. 644
20. Cairncross, pp. 254–5; MacDougall, pp. 90–1; Howard, p. 191
21. Hennessy, p. 425
22. Macmillan, *The Tides of Fortune*, p. 217
23. Gilbert, pp. 633–4; *HC* 6 December 1951, col. 2595; Young, *Britain and European Unity*, 1945–1992, p. 36; Nutting, *Europe will not Wait*, p. 37; *HC*, 12 February 1951, col. 48–50
24. Kilmuir, *Political Adventure*, pp. 185–7; Nutting, pp. 40–1
25. *HC*, 6 December 1951, cols. 2591–6, 2601–2, 2611; Foot, *Aneurin Bevan* 1945–1960, pp. 352–3
26. Dutton, *Anthony Eden*, p. 292; Churchill, *Europe Unite*, pp. 77–85
27. *HC*, 26 June 1950, col. 2052
28. Carlton, *Anthony Eden*, pp. 310–1
29. Lamb, *The Failure of the Eden Government*, pp. 63–5; Macmillan, *III*, pp. 468–72; Horne, *Macmillan, 1894–1956*, pp. 345–5; Kilmuir, *Political Adventure*, pp. 187–9
30. Macmillan, *III*, pp. 506–7; Moran, p. 354; Horne, p. 350; Carlton, pp. 313–4
31. Macmillan, *III*, p. 506; Seldon, pp. 413–4; Young, pp. 38–9, Dutton, pp. 295–9, 302, 311–3; Churchill, *Europe Unite*, pp. 310–21; Monnet, quoted in Denman, *Missed Chances*, pp. 185, 187
32. Gilbert, *Churchill, VII, The Road to Victory, 1941–1945*, pp. 1274, 1278
33. Nutting, p. 105
34. Dutton, p. 314; Rhodes James, pp. 352–3
35. Carlton, pp. 290–1; Shuckburgh, *Descent to Suez, Diaries 1951–56*, p. 32
36. Acheson, *Present at the Creation*, p. 597; Dutton, p. 330
37. Eisenhower, *Mandate for Change*, pp. 632, 198; Dutton, p. 335–6; Renwick, *Fighting with Allies*, p. 130; *The Times*, 7 October 1996; Hennessy, pp. 342–3

38. Rhodes James, p. 352; Shuckburgh, p. 27; Colville, p. 700; Maitland, *Diverse Times, Sundry Places*, p. 106
39. Deane, *The Evolution of Economic Ideas*, p. 187
40. Seldon, p. 559
41. *The Economist*, 13 February 1954; Howard, p. 203
42. Butler, p. 160; Howard, pp. 203–4; Williams, *Hugh Gaitskell*, p. 213; *The Economist*, 31 December 95; Seldon, pp. 561–2
43. *HC* 13 November 1951, col. 929; Shepherd, *Iain Macleod*, pp. 72–8; Fisher, *Iain Macleod*, pp. 80–6
44. Shepherd, pp. 93–4
45. Seldon, pp. 272–7
46. Macmillan, *III*, pp. 363–6; Horne, *Macmillan, 1894–1956*, pp. 332–3
47. Addison in Hennessy and Seldon (eds), p. 23
48. The *Spectator* 7 January and 4 February 1955; Gilmour, *Inside Right*, p. 134
49. Hennessy, pp. 440–3; Morgan, p. 90
50. Addison, *Churchill on the Home Front*, p. 416; Roberts, *Eminent Churchillians*, pp. 219–22
51. Addison, p. 416; *Spectator*, 4 March 1955
52. *HC*, 3 November 1953; Seldon, p. 187
53. Birkenhead, *The Prof in Two Worlds*, pp. 309–15
54. Moran, pp. 388–90; Seldon, p. 143–5
55. Butler, *The British General Election of 1951*, pp. 106–8; Macmillan, p. 363
56. Birkenhead, *Walter Monckton*, p. 276
57. Wigham, *Strikes and the Government 1895–1974*, p. 108
58. Roberts in *Eminent Churchillians*
59. *Spectator* 6 May 1955
60. Addison, *Churchill on the Home Front*, p. 413
61. Woolton, p. 380, Macmillan, p. 490
62. Roberts, pp. 253–4; Charmley, p. 160
63. Gilbert, *Never Despair 1945–1965*, p. 656; Wigham, p. 112
64. Wigham, *What's Wrong with the Unions?* p. 14; Wybrow, p. 160; D. Butler, *The General Election of 1955*, p. 163
65. Shepherd, p. 113; personal knowledge
66. Howard, p. 203; R. Butler, *The Art of the Possible*, p. 163
67. R. Butler, p. 173
68. Brittan, *The Treasury under The Tories, 1951–64*, p. 167; Howard, p. 190
69. Howard, p. 204; Ramsden, *Age*, p. 249
70. Soames, pp. 448–53; Moran, pp. 425–6; Seldon, pp. 419–21; Rhodes James, p. 392
71. Colville, p. 708; Sir Desmond Morton to I.G. March 1958

Chapter IV: Prelude to Suez

1. Margach, *The Abuse of Power*, pp. 105–6; Macmillan, p. 583; Pimlott (ed.), *The Political Diary of Hugh Dalton 1918–40, 1945–60*, pp. 657–8; Howard, *RAB*, pp. 107–8; Boyd-Carpenter, *Way of Life*, p. 123

2. Wybrow, *Britain Speaks Out, 1937–87*, pp. 7, 11, 20, 41, 43; Margach, p. 101; R. Churchill, *The Rise and Fall of Anthony Eden*, p. 197

3. Clark, *From Three Worlds*, p. 161; Margach, p. 101; Howard, p. 215

4. Rhodes James, p. 392; Howard, p. 215; private information; *Spectator* p. 461, 15 April 1955; D. Butler, pp. 185, 180; Ramsden, p. 287

5. Lamb, *The Failure of the Eden Government*, pp. 4–9; Pimlott (ed.), p. 659; Ramsden, p. 275

6. R. Butler, pp. 177–9; Robert Neild, in Gold (ed.), *Edward Boyle*, pp. 85–6; Brittan, *Steering the Economy*, pp. 200–2; *The Economist* 23 April 1955

7. D. Butler, *The British General Election of 1955*, p. 17; Craig (ed.), *British General Election Manifestos 1900–1974*, pp. 183, 189, 205; *Spectator*, p. 489, 22 April 1955, and pp. 524–5, 29 April 1955

8. Moran, p. 655; D. Butler, pp. 61, 77, 157; Ramsden, *The Making*, p. 176

9. Rhodes James, pp. 407–8; Ramsden, pp. 278–9; Carlton, p. 374; *HC*, 8 June 1955 cols 14–6; *Spectator*, p. 760, 17 June 1955; Moran, p. 667

10. Churchill, *Their Finest Hour*, p. 14; Dutton, pp. 126–7, 135; Nicolson (ed.), *Diaries and Letters, 1930–39*, p. 406

11. *Spectator*, p. 422, 8 April 1955; Ramsden, pp. 241, 265; D. Butler, p. 13

12. Avon, *Full Circle*, pp. 283–6; Wigham, *Strikes and the Government 1893–1914*, pp. 111–12

13. Lamb, pp. 24–8; Rhodes James, pp. 415–6; Dutton, pp. 270–1; *Spectator*, p. 785, 24 June 1955; Harry Douglas in the *Spectator*, pp. 480–1, 13 April 1956

14. Gilbert, p. 1142; Howard, pp. 215–6; Shepherd, *Enoch Powell*, pp. 109–10, 129–30; D. Butler, pp. 41–2

15. Shepherd, *Iain Macleod*, p. 101; Boyd Carpenter, pp. 123–5; Rhodes James, p. 411; Shuckburgh, *Descent to Suez*, pp. 277, 315; Dutton, p. 90

16. Clark, pp. 148–9; *Spectator*, pp. 408–9, 30 September 1955; pp. 436–7, 7 October 1955, pp. 481–2, 14 October 1955

17. R. Butler, pp. 179–81; Lamb, pp. 40–4; Williams, *Hugh Gaitskell*, p. 232; Brittan, pp. 198–203

18. Dutton, p. 278; Howard, p. 216; Lamb pp. 45–51; Williams, p. 233; Macmillan, *III*, pp. 688–9

19. Ramsden, p. 229; *Spectator*, p. 320, 2 September 1955

20. *HC* 29 July 1954, col. 756; Shuckburgh, pp. 75–6; Ramsden, pp. 263–5; Maudling, p. 65

21. Maitland, *Diverse Times, Sundry Places*, p. 59; Dutton, p. 480

22. Renwick, *Fighting with Allies*, pp. 143, 141

23. Kyle, pp. 56–7; Carlton, p. 365, 380–1

24. Trevelyan, *The Middle East in Revolution*, pp. 59–60; Dutton, pp. 372–3; Personal knowledge; Love, *Suez, The Twice-Fought War*, p. 250

25. Burns, *Between Arab and Israeli*, pp. 44; Rokach, *Israel's Sacred Terrorism*, p. 42; Nef, *Warriors at Suez*, p. 103; Dutton, p. 369

26. Burns, p. 63–4; Trevelyan, pp. 40–2; Nef, pp. 112–4, 176; Dalton, p. 370; Avon, *Full Circle*, p. 330; Macmillan, *III*, p. 652

27. Nef, p. 177; Love, p. 114; Carlton, p. 393; Trevelyan, pp. 56–8

28. Carlton, p. 393; Dutton, pp. 368–71

29. Nutting, p. 74; Denman, *Missed Chances*, p. 194

30. Lamb, p. 62; Denman, p. 196

31. Macmillan, *Riding the Storm*, p. 69; Lamb, pp. 68–70

32. Horne, *I*, pp. 363–4; Grant, *Delors*, pp. 62, 287; Denman, pp. 198–9

33. Young, *Britain and European Unity, 1945–1992*, pp. 45–9; Lamb, pp. 79–84

34. Barzini, *The Impossible Europeans*, p. 57; Denman, p. 199

35. Shuckburgh, p. 309; Macmillan, *III*, pp. 688–98; Eisenhower, *Mandate for Change*, p. 186; Rhodes James, p. 359

36. Macmillan, *III*, pp. 687, 693–4; Howard, p. 221; Ramsden, p. 288; Horne, *I*, pp. 373–6

37. Clark, *From Three Worlds*, pp. 152–4; Howard, pp. 222–3; Hailsham, *The Door Wherein I Went*, p. 128

38. Shuckburgh, p. 309; Shepherd, *Enoch Powell*, p. 125

39. Shuckburgh, p. 309; *Spectator*, p. 143. 3 January 1956

40. Margach, p. 106; Shuckburgh pp. 9, 42; Lamb, pp. 12–3; Rhodes James, p. 425; Clark, p. 155

41. Howard, p. 222; Lamb p. 13; Timmins, pp. 199, 537; Rhodes James, pp. 425–6; *Spectator*, pp. 35–6, 13 January 1956

42. Shuckburgh, pp. 324, 337; Nutting, pp. 86–9

43. Shuckburgh, *Descent to Suez, Diaries 1951–56*, pp. 327–32; Dutton, p. 307

44. Horne, *I*, pp. 379–80

45. Macmillan, *Riding the Storm*, pp. 6–15; Lamb, pp. 53–4

46. *Spectator*, p. 196, 10 February 1956; p. 239, 24 February 1956; Macmillan, *IV*, pp. 14–7

47. Lamb, pp. 55–8; Horne, *I*, pp. 381–4; *Spectator*, p. 741, 25 May 1956; pp. 515–6; 20 April 1956

48. Christopherson, *Capital Punishment and British Politics*, pp. 98–107, 126–38; *Spectator*, p. 236, 24 February 1956

49. Trevelyan, pp. 63–6; Love, p. 211; Nutting, pp. 28–32; Shuckburgh, pp. 340–1
50. Kyle, pp. 93–6; Nutting, pp. 32–3; Shuckburgh, pp. 343–5, Nicolson, *People and Parliament*, p. 115
51. Mitchell and Boehm, *British Parliamentary Election Results 1950–1964*, pp. 60, 123; Ramsden, *Age*, pp. 295–6; Wybrow, p. 45; Margach, p. 107
52. Clark, pp. 156, 161–2

Chapter V: The Temptation of Sir Anthony
1. Kyle, *Suez*, pp. 128–34; Nef, *Warriors at Suez*, pp. 261–3
2. Moggridge, *Keynes*, pp. 881–2; Kyle, p. 156; *Spectator*, 10 August 1956
3. Kyle, *Suez*, p. 155
4. Shepherds, *Enoch Powell*, pp. 118–22, 145–6
5. Nutting, *No End of a Lesson*, p. 47; Clark, p. 167, 170; Kyle, pp. 138–9; Nef, pp. 275–6, 291
6. Kyle, pp. 139–41
7. Clark, p. 170
8. Kyle, pp. 139, 168; Nef, pp. 285–6, 296–7
9. Moran p. 702; Avon, *Full Circle*, p. 440; Williams, *Hugh Gaitskell*, p. 280; Benn, *Years of Hope*, pp. 203–4
10. Williams, pp. 279–81; Moran, p. 150
11. Epstein, *British Politics in the Suez Crisis*, pp. 142–7, 202; Nef, p. 376
12. Ramsden, pp. 307–9; Nicolson, *People and Parliament*, pp. 116–7; Epstein, pp. 87, 97; Macmillan, *Riding the Storm*, p. 228
13. Thorpe, *Alec Douglas-Home*, p. 180–1; Nef, p. 315; Kyle, pp. 215–6, 234, 335, 203–4, 199
14. Kyle, p. 288
15. Gopal, *Jawaharlah Nehru*, pp. 273–8; Kyle, pp. 131, 55, 556
16. Avon, *Full Circle*, pp. 92–109, 114
17. Ghopal, p. 274; Cadogan Diaries, p. 462
18. Avon, pp. 134–8, 566; Dutton, pp. 373, 541, 394–5; Andrew, *Secret Service*, p. 495; Wright, *Spycatcher*, pp. 84–5, 160–1; Nef, pp. 41–2; Kyle, pp. 150–1; Urquhart, *Hammarskjold*, pp. 121–2
19. Avon, p. 71; Dutton, p. 389
20. Nef, p. 372; Kyle, pp. 249–50
21. Nutting, p. 93; Kyle, pp. 62–6; Rokach, *Israel's Sacred Terrorism, A Study based on Moshe Sharett's Personal Diary*, pp. 42–4
22. Horne, *Macmillan*, I, pp. 400–5; Nutting, pp. 47–8, 93–4
23. Nutting, pp. 95–6; Kyle, pp. 301, 601
24. Kyle, pp. 314–21, 327–31; Nef, pp. 342–8; Logan in *LRB*, 25 July 1991
25. Kyle, pp. 353–5; Rhodes James, pp. 532–6
26. Trevelyan, *The Middle East in Revolution*, p. 127; Kyle, pp. 396–7

27. Boardman, *The Glory of Parliament*, pp. 161–2; Trevelyan, p. 105; Clark, p. 200
28. Nef, p. 366; Kyle, pp. 401–3
29. Kyle, pp. 411–2, 464–5, 471–2; Horne, *I*, pp. 436–7, 440–3
30. Nef, p. 375; Shepherd, *Powell*, p. 148
31. Thomas, *The Suez Affair*, p. 9; Nutting, pp. 105–7, 122–3, 162; Gold (ed.), *Edward Boyle*, pp. 69–71; Dutton, p. 435
32. Shuckburgh, pp. 326–7; Nef, p. 154
33. Nutting, p. 50; Nef, p. 284
34. Hailsham, *A Sparrow's Flight*, pp. 285–90; Kyle, p. 341; BBC1, 22 October 1996; Shuckburgh, p. 362
35. Dutton, pp. 422–3; Shuckburgh, p. 365
36. Nicolson (ed.), *Harold Nicolson Diaries and Letters 1945–1962*, p. 313
37. Kyle, pp. 256–8; Horne, pp. 400–6, 418–24, 439–45; Dutton, pp. 408, 411, 439–42; Lloyd, *Suez 1956*, pp. 210–1
38. Thorpe, *Alec Douglas-Home*, p. 182
39. Kyle, p. 205
40. Alistair Forbes in the *Spectator*, 14 December 1996
41. Avon, *Full Circle*; Macmillan, *Riding the Storm*; Lloyd, *Suez 1956*, pp. 246–50
42. Kyle, pp. 426, 495; Foot and Jones, *Guilty 1957*
43. Thomas, p. 167
44. Carlton, pp. 454–6, 463; Dutton, pp. 420–1
45. Epstein, p. 142; Nicolson (ed.), pp. 315, 324; Clark, p. 210
46. Rhodes James, p. 597; Dutton, p. 423; Clark, p. 202; Shuckburgh, p. 365
47. *Spectator*, 7 December 1956; Scott Lucas, *Suez, the Americans, and the Overthrow of Anthony Eden*, p. 239; Lamb, p. 240
48. Personal knowledge; Nef, pp. 425–7
49. Lloyd, *Suez, 1956*, pp. 232–4; *HC* 3 December 1956, col. 884; 5 December 1956, cols. 1254–68
50. Lamb, pp. 292, 297–8; Ramsden, pp. 320–1; Rhodes James, pp. 589–91
51. Personal knowledge; *Spectator*, 21 December 1956
52. Kyle, pp. 517–8; Thomas, pp. 224–6; *HC*, 20 December 1956, col. 1518
53. Dutton, pp. 59, 3

Chapter VI: The Actor Manager

1. Macmillan, *Riding the Storm*, pp. 185, 182; Howard, p. 246
2. R. A. Butler, p. 194; Lloyd, p. 232; Horne, *I*, p. 447
3. Howard, p. 238; Kyle, pp. 507–8
4. Howard, pp. 239–41; Horne, *I*, pp. 454–6; Butler, *The Art of Memory*, p. 101; Rhodes James, pp. 599–600; Thorpe, *Alec Douglas-Home*, p. 188

5. Macmillan, pp. 202–3, 185–6; Cairncross (ed.), *The Robert Hall Diaries 1954–61*, p. 95; R. Butler, p. 196; Howard, pp. 249–50

6. *Spectator*, 25 January 1957; Macmillan, p. 196

7. Renwick, p. 161; Kyle, pp. 275, 467; Macmillan, p. 196

8. Renwick, p. 275

9. Young, pp. 50–1; Horne, *I*, p. 386; Renwick, p. 279; Lamb, p. 100

10. Dutton, pp. 309–10, Lloyd, p. 236

11. Horne, *II*, pp. 26, 33; Eisenhower, *The White House Years*, p. 123

12. Personal knowledge; Hailsham, *The Door Wherein I Went*, p. 149; Shepherd, *Powell*, p. 155

13. *Spectator*, 4 January 1957

14. Macmillan, p. 228; Horne, *II*, p. 38

15. Macmillan, pp. 228–30; Horne, *II*, pp. 37–9

16. Macmillan, pp. 209–10, 234–8; Horne, *II*, pp. 39–40

17. Clark, p. 207; Blake, p. 279

18. *Spectator*, 9 September 1958, 7 September 1956; Shepherd, *Iain Macleod*, pp. 112, 122–3

19. Shepherd, pp. 112, 122–7; Macmillan, p. 346; Middlemas: Politics in Industrial Society, p. 400; Cairncross (ed.), p. 158

20. *HC*, 9 April 1957, col. 982

21. Private information from Sir Frank Lee, (October 1961), Nigel Birch (October 1961) and Nicholas Davenport (June 1961); Cairncross (ed.), *The Robert Hall Diaries 1954–61*, pp. 121–2, 143–4

22. Maude and Powell, *Biography of a Nation* (1955)

23. Shepherd, *Powell*, pp. 129–30; Cairncross (ed.), pp. 144

24. Howard, p. 240; Cairncross (ed.), pp. 124, 144

25. Macmillan, pp. 350–1; Ramsden, *The Winds of Change*, p. 32

26. Rollings in Jones and Kandash (eds), p. 107

27. Brittan, *Steering the Economy*, pp. 209–10; *HC*, 25 July 1957, col. 643

28. Utley, *Enoch Powell*, p. 74; Shepherd, *Macleod*, p. 132; Shepherd, *Powell*, pp. 163–4

29. Macmillan, pp. 356–7; Brittan, pp. 216–7; Cairncross (ed.), pp. 126–7

30. Middlemas, *Power, Competition and the State, I*, p. 292; Cairncross (ed.), pp. ix, 121, 125; Brittan, pp. 212–7; Shepherd, pp. 169–72; *Spectator*, p, 410, 27 September 1957

31. Cmnd. 350, pp. 38, 29, 12.5; Pimlott, *Harold Wilson*, pp. 215–7; Macmillan, pp. 421–30; Horne, *II*, p. 67

32. Shepherd, pp. 172–7; Macmillan, pp. 364–5; Cairncross (ed.), p. 136; Boyd-Carpenter, pp. 137–9; Lamb, pp. 49–50

33. Shepherd, pp. 176–7; Macmillan, pp. 369–9

34. Boyd-Carpenter, p. 139; Dell, pp. 238–9; Horne, *II*, p. 73; Macmillan, p. 370

35. Middlemas, *II*, p. 294; Horne, *II*, pp. 73–4; Macmillan, p. 369; Shepherd, pp. 178–9

36. Shepherd, *Enoch Powell*, p. 129; Morgan, p. 174; Horne, *II*, pp. 75–8; Dell, *The Chancellors*, p. 223–41 'Chancellor Betrayed')
37. Utley, *Enoch Powell*, p. 72
38. Ibid, p. 72
39. Horne, *II*, p. 77
40. *HC*, 23 January 1958, cols. 1294–7
41. Shepherd, *Macleod*, pp. 134–6; Cairncross (ed.), p. 146
42. Feather to I.G., April 1962; Shepherd, *Macleod*, pp. 132–41; Wigham, pp. 118–23
43. Horne, *II*, pp. 78–9; Shepherd, pp. 138–9; Macmillan,, 713
44. Williams, pp. 299–300; Macmillan, p. 719; Hailsham, *The Door Wherein I Went*, p. 155
45. Hailsham, pp. 159–62; Walters, *Not Always with the Pack*, pp. 89–91; Ramsden, p. 48
46. Wybrow, p. 53; Horne, *II*, p. 88; Ramsden, pp. 36–7
47. Shepherd, *Macleod*, pp. 146–7; Ramsden, p. 37; personal knowledge
48. The *Spectator*, p. 480, 11 April 1997; Middlemas, *II*, 295; Horne, *II*, p. 141; Wybrow, p. 54
49. Butler and King, *The British General Election of 1959*, pp. 29, 31; private information
50. Macmillan, *IV*, pp. 505–11; Lamb, pp. 34–43
51. Macmillan, *IV*, p. 511
52. *HC*, 17 July 1958, col. 1560
53. Middlemas, *I*, pp. 231–2; Wigham, p. 126; *Spectator*, pp. 759–60, 13 June 1958; Feather to I.G., April 1962
54. I. G.'s Election address, central Norfolk, October 1962
55. Shepherd, *Macleod*, pp. 148, 145
56. Shepherd, pp. 145–6
57. Butler and King, pp. 14, 10, 32–3
58. Cairncross (ed.), 172, 178–9, 192, 194, 196; Brittan, pp. 220–6
59. Fisher, *Iain Macleod*, p. 134
60. Rhodes James, p. 608; Horne, *II*, pp. 146–8; Butler and King, p. 41
61. Hailsham, *The Door Wherein I Went*, p. 157; Williams, *Hugh Gaitskell*, pp. 309–13; Pimlott, *Harold Wilson*, pp. 222–3
62. Kandiah in Jones and Kandiah (eds.), p. 67
63. Hailsham: A Sparrow's Flight, p. 324; private information
64. Wybrow, p. 154; Boyd-Carpenter, p. 151
65. Personal knowledge
66. *Daily Mirror*, 25 July 1955

Chapter VII: Seeking a Rôle

1. Horne, *II*, p. 429; Macmillan, *VI*, p. 339; *Spectator*, p. 922, 14 December 1962
2. Horne, *II*, p. 181; *Spectator*, pp. 184–5, 14 August 1959
3. Bernard Levin in the *Spectator*, pp. 155–6, 7 August 1959; Lamb, pp. 237, 242

4. Macmillan, *IV*, pp. 733–8; Horne, *II*, p. 174
5. Private information; *HC*, 27 July 1959, cols. 193, 232–7; Levin in the *Spectator*, p. 156, 7 August 1959
6. Jones and Kandiah (eds), pp. 164–6; Shepherd, *Macleod*, p. 159
7. Shepherd, p. 151; Rhodes James, p. 344
8. Macmillan, *Pointing the Way*, p. 156; Shepherd, pp. 151, 225–6; the *Spectator*, p. 127, 31.1.1964
9. Jones and Kandiah (eds), p. 172; Thorpe, pp. 170, 197–9; Horne, *II*, pp. 396–7; Macleod to I.G. January 1961; Macmillan, *VI*, p. 318; Blake, p. 285
10. Denman, pp. 203–6; Maudling, pp. 67–73; Young, pp. 57–77
11. Young, p. 69
12. Macmillan, *V*, p. 213; Middlemas, *II*, p. 33; Young, p. 71
13. Denman, p. 208; Morris, *May–August 1960*, pp. 547–8; Dutton, *Anticipating Maastricht*, pp. 522–3; Soames to I.G., 17 October 1961
14. Horne, *II*, p. 258; Ball, *The Discipline of Power*, pp. 80–1; Cairncross (ed.), p. 265
15. *HC*, 31 July 1961, col. 929; Denman, pp. 215, 225
16. Ball, p. 83; Dutton, *Anticipating Maastricht*, pp. 534, 540
17. Young, p. 77; Howard, p. 296; Soames to I.G., 17 October 1961; Dutton, pp. 527–8
18. Lamb, pp. 433–42; Morgan, p. 227
19. M. Butler, *August and Rab*, p. 69; Lamb, p. 409; *Spectator*, p. 356, 23 March 1962
20. R. Butler, pp. 195–204; M. Butler, pp. 69–70; Howard, pp. 252–6, 263; Thatcher, *The Path to Power*, pp. 116–7
21. Butler, pp. 202–5; Howard, pp. 265–7
22. Shepherd, *Powell*, pp. 191–2, 199–200
23. Butler, pp. 205–7; Shepherd, *Macleod*, pp. 267–70; Williams, *Gaitskell*, pp. 385–6; Lamb, pp. 410–21
24. Lamb, p. 57; Cairncross (ed.), pp. 198–9, 207, 221–2, 231–7, 262; Horne, *II*, pp. 237–40
25. Horne, *II*, p. 240
26. Cairncross (ed.), p. 244
27. Cairncross (ed.), pp. 254, 260; Middlemas, *II*, pp. 36–7, 401, 410–1
28. Macmillan, *Pointing the Way*, pp. 360, 375
29. Cairncross (ed.), p. 244, 261; Brittan, pp. 257–9; Horne, *II*, pp. 247; Lee to I.G. 9 October 1961
30. Macmillan, p. 376; Brittan, pp. 253–7
31. MacDougall, *Don and Mandarin*, pp. 137–8
32. Gilmour, *Britain Can Work*, p. 11
33. Leruez, *Economic Planning and Politics in Britain*, pp. 95–9; Hennessy, *Whitehall*, p. 177
34. Thatcher, *The Path to Power*, p. 115; Tebbit, *Upwardly Mobile*, p. 74
35. Disraeli, *Vindication of the English Constitution*, p. 188
36. Whiteley, Seyd and Richardson, *True Blues*, p. 228

37. Hailsham, *The Door Wherein I Went*, pp. 151–2
38. Wybrow, pp. 62, 159; Butler and King, *The British General Election of 1964*, pp. 14–5
39. Personal knowledge; private information
40. Macmillan, *At the End of the Day*, p. 58; Shepherd, pp. 273–5
41. Macmillan, *VI*, p. 60
42. Shepherd, *Macleod*, p. 276
43. Timmins, *The Five Giants*, pp. 208–13; Shepherd, *Powell*, pp. 211–23
44. Shepherd, *Macleod*, p. 278
45. Horne, *II*, pp. 341–2; Howard, p. 291
46. Kilmuir, pp. 323–4; R. Butler, pp. 233–4; Horne, *II*, pp. 344–7
47. Shepherd, *Macleod*, pp. 129, 148–9, 253–5
48. Shepherd, pp. 294–5
49. Maudling, pp. 102–5; Brittan, pp. 273–5
50. Macmillan, p. 220; Thorpe, *Alec Douglas-Home*, pp. 239–40, 249; Lamb, p. 356; Renwick, p. 182
51. Brittan, p. 273–5, 280–2; Macmillan, *VI*, p. 349; Hailsham, *A Sparrow's Flight*, pp. 352–3; private information
52. Williams, pp. 406–10
53. Macmillan, *VI*, p. 140; Ramsden, p. 171
54. Prem. 11/3775. 23 August 1964; Macmillan, *VI*, pp. 348–55; Lamb, pp. 189–92
55. Schlesinger, *A Thousand Days*, p. 723; Lamb, pp. 297–8, 302–3; Macmillan, *VI*, p. 476.
56. Lamb, p. 303; Renwick, pp. 185–7; Thorpe, p. 251
57. Butt, *The Power of Parliament*, pp. 243–5; Lamb, pp. 310–9; Ball, pp. 106–7
58. Benn, *Out of the Wilderness*, pp. 6–7; personal knowledge; Butler and King, *The British General Election of 1964*, p. 79
59. Carrington, *Reflect On Things Past*, pp. 172–3; Margach, *The Abuse of Power*, pp. 122–3
60. Wright, *Spy Catcher*, pp. 193–4; *Spectator*, pp. 515, 518–20 16 April 1965; Margach, p. 123; *HC*, 7 March 1973, cols. 270–1
61. Lamb, p. 458
62. *HC*, 21 March 1963, cols. 720–42; Lord Denning's Report, Cmnd. 2152, pp. 54–5; Lamb, pp. 460–4; Howard, pp. 298–9; Morgan (ed.), *The Backbench Diaries of Richard Crossman*, pp. 989–93; personal knowledge
63. Pimlott, p. 290
64. *HC*, 17 June 1963, cols, 34–77, 99
65. The *Spectator*, pp. 8–9, 5 July 1965
66. Personal knowledge; Macmillan, pp. 405–6; Horne, *II*, p. 484; Wybrow, p. 67; R. Butler, p. 236; Horne, *II*, p. 532; Howard, p. 300.
67. Lord Denning's Report, pp. 1, 104–14; Macmillan, *VI*, pp. 443–4, 447

68. Denning, p. 101; personal knowledge; *Spectator*, p. 72, 19 July 1963; R. Butler, p. 236; Macmillan, pp. 446–50, 487

69. Sir H. Trevelyan to I.G. 14 October 1963; Schlesinger, p. 775; Horne, *II*, pp. 521–2; Macmillan, *VI*, p. 486; Renwick, pp. 190–1

70. Horne, *II*, pp. 539, 531; Macmillan, *VI*, p. 496

71. Horne, *II*, pp. 533–40; Thorpe, pp. 272–4; Macmillan, pp. 489–501

Chapter VIII: The War of the Macmillan Succession

1. R. Butler, p. 242; Ramsden, pp. 196, 198

2. Gilmour, *The Body Politic*, p. 77

3. Thorpe, pp. 260–1; Walters, *Not Always with the Pack*, p. 110; private information; Hailsham, *The Door Wherein I Went*, p. 221; Hailsham, *A Sparrow's Flight*, pp. 349–50 where he wrongly dates his meeting with Macmillan; see chapter seven

4. Walters, p. 111; Lord Fanshawe's discussion with Lord Margadale (formerly John Morrison) 5 July 1989

5. Private information; Goodhart, p. 191; Lord Fanshawe's discussion; Walters, p. 126

6. Howard, p. 290; Walters, p. 111; Goodhart, p. 191

7. Thorpe, pp. 273, 523; Howard, p. 302; Goodhart, p. 191; R. Churchill, *The Fight for the Tory Leadership*, pp. 81–2

8. Ramsden, p. 194; Churchill, p. 82; Prior, p. 33; Lord Fanshawe's discussion

9. Horne, *II*, p. 541; Maudling, p. 126; Shepherd, *Powell*, pp. 255–6; Home, *The Way the Wind Blows*, p. 181, Thorpe, pp. 277, 289

10. I.G.'s unpublished diary of the leadership struggle; G. Lewis: Lord Hailsham (forthcoming); Thorpe, pp. 276–9

11. Howard, p. 310; Notes of Sir John Richardson quoted in Lewis; Shepherd, *Powell*, pp. 255–6

12. Macmillan, *VI*, pp. 505–6

13. Shepherd, *Macleod*, pp. 311–2

14. Lewis, I.G.'s diary

15. I.G.'s diary; Lewis; Walters, pp. 124–5; R. Churchill, pp. 108–9

16. I.G.'s diary; R. Churchill, p. 109; Walters, p. 125

17. Home, p. 182; Walters, p. 127; Fisher, p. 237; Ramsden, p. 200

18. Home, p. 182; Hailsham, *Door*, p. 224; Thorpe, pp. 285–6, 295; Lewis

19. Ramsden, p. 198; Thorpe, pp. 294–5; I.G.'s diary; Lamb, p. 493

20. I.G.'s diary; Maudling, pp. 126–8; Prior, *A Balance of Power*, p. 31; Shepherd, *Macleod*, p. 316

21. I.G.'s diary; Lewis; Hailsham, *Sparrow*, pp. 353–4; Walters, p. 126

22. A. A. Milne, 'Disobedience'

23. I.G.'s diary

24. Goodhart, pp. 194–5

25. M. Butler, p. 79; R. Butler, p. 247

26. Fisher, p. 238; I.G.'s diary

27. Horne, *II*, pp. 555; Macmillan, *IV*, pp. 509–11; Howard, p. 316
28. Fisher, pp. 236–7; I.G.'s diary
29. The *Spectator*, pp. 65–7 17 January 1964; Shepherd, *Powell*, p. 257; Shepherd, *Macleod*, p. 360
30. Horne, *II*, pp. 553–4
31. Horne, *II*, p. 556; Thorpe, pp. 298–301
32. Horne, *II*, p. 531; I.G.'s diary; Thorpe, pp. 263, 267, 298–301
33. Thorpe, pp. 301–2; Horne, *II*, p. 555
34. Brogan, *The American Political System*, p. 227
35. Ramsden, p. 203; Thorpe, pp. 302–3
36. Churchill, p. 135; Prior, *A Balance of Power*, pp. 32–3; *The Whitelaw Memoirs*, p. 58; Shepherd, *Macleod*, pp. 322–4; Walters, p. 134
37. Horne, *II*, pp. 559–61; *Spectator*, p. 67
38. Horne, *II*, pp. 560–62; Gilmour in *LRB*, 27 July 1989
39. Enoch Powell to I.G. in 1987, a postscript to I.G.'s diary
40. Horne, *II*, p. 560; I.G.'s diary
41. Maudling, p. 129; I.G.'s diary; Walters, pp. 132–3
42. Thorpe, p. 312; Macmillan, *VI*, pp. 514–5
43. Pimlott, *The Queen*, p. 334; Boyd-Carpenter, pp. 178–9; Horne, *II*, p. 564; Macmillan, pp. 514–5
44. Shepherd, *Powell*, p. 260; M. Butler, p. 82; I.G.'s diary
45. Home, pp. 185–6, 215; I.G.'s diary; Shepherd, *Powell*, p. 259; Shepherd, *Macleod*, pp. 329–30, 334–7
46. Churchill, p. 135; Carrington, pp. 181–2; I.G.'s diary; Pimlott, *Wilson*, p. 305; Ramsden, p. 209
47. Macmillan, *VI*, pp. 506–7
48. I.G.'s diary; *Spectator* p. 67, 17 January 1964
49. Thorpe, p. 310. Horne, *II*, pp. 582, 617–9, 625–7

Chapter IX: Home and Heath

1. Thorpe, p. 321
2. Thorpe, pp. 257, 324; Pimlott, p. 306; See chapter eight above; Howard, p. 332; Horne, *II*, p. 518; personal knowledge; I.G.'s diary 19 January 1964
3. Thorpe, p. 338; White, *The Making of the President 1969*, p. 46
4. Evans and Novak, Lyndon B. Johnson, *The Exercise of Power*, pp. 326–7
5. Evans and Novak, p. 390; Thorpe, pp. 347–50; R. Butler, pp. 256–7; Howard, pp. 328–9
6. The *Spectator*, pp. 65–7, 17 January 1964; pp. 97, 101, 24 January 1997; Thorpe, pp. 344–5; Gilmour in the *Listener*, 30 July 1970; I.G.'s diary
7. Shepherd, *Powell*, pp. 257, 268–74; *Spectator*, pp. 457–9, 10 April 1964; p. 508, 17 April 1966
8. Bruce-Gardyne and Lawson, *The Power Game*, pp. 83–91; Butler and King, The British General Election 1969, p. 23

9. Shepherd, *Powell*, pp. 268–9; Home, pp. 189–215; Bruce-Gardyne and Lawson, *The Power Game*, pp. 98–9

10. Goodhart, pp. 196–8; Batt, *The Power of Parliament*, pp. 262–4; Morrison to Douglas-Home, 15 April 1964, PREM 11/5/54

11. Goodhart, p. 198; personal knowledge; Ramsden, pp. 217–9; Wigham, p. 132

12. *HC*, 4 April 1969, cols. 642, 697–8; 8 April, cols. 1004–5; Maudling, pp. 113–8; Pollard, *The Wasting of the British Economy*, pp. 43–4

13. Maudling, pp. 188, 130–1; Middlemas, *II*, p. 81; Brittan, p. 285

14. Maudling, pp. 130–1; *Spectator*, p. 503, 17 April 1964; private information, I.G.'s diary, 31 March, 16 April, 18 March

15. Macmillan to I.G. in the lobby, I.G.'s diary, 24 March 1964; Thorpe, pp. 353–4

16. personal knowledge

17. PREM 11/5006 19 December 1963; Ramsden, p. 215; Home, p. 187; Walters, p. 138

18. *Spectator*, p. 67, 17 January 1964; Timmins, pp. 202–3, 246–7; Clarke, pp. 288–9

19. Butler and King, p. 37; Wybrow, *Britain Speaks Out*, p. 70; Timmins, *The Five Giants*, p. 179; Butler and King, p. 38

20. I.G.'s diary 31 August 1966; Maudling, pp. 118–9; Brittan, pp. 284–6; Dell, pp. 301–3; Callaghan, *Time and Chance*, pp. 153–4

21. Craig, (ed.), *British General Election Manifestos 1959–1987*, p. 37

22. Campbell, *Edward Heath*, pp. 160–1; Butler and King, pp. 149–50; Matthew Coady in the *Daily Mirror*, 14 May 1964

23. Ramsden, p. 226; Butler and King, p. 148–9; D. Watt in the *Spectator*, pp. 465–6, 9 October 1964

24. Thorpe, p.366; the *Spectator*, p. 497, 16 October 1964; Butler and King, p. 147

25. Thorpe, 367, 371; Butler and King, pp. 147–8; Ramsden, pp. 227–8

26. Butler and King, pp. 123–4, 148–9; Howard, pp. 351–5; Thorpe, p. 368

27. Pinto-Duschinsky, *British Political Finance 1830–1980*, pp. 137–8

28. *Spectator*, p. 127, 31 January 1964

29. Pinto-Duschinsky in Hennessy and Seldon (eds), pp. 154–5; Skidelsky in Marquand and Seldon (eds), p. 53

30. Craig (ed.), p. 30

31. I.G.'s diary, 29 October 1964, 3 November 1964, 4 November 1964

32. Wilson, *The Labour Government 1964–70*, pp. 27–8; Callaghan, pp. 159–63; Pimlott, *Wilson*, pp. 350–2; MacDougall, pp. 152–3

33. Ball, *The Discipline of Power*, p. 93

34. Maudling, pp. 133–4; *HC*, 23 November 1900, col. 933; Brittan, pp. 296–8; Shrimsley, *The First Hundred Days of Harold Wilson*, p. 51; MacDougall, p 154

35. Campbell, p. 167

36. Goodhart, pp. 201–3; Ramsden, pp. 233–4
37. Margach, pp. 133–6; Thorpe, pp. 386–7
38. Home, pp. 219–20; I.G.'s diary, 5 July; Ramsden, p. 236; Goodhart, pp. 203–5
39. Walker, *Staying Power*, pp. 42–3; Campbell, p. 179; I.G.'s diary, 8 July, 22 July
40. Halcrow, *Keith Joseph*, p. 35
41. Churchill, *The Gathering Storm*, p. 437
42. Personal knowledge; Crossman, *Diaries of a Cabinet Minister I*, pp. 292–3
43. Crossman, pp. 253–4; Wilson, *The Labour Government, 1964–70*, pp. 150–1, 161–3
44. Kissinger, *The White House Years*, p. 933, Maudling, p. 142
45. Middlemas, *II*, p. 257; Ramsden, *The Making*, p. 242
46. Ramsden, *The Making*, p. 241; Campbell, pp. 202–4
47. *Spectator*, p. 435, 8 October 1965; Rhodes James, *Ambitions and Realities* pp. 93–5
48. Shepherd, *Macleod*, pp. 409–10; Shepherd, *Powell*, pp. 284–5, 318–9; Craig (ed.), p. 71
49. *Spectator*, p. 39, 14 January 1965
50. *Spectator*, pp. 71–3, 105, 21 and 28 January 1965; Thatcher, *The Path to Power*, p. 273
51. *Spectator*, p. 63, 21 January 1966
52. Clarke, *Hope and Glory*, p. 301
53. MacDougall, p. 167, *HC*, 17 November 1965, col. 1167
54. Craig, (ed.), p. 70
55. Butler and King, *The British General Election of 1966*, p. 101; Thorpe, p. 393; Ramsden, *Winds of Change*, p. 263; Shepherd, *Macleod*, p. 419
56. Callaghan, p. 192
57. Callaghan, pp. 192–3; Wilson, p. 297
58. Callaghan, pp. 196–290; Jenkins, *A Life at the Centre*, pp. 190–5
59. Campbell, p. 216; Prior, p. 55
60. Campbell, pp. 230–4; Pimlott, p. 435; personal knowledge
61. Wilson, p. 587; Pimlott, p. 483; Campbell, pp. 225–6

Chapter X: The Powellite Challenge

1. R. Butler, p. 202
2. Shepherd, *Powell*, p. 285; Cecil King, Diary 1970–1976, p. 248; personal knowledge
3. *One Europe*, pp. 9–11, 15–7, 12–4, 20–1
4. Utley, pp. 110–1
5. Shepherd, *Powell*, pp. 301–8; Utley, p. 112; Campbell, pp. 226–7; personal knowledge; I.G.'s diary, 6th May 1964
6. Shepherd, *Powell*, pp. 305–15; Utley, pp. 106–9
7. Letter to *The Times* 17 February 1968 by Ian Gilmour and David

Howell; Shepherd, pp. 305–7, 319; Utley, pp. 110–2; Campbell, pp. 228, 241; Pimlott, p. 388

8. Shepherd, p. 319
9. Whitehead, *The Writing on the Wall*, p. 32
10. Macmillan, *VI*, p. 506; Whitehead, p. 33
11. Shepherd, *Powell*, p. 319
12. Conservative Party Archives, EPG/66/70, 8 February 1960; Ramsden, *The Making*, pp. 260–2; Campbell, p. 235; Ridley, *My Style of Government*, pp. 3–4
13. Crossman, *II*, 106–7; Shepherd, *Powell*, pp. 323, 388; Cairncross (ed.), p. 1454; Macmillan, *IV*, p. 372; personal knowledge
14. Shepherd, *Macleod*, p. 429
15. Shepherd, *Powell*, pp. 323–4, 374
16. Foot, *The Rise of Enoch Powell*, pp. 67–72
17. Shepherd, *Powell*, pp. 286–91; Gilmour, *Inside Right*, pp. 134–5. At the time, members of One Nation sent their election address to their colleagues.
18. Shepherd, *Macleod*, pp. 494–8; Rhodes James, p. 164; Layton-Henry in Ball and Seldon (eds), *The Heath Government*, pp. 219–21
19. Hogg, pp. 369–70; Walker, p. 51; Shepherd, *Powell*, pp. 343–4; personal knowledge
20. Hogg, pp. 369–70; Shepherd, *Powell*, pp. 346–9; Foot, pp. 112–6; Rhodes James, pp. 182–4
21. Grigg, *The History of the Times, VI*, pp. 81–2; Gilmour, *Inside Right*, pp. 133–4; Shepherd, *Powell*, p. 356
22. Rhodes James, pp. 185–6; Shepherd, *Powell*, p. 345, 354, 361–3; Foot, pp. 111–2
23. Campbell, pp. 243–4; Thatcher, pp. 146–7; Whitelaw, pp. 81–2; Fisher, p. 297
24. Shepherd, *Powell*, p. 343
25. Campbell, p. 245; Shepherd, *Powell*, p. 375; Hogg, *Door*, p. 236
26. Shepherd, *Powell*, p. 118; Foot, pp. 118–9; Lane in Gold (ed.), p. 77
27. Heath in Gold (ed.), *Edward Boyle*, pp. 117–9; Rees-Mogg in ibid., pp. 122–3; Prior, p. 53; Lowe in Ball and Seldon (eds), pp. 211–3
28. Prior, p. 53; Ramsden, p. 246; Shepherd, *Powell*, pp. 286–90
29. Shepherd, *Powell*, p. 387; Horne, *II*, p. 76; Rhodes James, p. 208
30. Ramsden, p. 291; personal knowledge
31. Crossman, *III*, pp. 944–5; Beer, *Britain Against Itself*, pp. 42, 51
32. Wigham, p. 142; Beer, p. 53
33. Prior, pp. 48–9; cf. Howe, *Conflict of Loyalty*, p. 47
34. Campbell, pp. 228–30; P. Jenkins, *The Battle of Downing Street*, p. 102; Whitehead, pp. 31–2
35. Butler and Stokes, *Political Change in Britain*, pp. 168–9; 498–9; Rhodes James, p. 23; Butler and Duschinsky, *The British General Election of 1970*, pp. 46, 415
36. Ramsden, p. 271

37. Butler and Pinto-Duschinsky, p. 63
38. Butler and Duschinsky, pp. 46, 91; *Campaign Guide 1970*, p. 205; Lowe in Ball and Seldon (eds), p. 194. Unfortunately these sentences dropped out of the published document.
39. Fraser's Report on the 1970 election; personal knowledge; Ramsden pp. 300–3; Ramsden, *The Making*, pp. 275–6; Campbell, pp. 233, 264–5; Walker, *Staying Power*, p. 52; Shepherd, *Macleod*, p. 517
40. Shepherd, *Powell*, p. 388; Crossman, *III*, p. 799, 809, 813; Ramsden, *The Making*, p. 275
41. Crossman, *III*, 801, 809; Ramsden, p. 307; Hurd, *An End to Promises*, pp. 9–10
42. Unpublished passage of I.G.'s obituary of Iain Macleod, the *Listener* 30 July 1970; Fisher, pp. 303–4; Rhodes James, p. 8; Crossman, *III*, pp. 944–5
43. Personal knowledge; Thorpe, pp. 402–3
44. Shepherd, *Powell*, pp. 400–3; Rhodes James, pp. 276–8; Wood, (ed.), *Powell and the Election*, pp. 83–125; Prior, p. 59
45. Ramsden, pp. 314–7; Rhodes James, pp. 270–5; Hurd, pp. 25–6

Chapter XI: Heath's Rough Ride

1. Hurd, p. 31; Halcrow, *Keith Joseph*, pp. 39–44; Middlemas, *II*, p. 283; Hailsham, *Door*, pp. 287–8
2. Macleod to I.G., May 1974; *DNB*, 1961–1970, p. 705; Wigham, p. 165; *HC*, 7 July 1970, cols. 504–11; Shepherd, *Macleod*, pp. 531, 535; personal knowledge
3. Address by General de Gaulle to Members of both Houses of Parliament, 7 April 1960; P. Jenkins, *The Battle of Downing Street*, p. 140; Bagehot, *The English Constitution*, p. 4
4. Campbell, *Heath*, pp. 305–6; Cockerill, *Live from Number 10*, p. 171; Halcrow, p. 56
5. Timmins, pp. 299–300; Thatcher, pp. 168–72; Halcrow, p. 48; Thorpe, pp. 408–10
6. Rover, *Affairs of State, The Eisenhower Years*, p. 111
7. Whitehead, p. 56; Campbell, pp. 309–10
8. Barber, p. 78; Hennessy, *Cabinet*, p. 74
9. Hurd, p. 78; Campbell, *Edward Heath*, pp. 310–12; *Spectator*, p. 435 8 October 1965
10. Campbell, pp. 300–1
11. Cairncross in Ball and Seldon (eds), pp. 111–2, 115; Keegan and Pennant Rose, *Who Runs the Economy?* pp. 195–6; Shepherd, *Macleod*, pp. 332–3; *HC*, 10 November 1970, col. 219
12. Shepherd, *Iain Macleod*, pp. 532–3; Timmins, pp. 281, 300; Thatcher, pp. 179–84
13. *HC*, 27 October 1970, cols, 37–75
14. *Conservative Campaign Guide*, p. 423; Craig (ed.), p. 328; *HC* 10

November 1970, cols. 217–30, 260–5; Halcrow, p. 48; Gilmour, *Riot, Risings and Revolution*, pp. 439–40

15. Middlemas, *II*, pp. 323–4, 330, 332, 347; MacDougall, p. 187; Taylor in Ball and Seldon (eds), p. 170

16. Shepherd, pp. 480–1; Barber, p. 104; Middlemas, *II*, p. 309; Grigg, pp. 191–2

17. MacDougall, *Don and Mandarin*, pp. 189–90; Cairncross in Ball and Seldon (eds), pp. 125–6; Middlemas, *II*, pp. 305–10

18. Taylor in Ball and Seldon (eds), pp. 161–2

19. Wigham, pp. 165–6; Campbell, p. 369–70

20. Prior, p. 72; Thatcher, *What's Wrong with Politics*, pp. 6, 14; Gilmour, *The Body Politic*, pp. 146–7

21. Hailsham, *The Dilemma of Democracy*, p. 127; Middlemas, *II*, p. 277; Whitehead, p. 38; Wigham, p. 157; Taylor in Ball and Seldon (eds), pp. 162–3

22. Middlemas, *II*, pp. 316, 320–1

23. Grigg, *The Times*, p. 196; Taylor, in Ball and Seldon (eds), pp. 171–2; Ramsden, pp. 330–1

24. Taylor, p. 172

25. Whitehead, p. 73; Taylor, pp. 172–3; Campbell, p. 368; Middlemas, *II*, p. 263

26. Martin, *TUC*, p. 319; E. Wilson, *A Very British Miracle*, p. 11

27. Thatcher, *The Path to Power*, p. 206; Ridley, p. 4; Taylor in Ball and Seldon (eds), pp. 149–50, 144

28. Whitehead, pp. 80–1; Middlemas, *II*, pp. 315–6; Thatcher, *I*, pp. 213–5

29. Young, *Britain and European Unity, 1945–1992*, pp. 99–100; *Action Not Words*, p. 7; *A Better Tomorrow*, p. 29; George, *An Awkward Partner*, p. 49

30. Shepherd, *Macleod*, pp. 514–5; Ramsden, *The Making*, p. 276; Campbell, p. 248; Pimlott, p. 580

31. Denman, pp. 235–7; Campbell, pp. 353–60

32. Whitehead, pp. 59–60; Middlemas, *II*, p. 303; Denman, pp. 237–8; Young, p. 274

33. Whitehead, p. 65; Pimlott, p. 581

34. Young, *Britain and European Unity*, p. 114; R. Jenkins, pp. 318–9; Whitehead, pp. 65–6

35. Denman, p. 238; Pimlott, p. 581; R. Jenkins, pp. 322–3, 331

36. Ramsden, *Winds of Change*, p. 336; Campbell, pp. 399–400

37. Hurd, pp. 67–9; Ramsden, p. 335; Campbell, pp. 396–402; Whitehead, pp. 66–8

38. R. Jenkins, p. 329; Pimlott, pp. 589–90; Campbell, pp. 403–5; Denman, pp. 239–43

39. Denman, p. 241; Whitehead, p. 68; Young in Ball and Seldon (eds), pp. 277–8; Whitelaw, p. 95

40. Pimlott, p. 611

41. Pimlott, pp. 591–6; R. Jenkins, pp. 341–9; Whitehead, pp. 67–9; Wilson to I.G.
42. Hurd, pp. 25, 104; Grigg, p. 185
43. Clarke, p. 410; Grigg, p. 218
44. Whitehead, pp. 73–4; Prior, p. 73; Campbell, pp. 412–4
45. Maudling, pp. 160–1; Grigg, p. 220; Campbell, pp. 415–6; Whitehead, pp. 75–6
46. Campbell, pp. 414, 417–9; Taylor in Ball and Seldon (eds), pp. 177–8
47. Holmes, *Political Pressure and Economic Policy*, p. 73; Hurd, p. 103; Taylor, pp. 177–8; Reid, *Spectator*, 13 October 1989
48. Campbell, p. 420
49. Maudling, pp. 191, 263–5
50. Grigg, pp. 221–2, 209; Hoggs, *Door*, pp. 237–43; Maudling, pp. 28, 178; Arthur in Ball and Seldon (eds), p. 239
51. Personal knowledge
52. Private information
53. Maudling, pp. 184–5; Arthur, pp. 240–2; personal knowledge
54. Arthur, pp. 243–4; Maudling, pp. 186–7

Chapter XII: Undermining One-Nation
1. Campbell, p. 406; Hurd, pp. 7, 102
2. Cairncross, pp. 117–8; Whitehead, p. 84; Timmins, p. 307; Middlemas, *II*, p. 342; Ramsden, p. 351
3. Cairncross, pp. 116–7; Middlemas, *II*, pp. 344–5
4. Campbell, p. 446; Ramsden, pp. 350–1; Halcrow, pp. 50–1; Timmins, pp. 301–2; Maudling, pp. 332, 342; MacDougall, p. 189; Cairncross, pp. 117–8; Grigg, p. 223
5. Dell, pp. 385–6, 398–90; Cairncross, p. 132
6. Campbell, pp. 446, 449; Taylor in Ball and Seldon (eds), pp. 152–4; Walker, *Staying Power*, pp. 96, 110–1
7. *Evening Standard*, 25 May 1972; Norton, *Conservative Dissidents*, p. 92; Campbell, pp. 450–1
8. Thatcher, *The Path to Power*, pp. 220
9. Wigham, p. 101; Howe, *Conflict of Loyalty*, pp. 62–3
10. Whitehead, pp. 77–8, 80; Howe, pp. 63–4
11. Whitehead, pp. 78–9; Howe, pp. 64–5; Campbell, pp. 460–1; Taylor, pp. 175–6
12. Wigham, pp. 162–3; Taylor, p. 176; Whitehead, pp. 79–80
13. Campbell, p. 462
14. Wybrow, p. 160; Butler and Stokes, *Political Change in Britain*, p. 148
15. Taylor, p. 170; Campbell, pp. 463–4, 478; Maudling, pp. 163–5
16. Middlemas, *II*, p. 357; Haseler, *The Death of British Democracy*, p. 125
17. Haseler, *The Death of British Democracy*, p. 125; Taylor p. 162

18. Campbell, pp. 460, 472–6; Gilmour, *Inside Right*, pp. 236–8; Taylor, p. 180
19. Hurd, p. 105; Campbell, p. 479; Shepherd, *Powell*, pp. 427, 374; Grigg, p. 222
20. Thatcher, p. 224; Halcrow, p. 54; Howe, pp. 74–5; Norton, p. 119
21. Holmes, p. 87; Butler and Kavanagh, *The British General Election of February 1974*, p. 26
22. Wigham, p. 173–4; Campbell, pp. 531–4
23. *HC*, 6 March 1973, col. 248; Dell, p. 396; Cairncross in Ball and Seldon (eds), p. 109
24. Taylor in Ball and Seldon (eds), pp. 182–3; Middlemas, *II*, p. 360
25. Middlemas, *II*, pp. 359–61, 373; Whitehead, pp. 96–7; Hurd, pp. 87–8; Campbell, p. 538
26. Taylor in Ball and Seldon (eds), pp. 183–4; Campbell, pp. 537–8; Beer, p. 47
27. Vidal's intro to Shahak, *Jewish History, Jewish Religion*, p. vii; Kissinger, *The White House Years*, pp. 575–82; Kissinger, *Years of Upheaval*, p. 709; Riad, *The Struggle for Peace in the Middle East*, pp. 94, 152–4, 241–2, 252; Hill and Lord in Ball and Seldon (eds), pp. 301–2, 305–6
28. Kissinger, *Years of Upheaval*, p. 13; Thorpe, p. 434; Kissinger, *The White House Years*, pp. 933, 937, 141, 143
29. Campbell, pp. 539–40; Shepherd, pp. 536–40
30. Middlemas, *II*, pp. 377–8; Taylor in Ball and Seldon (eds), p. 184
31. Taylor, pp. 184–5; Middlemas, pp. 377–8
32. Middlemas, *II*, p. 378; Taylor in Ball and Seldon (eds), p. 185; Campbell, p. 570
33. Ball and Seldon (eds), p. 404; Wybrow, p. 105
34. Kavanagh in Ball and Seldon (eds), pp. 355–8; Ramsden, *The Making*, pp. 301–2; Hurd, p. 122; Butler and Kavanagh, *The British General Election of February 1974*, pp. 28–9
35. Prior, p. 91; Butler and Kavanagh, p. 66
36. Whitelaw, pp. 160, 164, 168; Pym, *The Politics of Consent*, p. 4
37. Arthur in Ball and Seldon (eds), pp. 253–8
38. I.G.'s diary, 17 January 1974
39. Campbell, p. 581; Howe, p. 79; Whitelaw, pp. 167–8
40. Whitelaw, pp. 167–70; Prior, p. 92
41. Campbell, p. 576–7; Kavanagh in Ball and Seldon (eds), pp. 359–60; Hurd, pp. 125–9; Walker, pp. 124–5; Howe, p. 784
42. I.G.'s diary 17 January 1974; Prior, p. 92; Ramsden, *Winds of Change*, pp. 372–3
43. Hurd, pp. 127–8
44. Kavanagh, in Ball and Seldon (eds), pp. 362–3
45. Ramsden, p. 377; Campbell, p. 604; Butler and Kavanagh, p. 107
46. Shepherd, pp. 441–5; Butler and Kavanagh,

47. Shepherd, pp. 446–7, 441; Pimlott, p. 611; King, *Diary 1970—1974*, p. 248
48. I.G.'s diary, 12 March 1974
49. Butler and Kavanagh, pp. 100–1, 116; Hurd, p. 134; Whitelaw, pp. 171–2; personal knowledge
50. Ramsden, pp. 380–1; Butler and Kavanagh, p. 260
51. I.G.'s diary 1 and 4 March 1974; Thatcher, *The Path to Power*, p. 239
52. *HC*, 15 November 1971, col. 48
53. Layton-Henry, in Ball and Seldon (eds), pp. 224–30, 234; Campbell, pp. 393–4; Hurd, p. 21; Ramsden, p. 362; Butler and Kavanagh, p. 208
54. *Sunday Times*, 7 July 1996
55. Skidelsky in Marquand and Seldon (eds), *The Ideas that Shaped Post-War Britain*, p. 60

Chapter XIII: In the Steps of St Francis

1. Halcrow, *Keith Joseph*, p. 56
2. Thatcher, *The Downing Street Years*, pp. 7, 14; Tebbit, *Upwardly Mobile*, p. 101
3. I.G.'s diary 8, 11, 13, 14, 16–9 March 1974; Campbell, p. 625
4. I.G.'s diary 12 March 1974; Campbell, pp. 625–6, 630
5. Butler and Kavanagh, *The British General Election of October 1974*, pp. 42–4, 52, 61–2; Campbell, pp. 633–4; I.G.'s Memo to Heath and Carrington, 25 March 1974; Heath to I.G. 1 April 1974; Lawson to Carrington 25 March 1974 and to I.G. 3 April 1974
6. Halcrow, pp. 71–5; Thatcher, *The Path to Power*, pp. 255–7; Prior, p. 97; Campbell, pp. 639–40
7. Butler and Kavanagh, *The British General Election of October 1974*, p. 95; *Putting Britain First*, p. 44
8. Thatcher, pp. 257–60; Gilmour, *Dancing with Dogma*, pp. 212–3; Lawson, *The View from No. 11*, p. 11
9. *Putting Britain First*, p. 3; Butler and Kavanagh, pp. 69, 101, 275
10. Butler and Kavanagh, pp. 124–9; Campbell, pp. 641–9; Prior, p. 98
11. Fowler, *Ministers Decide*, p. 7;
12. Personal knowledge; Campbell, pp. 663, 670; Halcrow, pp. 80–91; Thatcher, pp. 262–6
13. Campbell, pp. 101, 663–9; Shepherd, *The Power Brokers*, pp. 168–9; Critchley, *Heseltine*, p. 46; personal knowledge
14. Thatcher, pp. 277–80; Prior, p. 100; Howe, pp. 91–3; personal knowledge
15. Young, p. 92; Lawson, p. 13; Campbell, pp. 670–1
16. Wapshott and Brock, p. 140; Prior, p. 104
17. Thatcher, *The Path to Power*, pp. 292–93; Campbell, p. 676; private information
18. Walker, p. 132

19. Cosgrave, *Margaret Thatcher*, pp. 177–8; Halcrow, pp. 98–9; Cockett, *Thinking the Unthinkable*, p. 171
20. Thatcher, p. 291; Behrens: The Conservative Party from Heath to Thatcher, p. 54; Prior, pp. 103–4; Campbell, p. 682
21. Ziegler, *Wilson*, pp. 416, 447–8; Wilson, speech at Cardigan, 28 September 1974
22. Ziegler, pp. 413, 484, 486, 475–9
23. Whitehead, p. 189; Smith, *From Boom to Bust*, pp. 39, 19
24. *The Right Approach*, pp. 24, 21, 32, 37; Middlemas, *II*, p. 195; Thatcher, p. 317
25. Thatcher, *Path to Power*, p. 317; Howe, pp. 101, 105–6; *The Right Approach to the Economy*, pp. 1, 16–7; Norton, *Dissension in the House of Commons*, p. 435
26. Thatcher, pp. 330, 332; Ashford in Layton-Henry, (ed.), *Conservative Party Politics*, p. 109; Goodhart, *Full-Hearted Consent*, pp. 130–1, 190; Grigg, pp. 337–8
27. Thatcher, pp. 301, 319; Maudling, pp. 208–9, 224–6; personal knowledge
28. Thatcher, *Path to Power*, pp. 361–2
29. Bogdanor in Layton-Henry (ed.), pp. 85–9; Russel, *The Tory Party*, pp. 128–31; Norton, *Dissension in the House of Commons*, pp. 209–10; Thatcher, pp. 322–6
30. Layton-Henry in Layton-Henry (ed.), pp. 67–8; Thatcher, pp. 406–8; personal knowledge
31. Labour Party manifesto, 1974, p. 11
32. Behrens, p. 58; Campbell, p. 711
33. Whitehead, pp. 281–2
34. Young, *One of Us*, p. 131; Mrs Thatcher's Foreword to The Conservative Party Manifesto 1979, p. 5
35. Cockerell, *Live from Number 10*, pp. 247–9; Thatcher, p. 448
36. Whithead, p. 366
37. Thatcher, p. 461; Butler and Kavanagh, *The British General Election of 1979*, pp. 265, 316, 323; Campbell, p. 715; Wapshott and Brock, *Thatcher*, p. 161; Prior, p. 113
38. R. Jenkins, *European Diary 1977–81*, p. 449; Campbell, pp. 714–5
39. Ridley, pp. 25–6; Thatcher, *The Downing Street Years*, p. 28; Gilmour, pp. 7–8; Prior, p. 114
40. Halcrow, pp. 136–7; McSmith, Kenneth Clarke, pp. 69–70
41. Maudling, p. 209
42. This section is a brief summary of I.G.'s book, *Britain Can Work*, pp. 116–57
43. Cockett, *Thinking the Unthinkable*, p. 248; Keegan, *Mrs Thatcher's Economic Experiment*, pp. 119–23; Stephenson, *Mrs Thatcher's First Year*, p. 47; Prior, p. 12; Johnson, *The Economy under Mrs Thatcher 1979–90*, p. 48; Gilmour, *Dancing with Dogma*, pp. 21–2
44. Lawson, p. 37; Johnson, pp. 127–9; Gilmour, p. 22

45. Margaret Thatcher, speech at Birmingham Town Hall, 19 April 1979; Gilmour pp. 22–3

46. Thatcher, pp. 96–7; Smith, *Boom to Bust*, p. 176; Keegan, pp. 141–5; The Conservative Manifesto 1979, p. 277

47. Thatcher, p. 122

48. Whitehead, p. 376; Gilmour, p. 35

49. Howe, pp. 203–4; Johnson, p. 41; Wybrow, p. 159; Oliver, 'Whatever Happened to Monetarism', *Twentieth-Century British History, Vol. 8 No. 1*, 1997, p. 62

50. Prior, p. 122; Howe, pp. 202, 208, 473. For a full account of the ministerial differences at the 1981 budget, see Gilmour, *Dancing with Dogma*, pp. 36–53

51. Prior, p. 122; Howe, p. 198; Butler and Kavanagh, p. 31

52. Young, pp. 239–40; private information

53. Young, p. 240; *Changing Gear*, p. 4; Wybrow, p. 126

54. Stephenson, p. 12; Gilmour, p. 51; *Changing Gear*, p. 9; Halcrow, p. 150; Behrens, p. 110; Johnson, p. 227

55. Young, p. 110; Halsey, *British Social Trends since 1900*, pp. 192, 196; Butler and Kavanagh, *The British General Election of 1983*, p. 296

56. Letwin, *The Anatomy of Thatcherism*, p. 146–7; Boyson, *Centre Forward*, p. 47–8; Tebbit, *Upwardly Mobile*, p. 236

57. Crewe and King, *SDP*, pp. 133–45; Kavanagh, *Thatcherism and British Politics*, pp. 179–81

58. Carrington, pp. 348–71; Young, pp. 259–65; Critchley, *Boiled Sweets*, p. 180

59. Sked and Cook, *Post-War Britain*, p. 401; Harris, *Thatcher*, pp. 175–6; Young, p. 281

60. Gilmour, pp. 276–296; The Conservative Manifesto 1979, p. 30; Ashford in Layton-Henry (ed.), p. 113

61. Crewe and King, pp. 146–8; Timmins, p. 360; Critchley, p. 195

62. Gilmour, p. 145; Butler and Kavanagh,, p. 101

63. Holmes, *The First Thatcher Government*, p. 83

64. Statement on Economic Policy, University of Cambridge Faculty of Economics and Politics, *The Times*, 30 March 1981; Lawson, pp. 97–8; Howe, p. 209

65. e.g. PSBR for 1980–1 and 1981–2; Oliver, *Whatever Happened to Monetarism, in Twentieth-Century British History, Vol. 8, No. 1,* 1997, pp. 49–50, 57–8

66. Godley, in the *Observer*, 29 August 1982

Chapter XIV: The 'Economic Miracle', or From Slump to Slump

1. The Conservative Manifesto 1983, pp. 16, 24–5; Grimstone, *Privatisation, the Unexpected Crusade*, p. 23; Timmins, p. 381

2. The Conservative Manifesto 1983, p. 18; Timmins, p. 373

3. Butler and Kavanagh, pp. 217, 291, 293

4. *Observer*, 31 August 1980

5. Thatcher, p. 8
6. Thatcher, pp. 305–7; Gilmour in *Twentieth-Century British History, Vol. 5, No. 2*, p. 260
7. Thatcher, p. 306; Criddle in Seldon and Ball (eds), pp. 162–3; Ingle, *The British Party System*, pp. 82–3; Geoffrey Barker in the *Daily Telegraph* 17 June 1983
8. Norton in *Parliamentary Affairs, Vol. 42, Issue 1*, p. 56; Thatcher, p. 307
9. Barker in *Telegraph*, 29 July 1985; Lawson, pp. 432–3
10. Adeney and Lloyd, *The Miners Strike*, pp. 96–7; Walker, pp. 168–9, 172; Gilmour, pp. 104–5
11. Adeney and Lloyd, pp. 89–90; Goodman, *The Miners' Strike*, pp. 46–8; Sked and Cook, p. 450–2
12. E. Wilson, *A Very British Miracle*, p. 118; Lawson, p. 161; Ewing and Gearty, *Freedom under Thatcher*, p. 103; Walker, pp. 172–3
13. Walker, p. 184; Hammond, *Maverick*, p. 90; Gilmour, pp. 237–8; Wilson, p. 118
14. Howe, pp. 338–45; Ewing and Gearty, pp. 130–6; Gilmour, pp. 314–6
15. Wilson, p. 113
16. Stephens, *Politics and the Pound*, p. 31
17. Gilmour, *Dancing with Dogma*, p. 69; Tomlinson, *Public Policy and the Economy since 1900*, p. 346; Johnson p. 281; Smith, *The Rise and Fall of Monetarism*, p. 123
18. Keegan, *Mr Lawson's Gamble*, pp. 145–8, 186; Walker, p. 184; Gilmour, p. 73
19. Young, p. 502; Keegan, p. 186; Smith, p. 128
20. Smith, p. 80; Johnson, p. 58; *The Next Moves Forward*, p. 5
21. Wilson, p. 143–5; Johnson, pp. 148–9; Smith, p. 220
22. This paragraph is much indebted to discussions with Professor Wynne Godley.
23. S. Jenkins, *Accountable to None*, p. 31; Gilmour, p. 120
24. Lawson, p. 201; *Observer*, 2 July 1989; Crewe in Skidelsky (ed.), *Thatcherism*, p. 42; Butler and Kavanagh, *The British General Election of 1987*, p. 27; Riddell in Adonis and Hames (eds), p. 30
25. Thatcher, p. 677; Wilson, p. 89; Gilmour, p. 124; The Conservative Manifesto 1983, p. 17
26. Linklater and Leigh, *Not with Honour*, pp. 127–35; Ingham, *Kill the Messenger*, pp. 334–5; R. Harris, *Good and Faithful Servant*, pp. 130–3; Gilmour, pp. 233–4
27. Young, pp. 446–7
28. Young, p. 443; Harris, pp. 89–91, 144–50, 174–5; Gilmour, p. 232
29. Howe, pp. 471–2; Critchley, *Heseltine*, pp. 162–3; Lawson, p. 679
30. Howe, p. 472; Ingle, pp. 83, 85; Galbraith, *The Culture of Contentment, passim*
31. Thatcher, pp. 620, 418–21

32. Young, p. 496
33. Shepherd, *Powell*, p. 492; Garnett and Sherrington, 'UK Parliamentary Perspectives on Europe, 1971–1993'; *Journal of Legislative Studies, Vol. 2, No. 4,* 1996, pp. 394–5; Young, pp. 515–7
34. Lawson, p. 697; Healey, *The Time of my Life*, p. 534
35. Waller in Seldon and Ball (eds), p. 605; The Next Moves Forward, pp. 63, 51
36. Adonis in Adonis and Hames (eds), p. 161; Butler et al, pp. 26–7
37. Crewe in Skidelsky (ed.), p. 41; Young in *Conservative Century*, p. 439; *The Right Road for Britain,* (popular version), p. 4
38. *The Next Moves Forward*, p. 3; Butler and Kavanagh, *The British General Election 1992*, p. 29–30; *Daily Telegraph*, 1 June 1996
39. Crewe in Kavanagh (ed.), *The Thatcher Effect*, pp. 244–6; The Conservative Manifesto, p. 5; Crewe in Skidelsky (ed.), p. 41; Norton in *Parliamentary Affairs, Vol. 43, No. 1,* 1990, pp. 56–7
40. Lawson, pp. 111, 483–504
41. Ridley, *My Style of Government*, p. 2
42. HC, 15 March 1988, col. 993; HC, 21 March 1988, col. 109; HC, 14 March 1988, cols. 293–4
43. Lawson, p. 816; Keegan, p. 221; HC, 15 March 1988, cols, 993, 1008, 1012; Johnson, p. 297; Timmins, p. 450
44. Lawson, pp. 797–8; Keegan, pp. 228–9; Johnson, p. 208
45. Johnson, p. 208; HC, 16 March 1989, col. 293
46. Howe, p. 357; Gilmour, p. 323
47. Howe, pp. 572–3; McCormick in Dunleavy *et al* (eds), *Developments in British Politics 4*, pp. 273–5
48. Howe, pp. 691–2; Lawson, pp. 467, 898–9; Gilmour in *Twentieth-Century British History*, pp. 274–8; Denham and Garnett in *Contemporary Political Studies, I,* 1991, pp. 270–7
49. Thatcher, pp. 712; Howe pp. 586–90, 691; R. Harris, pp. 174–5; Lawson, pp. 1001–2
50. Thatcher, p. 714; Baker, *The Turbulent Years*, p. 296
51. Lawson, p. 995; HC, 24 October 1989, col. 686; Howe, p. 604; Thatcher, pp. 713, 717
52. Timmins, p. 442; Sked and Cook, pp. 522–3
53. Thatcher, pp. 647–8, 652; Butler *et al.* p. 32; Lawson, pp. 607, 583; Crewe in Skidelsky (ed.), p. 43; CMWY. 8449, pp. 37–9
54. Ridley, p. 133; Gove, *Michael Portillo,* p. 175
55. Butler *et al*, p. 151
56. Richard Shepherd MP, HC, 15 January 1988, col. 572
57. Butler and Kavanagh, *British General Election of 1992*, p. 31
58. HC, 31 October 1989, cols. 208–10; personal knowledge
59. Personal knowledge
60. Ridley, p. 241
62. Thatcher, pp. 850–5
63. Thatcher, pp. 858–60; Benn, *The End of an Era*, p. 614

64. *Lloyds Bank Economic Bulletin, Number 13*, February 1997, pp. 3–4
65. Crafts, *Britain's Relative Economic Decline 1879–1995*
66. *Timmins, p. 313; Joseph Rowntree Foundation: Report into Income and Wealth*, 1995; Gilmour in *Twentieth-Century British History*, p. 277
67. Perkin, pp. 486–7

Chapter XV: Drifting With Dogma
 1. Marr, *Ruling Britannia*, pp. 143–50
 2. Howe, p. 590; Junor, *The Major Enigma*, pp. 163, 158; Lawson, p. 711
 3. Anderson, *John Major*, pp. 280–1; Thatcher, p. 757
 4. Junor, p. 167; Gilmour, *Dancing with Dogma*, p. 277
 5. *Independent*, 23 April 1997
 6. Watkins, *A Conservative Coup*, p. 198
 7. Personal knowledge; Watkins, pp. 193, 202–5
 8. Junor, p. 205; Urban, *Diplomacy and Disillusion at the Court of Margaret Thatcher*, pp. 160–2
 9. Butler and Kavanagh, *General Election of 1992*, p. 39
10. Pearce, *The Quiet Rise of John Major*, p. 168
11. S. Jenkins, *Accountable to None*, p. 60
12. Butler, *et al*, pp. 180–1; S. Jenkins, pp. 59–60
13. Kavanagh and Seldon, *The Major Effect*, pp. 103, 173; *The Guardian Political Almanac 1993–4*, pp. 65, 68, 133; Timmins, p. 481
14. Major's speech at Northampton, Treasury Press Release, 27 October 1989; Employment Policy Institute Economic Report, September 1994; Smith, *From Boom to Bust*, p. 188
15. Denman, pp. 269–71; Stephens, pp. 199–203
16. Gallup Political and Economic Index, No. 377, January 1992, p. 2; Stephens, pp. 196, 283; *Campaign Guide 1992*, p. 12
17. Crewe in Kavanagh and Seldon, *The Major Effect*, p. 105; Shepherd, p. 198
18. Junor, p. 208; Stephens, p. 198
19. Ludlam in Ludlam and Smith (eds), *Contemporary British Conservatism*, p. 110; Stephens, pp. 200–4
20. Stephens, pp. 226–34
21. Stephens, pp. 234–6; Gilmour, p. 277
22. Stephens, pp. 240–55; Dell, pp. 548–9
23. Gilmour, pp. 335–6
24. Crewe in Skidelsky (ed.), *Thatcherism*, pp. 33–43; Heath *et al*, *Understanding Political Change*, pp. 171–82
25. Shepherd, *Macleod*, pp. 284–5; Gilmour, pp. 274–9; Kevin Phillips in the *International Herald Tribune* 12 June 1997
26. *Daily Telegraph*, 30 May 1994; *1997 Campaign Guide*, p. 752
27. Painter, *Marcel Proust, I*, pp. 260–1
28. S. Jenkins, *Accountable to None*, pp. 14–5

29. Scott, in *The Major Effect*, p. 337; Lister, ibid., pp. 355–6
30. Whiteley, Seyd and Richardson, *True Blues*, pp. 22–5, 42; Norton and Aughey, *Conservative and Conservatism*, pp. 212–4
31. McSmith, pp. 215–6
32. Renton, in *Guardian*, 14 May 1994
33. Gilmour, 'Will Major the Moderate Please Stand Up?', *Evening Standard* 23 May 1994; Shepherd, *Macleod*, p. 290
34. Ludlam, in Ludlam and Smith (eds), p. 116; Gove, Michael Portillo, p. 32; Timmins, p. 472
35. *HL*, 30 March 1993, cols. 759–60; Jenkins, p. 207; Lawson, p. 718; Ian Lang, quoted in Ludlam and Smith (eds), p. 17
36. S. Jenkins, *Accountable to None*; Marr, *Ruling Britain*; Mount, *The British Constitution Now*; Roy Jenkins in *Evening Standard*, 22 January 1997; Gilmour, *Dancing with Dogma*, pp. 177–8
37. Carr, *The Bolshevik Revolution, 1917–1923*, I, p. 84; Rousseau, *The Social Contract, Book III, Ch. XV*; S. Jenkins, pp. 9, 11, 60; Gilmour, pp. 179–80, 212
38. S. Jenkins, p. 102; Marr, pp. 87, 97; P. Foot in *London Review of Books*, 17 October 1996
39. Perkin, *The Rise of Professional Society*, pp. 478–88; Thatcher, *What's Wrong with Politics?*, p. 6; Mount, pp. 167–4; Gilmour, pp. 222, 198–9, 186–1
40. Thorpe, *Alec Douglas-Home*, pp. 399–401, 441–2; *Conservative Campaign Guide 1977*, pp. 518–20; Gilmour, pp. 220–4
41. Gilmour, *Evening Standard*, 23 May 1994
42. Denman, *Missed Chances*, pp. 272–4
43. Stephens, p. 321; Thatcher, *Path to Power*, p. 475; *Daily Telegraph*, 12 June 1995; Nigel Lawson in the *Daily Mail*, 14 June 1993
44. Hogg and Hill, p. 270; Stephens, pp. 323–4
45. Stephens, p. 322
46. Junor, p. 253; *Daily Telegraph*, 3 November 1995; Seldon in *The Major Effect*, p. 33
47. Riddell, Honest Opportunism, p. 22
48. *HC*, 10 March 1989, col. 1147
49. Nicholson, *Secret Society*, p. 9; *Daily Telegraph*, 20 May 1995; Simon Jenkins in *The Times*, 8 November 1995
50. *Independent*, 2 January 1997; *Guardian*, 11 January 1996
51. *HC*, 10 March 1989, col. 1147; *Independent*, 16 February 1996; *HC*, 26 February 1996, col. 606; Woodhouse, *Ministers and Parliament*, 278–91
52. Denman, *Missed Chances*, (1997 edition) pp. 274–6; *Daily Telegraph*, 22 May 1996; Major, speech on 'The Future of Europe', 19 June 1996
53. Lord Young, *Guardian*, 30 January 1996
54. Benn's Letter to his constituents in Bristol South East, 14 November 1970
55. Michael White, *Guardian*, 23 August 1996

56. *The Times*, 28 April 1997; *Guardian*, 3 April 1997; Stephens in *Financial Times*, 28–29 June 1997
57. *Independent*, 16 April 1997; *You Can only Be Sure with the Conservatives*, p. 19
58. Peter Kellner, *Observer*, 28 April 1996; also Kellner to I.G. 2 June 1997
59. Waldegrave in *Daily Telegraph*, 7 June 1997; R. McKibbin, *Very Old Labour*, in *London Review of Books*, 3 April 1997
60. Thatcher, *The Downing Street Years*, p. 7; S. Jenkins, *Accountable to None*, p. 8
61. P. Clarke, 'So Far, So-So', in *London Review of Books*, 6 June 1996
62. Anthony Bevin in the *Independent*, 31 May 1997
63. Waugh, in the *Sunday Telegraph*, 1 June 1997
64. Seldon, *Churchill's Indian Summer*, Gilbert, *The Wilderness Years, 1929–1935*

Bibliography

Acheson, Dean, *Present at the Creation: My Years in the State Department* (London: Hamish Hamilton, 1970)

Addison, Paul, *The Road to 1945: British Politics and the Second World War* (London: Jonathan Cape, 1975)

Churchill on the Home Front, 1900–1955 (London: Jonathan Cape, 1992)

Adeney, Martin and Lloyd, John, *The Miners' Strike 1984–5* (London: Routledge & Kegan Paul, 1986)

Adonis, Andrew and Hames, Tim (eds.), *A Conservative Revolution? The Thatcher–Reagan Decade in Perspective* (Manchester: Manchester University Press, 1994)

Amery, L. S., *My Political Life,* Vol. III: *The Unforgiving Years 1929–1940* (London: Hutchinson, 1955)

Anderson, Bruce, *John Major* (London: Fourth Estate, 1991)

Anderson, Sir John, *The Machinery of Government* (Oxford: Clarendon Press, 1946)

Andrew, Christopher, *Secret Service* (London: Heinemann, 1985)

Avon, Lord, *The Memoirs of the Rt. Hon. Sir Anthony Eden, K.G., P.C., M.C.,* Part 2: *1951–1957: Full Circle* (London: Cassell, 1960)

The Memoirs of the Rt. Hon. Sir Anthony Eden, K.G., P.C., M.C., Part 3: *The Reckoning* (London: Cassell, 1965)

Bagehot, Walter, *The English Constitution* (London: Oxford University Press, 1928)

Baker, Kenneth, *The Turbulent Years* (London: Faber & Faber, 1993)

Ball, George W., *The Discipline of Power: Essentials of a Modern World Structure* (London: Bodley Head, 1968)

Ball, Stuart and Seldon, Anthony (eds.), *The Heath Government 1970–1974* (London: Longman, 1996)

Barber, Anthony, *Taking the Tide: A Memoir* (Norwich: Michael Russell, 1996)

Barnes, John and Nicholson, David (eds.), *The Empire at Bay* (London: Hutchinson, 1988)

Barnett, Correlli, *The Audit of War* (London: Macmillan, 1986)

Barzini, Luigi, *The Impossible Europeans* (London: Weidenfeld & Nicolson, 1983)

Bassett, R., *Nineteen Thirty-One: Political Crisis* (London: Macmillan, 1958)

The Essentials of Parliamentary Democracy, 2nd edn (London: Cass, 1964)

Beer, Samuel, *Britain Against Itself: The Political Contradictions of Collectivism* (London: Faber & Faber, 1982)

Behrens, Robert, *The Conservative Party from Heath to Thatcher: Policies and Politics, 1974–1979* (Farnborough, Hants: Saxon House, 1980)

Benn, Tony, *Arguments for Democracy* (London: Jonathan Cape, 1981)

Out of the Wilderness: Diaries 1963–1967 (London: Arrow Books, 1988)

Against the Tide: Diaries 1973–79 (London: Arrow Paperbacks, 1990)

The End of an Era: Diaries 1980–90 (London: Arrow Paperbacks, 1994)

Years of Hope: Diaries, Letters and Papers, 1940–1962 (London: Hutchinson, 1994)

Birch, Nigel, *The Conservative Party* (London: Collins, 1949)

Birkenhead, Earl of, *The Prof in Two Worlds* (London: Collins, 1961)

Walter Monckton: The Life of Viscount Monckton of Brenchley (London: Weidenfeld & Nicolson, 1969)

Blackstone, Tessa and Plowden, William, *Inside the Think Tank: Advising Cabinet 1971–1983* (London: Mandarin, 1990)

Blake, Robert, *The Conservative Party from Peel to Thatcher*, 2nd edn (London: Fontana, 1985)

Boardman, Harry, *The Glory of Parliament* (London: George Allen & Unwin, 1960)

Booth, A. H., *British Hustings 1924–1950* (London: Frederick Muller, 1957)

Boothby, Robert, *The New Economy* (London: Secker & Warburg, 1943)

I Fight to Live (London: Victor Gollancz, 1947)

My Yesterday, Your Tomorrow (London: Hutchinson, 1962)

Boyd-Carpenter, John, *Way of Life* (London: Sidgwick & Jackson, 1980)

Boyson, Rhodes, *Centre Forward: A Radical Conservative Programme* (London: Temple Smith, 1978)

Brittan, Samuel, *The Treasury under the Tories, 1951–1964* (Harmondsworth: Penguin, 1964)

Steering the Economy, rev. edn (Harmondsworth: Penguin, 1971)

Brogan, D. W., *The American Political System* (London: Hamish Hamilton, 1943)

Bruce-Gardyne, Jock and Lawson, Nigel, *The Power Game* (London: Macmillan, 1976)

Bullock, Alan, *The Life and Times of Ernest Bevin*, Vol. II: *Minister of Labour, 1940–1945* (London: Heinemann, 1967)

Burns, Lt.-Gen. E. L. M., *Between Arab and Israeli* (London: George G. Harrap & Co., 1962)

Butler, David, *The British General Election of 1951* (London: Macmillan, 1952)

The British General Election of 1955 (London: Macmillan, 1955)

Butler, David, Adonis, Andrew and Travers, Tony, *Failure in British Government: The Politics of the Poll Tax* (Oxford: Oxford University Press, 1994)

Butler, David and Kavanagh, Dennis, *The British General Election of February 1974* (London: Macmillan, 1974)

The British General Election of October 1974 (London: Macmillan, 1975)

The British General Election of 1979 (London: Macmillan, 1980)

The British General Election of 1983 (London: Macmillan, 1984)

The British General Election of 1987 (Basingstoke: Macmillan, 1988)

The British General Election of 1992 (London: Macmillan, 1992)

Butler, David and King, Anthony, *The British General Election of 1964* (London: Macmillan, 1965)

Butler, David and Pinto-Duschinsky, Michael, *The British General Election of 1970* (London: Macmillan, 1971)

Butler, David and Rose, Richard, *The British General Election of 1959* (London: Macmillan, 1960)

The British General Election of 1966 (London: Macmillan, 1966)

Butler, David and Stokes, Donald, *Political Change in Britain: Forces Shaping Electoral Choice* (Harmondsworth: Penguin, 1971)

Butler, Mollie, *August and Rab* (London: Weidenfeld & Nicolson, 1987)

Butler, R. A., *The Art of the Possible: The Memoirs of Lord Butler, K.G., C.H.* (London: Hamish Hamilton, 1971)

The Art of Memory (London: Hodder & Stoughton, 1982)

Butt, Ronald, *The Power of Parliament* (London: Constable, 1967)

Cairncross, Alec, *Years of Recovery* (London: Methuen, 1985)

Cairncross, Alec (ed.), *The Robert Hall Diaries 1954–61* (London: Unwin Hyman, 1991)

Callaghan, James, *Time and Chance* (London: Collins, 1987)

Campbell, John, *Edward Heath: A Biography* (London: Jonathan Cape, 1993)

Carlton, David, *Anthony Eden: A Biography* (London: Allen Lane, 1981)

Britain and the Suez Crisis (Oxford: Basic Blackwell, 1988)

Carr, E. H., *The Bolshevik Revolution, 1917–23*, Vol. I (London: Macmillan, 1950)

Carrington, Lord, *Reflect on Things Past: The Memoirs of Lord Carrington* (London: Collins, 1988)

Chandos, Lord (Oliver Lyttelton), *The Memoirs of Lord Chandos* (London: Bodley Head, 1962)

Charmley, John, *Chamberlain and the Lost Peace* (London: Hodder & Stoughton, 1989)

A History of Conservative Politics 1900–1996 (London: Macmillan, 1996)

Chisholm, Anne and Davie, Michael, *Beaverbrook* (London: Hutchinson, 1992)

Christiansen, Arthur, *Headlines All My Life* (London: Heinemann, 1961)

Christoph, James, *Capital Punishment and British Politics: The British Movement to Abolish the Death Penalty, 1945–57* (London: George Allen & Unwin, 1962)

Churchill, Randolph, *The Rise and Fall of Sir Anthony Eden* (London: MacGibbon & Kee, 1959)

The Fight for the Tory Leadership: A Contemporary Chronicle (London: Heinemann, 1964)

Churchill, Winston, *Into Battle: Speeches* (London: Cassell, 1941)

Onwards to Victory: War Speeches (London: Cassell, 1944)

The Dawn of Liberation: War Speeches (London: Cassell, 1945)

'The Highroad of the Future', *Colliers Magazine*, 4 January 1947

The Second World War, Vol. I: *The Gathering Storm* (London: Cassell, 1948)

The Sinews of Peace: Post-War Speeches (London: Cassell, 1948)

The Second World War, Vol. II: *Their Finest Hour* (London: Cassell, 1949)

Europe Unite: Speeches 1947 and 1948 (London: Cassell, 1950)

The Second World War, Vol. IV: *The Hinge of Fate* (London: Cassell, 1951)

The Second World War, Vol. VI: *Triumph and Tragedy* (London: Cassell, 1954)

Clark, William, *From Three Worlds* (London: Sidgwick & Jackson, 1986)

Clarke, Peter, *Hope and Glory: Britain, 1900–1990* (London: Allen Lane, 1996)

Clayton, Joseph, *The Rise and Decline of Socialism in Great Britain, 1884–1924* (London: Faber & Gwyer, 1926)

Cockerell, Michael, *Live from Number 10: The Inside Story of Prime Ministers and Television* (London: Faber & Faber, 1988)

Cockett, Richard, *Thinking the Unthinkable: Think Tanks and the Economic Counter-Revolution 1931–1983* (London: HarperCollins, 1994)

Colville, Jock, *The Fringes of Power* (London: Hodder & Stoughton, 1985)

Conservative Party, *Annual Conference Reports*

Manifesto, Policy Documents and *Campaign Guides*

The Industrial Charter: A Statement of Conservative Industrial Policy (London: National Union of Conservative Party Constitutional Associates, 1947)

The Right Approach: A Statement of Conservative Aims (London: Conservative Central Office, 1976)

Cooper, Duff, *Old Men Forget: The Autobiography of Duff Cooper* (London: Rupert Hart-Davis, 1953)

Cosgrave, Patrick, *Margaret Thatcher: Prime Minister* (London: Hutchinson, 1978)

Cowles, Virginia, *Looking for Trouble* (London: Hamish Hamilton, 1941)

Crafts, Nicholas, *Britain's Relative Economic Decline* (1997)

Craig, F. W. S. (ed.), *British General Election Manifestos 1900–1974*, rev. edn (London: Macmillan, 1975)

British General Election Manifestos 1959–1987, 3rd edn (Aldershot: Dartmouth, 1990)

Crewe, Ivor and King, Anthony, *SDP: The Birth, Life and Death of the Social Democratic Party* (Oxford: Oxford University Press, 1995)

Cripps, Stafford et al., *Problems of a Socialist Government* (London: Gollancz, 1933)

Critchley, Julian, *A Bag of Boiled Sweets: An Autobiography* (London: Faber & Faber, 1994)

Heseltine: The Unauthorised Biography (London: André Deutsch, 1987)

Cross, Colin, *Philip Snowden* (London: Barrie & Rockliffe, 1966)

Crossman, Richard, *The Diaries of a Cabinet Minister*, 3 vols. (London: Hamish Hamilton, 1975–7)

Daalder, Hans, *Cabinet Reform in Britain 1914–1963* (Oxford: Oxford University Press, 1964)

Dalton, Hugh, *The Fateful Years: Memoirs, 1931–1945* (London: Frederick Muller, 1957)

High Tide and After: Memoirs, 1945–1960 (London: Frederick Muller, 1962)

Davies, A. J., *We, the Nation: The Conservative Party and the Pursuit of Power* (London: Little, Brown, 1995)

Deane, Phyllis, *The Evolution of Economic Ideas* (Cambridge: Cambridge University Press, 1978)

Dell, Edmund, *The Chancellors: A History of the Chancellors of the Exchequer 1945–90* (London: HarperCollins, 1996)

Denman, Roy, *Missed Chances: Britain and Europe in the Twentieth Century* (London: Cassell, 1996)

Denning, Lord, *Lord Denning's Report: Presented to Parliament by the Prime Minister* (London: HMSO, 1963) (Cmnd. 2152)

Dilks, David (ed.), *The Diaries of Sir Alexander Cadogan, O.M., 1938–1945* (London: Cassell, 1971)

Disraeli, Benjamin, *A Vindication of the English Constitution, In a Letter to a Noble and Learned Lord* (London: Saunders & Otley, 1835)

Dunleavy, Patrick, Gamble, Andrew, Holliday, Ian and Peel, Gillian (eds.), *Developments in British Politics 4* (London: Macmillan, 1993)

Durham, Martin, 'The Thatcher Government and the Moral Right', *Parliamentary Affairs*, Vol. 42, No. 1 (1989)

Dutton, David, 'Anticipating Maastricht: The Conservative Party and Britain's First Application to Join the European Commuity', *Contemporary Record*, Vol. 7 (1993)

Anthony Eden: A Life and Reputation (London: Edward Arnold, 1997)

Ehrman, John, *The Younger Pitt*, Vol. III: *The Consuming Struggle* (London: Constable, 1996)

Eisenhower, Dwight D., *The White House Years*, Vol. I: *Mandate for Change 1953–1956* (London: Heinemann, 1963)

Epstein, Leon D., *British Politics in the Suez Crisis* (London: Pall Mall Press, 1964)

Evans, Rowland and Novak, Robert, *Lyndon B. Johnson: The Exercise of Power* (London: George Allen & Unwin, 1967)

Ewing, K. D. and Gearty, C. A., *Freedom under Thatcher: Civil Liberties in Modern Britain* (Oxford: Clarendon Press, 1990)

Feiling, Keith, *The Life of Neville Chamberlain* (London: Macmillan, 1946)

Fisher, Nigel, *Iain Macleod* (London: André Deutsch, 1973)

Foot, Michael, *Aneurin Bevan*, Vol. II: *1945–1960* (St Albans: Paladin, 1975)

Foot, Michael and Jones, Mervyn, *Guilty, 1956* (London: Victor Gollancz, 1957)

Foot, Paul, *The Rise of Enoch Powell: An Examination of Enoch Powell's Attitude to Immigration and Race* (Harmondsworth: Penguin, 1969)

Fowler, Norman, *Ministers Decide: A Personal Memoir of the Thatcher Years* (London: Chapman, 1991)

Galbraith, John K., *The Culture of Contentment* (London: Sinclair-Stevenson, 1992)

Garnett, Mark and Sherrington, Philippa, 'UK Parliamentary Perspectives on Europe 1971–1993, *Journal of Legislative Studies*, Vol. 2 (1996)

George, Stephen, *An Awkward Partner: Britain in the European Community*, 2nd edn (Oxford: Oxford University Press, 1994)

Gilbert, Martin, *Winston S. Churchill*, Vol. V: *1922–1939* (London: Heinemann, 1976)

Winston S. Churchill, Vol. V: *Companion*, Part 2: *The Wilderness Years, 1929–1935* (London: Heinemann, 1985)

Winston S. Churchill, Vol. VII: *The Road to Victory, 1941–1945* (London: Heinemann, 1986)

Winston S. Churchill, Vol. VIII: *Never Despair, 1945–1965* (London: Heinemann, 1988)

Gilmour, Ian, *The Body Politic*, rev. edn (London: Hutchinson, 1971)

Inside Right: A Study of Conservatism (London: Hutchinson, 1977)

Britain Can Work (Oxford: Martin Robertson, 1983)

Dancing with Dogma: Britain under Thatcherism (London: Simon & Schuster, 1992)

Riot, Risings and Revolution: Governance and Violence in Eighteenth-Century England (London: Hutchinson, 1992)

'The Thatcher Memoirs', *Twentieth-Century British History*, Vol. 5, No. 2 (1994)

Gold, Ann (ed.), *Edward Boyle: His Life by His Friends* (Basingstoke: Macmillan, 1991)

Goodhart, Philip, *Full-Hearted Consent: The Story of the Referendum Campaign and the Campaign for the Referendum* (London: Davis-Poynter 1976)

Goodhart, Philip and Brunston, Ursula, *The 1922* (London: Macmillan, 1973)

Goodman, Geoffrey, *The Miners' Strike* (London: Pluto, 1985)

Gopal, Sarvepalli, *Jawaharlal Nehru*, Vol. II: *1947–1956* (London: Jonathan Cape, 1979)

Gove, Michael, *Michael Portillo: The Future of the Right* (London: Fourth Estate, 1995)

'Gracchus', *Your M.P.* (London: Victor Gollancz, 1944)

Grant, Charles, *Delors: Inside the House that Jacques Built* (London: Nicholas Brealey, 1994)

Grigg, John, *The History of The Times*, Vol. VI: *The Thomson Years 1966–1981* (London: Times Books, 1993)

Grigg, P. J., *Prejudice and Judgement* (London: Jonathan Cape, 1948)

Grimstone, Gerry, 'Privatisation: The Unexpected Crusade', *Contemporary Record*, Vol. 1, No. 1 (Spring 1987)

Hailsham, Lord (see Hogg, Quintin)

Halcrow, Morrison, *Keith Joseph: A Single Mind* (London: Macmillan, 1989)

Halsey, A. H. (ed.), *British Social Trends since 1900: A Guide to the Changing Social Structure of Britain*, 2nd edn (Basingstoke: Macmillan, 1988)

Hammond, Eric, *Maverick: The Life of a Union Rebel* (London: Weidenfeld & Nicolson, 1992)

Hancock, W. K. and Gowing, M. M., *British War Economy* (London: HMSO, 1949)

Hanson, A. H., *Parliament and Public Ownership* (London: Cassell for the Hansard Society, 1961)

Harris, José, *William Beveridge* (Oxford: Clarendon Press, 1977)

Harris, Kenneth, *Thatcher* (London: Fontana, 1989)

Harris, Robert, *Good and Faithful Servant: The Unauthorized Biography of Bernard Ingham* (London: Faber & Faber, 1990)

Harrison, Martin, *Trade Unions and the Labour Party since 1945* (London: George Allen & Unwin, 1960)

Harvey, J. (ed.), *The Diplomatic Diaries of Oliver Harvey, 1937–1940* (London: Collins, 1970)

Haseler, Stephen, *The Death of British Democracy: A Study of Britain's Political Present and Future* (London: Elek, 1976)

Haxey, Simon, *Tory M.P.* (London: Victor Gollancz, 1939)

Hayek, F. A. von, *The Road to Serfdom* (London: G. Routledge & Sons, 1944)

Healey, Denis, *The Time of My Life* (London: Michael Joseph, 1989)

Heath, Anthony et al., *Understanding Political Change: The British Voter, 1964–1987* (Oxford: Pergamon, 1991)

Hennessy, Peter, *Cabinet* (Oxford: Basil Blackwell, 1986)
  Whitehall (London: Secker & Warburg, 1989)
  Never Again: Britain 1945–51 (London: Jonathan Cape, 1992)

Hennessy, Peter and Seldon, Anthony (eds.), *Ruling Performance: British Government from Attlee to Thatcher* (Oxford: Basil Blackwell, 1987)

Hoffman, J. D., *The Conservative Party in Opposition, 1945–51* (London: MacGibbon & Kee, 1964)

Hogg, Quintin, *The Case for Conservatism* (Harmondsworth: Penguin, 1947)

The Purpose of Parliament (London: Blandford Press, 1947)

The Door Wherein I Went (London: Collins, 1975)

The Dilemma of Democracy (London: Collins, 1978)

A Sparrow's Flight: The Memoirs of Lord Hailsham of St Marylebone (London: Collins, 1990)

Hogg, Sarah and Hill, Jonathan, *Too Close to Call: Power and Politics – John Major in No. 10* (London: Little, Brown & Co., 1995)

Hollis, Christopher, *Along the Road to Frome* (London: George G. Harrap & Co., 1958)

Holmes, Martin, *Political Pressure and Economic Policy: British Government 1970–1974* (London: Butterworth, 1982)

The First Thatcher Government, 1979–1983: Contemporary Conservatism and Economic Change (Brighton: Harvester Wheatsheaf, 1985)

Home, Lord, *The Way the Wind Blows: An Autobiography* (London: Collins, 1976)

Horne, Alistair, *Macmillan*, Vol. I: *1894–1956* (London: Macmillan, 1988)

Macmillan, Vol. II: *1957–1986* (London: Macmillan, 1989)

Howard, Anthony, *RAB: The Life of R. A. Butler* (London: Jonathan Cape, 1987)

Howe, Geoffrey, *Conflict of Loyalty* (London: Macmillan, 1994)

Hume, David, 'Of Commerce', in *Essays: Moral, Political and Literary*

Hurd, Douglas, *An End to Promises* (London: Collins, 1979)

Ingham, Bernard, *Kill the Messenger* (London: HarperCollins, 1991)

Ingle, Stephen, *The British Party System* (Oxford: Basil Blackwell, 1987)

Jenkins, Peter, *The Battle of Downing Street* (London: C. Knight, 1970)

Jenkins, Roy, *European Diary, 1977–1981* (London: Collins, 1989)

A Life at the Centre (London: Macmillan, 1991)

Jenkins, Simon, *Accountable to None: The Tory Nationalization of Britain* (London: Hamish Hamilton, 1995)

Johnson, Christopher, *The Economy under Mrs Thatcher 1979–1990* (Harmondsworth: Penguin, 1991)

Jones, Harriet and Kandiah, Michael (eds.), *The Myth of Consensus: New Views on British History, 1945–1964* (Basingstoke: Macmillan, 1996)

Junor, Penny, *The Major Enigma* (London: Michael Joseph, 1993)

Kavanagh, Dennis, *Thatcherism and British Politics: The End of Consensus?*, 2nd edn (Oxford: Oxford University Press, 1990)

Kavanagh, Dennis and Seldon, Anthony (eds.), *The Thatcher Effect: A Decade of Change* (Oxford: Clarendon Press, 1989)

The Major Effect (London: Macmillan, 1994)

Keegan, William, *Mrs Thatcher's Economic Experiment* (London: Allen Lane, 1984)

Mr Lawson's Gamble (London: Hodder & Stoughton, 1989)

Keegan, William and Pennant-Rea, Rupert, *Who Runs the Economy?* (London: Temple Smith, 1979)

Kelf-Cohen, R., *Nationalisation in Britain: The End of a Dogma*, 2nd edn (London: Macmillan, 1961)

Keynes, J. M., *Essays in Persuasion* (London: Macmillan, 1931)

Kilmuir, Earl of, *Political Adventure: The Memoirs of the Earl of Kilmuir* (London: Weidenfeld & Nicolson, 1964)

King, Anthony (ed.), *Why is Britain Becoming Harder to Govern?* (London: BBC Publications, 1976)

King, Cecil, *The Cecil King Diaries 1970–1974* (London: Jonathan Cape, 1975)

Kissinger, Henry, *The White House Years* (Boston: Little, Brown, 1979)
Years of Upheaval (Boston: Little, Brown, 1982)

Kyle, Keith, *Suez* (London: Weidenfeld & Nicolson, 1991)

Lamb, Richard, *The Failure of the Eden Government* (London: Sidgwick and Jackson, 1987)
The Drift to War, 1922–1939 (London: Bloomsbury, 1991)
The Macmillan Years 1957–1963: The Emerging Truth (London: John Murray, 1995)

Lawson, Nigel, *The View from No. 11: Memoirs of a Tory Radical* (London: Bantam, 1992)

Layton-Henry, Zig (ed.), *Conservative Party Politics* (London: Macmillan, 1980)

Leigh, David and Vulliamy, Ed, *Sleaze: The Corruption of Parliament* (London: Fourth Estate, 1997)

Leruez, Jacques, *Economic Planning and Politics in Britain*, trans. Martin Harrison (London: Robertson, 1975)

Letwin, Shirley, *The Anatomy of Thatcherism* (London: Fontana, 1992)

Lewis, G., *Lord Hailsham* (London: Jonathan Cape, 1997)

Linklater, Magnus and Leigh, David, *Not with Honour* (London: Sphere, 1986)

Lloyd, Selwyn, *Suez 1956* (London: Jonathan Cape, 1978)

Love, Kenneth, *Suez: The Twice-Fought War* (New York: McGraw-Hill, 1969)

Ludlam, Stephen and Smith, Martin (eds.), *Contemporary British Conservatism* (Basingstoke: Macmillan, 1996)

McCallum, R. B. and Readman, Alison, *The British General Election of 1945* (London: Oxford University Press, 1947)

MacDougall, Donald, *Don and Mandarin: Memoirs of an Economist* (London: John Murray, 1987)

Macleod, Iain, *Neville Chamberlain* (London: Frederick Muller, 1961)

Macleod, Iain and Maude, Angus (eds.), *One Nation: A Tory Approach to Social Problems* (London: National Union of Conservative Constitutional Associations, 1950)

Macmillan, Harold, *The Middle Way: A Study of the Problem of Economic and Social Progress in a Free and Democratic Society* (London: Macmillan, 1966)

Memoirs, Vol. III: *Tides of Fortune, 1945–1955* (London: Macmillan, 1969)

Memoirs, Vol. IV: *Riding the Storm, 1956–1959* (London: Macmillan, 1971)

Memoirs, Vol. V: *Pointing the Way, 1959–1961* (London: Macmillan, 1972)

Memoirs, Vol. VI: *At the End of the Day, 1961–1963* (London: Macmillan, 1973)

McSmith, Andy, *Kenneth Clarke: A Political Biography* (London: Verso, 1994)

Maitland, Donald, *Diverse Times, Sundry Places* (Brighton: Alpha Press, 1996)

Margach, James, *The Abuse of Power* (London: W. H. Allen, 1978)

Marquand, David, *Ramsay MacDonald* (London: Jonathan Cape, 1977)

Marquand, David and Seldon, Anthony (eds.), *The Ideas that Shaped Post-War Britain* (London: Fontana, 1996)

Marr, Andrew, *Ruling Britannia: The Failure and Future of British Democracy* (London: Michael Joseph, 1995)

Martin, Ross, *TUC: The Growth of a Pressure Group 1968–1978* (Oxford: Clarendon Press, 1980)

Maude, Angus (ed.), *The Right Approach to the Economy* (London: Conservative Political Centre, 1977)

Maude, Angus and Powell, Enoch, *Biography of a Nation: A Short History of Britain* (London: Phoenix House, 1955)

Maudling, Reginald, *Memoirs* (London: Sidgwick & Jackson, 1978)

Medlicott, William, *Contemporary England, 1914–1964* (London: Longmans, 1967)

Michie, Jonathan (ed.), *The Economic Legacy 1979–1992* (London: Academic Press, 1992)

Middlemas, Keith, *Politics in Industrial Society* (London: André Deutsch, 1979)

Power, Competition and the State, Vol. I: *Britain in Search of a Balance, 1940–61* (Basingstoke: Macmillan, 1986)

Power, Competition and the State, Vol II: *Threats to the Postwar Settlement: Britain, 1961–74* (Basingstoke: Macmillan, 1990)

Power, Competition and the State, Vol. III: *The End of the Postwar Era: Britain since 1974* (Basingstoke: Macmillan, 1991)

Orchestrating Europe: The Informal Politics of the European Union, 1973–1995 (London: Fontana, 1995)

Middlemas, Keith and Barnes, John, *Baldwin: A Biography* (London: Weidenfeld & Nicolson, 1969)

Miliband, Ralph, *Parliamentary Socialism: A Study in the Politics of Labour* (London: George Allen & Unwin, 1961)

The State in Capitalist Society (London: Quartet Books, 1973)

Mitchell, B. R. and Boehm, Klaus, *British Parliamentary Election Results, 1950–1964* (Cambridge: Cambridge University Press, 1966)

Moggridge, D. E., *Maynard Keynes: An Economist's Biography* (London: Routledge, 1992)

Moran, Lord, *Winston Churchill: The Struggle for Survival 1940–1965* (London: Constable, 1966)

Morgan, Janet (ed.), *The Backbench Diaries of Richard Crossman* (New York: Holmes & Meier Publishers, 1981)

Morgan, Kenneth, *The People's Peace: British History 1945–1989* (Oxford: Oxford University Press, 1990)

Morris, C. J., 'May–August 1960', *Contemporary Record*, Vol. 5, No. 3 (Winter 1991)

Morton, J. B., *A Bonfire of Weeds* (London: Jonathan Cape, 1939)

Mount, Ferdinand, *The British Constitution Now: Recovery or Decline* (London: Heinemann, 1992)

Neff, Donald, *Warriors at Suez: Eisenhower Takes America into the Middle East* (New York: Linden Press/Simon & Schuster, 1981)

Nicholas, H. G., *The British General Election of 1950* (London: Macmillan, 1951)

Nicholson, Emma, *Secret Society: Inside – and Outside – the Conservative Party* (London: Indigo, 1996)

Nicolson, Harold, *Diaries and Letters, 1930–1939* (London: Collins, 1966)

Diaries and Letters, 1945–1962 (London: Collins, 1968)

Nicolson, Nigel, *People and Parliament* (London: Weidenfeld & Nicolson, 1958)

Norton, Philip, *Conservative Dissidents: Dissent within the Parliamentary Conservative Party 1970–74* (London: Temple Smith, 1978)

Dissension in the House of Commons, 1974–1979 (Oxford: Clarendon Press, 1980)

'"The Lady's not for Turning", But What about the Rest? Margaret Thatcher and the Conservative Party 1979–1989', *Parliamentary Affairs*, Vol. 43, No. 1 (1990)

Norton, Philip and Aughey, Arthur, *Conservatives and Conservatism* (London: Temple Smith, 1981)

Norton-Taylor, Richard, Lloyd, Mark and Cook, Stephen, *Knee Deep in Dishonour: The Scott Report and Its Aftermath* (London: Victor Gollancz, 1996)

Nutting, Anthony, *Europe Will Not Wait: A Warning and a Way Out* (London: Hollis & Carter, 1960)

No End of a Lesson: The Story of Suez (London: Constable, 1967)

Oliver, Michael, 'Whatever Happened to Monetarism?', *Twentieth-Century British History*, Vol. 8, No. 1 (1997)

Orwell, S. and Angus, Ian (eds.), *The Collected Essays, Journalism and Letters of George Orwell*, Vol. I: *An Age Like This, 1920–1940* (Harmondsworth: Penguin, 1970)

The Collected Essays, Journalism and Letters of George Orwell, Vol. III: *As I Please, 1943–1945* (Harmondsworth: Penguin, 1970)

Painter, George D., *Marcel Proust: A Biography*, Vol. I (London: Chatto & Windus, 1959)

Pearce, Edward, *The Quiet Rise of John Major* (London: Weidenfeld & Nicolson, 1991)

Perkin, Harold, *The Rise of Professional Society: England since 1880* (London: Routledge, 1989)

Pimlott, Ben, *Hugh Dalton* (London: Papermac, 1986)
   Harold Wilson (London: HarperCollins, 1992)
   The Queen: A Biography of Queen Elizabeth II (London: HarperCollins, 1996)

Pimlott, Ben (ed.), *The Political Diary of Hugh Dalton 1918–40, 1945–60* (London: Jonathan Cape in association with the London School of Economics, 1986)
   The Second World War Diary of Hugh Dalton, 1940–45 (London: Jonathan Cape in association with the London School of Economics, 1986)

Pinto-Duschinsky, Michael, *British Political Finance 1830–1980* (Washington: American Enterprise Institute for Public Policy Research, 1981)

Pollard, Sidney, *The Wasting of the British Economy: British Economic Policy 1945 to the Present* (London: Croom Helm, 1982)

Prior, James, *A Balance of Power* (London: Hamish Hamilton, 1986)

Pym, Francis, *The Politics of Consent* (London: Hamish Hamilton, 1984)

Ramsden, John, *The Making of Conservative Party Policy: The Conservative Research Department since 1929* (London: Longman, 1980)
   The Age of Churchill and Eden, 1940–1957 (London: Longman, 1995)
   'That Will Depend on Who Writes the History: Winston Churchill as His Own Historian', Inaugural Lecture, 1996
   The Winds of Change: Macmillan to Heath, 1957–1975 (London: Longman, 1996)

Renwick, Robin, *Fighting with Allies: America and Britain in Peace and War* (Basingstoke: Macmillan, 1996)

Rhodes James, Robert, *Ambitions and Realities: British Politics, 1964–70* (London: Weidenfeld & Nicolson, 1972)
   Anthony Eden (London: Weidenfeld & Nicolson, 1986)
   Bob Boothby: A Portrait (London: Hodder & Stoughton, 1991)

Rhodes James, Robert (ed.), *Chips: The Diaries of Sir Henry Channon* (London: Weidenfeld & Nicolson, 1967)

Riad, Mahmoud, *The Struggle for Peace in the Middle East* (London: Quartet Books, 1981)

Riddell, Peter, *The Thatcher Era and Its Legacy* (Oxford: Basil Blackwell, 1991)
   Honest Opportunism: The Rise of the Career Politician (London: Hamish Hamilton, 1993)

Ridley, Nicholas, *My Style of Government: The Thatcher Years* (London: Hutchinson, 1991)

Robbins, Lord, *Political Economy, Past and Present: A Review of Leading Theories of Economic Policy* (London: Macmillan, 1976)

Roberts, Andrew, *The Holy Fox: A Biography of Lord Halifax* (London: Weidenfeld & Nicolson, 1991)

Eminent Churchillians (London: Weidenfeld & Nicolson, 1994)

Rokach, Livia, *Israel's Sacred Terrorism: A Study Based on Moshe Sharett's Personal Diary and Other Documents* (Belmont, Mass.: Association of Arab-American University Graduates, 1980)

Rovere, Richard H., *Affairs of State: The Eisenhower Years* (New York: Farrar, Straus & Cudahy, 1956)

Russel, Trevor, *The Tory Party: Its Politics, Divisions and Future* (Harmondsworth: Penguin, 1978)

Schlesinger, Arthur, *A Thousand Days: John F. Kennedy in the White House* (Boston: Houghton Mifflin, 1965)

Schumpeter, Joseph, *Capitalism, Socialism and Democracy*, 3rd edn (London: George Allen & Unwin, 1950)

Scott Lucas, W., 'Suez, the Americans and the Overthrow of Anthony Eden,' *LSE Quarterly* (Autumn 1987)

Searing, Donald, *Westminster's World: Understanding Political Roles* (Cambridge, Mass.: Harvard University Press, 1994)

Seldon, Anthony, *Churchill's Indian Summer: The Conservative Government, 1951–55* (London: Hodder & Stoughton, 1981)

Seldon, Anthony and Ball, Stuart (eds.), *Conservative Century: The Conservative Party since 1900* (Oxford: Oxford University Press, 1994)

Shahak, Israel, *Jewish History, Jewish Religion: The Weight of Three Thousand Years* (London: Pluto Press, 1994)

Shepherd, Robert, *The Power Brokers: The Tory Party and Its Leaders* (London: Hutchinson, 1991)

Iain Macleod (London: Hutchinson, 1994)

Enoch Powell (London: Hutchinson, 1996)

Shinwell, Emanuel, *Conflict without Malice* (London: Odhams Press, 1955)

Shrimsley, Anthony, *The First Hundred Days of Harold Wilson* (London: Weidenfeld & Nicolson, 1965)

Shuckburgh, Evelyn, *Descent to Suez: Diaries 1951–56* (London: Weidenfeld & Nicolson, 1986)

Sked, Alan and Cook, Chris, *Post-War Britain: A Political History*, 4th edn (Harmondsworth: Penguin, 1993)

Skidelsky, Robert (ed.), *Thatcherism* (London: Chatto & Windus, 1988)

Smith, David, *The Rise and Fall of Monetarism: The Theory and Politics of an Economic Experiment* (Harmondsworth: Penguin, 1987)

From Boom to Bust: Trial and Error in British Economic Policy (Harmondsworth: Penguin, 1992)

Snowden, Philip, *An Autobiography*, 2 vols. (London: I. Nicholson & Watson, 1934)

Soames, Mary, *Clementine Churchill* (London: Cassell, 1979)

Somervell, D. C., *Stanley Baldwin: An Examination of Some Features of Mr. G. M. Young's Biography* (London: Faber & Faber, 1953)

Stephens, Philip, *Politics and the Pound: The Conservatives' Struggle with Sterling* (London: Macmillan, 1996)

Stephenson, Hugh, *Mrs Thatcher's First Year* (London: Jill Norman Ltd, 1980)

Stewart, Michael, *Keynes and After*, 3rd edn (Harmondsworth: Penguin, 1986)

Strang, Lord, *Home and Abroad* (London: André Deutsch, 1956)

Stuart, James, *Within the Fringe: An Autobiography* (London: Bodley Head, 1967)

Swinton, Earl, *Sixty Years of Power: Some Memories of the Man Who Wielded It* (London: Hutchinson, 1966)

Taylor, A. J. P., *The Origins of the Second World War* (London: Hamish Hamilton, 1961)

Tebbit, Norman, *Upwardly Mobile* (London: Futura, 1989)

Templewood, Lord, *Nine Troubled Years* (London: Collins, 1954)

Thatcher, Margaret, *What's Wrong with Politics?* (London: Conservative Political Centre, 1968)
  The Downing Street Years (London: HarperCollins, 1993)
  The Path to Power (London: HarperCollins, 1995)

Thomas, Hugh, *The Suez Affair*, rev. edn (London: Weidenfeld & Nicolson, 1986)

Thomson, Malcolm, *David Lloyd George: The Official Biography* (London: Hutchinson, 1948)

Thorpe, D. R., *Selwyn Lloyd* (London: Jonathan Cape, 1989)
  Alec Douglas-Home (London: Sinclair-Stevenson, 1996)

Timmins, Nicholas, *The Five Giants: A Biography of the Welfare State* (London: HarperCollins, 1995)

Tomlinson, Jim, *Public Policy and the Economy since 1900* (Oxford: Oxford University Press, 1990)

Trevelyan, Humphrey, *The Middle East in Revolution* (London: Macmillan, 1970)

Urban, George R., *Diplomacy and Disillusion at the Court of Margaret Thatcher: An Insider's View* (London: I. B. Tauris, 1996)

Urquhart, Brian, *Hammarskjöld* (London: Bodley Head, 1973)

Utley, T. E., *Enoch Powell: The Man and His Thinking* (London: William Kimber, 1968)

Viereck, Peter, *Conservatism Revisited* (London: John Lehmann, 1950)

Walker, Peter, *Staying Power: An Autobiography* (London: Bloomsbury, 1991)

Walters, Dennis, *Not Always with the Pack* (London: Constable, 1989)

Wapshott, Nicholas and Brock, George, *Thatcher* (London: Futura, 1983)

Watkins, Alan, *A Conservative Coup: The Fall of Margaret Thatcher* (London: Duckworth, 1991)

Watson, George, *Politics and Literature in Modern Britain* (London: Macmillan, 1977)

Watt, Donald Cameron, *How War Came: The Immediate Origins of the Second World War, 1938–1939* (London: Heinemann, 1989)

Waugh, Evelyn, *The Diaries of Evelyn Waugh* (Harmondsworth: Penguin, 1979)

Wheeler-Bennett, Sir John, *John Anderson, Viscount Waverley* (London: Macmillan, 1962)

White, Theodore, *The Making of the President, 1968* (London: Jonathan Cape, 1969)

Whitehead, Phillip, *The Writing on the Wall: Britain in the Seventies* (London: Michael Joseph, 1985)

Whitelaw, William, *The Whitelaw Memoirs* (London: Aurum, 1989)

Whiteley, Paul, Seyd, Patrick and Richardson, Jeremy, *True Blues: The Politics of Conservative Party Membership* (Oxford: Clarendon Press, 1994)

Whiteside, Noel, *Bad Times: Unemployment in British Social and Political History* (London: Faber & Faber, 1991)

Whitfield, J. H., *Machiavelli* (Oxford: Basil Blackwell, 1947)

Wigham, Eric, *What's Wrong with the Unions?* (Harmondsworth: Penguin, 1961)

Strikes and the Government 1893–1974 (London: Macmillan, 1976)

Williams, Francis, *A Prime Minister Remembers: The War and Post-War Memoirs of the Rt. Hon. Earl Attlee* (London: Heinemann, 1961)

Williams, Philip, *Hugh Gaitskell* (London: Jonathan Cape, 1979)

Wilson, Edgar, *A Very British Miracle: The Failure of Thatcherism* (London: Pluto Press, 1992)

Wilson, Harold, *The Labour Government 1964–1970: A Personal Record* (London: Weidenfeld & Nicolson, 1971)

Wood, John (ed.), *Powell and the 1970 Election* (Kingswood: Elliot, 1970)

Woodhouse, Diana, *Ministers and Parliament: Accountability in Theory and Practice* (Oxford: Clarendon Press, 1994)

Woolton, Lord, *Memoirs* (London: Cassell, 1959)

Wright, Peter, *Spycatcher* (New York: Viking, 1987)

Wybrow, Robert, *Britain Speaks Out, 1937–87: A Social History as Seen through the Gallup Data* (Basingstoke: Macmillan, 1989)

Young, Hugo, *One of Us: A Biography of Margaret Thatcher*, rev. edn (London: Pan in association with Macmillan, 1990)

Young, J. W., *Britain and European Unity, 1945–1992* (Basingstoke: Macmillan, 1993)

Ziegler, Philip, *Wilson: The Authorised Life of Lord Wilson of Rievaulx* (London: Weidenfeld & Nicolson, 1993)

Index